Georgetown University Round Table on Languages and Linguistics 1992

Language, Communication, and Social Meaning

James E. Alatis, *Editor*

Georgetown University Press, Washington, D.C.

Bibliographic notice

The title of the series includes the year of a Round Table and omits both the monograph number and the meeting number, thus: *Georgetown University Round Table on Languages and Linguistics 1992,* with the regular abbreviation *GURT '92*. Full bibliographic references should show the form:

Pike, Kenneth L. 1993. A brief update on my interest in relating language to philosophy. In: Georgetown University Round Table on Languages and Linguistics 1992. Washington, D.C.: Georgetown University Press.

Printed in the United States of America

Library of Congress Catalog Number: 58-31607
ISBN 0-87840-127-X
ISSN 0186-7207

TO KENNETH L. PIKE
WHOSE PIONEERING WORK IS REFLECTED IN THE THEMES OF THIS MEETING

Contents

Acknowledgments and Permissions

The following publishers have generously given permission to reprint the following pages. The author and title of the article in which these pages appear are given in brackets.

Walker, R., et al. 1991. Assoziationen Deutsch fur die Mittelstufe, pages 169–70. New York: McGraw-Hill, Inc. [Kramsch, Claire. The dialogic emergence of culture in the language classroom.]

Ashmore, Malcolm. 1989. The Reflexive Thesis, page 227. Chicago: University of Chicago Press. [Swales, John M. Discourse community and the evaluation of written text.]

Spack, Ruth. 1988. The author responds to Johns... TESOL Quarterly 22.707-08. Alexandria, VA: Teachers of English to Speakers of Other Langauges, Inc. [Swales, John M. Discourse community and the evaluation of written text.]

The following corporations have generously given permission to use quotations from their advertisements for use in *Information flow in written advertising* (Peter H. Fries). The product name follows in parentheses.

CPC International Inc. (Niagara Professional Finish)
Canon USA (Canon Color Laser)
Chesebrough-Ponds (Cutex 'Strong Nail' Nail Strengthener)
Chrysler Motor Corporation (Jeep Eagle)
Corning Incorporated (Corning PhotoGray Extra Lenses)
COSMAIR, Inc. (L'Oreal Avantage and L'Oreal Creme Conditioner)
Hyundai Motor America (Sonata GLS V 616)
James River Corporation (Brawny Paper Towels)
Kraft General Foods (Shake'N Bake)
Nissan Motor Corporation in USA (Nissan)
Reynolds Metals Company (Reynolds Oven Cooking Bags)
Sunshine Biscuits Inc. (Sunshine Cookies and Crackers)

Welcoming Remarks

James E. Alatis
Dean, School of Languages and Linguistics, Georgetown University
Chair, Georgetown University Round Table on Languages and Linguistics 1992

Good evening, ladies and gentlemen. My name is James E. Alatis and I am Dean of the School of Languages and Linguistics and Chair of the Georgetown University Round Table on Languages and Linguistics. At an institution that is more than two hundred years old, and at a conference well into its fourth decade, we are guided by certain traditions. These traditions determine the format of our opening session and assign three important responsibilities to the Chair of the Round Table, which I consider it a privilege to perform. On the first night of the Round Table, the Chair welcomes participants, thanks organizers, and introduces speakers. Perhaps I am unduly suspicious, but since I have been chair of the Round Table, it seems the terms 'brief' and 'short' have cropped up as the ubiquitous modifiers of these duties. Or perhaps these people just know me too well. Short or long, brief or verbose, it is my great pleasure to welcome you to the campus, to the Leavey Center, and to the Round Table meeting. For those of you who are new to the Round Table meeting and to Georgetown, I should warn you that, perhaps influenced by our neighbor, the federal government, we use a lot of acronyms here. For example, the School of Languages and Linguistics is the SLL, the Intercultural Center is known as the ICC, the Georgetown University Sailing Team is, that's right, GUST, but, by far, the most important for the next few days is GURT, the Georgetown University Round Table. This, the forty-third GURT meeting, has as its theme, 'Language, Communication, and Social Meaning.'

The Round Table meeting each year gathers leaders in languages and linguistics to campus to share the results of their research and offer their viewpoints. I have been pleased and proud to be associated with GURT since 1966, when I first came to campus. As good, as substantive, as well-planned and executed as the previous Round Tables have been, I assure you that no previous GURT surpasses the promise of our current meeting. For the next three days, we shall have the opportunity to listen to scholars of international stature, who are in great demand around the world as speakers, researchers, lecturers, and consultants. Some have traveled a great distance, others have had to juggle demanding commitments to be here, and I would like to express my gratitude to each and every one of them for their support of the Round Table. Because the Round Table has been able to maintain a reasonable size, we shall also have the opportunity to discuss and comment upon the presentations. This is a welcome element for a meeting devoted to communication. I would encourage you to take advantage of these opportunities, either during the question period following the presentations, or more informally, during the coffee breaks. As accomplished as our speakers are, they realize that they have as much to gain from these exchanges as do you. Over the years, I have asked questions both naive and preposterous, and though I have been growled at a few times, I have never been bitten.

A moment ago, I promised you a magnificent meeting and it is a promise on which I am confident we shall deliver. As you saw from the GURT announcements and the meeting program, we have wonderful plenary speakers, concurrent sessions, and panel discussions. However, this meeting did not come together as a result of the big bang theory, nor did it evolve gradually over the centuries, and it was only indirectly created by God. It took hard work, organizational ability, and knowledge of diverse fields of linguistics to bring the GURT together. My Hellenic hubris and penchant for hyperbole aside, the GURT's greatness is not because I am chair, but rather because groups of people been working on the theme and schedule of this meeting for more than a year. And it is to these people that I would now like to turn.

First, and most importantly, I would like to express a thousand thanks to Carol J. Kreidler, the Round Table coordinator. In the four years that she has been handling this daunting task, I have come to expect miracles. This year has been no exception because Carol took on another modest responsibility in her spare time. She is now Director of our Division of English as a Foreign Language, a program with an enrollment of approximately 200 students. Yet, nothing fell between the cracks. She was always available to listen patiently to my wild ideas and performed the impossible as a matter of routine. In short, without her care and attention, we would not have a conference. And so, as a very modest token of gratitude, on behalf of everyone here, I would like to present roses to Carol with our thanks and best wishes.

As magnificent as Carol has been, even miracle workers need some assistance. This year, the GURT was organized with the help of a number of our graduate students. Over the course of the year, they devoted countless hours to our meeting. They brought to their task enthusiasm for the field, coupled with wonderful organizational abilities. We simply could not have done it without them. Their names appear on the covers of your programs, and I think it appropriate to recognize them now for all they have done and, as our meeting progresses, for all that they will do. They are Yu-chen Fan, Rebecca Freeman, Minako Ishikawa, Kenneth Kidd, Lourdes Pietrosemoli, and Carolyn Straehle. I think a round of applause is in order.

Many of you here this evening also participated in the Round Table pre-sessions. These pre-sessions have allowed the Round Table over the years to include a special focus on topics which otherwise could not be addressed through our regular program. What began quite informally many years ago have developed into sophisticated sessions worthy of any conference on languages and linguistics. I attended several over the course of the day and would like to offer my sincere congratulations to the organizers, presenters, and participants on a job well done. It is my sincere wish that the GURT will continue to be a welcome venue for these sessions in the future.

As I noted a few moments ago, people who know me have urged me to be brief. They have made a point of observing that my pleasant duty of welcoming you, thanking our organizers, and introducing our speakers should leave time for the speakers to speak. Thus chastised, and with apologies to anyone I may, in my haste, have left out, I would now like to move to another important Round Table tradition—the presentation of the Dean's Medal.

Presentation of the Dean's Medal to Kenneth L. Pike

James E. Alatis
Dean, Georgetown School of Languages and Linguistics
Chair, Georgetown University Round Table on Languages and Linguistics 1992

In the past, the Round Table has been an occasion during which the School of Languages and Linguistics has recognized distinguished achievements in the fields of language and linguistics with the award of the Dean's Medal. Previous recipients have included Henry and Renee Kahane and John Bissell Carroll. Although intended to honor them, their presence at the Round Table and their acceptance of the medal has, in fact, honored the medal and the University which awards it. This year is no exception as the School and Round Table recognize the lifetime of accomplishment of one of the field's most distinguished members: Kenneth L. Pike.

A man of great insight and a man of great faith, Kenneth Pike has devoted his scholarship to the service of others. Because he has done so much for so many, it is indeed difficult to gauge his impact on our field. Thousands of students and scholars have benefitted from his seminal publications. Still others have been fortunate to attend the Summer Institute of Linguistics; he was the Institute's first President and still provides great leadership. His more than thirty years with the University of Michigan influenced an entire generation of students, who, in turn, have sparked an interest in Kenneth Pike's work around the world.

Kenneth Pike's selflessness, accomplishments, and devotion to principle have brought him numerous honors and assignments. He has numerous honorary degrees, including one from Georgetown, he is an honorary professor at three universities in Peru, and he has been elected to the National Academy of Sciences and American Academy of Sciences. He was elected President of the Linguistic Society of America and the Linguistic Association of Canada and the United States.

A man of great peace and humility, Kenneth Pike has been an honored lecturer in more than forty-two countries around the world. He has resisted trends and fads in the field, adopting a far more holistic approach to the understanding of language and its function in culture. His work on Phonetics and Phonemics, Rhetoric, Tagmemics, and Grammatical Analysis are standard references in the field. Although he has authored more than a dozen major books, if his only publication were *Language in Relation to a Unified Theory of the Structure of Human Behavior*, then he would still be recognized as one of our field's most distinguished contributors. He has been accurately described as the world's greatest living phonetician.

Georgetown is a Jesuit university. The motto of the Jesuits is 'Ad majorem Dei gloriam.' But such a motto is also appropriate to Kenneth Pike, whose distinguished record of teaching and scholarship has been devoted to the greater glory of God. And so, it is with great respect and gratitude that Georgetown University, the School of Languages and Linguistics, and the Round Table recognize Kenneth Pike and wish him many years of continued success and distinction. I am also pleased to announce that the published proceedings of the Round Table will be dedicated to Kenneth Pike, whose pioneering work is so clearly reflected in the themes of our meeting.

As an aside, you should know that Kenneth Pike will deliver his paper at 2:00 on Wednesday. I am confident I speak for everyone here when I say how much we are looking forward to an update on your interest in relating language to philosophy. Thank you.

M.A.K. Halliday: An introduction

James E. Alatis
Dean, School of Languages and Linguistics, Georgetown University
Chair, Georgetown University Round Table on Languages and Linguistics 1992

This evening, we depart somewhat from tradition by having two opening addresses, by two very distinguished scholars, from two different linguistic perspectives. One, Professor M.A.K. Halliday, is British; the second, Professor Dell Hymes, is an American. Although I am not privy to both their papers, I suspect that anyone expecting a showdown or debate will be sorely disappointed. To be sure, these gentle men have approached their fields from differing traditions, but as is the case with all true scholars, they see that there is a great deal more that links them than separates them.

Our sequence of speakers is alphabetical. Professor Halliday was born in Leeds in 1925. His B.A. was awarded by the University of London in Chinese language and literature. Following study in China, he received his Ph.D. from Cambridge in 1955. He has held teaching appointments at Cambridge, Edinburgh, and London, where, until 1970, he was Professor of General Linguistics. From 1973 to 1975, he taught at the University of Illinois. He next became Professor and Department Head at the University of Sydney, retiring in 1987. His ensuing activities have stretched our definition of retirement and have included a year at the National University of Singapore. He is currently Visiting Professor at International Christian University in Tokyo.

Throughout his career, he has been much sought after as a visiting faculty member. He has been on the faculty of the LSA's Summer Linguistic Institutes on three occasions and has been a visiting faculty member at Yale, Brown, and the University of California at Irvine. His honorary degrees and prestigious awards are well deserved and too numerous to mention. His research on semantics and the grammar of modern English, text linguistics and register variation, the educational applications of linguistics, and text generation in artificial intelligence have resulted in important publications which are considered among the most authoritative in the field. This evening, Professor Halliday will address 'The Act of Meaning.' Ladies and gentlemen, please join with me in welcoming our distinguished speaker to the podium.

The act of meaning

M.A.K. Halliday
International Christian University, Tokyo

I

If I had been choosing a title after finishing this paper, instead of before writing it as one always has to do, I should probably have sought a wording that was more suggestive of the power of language, because this was the motif that tended to emerge most strongly as I wrote. Ideally, perhaps, I should have needed to introduce this second motif alongside the original wording, so as to bring out the inevitable connection between the two. The power of language is vested in the act of meaning.

Many years ago, I wrote somewhere that the act of meaning is a social act; and so it is. It is also a biological act; and it is also a physical one. But these components are related, in a logical and also in a historical sequence. The history of western thinking, in the centuries following Galileo, often seems like a struggle to come to terms, one by one, with these differing and increasingly complex types of phenomena: first the physical, then the biological, then the social; and it seems to have taken three or four generations to crack each new code.

You may well object that nothing could be more complex than the phenomena of the physical universe. Certainly in understanding them physicists are involved in quite staggering efforts of integration and of abstraction; and we are no nearer 'the end of physics' now than we ever were—or than the end of linguistics or the end of any other branch of knowledge. Or, if we are, this is, as Schaffer (1991) has convincingly shown, a cultural closure, not a physical one: a limitation on our own ways of knowing, not on what there is to be known. But in another sense, physical systems-and-processes—that is, physical phenomena construed as the domain of systematic knowledge—are simpler to apprehend, because we are able to interpret them purely as physical; whereas biological systems-and-processes are not just biological—they are also physical. And when we turn to social phenomena, these are not just social; they are social, and biological, and physical. The consequence is that, by this time, we no longer know an INSTANCE when we meet one. When one is confronted with social processes, what is a fact any more?

And this problem of instantiation—of the relation between observable phenomena and the system that, in some sense, 'lies behind' them—becomes still more formidable when we reach phenomena of the fourth type, namely those of meaning, or semiotic ones, which are (the pattern is familiar!) at once also social, and also biological, and also physical. While we may criticize Saussure for having failed to solve this problem (that of the nature of parole and its relation to langue), we should rather give him credit for having problematized it in the first place, as Culler did (1977). This failure to construe the link, in semiotic systems-and-processes, between the INSTANCE—the act of meaning, in other words—and the SYSTEM (prototypically, a language) has haunted our late twentieth century linguistics, which has oscillated wildly between system and instance, creating a massive disjunction between the two. In the 1960s, if you dared to mention the text, you were dismissed as 'data-oriented'; while in the 1980s if you ventured to refer to the system, you were attacked for 'totalizing'. But combining being data-oriented with totalizing is a useful recipe for understanding things; we sometimes call it scientific method.

So there is a gradient here, a cline of difficulty, as we move from physical to biological to social to semiotic systems; as we move along this cline we get further away from anything we can recognize as effects following from causes, causes leading to effects. But there is also another cline, that of ever-increasing risk, as we move towards the more distinctively human processes. Already in the eighteenth century people felt threatened when scientists applied the methods of the physical sciences to biological systems, systems with life in them; and they—or their descendants—became more uncomfortable some three or four generations later when these same methods began to be applied to social systems, which have not only life but also value. Small wonder, then, that many react with dismay when the domain of science starts encroaching on those which are the most human systems of all, namely semiotic systems—which have not only life, and not only value, but also meaning.

It is threatening, no doubt, to discover that there are processes beyond our conscious control in those very acts of consciousness by which our own selves are most clearly defined. Linguists often start their papers with the formula 'You're not going to like what I say'; no doubt this is partly because they are hoping to establish a claim for originality, as one has to do in order to gain tenure in these difficult times, but we do not hear this, as far as I can tell, from scientists or mathematicians—because it is also a spell, a call for protection against the dangers of apprehending the forces of meaning. The danger lies in relating the instance to the system, because that is the source of the power. You are safe in studying the system (as linguists traditionally did), because you do not reveal it at work in the form of text. You are safe in studying the text, as a philologist or student of style or of discourse, because you do not let it display the power of the system. But if you put the two together the text is revealed for what it is, an act that has meaning because it is not sui generis; it is the actualizing of a potential, by means of processes that are patterned—and therefore, in an important sense, predictable. So there is an emotional gradient here as well as an intellectual one. We resist being told how much of what we 'choose' to say is programmed, either as ready-made pieces of wording, as Pawley (1985) made clear, or in the probability profiles revealed by large-scale quantitative studies (Nesbitt and Plum 1988; Halliday and James 1993). Yet no child could learn a mother tongue if it was not characterized by massive regularities of these two complementary kinds.

Now a physical system is a physical system. But a physical theory is a semiotic system: a 'system of related meanings', as Lemke (1990a) describes it. We gain our understanding of physical phenomena—of phenomena of any kind, in fact—by using the special powers of a semiotic system to transform them (cf. Matthiessen 1991). The seventeenth century 'founders of modern science' were aware of this power that language had, and were inclined to be somewhat suspicious of it, believing that phenomena were often distorted in the process of being transformed into meanings. Hence they took seriously Francis Bacon's cautions against what he called the 'idols of the marketplace' (idola fori), one of the four kinds of idol that he felt impeded scientific thinking. The idola fori were the misconceptions that arose, in the words of Dijksterhuis (1986:398):

> from the thoughtless use of language, from the delusion that to all names there must correspond actually existing things, and from the confusion of the literal and the figurative meaning of a word; ...

The physical scientists' defence against this semiotic idolatry turned out to be one of the ironies of modern semohistory. While they were committed to producing a 'language of science' that would be free of ambiguity and metaphor (cf. Coetzee 1981), Newton and his successors developed a form of discourse that was almost certainly the most highly metaphorical the world had yet encountered, with all the ambiguity that that connotes. But the metaphor they were awary of was metaphor in its canonical sense, the metaphoric use of the lexis; whereas the metaphor they created in their own discourse is a metaphor that lies in the grammar (Halliday 1988; Martin 1990a; Halliday and Martin 1993).

Meanwhile in the centuries that followed, the notion of the power of language tended to recede into the background. The scientists got on with the business of doing science; and the linguists got on with the business of describing language, within their own definition of the task—for example, in England, the study of phonetics and spelling reform. For Saussure the only significance of an act of meaning—or 'act of speaking', acte de parole—was as a piece of evidence for the system, not as a constitutive act. It is striking, therefore, to find that this motif, that of the power of semiotic processes, has reemerged as a major theme in the late twentieth century. It has reemerged, in fact, from a number of different directions, so that it is not easy to present a brief yet coherent account. But let me try and enumerate some of the contexts in which the power of language is proclaimed, giving examples from the work that I am familiar with (which is, obviously, only a small portion of the whole).

We may perhaps identify five general headings: (1) language as means of access; (2) language as ideology; (3) language and social inequality; (4) language as metadiscourse (in the construction of reality); (5) language as model (for understanding systems of other kinds).

II

1 Language as means of access. The notion that language provides a means of access to particular domains, or spheres of social action, has been familiar since the 1960s: from the work of Gumperz and Hymes, in relation to functional varieties or 'registers', and from Bernstein's work in relation to codes. I shall come back to Bernstein under another heading; the common factor here is that the mode of access is some VARIETY of a language. Opening up access, in this semiotic sense, is now seen as a central task of language education. Jay Lemke's important book on science education is called *Talking Science*, and subtitled *Language, learning, and values*. Britain now has a National Curriculum, and the teacher education materials on Curriculum by Ronald Carter and his 'Language in the National Curriculum' colleagues put in the foreground the learner's access to knowledge through language. Most 'linguistic' of all are the Australian genre-based curricula, especially those produced for the New South Wales Disadvantaged Schools Program under the leadership of J.R. Martin. These last are based explicitly on the view that in order to access knowledge of any kind you have to control the semiotic resources which construe that knowledge; and furthermore, that only by redesigning the curriculum around those resources—the generic construction, the discourse semantics, and the lexicogrammar of the registers involved—can educators hope to open up to the learners the various discourses that make it possible to participate in the democratic political process (Lemke 1990a; Carter et al. 1990; Christie et al. 1991–92; New South Wales Disadvantaged Schools Program 1990–; Matthiessen 1993).

Work of this kind would not easily derive from, or reconcile with, a correspondence notion of language, the view that language is doing no more than reproducing a cognitive model of experience. Rather, it assumes a constructivist interpretation, whereby language actively construes human experience, from the 'commonsense' constructions of the everyday mother tongue to the highly elaborate edifices of the disciplines as they are taught and researched in schools and universities. In this perspective, the grammar of every natural language is (among other things) a theory of human experience; it is through our acts of meaning that we transform experience into the coherent—though far from consistent—patchwork that we learn to project as 'reality'.

2 Language as ideology. In other words, activities such as these presuppose a Whorfian view of language, at least in terms of my perceptions of what Whorf was saying, which have always been different from the received interpretation of Whorf's views in the United States. Let me quote from a recent paper by Alan Rumsey, entitled *Wording, meaning, and linguistic ideology* (1990:346):

> In common with Whorf, I believe that the best way to study the relationship between language structure and other aspects of social life is by looking for what he called 'fashions of speaking': global complexes of features that 'cut across the typical grammatical classifications, so that such a 'fashion' may include lexical, morphological, syntactic and otherwise systemically diverse means coordinated in a certain frame of consistency' (Whorf 1956:158).
>
> To what did Whorf seek to relate such 'fashions'? Most of the research that has been done on the so-called Sapir–Whorf hypothesis has been about language and PERCEPTION or 'cognitive processing' (cf. Lucy 1985). For present purposes, a better reading of Whorf is the revisionist one in Silverstein (1979), which takes him to be addressing himself to the Boasian problem of the relation between language as 'primary ethnological phenomenon' and the 'secondary rationalization' in terms of which speakers of the language understand it to operate (Boas 1974:23 fl.).

Rumsey finds 'a certain kind of ideology developing "in conjunction with" certain kinds of language structures', a relationship which he characterizes as a dialectical one. The 'frame of consistency' treated in his paper is one which relates certain cohesive devices to the grammar of reported speech, in English and in Ungarinyin; so here the dialectic is between language structures and 'commonsense notions about the nature of LANGUAGE in the world' (my emphasis); but for Whorf they could be commonsense notions about any aspect of the world. Other examples of such 'frames of consistency' will be found in the work of Martin on Tagalog (Martin calls them 'grammatical conspiracies'), and of Hasan on Urdu; the syndrome of features of transitivity and theme that developed in Early Modern English, first identified by Mathesius, would also constitute such a frame of consistency (Martin 1988; Hasan 1984; Halliday 1990).

Language neither drives culture nor is driven by it; the old questions about which determines which can be set aside as irrelevant, because the relation is not one of cause and effect but rather (as Firth saw it, though not in these words) one of realization: that is, culture and language co-evolve in the same relationship as that in which, within language, meaning and expression co-evolve. Thus above and beyond the random, local variation between languages that was the subject matter of earlier typological studies, we may expect to find nonrandom variation realizing different construals of reality across major alternations in the human condition. But given that language and culture evolve together in this kind of relationship, it is inevitable that language will take on an ideological role. It has been accepted for some time that race and gender are constructed in language; and the 'critical linguistics' developed by Roger Fowler and his colleagues in the late 1970s sought to ground this recognition in a deeper awareness of the role of GRAMMAR in such constructions—for example by examining the grammar of politically divergent texts which were reporting on one and the same racially charged event (Fowler et al. 1979). Within the same period, feminist studies of language moved on from gender pronouns and expressions of uncertainty to take account of the divergent roles in the grammar of transitivity taken up by female and male characters in popular romantic fiction (Thwaite 1986). Interestingly, this level of interpretation has now become generally accessible; see for example the article 'Romance in Cartlandia' by Peter Thomas in the *Guardian Weekly* of 29 March 1992. One can now cite numerous studies of the construction of ideology through acts of meaning (as examples, Kress and Hodge 1979, 1988; Threadgold et al. 1986; Threadgold and Cranny-Francis 1990; Van Leeuwen 1989; Lemke 1990b; Thibault 1988); and it is a central concern of the Australian journal *Social Semiotics*.

3 Language and social inequality. And it is what Bernstein was telling us about some 25 years ago. In a hierarchically ordered society there are likely to be major SEMIOTIC disjunctions between different levels in the hierarchy. Social classes are construed in language; hence they are validated (naturalized), reinforced, and transmitted in language; thus, language is functioning as an agency of social inequality. Bernstein's ideas got distorted even more than those of Whorf—partly because they are very threatening: if acted upon, they could disrupt the social order. But they are also difficult to grasp; and I think that this is because the phenomena he was observing, that he referred to as codes (or more fully as 'socio-linguistic coding orientations'), fall squarely in the problematic middle ground between the system and the instance—between the meaning POTENTIAL of language and the instantiated ACT OF MEANING. Such codes, in other words, do not form distinct linguistic systems (they are not different languages); but nor are they particularities of performance (either in the Chomskyan or in the Hymesian sense). Bernstein did once try to locate them with reference to a competence/performance dichotomy, but he soon abandoned this as a mistake; rather, such phenomena neutralize these distinctions, and force us to realize that the 'system' and the 'instance', by whatever names we choose to call them, are not in fact different phenomena—they are one and the same phenomenon seen by different observers.

Let me use my favourite analogy here, that of the climate and the weather. Certain changes seem to be taking place around us today, quite serious ones, like global warming; but are these changes perturbations in the climate, or are they variations in the weather pattern? If you ask that question, it makes it seem as if there are two possible classes of event; but there are not. What the question means is, will I understand these changes better if I view them from the standpoint of a climate observer, or from the standpoint of a weather observer? We shall probably need both perspectives; but in any case, climate and weather are not different phenomena; they are different observational time depths. So it is with language: the language system, and the language instance or act of meaning, are one phenomenon, not two; and codes, like Whorf's fashions of speaking, have to be observed in both perspectives.

Hasan has interpreted Bernstein's codes, in semiotic terms, using the concept of semantic variation. This is different from functional, or register, variation in one critical respect: in semantic variation there is a higher level constant—we can talk of semantic 'variants'; whereas in register variation there is not. Registers are ways of doing different things; there is no level of interpretation at which, say, technocratic discourse and casual conversation become signifiers of a common signified. With codes there is; and in this respect, codes resemble social dialects; but whereas social dialects (like dialects in general) realize their higher level constant in the semantic system (that is, within language itself), codes come together only OUTSIDE of language, in the culture. It is only at an abstract level in the context of culture that different codes can be seen to realize a common 'signified'.

Following up Bernstein's work two decades later, Hasan and her colleagues analysed semantically over 20,000 messages of spontaneous conversation between mothers and their preschool children in the home, and subjected the results to a detailed cluster analysis. The analysis showed significant differences in the patterns of meaning that were adopted, respectively, by mothers of boys and mothers of girls. Their discourse did not constitute two different language systems (two climates); they were all native speakers of Australian English. Nor, on the other hand, were they just random fluctuations in the semiotic weather. They were different codes—that is, consistent orientations to different ways of meaning, which construed boys and girls as different social beings. And the same study—same analysis, same data, same program—showed up other differences, equally significant both ideologically and statistically, between mothers from the working class and mothers from the middle class. And the children's own part in the dialogues revealed very clearly—not by direct imitation of the mothers, which would make no sense, but by a deeper semiotic resonance in their grammar—that they were, at 3½ years old, paid-up members of the social bond (Hasan 1990; Hasan and Cloran 1990).

4 Language as metadiscourse. There are three parts to this: construing experience, enacting interpersonal relations, creating a semiotic level of reality. In the 1960s, in what I called the 'metafunction' hypothesis, I suggested that the content plane of language—the lexicogrammar and its higher level ordering as semantics—could be best understood as simultaneously constructing meanings of three different kinds: meaning as reflection—construing human experience; meaning as action—enacting interpersonal relationships; and meaning as texture, which I saw as having an enabling function with regard to the other two (Halliday 1967/68).

The centrepiece in the grammar of experience is the transitivity system. Davidse has shown, in her comprehensive *Categories of Experiential Grammar* (1991), how the transitivity system of English construes experience for those for whom it serves as mother tongue. For most recent generations, until the very recent ones, this has meant the Anglo-Celtic peoples; and I include '-Celtic' here, not just to recognize that the Celts now largely have to make do with English, or with French, but to make the substantive point that, from the more cryptotypic aspects of the grammar, it seems clear that Celtic semogenic resources have contributed significantly to the semantic potential of these two languages. The transitivity system has also figured prominently in French work in functional grammar and semantics, notably that of Bernard Pottier; and its role in reality construction is central to the thinking of Claude Hagège (e.g. Hagège 1985). And perhaps I might pay respect here to another distinguished Francophone colleague, the late Algirdas Greimas, who died only a few weeks ago. Greimas was convinced, though from a different point of departure, of the essential unity of language and experience. Fabbri wrote of him (1992:21):

> On sait que, pour Greimas, langues (naturelles) et monde (naturel) ne sont pas séparés mais au contraire entrelacés comme dans un monogramme. Il s'agit pour lui de macrosémiotiques dans lesquelles les catégories du signifiant mondain sont les mêmes que celles qui constituent le plan du contenu du langage ...

A very natural framework for modelling transitivity structures is one based on processes and participant roles, along with some third category of circumstantial elements. Martin has proposed, for Tagalog, an alternative interpretation of transitivity, one based on orientation. There can be more than one way of construing experience in grammar, and we may need a different grammatics to bring out the complementarities involved (Halliday 1967/68; Martin, in press).

But the full creative power of an act of meaning arises from the fact that language BOTH construes AND enacts. It is not only a way of thinking about the world; it is also, at one and the same time, a way of acting on the world—which means, of course, acting on the other people in it. There has always been a place in studies of grammar for a few very general interpersonal systems such as mood; recently, however, not only have these systems come to be interpreted more theoretically, but also other kinds of interpersonal meaning have been brought under attention (e.g. Martin 1990b; Butler 1988).

Martin talks of 'interpersonal grammatization', and it has always seemed to me that interpersonal systems such as those realized by intonation (in many languages, such as English) should be understood as the enactment of social meaning through the systemic power of the grammar. The role of interpersonal grammar in learning is foregrounded in Lemke's work (e.g. 1988). In my view one of the significant facts about children's language development, in the context of language education, is that so many grammatical resources—including those which will eventually function overwhelmingly in experiential contexts—are developed first in the interpersonal domain. For example, at the time of transition from protolanguage to mother tongue (roughly, 1½–2 years old), a child may learn to give information that is not known to the listener (as distinct from rehearsing experience that has been shared) when he has hurt himself and needs to gain sympathy (Painter 1984); children typically first learn the logical semantics of conditionals in the context of threats and warnings (Phillips 1986), and they first master grammatical metaphor in the form of interpersonal metaphors of mood and modality (Halliday in press).

But this conjunction of the experiential and the interpersonal depends in turn, for its efficacy as discourse, on meaning of a third kind, the creation of texture. Matthiessen (1992; cf. also 1991) interprets and explains this as the grammaticizing of the semiotic process itself. The grammar creates its own 'world three'—not quite in Popper's sense—which is a world that is made of meaning, the semiotic counterpart of our worlds of reflection and of action.

5 Language as model. Some time ago I started using the term 'grammatics' to refer distinctively to grammar as a theoretical pursuit: grammatics as the study of grammar, parallel to linguistics as the study of language—but more especially applying the term to grammatical theory used as a source of explanation. Like all theories, a theory of grammatics is a semiotic system; but with the special characteristic that the phenomena it is designed to explain are themselves also semiotic systems—languages. Traditionally, linguists have usually tried to model their theories on theories that were designed to explain systems of other kinds; but in semiotics (which is not a discipline, but a thematic organization of knowledge like mathematics) all phenomena are being investigated and interpreted as systems of meaning, and this makes it possible to use grammatics as a way of explaining them. The most immediately accessible are other, nonlinguistic, semiotics such as forms of art: not just literature, which can naturally be apprehended through the grammar (by means of a grammatics) because it is made of language (cf. Butt 1984, 1988; Gregory 1985; Threadgold 1988), but also performance (dance and drama), music, and forms of visual art. Michael O'Toole (1989, in press) uses grammatics for his investigations of painting, architecture, and sculpture; Steiner (1988) and Van Leeuwen (1988) for music; and Paul Thibault (1991), starting from narrative theory, exploits grammatics as a resource for integrating the text into a broader framework of 'social semiotics as praxis'.

But it is now being suggested that some PHYSICAL systems might be better understood if they could be modelled 'as if' they were semiotic ones. This motif began to appear some time ago in the writings of post-quantum physicists, perhaps in conjunction with their renewed interest in the language of their own science; and as far as I can tell it seems to have an interpretation on two different levels: (1) that some physical systems INCORPORATE semiotic ones (e.g. Prigogine and Stengers' example of the communication among molecules that is necessary for them to operate as a 'chemical clock'—and compare, in biology, communication among the eggs in a clutch getting ready to be hatched); and (2) that some physical systems ARE semiotic (e.g. Bohm's interpretation of the speed of light as the maximum speed of propagation of a signal) (Prigogine and Stengers 1982:147–8; Bohm 1980:123). In either case, the critical event is an act of meaning. A physical system is no longer 'just' a physical system. But, by the same token, a grammatics is no longer just a theory of grammar.

III

So in the past generation we seem to have rediscovered something of the power of language, recognizing that an act of meaning is not the coding and transmitting of some pre-existing information or state of mind, but a critical component in a complex process of reality construction—critical in that on the one hand it is itself one part of reality, and on the other hand it is a metaphor for some other part. Semiotic systems, while they are COMPONENTS OF human experience, along with physical, biological, and social ones, are also THEORIES ABOUT that experience (including about themselves, there being no constraint on their reflexivity (Lemke 1984)). That is their metaphorical aspect; and it is the success of that metaphor, in one's semiotic acts, I think, that determines how effective one's discourse is going to be.

This power of the act of meaning would not have been news to the sophists in ancient Athens, who constructed their grammatics in order to find out how language could persuade people of something even when it was not true. Or to the founders of modern science, who tried to design their language so that it would open up for them the gateway to new knowledge. And of course it is no news to my copresenter tonight, Dell Hymes, who has proclaimed not only the power of language but also the need for a grammatics with which to apprehend it—as he said, writing about attaining the 'joy and understanding' of Native American verbal art, 'If we do not deal with the means, we cannot possess the meanings' (Hymes 1981:5).

Nevertheless we cannot help noticing a contradiction here. In fact, relatively few of those concerned, however much they may be aware of, and may even celebrate, the power of the act of meaning, have actively tried to 'deal with the means' of its achievement. Unlike the works I have been citing in this paper (which do), most studies in semiotics—including what we might call 'applied semiotics'—do not engage seriously with language; and many explicitly deny that it is relevant to do so. When physical scientists comment on language, they often seem content to treat it at the level of the eighth grade.

To be fair to those scientists, this is partly, I think, because they are aware that we—the linguists—have still not cracked the code of systems of this fourth order of complexity, semiotic systems. We do not yet fully understand the nature of our own fundamental abstractions, those of realization and instantiation, nor the complex multiple relationship that holds between them. And for our other colleagues there is probably a further reason: that much of what we are able to tell them tends to be rather discouraging—like Bacon with his idola fori, we are obsessed with language doing its worst. We even hold conferences on lying.

I should plead guilty here too: in my paper at AILA in 1990 I particularly emphasized how the power of language functions to create and maintain all kinds of inequalities and hegemonies—not only citing the familiar examples of social class and sex (or 'gender' as we now call it, in a ritual bow to these same idols), but also suggesting how our language locks us in to the twin myths of endless growth and of our own status as the lords of creation (myths of growthism and lordism, if you like these -istic terms). I stressed these inequalities, these antidemocratic fashions of meaning; and I did this so as to show that we need to learn to think grammatically, to become aware of such cryptotypic effects in our everyday 'commonsense' language, if we want to continue to prosper as a species, or even if we want to survive.

So let me end this evening by turning over the coin, and proclaiming instead the democratic potential of our familiar semogenic resources. Our transitivity systems, for example, seem at first sight to be dominated by this apparently immutable hierarchic scale of animacy, privileging humanity over the rest of creation and, within humanity, the generalized human male. But the semantic space construed by transitivity is an elastic space; these are tendencies—they are not categorical, which means they can be reversed, or subverted. This is possible because when you override them, it does not force a reinterpretation; compare my example of *what the forest is doing*, which can be interpreted as an effective material process with *the forest* as Actor (and, potentially, as Agent, depending on what follows). [A categorical system is one you cannot subvert. Here, if you produce an 'illicit' combination, it simply gets co-opted—that is, reinterpreted according to the category, or one of the categories, in question. Thus in English, in mental processes (only), the distinction of '+/- consciousness' is categorical; hence if I ask what the forest is thinking, or what the forest knows, the forest is thereby co-opted into the class of conscious beings—or else the process itself is metaphorized into something else, as in *what the forests are now seeing* is total destruction.] Interestingly, it is in symbolic processes that humans lose any such privileged status: any entity is equally acceptable as a signal source, e.g. *that rock formation tells you that the whole region was uplifted*.

We can also subvert the process by which the code barrier limits access to educational knowledge. (I do not think, by the way, that there is any significant difference, in this respect, among the various English-speaking countries. The British are always cited as uniquely class-ridden, but this is because they wear their classes on their sleeves, whereas over here the pattern is more covert—I think Paul Fussell is one who has made this point. But the same barriers are in place.) Since the disjunction between educational knowledge and commonsense knowledge is construed in the grammar, it can also be deconstrued in the grammar. Simply by spreading knowledge about language ('KAL', as it is called in the British work) one can do much to demystify educational discourse; but one can also use the grammar as a resource in order to bridge—or even to close—the gap.

Two strategies suggest themselves. One, to provide stepping stones from 'common sense' to technicality and grammatical metaphor within the experiential component of the grammar—agnate forms of discourse that form a gradation from the one to the other. The other strategy is to map more learner-friendly interpersonal meanings into the educational discourses. You have to be careful, in that second case, to avoid what Martin calls 'childism' (1989); but I think it can be done.

In any case the disjunction is partly a matter of our own failure to understand the nature of commonsense knowledge, knowledge as construed—and learnt by children—in the language of daily life. Of course, children have to relearn a great deal once they come into school—they have to systematize and technicalize their own construction of experience; but that is no reason why we should not recognize how much they knew before they came. Ruqaiya Hasan's study of 'Rationality in everyday talk between mothers and children' shows the many forms of reasoning that are deployed in everyday discourse in the home; the 3-year-old's grammar has plenty of varied resources for constructing sequences of argument (Hasan 1992). What Hasan has shown is that different kinds of rationality are functional in different social contexts. Moving into the discourse of education is not a matter of transcending some opposition between nonrational and rational; it means recognizing the contexts in which different forms of rationality are deployed.

If we compare the discourses of today with those of a century ago, we become aware of the potential that the system has for change. This is a potential, of course, that has to be actively taken up, if we want it to change in a particular direction: taken up not by legislation or decree, but by changing our own habits of meaning, towards different frames of consistency. The semantic space can always be expanded; as I said before, it is an elastic space, indefinitely malleable—and semiotic growth, growth in meaning potential, is one kind of growth which does not use up natural resources or engender polluting side effects!

The system of language is always in transition—because every act of meaning transforms it, however microscopically, from what it was into something else. You cannot redesign it; but you can nudge it along by the innumerable small momenta (a phrase of Whorf's I never tire of repeating) of thoughtful acts of meaning. You can even reverse the marking, up to a point, as protagonists of the cause of women have done with English personal pronouns. This is because there is no insulation between the system and the text; the system is the text, only (as I put it earlier) it is being observed from a different time depth. Hence it is in the act of meaning that the power of language resides; and that is what makes linguistic systems, in the last resort, subject to the democratic process.

REFERENCES

Bohm, David. 1980. Wholeness and the Implicate Order. London: Routledge and Kegan Paul [Ark Paperbacks, 1983].

Butler, Christopher S. 1988. Politeness and the semantics of modalized directives in English. Linguistics in a Systemic Perspective, ed. by James D. Benson, Michael J. Cummings, and William S. Greaves. Amsterdam: Benjamins.

Butt, David. 1984. The Relationship between Theme and Lexicogrammar in the Poetry of Wallace Stevens. Macquarie University. Ph.D. thesis.

Butt, David. 1988. Ideational meaning and the existential fabric of a poem. New Developments in Systemic Linguistics, Vol. 2: Theory and application, ed. by Robin P. Fawcett and David J.

Young. London and New York: Pinter.
Carter, Ronald, et al. 1990. Language in the National Curriculum. Department of English Studies, University of Nottingham.
Christie, C., et al. 1991–92. Language as a Resource for Meaning, Series 1–4. Sydney: Harcourt Brace Jovanovich.
Coetzee, J.M. 1981. Newton and the ideal of a transparent scientific language. Journal of Literary Semantics.
Culler, Jonathan. 1977. Saussure. Glasgow: Collins (Fontana Modern Masters).
Davidse, Kristin. 1991. Categories of Experiential Grammar. University of Leuven. Ph.D. thesis.
Dijksterhuis, E.J. 1961. The Mechanization of the World Picture. London: Oxford University Press [Princeton, NJ: Princeton University Press, 1986].
Fabbri, Paolo. 1992. Pertinence et adéquation. Limoges: PULIM, Université de Limoges (Nouveaux Actes Sémiotiques 19).
Fowler, Roger et al. 1979. Language and Control. London: Routledge and Kegan Paul.
Gregory, Michael J. 1985. Linguistics and theatre—Hamlet's voice: Aspects of text formation and cohesion in a soliloquy. Forum Linguisticum 7.
Hagège, Claude. 1985. L'homme de paroles: Contribution linguistique aux sciences humaines. Paris: Fayard.
Halliday, M.A.K. 1967. Intonation and Grammar in British English. The Hague: Mouton (Janua Linguarum Series Practica 48).
Halliday, M.A.K. 1967/68. Notes on transitivity and theme in English, Parts 1–3. Journal of Linguistics 3.1, 3.2, 4.2.
Halliday, M.A.K. 1988. On the language of physical science. Registers of Written English: Situational factors and linguistic features, ed. by Mohsen Ghadessy. London and New York: Pinter.
Halliday, M.A.K. 1990. New ways of meaning: A challenge to applied linguistics. Journal of Applied Linguistics (Greek Applied Linguistics Association) 6.
Halliday, M.A.K. In press. Towards a language-based theory of learning. Linguistics and education.
Halliday, M.A.K., and Z.L. James. 1993. A quantitative study of polarity and primary tense in the English finite clause. Techniques of description: Spoken and written discourse, ed. by John M. Sinclair et al. London and New York: Routledge.
Halliday, M.A.K., and J.R. Martin. 1993. Writing Science: Literacy and discursive power. London and New York: Falmer Press.
Hasan, Ruqaiya. 1984. Ways of saying, ways of meaning. The Semiotics of Culture and Language, Vol. 1, ed. by Robin P. Fawcett et al. London and Dover, NH: Pinter.
Hasan, Ruqaiya. 1990. Semantic variation and sociolinguistics. Australian Journal of Linguistics 9.2.
Hasan, Ruqaiya. 1992. Rationality in everyday talk: From process to system. Directions in Corpus Linguistics: Proceedings of Nobel Symposium 82, Stockholm 4–8 August 1991, ed. by Jan Svartvik. Berlin: Mouton de Gruyter.
Hasan, Ruqaiya, and Carmel Cloran. 1990. A sociolinguistic interpretation of everyday talk between mothers and children. Learning, Keeping and Using Language: Selected papers from the Eighth World Congress of Applied Linguistics, Sydney 16–21 August 1987, Vol. 1, ed. by M.A.K. Halliday, John Gibbons, and Howard Nicholas. Amsterdam: Benjamins.
Hymes, Dell. 1981. 'In vain I tried to tell you': Essays in Native American ethnopoetics. Philadelphia: University of Pennsylvania Press.
Kress, Gunther, and Robert Hodge. 1979. Language as Ideology. London: Routledge and Kegan Paul.
Kress, Gunther, and Robert Hodge. 1988. Social Semiotics. London: Polity Press.
Lemke, Jay L. 1984. Semiotics and Education. Toronto: Victoria University (Toronto Semiotic Circle Monographs, Working Papers and Prepublications).
Lemke, Jay L. 1988. Genres, semantics and classroom education. Linguistics and Education 1.1.
Lemke, Jay L. 1990a. Talking Science: Language, learning, and values. Norwood, NJ: Ablex (Language and Educational Processes).
Lemke, Jay L. 1990b. Technical discourse and technocratic ideology. Learning, Keeping, and Using

Language: Selected papers from the Eighth World Congress of Applied Linguistics, Sydney 16–21 August 1987, Vol. 2, ed. by M.A.K. Halliday, John Gibbons, and Howard Nicholas. Amsterdam: Benjamins.

Martin, J.R. 1988. Grammatical conspiracies in Tagalog: Family, face and fate. Linguistics in a Systemic Perspective, ed. by James D. Benson, Michael J. Cummings, and William S. Greaves. Amsterdam: Benjamins.

Martin, J.R. 1989. Factual Writing: Exploring and challenging social reality. Oxford: Oxford University Press.

Martin, J.R. 1990a. Literacy in science: Learning to handle text as technology. Literacy for a Changing World, ed. by Frances Christie. Hawthorn, Victoria: Australian Council for Educational Research.

Martin, J.R. 1990b. Interpersonal grammatization: Mood and modality in Tagalog. Philippine Journal of Linguistics 21.1.

Martin, J.R. In press. Transitivity in Tagalog: A functional interpretation of case. Meaning and Choice in Language, Vol. 2: Grammatical Structure, ed. by Margaret Berry, Christopher S. Butler, and Robin P. Fawcett. Norwood, NJ: Ablex.

Matthiessen, Christian. 1991. Language on language: The grammar of semiosis. Social Semiotics 1.2.

Matthiessen, Christian. 1992. Interpreting the textual metafunction. Advances in Systemic Linguistics: Recent theory and practice, ed. by Martin Davies and Louise Ravelli. London and New York: Pinter.

Matthiessen, Christian. 1993. Register in the round: Diversity in a unified theory of register analysis. Register Analysis, ed. by Mohsen Ghadessy. London and New York: Pinter.

Nesbitt, Christopher, and Guenter Plum. 1988. Probabilities in a systemic grammar: The clause complex in English. New Developments in Systemic Linguistics, Vol. 2: Theory and application, ed. by Robin P. Fawcett and David J. Young. London and New York: Pinter.

New South Wales Disadvantaged Schools Program. 1990–. Write it Right. Erskineville, N.S.W.: Department of Education and N.S.W. Education and Training Foundation.

O'Toole, Michael. 1989. Semiotic systems in painting and poetry. A Festschrift for Dennis Ward, ed. by M. Falchikov, C. Poke, and R. Russell. Nottingham: Astra Press.

O'Toole, Michael. In press. A systemic-functional semiotics of art. Meaning and Choice in Language, Vol. 3: Discourse in Society, ed. by Peter H. Fries and Michael J. Gregory. Norwood, NJ: Ablex.

Painter, Clare. 1984. Into the Mother Tongue: A case study in early language development. London and Dover, NH: Pinter.

Pawley, Andrew. 1985. On speech formulas and linguistic competence. Lenguas Modernas (Universidad de Chile) 12.

Phillips, Joy. 1986. The development of modality and hypothetical meaning. Working Papers 3. University of Sydney Linguistics Department.

Prigogine, Ilya, and Isobel Stengers. 1982. Order out of chaos: Man's new dialogue with nature. London: Heinemann [Fontana Paperbacks, 1985].

Rumsey, Alan. 1990. Wording, meaning, and linguistic ideology. American Anthropologist 92.2.

Schaffer, Simon. 1991. Utopia limited: On the end of science. Strategies 4/5.

Steiner, Erich. 1988. The interaction of language and music as semiotic systems: The example of a folk ballad. Linguistics in a Systemic Perspective, ed. by James D. Benson, Michael J. Cummings, and William S. Greaves. Amsterdam: Benjamins.

Thibault, Paul. 1988. Knowing what you're told by the agony aunts: Language function, gender difference, and the structure of knowledge and belief in the personal columns. Functions of Style, ed. by David Birch and Michael O'Toole. London and New York: Pinter.

Thibault, Paul. 1991. Social Semiotics as Praxis: Text, social meaning making and Nabokov's 'Ada'. Minneapolis: University of Minnesota Press.

Threadgold, Terry. 1988. Stories of race and gender: An unbounded discourse. Functions of Style, ed. by David Birch and Michael O'Toole. London and New York: Pinter.

Threadgold, Terry, et al. (eds.) 1986. Semiotics—Ideology—Language.Sydney: Sydney Association

for Studies in Society and Culture.
Threadgold, Terry, and Anne Cranny-Francis (eds.) 1990. Feminine/Masculine and Representation. Sydney: Allen and Unwin.
Thwaite, Anne. 1986. Transitivity and gender in two texts from popular fiction. University of Sydney Linguistics Department: ms.
Van Leeuwen, Theo. 1988. Music and ideology: Towards a sociosemantics of mass media music. Working Papers 2. Sydney: Sydney Association for Studies in Society and Culture.
Van Leeuwen, Theo. 1989. Changed times, changed tunes: Music and ideology of the news. Australian Television: Programmes, pleasures and politics, ed. by John Tulloch and George Turner. Sydney: Allen and Unwin.

Dell Hymes: An introduction

James E. Alatis
Dean, School of Languages and Linguistics, Georgetown University
Chair, Georgetown University Round Table on Languages and Linguistics 1992

Our second speaker this evening is Dell Hymes. Professor Hymes was born in Portland, Oregon, in 1927. He received his B.A. from Reed College and his Ph.D. in Linguistics from Indiana University. An anthropologist and linguist, he has held faculty appointments at Harvard, the University of California at Berkeley, the University of Pennsylvania, and the University of Virginia in departments and disciplines such as: anthropology, linguistics, folklore, sociology, and education. During a period of temporary madness or temporary glory, he also served the University of Pennsylvania as Dean. He has been a Fellow of the Guggenheim Foundation, the American Council of Learned Societies, the Center for Advanced Study in the Behavioral Sciences, the National Endowment for the Humanities, and the American Folklore Society. So clearly, he is quite a fellow. His major publications include *Language in Culture and Society*, *Language in Education*, and *Foundations in Sociolinguistics*. He is considered by many, along with such other great scholars as Dr. Charles Ferguson, to be among the founders of sociolinguistics in the United States. It is my great honor therefore to introduce and welcome Professor Dell Hymes, who will speak on 'Inequality in Language: Taking for Granted.'

Inequality in language: Taking for granted

Dell Hymes
University of Virginia

1 Preface. I will focus on social meaning involved in evaluations of languages and what can be said in them, more particularly, with the dialectic between actual and potential ability.[1]

Many address these issues, not least those concerned with literacy and bilingual education, with the Official English movement, and the like. Recent experiences have brought this aspect of social meaning home to me anew. I want to suggest that we are not always entirely frank and consistent in dealing with social meaning in situations of inequality. Let me do this by considering three aspects of inequality in turn. Each involves a kind of a taking for granted.

One aspect has to do with potential equivalence, as something we may take for granted and forget to say. A second has to do with equating what is potential with what is actual ability. A third has to do with oral narrative.

I will talk in terms of 'language'. Most people do, including linguists, and the issue of inequality is historically associated first of all with the notion of 'language'. The true subject, of course, is not 'language' alone, but repertoire—the mixes of means and modalities people actually practice and experience. Study of communicative repertoires makes the question of inequality all the more salient, if only because it inescapably involves choice among alternatives. Much of what I say is a recollecting of things already known, but often enough, it seems, left out of account.

2 Potential equality. Linguists tend to take for granted that languages, and varieties of language, are (POTENTIALLY) equal. That users of any have a right to life, liberty (autonomy), and the pursuit of meaning.

This assumption is foreign to many outside the field. Its foreignness is clear

---

[1] This paper is based on a lecture in memory of Nessa Wolfson, sponsored by the Wolfson family, and the Graduate School of Education of the University of Pennsylvania. The lecture was given October 25, 1991, and its text has appeared in the Working Papers in Educational Linguistics, prepared by graduate students in the Educational Linguistics program of the School, Vol. 8, No. 1 (1992).

to those who work with and on behalf of minority languages. Within 'theoretical' linguistics, the matter is not likely to arise. If it does, the focus is on potentiality. That has a history.

Linguistics is rather recent as a separate discipline. The Linguistic Society of America was founded only in 1924. Many of its founders were conscious of a need to dispel misconceptions about language. They were conscious of working against popular, even learned, conceptions about language, conceptions which relegated many languages, especially unwritten ones, to 'primitive' status, as lacking sufficient vocabulary, or even regularity of grammar, or at least as deficient in some respect. Much of the general linguistics of the time appeared a projection of acquaintance with the languages of one region, Europe. To combat such preconceptions was an important part of the mission of linguistics itself. Boas, Bloomfield, Sapir, Whorf, and others took it as part of their mission.

This egalitarian perspective was extended to varieties within a language. It was clear that many notions of correctness had grown up, even been invented, in the course of instructing an aspiring middle class in verbal manners. Seen against the history of the language, and against other languages around the world, many preferences of pronunciation, or construction, were arbitrary. Many explanations of preferences were secondary rationalizations. The choice of a standard had little to do with intrinsic qualities, much more to do with politics, class, and location.

In sum, structural differences among languages were not to be ranked on a scale of superiority. Differences within a language had social meaning for its users, and might be ranked by them, but such rankings were not intrinsic to the linguistic features themselves. They were the result of secondary association. One and the same pronunciation of 'bird' [båid] might be stigmatized in New York City, admired in Charleston. Diversity of structure went together with equivalence of function.[2]

The great, liberating consequence of this was to sever the age-old connection between verbal trappings and personal worth. Character does not come in one accent alone; intelligence has many voices.

We take this so for granted within linguistics that we may forget to teach it. I remember some years ago in an anthropology course at Penn, when a question revealed that a student had just those notions about 'primitive' languages that, one assumed, the labors of Boas, Bloomfield, and Sapir had driven from the land. I had said nothing about them in class. Were it not for the chance of a question, that student (and others?) would have passed through the class with such notions intact.

The truth is that we must never take for granted that what we take for granted is known to others. ELEMENTARY ASSUMPTIONS OF LINGUISTICS CAN BE LIBERATING FOR THOSE TO WHOM THEY ARE UNKNOWN. The task of confronting

---

[2] Cf. discussion in the opening pages of Hymes 1966.

misconceptions about the status of languages, as languages, may never be over. A victory which seems old, won in the past, by those such as Boas and Sapir and Bloomfield, continues to need to be won. In the United States there are those, progressive to the core, who are surprised that someone they know studies 'Indian languages'. Are they really languages, our daughter was asked by such a person. With regard to the languages of the Aborigines in Australia, Blake (1991:vii) reports: 'Even among highly educated people the question is still asked, "Do these people have real, full languages?". The book is intended to illustrate at least that this is the case, and to encourage further inquiry.'

Wherever there is a variety of English that differs from a certain standard, there will be those who will see it not as different but as deficient. The burgeoning creativity of those in Africa and Asia and the Pacific, replanting English, cross-breeding English: their novel integrations of resources add color and beauty to the world, to those who can see them as configurations of their own (cf. Kachru 1990).

The same kind of task may continue to be true indefinitely with what can be called the 'hidden injuries of accent'. I have argued in the past that even if everyone spoke a recognizable standard English, there would be those who would create a hierarchy out of adverbs, and lament the decline of the language. We are far from so recherché a state.

Students may come to a class in sociolinguistics, believing their normal speech intrinsically inferior, and leave with that sense of stigma never having become known.

[Last spring my wife Virginia took on a large undergraduate class in sociolinguistics. The size of the class was frustrating; the students were mostly anonymous faces. She decided to ask each student to write a journal, which she would read and respond to. The journals disclosed personal experiences and beliefs as to difference and deficiency, right and wrong, that would otherwise have been invisible. The journals disclosed effects of the course as well. Learning about diversity from the standpoint of linguistics made a difference to some, who could now separate what was socially necessary for them to use from prejudice against other forms of speech, including their own. It made a difference to one student just to learn that what she and her family spoke was called 'Highland Southern', that it had a name. A name added identity, a degree of legitimacy.]

Linguistic assumptions may come to be taken for granted without our realizing it. This was brought home to me recently by a colleague who works in the Caribbean. He stressed continuing prejudice in education against Jamaican Creole, the continued dominance of the view that only standard English counts, how that effects what is done and who can do it. That should not have surprised me. But study of pidgin and creole languages has grown immensely. Thirty years ago there were only a few scholars and significant studies. Now even a specialist can hardly keep track of the literature, and it influences other branches of linguistics. Languages once of interest to few are accepted as worthy of study by all. Even a specialist can forget that such legitimacy once had to be fought for within the field, and, outside, still does.

In our own classes there are likely to be students with kinds of misconception we tend to forget, and for whom common practices of teaching and evaluation may be harmful. Indeed, we may have to face in our society an increasing authoritarianism, as in England. Here, as there, there may not only be practiced, but mandated, the costly policy of teaching a single standard that Harold Rosen protests in a recent essay, 'The nationalisation of English' (1991). Diversity of accent may be accepted in principle; so may the appropriateness of different styles to different situations. Yet the practice may be oppressive, Rosen argues, if there is no allowance for contestation and negotiation.

Insofar as the issue is the primacy of (standard) English there is really no issue except a symbolic one, or perhaps a covert one. Students do recognize their social system, and that in it one language, and a version of that language, not their own, is firmly in place, with a social meaning for others that may not be their own (Edelsky 1991:chapter 2). Still, it makes a difference if one recognizes the circumstances, does not 'misrecognize' them, understands that they might be otherwise. (cf. Bourdieu 1991).

In this context one should note the widespread assumption that the brain has room for command of only one language. If that were true for Americans, they would have to be classed as biologically deficient, since multilingualism is a NORMAL accomplishment in most of the world. And the frequent opinion that language is divisive. Difference of language is not in itself divisive, although of course it can become the symbol of conflict in certain economic and political circumstances. A good way to make a language a symbol of conflict is to repress it.

3 Actual inequality. As linguists, we often act as if the kind of equality just discussed is the whole of the story, as if the potential is the actual. Rankings of languages, and of features of languages, are secondary and arbitrary. Where differences exist, what matters is (a) relativity and (b) potential equality (or equivalence). As to abilities, the preferred image, the representative anecdote, is that of Chomskian theory, the amazing unfolding ability of the growing child.

Each of these involves an equation of the potential with the actual. The ideal picture is poignant against the realities of our world, where pregnant women may not have enough to eat, and where judgments of subordination can be enforced.[3]

We may shut out findings that suggest actual inequality. Our methodological relativism—all languages are equal in the sight of science—is translated into the ideology that all languages are equal in the sight of humankind, or should be. Of course they should be when the evaluation is based on unfamiliarity or prejudice. But people often know perfectly well that they can accomplish some

---

[3] These points about the Chomskian representative anecdote, and its poignancy, first came to me in preparing a paper in 1967 for a conference on language and education.

things in one language or variety that they cannot in another. Sometimes the reason is a secondary prejudice, a matter of acceptability. Even then knowledge that the privileging of one pronunciation or style over another is arbitrary does not remove the privilege. And sometimes the reason is truly a matter of what can be done. Any language has the potential to become a language in which scientific medicine is practiced. Most languages do not now have the vocabulary, discourse patterns, and texts.

The projection of actual equality echoes an older time, and the rise of linguistics in the nineteenth century. The origin and history of peoples was a nineteenth century preoccupation. Linguistics rose to intellectual prominence through its success in tracing common origins backward, subsequent diversification forward. The implicit picture was of the peopling of the world by groups marked by a single, autonomous language.

This implicit picture has continued well into this century. It was the unstated premise of earlier discussions of linguistic relativity. The Hopi language could shape the Hopi view of the world because, it was implied, it was the only language the Hopi learned and used. The language was autonomous. Whatever came to expression in it, or did not, had its origin and explanation among the Hopi.

We all know that the world we live in is one in which communities with a single, autonomous language are scarce. Since the emergence of what Immanuel Wallerstein calls 'the world-system', the great process affecting languages has not been separation and diversification, but contact and reintegration. Of course there has always been multilingualism, and, within a monolingual group, a plurality of styles or registers. Ways of using language have always been defined in relation to each other, have always been potentially in competition with each other. This has become the general case. Not only varieties, but most languages themselves probably now are alternatives within a repertoire. Most are not autonomous. What they can express is partly a function of their niche within the ecology of a community and larger society, influenced by policies and funding for schools, resources for printing, and the like.

When I entered linguistics, the rightness of the equality of all languages was so certain that it was believed, and argued, that one could express anything in any language, translate anything into any language, that all languages were equally complex. Not that one had evidence. The statements were simply consistent with, elaborations of, an insurgent and triumphant world view.[4]

These statements were felt consistent with a belief in the cognitive relativity

[4] Such statements continue to be made. A manuscript I read recently (December 1991) had several, including the claim that five-year-old children arrive at school knowing 95% of the rules of their language. Is there an agreed-upon count of the number of rules of English, of any language? A book that assumes equivalence between potential and actual equality has just had a second edition (Aitchison 1990). It does so in the name of equality. My point is that we can not expect to achieve greater equality by claiming as true what no one knows, and denying actualities of which many have experience.

of languages. In effect, different structures, different styles, but with equivalence of function. We took delight in differences, in surprises, in the wonderful way another language might do something.[5]

Some of you may have entered linguistics as, or since, another world view became triumphant, so that for a while, it was believed and argued that there are essentially no cognitive differences, that differences of structure are superficial and without significant effect. Linguistic relativity, which had seemed obviously true, came to seem obviously wrong. Whorf, whose name had became attached to the notion, had seemed important and interesting, if not necessarily right; now he seemed naive (and to some still does).

One of the rewards of living a long time in the same line of work is that people bring back the tunes, the golden oldies, of one's youth. Now the study of metaphor and cognitive bases for grammar and language lend a certain respect to Whorf (Lakoff 1987, Langacker 1987, 1990, 1991; Lucy 1991). Emphasis on difference once made Whorf seem bad, to Joshua Fishman and others, insofar as difference might imply incapacity. Now for Fishman emphasis like that of Whorf on difference reinforces respect for minority languages and Whorf has a role to play (Fishman 1982). Peter Mühlhäusler and Rom Harré (1990) find it perfectly obvious that Whorf's claims are true for the individual, who internalizes particular kinds of social meaning in learning the person-marking of a language.[6]

Perhaps one can live long enough to see accepted within the core of linguistics the consequences of a world of only partly autonomous languages, and varieties of language. A world in which the development of a given language or variety for a certain purpose may have a cost which will not be met. In which it is recognized that the same language name does not entail the same means and abilities. In which it is recognized that the dimensions which govern the development of pidginization and creolization govern the development of all languages.

The historically derived character of ANY language has to do with (Hymes 1971:83):[7]

- Scale of linguistic means, having regard both to outer form (simplification, complication) and inner form (reduction, expansion) in its various levels and domains;

- Provenience of linguistic means, that is, confluence of traditions;

---

[5] An explicit statement is found at the end of Sapir and Swadesh (1946).

[6] For extended and thoughtful discussion of the current state of the subject, see Lucy 1991 and three books expected this year (Lucy 1992a, 1992b, 1992c).

[7] What follows generalizes to all languages the characteristics of pidginization and creolization, as indicated by a survey of information two decades ago (Hymes 1971: 83). It was a point of that essay that pidgins and creoles were complex configurations of processes more widely shared.

- Scope of social role (restricted, extended), having to do with use within a group as primary or secondary means of communication, and between groups as well.

- Contexts, with regard to selection and channeling of its use; motivation and identification on the part of persons involved; the communicative repertoires of the persons involved; relations to other linguistic norms.

Contact and integration within a repertoire entails change in one or more of these dimensions. Since the emergence of a 'world-system', hardly any language has escaped such change. Some have expanded, some contracted, in use and consequently in means as well. A wide range of processes—standardization, pidginization, creolization, obsolescence—are aspects of a general history. It will take some time to develop adequate pictures for all this, an understanding comparable to that achieved for 'genetic' diversification. But at least it is clear that the potential equivalence of all languages, and users of language, is not adequate as a picture.

The social meaning of language, in other words, of a language, is a function not only of immediate context, but also of PERSISTENT context. Over time some possibilities of meaning, expressive as well as referential, poetic as well as pragmatic, have been cultivated, and others not. The means are at hand for indicating and shaping some kinds of meaning, and not for others. Some kinds of expression have a cost that others do not. Means of speech are sometimes evaluated in terms of characteristics that are not secondary but INTRINSIC.

This is so even under conditions of primacy and autonomy. Languages, varieties, verbal repertoires adapt and evolve, developing some means and meanings and not others. In an important sense Navajo over time became a language better suited for dealing with the American Southwest, not so apt for snow, more fit for maize, more fluent for the kind of cosmology expressed in Pueblo tradition. Every translator knows that there are things that can be done in one language that cannot be done in another. It is only if one divorces meaning from form that one can claim that there is completeness of translation. Given pages enough and time, that meaning, that effect, that takes one line in the original can be explained. But still the meaning is not the same. Meaning is partly a matter of means. Elaboration, explanation substitute or insert the meaning of a different genre. What was funny or trenchant or compelling in the sound profile of a single line is not as a disquisition. The hearer or reader is changed into a student of a text, no longer an active participant in immediate recognition. Intrinsic difference is all the more the case when a language or variety is socially constrained.[8]

---

[8] For example, the obsolescent language, East Sutherland Gaelic, closely studied by Nancy Dorian (1981; cf. Dorian 1989). Cf. also what Bloomfield reported about the Menomini, White Thunder (Hymes 1974, Ch. 3:71ff). The example is taken up more fully in the original article of 1967, and in somewhat different form as the beginning of Ch. 2 of my *Toward linguistic competence*

And as everyone knows in daily life, and especially those in the work of education, it is a fallacy to equate the resources of a language to the resources of (all) users. Knowing English may still leave someone inferior as a narrator to someone in a Native American or African American language tradition. Every community is diverse in relative command of the possibilities of the language(s) available. When one considers literacy, we are likely to live in a world in which almost everyone is 'literate' in some sense, yet command of literacy is cruelly stratified—often because the conditions under which they are introduced to literacy perpetuate inequality (Hymes 1987b), sometimes because the kind of literacy expected may alienate them from their communities (Edelsky 1991:Ch. 8, 'Risks and possibilities of whole language literacy: alienation and connection').

One must be willing to recognize that lack of equivalence is endemic to the world. (Stigmatizing those who call attention to it (Whorf, Bernstein) is not a help.) The help that is needed is to describe and compare such cases, develop the ability to recognize and analyze recurrent types of case, and to address what can be done. An important part of that help can come from those who necessarily address the actual inequalities of minority languages and language learners. If human beings are not only language-using animals, but also goaded by the spirit of hierarchy, as two elements of Kenneth Burke's definition have it, then there will never be a lack of need for such work.

4 Oral narrative. These two aspects of our language situation, potential and actual, come together in narrative. Every community has narrative. Evidently it rests on an ability inherent in human nature, that is possible everywhere, perhaps as an aspect of the ability for language itself.

Like much of language, much of the organization of oral narrative is out of awareness. My late colleague Nessa Wolfson made a pioneering contribution in this respect, tracing use of the conversational historical present. Everyone is aware that a change into the present tense may dramatize what is said, convey in English immediacy. Instead of *And then I saw ...* , *And then I see ...* What had not been realized was that some occurrences can not be explained that way. That whatever else may be the case, switching into and out of the historical present marks the beginning and end of a part of what is being said. The changes themselves segment the story. It can be a device for giving narrative organization, unconsciously so.

Some years ago my wife Virginia and I independently analyzed a narrative Nessa had recorded. We did so in the light of other forms of unconscious patterning that we had found in Native American languages. She encouraged us in this. I would like to share with you now an analysis of one of her favorite examples (Wolfson 1982:25–7; 1989:140). We refer to it by its first line *She's a widow.*

1984 [1973]).

Let me note that this analysis is the last of several. Some narratives follow an obvious pattern throughout, but many do not. They make use of principles shared with other stories, but a somewhat individual use, having rhythms partly their own, an architecture that varies and emerges. One has to live with such a story for a while, become sensitive to its details and themes, try alternative ways of being true to both. A given analysis may be only one of a series of approximations. This analysis does seem to recognize every detail, to be consistent, to show a coherent development of themes.

To recognize the patterning of oral narratives, one must start with their lines and the ways in which lines constitute verses. One must go on to recognize relations among verses that constitute larger rhetorical forms. This is the step that few so far have taken.

The story is presented here in two forms. The first is the form in which it was published as part of the evidence for the conversational historical present—a continuous sequence of prose (Wolfson 1982:25–7; 1989:140). The second presents the story as a sequence of lines.[9]

The shape of the sequence is indicated by certain conventions. One or more lines go together in what can be called a VERSE. The first (or only) line of a verse is flush left. Verses go together in what can be called a STANZA. Between stanzas there is a space. Stanzas go together in what can be called a SCENE. A scene is identified by lowercase Roman numerals at the margin.

So far there appear to be two basic types of organization. In many cases, the unmarked, or default, relation among elements is that of sets of two and four, For other traditions, the unmarked relation is that of sets of three and five. English communities are not uniform. Traditional stories from the British Isles may use two and four. Story tellers in the United States typically use three and five.

It seemed at first that this narrative might use relations of two and four, with four scenes overall. Possible parallels in the opening of stanzas suggested as much. Further review brought awareness of separation of parts of a conversational exchange at two points; of failure to recognize two lines marked by initial capitalization and final period as verses; and of failure to grasp that parallel remarks about 'making everything up' were ending points of parallel sections. All this fell into place when the narrative was seen as having five scenes, whose internal relations were three and five.

In traditions whose unmarked pattern is three and five, there is often a striking rhetorical relation. It occurs in widely separated languages, in the Chinookan family of the Pacific Northwest, in songs in the Kalevala tradition of Finnish, and in northeast Philadelphia English. The relation is one of

---

[9] Neither Virginia nor I have heard the tape of the narrative. We have worked from the text as presented in Nessa's dissertation, and as published in her monograph (1982:25-7), and in a later article (1989:140). In doing so, Virginia particularly has paid scrupulous attention to the details of the transcription. Commas, periods, and capitalization have been consistently used as indications of verses in the light of her experience with a variety of English oral narratives.

INTERLOCKING. In a sequence of five elements, the first three may go together as one sequence of action, and the last three go together as well. The third element is a pivot, simultaneously ending one sequence and beginning another. In the arithmetic of such narratives, 3 + 3 can equal 5.

The relation of interlocking holds throughout *She's a widow*. It does so at several levels. At the level of the whole story, the five scenes interlock. The first three state a situation, report an opportunity and strategy, and reach an outcome, acceptance of the bid. At the same time, the third scene initiates three steps of acceptance: of price, certificates, date of settlement.

(Notice that each of these scenes comes round at the end to the theme of acceptance, and that the third and fourth do so in parallel fashion. Coming round to a recurrent ending point is sometimes decisive for analysis.)

The stanzas within all scenes but the first (lines 1–5) are linked by interlocking as well. Thus, the second scene (lines 6–59) has five stanzas. The first two are marked initially in terms of summertime (AB), and the last two are marked finally in terms of 'making up a lot of things/everything' (DE). The first pair bring in the realtor and the narrator; the last pair bring in the narrator's wife in conversation with the realtor. These two pairs of stanzas are linked by a pivot, (C). In this central stanza the narrator finds out the true amount that had been bid for the house. That discovery is the outcome for the stanzas in which he becomes involved in an effort to buy the house. The discovery evidently also alerts him to a possible plan and is the onset of the stanzas in which he initiates it. In sum, stanza (C) is at one and the same time the outcome of one series of three stanzas (ABC), and the onset of another (CDE).

The third and fourth scenes (lines 60–84, 85–103) each consist of pairs of conversational exchange. In each there are four pairs of conversational exchange, followed by a later call and an acceptance. In each the third pair is pivotal. The narrator's wife (in iii) or the narrator (in iv) states a condition. The condition is an outcome of what has so far occurred and an onset of the conclusion to follow. In both scenes the next (fourth) pair has the realtor say that the widow will not go for it. The final (fifth) pair has a subsequent call and acceptance. Again, we have AB(C)DE.

The fifth scene (lines 104–42) turns on dates. Its first stanza has the narrator say he will try to get January, rather than October. Its second stanza has him change the agreement that way and insist. Its third stanza has the widow refuse January. All that is a unified sequence of three stanzas. The conclusion of one three-part sequence proves again to be the onset of another. The next (fourth) stanza is a response and a next step to the refusal of January. It itself begins with a three part sequence, ringing changes on months and dates:

So then my next date was December,
    and she went to November,
        and I finally pushed her to November 18th

and the third line, concluding that sequence of dates, initiates a further sequence and outcome within the verse:

> and I finally pushed her to November 18th
>   and that's where we got it,
>   and, uh, she did back off.

The first outcome is arrival at a third date, the second and final outcome is refusal yet again.

A further word on the organization of this final scene. It is not surprising to find a scene organized as pairs of verses throughout, as is the case with scenes [iii] and [iv]. It does seem surprising to find just the last three stanzas of a scene consisting of pairs. The first stanza has three verses, the second five, and clearly so. Just the first three verses are interchange between the narrator and his cousin. Just the next five verses are interchange between the narrator and the realtor.

Although the earlier and later stanzas of the scene differ in type of patterning of verses (three and five for (AB), two for (CDE)), the principle of change of stanza with change of participants is constant. It informs the pairs of verses also. Just the next two verses (C) involve the realtor and the widow. And their outcome—

> So he took it back to her
>   and she called the deal off.
> She wouldn't accept January

is a third step, and outcome, in sequence with the opening stanzas.

In the next two verses (D) the participants change yet again. Now it is just the narrator and the widow who are involved. The two verses have indeed a strong marker of beginning, for this narrator, not just 'So' but 'So then' (cf. line 104, where 'So then' begins the scene as a whole). And the verses are internally linked by repetition of the words, and topic, 'back off'.

At the level of steps of action, also, if 'She wouldn't accept January' (C) is the first step in a sequence of responses to the narrator's proposed settlement date, for her to back off (D) is a second.

The third step comes in the next pair of verses (E). Its conclusiveness is signaled by 'finally', and flat statement of final date:

> She FINALLY went—
>   we settled at November 18th.

Pairing is an obvious pattern when what is narrated is conversational exchange, as in scenes [iii] and [iv]. The pairing in scene [v] may be something of a change of pace, for intensification of effect. Certainly each of the pairs is a step in the action of the whole. As noted, the first three stanzas have an outcome in the first pair, the first refusal. The narrator undertakes to try to get

January, insists on January to the realtor, January is refused. At the same time the pair of verses containing the refusal is the start of a second three-step sequence, refusal, backing off, acceptance. Each step is evidently a point of structure at the level of stanza.

The last two lines return the story to the present. No more widow, realtor, cousin, or wife, or house to be bought. The lines seem to address the hearer of what has gone before, almost explicitly, changing what is said from a story to direct conversation, but at the same providing a final twist to all that has been recounted. Perhaps it is not an accident that the lines rhyme (*now* ... *now*), analogous to a closing Shakespearean couplet, or to the formal words which return a Native American myth to the present.

5 On alternation of tenses. The analysis of the narrative, and especially the analysis of the last scene and its last three stanzas, gains further point and support by attention to the use of tenses.

Use of the conversational historical present in relation to past and general present was indeed the focus of Wolfson's treatment of the narrative. Other writers have returned to the long-standing notion of the historical present as in itself expressive. Johnstone (1990:82–3) notes Schiffrin's claim (1981) that the historical present is an evaluative device, and advances the hypothesis that in her own data from Fort Wayne there is an evaluative role restricted to 'the say/go system' (that is, to the use of certain verbs in attributing dialogue). She cites a story in which, whenever there is a tense difference in attributing discourse, it is the authority figure (police officer) whose words have the marked form, nonpast for a past event; the nonauthority figure always has the unmarked past tense.

This story from Philadelphia is one source of Wolfson's finding that neither tense is marked in itself, that what is marked is the switch, that indeed the past may be the marked tense. Discovering the organization of the story in terms of verses, stanzas, and scenes underscores her observation.

The short introductory scene begins with the general present (twice) and then has the past (twice). The second scene is entirely in the past for its first stanza (A), the past, general present, and past for the second stanza (B), the past, general present, and past for the third stanza (C). Its fourth stanza (D) begins in the past (twice) and then introduces a convention of the narrator, namely, that COMMUNICATIVE ACTS ARE IN THE PRESENT TENSE (*calls*, *figure* (followed by quoted thought), *gets on the phone*, *says*). It is the third and fifth verses of this stanza, an INTERMEDIATE AND CLOSING CULMINATION, that have past tense (*told*, *made up*). The fifth stanza (E) has two verbs of saying, then like the fourth closes in the past (*made up*).

The central scene [iii] has five pairs of verses. Its first four pairs are verbal exchanges between the realtor and the narrator's wife. All use *says*. The fifth pair is the outcome, the first of what are to be three outcomes of the theme of the story, acceptance, and its two verbs are in the past (*got*, *was accepted*).

The fourth scene follows the model of the third. There are four pairs of verbal exchange, all in the present, and a fifth pair for the outcome, acceptance. Here the fifth pair is also in the present (*get a call*), and quoted speech (*Okay, she's accepted*). The present tense of *get a call* cannot be explained as communicative, because of the contrast with *got a call* at the end of the preceding scene. It seems that the present tense becomes so much the unmarked tense that it carries through the whole scene and into the next. For the fifth scene begins by repeating *get*, followed by non-communicative verbs now also in the present: *do, picks up, take, goes, walk in, sign* as well as *says*.

The present tense continues through the end of the second stanza (B) save for one verb not in the present. Wolfson observes (1982:36) that it expresses the real estate agent's astonishment when he discovers that the date was changed (*all of a sudden he looked at the agreement*).

The remainder of the story is in the past tense. That highlights the narrator's last assertive demand (*Deal's off* (line 128)). This ultimatum is parallel to the final demand in each of the preceding two scenes. In those two scenes [iii, iv] the demand comes at the end of the fourth stanza. Here it comes at the end of the second.

What follows in all three scenes (iii, iv, v) has to do with acceptance. In [iii] and [iv] acceptance is quickly told in a single pair of verses, short and sweet as it were. Scene [v] might have ended that way as well. When relations of three and five prevail, a third stanza is often a concluding stanza. But given the immediate acceptance in the preceding scenes, here the third stanza (C) is a surprise, a true complication, a bit of last minute suspense. The drama is expressed, not by tense change, however, but by position and elaboration.

There are three steps. Stanza (C) reports refusal to accept, stanza (D) a backing off, stanza (E) acceptance at last.

The sequence of past tenses in these lines can be taken as equivalent structurally to the concluding past tense of scene [iii]. In the context of these last three scenes, then, it is the present tense of stanza (E) at the end of scene [iv] that stands apart. As suggested above, the present tense at the end of scene [iv] is not an expressive change, but part of a continuity of line, not a sforzando, as it were, but a sostenuto. The present tense has become, locally, the unmarked tense.

All this indicates that the expressive or evaluative role of tense change should be interpreted in relation to specific narrators, even specific narrations, and that interpretation of tense change may depend upon a structure of lines, verses, stanzas, and scenes.

6 Overview. We see here a thoroughgoing shaping of personal experience. A mode of shaping which in a myth by the last Kathlamet Indian able to recount myths undergirds and articulates a wrenching vision of the end of a people. A mode of shaping, which, perceived, gives point and proportion to what seemed to lack it, revealing meaning through implicit relations.

Perhaps more than anything else, oral narrative is an indication of the relation between potential and actual in language, the dialectic between potential equality and actual inequality. Every normal child may be born with the potentiality for such shaping, but not every community gives such shaping the same place. Oral narrative is central to a traditional Native American community, marginal perhaps to ours. Evidence there of the nature and shaping of the world, here something that can be dismissed as 'anecdote'. Even when languages survive, there may be no one who any longer has the old skills, or is encouraged to develop them anew. In this aspect of language, many communities may have been richer before Columbus than they and many of us are now.

Too little is known of the life of oral narrative to say very much. All one can say is that it appears likely that language carries with it everywhere the possibility of giving experience the form of story, richly shaped, by means of equivalences and internal relations that make it a kind of poetry. The one universal definition of poetry is organization in terms of lines. That is what we see in this narrative recorded by Nessa. When it comes to the possibility of poetry, Homer walked with the Macedonian swineherd, Li Po with the headhunting savage of Assam.[10] Recognition of this dimension of narrative may make it possible to find more meaning in, give more weight to what is sometimes dismissed as gossip or anecdote, yet is the only articulate form some experiences and lives achieve. Recognition of this dimension shows narratives from Native American communities, dismissed by some as repetitively dull, to be works of art. The working out of this dimension of narratives recorded in the past can be part of repatriation (Hymes 1991). Where a tradition has been lost, we can at least bear witness to what has been lost and help redeem its worth for its descendants.

We can indeed enable participants in traditions to take up such analysis themselves. Such analysis depends upon a linguistic perspective, a close attention to linguistic features and relations, to covariation of form and meaning, but it is a use of linguistic perspective that can be shared, that can be given away. To notice tone groups and intonation contours, to notice recurrence of particles, to notice groupings of turns at talk, to build up a ground sense of how resources such as these are deployed—to do that does not require a graduate degree, but a degree of training.

In sum, there lies ahead a vast work, in which members of narrative communities can share, the work of discovering forms of implicit patterning in oral narratives, forms largely out of awareness, RELATIONS grounded in a universal POTENTIAL, whose ACTUAL realization varies. To demonstrate its presence can enhance respect for, appreciation of the voices of others.

Such discovery does not guarantee that what is said is true or admirable, but it CONTINUES THE TRADITION of discovering in the oral what had not been recognized, relationships, order, and values thought to be restricted to the written. Oral varieties have not only grammar and regularity of change; their narratives have shape, often a thoroughgoing architecture.

---

[10] To adapt Sapir's well-known sentence about linguistic form (1921:219).

7 Elementary linguistics. The possibility of sharing brings up again the opening suggestion that a program in linguistics, socially concerned, should attend to the dialectic of potential and actual. There are many established varieties of linguistics. I would like to suggest one more.

One often thinks of branches of linguistics in terms of the study of groups of languages: Germanic, Romance, Chinese, Finno-Ugric, Athapaskan, Niger-Congo (including Bantu), etc. Sometimes one thinks of the study of types of language, such as tone languages, ergative languages, pidgins and creoles, or the study of aspects of language, such as phonology, semantics, historical linguistics. If there is any simple contrast, probably it is that between 'theoretical linguistics' and 'applied linguistics'.

These two labels can be misleading. Those who work with practical situations do not merely apply the findings of 'theoretical linguistics', for the simple reason that 'theoretical linguistics' does not take into account much of what needs to be known. It abstracts from social life altogether, or, if it models social life, abstracts from its actual patterns, often in an a priori way. Practical situations require a knowledge of language in use, and in terms of the situation itself. They require description of features of language and features of social life together. Application is not a matter merely of implementation, but a matter of acquiring new knowledge. Practical problems are a point of integration, of emergent configurations, if you will, a point on which an adequate theory of language in use will depend.

Beyond this contrast between 'theoretical' and 'applied', there is what one might call 'elementary linguistics'. It is the linguistics someone needs, not to write a grammar, but to read one. To recognize that two transcriptions of a word in a language of concern are not significantly different. To discern that something has recurred in a conversation or a narrative. It is the linguistics that every student of human life should know, that one would like everyone to know, the linguistics that should be part of general education, indeed, of elementary education.

Such a linguistics would be equivalent to elementary 'literacy' in linguistics. It would give a grasp of the sounds and forms of language in general. It would enable those not linguists to make use of material of concern to them.[11] It

[11] This past summer (1991) I received a letter from Coos Bay, Oregon, from the man in charge of cultural heritage for the Confederated Tribes of Coos, Lower Umpqua, and Siuslaw Indians. He knew that almost forty years ago I had sought out the last speakers of those languages, and learned something at least of Siuslaw. We drove down. He himself (Donald Whereat) was a Coos descendant, and knew nothing of the language, but he had systematically gathered together everything that had been done and was known about the language, including correspondence among those who had studied it. He was without illusions or ideology. He simply needed help in understanding what he had gathered—to begin with, the differences in the symbols used by two linguists at different times to write the language.

Virginia undertook to provide him first with an understanding of the sounds of his own English, and then, through that, with an understanding of the respects in which the sounds of Coos different. He could have learned the symbols, the logic of their presentation in a chart, and

would enable them to recognize in narratives points of recurrence and relations of shape. It would enable students at leading universities to understand that when someone says *fightin*, they have not dropped a *g*, but substituted one sound for another, an alveolar nasal for a palatal velar. It would mean not having to start over again from scratch in every course about language at a leading university. It would meant not having to explain the term *aspect* to speakers of a language (English) in which it is pervasive. It is a linguistics that would enable people who can recognize and name so much of what is around them to recognize and name the elements of that which makes naming possible, language itself. And to approach the many social aspects of language, literacy, bilingualism, ethnic identity, and the like, in realistic terms.

Such an elementary linguistics would involve values that have been earned by experience: understanding the potential equality of all languages; understanding the secondary origin of most social meaning and evaluation of varieties of language; understanding as well that disparate historical circumstances shape languages differently, affecting what can actually be done with their resources now.

Elementary linguistics is ultimately a contribution to the well-being of linguistics itself, no doubt, but it is first of all a contribution to society. And it is where linguistics is undertaken to contribute to society that one can most hope for that contribution to be made.

Linguistics is so fascinating that it is easy to forget its connections with the world around it. It is where linguistic work is connected with practical problems and the circumstances of actual communities that one is most likely to realize the need to stress the potential equality/equivalence of all languages, grounded in human nature. To recognize the actual inequalities that obtain. To be brought face to face with the difference it can make to share with others understandings linguists may take for granted.

Many branches of linguistics are in such a position. Their day-to-day experience can be linked to a general good, a humanistic goal, the understanding of the actual life of language, and the sharing of that understanding with others.

REFERENCES

Aitchison, Jean. 1990. Language change: progress or decay? 2nd ed. Cambridge Approaches to Linguistics. Cambridge: Cambridge University Press.

Blake, Barry J. 1991. Australian aboriginal languages. A general introduction. 2nd ed. St. Lucia: University of Queensland Press. [Distributed in the USA and Canada by International Specialized Book Services, Inc., 5602 N.E. Hassalo St., Portland Oregon, 97213-3640.]

Bourdieu, Pierre. 1991. Part II, 'The social institution of symbolic power', esp. Ch. 3, 'Authorized language': The social conditions for the effectiveness of ritual discourse. Language and symbolic power. Oxford: Polity Press; Cambridge: Harvard University Press.

---

the descriptive terms, at any time in his life. It was almost an accident that he reached someone to share the information with him. There must be many such instances of alienation from knowledge of one's own heritage for lack of elementary linguistics.

Dorian, Nancy. 1981. Language death: The life cycle of a Scottish Gaelic dialect. Philadelphia: University of Pennsylvania Press.

Dorian, Nancy (ed.) 1989. Investigating obsolescence. Studies in language contraction and death. Cambridge: Cambridge University Press.

Edelsky, Carole. 1991. With literacy and justice for all. Rethinking the social in language and education. Critical Perspectives on Literacy and Education. London: The Falmer Press.

Fishman, Joshua A. 1982. Whorfianism of the third kind: Ethnolinguistic diversity as a worldwide societal asset. Language in Society 11.1–14.

Hymes, Dell. 1966. Two types of linguistic relativity (with examples from Amerindian ethnography). Sociolinguistics, ed. by William Bright, 114-67. The Hague: Mouton.

Hymes, Dell. 1967. On communicative competence. Research planning conference on language development in disadvantaged children, June 1966. New York: Yeshiva University. 116. [Published as: Hymes, Dell. 1971. On linguistic theory, communicative competence, and the education of disadvantaged children. Anthropological perspectives on education, ed. by Murray L. Wax, Stanley A. Diamond, and Fred Gearing, 51–66. New York: Basic Books.]

Hymes, Dell. 1971. Introduction, Part III. Pidginization and creolization of languages, ed. by Dell Hymes, 65–90. Cambridge: Cambridge University Press.

Hymes, Dell. 1974. Foundations in sociolinguistics. Philadelphia: University of Pennsylvania Press.

Hymes, Dell. 1980. Language in education. Washington, DC: Center for Applied Linguistics.

Hymes, Dell. 1984. Vers la compétence de communication. Langue et Apprentissage des Langues. Paris: Hatier-Credif.

Hymes, Dell. 1987a. A note on ethnopoetics and sociolinguistics. Working Papers in Educational Linguistics 3, 2.i–xxi. Philadelphia: Graduate School of Education, University of Pennsylvania.

Hymes, Dell. 1987b. Foreword. The future of literacy in a changing world, ed. by Daniel Wagner, xi–xvii. Oxford and New York: Pergamon Press.

Hymes, Dell. 1991. Custer and linguistic anthropology. Journal of Linguistic Anthropology 1.5–11.

Johnstone, Barbara. 1990. Stories, community, and place. Bloomington: Indiana University Press.

Kachru, Braj. 1990. World Englishes and applied linguistics. Learning, keeping, and using language. Selected papers from the Eighth World Congress of Applied Linguistics, Sydney, 16–21 August 1987, 203–29. Amsterdam/Philadelphia: John Benjamins.

Lakoff, George. 1987. Women, fire, and dangerous things: What categories reveal about the mind. Chicago: University of Chicago Press.

Langacker, Ronald W. 1987. Foundations of cognitive grammar. Vol. I: Theoretical prerequisites. Stanford: Stanford University Press.

Langacker, Ronald W. 1990. Concept, image, and symbol. The cognitive basis of grammar. Cognitive Linguistics Research 1. Berlin and Hawthorne, NY: Mouton de Gruyter.

Langacker, Ronald W. 1991. Foundations of cognitive grammar. Vol. II: Descriptive application. Stanford: Stanford University Press.

Lucy, John A. 1991. Empirical research and linguistic relativity. Paper prepared in advance for symposium, 'Rethinking linguistic relativity' (May 3–11, 1991), sponsored by Wenner-Gren Foundation for Anthropological Research.

Lucy, John A. (ed.) 1992a. Grammatical categories and cognition: A case study of the linguistic relativity hypothesis. Cambridge: Cambridge University Press.

Lucy, John A. (ed.) 1992b. Language diversity and thought: A reformulation of the linguistic relativity hypothesis. Cambridge: Cambridge University Press.

Lucy, John A. (ed.) 1992c. Reflexive language: Reported speech and metapragmatics. Cambridge: Cambridge University Press.

Mühlhäusler, Peter, and Rom Harré. 1990. Pronouns and people: The linguistic construction of social and personal identity. Language in Society 15. Oxford: Basil Blackwell.

Rosen, Harold. 1991. The nationalisation of English. International Journal of Applied Linguistics 1.104–17.

Sapir, Edward. 1921. Language. New York: Harcourt Brace.

Sapir, Edward, and Morris Swadesh. 1946. American Indian grammatical categories. Word 2.103–12. [Reprinted in: Hymes, Dell (ed.) 1964. Language in culture and society. New York:

Harper and Row.]

Schiffrin, Deborah. 1981. Tense variation in language. Language 57.45–62.

Wolfson, Nessa. 1982. CHP. The conversational historical present in American English narrative. Topics in Sociolinguistics 1. Dordrecht/Cinnaminson: Foris Publications.

Wolfson, Nessa. 1989. The conversational historical present. Analyse grammaticale de corpus oraux. LINX 21, 1.135–50. [Université de Paris-X-Nanterre, Centre de Recherches Linguistiques, Bâtiment F. 514,200, avenue de la République, 92001 Nanterre CEDEX, France.]

Wolfson, Nessa, and Joan Manes (eds.) 1985. Language of inequality. Contributions to the Sociology of Language, 36. Berlin, New York, and Amsterdam: Mouton.

Language transfer and levels of meaning potential in Malaysian English

Peter H. Lowenberg
San Jose State University

Malaysian English is one of the 'nonnative varieties' of English (Kachru 1986) which have developed in many of the multilingual former colonies of Britain and the United States (e.g. Nigeria, Kenya, India, and the Philippines). In these African and Asian nations, English was introduced during the colonial era and, to varying degrees, continues to be widely used as a second language in a broad range of INTRAnational domains, including government administration, law, education, business, the mass media, and literature.[1] The use of English in these settings by nonnative speakers in the absence of native speakers, in non-Western sociocultural contexts, and in constant contact with other languages has led to the development of these nonnative varieties, which are marked by systematic differences from the 'native-speaker' varieties (e.g. British and American English) in the forms and functions of English at all linguistic levels, from phonology through discourse.

Not surprisingly, many of these differences result from TRANSFER into English of linguistic features from other languages in these multilingual speakers' verbal repertoires (Kachru 1986). Past research on these varieties, including Platt and Weber (1980), Wong (1982, 1983, 1991), Trudgill and Hannah (1985), and even a footnote in Selinker's (1972) landmark paper on interlanguage, has generally treated such transfer as no different from the transfer that occurs, often as a compensatory strategy, in all nonnative language acquisition. Such a conclusion is no doubt warranted with regard to the millions of speakers of nonnative varieties who never gain much profiency in ANY variety of English, native-speaker or nonnative.

---

[1] A more extensive list of African and Asian countries where English has some official status in one or more of these domains also includes Bangladesh, Botswana, Brunei, Cameroon, Ethiopia, Fiji, The Gambia, Ghana, Lesotho, Liberia, Malawi, Malta, Mauritius, Myanmar (formerly Burma), Namibia, Nauru, Pakistan, Seychelles, Sierra Leone, Singapore, South Africa, Sri Lanka, Sudan, Swaziland, Tanzania, Tonga, Uganda, Western Samoa, Zambia, and Zimbabwe (McCallen 1989:7–9, *Britannica Book of the Year 1992*:760–763).

However, transfer is also frequently used by speakers of nonnative varieties who are extremely proficient not only in their own nonnative variety, but in a native-speaker variety as well. Among these speakers, rather than an acquisition strategy, transfer is used as a strategy of enrichment for 'adapting an alien code to the sociocultural context of use' (Sridhar 1985:52–53).

This paper will examine the forms and functions of this latter type of transfer in the English of Malaysia. After a brief introduction to the historical and contemporary sociolinguistic contexts in which English has developed and is used in Malaysia, the paper will focus on how transfer from Malaysian English speakers' other languages serves a number of communicative functions along an extended style range, from a formal, Standard Malaysian English to extremely colloquial subvarieties. Particular attention will be given to what Kachru (1987) calls the 'bilingual's creativity': novel ways in which features from English and other languages are combined to enhance the 'meaning potential' (Halliday 1978) of English to a degree not possible in the traditional, monolingual varieties of English.

Examples of this transfer come from both primary written and spoken data, and from the growing body of Malaysian English literature, the latter demonstrating that these types of transfer are indeed recognized by the educated Malaysians who write and read this literature.[2]

Historical and sociolinguistic context. The sociolinguistic setting of contemporary Malaysian English began to develop during the British colonization, from the late eighteenth until the mid-twentieth centuries, of the Malay Peninsula, and of present-day Sabah and Sarawak, which occupy most of the western half of the island of Borneo. When the British arrived, the population of the region was primarily Malay, though other ethnic groups had long been present, including at least 3,000 Chinese in Penang. The initial colonial period, during which the British developed their primary commercial centers at Penang, Malacca, and Singapore, along the west coast of the Malay Peninsula, saw large-scale immigration from Southern China into these centers (Hirschman 1985). With subsequent increased British development of the region came further immigration of Chinese and of South Asians from India and Ceylon (present-day Sri Lanka) to fill the growing need for labor for which the Malay population was insufficient (Thomas 1983). Large numbers of the Chinese came to work as indentured laborers in the tin mines, while many South Asians were recruited to work on the expanding rubber and coffee plantations and on construction of a railroad. However, over time, large populations of both Chinese and South Asians migrated to the coastal cities (Platt and Weber 1980).

---

[2] The value of literary data as a supplementary source in linguistic analysis has been demonstrated convincingly by Lakoff and Tannen (1984) and by Tannen (1989). In Malaysia, literature has been analyzed by the anthropologist David Banks (1986:13) as useful 'social science data' which can 'redress the tendency of anthropologists ... to disregard the informed opinion of local intellectuals.'

As a result of these immigrations, the population of the area constituting present-day Malaysia became and remains extremely multi-ethnic, including, in Malaysia's 1991 estimated population of 18.2 million, 61.4% indigenous groups, mostly Malay; 30.0% Chinese; and 8.1% South Asian (*Britannica Book of the Year 1992*). The dominant languages spoken by this diverse population have traditionally been and remain Hokkien, Cantonese, and Hakka by the Chinese, Tamil by the South Asians, and Malay by the ethnic Malays (Le Page 1962, Platt and Weber 1980, Asmah 1985).

In addition to these languages, from the beginning of the nineteenth century, English was taught and then used as the medium of instruction of schools in the urban centers. Largely as a result of these schools, English became the dominant language of power among an urban, multi-ethnic, non-European elite who became increasingly involved in the day-to-day administration and commerce of the colony (Platt and Weber 1980, Platt, Weber, and Ho 1983; Hirschman 1985). After independence in 1957, English remained the primary language of instruction until the 1970s and early 1980s, when it was officially replaced by Malay (Watson 1984, Clutterbuck 1985). However, English is still widely used by the current Malaysian elites from the three major ethnic groups, most of whom received their education in the old English-medium schools and are still quite proficient in English (Augustin 1982, Le Page 1984). It is this community of English-proficient Malaysians whose transfer from other languages into English will now be discussed.

Standard English: Functions of lexical shifts from Malay. At the level of Standard Malaysian English,[3] transfer from other languages has been primarily lexical (Tongue 1979, Platt and Weber 1980, Augustin 1982, Wong 1982). This lexical borrowing has been largely attributed to the filling of what Richards (1979) calls 'lexical gaps', for which other varieties of English have no denotatively equivalent terms (Tongue 1979, Platt and Weber 1980). Examples of such borrowings from Malay are shown in (1) and (2).

(1) The residents will repair the roofs on a *gotong-royong* basis (*The Malay Mail*, January 12, 1988).

(2) I have often been criticised by my friends for easily bowing down to apologise, but I will always do so—it is required by both our religion and *adat* (from a political speech, *New Straits Times*, April 27, 1987).

---

[3] Standard English, like other 'standard' languages, has always been extremely difficult to delimit. In this paper, based on Trudgill (1983), Tay and Gupta (1983), and Tickoo (1991a), the standard model of a variety of English, native or nonnative, is operationally defined as the linguistic forms of that variety that are normally used in formal speaking and writing by speakers who have received the highest level of education available in that variety. Standard English is the accepted model for official, journalistic, and academic writing; for public speaking before an audience or on radio or television; and for use as a medium and/or subject of instruction in the schools. For further discussion of features of Standard Malaysian English, see Lowenberg (1989).

Both of these italicized terms refer to institutions with characteristics unique to Malay-speaking Southeast Asia: *gotong-royong* to a form of communal cooperation, and *adat* to a body of traditional law.

However, the impact on English of transfer from other languages is more evident in what Richards (1979) terms 'lexical shifts', where borrowings replace English words or phrases which are denotatively, but not connotatively, equivalent. The most striking of these lexical shifts are what Paine (1981:14) has called BANNER WORDS: 'single words or phrases ... that are likely to induce a proposition by inference.' Examples of such banner words in American English are *democracy* and *freedom fighters*, which trigger in most Americans complex schemata of values and associations that politicians repeatedly appeal to when seeking popular support (Parkin 1984, Geis 1987).

In Malaysian English, such banner words are most often transferred from Bahasa Malaysia, a variety of Malay that has become Malaysia's national and, despite resistance from many non-Malays, sole official language (Watson 1984, Clutterbuck 1985, Means 1991). An example occurs in (3), where the Malay word *Merdeka* signifies achievement of independence from colonial rule (August 31, 1957).

(3) Earlier, speaking at the opening of the Sekolah Kebangsaan Lumut, he suggested that certain old schools built before *Merdeka* be turned into museums to motivate pupils (*New Straits Times*, March 20, 1989).

This use of *Merdeka* in Malaysia's leading English-language newspaper, the *New Straits Times*, which is owned by the ruling political party and is circulated nationwide (Means 1991), tends to associate the entire concept of Malaysian nationhood with the language of the ethnic Malays. In contrast, the English equivalent, *independence*, would denote the same concept without making any group or their language predominant.

The banner word most frequently appearing in the Malaysian English-language press is *Bumiputera* (literally, 'sons of the soil'). This borrowing refers to people considered indigenous to Malaysia, predominantly the ethnic Malays, but also officially includes other ethnic groups, especially in Sabah and Sarawak, who are neither Malays nor descendants of Chinese or South Asian immigrants. Continuing a policy initiated by the British colonizers to appease local Malay rulers (Watson 1984, Means 1991), *Bumiputera* is today most often used in the context of a large number of land tenure, political, employment, investment, and educational programs which favor these indigenous peoples in order to elevate their economic status to parity with urban Chinese and South Asian Malaysians, many of whose families became quite wealthy during the colonial and immediate post-colonial eras (Clutterbuck 1985, Davey 1990, Means 1991).[4] The word

---

[4] According to amendments in 1971 to the National Sedition Ordinance, the mass media are prohibited from any discussion of these special rights of *Bumiputeras* (Means 1991).

Bumiputera's roots in Sanskrit, long considered the most classical and scholarly language of the Malay Archipelago (Alisjahbana 1976), tend to neutralize this deliberate inequity in official policy while lending it nationalistic legitimacy.[5] The frequency with which *Bumiputera* is used is demonstrated by its following four occurrences in the *New Straits Times* during a six-day period: in a news report (4), in employment advertisements (5 and 6), and in an announcement of scholarship opportunities (7).

(4) In addition, *Bumiputera* equity participation in the corporate sector increased from 4.3 per cent in 1971 to 17.8 in 1985, although half of it was held through Government agencies and trustees ... (*New Straits Times*, March 22, 1989).

(5) OFFICE COORDINATOR wanted. Varsity/college graduate (any discipline). Male/female. *Bumiputera.* Sociable, able to mix well with people, fluent in English ... (*New Straits Times*, March 25, 1989).

(6) PRECISION TUBE PRODUCT requires ... 2) *Bumiputera* female Secretary with secretarial qualifications. 2 years experience and fluent in English (*New Straits Times*, March 20, 1989).

(7) *Bumiputera* students, including those who are pursuing Matriculation Courses in any local Universities, are encouraged to apply (*New Straits Times*, March 25, 1989).

Though, as noted above, *Bumiputera* officially includes not only Malays but also many other indigenous ethnic groups, its range is, in fact, frequently restricted to just the Malays, as indicated in the political speech reported in (8).

(8) Deputy Prime Minister Ghafar Baba has been appointed the head of a high-powered committee to review the New Economic Policy (NEP) and formulate a new policy to help *Bumiputeras* own 50 per cent of the nation's wealth by the year 2000 ... Encik Ghafar said the new policy was expected to 'give *Malays* equality with the other races in the real sense of the word' ... 'I need the support and prayers of all *Bumiputeras* in this venture to improve the well-being of *the race*,' he added (*New Straits Times*, March 23, 1987).

Equally significant is the explicit exclusion from Bumiputera status of

[5] Kachru (1992) reports that the word *Bumiputera* has the same exclusionary function in parts of India. In Malaysia's neighbor Indonesia, another Sanskrit-based word, *Pribumi* 'first on the soil', is used to favor indigenous people over descendants of Chinese and other immigrants in a similar series of economic and educational programs (Wickman 1983).

'immigrant races'—Malaysians of Chinese or South Asian descent (Clutterbuck 1985:377)—many of whose families have lived in the region for several generations if not centuries (Hirschman 1985). Malaysians with these backgrounds are defined by the government as a single population with fewer rights and privileges than the *Bumiputeras* by being officially designated *non-Bumiputeras* (Asmah 1985:19), as in (9).

(9) Foreign ownership decreased from 61.7 per cent to 25.5 while *non-Bumiputera's* [sic] increased from 34 per cent to 56.7 (*New Straits Times*, March 22, 1989).

Bumiputera and *non-Bumiputera* thus function to exclude Chinese, South Asian, and at times, as indicated in (8), even indigenous Malaysians from a number of rights and privileges enjoyed by their Malay compatriots.

However, in other contexts, another banner word from Bahasa Malaysia, *rakyat* 'the people', is often used to INclude these very groups in order to promote among them the perception of a shared national identity with the Malays. In traditional Malay, *rakyat* meant the rural 'common people' (Watson 1984), but in contemporary Bahasa Malaysia, and Malaysian English, it often refers to all of 'the Malaysian people', as in (10).

(10) Victory belongs to both sides, to the *rakyat* and to the system ... (*New Straits Times*, December 17, 1983, in Rinn-Sup Shinn 1985:217).

The use of *rakyat* rather than the English word *people* in discourses of this type subtly defines in English the entire multiethnic population of Malaysia in terms of the language of the ethnic Malays.

Even when used in its traditional sense of only the rural population, *rakyat* still attributes a common identity with Malays to large numbers of non-Malays, especially Chinese, who live and work in the villages of Peninsular Malaysia (Carstens 1986:1–11), and to most of the population of Sabah and Sarawak. This is illustrated in (11), which reports on a political address given by an ethnic Malay official in Sarawak, where in 1978–79 only 19.8% of the population were Malays (*Europa Year Book 1987*).

(11) Datuk Taib thanked the gathering for supporting him and his policies and urged all to work for the *rakyat* to ensure the Fifth Malaysia Plan was successfully implemented (*New Straits Times*, January 24, 1985).

Similarly, though not employing such banner words as *Bumiputera* and *rakyat*, (12) from neighboring Sabah, where in 1978 only 5.1% of the population were ethnic Malays (*Europa Year Book 1987*), likewise demonstrates the use of lexical transfer from Bahasa Malaysia to English in order to promote a shared identity with Malays.

(12) A night to remember. '*Mengalai begitu dong*!' says the expert to one of the *makchiks*. The sporting *neneks* sang and '*mengalaid*' through the night (*Sabah Times*, June 20, 1980:13).

This is the caption to a photo accompanying a feature English-language article in the women's section of a major newspaper in Kota Kinabalu, the capital of Sabah. The article describes an in-service training course for elderly midwives from remote villages in Sabah. Of particular interest here are the words *nenek* and *makchik*, affectionate Malay terms for 'grandmother' and 'older woman', respectively. In this article, these Malay words refer to women who are not ethnically Malay, thereby defining them in English in the terms of the nationally dominant Malays.[6]

As with *non-Bumiputera* in (9), the transfer of banner and other words from Bahasa Malaysia into the English-language press in (10–12) serves to define large non-Malay populations in Malay terms.[7] This encoding of the relative status of other ethnic groups through the language of the politically most powerful group, the Malays, illustrates an observation by Tromel-Plotz (1981:76 in Kachru 1986:23), that 'only the powerful can define others and make their definitions stick. By having their definitions accepted they appropriate more power.' From a broader perspective, the use of borrowings such as *Bumiputera* and *rakyat* in English, alternately to exclude and to include non-Malays in a Malay-dominated society, illustrates Halliday's observation (this volume) that language both CONSTRUES and ENACTS social realities.[8]

Colloquial English: Code mixing and code switching. In the more colloquial subvarieties of Malaysian English, transfer from other languages expands from lexical borrowings to more extensive code alternations, and the

---

[6] The word *mengalai* is glossed in the article as meaning 'to disco' in this context. *Mengalai begitu dong* can be translated as 'dance like this'.

[7] That non-Malays are sensitive to these functions of Bahasa Malaysia is indicated by Llamzon's (1978:90) observation that

> the feeling is prevalant, though frequently unexpressed, that the language is still very much identified with a group; that Bahasa Malaysia is unable to transcend the narrow confines of its ethnic identity; that the propagation of the language is nothing more than an attempt on the part of its native speakers to assert their superiority and heighten rivalry and competition by placing the other groups in the country at a disadvantage.

[8] From this perspective, borrowings for purposes of exclusion, such as *Bumiputera* and *non-Bumiputera*, could be functioning as exponents of what Fasold (1984:3, based on Fishman 1968) terms NATIONISM, the 'pragmatic problems of governing', particularly in 'general government administration and education'. In contrast, the function of borrowings for purposes of inclusion, such as *rakyat*, would be to promote NATIONALISM, 'feelings that develop from and support nationalities' (Fasold 1984:3, also based on Fishman 1968).

pragmatic functions of transfer become more affective and interpersonal.[9] In the examples in (13), from informal letters written between English-medium-educated ethnic Malay students attending universities in the United States, the code shifts appear to foreground feelings of friendship, rapport, and intimacy.[10]

(13) I'm trying to study, *tapi tak boleh.*
'I'm trying to study, but I can't'

Charleston is so boring *kalau you tak ada.*
'Charleston is so boring when you're not here'
(Meedin 1985:18)

The extended dinner-time conversation in (14) also occurred among English-medium-educated ethnic Malay university students in the United States.[11]

(14) Shah: *Apa you tengok tu*?
'What are you watching?'

Zainal: *Airwolf.*

Shah: Ah, *sudah* ... News in five minutes ...
'Ah, it's over'
News *sekarang*? Oh, I'm sorry.
'News now?'
See, in Texas it's different. Uh, prime time starts at seven.

Zainal: Seven?

Shah: And then, you know, the news is at ten, and then they have *Nightline*, and then they have *Johnny Carson Show* at 10:30.

Zainal: I haven't been to Texas.

---

[9] Unlike the banner words discussed earlier, in the more colloquial subvarieties of Malaysian English, transfer occurs not just from Bahasa Malaysia, but also from several of the other widely used ethnic languages, including Tamil and several varieties of Chinese (Platt and Weber 1980, Wong 1982). The examples in this discussion, however, largely involve transfer from Malay.

[10] Markers of colloquial Malay in (13) are *tapi* 'but' and *tak* 'not' instead of Standard Bahasa Malaysia *tetapi* and *tidak*, respectively. Another marker of informality is the use of English *you* in place of a number of second-person personal pronouns available in Malay (Hussain 1979).

[11] Unpublished data collected by Noor Liza Mohd Isa, Department of Linguistics, Georgetown University.

Shah: Texas is a very simple state. Very, very wealthy state ... extremely wealthy ... Well, to me, anyway, I can see the wealth ... *Sana macam* shopping mall ... they've got
'There is a type of'
exclusively *orang kaya punya*, and uh, parking, valet
'rich people'
parking ... you want to go shopping, valet parking ... when you *masuk*, red-carpet ... you *masuk ke dalam*,
'enter' 'go inside'
my God, they, that's expensive place *lah*, and,
(emphatic particle)
see there, in Texas, even the rich people there *pakai*
'wear'
jeans and cowboy shirt, but then they wear custom-made cowboy shoes, you know. To have a cowboy boot custom-made costs you about $1500, $1800.

Liza: Why is it so expensive?

Shah: Custom-made.

Liza: Yeah ... but in Malaysia ...

Shah: *Itu janganlah* compare! *Janganlah gitu*!
'Don't compare like that! Don't do that'

The initial question in this exchange is in Malay, but the conversation then shifts to English, with occasional Malay borrowings, as Shah completes a descriptive account about shopping malls in Texas. However, in admonishing Liza not to compare the prices of boots in Texas with those in Malaysia, Shah shifts back to Malay. These exchanges in (13) and (14) both suggest that changes in the type of alternation between languages can coincide with changes in speakers' pragmatic intentions.

A particularly frequent marker of colloquial Malaysian English in (14) is the emphatic particle *lah* (sometimes *la*) as in *that's expensive place lah*, which is commonly used to foreground familiarity and rapport in informal conversations among close friends or intimates. This particle, which is also a marker of colloquial Singapore English, has been posited by some scholars as originating in Hokkien and by others as coming from Malay, but it is now ubiquitous in colloquial Malaysian English by speakers from all ethnic backgrounds (Richards and Tay 1977, Kwan-Terry 1978, Bell and Peng Quee Ser 1983).

This use of *lah* frequently appears in Malaysian English literature, as in (15), from a short story, set in Kuala Lumpur, about two Tamil-speaking Malaysian university students of Ceylonese descent who are planning to exchange secret love letters during the upcoming school vacation.

(15) ... Rukumani asked Devanayagam, 'This time you think you can write or not? Can send to Amy's house, *what*. My mother likes her mother. I can easily go there to get your letters. Can just put "Miss Amy Wong". She knows your writing and won't open.'

'I think so can,' replied Devanayagam, 'but helluva difficult, man. See *ah*, my sisters brothers all, running all over the house and if I write they all ask if I'm learning and want to look. Also *ah*, if I go post office that clerk at the post office can see me. He's a joker, so sure to tell my father I send love letters. But still try *lah*!' (Siew Yue Killingley, *Everything's Arranged*, in Fernando 1968:195–205).

In addition to *lah*, the particles *ah* and *what*, which serve similar functions of marking familiarity and rapport, also occur in (15), along with the dropping of pronouns made redundant by context, which occurs both in Malay and several varieties of Chinese (Platt and Weber 1980).

That these two university students are also proficient in Standard Malaysian English is indicated in Rukumani's letter in (16), written to Devanayagam later in the story, when they have been apart for some time.

(16) Dearest Deva,

I think of you very often but maybe you have forgotten me. I received your letter about your proposed marriage. If you agree to that I cannot do anything to prevent it and I hope you will be very happy. But I shall never forget you and hope that spiritually we shall remain close like brother and sister ...

The absence of code mixing or transfer from other languages in (16) may result from the change in channel of communication from speaking in (15) to writing in (16). Nevertheless, in the context of this short story, Rukumani's code switch from colloquial to Standard English in these two passages dramatically emphasizes for the reader an emotional distance that has now developed between her and Devanayagam.

In contrast to the highly educated Rukumani and Devanayagam, for Malaysians with little or no formal education, the colloquial variety often comprises the entire repertoire of English (Platt and Weber 1980). This is illustrated by K.S. Maniam's short story *Ratnamuni*, narrated in the first person by an uneducated South Indian immigrant to Malaysia, which appears entirely in colloquial Malaysian English, as illustrated in (17).

(17) *Cheenan*, *Malai*, white *tuan*, I don't know, *ayah Kling* like me look for children like gold. She all holiness praying for more holiness. Govindan, the crooked-tongue, said: 'Your wife is

another *avayar* building steps to heaven' (K.S. Maniam, in Fernando 1981:34–63).

Malay words in this passage include *tuan* 'mister', *ayah* (a term of respect), and *kling* (a pejorative term for Indians). However, the author marks the narrator's ethnic identity through the other borrowings, which are transferred from Tamil: *Cheenan* 'Chinese', *Malai* 'Malay', and *avayar* 'a woman saint'.[12]

Both this ethnicity and the informality of this narrative are marked in (18), from the same story.

(18) *Repot-kepot*, ayah. I cannot tell straight. This Bedong I stay all my life I did not come straight ...

Destination-mastination. This land here I can hold in the palm of my hand. The loin-cloth of the Big Country ... I am *Hanuman*, the rowing monkey for them.

Here the narrator's Indianness is marked by reference to 'the Big Country' and to *Hanuman*, the monkey deity who is a central figure in the Hindu epic *Ramayana*. The novel constructions *repot-kepot* (*repot* is a Malay word meaning 'nuisance or bother') and *destination-mastination* illustrate a creative form of partial reduplication that signals informality in Malay and in several Indian languages; in other nonnative varieties of English, as in Indian English *petrol vetrol* (Kachru 1983); and even in the native-speaker varieties of English, as in American *helter-skelter* and *higgledy-piggledy*.

Another written genre popular in Malaysia in which colloquial Malaysian English is frequently used is the cartoon or comic book, as in (19) and (20), in which a popular syndicated cartoonist examines the 'ups and downs of married life' (Lat 1978:116).[13]

(19) *bila saya bilang* ... DARLING I LOVE YOU! *Tapi dia jawab* OH, SHUT UP YOU! Somebody told me *dia ada lain perempuan*. 'I said DARLING I LOVE YOU! But she answered OH, SHUT UP YOU! Somebody told me you have another woman.'

(20) And about the husband who asked for trouble ... *Saya pulang ke rumah cukup senang hati*, but my *ternampak* lipstick on my *pipi*. 'And about the husband who asked for trouble ... I came home

---

[12] I am grateful to Sundari Naidu for assisting me with the English glosses for these borrowings.

[13] The colloquial tone of these passages is marked by the use of informal Malay constructions, including *tapi*, as in (13), and *jawab* 'answer' instead of *menjawab* (Hussain 1979). The code mixing in (19) is also marked by the construction *lain perempuan* 'another woman', which appears to be influenced by English syntax; this phrase would be *perempuan lain* in Standard Bahasa Malaysia (Abdul Wahab, personal communication).

feeling happy, but my, there was lipstick on my cheek.'

Both of these examples are marked by extensive code mixing, the primary intent of which appears to be engaging the reader's involvement in the episodes by conveying humor through a shared bilingual repertoire.

Conclusion. The discussion and examples in this paper illustrate only a few of the forms and functions of language transfer that contribute to the meaning potential of Malaysian English across its entire style range. At the level of Standard English, where transfer is primarily lexical, borrowings from Bahasa Malaysia can be used to foreground or to neutralize particular identities, statuses, and privileges. At the more colloquial range of Malaysian English, transfer includes not only borrowing but also code mixing and switching as bi- and multilingual speakers and writers draw from their entire linguistic repertoires to foreground informality, familiarity, rapport, humor, and again, ethnic identity.

However, the significance of the forms and functions of transfer presented in this paper stems from their occurrence not only in Malaysian English but in all nonnative varieties of English that have been described to date, including Philippine English, Singapore English, Indian English, Sri Lankan English, and numerous varieties in western, eastern, and southern Africa (cf. bibliography in Platt, Weber, and Ho (1984) for a comprehensive list of studies concerning these other nonnative varieties). As in Malaysian English, research in all of these other varieties is revealing that such transfer often is not a compensatory strategy of second language acquisition but rather results from the acculturation of English by highly proficient nonnative speakers to fit strategies of communication in specific non-Western, multilingual sociocultural contexts of use.

These findings ultimately have important implications that go beyond English to our basic notions of what constitutes 'a language' and 'a speaker of a language'. Descriptions of particular languages—whether within the paradigms of structural, generative, or more functional, variationist approaches—have heretofore generally sought to capture the linguistic knowledge shared by largely monolingual native speakers of those languages. However, as Kachru (1985:26) has observed, 'what is needed is recognition of the fact that traditional bilingual societies cannot be viewed from the perspective of a monolingual society.' Rather, in such communities as those in which nonnative varieties of English have developed, Ferguson (1982:viii) suggests, 'in describing a particular language or language variety, it is necessary to identify its users and to locate its place in the verbal repertoires of the speech communities in which it is used.'[14] As has been demonstrated in this paper, instances of code alternation and transfer, whether lexical borrowing, code mixing, or code switching, cannot

---

[14] Hymes (1984:44) goes a step further in proposing that this concept of verbal repertoire should be 'the central scientific notion' in language description.

be accurately interpreted without reference to the relative status and functions of the languages in these communities' total linguistic repertoires. Continued research on nonnative varieties of English will not only provide further insights about these varieties, but will also sharpen our understanding of the complex communicative strategies that have developed among multilinguals around the world.

REFERENCES

Alisjahbana, S. Takdir. 1976. Language planning and modernization: The case of Indonesian and Malaysian. The Hague: Mouton.

Asmah Haji, Omar. 1985. Patterns of language communication in Malaysia. Southeast Asian Journal of Social Science 13, 1.229–50.

Augustin, John. 1982. Regional standards of English in Peninsular Malaysia. New Englishes, ed. by John B. Pride, 248–58.

Bell, Roger T., and Larry Peng Quee Ser. 1983. 'To-day *la*?' 'Tomorrow *lah*!'; the LA particle in Singapore English. RELC Journal 14, 2.1–18.

Banks, David J. 1986. Islam and political change in rural Malay society: Shahnon Ahmad's novels as data. Cultural identity in northern Peninsular Malaysia, ed. by Sharon A. Carstens, 13–28. Athens, OH: Ohio University Center for International Studies.

Britannica Book of the Year 1992. 1992. Chicago: Encyclopedia Britannica.

Carstens, Sharon A. (ed.) 1986. Cultural identity in northern Peninsular Malaysia. Athens, OH: Ohio University Center for International Studies.

Clutterbuck, Richard. 1985. Conflict and violence in Singapore and Malaysia, 1945–1983. Boulder, CO: Westview Press.

Davey, William G. 1990. The legislation of Bahasa Malaysia as the official language of Malaysia. Perspectives on official English: The campaign for English as the official language of the USA, ed. by Karen L. Adams and Daniel T. Brink, 95–103. Berlin: Mouton de Gruyter.

Europa Year Book 1987. 1987. London: Europa Publications Limited.

Fasold, Ralph. 1984. The sociolinguistics of society. Oxford: Basil Blackwell.

Ferguson, Charles A. 1982. Forward. The other tongue, ed. by Braj B. Karchru, 1st edn., vii–xi. Urbana: University of Illinois Press.

Fernando, Lloyd (ed.) 1968. Twenty-two Malaysian stories. Singapore: Heinemann Educational Books.

Fernando, Lloyd (ed.) 1981. Malaysian short stories. Kuala Lumpur: Heinemann Educational Books.

Fishman, Joshua. 1968. Nationality-nationalism and nation-nationism. Language problems of developing nations, ed. by Joshua Fishman, Charles Ferguson, and Jyotirindra Das Gupta, 39–52. New York: John Wiley and Sons.

Geis, Michael L. 1987. The language of politics. New York: Springer-Verlag.

Halliday, M.A.K. 1978. Language as social semiotic: The social interpretation of language and meaning. Baltimore: University Park Press.

Hirschman, Charles. 1985. The society and its environment. Malaysia: A country study, ed. by Frederica M. Bunge, 67–127. Washington, DC: Foreign Area Studies, the American University.

Hua Wu Yin. 1983. Class and communalism in Malaysia. London: Marram Books.

Hussain, Khalid M. 1979. Kamus dwibahasa: Bahasa Inggeris—Bahasa Malaysia. Kuala Lumpur: Dewan Bahasa dan Pustaka.

Hymes, Dell. 1984. Sociolinguistics: Stability and consolidation. International Journal of the Sociology of Language 45.39–45.

Kachru, Braj B. 1983. The Indianization of English. New Delhi: Oxford University Press.

Kachru, Braj B. 1985. The bilingual's creativity. Annual Review of Applied Linguistics, 6.20–33.

Kachru, Braj B. 1986. The alchemy of English. Oxford: Pergamon Press. [Reprinted, 1990, Urbana: University of Illinois Press.]

Kachru, Braj B. 1987. The bilingual's creativity: Discoursal and stylistic strategies in contact literatures. Discourse across cultures: Strategies in world Englishes, ed. by Larry E. Smith, 125-40. New York: Prentice Hall.

Kachru, Braj B. 1992. Meaning in deviation: Toward understanding non-native English texts. The other tongue. 2nd edn., ed. by Braj B. Kachru, 301-26. Urbana: University of Illinois Press.

Kwan-Terry, A. 1978. The meaning and the source of the 'la' and 'what' particles in Singapore English. RELC Journal 8, 2.22-36.

Lakoff, Robin Tolmach, and Deborah Tannen. 1984. Conversational strategy and metastrategy in a pragmatic theory: The example of *Scenes from a marriage*. Semiotica 49, 3-4.323-46.

Lat. 1978. Lat's lot (2nd collection). Kuala Lumpur: Berita Publishing Sdn. Bhd.

Le Page, Robert B. 1962. Multilingualism in Malaya. Symposium on multilingualism. [Proceedings of the second meeting of the Inter-African Committee on Linguistics, July 16-21, 1962, Brazzaville] London: Committee for Technical Cooperation in Africa.

Le Page, Robert B. 1984. Retrospect and prognosis in Malaysia and Singapore. International Journal of the Sociology of Language 45.113-26.

Llamzon, Teodoro A. 1978. English and the national languages in Malaysia, Singapore, and the Philippines: A sociolinguistic comparison. Cross Currents 5, 1.87-104.

Lowenberg, Peter H. 1988. Malay in Indonesia, Malaysia, and Singapore: Three faces of a national language. With forked tongues: What are national languages good for? ed. by Florian Coulmas, 146-79. Ann Arbor: Karoma Publishers.

Lowenberg, Peter H. 1989. Testing English as a world language: Issues in assessing nonnative proficiency. Georgetown University Round Table on Languages and Linguistics 1989, ed. by James E. Alatis, 216-27. Washington, DC: Georgetown University Press.

McCallen, Brian. 1989. English: A world commodity. London: The Economist Intelligence Unit.

Means, Gordon P. 1991. Malaysian politics: The second generation. Singapore: Oxford University Press.

Meedin, Hafriza. 1985. Code-switching, Malaysian style. Unpublished manuscript. Department of Linguistics, Georgetown University.

Noss, Richard B. (ed.) 1983. Varieties of English in Southeast Asia. Singapore: SEAMEO Regional Language Centre. [Anthology Series 11]

Paine, Robert. 1981. When saying is doing. Politically speaking, ed. by Robert Paine, 9-23. Philadelphia: Institute for the Study of Human Issues.

Parkin, David. 1984. Political language. Annual Review of Anthropology, 13.345-65.

Platt, John, and Heidi Weber. 1980. English in Singapore and Malaysia. Kuala Lumpur: Oxford University Press.

Platt, John, Heidi Weber, and Mian Lian Ho. 1983. Singapore and Malaysia. Amsterdam and Philadelphia: John Benjamins. [Volume 4 in Varieties of English around the world.]

Platt, John, Heidi Weber, and Mian Lian Ho. 1984. The new Englishes. London: Routledge and Kegan Paul.

Richards, Jack C. 1979. Rhetorical and communicative styles in the new varieties of English. Language Learning 29, 1.1-25.

Richards, Jack C., and Mary W. J. Tay. 1977. The *la* particle in Singapore English. The English language in Singapore, ed. by William Crewe, 141-56. Singapore: Eastern Universities Press.

Selinker, Larry. 1972. Interlanguage. International Review of Applied Linguistics 10.209-31.

Shinn, Rinn-Sup. 1985. Government and politics. Malaysia: A country study, ed. by Frederica M. Bunge, 185-231. Washington, DC: Foreign Area Studies, The American University.

Sridhar, Kamal K. 1985. Sociolinguistic theories and non-native varieties of English. Lingua 68.85-104.

Tannen, Deborah. 1989. Talking voices: Repetition, dialogue, and imagery in conversational discourse. Cambridge: Cambridge University Press.

Tay, Mary W. J., and Anthea Fraser Gupta. 1983. Towards a description of Standard Singapore English. Varieties of English in Southeast Asia, ed. by Richard Noss, 173-89. Singapore: SEAMEO Regional Language Centre. [Anthology Series 11]

Thomas, R. Murray. 1983. Malaysia: Cooperation versus competition—or national unity versus favored access to education. Politics and education: Case studies from eleven nations, ed. by R. Murray Thomas, 149–68. Oxford: Pergamon Press.

Tickoo, Makhan L. (ed.) 1991. Languages and standards: Issues, attitudes, and case studies. Singapore: SEAMEO Regional Language Centre. [Anthology Series 26]

Tongue, R.K. 1979. The English of Singapore and Malaysia. 2nd rev. edn. Singapore: Eastern Universities Press.

Tromel-Plotz, Senta. 1981. Languages of oppression (review article). Journal of Pragmatics 5.67–80. [Cited in Kachru 1986]

Trudgill, Peter. 1983. Sociolinguistics: An introduction to language and society (rev. edn.). Harmondsworth, Middlesex: Penguin.

Trudgill, Peter, and Jean Hannah. 1985. International English: A guide to varieties of standard English. 2nd edn. London: Edward Arnold.

Watson, J.K.P. 1984. Cultural pluralism, nation-building and educational policies in Peninsular Malaysia. Language planning and language education, ed. by Chris Kennedy, 132–50. London: George Allen and Unwin.

Wickman, Stephen B. 1983. The economy. Indonesia: A country study, ed. by Frederica M. Bunge, 119–74. Washington, DC: Foreign Area Studies, The American University.

Wong, Irene F.H. 1982. Native speaker English for the third world today? New Englishes, ed. by John B. Pride, 261–86. Rowley, MA: Newbury House.

Wong, Irene F.H. 1983. Simplification features in the structure of colloquial Malaysian English. Varieties of English in Southeast Asia, ed. by Richard B. Noss, 125–49. Singapore: SEAMEO Regional Language Centre. [Anthology Series 26]

Wong, Irene F.H. 1991. Models for written English in Malaysia. Languages and standards: Issues, attitudes, and case studies, ed. by Makhan L. Tickoo, 97–108. Singapore: SEAMEO Regional Language Centre. [Anthology Series 26]

Meaning, means, and maintenance

Kamal K. Sridhar*
State University of New York, Stony Brook

1 Introduction. The language scene in India provides a unique mosaic of linguistic diversity and heterogeneity. Bilingualism is a natural state of behavior in India. As Pandit (1972) explains it, a Gujarati spice merchant settled in Bombay can simultaneously control five or six languages. Such a merchant will speak Gujarati in his family domain, Marathi in a vegetable market, Hindi with the milkman, Kacci and Konkani in trading circles, and even English on formal occasions. Such a person may be poorly rated in the area of implicit knowledge of linguistic rules of these languages, but in terms of verbal linguistic ability, he can easily be labelled a multilingual, fairly proficient in controlling different life situations with ease and skill.

Historical reasons contributed to the linguistic reorganization of India, with 12 major language areas, each identified by a distinct language being spoken by the majority of the people in that region. Apart from the dominant regional language, every region is inhabited by several types of minority language speakers, for example, speakers of tribal languages, migrant language speakers, religious minorities, etc. The intensity of minority language speakers varies from one state to another, ranging between 5% in Kerala to 84.5% in Nagaland. These minority speakers tend to maintain their native languages, at least in the home domain (Pandit 1977, 1978; Srivastava 1988, Mohanlal and Dua 1983). They do so for maintaining ethnic separateness as well as for separating the home life from public life. The minority community acquires the language of the host community for survival purposes (e.g. for communicating with neighbors and colleagues, for jobs, etc.).

For this reason, in spite of mass illiteracy, a societal type of bilingualism/multilingualism (e.g. the case of the Gujarati spice merchant) has become the life and blood of India's verbal repertoire. It is this type of bilingualism that needs to be investigated further.

It is also often claimed that a distinctive feature of Indian bilingualism is its

* The author would like to thank Ms. Hema Shah for helping collect the Gujarati data and the Gujarati community for their participation.

stability, that is, speakers of Indian languages tend to maintain their languages over generations and centuries, even when they live away from the region where it is spoken (Agnihotri 1979, Bhatia 1981, Gambhir 1981, Moag 1978). Although this claim has not gone unchallenged, especially with reference to the loss of some tribal languages (Chakledar 1981, Ekka 1979, Mahapatra 1979), there is enough evidence of long-range maintenance to warrant a detailed study of this phenomenon. The migrant speech communities continue to speak their own language in the home domain. Through their mother tongues, they endeavor to maintain their ethnic boundaries. Since both the migrant speech community and the host community agree on limited separation, this results in cultural pluralism. Thus, while the migrant speech community retains its native language as an effective device for ethnic separateness and survival, it may acquire the language of the host community as a job-select language. Such cases of partial shift rather than total assimilation are seen all over India (e.g. the Tamil-speaking Palghat Iyers settled in Malayalam-speaking Kerala (Subramoniam 1977); the Saurashtri-speaking Gujaratis settled in Tamil Nadu (Sharma 1977); the Marathi speakers in Tamil Nadu; the Telugu speakers in Kannada-speaking Karnataka, the Bengalis settled in Hindi-speaking New Delhi (Mukherjee 1980); to mention just a few), thereby providing a case of societal bilingualism. (For a detailed description of Indian bilingualism/multilingualism, readers are referred to Kachru 1986; Sridhar 1985, 1989; Srivastava 1977, 1988).

Several explanations have been offered for this maintenance. In addition to 'group internal' factors such as maintenance of social ties, kin relationships ('a continuous link between the out-of-the-state community and the home-based community'), Gumperz and Wilson (1971) have proposed 'ethnic separateness of home life', that is, a strict separation between the public and private (intra-kin) spheres of activity, as the central variables. The crucial question, as Southworth and Apte (1974) rightly point out, is why 'ethnic separateness' is so critical in South Asia as compared to other parts of the world. They also offer a partial answer by noting that the groups who have maintained their linguistic separateness are for the most part 'rather small groups who could be said to have some particular reason for remaining separate', such as prestige (e.g. Brahmins), particular occupational identification (e.g. goldsmiths, tailors), or enforced separation (e.g. in the case of traditional untouchables).

Coming from a traditionally multilingual-pluricultural society, and given the fact that English is not a new language, would Asian Indians in the United States follow a different pattern of maintenance? As post-1965 immigrants, the so-called 'new ethnics' (Fisher 1980; Saran and Eames 1980), they are here under different conditions compared to the earlier immigrants (Fishman 1966). They are neither victims of war nor victims of religious/political persecutions. They tend to be better educated and technically qualified, which helps their entry into the American middle class without much hardship. Their culture and even complexion is so different from the mainstream Judeo-Christian/European traditions that their assimilation is likely to be at best partial. In addition to ethnic separateness of home life, other variables such as proficiency in English before arrival in the United States, frequent code-mixing and switching in English, and access to the home country through rapid transport and telecommunications are being explored in this study as contributors to language maintenance.

2 Theoretical basis. The theoretical basis for this study is that of Fishman (1966), which involves three major topical subdivisions: (a) habitual language use at more than one point in time or space under conditions of intergroup contact; (b) antecedent, concurrent, or consequent psychological, social, and cultural processes and their relationship to stability or change in habitual language use; and (c) behavior toward language in the contact setting, including directed maintenance or shift efforts. Given that the topic of language maintenance and/or shift among Asian Indians in the United States is being studied for the first time here and given the recency of the migration of this group, comparison across time is obviously not possible. However, comparison across space has been attempted with reference to migrant groups within and outside India. Keeping the above factors in mind, data through the medium of a written questionnaire and through participant-observation was collected from several Asian Indian language communities, for example, the Kannadigas, the Gujaratis, and the Malayalees. Research data from several other Asian Indian language communities is being collected. I have already discussed the data from the Kannadigas in an earlier study (Sridhar 1988). The present study focusses on the Gujaratis. The reasons behind the choice of this community are several. The major reasons are as follows:

1. It is the second largest Asian Indian community in the United States after the Hindi speakers.
2. It has pioneered as a migratory community, and there are Gujarati migrant populations in India as well as outside India, for example, Kenya, England, Canada, etc.
3. It has been the focus of investigation in several areas of the world: Kenya (Neale 1974); Britain (Clark, Peach and Vertovec 1990; Desai 1963; Mercer and Edwards 1978; Patel 1972 to mention just a few).
4. The members of this community are spread across a wide range of educational and socioeconomic statuses.

It is also interesting to note that most studies on this community point out that the Gujaratis continue their traditional way of life, adapting to circumstances but retaining the core values of their culture.

A 43-item questionnaire written in Gujarati was mailed to 100 families in the New York/New Jersey area. A total of 91 families responded, but three of the questionnaires were from recently married couples. Since we are interested in collecting data from second-generation populations, these three respondents were excluded. Responses from 88 Gujarati families thus form the corpus for this study. The questions asked for different types of information in order to be able to document the patterns of language use among the first- and second-generation immigrants to see if there are factors that can be isolated as those that contribute to maintenance and/or shift. The data collected falls under the following categories: (1) background information and profile of the community; (2) opportunities for language maintenance in the New York/New Jersey area; (3) maintenance of ethnic rootedness and culture; (4) parents' use of the language; (5) parents' attitude to the native language; (6) children's proficiency or lack of it in the ethnic language; and finally, (7) the children's attitude toward the ethnic tongue. In the section below, a brief profile of the community is presented. References to an earlier study on language use among Kannadigas (Sridhar 1988) is also cited to provide a comparative perspective on language use among Asian Indians.

3 Profile of Gujaratis in the New York City area. Compared to their compatriots the Kannadigas from Karnataka, South India (Sridhar 1988), the members of this community are spread across a wider spectrum of educational qualifications and professions. The highest degree for the Kannadigas is MA/professional (65%), while only 35% of the Gujaratis reported their highest degree as MA/professional. The community is spread across a wide range of professions and occupations. In the professional category (doctors, lawyers, etc.), Gujaratis report 37.7% (cf. Kannadigas 78%). Half of the subjects (50%) report that they are employed in 'jobs' (factory workers, clerical workers, telephone operators, etc.). Gujaratis are thus a more heterogeneous group in terms of education and occupation. Both groups are similar in terms of their educational background. Both groups attended English-medium colleges back home in India (Gujaratis 94%, Kannadigas 95%); though at the high school level, there is a marked difference between the two groups—more Gujaratis attended Gujarati-medium schools (96%) than Kannadigas attending Kannada-medium schools (80%). These figures are important in documenting their exposure to and familiarity with English, and how comfortable they feel using English. Also, these figures are significant from the point of view of their contribution to the respondents' linguistic repertoire. Their urban background and education through the English medium is suggestive of a higher level of proficiency in English. The fact that in most families both husband and wife are educated and work outside the home suggests the possibility of frequent code-switching between English and the home language, even in informal domains (Kachru 1978, Sridhar 1978, Sridhar and Sridhar 1980, Sridhar 1982). One effect of this code-switching pattern is that the pattern of 'ethnic language at home—English outside' found in traditional immigrant homes (e.g. the Gujaratis) may not be as strongly present in the Kannada families. Instead, the children are likely to be exposed to linguistic input that is largely a mixture of English and Kannada. Also, since more females in the Gujarati sample were educated through the Gujarati medium even at the college level, the chances for ethnic tongue maintenance are stronger.

Another set of data that is interesting for our purposes is data relating to the question of citizenship. A slightly higher percentage of the Kannadigas have taken up American citizenship (males: 45%, females: 25%) as compared to the Gujaratis (males: 27.7%, females: 22.9%). These figures are significant in that they allow us to see if taking up American citizenship can be equated with more assimilation, and therefore, more shift. Does maintaining Indian citizenship translate into more patterns of maintenance? These questions can be answered only by future studies on these two groups.

A number of questions dealing with opportunities for using the native language were included in the questionnaire, and the data are summarized below.

4 Opportunities for language maintenance in the New York City area. It is interesting to note that extensive 'support groups' exist for both communities. Each group reports having between 11 and 34 families in the area that speak their language. The families get together often on weekends and during Indian festivals. Both groups report attending the social events arranged by their respective organizations (Kannada Koota, and the Gujarati Samaj). These events include picnics, entertainment programs, youth conferences, etc. These data are significant in that they indicate a high degree of social interaction which often results in the use of the ethnic tongue. Data on the presence of friends and relatives is complemented by information on frequency of interaction among the families.

Regarding patterns of interaction, 77.6% of the Gujarati parents indicated that they interact mostly with other Gujaratis (cf. Kannadigas 42.9%). Their pattern of socialization is instructive for its implications for language and ethnic maintenance, for studying the process of acculturation and assimilation, and for gaining insights into the process of remaining bilingual. The socialization pattern indicates that both groups are very much rooted in their ethnic culture and traditions, though the Gujaratis are more traditional and interact mostly with other Gujaratis. The Kannadigas, on the other hand, are more cosmopolitan and interact with Kannadigas and other Indians. What was surprising was that neither group interacts with Americans. Very few in the Kannada group indicated that they invite Americans to their homes, while none of the Gujaratis indicated inviting Americans to their homes.

This lack of assimilation is consistent with other behaviors and attitudes. Most Asian Indians are not very fond of American sports, they are still very heavily rooted in their home culture, as is evidenced by the set of data indicating their preference for Indian food, their participation in all types of ethnic events; for example, visits to the Hindu temple and frequent visits with relatives and friends in the area. Most families frequently visit India and often entertain lots of visitors from India. These patterns of socialization indicate that the two communities are providing ample opportunities and avenues for maintenance of the ethnic tongue(s). Since the major aim of this study is to document, in as much detail as possible, the patterns of language use in the first generation, several items on the questionnaire focussed on the parents' use of the ethnic tongue and English in both formal as well as informal domains.

5 Parents' use of the language. Most Gujarati parents reported that when their friends visit them, the conversation is mostly in the ethnic tongue: 55.7% (cf. 19% for Kannadigas). The Gujaratis do not use much English in this domain, only 38% indicated using Gujarati mixed with English (cf. 57% for Kannadigas). A similar pattern of language use is found in phone conversations (Gujarati mostly: 57.3%, Kannada mostly 42.9%; Gujarati mixed with English: 42.6%, Kannada mixed with English: 57.1%). These findings are consistent with studies of Kannadigas in New Delhi (Satyanath 1982), and Gujaratis in England, Kenya, Uganda, etc. This is pretty much the pattern in urban India, with most groups reporting a code-mixed variety with English slowly moving into the home domain (Mukherjee 1980, Satyanath 1982, to cite just a few).

In writing letters to friends and relatives back home, an interesting pattern of language usage emerges. Gujarati and Kannada are the almost exclusive choices of language when the addressee is the respondent's mother (Gujarati: 90.8%, Kannada: 94%). The reason for the overwhelming use of the ethnic tongue is that most mothers of this generation may not be educated, and are thus monolingual in the ethnic tongue. The pattern changes when corresponding with father, siblings, and friends, where a code-mixed variety with English is often used.

Against this background of parental use of the native language and English, it would be interesting to compare the patterns of language use among the children. It is important to keep in mind here that the data reported is based on the parents' report rather than actual samples of children's language use. The validity of parents' reports was confirmed by the researcher in informal observations, though a more direct study is certainly needed. A distinctive feature of the present study is the attempt to present a detailed description of the nature and extent of the children's proficiency in the ethnic tongue.

6 Children's use of the ethnic tongue. First of all, the parents were asked whether their children understood the variety of native language spoken in everyday conversations (e.g. when discussing foods, friends, holidays, etc.). The parents were unanimous in pointing out that their children can understand the ethnic tongue where day-to-day matters are discussed. Probed in a subsequent question about how well their children can speak the ethnic tongue, the responses indicate that majority of the first-born children and a slightly lesser percentage of the second children have this capacity. With regard to speaking ability, this skill was subdivided into four types of behavior ranging from minimal lexical competence (a score of 1 was given for responses in this category) to native-like competence (a score of 4 was given to this category), with two intermediate categories (scores of 2 and 3 were assigned to responses in this category). The results for the two groups are as follows:

	Child 1	Child 2	Child 3
Gujarati	6.1	5.5	5.5
Kannada	2.4	2.1	1.5

It is often observed that the older children in first-generation immigrant families are more proficient in the ethnic language than their younger siblings. This claim seems to be supported here. There may be several explanations for this. Parents have greater control over the linguistic input directed at the first born. Also, presence of older siblings whose language is increasingly affected by the mainstream language may make the younger child's control over the ethnic tongue less secure.

There were several other questions relating to the children's competency in the native tongue. Asked about the language the children chose when responding to parents, the majority of the parents indicated that their children responded in a code-mixed language. When asked if the children seem to be using the ethnic tongue more with grandparents, rather than with parents, the responses were as follows:

	Gurati	Kannada
More with grandparents	45.1	85.7
About the same	35.4	9.5

Once again, this could be due to the fact that the grandparents may not necessarily be educated in English (this is more true of grandmothers in that generation).

The litmus test of maintenance is of course the use of the ethnic tongue by younger generations among themselves. There were a few questions that attempted to explore the children's attitude to the ethnic tongue. As a background for this, parents were asked if the children got together with other children from their cultural group on their own. Not surprisingly, the children's pattern of socialization is much more assimilatory than that of their parents. They get together with children from different language and cultural backgrounds. On a subsequent question about the language used when they get together with other children from their language backgrounds, the Gujarati children tend to use more Gujarati (55.2%), the Kannada children use mostly English (90.5%). The use of more English by Kannada children is consistent with the findings of Satyanath's (1982) study, where Kannada-speaking children growing up in New Delhi tend to use the language of the majority (Hindi and English) outside the home domain. The Gujarati children, on the other hand, tend to use more Gujarati, which is supported in the studies on this community by Mercer and Edwards (1978), Neale (1974), Desai (1963), and others who have looked at this community in some detail. The children do have a positive attitude about being spoken to in the native language. Asked how the children feel about their talking to them in the native language 65.5% of the Gujarati parents (cf. 94.7% of the Kannada parents) indicated that the children don't mind; and 'they like it' was chosen by 57.1% of the Gujarati parents (cf. 26.3% of the Kannada parents). (Note: some parents chose more than one response, hence the figures add up to more than 100%). Very few parents indicated that the children ask to be spoken to in English. Asked about their (the parents') opinion on the future of their language in the United States, 'It will be maintained by a few number of people' was chosen by 86% of the Gujaratis (cf. 100% Kannadigas). When probed in a subsequent question about the possibility of their language not surviving after the present generation, few agreed with this fatalistic proposition. The parents are realistic enough to recognize that their languages should be maintained for inter-ethnic communication. They wish that their children would learn the language and several Gujarati parents indicated that they are willing to take an active part in promoting their language. Probably this explains the existence of several bilingual programs in New Jersey (specifically in Union City and Jersey City).

7 Summary and conclusion. The study is far from complete. As more data becomes available and analyzed, a more representative pattern would emerge. Some broad generalizations regarding maintenance/shift are, however, attempted:

1. Like the Gujarati spice merchant mentioned in the beginning of the paper, the children of Asian Indian immigrants may NOT have implicit knowledge of linguistic rules for their native language; nevertheless, they are not completely monolinguals either.

2. Code-mixing and code-switching are a way of life in India. In previous case studies, evidence such as code-mixing/switching have been used to support claims of language shift, and sometimes even attrition. 'Selective adaptation' or 'accommodation without assimilation' seem to be more appropriate terms for describing these communities.

3. Gibson (1988) claims the following regarding the second- and third-generation Punjabi-Americans in Valleyside, California, which seems to be appropriate here. In Gibson's words, ' ... Parents firmly instruct their young to add what is good from majority ways to their own but not to lose what is significant about their Punjabi heritage. Young people, for their part, adopt more of the majority group's values than their parents would like, but still they resist assimilation, like their parents, resent the pressures on them to change' (1988:198).

4. And finally, it seems to me that the term MAINTENANCE, and thereby, by extension, the term SHIFT, needs to be redefined. Complete maintenance seems to be an unlikely proposition, since it does not exist even

in India. Most bilinguals/multilinguals are not literate in either of their languages, neither do they use all the languages in their repertoire in all the domains. It is precisely this kind of bilingualism/multilingualism that needs to be studied, and maintenance and shift defined within these parameters. This paper is a modest attempt in this direction.

REFERENCES

Agnihotri, Ramakant K. 1979. Process of assimilation: A sociolinguistic study of Sikh children in Leeds. Unpublished doctoral dissertation. England: York University.

Bhatia, Tej K. 1981. Trinidad Hindi: Three generations of a transplanted variety. Studies in the Linguistic Sciences. 11, 2.135-50.

Chakledar, S. 1981. Linguistic Minority as a Cohesive Force in Indian Federal Process. Delhi: Associated Publishing House.

Clark, Colin, Ceri Peach, and Steven Vertovec (eds.) 1990. South Asians Overseas: Migration and Ethnicity. Cambridge: Cambridge University Press.

Desai, Rastimi. 1963. Indian Migrants in Britain. London: Oxford University Press.

Ekka, Francis. 1979. Language loyalty and maintenance among the Kuruxs. Language Movements in India, ed. by E. Annamalai, 99–106. Mysore: Central Institute of Indian Languages.

Fisher, Maxine. 1980. The immigrants of New York City. Columbia, MO: South Asia Books.

Fishman, Joshua A., V.C. Nahirny, J.E. Hofman, and R.G. Hayde (eds.) 1966. Language Loyalty in the United States. The Hague: Mouton.

Gambhir, Surendra. 1981. The East Indian speech community in Guyana: A sociolinguistic study with special reference to Koine formation. Unpublished doctoral dissertation. University of Pennsylvania.

Gibson, Margaret A. 1988. Accommodation without Assimilation. Ithaca: Cornell University Press.

Gumperz, John J., and Robert Wilson. 1971. Convergence and creolization: A case from the Indo-Aryan Dravidian border. Pidginization and Creolization of Languages, ed. by Dell Hymes, 151–67. Cambridge University Press.

Kachru, Braj B. 1978. Toward structuring code-mixing: An Indian perspective. Aspects of Sociolinguistics in South Asia. International Journal of the Sociology of Language 16.27–46.

Kachru, Braj B. 1986. The Alchemy of English. Oxford: Pergamon Press.

Kachru, Braj B., and S.N. Sridhar (eds.) 1978. Aspects of Sociolinguistics in South Asia. Special issue of the International Journal of the Sociology of Language 16.

Mahapatra, B.P. 1979. Santhali language movement in the context of many dominant languages. Language Movements in India, ed. by E. Annamalai, 107–17. Mysore: Central Institute of Indian Languages.

Mercer, N., and D. Edwards. 1978. Communication and Context. Open University Press, Milton Keynes.

Moag, Rodney F. 1978. Linguistic adaptations of the Fiji Indians. Rama's Banishment: A Centenary Volume on the Fiji Indians, ed. by V. Mishra, 112–38. Heinemann: Australia.

Mohanlal, Sam, and Hans Raj Dua. 1983. Maintenance of Hebrew among the Jews in Cochin: A case study of language use. To Greater Heights, Vol. II, ed. by D.P. Pattanayak and E. Annamalai, 436–51. Mysore: Central Institute of Indian Languages.

Mukherjee, Aditi. 1980. Language maintenance and language shift among Panjabis and Bengalis in Delhi: A sociolinguistic perspective. Unpublished doctoral dissertation. Delhi: University of Delhi.

Neale, Barbara. 1974. Language use among the Asian communities. Language in Kenya, ed. by W.H. Whitely, 263–318. Nairobi: Oxford University Press.

Pandit, Prabodh B. 1972. India as a Sociolinguistic Area. Gune memorial lectures. Ganesh Khind: Poona University Press.

Pandit, Prabodh B. 1977. Language in a plural society. New Delhi: Devraj Chenana Memorial Committee.

Pandit, P.B. 1978. Language and identity: The Panjabi language in Delhi. International Journal of the Sociology of Language 16.93–108.

Patel, N. 1972. A Passage from India. Society 9.25–63.

Saran, Paramatma, and Edward Eames. 1980. The new ethnics: The Asian Indians in the U.S. New York: Praeger.

Satyanath, T.S. 1982. Kannadigas in Delhi: A sociolinguistic study. Unpublished doctoral dissertation. Delhi: University of Delhi.

Sharma, P.G. 1977. Indian bilingualism. Indian Bilingualism, ed. by P.G. Sharma and S. Kumar, 3–16. Agra: Central Hindi Institute.

Southworth, Franklin C., and Mahadev L. Apte. 1974. Introduction. Contact and convergence in South Asian languages. International Journal of Dravidian Linguistics, ed. by Franklin C. Southworth and Mahadev L. Apte, 3, 1.1–20.

Sridhar, Kamal K. 1982. English in a South Indian Urban Context. The Other Tongue, ed. by Braj B. Kachru, 141–53. Urbana: University of Illinois Press.

Sridhar, Kamal K. 1985. Bilingualism in South Asia (India): National/regional profiles and verbal repertoires. Annual Review of Applied Linguistics 6.169–86.

Sridhar, Kamal K. 1988. Language maintenance and language shift among Asian Indians: Kannadigas in the NY area. International Journal of the Sociology of Language 69.73–87.

Sridhar, Kamal K. 1989. English in Indian Bilingualism. New Delhi: Manohar.

Sridhar, S.N. 1978. On the functions of code-mixing in Kannada. International Journal of the Sociology of Language 16.109–17.

Sridhar, S.N. and Kamal K. Sridhar. 1980. The syntax and psycholinguistics of bilingual code-mixing. Canadian Journal of Psychology 34, 4.409-18.

Srivastava, Ravindra N. 1988. Societal bilingualism and bilingual education: A study of the Indian situation. International Handbook of Bilingualism and Bilingual Education, ed. by Christina B. Paulston, 247–74. New York: Glenwood Press.

Srivastava, R.N. 1977. Indian bilingualism: Myth and reality. Indian Bilingualism, ed. by P.G. Sharma and Suresh Kumar, 57-87. Agra: Central Institute of Hindi.

Subramoniam, V.I. 1977. A note on the preservation of the mother tongue in Kerala. Indian Bilingualism, ed. by P.G. Sharma and Suresh Kumar, 21–38. Agra: Central Institute of Hindi.

Contested conventions in writing about the law

Courtney B. Cazden
Harvard Graduate School of Education

At the 1972 Georgetown University Round Table on Bilingualism and Language Contact, Dell Hymes used his time on the program to introduce Susan Philips, then a doctoral student, who reported her research on participant structures in classrooms and community on the Warm Springs Reservation. Similarly, I am introducing Judith Diamondstone's doctoral research on how arguments for a classroom mock trial got written in one seventh grade classroom by placing it in a larger scene of contested conventions in writing about the law.

In his conceptualization of written discourse conventions for the *Annual Review of Applied Linguistics*, Atkinson (1990) identifies three functions of these conventions: cognitive, social, and textual. Omitted from Atkinson's excellent analysis is their function in regulating the meanings that can be expressed.

Conventions are routinely contested in classrooms when newcomers to a way of writing struggle to learn, or resist such learning. They are also contested when writers—students or professionals—violate norms in order to express meanings that conforming to the conventions does not allow. It is especially interesting when conflicts about writing in the classroom can be related to conflicts over writing in some larger domain of social life.

Our case material that suggests such a relationship comes from writing about the law. We are not specialists in the law, and so can only refer to contested legal conventions when discussions of them surface in general periodicals and books.

One set of examples comes from the existence of two competing manuals prescribing the form of legal citations that differ in features of legal register (T.O. 1992). The older manual, *The bluebook: A uniform system of citation* (the '*Bluebook*'), now in its fifteenth edition, is published by a consortium of four Ivy League law reviews (Columbia Law Review Association 1991). The new competitor, first published in 1989, is the University of Chicago's 1989 *Manual of legal citation* (the '*Maroonbook*').

The *Maroonbook* is one-fifth the length and lays out a much simpler citation system. In recommending it, the Honorable Richard Posner (1986:1349), judge of the United States Court of Appeals for the Seventh Circuit, challenges the

Bluebook's hegemony (in his words) and severely criticizes it for creating 'an atmosphere of formality and redundancy in which the drab, Latinate, plethoric, euphemistic style of law reviews and judicial opinions flourishes'. One of his examples, which becomes a point of conflict in the classroom in Diamondstone's case study, is the conventional insistence on referring to parties in a case by role titles—plaintiff, defendant, etc.—rather than by their personal names.

A more interesting set of examples is found in the writings of prominent minority law professors where more than register features are at issue. As described by Jon Weiner (1989:246) in a column in *The Nation*, 'Law profs fight the power':

> [S]omething genuinely new is happening in the world of minority legal scholarship: A body of work is appearing that is radically different from the typical law review fare, not only in content but also in form.

One example is an article by Charles Lawrence in the *Stanford Law Review* (1987:317) arguing for legal recognition of unconscious racism. It begins with the kind of personal narrative that, in Weiner's (1989:246) words, 'has become a hallmark of the new minority scholarship':

> It is 1948. I am sitting in a kindergarten classroom at the Dalton School ... It is circle time ... and the teacher is reading us a book ... The book's title is *Little Black Sambo*.

One and one-half pages later, the article starts again:

> This article reconsiders the doctrine of discriminatory purpose that was established by the 1976 decision, *Washington v. Davis* (1987:318).

Even more complex in form is Patricia Williams's new book, *The Alchemy of Race and Rights: Diary of a Law Professor* (1991). Juxtaposed throughout Williams's book are a variety of genres, including technical discussions of her field of contract law; tales of her great-great-grandmother's life in slavery; a personal narrative of her rage when, pushing the buzzer on the locked door of a Benetton store on New York's Madison Avenue, the clerk refused to let her in; and her later rage when a law review editor radically edited her account of the incident for an invited symposium on 'Excluded Voices', while assuring her his editing was not censorship, 'just a matter of style'.

The problem—for all writers, student and professional alike—is that matters of style can entail matters of significant meaning. As Richard Delgado, like Williams, from the University of Wisconsin Law School, explains (in Weiner, 1989:248):

> The debate is about voice, about making everybody speak one language ... The whole idea of the dominant legal discourse is to limit the range of what

you can express, the range of argument you can make.

In the words of Matsuda, from the University of Hawaii Law School (in Weiner, 1989:246):

> Mainstream legal scholars write as if there's only one way of knowing the world. They all write with the same universal authoritative voice. But when you read Chuck Lawrence and Pat Williams ... [s]cholarship for them is not an abstract intellectual process divorced from experience.

Conflicts between voices that express more abstract process or more connection to personal experience also become contested among Diamondstone's student writers.

The implication for teachers is not that conventions needn't be learned. It is undoubtedly not accidental that Lawrence and Williams are now faculty members in prestigious law schools; and they undoubtedly 'paid their dues' by writing more conventionally on the way there. What Henry Widdowson said in his second talk at the Georgetown University Round Table on Languages and Linguistics 1992 about learning a second language is also good advice for learning second registers or discourses: 'If you want to beat them, join them first'.

But teachers should be aware that written discourse conventions are social constructions and not in any sense 'natural'. Being aware that there are conflicts about them in the adult world should help teachers consider more seriously the problems in learning and conforming to them that arise between teacher and students or—as in Diamondstone's case study—among students themselves. And, especially with older students, critical awareness of relationships between forms and meanings can be an important objective of the writing curriculum itself.

Such critical language awareness is the focus of work by a group of applied linguists at Lancaster University (Clark and Ivanič 1991; Fairclough 1989). A simplified version of their model of language is shown in Figure 1 (from Clark and Ivanič 1991:169).

In Diamondstone's case study, the text the students are composing is Layer 1; the classroom interactions in which these texts are produced (not analysed here) are Layer 2; and the conventions being contested by the participants are part of Layer 3 (as well as, I would add, other class, race, and culture influences on the participants, as Diamondstone suggests in her analysis). About conventions, Clark and Ivanič (1991:171) say:

> Layer 3, 'socio-historical context' represents the way in which discourse conventions for particular types of writing are shaped by dominant views of the nature of knowledge and the assumed relations between readers and writers of this type of discourse. In our view, these conventions are not fixed for all time, but are part of the continual struggle over meaning.

(Parenthetically, it seems to me that in discussions of nondialectal language variation, it is harder and harder to control how a set of terms—REGISTER, GENRE, DISCOURSE, STYLE, plus the admittedly vaguer VOICE—divide up the semantic field.)

Figure 1. A critical view of language: Consciousness-raising about the writing process (from Clark and Ivanič 1991:169).

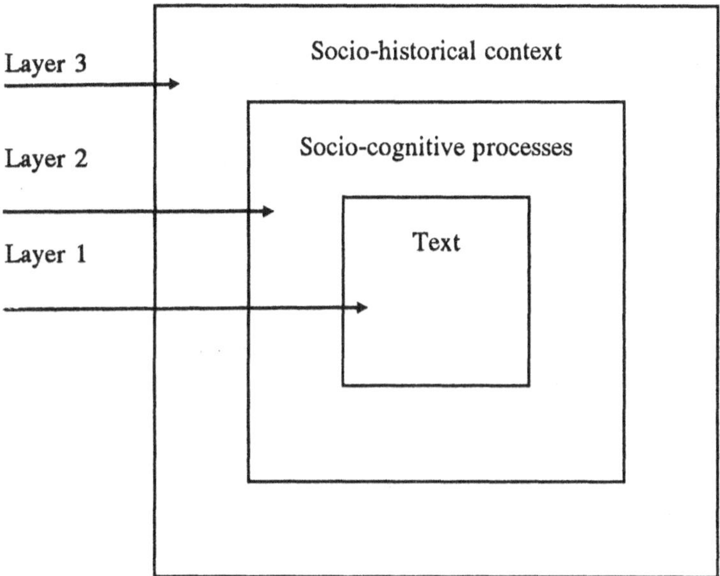

REFERENCES

Atkinson, Dwight. 1990. Annual review of applied linguistics, 57–76. New York: Cambridge University Press.

Clark, Romy, and Roz Ivanič. 1991. Consciousness-raising about the writing process. ed. by C. James and P. Garrett, 168–85. Language awareness in the classroom. New York: Longman.

The Columbia Law Review Association. 1991. The bluebook: A uniform system of citation. Cambridge, MA: The Harvard Law Review Association.

Fairclough, Norman. 1989. Language and power. New York: Longman.

Lawrence, Charles R. III. 1987. The id, the ego, and equal protection: Reckoning with unconscious racism. Stanford Law Review 39.317–88.

T.O. 1992. Maroonbook: Will clarity triumph? The University of Chicago Magazine 84, 3.12–13.

Posner, Richard. 1986. Goodbye to the bluebook. The University of Chicago Law Review 53.1343–52.

University of Chicago Law Review. 1989. The University of Chicago manual of legal citation [The 'Maroonbook']. Chicago: Author.

Weiner, Jon. 1989. Law profs fight the power. The Nation September 4, 11.246–48. [Reprinted in J. Weiner. 1991. Professors, politics and pop. London and New York: Verso.]

Williams, Patricia. 1991. The alchemy of race and rights: Diary of a law professor. Cambridge: Harvard University Press.

Register or relevance? Seventh grade students write arguments for a mock trial

Judith Diamondstone*
Harvard Graduate School of Education

The following study is drawn from observations of a progressive pedagogy, designed to introduce middle-grade students to the discourse and procedures of the law as well as to African Americans' contribution to civil rights struggles in this country. However, the focus here is on constraints on social innovation. During a small-group writing activity, several students imposed their own formal criteria for legal arguments on an African American peer, who overlooked courtroom conventions and included her own perspective in her writing. Ironically, the professional orthodoxies for legal scholarship are changing, as minority legal scholars have opened the question of what counts as legal text in leading law journals. Exploiting the conventions of their discipline, these scholars have argued for and included presentations of their own experience (Cazden 1992). The following study raises concerns germane to the project of broadening access to academic and professional literacies, particularly in heterogeneous classrooms situated in a rapidly changing world.

In the spring of 1987, a talented African American social studies teacher coordinated a mock trial of the school desegregation case, Brown v. the State of Kansas Board of Education, that was decided by the Supreme Court in 1954. His seventh grade students represented the plaintiff, Linda Brown, an African American child who was not allowed to attend a White school in her own neighborhood; his eighth grade represented the State of Kansas Board of Education. A competition between the two grades was set up for a social studies conference that simulated both Supreme Court and lower court procedures; a panel of parents acted as judges.

I was an observer in that classroom, and focus here on four students who were writing closing arguments for the plaintiff, Linda Brown. Two (Nora and Jodi) were Anglo girls and considered expert writers by both teacher and peers;

* This research has been supported by grants from the Carnegie Corporation to Michael Cole, the Spencer Foundation to Courtney Cazden, and a Mellon Dissertation Fellowship through the Literacies Institute, Newton, MA.

one (Tanya) was an African American girl; and one (Derek) an African American boy. The texts produced by these students show that they had different notions of what a good text might be in this situation. Nora and Jodi adhered to the register of courtroom argument. Tanya made her contribution at the level of content. As an African American female student about the same age as Linda Brown, her experience linked her to the civil rights legacy and to this case in particular. Derek, who was also African American, wanted his writing to sound authoritative and allied himself with Nora and Jodi.

As a result, after working together for a couple of months, three of the students (Nora, Jodi, and Derek) produced texts that were schematically sophisticated but lacked moral fervor, while Tanya wrote texts that were highly keyed to the experience of African Americans and the effects of racism but not to courtroom discourse. Tanya's peers perceived her texts to be inappropriate and thus rejected them.

I examine here two sets of transcripts, both comparing written text with the revisions made on it. In the first, Tanya writes a text that her peers revise; in the second, Tanya's peers write a text FOR her, which she significantly modifies when she speaks the text from memory at a whole-class rehearsal. In analyzing these texts, I will draw on background material from the classroom, many conversations with the teacher, and interviews with the four students that I conducted last summer before their senior year in high school.

The first set of transcripts was produced from an audiotape of the students' first session together in late January 1987. The students probably discussed their plans before they turned the tape recorder on. The transcript begins when the students presented, in a prearranged sequence, what they had composed so far. The following is an excerpt of the interaction over Tanya's turn when she presented her first draft.

N=Nora T=Tanya D=Derek ?=unidentified

Transcript excerpt from segment 1, first taped session, January 1987

N: And then Tanya's going to do the third part
T: (off mic) really great
N: REALly great
T: (into mic) You know? really great!
(aside; off mic) You want me to read this?—[Can I just??
D: [Just [read it Tanya.
?: [Doesn't matter.
T: (into mic) All right. I'm doing, you know, I'm like switching the tables around? All right. Your Honor, my name is Counselor Tanya White? (fast and breathless) As you know Linda Brown had to walk several blocks to get to her Negro school. On her way she had to walk past a White school in her own neighborhood. She could not go to that school because of the color of her skin. (breath) Y'you don't want me to put,

put yourself in her position, like switch it around?
?: No.

Tanya's text, extracted from the interaction, follows:

> Your Honor, my name is Counselor Tanya White? As you know Linda Brown had to walk several blocks to get to her Negro school. On her way she had to walk past a White school in her own neighborhood. She could not go to that school because of the color of her skin.

About seven minutes after Tanya presented her text, Nora and Jodi revised it over her objections. Below is an excerpt from a 1.5 minute sequence, when the edits were imposed. Edits made by Nora or Jodi are numbered and appear in small capitals. Phrases of uncertain authorship are bracketed: they may have been in Tanya's original text although she didn't speak them aloud, or they may have been added by Nora in her reading of the text—Tanya kept saying that Nora couldn't read her handwriting. Overlapping turns are indicated with curly braces. Ellipsis points indicate omitted phrases and turns.

Transcript excerpt from segment 5 first taped session (cont.)

Nora: Your Honor, My name is Counselor Tanya White, [AND I AM LINDA BROWN].... As you know Linda Brown had to walk several.... FORGET AS YOU KNOW... *1.
Jodi: THE PLAINTIFF *2
Nora: ....THE PLAINTIFF HAS *3 TO WALK... several blocks to get to her Negro school and then on her way she has to walk past a White school—No... In her neighborhood there is...
Jodi: IN HER NEIGHBORHOOD {THERE IS A WHITE SCHOOL
Nora: {THERE IS A WHITE SCHOOL *4. Because it's not on her way she had to walk past a White school in her neighborhood.]

Changes made by Tanya's peers on Tanya's text.

1. 'As you know' was rejected.
2. 'Linda Brown' was changed to 'The plaintiff'.
3. 'HAD to walk ... ' was changed to 'HAS to walk ... '.
4. 'ON HER WAY she had to walk past a White school IN HER NEIGHBORHOOD' was changed to 'IN HER NEIGHBORHOOD THERE IS a White school she had to walk past every day'.

An explanation of the edits follows:

1. *As you know* was rejected. *As you know* implicates the audience in the speaker's point of view, establishing that what the speaker is about to

present is shared knowledge.

2. *Linda Brown* was changed to *the plaintiff. Linda Brown* is a more familiar address, and like *as you know*, reduces the distance between the attorney arguing for Linda Brown and the judging audience. In contrast, *The plaintiff* maximizes social distance and formalizes the presentation.
3. The change from *had* to *has* seems less significant than the others, since Nora herself uses past tense later.
4. In Tanya's version of the sentence, *On her way she had to walk past a White school in her own neighborhood*, events unfold through the experience of the subject, *she*, in the main clause. The description of place (the White school) is subordinated to the narration of events and experience.

In Nora and Jodi's version, *In her neighborhood there is a White school she had to walk past every day*, there is no subject in the main clause; a subject *she* appears in a dependent clause at the end. The focus is on objects and features, rather than on the walking experience, and the copula asserts the way things are, removed from anyone's sympathies. The speaker and subject are distanced in a world that is objectified. In short, the sentence is written in expository mode.

To summarize, Tanya wrote a narrative argument from Linda Brown's point of view, implicating the audience in her position with the phrase *as you know*. Her sentence puts the judges in Linda Brown's shoes. Her peers, especially Nora, preferred a more formal, expository argument, distanced from the audience and from everyday experience.

The second set of transcripts was produced from audiotape recordings of small-group sessions and a whole-class rehearsal about one month later. Throughout the interim month, Tanya's peers continually rejected her texts. When Tanya tried to rewrite what they wrote, her peers rejected her revised texts and, on several occasions, wrote a completely different one for her. The text I examine here is the last one written for her and the one that she actually performed at the mock trial. It is based on an experiment designed by Kenneth Clarke to show the psychological effects of segregation by testing children's identification with black and white dolls. Clarke's work was mentioned in the now famous Footnote #11 of the Supreme Court's decision (Kluger 1977: 705–706).

Space does not permit an examination of the session when the text was actually composed; however, an analysis would show that all of the lines were composed either by Nora or Jodi, although both Derek and Tanya actively contributed to the session. Tanya, for instance, knew about the doll experiment; she knew the name of the psychologist who performed it, Kenneth B. Clarke, which Nora did not know, and she retrieved a book from the classroom which Nora may have referred to when she was writing the questions that were asked in the experiment. Thus, Tanya showed keen interest in presenting this evidence.

The text in Figure 1 was extrapolated from the taped session when it was composed and from taped rehearsals. It represents the text as it was constructed for Tanya by her peers. I have divided it into constitutive parts, which I have labeled. The text was reconstructed from transcripts of sessions composing it and rehearsals, February 23–26, 1987.

Figure 1. Text written for Tanya by her peers: The doll case argument.

Formal introduction.

May it please the court, my name is Tanya White, Counselor for the plaintiff in this action.

Theme and causal link to client's claim.

We have valid proof that Negro people feel inferior AS A RESULT OF SEGREGATION.

Description of doll experiment.

A man named Kenneth B. Clarke, a 37-year old psychologist performed an experiment to prove this point. He purchased four identical dolls, two white and two Negro. He asked children between the ages of three and seven these questions: Give me the white doll. Give me the black doll. Give me the Negro doll. Seventy-five percent of these children gave him the correct doll. Then he asked these questions: Give me the good doll. The children gave him the white doll. Give me the bad doll. The children gave him the Negro doll. Give me the doll that you like the best. They gave him the white doll.

Evaluation of experiment.

Throughout these tests the Negro children showed an unmistakable preference for the white doll. They identified the Negro doll as the bad doll, thus rejecting the doll of their own race.

Restatement of causal link to client's claim.

THIS CAN ONLY BE CAUSED BY SEGREGATION IN SCHOOLS.

Response to opposing argument.

Rhetorical device (a question implying the negative).

Is this what we want for our country?

Statement of opposing argument.

This is what the [defendant] calls [protecting] the culture of Negroes.

The schema shows a good grasp of what counts as a legal argument. Evidence must be presented so that its relevance to the client's case is made explicit: The findings of the doll experiment are attributed to segregation twice—at the beginning and end of the description of the experiment. In addition, the students anticipated and addressed their opponent's argument.

A reading of the text, however, shows the effect of its schematic organization as somewhat superficial. The doll study was designed to show that Negro children felt inferior, but there was no experimental evidence that their preference for white dolls had anything to do with segregation. The students stated a causal link without saying how or why the findings of the experiment resulted from segregation.

Tanya had several chances to rehearse the text that was written for her—with her group and at a whole-class rehearsal. Whenever she tried to read what Nora and Jodi had written, she stumbled over unfamiliar phrases, such as *unmistakable preference* and *thus rejecting* ... No one explained what they meant or why particular features of the text had been included. At a second whole-class rehearsal, when Tanya claimed she had left her text at home, she was asked by the teacher to tell a visiting lawyer what she was going to say.

A=Teacher T=Tanya S=Student

Transcript of Tanya speaking the doll case argument from memory.
Evening of February 26, 1987 (with Attorney Enrich).

A: Tanya, can you remember your part? You don't have your cards.
T: No.
A: Ok, can you remember SOME of your part?
T: Very little.
A: Say, uh, Tanya, can you please tell Mr. Enrich at least WHAT you're going to be saying during the opening.
T: Ok. You want me to say what I can remember? (Into mic) I'm sorry I'm late, um. Well, I'll be doing the doll case, with Dr. Kenneth B. Clarke? And um, I explain the doll case. And um, you know, I prove—Huh?
S: Tell him what the doll case is.
T: It's a um, it's a an ex it's experiment that proves that Negro children feel inferior compared to White children. And um, in the case, in the it, it, y'know the experiment is proven, by because um, he asked, the doll y'know, he asked children these questions, like, give me the Negro doll, give me the white doll, or give me the black doll? but seventy-only seventy-five percent? of, no seventy-five percent of the children answered the, gave the correct answer. But when he asked, give me the doll that you like the best? right? The, all the Negro children said, picked the white dolls. They identified, the Negro doll, as the doll, as the bad doll, and, the experiment is proven.
A: That will go in between, um, those last statements. ok? Now can we have the closing statement? Then we'll get to questions.

The text, extracted from the interaction, is presented in Figure 2, divided into constitutive parts, with false starts and self-corrections removed. Some features of Tanya's text contrast with the version composed by her peers simply by virtue of its being spoken. It is less detailed, it includes false starts and self-corrections, and it omits words the speaker could not pronounce.

Other features are more typical of written texts. The theme is stated in expository mode in the detached, authoritative register that the copula and the passive tense achieve (*It's an experiment that proves ...*; *the experiment is proven*). It is integrated—there are more hypotactic than paratactic connectors (2:1).

Figure 2. Tanya's text.

Introduction.

Well, I'll be doing the doll experiment with Dr. Kenneth B. Clarke. And um, I explain the doll case ...

Theme.

It's an experiment that proves that Negro children feel inferior compared to White children.

Description of doll experiment.

In the case the experiment is proven because he asked these questions, like, give me the colored(?) doll, give me the white doll, give me the black doll? Seventy-five percent of the children gave the correct answer. But when he asked, give me the doll that you like the best? Right? All the Negro children said the white doll.

Conclusion.

They identified the Negro doll as the bad doll, and the experiment is proven.

But it is also significantly different from the text that was written for her. Below, Tanya's theme sentence is compared with the original.

From text composed by peers:

> We have valid proof that Negro people feel inferior AS A RESULT OF SEGREGATION.

From text spoken by Tanya:

> It's an experiment that proves that Negro children feel inferior COMPARED TO WHITE CHILDREN.

Tanya changed the final clause in the written text, *as a result of segregation*, to the clause *compared to White children*. In fact, Tanya's spoken text makes no reference at all to segregation in schools, which is what her client's case is all about.

Her version of the doll experiment falls under the theme of interracial experience—specifically, on the feelings of children. Either she didn't go far enough in memorizing the text written for her, or she stopped where she did because her text achieved the purpose she had for it. The latter inference is supported by an interview I had with Tanya last summer, four years after the mock trial.

During that interview, I had shown Tanya the transcript from the first small-group session. After discussing why she thought the others had rejected her text, I asked her, of all the texts written for her or that she wrote herself, which one she wished she could have performed. She said she would have combined both the first text, the one about Linda Brown displayed at the beginning of this paper, with the doll experiment, because the first, which tried to put the judges in Linda Brown's shoes, led right up to the findings of the doll study. In her words, 'This [the first text] is just getting straight to the point of what the doll case ... it it's telling THEM, you know, what, you know, what actually does ... another race feel towards your own; towards, you know, another race, what exactly is going down ... '

Perhaps in presenting the doll experiment from memory, Tanya did not place her text in the framework of courtroom argument because she was so invested in the moral implications of the study. As her peers were listening for form, Tanya was listening for meaning. In any case, the students had different notions of what should count as a text in this particular situation.

What was the situation? The students were acting as lawyers arguing in a format that combined juridical proceedings with specific educational objectives. Their audience was broad, including parents and visiting lawyers. The official criteria for judging the students included not only understanding the material but performing it. Finally, the teacher introduced unofficial goals. He encouraged the students to bring their own perspective, 35 years after the litigation, into their arguments. The teacher's goals disrupted the constraints of the simulation. In short, the students were more free to determine the kind of text that would work than institutions ordinarily allow, and more free than Tanya's peers were willing to accept.

In a situation so ripe with possibilities, it is not surprising that the students interpreted the task differently. The interview transcripts indicate that for Nora and Jodi, the mock trial was first of all a competition with the eighth grade and, by implication, an exercise for school, where so often formal criteria matter more than content. For Tanya, the mock trial was an introduction to Black history, and, by implication, an invitation to contribute her own knowledge of African American experience. Regrettably, the students' different interpretations of the task interfered with the educational potential of the project.

What would have been necessary for the students to have learned from one another? What kind of support would be required for those students who have a quick grasp of register and facility with form to attend to meanings that refer to experience they're not familiar with? Or for a student who is morally committed to acquire a register that may make those commitments sound strange? Here, the research literature advises teaching students how to collaborate, how to ask good questions, how to take turns teaching each other, and it cautions teachers not to leave students to their own devices but to intervene directly.

How did the teacher intervene? The teacher had a powerful influence on the students, according to their own account, and visited the small-group sessions periodically. He strongly supported Tanya, not least by insisting that she take a leading role in the mock trial. But he also validated the expertise that Nora and Jodi brought to the group. He acknowledged the status of the experts, and he did not intervene on Tanya's behalf when she had conflicts with them.

How can we make sense of the apparent contradictions in the teacher's actions? As an African American who had attended schools where no one 'gave a damn,' this teacher saw himself as an authority on moral and holistic education, but not an authority on academic writing (which he had problems with himself the following year as a master's student at Harvard [Diamondstone 1992]). And as a Black teacher in a White school district, he was contradictorily positioned: when dealing with the class, he had to mute his personal agenda for radical social change; when he interacted with the African American students, he articulated the contradictions they faced and gave them opportunities to try out the choices they had in front of them.

If we take a Habermasian view of the classroom as supporting more ideal communicative situations than the real world affords, then this case study shows the complexities of achieving them in a classroom heterogeneous in academic abilities and race.

REFERENCES

Cazden, Courtney B. 1992. Contested conventions in writing about the law. Georgetown University Round Table on Languages and Linguistics 1992, ed. by James E. Alatis. Washington, DC: Georgetown University Press.

Diamondstone, Judith D. 1992. Walking that walk, talking that talk: Learning to collaborate. Students teaching, teachers learning, ed. by N.A. Branscombe, D. Goswami, J. Schwartz, 179-91. Portsmouth, NH: Boynton/Cook.

Kluger, Richard. 1977. Simple justice: The history of Brown v. Board of Education and Black America's struggle for equality. New York: Random House.

Contexts for meaning

Ruqaiya Hasan
Macquarie University, Australia

1 Introduction. Let me begin this paper by problematising the relation between 'language' and 'communication', two of the three terms that form the theme of this Round Table. I will present a reinterpretation of this relation, which in my opinion has important implications for the interpretation of the third term in the Round Table theme, viz., 'social meaning'. My claim will be that ALL meaning is social. If so, then the modifier 'social' in the expression 'social meaning' is either a tautology, or worse still it is a potential source of what Bourdieu (1977) refers to as 'méconnaissance', misleading us into thinking that meanings could be other than social. I will suggest that the current interpretation of 'social meaning' particularly as that term is used in sociolinguistics today is theoretically inadequate. Belief in the validity of this term leads to a refusal to recognise certain kinds of linguistic variation whose ideological power is, thus, permitted to remain invisible and entrenched, while the study of language in society is prevented from a deeper understanding of how language is used for the living of life, how it acts in the creation, maintenance, and alteration of human relations, which range from consensus to conflict, from cooperation to exploitation, and from accommodation to submission.

I shall begin my paper by presenting in section 2 a partial history of how the relation between language and communication has typically been conceptualised in the dominant strands of modern linguistics. Thanks particularly to the seminal work of Labov (1972), we are familiar with some of the shortcomings of that conceptualisation. However, it is my belief that Labov's own methodology for bringing language and communication together is not free of problems. Section 2 of this paper concludes by developing this view. Section 3 presents an account of the relation between language and communication which derives from certain divergent strands of modern linguistics; more specifically, it represents the position taken by systemic functional linguistics as that theory has evolved over the years. In section 4, I turn to the notion of social meaning to see how this concept compares with the view of linguistic meaning presented in section 3. In section 5, I discuss some results of a research in linguistic variation which I have conducted at Macquarie University chiefly with the help of my colleague, Carmel Cloran. My aim in presenting the findings of this research is to indicate how the reinterpretation of communication and language enhances the scope of sociolinguistics.

2 Language and communication. Returning to language and communication, I suggest that in fact these terms foreground once again the dichotomy invested in that extraordinary Saussurian pair LANGUE and PAROLE—extraordinary because surely there is no other pair of terms in modern linguistics that has been christened and rechristened at the altar of so many different linguistic theories. We have met the pair some time under the guise of SYSTEM and PROCESS, or as LANGUAGE SYSTEM and LANGUAGE USE, some time as COMPETENCE and PERFORMANCE, or as LANGUAGE and SPEAKING or as LANGUAGE and SPEECH, some time as the POTENTIAL and the ACTUAL, and some time as just LANGUAGE and COMMUNICATION—as in the theme of this Round Table. I certainly do not intend to imply that the relations of the terms to each other remain identical across theories: Each reexploration represents a somewhat different conceptualisation of the two terms; yet, there still remains a good deal in common even across very distinct theories, and from this, one may be entitled to draw certain conclusions.

For example, the reiterated affirmation of this binary division points, at the least, to a conviction among linguists that in order to understand the nature of verbal semiosis, it is necessary to recognise the separateness of these two aspects of the overall experience of human language. But it probably points to something else as well: it shows, perhaps, that we have not yet fully worked out all the significant relations between the two terms—we have not yet 'cracked the code', as Halliday put it in his talk. That is why decade after decade, theory after theory, the terms need to be revisited, reexplored, and reconceptualised. And because linguistic theories since Saussure have agreed in emphasising the distinction between langue and parole, foregrounding their separateness, it seems only reasonable to suggest that what has remained unclarified, what has been pushed in the background and so has forced linguists to revisit the concepts, is some relation that undermines this claim of simple separateness between language and communication.

The history of linguistics lends further credence to this view: from time to time, linguists have argued that language and communication are not just two separate aspects, simply needing to be divorced from each other in the interests of doing true linguistics; they have at least hinted at some positive relation that ties the two together, thus throwing doubt on the wisdom of emphasising only half of the truth, namely their separateness. It is not fanciful to suggest that it is here—in the examination of the nonseparateness of langue and parole—that we might be able to find a more satisfactory interpretation of the mutual relationship between the first two terms of the theme of this Round Table.

What are these relations of nonseparateness, and who advocated them? Surprising as the claim may sound, their first advocate was the great master himself, who while insisting on the importance of the distinction between langue and parole also drew attention to their interdependence: it was Saussure

(1966:18–19) who claimed that

> language is necessary if speaking is to be intelligible and produce all its effects; but speaking is necessary for the establishment of language, and historically, its actuality always comes first. How would a speaker take it upon himself to associate an idea with a word-image if he had not first come across the association in an act of speaking? Moreover, we learn our mother language [sic] by listening to others; only after countless experiences is it deposited in our brain. Finally, speaking is what causes language to evolve ... Language and speaking are then interdependent; the former is both the instrument and the product of the latter. But their interdependence does not prevent their being two absolutely distinct things. (cf. also Saussure 1983:19).

The distinction between these two 'things' appeared so absolute to Saussure (1966:19–20) that he despaired of the possibility of studying them together within the same theoretical framework:

> We must choose between two routes that cannot be followed simultaneously; they must be followed separately. One might IF REALLY NECESSARY apply the term linguistics to each of the two disciplines and speak of a linguistics of speaking. But that science must NOT BE CONFUSED WITH LINGUISTICS PROPER, WHOSE SOLE OBJECT IS LANGUAGE. (emphasis added)

I do not quote these passages because I agree with everything Saussure has to say, but because such passages show that the original architect of the famous dichotomy did not simply insist on the separateness of language and communication, he also recognised certain strong positive relations that tied the two together. The problem of how to describe the mutually supportive relations of language and communication engaged the attention of some of the best-known European linguists: Mathesius, Hjelmslev, and Firth. Mathesius attempted a functional explanation, and amongst his peers came closest to devising a dialectic approach (Mathesius 1964, Daneš 1987); Hjelmslev (1961) attempted to unite system and process by creating analogous categories for their description within the same analytical framework, and by other such formal means (Hasan in press; Martin in press); Firth (1957), inspired by Malinowski's ethnographic studies, turned to the notion of context as a solution to the problem. But with the rise of the dominant model of the sixties in the United States, these views either lost salience or were pejoratively dismissed, hardly ever receiving a fair interpretation. This was only to be expected since none of these linguistic frameworks shared the fundamental assumptions of the transformational grammar (TG) of the sixties. Let me turn briefly to this dominant model, then, in order to see how language and communication fared there.

It is commonly believed today that Saussure's language (langue) and speaking (parole) are interchangeable with Chomsky's competence and performance. There certainly are some similarities between the two linguists: Both assume the homogeneity of langue/competence; both prioritise langue/competence as the object of true linguistics; and both concede (reluctantly?) the possibility of studying parole/performance so long as it stays somewhere beyond the fringes of 'linguistics proper'.

However, in the context of the present discussion there are important differences as well: note for example that Chomsky perceives little positive relation between language and communication. In this, he is far more logical than is Saussure in his recommendations: the idea of language as 'the product' of communication MUST remain foreign to the conception of language as a mental organ. In a model where details of formal structure itself—rather than the human capacity for verbal semiosis—is treated as innate, language change and language variation must pertain only to 'surface' matters; and there can only exist an irreversible temporal linearity between language and communication: one can view language as an 'instrument' for communication, one can point out that the nature of this instrument is not perfectly reflected in communication, but one can hardly concede that language is the 'product' of communication or that communication plays any significant part in shaping or evolving language.

Unlike Chomsky, Saussure thought of language as 'essentially social'—an assumption shared by Mathesius, Hjelmslev, and Firth, which brings them closer to the spirit of Saussure's approach. And while Saussure saw communication as 'psychophysical', he still thought of it as rooted in this socially created language. So he could grant an interdependence between langue and parole—and he did so with a clear voice. But it is precisely this step together with his conception of 'linguistics proper' which leads to contradictions.

As I see it, Saussure's position embroils him in theoretical incoherence, whereas Chomsky's claims are lacking in observational adequacy: the empirical fact is that language, in a nontrivial sense of that term, is not homogeneous. Synchronically, it shows variation; and diachronically, it is subject to change. A linguistics that cannot explain why intuitions about the well-formedness of a sentence differ across the various historical stages of a particular language is inadequate in terms of its own goals, its own standards of evaluation. So language and communication are, in the end, problematic notions for both the structuralist formal models, but the nature and origin of the problems is not the same. This analysis is relevant to my critique of sociolinguistics as practised today, as the closing remarks in this section will show.

It is not necessary to repeat here Labov's masterly critique of these two linguistic theories. This critique did not dwell on the differences between the two models; it focused, instead, on what lay in common between the Saussurean and Chomskyan conceptions of 'doing linguistics'. Weinreich, Labov, and Herzog (1968) and Labov (1972) forcefully and convincingly brought to our attention the problems and paradoxes that inhere in the assumption of linguistic homogeneity and in the attempt to study language in isolation from communication. The name of Labov is rightfully associated with this sociolinguistic turn. It was Labov (1972:184) who presented evidence of 'orderly heterogeneity' in language and skillfully demonstrated 'the use of the present to explain the past'; it was from him that we learnt that no study of language is viable except in its social context; that 'the basic data for any form of general linguistics would be language as it is used by the native speakers communicating with each other in everyday life.'

It was not that Labov was the first to have stumbled upon these profound truths: the ideas were well accepted by many even in America. What carried greater conviction was the particular combination of careful empirical research and theoretical reflection which Labov brought to his discourse of the late sixties. At that point in the history of linguistics, it seemed as if a major step was about to be taken in creating a linguistics which would pay due respect to the interdependence of language and communication while still acknowledging their specificity. Saussure had declared 'we must choose between two routes', because in his opinion both could 'not be followed simultaneously'. For a moment, it seemed that Saussure was to be proved wrong: linguistics was to become an integrated study of both language and communication. It is not my intention to underestimate the importance of Labov's work when I say that these promises remained promises; the expectations did not turn into reality. What actually happened was something rather different: Sociolinguists ended up doing diachrony by synchrony, and sociolinguistic variation was carefully restricted to surface phenomena (Hasan 1989). Let me explain what I mean by these claims.

Labovian sociolinguists—and the name of Labov stands here for all who follow his methodology, which in practice amounts today to most mainstream sociolinguists most of the time—study language change by describing what could justifiably be seen as a particular état de langue, and confronting it with a similar description of another specific état de langue. True that the Labovian état de langue in contrast to Saussure's langue and Chomsky's competence displays 'orderly heterogeneity' since what forms the basis of description is 'language ... used by the native speakers communicating ... in everyday life', but the problem of creating a linguistics of human verbal semiosis such that it provides a viable description of the relation of interdependence between language and communication is not resolved simply by using naturally occurring language as the data against which the observational adequacy of our claims may be checked. Certainly the use of such data is a large step in this direction and Labov must be thanked for turning the tide against navel gazing in favour of audiotaping, but this step by itself is not tantamount to creating an integrated linguistics of language and communication.

In one respect these studies of diachrony via synchrony are disturbingly like traditional philological studies: the study of LANGUAGE change is here transmuted into the study of the stages of ITEM change. Thus one examines how a particular consonant gives way to another consonant; how one vowel, over time, becomes another; one 'word-image' acquires another phonological shape. Whatever the faults of the Saussurean views on language change, his criticism of this mode of describing language change was cogent, and we might be well advised not to disregard them. Accounts of such atomistic changes can hardly be expected to reveal the nature of the massive interaction between communication and language that has to be postulated to account for their interdependence.

Where Labov came nearest to integrating the two perspectives was in the observation that synchronic variation and diachronic language change are two facets of the same phenomenon. This is a valuable insight, but the effectiveness of this insight is compromised by Labov's view of synchronic variation: we are told that synchronic variation, particularly of the sociolinguistic kind, is relevant only to social meaning. It concerns the HOW, not the WHAT of saying: what Labov refers to as 'referential meaning'—the real stuff of linguistic meaning that constitutes SEMANTICS (Weiner and Labov 1983)—is said to fall outside synchronic variation; there is no social variation in 'semantics proper'. But if so, what mechanism do we have for diachronic semantic change? We could say—following the logic of autonomous linguistics—that change and variation in language are limited to surface phenomena, not reaching the deeper level of semantics.

Ironically, we do not need to go far in search of arguments to refute this kind of claim: Labov's own arguments used against the claim of linguistic homogeneity will do beautifully! It might be argued that the Labovian methodology for the study of language in society is the best we have at present; this may be so, but it can hardly be a reason for stopping one from suggesting that we need something better. Saussure restricted linguistics to the study of language alone, thus denying the possibility of combining the two perspectives; Labovian methodology allows us to describe both but only up to a point: its acceptance of some of the basic assumptions of a model that treats language as an asocial and arbitrary system (Gardin and Marcellesi 1987) prevents it from providing a consistent framework for studying the interdependence of language and communication. Saussure conceptualised this interdependence in terms of determination: language as not only an 'instrument' but also the 'product' of communication. The metaphor of determination highlights causality, and the causal perspective is, to use Markova's terms, perforce 'monological' because it is a perspective in which two 'things' are brought together in a cause–effect logic (Markova 1988). This is what militates against devising a linguistics which will account for both simultaneously.

To achieve this we need to adopt a 'dialogical' perspective, which emphasises the cogenesis of communication and language: instead of seeing them as two independent things which come together by what one does for the other, the cogenetic perspective emphasises the fact that in a rather important sense the two are inherently united; one does not determine the other: they coevolve. If we are to create a linguistics that follows the 'two routes' of language and communication 'simultaneously', then we must at one and the same time see language as a system that underlies communication, and communication as the impetus for the genesis of that system. It is this perspective that will explain why the structure of language is as it is and why language is able to meet the communicative needs of its speakers to the extent that it does.

3 Communication and language: A functional perspective. In order to create integrated linguistics, we need to interpret the term communication in a specific way. As it happens, the interpretation that is needed is not a new one: the view is, in fact, widely accepted that communication is not merely 'uttering ... noises of certain types, belonging to and as belonging to, a certain vocabulary, conforming to and as conforming to a certain grammar' (Austin 1978:95); rather, communication is first and foremost an act of meaning, an exercise in intersubjectivity. But an explicit acceptance of this view raises an important question: what forms the basis of intersubjectivity, what makes the act of meaning possible? Dominant linguistics has an ideological commitment to the uniqueness of individuals, which leads it to insist that meanings are in speakers; however, the postulate of intersubjectivity demands that, for any communication to occur, meanings must be across speakers—they must be shareable and shared.

But if meanings are specific to individuals, then on what basis can there be any sharing? One answer has been to cite shared context as the basis for intersubjectivity. But where there is an assumption of the purely individual nature of meaning, the viability of this answer will itself demand a particular view of context: it will imply that context is something concrete and physical whose recognition calls for nothing other than the physical senses, and the 'vocables' are simply 'names' for the elements of this physiologically accessible context. The grandiose catch-all label of shared world knowledge—as if the world was as free of variation as language—is not unmotivated. If we can assume that by virtue of being human, we all apprehend the same 'things', and that the 'vocables' of a language are names for these things, this helps explain the currency value of the vocables in the exchange of meaning. By these steps, language becomes nomenclature, semantics is restricted to being referential, and the notion of reference is reduced to a variety of association or correspondence.

Much has been written against the 'view that every meaningful word is a name and that every sentence is a description' (Baker and Hacker 1985:13), and clearly this is not the right place to pursue this lengthy debate. The point, however, needs to be made emphatically—and has been made, amongst others, by Bernstein, Gumperz, Halliday, and Hymes—that context in the sense of 'occasion for talk' (Hasan in press; Martin in press) cannot be seen as a concrete, physical construct: it is itself semiotically constituted, and by this I mean two things. First, it is not the physical phenomena themselves but their interpretation in a community that is relevant to our 'perception' of the nature of context; and secondly the identity of some context as this occasion of talk or that is, in the last resort, defined by the linguistic meanings being exchanged. So, for example, if while I am browsing in a shop, a shop assistant says to me *Can I help you?*, this broaches a context of shopping; if my reply to this is *No, thank you. I am only looking.*, this redefines the context as not an occasion for shopping talk: the concrete physical situation has remained virtually unaltered, but two distinct contexts have been 'recognised' by the speakers largely on the basis of what is said.

Simple as in many ways this example is, it hopefully succeeds in making the point that the idea of a language-independent shared context as the explanation for the possibility of the exchange of (individual-internal) meanings poses serious problems: it appears that the sharing of meaning is itself essential to one's perception of context. So, instead of equating context with concrete, physical phenomena—with material situational setting (Hasan 1973)—it is best to think of it as part of a theory of how speakers and addressees position and reposition their world by their acts of meaning. And the word 'meaning' as used here refers to a more complex notion than the relation of naming or correspondence. The act of meaning, which is to say communication, is not isolated items of the lexicon or single simple sentences: the act of meaning is in fact TEXT. 'The *text* is the linguistic form of social interaction. It is a continuous progression of meaning' (Halliday 1975:37). This implies that it is the text that identifies the nature of its context. To claim that context is known by text is to say with Hymes that language in use reconstitutes context: communication as exchange of meaning is an on-going record of the contexts being 'created'. This turns context into a semiotic construct whose value and identity is known by the meanings that are meant: context and text are really two sides of the same coin—two functives of the same function of semiosis. The signified context and the signifying meanings in the shape of text are related to each other by realization. This is an interesting conclusion: it implies that the nature of context can be revealed in the act of meaning itself.

So what do contexts look like when seen through linguistic meanings? Granted that each occasion of talk is distinct from every other, is there anything in common across these myriad individual contexts? We are familiar with certain frameworks, such as that of Hymes' (1968), which identify contextual parameters that are relevant at an abstract level to every occasion of talk. These share a good deal with the Hallidayan framework, which builds on the work of Malinowski and Firth. Most readers will be familiar with Halliday's notion of context of situation as a tripartite construct consisting of TENOR (i.e. the nature of social relations between speakers), FIELD (i.e. the nature of the social action engaging the speakers), and MODE (i.e. the semiotic organisation of social action and social relation). My aim is to highlight certain, perhaps not well-understood aspects of this conceptualisation.

In the sixties, Halliday's framework did not differ very significantly from that of Hymes: Halliday's three contextual parameters differently aligned most of the contextual features that Hymes divided into seven. But even at this early stage one difference was noticeable: from the very beginning, Halliday has attempted to relate context of situation to the wordings of the text (Halliday, McIntosh, and Strevens 1964:74–110). With the development of the functional perspective (Halliday 1970; 1975; 1977; 1985; 1991; Halliday and Hasan 1989), this aspect of his approach has become increasingly explicit: Halliday argues a 'natural' (i.e. nonarbitrary) relation between the structure of context and the organisation of language. Given the claim about the semiotic nature of context, this is a significant development, and it may be helpful at this point to spell out the steps in this argument.

Consider first two well-recognised facts about texts: each text is an 'individual'; each has a distinct identity, in the sense that it is not the replication of any other text. And no text can be a complete record of all the meanings possible in a language; its meanings will be a 'selection made by the speaker from the options that constitute the *meaning potential*' (Halliday 1975:37; italics in original). The claim that text is a selection, an instantiation of the meaning potential, is important for three reasons. First, it is a claim that a text is interpretable only in light of the systems as they are shared by the speakers. This does not mean that everything in the text necessarily conforms to such system(s). As Sinclair (1991:492) points out, 'language users use the regular patterns as jumping off points, and create endless variations to suit particular purposes. The variations are not random, but are rule governed, like the underlying patterns.' The underlying patterns are what constitutes the meaning potential. The idea of language as system is essential to even recognise variation: Concepts such as 'same', 'different', and 'original' are unintelligible without some idea of what is POSSIBLE and what is TYPICAL in some environment. This sense of the possible underlies the postulate of language as a meaning potential.

To sum up this point, human language acts as a resource, a meaning potential, whose actualisation in texts is a necessary condition for the construal of contexts, if contexts are semiotic in nature. Secondly, if despite being an 'individual' each distinct text reveals the abstract structure of context, then this argues that over and above those specificities of meaning which individualise texts, it is possible to recognise a more abstract level of meaning, as some type of meaning rather than a specific element of meaning. The capacity of different individual texts to construe context indicates that what is relevant to the construal of context is the abstract types of meaning. This takes us to the third point: if we say that every text 'has' these categories of meaning, we must imply that the entire meaning potential can be described in terms of this abstract organisation. Otherwise individual texts that are only a selection from it, an actualisation of it, could logically not display within them these categories of meaning. We conclude then that it is a characteristic of the meaning systems of human language—the meaning potential as a whole—that it will make possible the construal of the field, the tenor and the mode of speakers' discourse.

This returns us to the original claim: the meaning system of human language is not arbitrary; it is functionally specialised with respect to context. But this in its turn, poses a further question: what is the explanation for the presence of this functional organisation in the meaning potential of human language? It seems that the choice of answers is limited: either we must maintain that linguistic meanings are as they are because they are the signifier of the context of social interaction, or we must rely on serendipity. Systemic functional linguistics adopts the first solution, thus subscribing to the view that the cultural systems of a community are created, maintained, and altered by its semiotic systems: they enter into the cycle of semiosis. Just as text is an instantiation of the meaning potential of language, so also context of situation is an instantiation of the context of culture: a particular context of situation is interpreted by reference to the underlying system—that is, context of culture; and just as the text's meaning selection realizes the context of situation, so the meaning potential of the language as a whole realizes the context of culture.

The functional specialisation of the meaning potential is explained by this semiotic relation between language and context. The meaning system of human language is organised the way it is since language and context are semiotically united: linguistic meaning construes context, and context activates linguistic meaning. This dialectic between linguistic meaning and social context is one important part of Halliday's claim about the functional nature of language. However, the full significance of this claim can be understood only when a critical question is raised and answered: how are linguistic meanings produced? What part, if any, does the form of language play in the production of linguistic meanings?

In formal models, linguistic meaning is some glorified variety of the naming relation. This assumes that things, properties, processes, etc., can be itemised, and their boundaries identified, without any semiotic mediation. The forms of language—its lexicon and syntax—are simply labels to refer to 'what there really is'. Given these assumptions, it is logical for such models to present the relation between meaning and form as arbitrary, arising purely from conventional association. These views are incompatible with a semiotic view of context: in an account of language as social semiotic, it is incoherent to suggest that we can know without semiotic mediation 'what there REALLY is'; according to this approach, what we are destined to consider real in the living of life is at least as much semiotically construed as it is sensuous, with the significant difference that only the semiotically construed has any value for exchange. So far as interaction is concerned, the currency value of private, unsharable sensuous experience is nil. Linguistic meaning is an interface between the world as we experience it and the interpretation of that world as it is construed by the form of language (Matthiessen 1991).

In an important sense, then, the abstract relation of coding which links context and meaning is recapitulated in the relation between meaning and wording. So with some oversimplification it may be claimed that context is realized as meaning; meaning is realized as wording, or lexicogrammar. The creative power of language resides largely in the lexico-grammar, for it is the lexicogrammar that produces meaning, and this is tantamount to producing semiotic constructs of reality. It is through the realizational relation between meaning and wording that the world of human experience enters into discourse.

Given this stance, the relation between meaning and form cannot be that of conventional association between the name and what the name names, since neither meaning nor form can be said to precede the other: they coevolve, just as culture and meaning potential, and context and text, coevolve. This is the heart of Halliday's functional hypothesis, according to which the higher linguistic strata—those of meaning and wording—are functionally organised with respect to context: the form of human language is as it is since it coevolves with the meanings which coevolve with the community's contexts of social interaction. This is what links the social existence of speakers to their verbal syntagms confirming the functional, nonarbitrary nature of the higher levels of linguistic organisation.

An attractive aspect of Halliday's functional hypothesis is that it is open to empirical examination. To begin with, if context is a semiotic construct realized by meanings as construed by wording, then in texts as its realization there will exist evidence of what the abstract form of context is like: a hypothesis about the abstract nature of context would be seen as viable ONLY IF the meanings of the text will bear testimony to it.

Leaving metaphors aside, what would count as evidence for the functional hypothesis? In systemic functional linguistics this is taken to mean that the abstract organisation of each of these levels of linguistic description would echo the organisation of the other two. So, for example, if Halliday claims that context is a semiotic construct consisting of three abstract parameters, this can be rewritten as a claim that the higher strata of meaning and wording display a similar organisation. So given the tripartite structure of context, if it is taken as the starting point, then the linguistic levels of meaning and wording should also be describable as comprising three subsets—or clusters of the system—such that they would possess the following properties:

1. Each specific contextual parameter would be realizationally related to a specific cluster of meaning system; this implies that meanings are functionally specialised vis-à-vis context.

2. Each such cluster would in turn be realizationally related to a specific cluster of lexicogrammatical system; this implies that the lexicogrammar is functionally organised with respect to context-realising meaning systems.

The claim of systemic functional linguistics is that indeed such a fractal organisation does exist at the higher levels of language. To appreciate these claims, it is necessary to understand the concept of system.

The three notions fundamentally relevant to the understanding of system are the POTENTIALITY of CHOICE in some ENVIRONMENT: a system 'is a' set of interlocking options which represent what is 'possible', the potential, under some explicitly specified condition. To take a fairly obvious example, in the environment of interrogative, that is, where a clause 'has' the feature interrogative, there exists the potential of choosing between the features polar (construing typically demand for confirmation: *Is it?* or *Isn't it?*) or nonpolar (typically construing demand for information: *Why / Where / When did you?*). To say that the level of meaning has a tripartite systemic organisation is to maintain also that the choice of options in one system is relatively independent of choices in the other two: the choice of polar v. nonpolar from the system of MOOD is not constrained by the choice of transitive v. intransitive from the system of

TRANSITIVITY. (*Are you going?, Did you see him?, Where did you go?, Whom did you see?*) And each of these lexico-grammatical systems construes a specific system of meaning which is realizationally linked to some specific contextual parameters. For each contextual parameter, there is, as it were, a minisemantics and for each system of meaning, a mini-lexicogrammar. These points can be illustrated by using the information in Table 1, where the contextual features and some of the realizing systems of meaning and wording are tabulated.

But before that, let me make two points. First, realization is not a simple relation of replication (Halliday 1991, 1992); the requirement of a strict one-to-one correspondence contradicts the need for the recognition of distinct strata as distinct orders of abstraction (Hasan in press). Second, talking about systems of meaning and wording is crucially different from talking about isolated individual elements of meaning or wording: characterising a system of meaning or wording as a whole is to deal with categories of a higher level of abstraction, as was pointed out earlier. To take an example, instead of being concerned with a specific meaning, for example *statement*, we are concerned with a system of meaning, for example *speech role exchange*, whose specific terms are *statement, question, command, acceptance*, etc., amongst others. Similarly, the concern is not with an isolated entry in the lexicon such as *pain*, but with the systems of the lexicon as significative resource; nor are we concerned with specific structures such as declarative clause, but rather with the mood system as a whole.

Let me turn now to Table 1 to provide a brief illustration of how a contextual parameter, a category of meaning, and a category of wording are realizationally related. In each case I shall restrict myself to using as examples only part of the social facts relevant to the contextual parameter under focus and the meaning–wording systems which construe it. We can begin with tenor, and within tenor with that aspect of social relation which translates into a sense of our rights and obligations as interactants in the same social activity. Obviously the modality choices are relevant in the construal of this aspect of tenor, but the system of speech role exchange is equally important, if not more so (Halliday 1985; Matthiessen and Halliday 1992). The choices available here are those of demanding or giving, and what is demanded or given could be either information or service. If the speech role of demanding service is adopted, further choices become available, such as direct order (*Cook those potatoes!*) or consultative order (*Could you cook those potatoes?*), or assertive desiderative order (*I'd like you to cook those potatoes*), and so on. (Both the examples and the terminology are simplified; cf. Hasan 1989 for a more detailed example of part of the semantic system of speech role exchange.)

Which of the options is chosen is relevant to what social relation already exists between the speakers and/or what social relation the speakers wish to construe now. These systemic meaning options are lexicogrammatically realized as choices in mood, with such options as imperative (*Cook those potatoes!*), or interrogative (*Could you cook those potatoes?*), or declarative (*I'd like you to cook those potatoes.*), and so on. It is not the case that every text will 'have' in

Table 1. Metafunctional resonance: The cogenesis of context, meaning, and wording.

Metafunction	Contextual Variable	Meaning System	Wording System
interpersonal	social relation (= TENOR)	role exchange; assessment of probability, obligation	mood system (e.g. declarative v. interrogative...); systems of modality, modualation
experiential	social action (= FIELD)	states of affairs classification of phenomena	transitivity system (e.g. material v. verbal...); lexical systems ...
logical		relations of states of affairs relations of phenomena	expansion, project systems modification ...
textual	semiotic organisation (= MODE)	point of departure; news focus points of identity, similarity	thematic, information systems phoricity, lexical field

it an imperative or an exclamative; simply that typically communication involves making some choice from this system. I shall refer to the cluster of systems of meaning which construes the tenor of discourse as INTERPERSONAL MEANINGS, and to that cluster of systems of the lexicogrammar which construe such meanings as INTERPERSONAL LEXICO-GRAMMAR. The contextual parameter of tenor, interpersonal meanings, and interpersonal lexicogrammar are related to each other functionally. The INTERPERSONAL METAFUNCTION of language consists in this relation. To say that human language 'has' interpersonal metafunction is to say that in every language there is a set of lexicogrammatical systems which construes systems of meaning that contribute to the production, maintenance, and alteration of social relations between interactants, and to making the 'inner self' of the speakers accessible intersubjectively.

The system of meanings to which Table 1 refers as 'states of affairs' concerns goings on: doing, sensing, saying, being, which imply the involvement of participants such as 'doer', 'done-to' etc., and circumstances such as those of time, place, manner, etc. This is one of the systems of meaning that is relevant to the construal of social action. For example, *Cook the potatoes in boiling salted water for 20 minutes until soft* construes part of the social action of instructing someone how to cook something. Lexicogrammatically, such meanings are realized by choices in the system of transitivity and by 'lexical' reference as is perhaps evident from this example. The type of meaning that (partially) construes social action, and that is itself construed by transitivity and lexical reference may be referred to as EXPERIENTIAL. However, social action is not typically construed simply by reference to 'simples': speakers also need to refer to complex entities and complex states of affairs—for example not just *water* but *salted water*; not just *salted water* but *boiling salted water*; not just *Cook potatoes ...* , but also *Cook potatoes ... until soft*. What is achieved here is greater specificity through relating things to properties and some state of affairs to some other(s).

The meaning systems that form the basis of such relations are known as LOGICAL meanings and they are construed by LOGICAL LEXICOGRAMMAR, for example, systems of expansion and projection (Halliday 1985). The logical and experiential systems of meanings and wordings are together active in the construal of social action. The relation that links logical experiential meanings and wording to the contextual parameter of social action is referred to as the ideational metafunction of language. The recognition of the IDEATIONAL METAFUNCTION of language is a recognition of the fact that in every language there exist systems of wording which construe meanings, that in turn form the expression of the speakers' experience of the world, both the external world of sensuous experience and the internal one of imagination, cognition, reflection, etc.

Turning to the third contextual parameter, it is difficult to illustrate briefly—and without trivialisation—how linguistic meanings construe the semiotic organisation of human relation and action. What is at issue is the ongoing organisation of the interpersonal and ideational meanings into an accessible flow of communication. This involves the identification of the temporal phenomena that are entering into the discourse as the same happening or entity, for example *the potatoes ...* , (i.e. definite, identified as same individuals rather than just any members of the class *potato*), or indicating differing degrees of similarity, for example *another potato* (identical class but distinct member), or *some onions* (distinct classes which pertain to the same general domain). Additionally, it involves judgements of what information is accessible from what source; for example using the expression *the potatoes* where there has been no previous mention of potatoes, as opposed to in a recipe as in the original example where the ingredients mention *new potatoes 1 lb.* The semiotic organisation of information also involves decisions about what needs foregrounding: compare *Into the salted boiling water drop the peeled potatoes ...* as opposed to *The potatoes should be cooked in ...* , as opposed to *Cook the potatoes in ...* Each of these expressions is grammatical so far as the individual clause is concerned, but the textual environment in which one is more likely to occur than the others will be governed by such considerations as how topic is to be organised. The inability to make appropriate judgements for the semiotic organisation of interpersonal and ideational meanings so as to make communication easily accessible to one's addressee is one of the underlying problems of what is known as 'disordered communication'. The lexicogrammatical systems which construe such meanings are those of phoricity, lexical-field formation, theme and information-focus development. Such meanings and wordings together construe the mode of discourse, and their relation is recognised as the textual metafunction of language.

Just as there is no social context that consists simply of social action or of social relation or of semiotic organisation, so also there is no text which displays just one kind of meaning, just one kind of wording: the three metafunctions operate in unison. So *Cook the potatoes in salted boiling water until soft* 'has' interpersonal meaning; it has an exhortative command realized as a jussive imperative. It also 'has' an experiential meaning, displaying a state of affairs that involves acting on something realized as material process *cook* and goal *the potatoes*, and so on. The logical and textual meanings and wordings of the syntagm in question have already been briefly alluded to. The grammar of a language is a device for the calibration of the distinct metafunctional strands into one and the same syntagm. So we do not have texts and/or messages that are simply interpersonal, or ideational, or textual: they are functional in all three ways at once. In this respect, the systemic functional concept of metafunction is significantly different from that of, say, Bühler, to whom most ideas about linguistic functionalism can be traced (Dirven and Fried 1987). Bühler's functions, unlike the systemic functional metafunctions, were mutually exclusive. The discussion in this section is not presented as an account of functionalism in systemic functional linguistics: this is a large issue that cannot be developed here (cf. Halliday and Hasan 1989; Hasan and Perrett in press). It was necessary to bring in the notion of the functional organisation of language and the simultaneity of metafunctions in order to pave the way to a reinterpretation of the relations of language, communication, and social meaning. This will be the concern of the next section.

4 Functionalism and social meaning. Although I have presented a highly condensed account in the previous section, it hopefully does suggest that linguistic form is functionally organised with respect to systems of meaning and systems of meaning with respect to the context of communication. Let me clarify what the acceptance of this approach implies for a revised understanding of the relations of the three terms in the theme of this Round Table. First, take the claim of cogenetic relation which links context, communication, and language. This is an attempt to do justice to the specificity of communication and language while also recognising their deep interdependence. It is implied in this claim also that functionalism is not an attribute of any one level of language; it is neither intrinsic nor extrinsic: it is a relation that links the material conditions of human social existence to human verbal semiosis. This is why the resonance of the metafunctional principle is felt through the context of communication to language use through to language system. This perspective is capable of explaining why the potential for being useful inheres in human language: language is able to meet the needs of its speakers because the wordings and meanings of a language are not arbitrary with respect to the community's living of life. Society, in a very real sense, is operative 'in' language just as much as language is operative 'in' society. If we find 'the reflection of social processes in linguistic choices', this is because the roots of communication are in the social living of life, and because the form that human communication takes is text, and because text is to language as an instance is to a system. It is only in this kind of approach that doing sociolinguistics can equal doing linguistics.

Saussure had doubted the possibility of creating a linguistics which would at once respect the distinct identity of language and communication and yet illuminate their deep interdependence: it seems to me that the functional approach I have described here goes a considerable way towards meeting that challenge. This resolution is made possible in fact by following Saussure's hint—by taking him more seriously than he took himself when he suggested that linguistics was a species of semiology, concerned with one semiotic system among many others in the community. But whereas Saussure thought of the various semiotic systems as simply copresent, systemic functional linguistics attempts to integrate language as a semiotic system with other semiotic systems in a community. It is clear that the claim of cogenesis itself rests on that of the semiotic relation of coding which integrates the context of culture and situation with language and communication. In taking this step we have found it necessary to reject Saussure's entirely sequential way of looking at communication and language (cf. quotations in section 2).

By these steps we have arrived at a point in this discussion where the concept of 'social meaning' can be reviewed. The relation of semiotic construal of context, communication, and language denies the possibility of recognising a causal determinative relation between these terms. Clearly, in a linguistics of this kind, those referential theories of meaning are unacceptable where every word names some preidentified thing and every sentence mirrors some actual state of affairs. I argued in section 3 that the construal of context calls for interpersonal, ideational, and textual meanings, and that all three types of meaning are construed simultaneously by lexicogrammar. If so, then there seems no justification for claiming that the linguistic level of meaning—its semantics—is just referential and that other kinds of meaning can be excluded from semantics.

From a functional point of view, all three kinds of meaning are equally socially motivated, and together they constitute the semantic level of language. This removes the justification for making a distinction between meaning that is social and meaning that is semantic. It might be argued that the concept of social meaning is required because the attitudes of the community valorise something which in itself has no meaning, namely, the phonological variants. I do not find this very convincing. In the first place, variation invites valorisation; phonological variation is no exception to this rule. Second, it would be an error to give the impression that if VALUE in the sense of prejudice or praise is attached to meanings—and it certainly is—this is because these values INHERE in the nature of those meanings in some nonsocial natural way just as gravity inheres in matter.

Nothing could be further from the truth: the valorisation of meanings depends on the attitudes of the community as much as the valorisation of the phoneme does. Our failure to recognise this is not activated by some scientific principle; it simply confirms the power of ideology. So to single out the valorisation of phonological variation as social meaning and to claim that it is this meaning that is the true concern of sociolinguistics is to deny the possibility that meanings are subject to valorisation. This leaves our ideological allegiances unexplored; it encourages simplistic solutions to highly complex problems—one example is the unqualified claim about the equality of languages (cf. Hymes this volume), another is to say that semantic variation is not social (Weiner and Labov 1983), and if someone attempts to record its social nature, this is simply because such researchers are prejudiced, or their linguistic techniques are inferior.

These attitudes to semantic variation leave us with a serious problem: if it is believed that in a complex society such as ours, phonological variation is 'functional' in the sense of being practically useful (Weinreich, Labov, and Herzog 1968:101), then how is the absence of the variation in meaning to be explained? Since meaning is what our social universe is made of, why would there be no variation here? Why would there be no valorisation? In the following section I present the findings of a research in semantic variation to show not only that semantic variation is a possibility but that it is an actuality, and that in a manner of speaking this variation is 'functional': it plays an important part in maintaining the inequalities of our 'egalitarian' societies.

5 Semantic variation: The ideological power of meaning and wording.

The details of the research, one fragment of which I discuss here, are provided in Hasan (1989; 1991) and Hasan and Cloran (1990). These research projects were financed by the Australian Research Council and Macquarie University; their main concern was to explore how and if participation in everyday talk establishes ways of learning. The data for the first phase of this research consisted of some 100 hours of naturally occurring dialogues between 24 Australian-born mother–child dyads, who were native speakers of English.

My colleague Carmel Cloran conducted a semantic analysis of over 20,000 messages from this large collection of dialogues; the framework for the analysis was provided by semantic networks prepared by Hasan. The subjects were equally distributed for social class and child's sex; the mean age of the children was 3 years 8 months. Social class ascription was on the basis of the degree of power and autonomy in place of work: 12 of the families belonged to higher autonomy professions (HAP) (e.g. bank managers, doctors, university teachers, etc.), and 12 belonged to lower autonomy professions (LAP) (e.g. council truck driver, factory worker, unemployed).

The analysed data was statistically processed using a Principal Components procedure. The input consisted of the frequency of certain semantic choices expressed as a percentage of a relevant higher order category for each subject; the set of semantic choices used as input in any one processing was contextually and/or semantically related, for example the semantic choices in making commands, giving reasons, and challenging and/or supporting are relevant to the construal of the context of control. The statistical procedure assigns a positive or negative loading to each input feature. The higher this loading the more likely (if loading is positive) or unlikely (if loading is negative) the occurrence of the feature would be in the high-scoring subjects. The successive overall clustering of these features as a whole accounts for degrees of variance in the data. Only those features are relevant to this variance which reach a certain degree of loading; if the loading of some feature goes below this point, this indicates the comparative irrelevance of that particular feature to the variance in the data from the point of view of that cluster. Each subject is assigned an overall score on the basis of each such cluster. Table 2 displays the first such clustering, called PC1, which accounts for 45.00% variance in the data. The input features consist of some semantic choices relevant to maternal control.

The majority of the features in Table 2 are semantic choices in making command (C), two are features of reason (R), Q(explain) stands for challenge and S(supportive) for supportive comments. Table 2 claims that high-scoring mothers would be highly likely to make indirect (e.g. *Could you take this stuff to your room?*) and suggestive commands (e.g. *We'll get dressed. How about taking this stuff to your room now?*). The features indirect and suggestive are in systemic contrast with direct commands (e.g. *Take this stuff to your room*) and impositions (e.g. *You will take this stuff to your room now.*), with the implication that those who score high on the former two must score low on the latter, and vice versa. So mothers who score low on indirect and suggestive are highly likely to make direct commands or impositions. High-scoring mothers are also highly likely to make elaborated commands, where the command is related to some other message which expresses a condition, concession, etc. as in *Could you stir the mixture as I pour the milk in?* High-scoring subjects are also reasonably likely to make prefaced commands, where the command is projected (Halliday 1985) as a locution, desire, or idea, etc. as in *I want you to stir the mixture as I pour the milk in*, where the command to stir the mixture is projected as the speaker's desire. I ignore C(action) since its loading is not criterial on PC1.

Table 2. Socio-semantic variation in maternal control.

Features	PC1
C [indirect]	0.84
S [supportive]	0.83
C [suggestive]	0.82
C [elaborated]	0.77
R [logical]	0.64
R [elaborated]	0.62
Q [explain]	-0.50
C [action]	0.34
C [prefaced]	0.44
Eigenvalue	4.04
Percent variance	45.00
(p (H > L) <.0002)	

Turning to reasons, high-scoring mothers are very likely to give logical reasons—reasons that are grounded in the physical nature of the universe, for example, *(Don't touch that) because it's hot.* Such reasons contrast with reasons whose grounding is social. Social reasons range from convention, for example, *because that's how we do it* to threat; for example, *because I'll hit you.* So PC1 scores indicate that the low-scoring mothers are very likely to give social reasons. High-scoring mothers are also very likely to give elaborated reasons, as in *because it's Rebecca's doll and if you break her she'll [i.e. Rebecca] will be very upset.* Q(explain) refers to a why-question, which when addressed to the child by the mother in the context of control is seen as a challenge. For example when Karen refuses to comply with the mother's order to kiss her goodnight, the mother says *You're not gonna kiss me? Why?* This feature has a negative loading, with the implication that high-scoring mothers are not likely to challenge their children in the context of control. The remaining feature S(supportive) refers to such remarks as *I know you'll understand*, which express confidence in the child's ability to act 'reasonably', 'judiciously', etc., and this feature has a high positive loading, implying that high-scoring subjects are highly likely to issue supportive statements in the context of control.

The statistical procedure assigns an overall score to each subject. Figure 1 identifies the position of the 24 mothers by reference to their scores on PC1 and PC2.

In Figure 1, the location of mothers is determined on the vertical axis by reference to their scores on PC2, so high scorers are placed at the top and low ones at the bottom end of the vertical axis. My concern here is not with PC2, so this axis will not be discussed. The mothers' position on the horizontal axis is relevant to the present discussion as this position is determined by reference to their scores on PC1. On this axis, the leftmost point indicates the lowest score.

Figure 1. The reflection of social hierarchy in semantic choices.

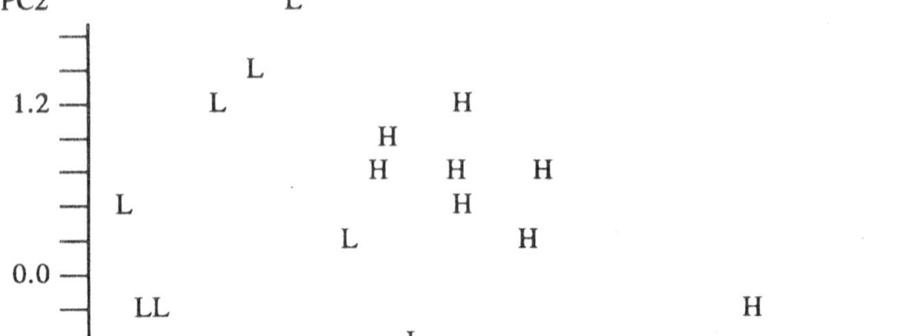

viz. -1.40, and the rightmost, the highest, viz. 2.10. So the lower the mother's score on PC1, the more to the left her location would be in Figure 1, and the higher her score, the further to the right she would be positioned.

The letter H in Figure 1 indicates a HAP mother, the letter L a LAP one, and it is quite clear from the figure that the HAP mothers are the ones who have, on the whole, scored higher than the LAP mothers on PC1. This should not be taken as a claim that HAP mothers INVARIABLY act this way any more than the high frequency of r-fulness could be taken to imply that speakers of a rhotic dialect invariably produce /r/. What is being identified is a fashion of speaking, a coding orientation which occurs significantly often to become associated with a particular social group. Nor am I claiming that every single mother in these two social groups will behave in conformity with the group's practices. My claim is simply that in the context of control, there is far greater likelihood of a HAP mother than of a LAP mother displaying orientation to the cluster of meanings identified by PC1 ($p\ (H > L) < .0002$). A cluster analysis of the data produced the same results.

But what is the interpretation of this result? What does it mean to say that HAP mothers control their children's behaviour by giving indirect or suggestive commands? To interpret the results of PC1 we need to ask what principles governing behaviour are indicated by this semantic orientation: what is the representation of these habitual meaning selections in the interactants' consciousness? What experience of the world is construed by this fashion of speaking?

The semantic features' indirect and suggestive command underplay the speaker's privilege to command; they permit a sense of discretion to the addressee. It is important to point out that neither group of mothers is willing to 'let the child get away with it': in the majority of cases both groups get the children to act in the way that the MOTHERS desire. But for the HAP child the mother's power remains invisible, whereas the LAP child is left in no doubt whatever about the mother's power to get him to act as she thinks best. When it comes to reason, we find a similar pattern: a 'logical' reason that is grounded in the physical nature of the world appears to have an objective character; the effectiveness of a social reason such as threat, convention, or bribe resides once again in the position of the reason-giver vis-à-vis the addressee. The HAP mother's authority remains 'safely' masked; the LAP mother's authority is flagrantly obvious.

Commands and reasons with the semantic feature elaborated possess greater verbal specificity. The greater the degree of empathy between the speaker and addressee, the less need there would be for verbal specificity. A higher degree of elaboration implies that the speaker is less willing to assume shared knowledge with the addressee. The interactants are thus construed as individuals 'in their own right', with thoughts, beliefs, and feelings that are inaccessible to others without their saying. This interpretation of elaboration is further supported by the fact that mothers given to elaboration are also those whose commands tend to be prefaced. A preface such as *I'd like you to ..., Do you think you could ...*, etc. is making one's own subjective position verbally explicit or seeking the addressee's subjective position. That is to say, the speaker is not willing to assume or allow shared knowledge of the conversational other's subjectivity. The HAP child is thus socio-semiotically produced as an individual with his own unique subjectivity, the sharing of which is in his personal discretion.

This granting of unique individuality, the masking of maternal power, and the granting of discretion combine to produce a sense of the world under one's control, where the external control on the child's actions is rendered invisible, its motivation being presented as either above human manipulation (reasons are 'logical', guided by 'unavoidable rational principles') or as self-regulated (the child has discretion and own judgement). The LAP child is socio-semiotically produced as someone whose experience of the collectivity is an aspect of his subjectivity, the sharing of which does not depend on his personal discretion; the control on the child's action is quite visibly external. The power that controls his actions is derived from the speaker's social position vis-à-vis the addressee. But this position itself is not unique to the speaker: it is the condition of being a mother—a status recognised by the community—which gives the speaker greater discretion than the child. The child's actions are quite clearly under the control of this greater power.

When a couple of decades ago Bernstein (1971) drew attention to the variation in coding orientation he was, in my view, unfairly attacked as displaying social class prejudice. In the flurry of the debate a rather interesting issue got lost. Let me point to that issue by taking the two pictures I have presented here—one created by HAP fashions of speaking, the other created by LAP fashions of speaking. It is ironic that I can be accused of prejudice against the LAP group, only if the snobbishly smug assumptions of my hypothetical accuser are accepted; for the accusation of prejudice against the LAP group will hold ONLY IF it is granted that the HAP ways of meaning are indeed the better ways of meaning. I submit that this is by no means a necessary assumption in the description of socio-semantic variation than it is in describing stigmatized accents as different from privileged ones. This raises the question: on what basis do we valorise human behaviour, particularly of the semantic type, which underlie our beliefs, ideas, etc? I am forced to agree with the claim that 'the ideas of the ruling class are in every epoch the ruling ideas, that is, the class which is the ruling MATERIAL force of society, is at the same time its ruling INTELLECTUAL force' (Marx and Engels 1970:64; emphases in original). That means that there is at least as much, if not far more, prejudice in granting the superiority of HAP behaviour than there is in describing LAP behaviour as different! The unquestioned assumption that the HAP construal of social consciousness is in fact natural is capable of being far more pernicious because it is not even perceived as prejudice. Later I will argue that this assumption has a role in our society, but for the present let me ask: how is this orientation to meaning on the part of these two groups functional in a complex industrial society which, claiming to be egalitarian, bristles with inequality? Here is a speculative answer.

Higher autonomy professions' ways of behaving appear highly functional in the HAP station of life: if you have sufficient autonomy so that you can make significant decisions about your environment, and you can use others as the instrument for the execution of those decisions, then you are in a position of control; you are controlling others' actions in order to get them to do things you consider 'reasonable'. When control is invisible, when reasons are 'in the nature of things', the chances of open conflict are reduced. In my data HAP children cry; they complain; they even retaliate symbolically; but they seldom challenge the mother's authority, and they certainly do not directly reject their mother's commands. From the point of view of middle-class ideology, the HAP mother is polite, she is 'reasonable', she gives the child a positive face, and so on. But let us not forget that her behaviour is well suited to efficient subjugation, where the subjugated becomes a willing accomplice in his own subjugation. This is true power, and for an apprenticeship to the middle-class stations in life, its functional value can hardly be questioned!

But what about the other side of the picture? There are contradictory messages in the control practices of the LAP group, one which celebrates the power of authority and the need for obedience, and another which lays authority bare as an open target for attack. One might ask: how can a flagrant parading of authority be functional? I am inclined to suggest that it depends on who you are, what degree of autonomy you possess, how far you control, and how far you are yourself controlled. It is certainly true that in most societies the autonomy of members will vary from context to context: one could be more autonomous with respect to some, less with respect to others. Nonetheless, some of us may be less autonomous with respect to a good proportion of the community's contexts, and the LAP subjects in my research belong to that category.

Under these conditions, the maintenance of social existence will involve entering in relations of submission—relations that are independent of our will, relations the basis of which lies in the other's power. The recognition of authority could then be criterial; the inculcation of the idea that the nature of control is external would be an entirely beneficial perspective. If authority is visible, if the source of control is tangible, one can hit back: in my data LAP children defy the mother, they reject the mother's commands, they challenge her authority, they are willing to 'take her on' physically. If the views presented here are accepted, it would seem that a tension exists in our society: middle-class practices are geared to maintaining hierarchy by making subjugation invisible; working-class practices are geared to challenge subjugation. And it is here that we can highlight the function of an unquestioned belief in the superiority of the middle-class practices.

The positive evaluation of the middle-class practices makes any divergence from those practices questionable. Logicality, rationality as we understand these terms are fashioned to fit middle-class practices; it is not that members of the middle-class never submit to authority or that they never support acts of violence—it is significant that our sense of outrage at violence or exercise of authority is itself so selective, so self-serving! Similarly, the importance of collectivity is not absent from middle-class contexts; where it is to be disregarded is in the context of 'self-fulfillment': 'I' before 'we', as Bernstein pointed out. This supports the highly valued 'free competition'—a principle extraordinarily well understood by the middle classes. The higher valorisation of middle-class practices is a powerful deterrent to challenge.

I am aware of the provocative nature of my comments, so for good measure let me close this discussion of socio-semantic variation by saying that the examination of this kind of variation is a key to the conflicting ideologies in our modern complex societies; its recognition is a challenge to our facile belief in the benevolently egalitarian nature of the society we live in; and that at this moment in the history of the world when we are rather inclined to congratulate ourselves on the continued success of our economic order, on our admirable democracies, the need is more urgent than ever before to pay attention to the challenge which the sociolinguistics of semantic variation is capable of revealing. A sociolinguistics that is able to reveal the power of language and communication in the creation, maintenance, and alteration of the world we live in demands a theory of meaning that goes beyond meaning as correspondence to facts. But such a theory of meaning demands a recognition of linguistic functionalism—not the simplistic variety which atomistically examines the usefulness of items, forms, and devices, but a functionalism of the kind which explores the deep interdependence between communication and language.

6 Synopsis. In this paper I have argued that current conceptions of the relationship between language and communication are flawed, and flaw our understanding of the scope and power of human language. I have argued that communication is the act of meaning, characterised by intersubjectivity. To account for intersubjectivity we need to grant the semiotic nature of context, which in turn implies a cogenetic relation between context and linguistic meanings. If context is a semiotic construct, linguistic meanings cannot be seen as a naming relation linking the form of language to the world of experience. Linguistic meanings are construed by lexicogrammar. From the semiotic nature of context and from the construal relations of context, meaning, and wording flows the metafunctional hypothesis. This approach puts in doubt the division of linguistic meaning into social and semantic. It permits us to recognise the possibility of semantic variation, thus revealing to us the power of our communication in the creation, maintenance, and change of the social world in which we live.

REFERENCES

Austin, J.L. 1980. How to do things with words, ed. by J.O. Urmson and Marina Sbisà [with corrections and new index]. Oxford: Oxford University Press.

Baker, G.P., and P.M.S. Hacker. 1988. Wittgenstein: Rules, grammar and necessity: Vol. 2 of An analytical commentary on the Philosophical Investigations. London: Blackwell.

Bernstein, Basil. 1971. Class, codes and control, Vol. 1: Theoretical studies towards a sociology of language. London: Routledge and Kegan Paul.

Bourdieu, Pierre. 1977. Outline of a theory of practice, trans. by R. Nice. Cambridge: Cambridge University Press.

Daneš, F. 1987. On Prague School functionalism in linguistics. Functionalism in linguistics, LLSEE Vol. 20, ed. by Rene Dirven and Vilem Fried, 3–38. Amsterdam: Benjamins.

Dirven, René, and Vilém Fried. 1987. Functionalism in linguistics. LLSEE Vol. 20, ed. by Rene Dirven and Vilem Fried. Amsterdam: Benjamins.

Firth, J.R. 1957. Papers in general linguistics 1934–1951. London: Oxford University Press.

Gardin, B., and J.B. Marcellesi. 1987. The subject matter of sociolinguistics. Sociolinguistics: An international handbook, Vol. 1, ed. by Ulrich Ammon, Norbert Dittmar, and Klaus J. Mattheier, 16–25. Berlin: de Gruyter.

Halliday, M.A.K. 1970. Language structure and language function. New Horizons in linguistics, ed. by John Lyons, 140–65. Harmondsworth: Penguin.

Halliday, M.A.K. 1975. Language as social semiotic: Towards a general sociolinguistic theory. The First LACUS Forum, ed. by Adam Makkai and Valerie Becker Makkai, 17–46. Columbia, SC: Hornbeam Press.

Halliday, M.A.K. 1977. Text as semantic choice in social context. Grammar and descriptions, ed. by Teun A. van Dijk and János S. Petöfi, 176–225. Berlin: de Gruyter.

Halliday, M.A.K. 1985. Introduction to functional grammar. London: Edward Arnold.

Halliday, M.A.K. 1991. The notion of 'context' in language education. Language education: interaction and development, ed. by Thao Le and Mike McCausland, 1–26. Launceston: University of Tasmania.

Halliday, M.A.K. 1992. How do you mean? Recent advances in systemic linguistics, ed. by Martin

Davies and Louise Ravelli. London: Pinter.

Halliday, M.A.K., Angus McIntosh, and Peter Strevens. 1964. The linguistic sciences and language teaching. London: Longmans.

Halliday, M.A.K., and Ruqaiya Hasan. 1989. Language, context and text: Aspects of language in a social-semiotic perspective. Oxford: Oxford University Press.

Hasan, Ruqaiya. 1973. Code, register and social dialect. Class, codes, and control Vol. 2: Applied studies towards a sociology of language, ed. by Basil Bernstein, 253–92. London: Routledge and Kegan Paul.

Hasan, Ruqaiya. 1989. Semantic variation and sociolinguistics. Australian Journal of Linguistics 9, 2.221–76.

Hasan, Ruqaiya. 1991. Questions as a mode of learning in everyday talk. Language education: interaction and development, ed. by Thao Le and Mike McCausland, 70–119. Launceston: University of Tasmania.

Hasan, Ruqaiya. (in press) The conception of context in text. Discourse in society: Systemic functional perspectives, ed. by Peter H. Fries and M. Gregory. Norwood, NJ: Ablex.

Hasan, Ruqaiya, and Carmel Cloran. 1990. A sociolinguistic interpretation of everyday talk between mothers and children. Learning, keeping and using language, Vol. 1: Selected papers from the 8th World Congress of Applied Linguistics, Sydney 16–21 August 1987, ed. by M.A.K. Halliday, John Gibbon, and Howard Nicholas, 67–100. Amsterdam: Benjamins.

Hasan, Ruqaiya, and Gillian Perrett. (in press) Learning to function with the other tongue: A systemic functional perspective on second language teaching. Perspective on pedagogical grammars, ed. by Terence Odlin. New York: Cambridge University Press.

Hjelmslev, Louis. 1961. Prolegomena to a theory of language, trans. by Francis J Whitfield. (rev. Eng. edn.) Madison: University of Wisconsin Press.

Hymes, Dell H. 1968. The ethnography of speaking. Readings in the sociology of language, ed. by Joshua A. Fishman, 99–138. The Hague: Mouton.

Labov, William. 1972. Sociolinguistic patterns. Philadelphia: University of Pennsylvania Press.

Markova, Ivana. 1988. A three step process as a unit of analysis in dialogue. The dynamics of dialogue, ed. by I. Markova and Klaus Foppa, 129–46. New York: Harvester.

Martin, J. R. (in press) The English text. Amsterdam: Benjamins.

Mathesius, Vilem. 1964. On the potentiality of the phenomena of language. A Prague School reader in linguistics, compiled by Josef Vachek, 1–32. Bloomington: Indiana University Press.

Matthiessen, Christian. 1991. Language on language: The grammar of semiosis. Social Semiotics 1, 2.69–111.

Matthiessen, Christian, and M.A.K. Halliday. MS. Systemic functional grammar. Current approaches to syntax, ed. by F. Peng and J. Ney. Amsterdam and London: Benjamins and Whurr. (avail. from Matthiessen, Dept. of Linguistics, Sydney University).

Marx, Karl, and Friedrich Engels. 1970. The German ideology, Part one, ed. and intro. by C.J. Arthur. London: Lawrence and Wishart.

Saussure, Ferdinand de. 1966. Course in general linguistics, trans. by Wade Baskin. New York: McGraw-Hill.

Saussure, F. de. 1983. Course in general linguistics, trans. and ann. by Roy Harris. London: Duckworth.

Sinclair, John M. 1991. Shared knowledge. Linguistics and language pedagogy: The state of the art. Georgetown University Round Table on Languages and Linguistics 1991, ed. by James E. Alatis, 489–500. Washington, DC: Georgetown University Press.

Weiner, E.J., and William Labov. 1983. Constraints on the agentless passive. Journal of Linguistics 19.29–58.

Weinreich, Uriel, William Labov, and Marvin I. Herzog. 1968. Empirical foundations for a theory of language change. Directions from historical linguistics: A symposium, ed. by P. Lehman and Y. Malkiel, 97–195. Texas: University of Texas Press.

Language, communication, social meaning, and social change: The challenge for teachers

Sandra J. Savignon
University of Illinois at Urbana-Champaign

The theme of the 1992 Georgetown Round Table is provocative: language, communication, and social meaning. Michael Halliday and Dell Hymes have honored us with their participation. Both theorists have long held linguistic form and social meaning to be inseparable, Hymes with his notion of communicative competence, Halliday with his representation of meaning potential and the elaboration of functional grammar. Their theoretical models have contributed remarkable insight into the business of language and language use, insight that is vital to understanding the process of language learning.

With these theoretical constructs as backdrop, I have chosen to focus on teachers, both past and present, and the challenge not only of language, communication, and social meaning, but the challenge of social change. In choosing to focus on teachers I acknowledge a lifelong engagement with teaching. A researcher who has remained at heart a teacher, I feel almost daily the pull between wanting to teach and wanting to learn. No matter how long one has been teaching, there remains much to learn. We live in a time of accelerating change, on the world front, on the national front, on the home front. Roles and identities are no sooner asserted than they are questioned, reexamined. Fresh perspectives and changing worldviews bring new understanding. All the more in a world of change, teachers are challenged to remain learners.

My focus on teachers serves also to reaffirm the essential link between linguistics and education. Linguistics has to do with language and with language awareness. Language awareness includes recognition of linguistic resources and an understanding of how language is used to negotiate and create meaning. Language awareness includes recognition of the forms and manner of discourse and an understanding of language power. Language awareness also includes recognition of language rights in a multicultural, multilingual society.

Language is not simply a means of communication. Language IS communication. And communication both determines and is determined by social meaning. Social meaning is shared meaning, community meaning. Social meaning thus mirrors social change. Societies change. Meanings change.

Language, then, is culture in motion, a system of meanings that at once responds to and influences social change.

Contemporary multidisciplinary perspectives on language use, and richer description of language use by learners—at home, in the community, and in the classroom—bring with them new insights into language learning. Language learning is seen to be inseparable from socialization. In learning how to mean, one is learning to take one's place in society. Where there are options, there may be uncertainty and conflict regarding roles and expectations. Social change, community change, comes not without controversy. By definition, socialization in a community with a goal of democracy includes the ability to understand and participate in social change.

The challenge for teachers is thus dual: to remain a learner, attentive to social change, and at the same time enable others to more effectively interpret and participate in that change.

Language. Asked to describe what language is, teachers might well begin with words such as lexicon, phonology, and syntax. Or they might use lay terms—vocabulary, pronunciation, and grammar. For centuries, LANGUAGE TEACHING in academic settings has been synonymous with GRAMMAR TEACHING. The focus of language classrooms and materials around the world, grammar study remains for many synonymous with language study.

This kind of language teaching is what many who are second or foreign language teachers often do best. A long and rich tradition of grammar teaching as language teaching sustains today the centrality of grammatical analysis in most language teacher education programs. Teachers typically take satisfaction in illustrating and explaining points of grammar and engaging learners in exercises and drills to test their understanding. Where learners have a native or first language in common, translation in some form or another remains a familiar and favored activity.

Viewed within the historical context of academic language teaching, this emphasis on grammatical analysis is anything but surprising. The most prestigious if not the only languages taught in schools for many centuries were Greek and Latin. Study of these classical languages was valued in particular for the analytical skills such study was presumed to develop, not unlike the skills or muscles developed by a ballerina at the barre. In addition, the translation of ancient texts provided learners with models of moral and artistic merit. When modern languages were finally accepted into European and American public school curricula, teachers eager to assert standards and rigor took care to teach French, German, and English on the pattern of grammar analysis and translation followed by their colleagues in Greek and Latin. Nonetheless, modern language study was held in low esteem. In the United States, French was considered a suitable diversion for young ladies, along with dance and embroidery, while their brothers went to school and studied the classics. In England, when French and other modern language degree programs were established at Cambridge and Oxford at the end of the nineteenth century, they were considered 'soft options.'

The quest for respectability served to squelch reform efforts to teach the spoken language, and philology took its place.

In an interesting account of this period in England, Howatt (1984) notes that the success of women students in modern language programs, in particular, was not without consequence. In reaction, philology soon became a favored focus for men students and assumed a position of prestige and favor. Parallel developments in the United States and other countries, both Western and non-Western, help to explain prevailing patterns of power and prestige. Such historical perspective is helpful in understanding the opposition often encountered today by those who seek curricular reforms, reforms that challenge the canon of literary texts, promote the study of contemporary language varieties and language policy, and reflect up-to-date second language acquisition theory in their instructional programs.

Communication. Increasingly, contemporary discussion of language teaching goes beyond grammar to include reference to communication. And there is likely to be some emphasis on learner involvement. Favored teaching methods today are said to be interactive, to involve the interpretation, expression, and negotiation of meaning. As the Western world emerged from the 1960s, a decade marked with student protest and demands for relevance, increased learner participation seemed both reasonable and possible. Learner interest also lent support to a new emphasis on oral communication. Communicative approaches were further bolstered by second language acquisition research findings that affirmed the role of exploration and error in the development of communicative competence.

We congratulate ourselves today on seeing language as communication, on adopting a perspective that considers roles and range in both written and spoken discourse. However, we should not so simplify history that we fail to acknowledge the recurring theme of communication in centuries past. This year of 1992 marks the 400th anniversary of the birth of Comenius (1592–1670), a European educator and philosopher well known in the history of language teaching. Comenius is often cited for his objection to the method of language teaching that had resulted from the teaching of skills of grammatical analysis in the Middle Ages. The preoccupation with grammatical analysis had grown so that by the Renaissance it was viewed as a method for actually teaching the language. In his words, 'Youngsters are held captive for years, overcome with an infinite number of grammar rules—long, entangled, obscure, and generally useless'. He goes on: 'The first immutable law of teaching is that form and meaning in language should always go together and that learners should express in words only those things they understand ... He who speaks without understanding, chatters like a parrot in a cage' (Comenius 1665, my translation).

In the nineteenth century, proponents of the Natural Method—language learning through language use—would rediscover Comenius. Proponents of the Natural Method spurned both phonetic and grammatical analysis. They also rejected translation, which by the end of the eighteenth century had become the basis of language teaching. Denying that explanation was a necessary part of teaching, they claimed that learners should be allowed to discover for themselves how to function in their new language. The following words were written in 1870 by N. M. Petersen:

> With respect to method, the artificial one must be given up and a more natural one must take its place. According to the artificial method, the first thing done is to hand the boy a grammar and cram it into him piece by piece, for everything is in pieces; he is filled with paradigms which have no connection with each other or with anything else in the world ... On the other hand, the natural method of learning languages is by practice. That is the way one's native language is acquired (Petersen 1870:297–298).

Thirty-four years later, the Danish linguist Otto Jespersen would cite these words and conclude: 'It is now half a century ago since N.M. Petersen uttered these golden words, and still the old grammar-instruction lives and flourishes with its rigmaroles and rules and exceptions' (1904:111). 'Language is not an end in itself,' he wrote, 'it is a way of connection between souls, a means of communication' (1904:4).

Today, of course, many of the methods and texts that claim to be communicative fall short of what Jespersen had in mind. Structurally focused materials said to promote 'mastery' are often concerned more with form than with 'communication between souls.' So-called 'communication practice drills' are identified in materials that remain little changed from their audiolingual days. And grammar instruction lives and flourishes with reassertion of concern for 'accuracy,' where the 'ideal native speaker' is said to set the norm.

Interestingly, research in second language acquisition itself has served to sustain the supremacy of the sentence. The emphasis on morphosyntactic features characteristic of most SLA research has eclipsed thoughtful attention to less quantifiable but more communicative values of language learning. In foreign language teaching in the United States we used to speak of cross-cultural awareness. Exchange programs and study abroad were valued for their contribution to international understanding. Literary competence was considered a reward of language study. Today in our professional journals and conferences, these broader, more humanistic perspectives are often missing. In their place, we have reports of studies with conflicting findings having to do with 'input,' 'corrective feedback', and learner 'acquisition'. The very use of the term 'acquisition' suggests that language is something static, to be acquired, as opposed to a way of meaning that must be learned.

The conviction that study of the acquisition of selected morphosyntactic features will lead to discovery of the 'best' classroom teaching method is reminiscent of the initial enthusiasm in the 1960s for computer-aided instruction. New computer technology was seen to make possible the ideal language learning program. Research money and many, many hours of effort went into defining a sequence of morphosyntactic development and designing programs based on learner error analysis and behaviorist principles of learning. The efforts have since been abandoned. In the meantime, however, language learners around the world continued to go about the business of learning, often in idiosyncratic and highly successful ways, both inside and outside the classroom. For a majority of the successful learners, bilingualism is the norm.

Social Meaning. If communication has been a recurrent theme in language teaching, social meaning, on the other hand, adds new dimension. Social meaning as a theoretical construct has been much discussed. However, the relation of the construct to issues of educability and educational systems awaits elaboration and action. There has been talk of language and education, but there has been little exploitation of the construct of social meaning in teacher education, curriculum, and teaching materials. In a world of diversity and change, a curriculum designed for a monolingual, monocultural society takes on new social meaning. The unprecedented spread of English language learning and teaching throughout the world challenges programs, materials, and language assessment. Inclusion of social meaning in discussions of language teaching inevitably raises issues of standards, norms, appropriacy. Whose manner of expression is held to be the norm? How mutual is mutual intelligibility? Whose interpretations are said to set the standard? In a world of multicultural challenge and changing perspectives, normative education and universal schooling have met head on.

Within the United States, where the language taught is other than English, cultural or cross-cultural competence remains an incidental goal. Despite the contributions to language as culture theory of Michael Halliday and Dell Hymes, the American FL profession has continued to treat culture as a 'fifth skill,' following and seemingly distinct from so-called 'language skills' of listening, speaking, reading, and writing. Language textbooks, test formats, and teacher manuals all reflect this view. Maintenance of a structurally driven discrete point tradition in language teaching requires an adjustment in any representation of communication as both variable and embedded in social context. Formulaic, simplified texts continue to stand as 'context' for the presentation of grammatical forms. Social meaning is absent. In contrast, the teaching of English as a second language within the United States assumes learner acculturation. From the beginning of instruction, texts offer examples of American ways of expressing and interpreting meaning. These ways are presented as models appropriate for learners to follow. And the contexts represented may provide indication of the anticipated social role to be played by the nonnative language learner.

Within the foreign language teaching profession, initiatives in communicative language teaching have been criticized for their lack of attention to formal accuracy, much in the same way that immersion programs in Canada have been criticized for failing to produce morphosyntactically native-like speakers of French. A persistent focus on morphosyntactic features of oral expression, moreover, has served further to limit attention to interpretive skills, listening and reading strategies that provide access to culturally authentic texts and a surer basis for continued language learning.

Not only within the United States and Canada but in all parts of the world, the social meaning of language teaching itself has a decided influence on curricula, methods, and goals. Who teaches what languages to whom? And to what end? In formerly colonized Third World countries, socialization for an educated elite continues to mean learning the language of the colonizer. Textbooks are key in establishing the meaning of the learning. As the mediator between teacher and learner, texts convey the social values of the curriculum. As English increasingly becomes the language of both international and intranational communication—in business, in politics, in scientific research—there is undeniable assertion of power in the use of the terms 'native' and 'nonnative' speaker. With nonnative users of English currently outnumbering native users by more than two to one, so-called native speaker norms are challenged as a goal for learners.

Exploration of options and outcomes in language teaching similarly takes place within a social context. There is politicization of research designs as well as of the interpretation of findings. Economic and political pressures assert majority linguistic or cultural values. North American examples of the latter include the controversy in Canada over the success of French immersion and, in the United States, the continuing debate over the goals and practice of bilingual education. In mainstream American culture, the low social value and even the stigma of using a language other than English is reflected in the limited success of what continue to be called 'foreign' language programs, limited in terms of both length of study and learner attainment.

Language assessment measures have long played a major role in shaping program and materials design. Examinations are a key tool in social policy. From the time Napoleon first used national examinations to select civil servants, examinations have been used to define social values. The content, format, and evaluation of such examinations were the responsibility of a self-ordained group of judges with an understandable interest in self-preservation. By the mid-nineteenth century, a system of public examinations controlled by the universities was well established. Howatt (1984:133) describes the impact on secondary school language curricula in England:

> The 'washback effect' of these examinations had the inevitable result of determining both the content of the language teaching syllabus and the methodological principles of the teachers responsible for preparing children to take them. Though public examinations did not create the grammar-translation method, they fixed its priorities.

A similar phenomenon occurred in the United States with the widespread post-World War II application of psychometric theory to language testing. A concern with 'objective,' 'scientific' measurement of language proficiency began to grow in the 1950s and on into the 1960s, a decade John Clark (1972), former test consultant with Educational Testing Service (ETS), has described as the 'golden age' of standardized test development. Under contracts from the United States Office of Education, two major standardized test batteries were developed: the Modern Language Association (MLA) Foreign Language Proficiency Tests for Teachers and Advanced Students and the MLA Cooperative Foreign Language Tests. Never since has there been such a large-scale effort to establish norms for language study in American schools.

It was during this same period that the Test of English as a Foreign Language (TOEFL) was launched. Developed to test the English proficiency of foreign students applying for admission to American colleges and universities, the program was initially funded with grants from government and private agencies and attached administratively to the MLA. In 1965, ETS assumed responsibility for program operation, and its offices were moved to Princeton, New Jersey.

The TOEFL and MLA language tests have served not only to evaluate learners and programs but to shape language programs and materials around the world. Alas, in making claims of objectivity and promoting standardization, they ignore all that Halliday and Hymes have shown us about the multidimensional, context-embedded, social nature of language. Interpreting texts from multiple perspectives reveals ambiguity, underscores the negotiative nature of communication. Language skills are social skills, whatever the context of situation. Interpretation and self-expression involve reflection on that context. Recognition of language varieties and of the rights of language communities to identify and affirm their own needs and norms is an affirmation of social meaning. On the other hand, language tests that fail to represent the contextualized, negotiative nature of communication cannot be said to encourage such affirmation.

When considering social meaning, teachers must also consider the issue of appropriacy in their own classroom style. Local norms offer considerable variety in this respect. Teachers may be mentors, coaches, and even friends for learners. They often are also task masters and judges. Teachers need to understand their options; and they need to see their role as dependent as much on the learners' expectations and interpretation as on their own intent. Roles are negotiated.

Novice teachers sometimes learn this lesson the hard way. In her novel, *China Men*, Maxine Hong Kingston tells the story of a lesson gone awry. Baba, a young teacher in rural China, has a love and respect for language and for literature. A conscientious and demanding teacher, he is eager to share his joy with the boys in his charge.

> At mid-afternoon, he told the students that they had been working so hard, he would treat them: he'd give them the first line of a couplet, and they could finish it almost any way they pleased. He read many examples in order to inspire them. But boredom drained their eyes. The word poetry had hit them like a mallet stunning cattle ... He pressed onward, ... 'Now I'll give you a first line that establishes the season and place, he said. 'You find the second line. You can write about an animal, a plant, a battle strategy,

the climate, a cloud ... '

'I don't get it.' We don't understand you.' 'You don't explain clearly.'

'Take a guess,' he suggested. 'Taking a guess is the same as making up a story.'

'That doesn't make sense.' 'We don't understand.' 'You're making things up because you don't know the answers' ...

'Explain,' said the students.

The boys spoke in the brute vulgate, and he saw that he had made a bad mistake translating literature into the common speech. The students had lost respect for him; if he were so smart, he would not speak like them. Scorn curled their lips and lifted their eyebrows. 'Explain,' they demanded without standing up for recognition. (1989:36–37).

Inexperienced and idealistic, Baba sought to engage his learners, to impart to them his love of language by speaking to them in the way they spoke to one another. Instead, he had lost them. They no longer respected him as their teacher. Classroom style and manner of teaching hold social meaning. Negotiation of that meaning is an ongoing, dynamic process. Tradition and the expectations of the participants influence the nature of the negotiation. As they face a classroom of learners, teachers must ask themselves WHOSE norms hold? WHOSE culture? and for WHAT? What message does the textbook send about the value and purpose of language study? What does the curriculum say about social values, about how the members of a society see themselves and see others? In addressing these questions of social meaning, teachers confront issues of social change.

Social change. Every society has rules for participation in social events. And these rules shape language development, social identity, and self-expression. Language also serves to identify and challenge established social rules. Michael Halliday has defined meaning potential as the range of variation available to the speaker. A linguistic act is not only a use of the potential of the language system. A linguistic act is a social and cultural act, an expression of who we are and what we value (Halliday 1977). Language experience provides options, expands the range of what speakers can do, of what they can mean. Hegemony comes at the expense of diversity. Options are narrowed, choice is restricted.

Where the communicative competence defined by Dell Hymes is a goal for language learners, the focus is on learner meaning and learner empowerment. Language learning is viewed in a context of social development. The communicative perspective of my own research interests in language learning, and the language as culture approach I have followed in curriculum design and teaching (Savignon 1972, 1983), have reflected my early educational interests in social and political science. If I had not been born a girl, these same interests may not have led me to language teaching. Inasmuch as my experience is illustrative of social change, let me explain.

My elementary and secondary school years were spent in a laboratory school on the campus of what was then called the Illinois State Normal University. Our teachers were a select group, teachers of teachers. Many of them were women. Student initiative was encouraged, and we enjoyed library, audio-visual, and other resources beyond those available in most public schools at the time. My program of studies included math, science, literature, Latin, French, history, and home economics. Freshman girls were required to learn how to make a dirndl skirt and eggs à la goldenrod. Only college-bound senior boys enrolled in physics. My mother was a wife and homemaker. Showing a proper mother's concern for the social success of her tall, adolescent daughter with clear intellectual interests, she cautioned, 'Don't speak up in class or the boys won't like you.'

Things went well. I didn't speak up too much and my steady boyfriend was the captain of the basketball team. But I did end up the class valedictorian. My classmate Steve was salutatorian. Miss Stroud, our senior class adviser, planned our commencement program. Sandra would speak of the past, our rich literary and artistic heritage. Steve would look to the future, science and adventure in the years ahead.

My college major was social studies. French was always an easy subject and I went on to develop my ability through a year of study in Grenoble. My dream was a career in foreign diplomacy. My father encouraged me to seek a teaching certificate, 'always a good insurance policy for a woman,' he reasoned. I followed the rules and was engaged to be married in June after my graduation.

That I went on to do graduate studies was in no way a reflection of any professional expectations or ambitions. I had never even seen a woman college professor, much less aspired to be one. The encouragement of my academic adviser, along with a Woodrow Wilson Fellowship, framed my future in ways I could not have imagined. Launched on a program of philology and literary criticism, the only graduate option then available in French, but still holding to my socio-political interests, I sought to include a minor in political science. 'No way,' said the professor who had given me an A in his upper division course in American political analysis. 'I don't accept women graduate students.' So it happened that I chose a minor in linguistics. My good fortune was that Illinois had one of the best linguistics programs in the United States. My first professor, Kenneth Hale, initiated me in the analysis of Papago field data. Eventually I would forsake French literary studies for psycholinguistics and second language acquisition.

I recount this story because it is mine, and because it colors my interpretation of the world and helps to define what I can mean, how I can mean. Language learning is embedded in socialization. Important contributions to the analysis of gender differences in language use by Elinor Ochs, Deborah Tannen, Cheris Krammarae, and others have helped me to understand how, as a woman, I have come to interpret, express, and negotiate meaning as I do. Through the insights they have provided, I have come to see more clearly cultural differences in style for what they sometimes are—differences not in intent but in means of expression. Differences in style and manner of expression are okay. Even in professional settings—the classroom, committee meetings, and conferences—I can be myself and not feel I should try to be one of the boys. It also helps to have a few more women colleagues with whom to exchange experiences, and I am pleased when I see women assume roles traditionally assigned to men, for example, as heads of academic units and as plenary speakers at professional meetings.

I have also come to better understand power asymmetry and self-disenfranchisement. Not all participants in negotiation are equal, and assertion of rights comes more easily to those in positions of power. Dominant groups have an advantage in working out meanings with which they are comfortable. Recognition of established differences in socialization brings with it a sense of place, along with a better appreciation of what is needed to promote change. And having known how it feels to be shut out, to have a voice muffled, if not silenced, I am better able to understand the feelings of others who seek self-expression, affirmation of self-worth.

Ours is a time of marked social change. In our communities, in our workplaces, and in our schools, diminishing resources and shifting ethnic, racial, and linguistic balance bring a growing sense of inequity and disarray. In the United States, business executives blame the Japanese for a stalled economy, politicians increasingly cite the poor, a disproportionate number of them black or Hispanic, as a drain on the national coffers, and a powerful and articulate lobby is demanding that English be declared the national language.

As cultural and linguistic values are argued, incidents of cultural, ethnic, racial, and sexual violence increase. When they do not occur, they are imagined. A recent hotel review in the *New York Times* (February 14, 1992) begins as follows:

> The bar in New York City's Mark hotel is small, dimly lighted and as cozily intimate as a private club. So intimate that the Frenchman in aviator glasses, black jeans, and a jacket with Mickey Mouse stitched under a 'Euro Disney' logo felt free to slide his chair to a corner table occupied by two women. 'May I eat off your plate?' he murmured in a thick Parisian accent, smoke curling up from his Gauloise. He helped himself to a thick slice of goat cheese quesadilla and munched ingratiatingly.
>
> Even the nicest Upper East Side hotels are not safe from creeping Eurotrash. My friend and I had checked into the Mark for a quiet, self-indulgent girls' weekend of room service folly, a kind of Thelma-and-Louise adventure. Fortunately for the Frenchman, we had not packed firearms.

Funny? Offensive? A sign of the *Times*? Meanwhile, students at the West Side Academy, a middle school attached to P.S. 75 in Manhattan, write essays to express their thoughts on the murder of a black youth who was looking for a used car in the largely white Bensonhurst section of Brooklyn. 'I feel all this violence and anger and racism, it disturbs me,' the teacher tells the class, all of whom are black or Hispanic. 'But that's good. It shows me the truth' (*New York Times*, February 15, 1992).

The violence felt within our communities is echoed in our international relations. Not long ago, Senator Hollings responded to reported comments by a Japanese official that many Americans are lazy and lack a work ethic. He is quoted has having told an assembly of workers in South Carolina that they 'should draw a mushroom cloud and put underneath it, 'Made in America by lazy and illiterate workers and tested in Japan.' He called his remark a joke, and when reporters conveyed to him the controversy he had raised, he responded, 'I'm glad I said it, glad I said it' (*New York Times*, March 5, 1992). No matter that the Japanese official had been misquoted in the American press, his comments taken out of context.

On a more upbeat note, Senators Al Gore and Barbara Mikulski have organized a series of monthly seminars for senators and their families on 'gender dynamics'. Debate over Senate response to sexual issues raised by the hearings for Supreme Court nominee Clarence Thomas prompted the series. The first seminar was led by Carol Gilligan of the Havard Center for Gender Studies, author of *In a Different Voice*. The second seminar was led by Georgetown professor of linguistics Deborah Tannen, author of the best-selling book *You Just Don't Understand* (*New York Times*, March 7, 1992). The national controversy sparked by the reaction of an all-male Senate committee to testimony by Anita Hill, and the widespread popular appeal of Tannen's work, focus attention on social meaning and the process of social change. Debate continues over what HE said and what SHE said, what HE meant, and what SHE meant. Interpretation reflects as much the experience and expectations of the interpreter as the words and intonations of the speakers.

In the midst of upheaval, the expression of cultural values that challenge those of a dominant, privileged elite, the monthly review *New Criterion* claims to reaffirm mainstream values. In the words of the letter of solicitation sent out to new subscribers, *New Criterion* is 'one magazine that tells you what is right and what is wrong with our cultural life today.' 'Dear Reader,' begins the letter,

> Do you have the feeling nowadays that something has gone terribly wrong with the arts? Do you sometimes have the impression that our culture has fallen into the hands of the barbarians? Does it make you angry when you see museums putting on shows that are trivial, vulgar, and politically repulsive? Are you appalled when leading universities abandon the classics of Western thought for the compulsory study of 'third world' propaganda?

Houston Baker, newly elected and the first black president of the Modern

Language Association of America, reprinted the text of the *New Criterion* letter in the Spring 1992 *MLA Newsletter*, and I am indebted to him for bringing it to my attention. In reacting, Baker (1992:3) gives full expression to his rage:

> Who speaks here is a black man in America who is terribly honored to have received awards in the humanities, honorary degrees from colleges and universities, writers' and teaching awards, and the label of 'left' adversary to white male dominance. Who speaks and writes here—out of the most humanistic of motives—is a black man who feels that [this] type of nauseating verbiage is the last breath of white, male, Western anxiety engaged in a sputtering attempt to put out conflagrations that those of us who call ourselves NEW PEOPLE in no way started.'

Ours is a time of change, marked by anxiety and struggle. We move through zones of uncertainty. Whose cultures will survive? What literature will remain? However imperfectly, can we learn to listen to the voice of the other? Can we find peace in pluralism?

Conclusion. The challenge to teachers is clear. For so long as there have been languages, there have been language learners. And for so long as there have been learners of language, there have been teachers of language. Whether they are children or adults, whether the language they are learning is their first, second, or third, learners need teachers. The best teachers provide a model for learners. They engage and guide them in their efforts at self-expression. Teachers interpret and respond to learners. They know and understand learner limitations. Above all, good teachers challenge learners.

Language is communication, communication rich with social meaning. Program development, teacher education, and program evaluation should begin with an understanding of language as communication, language as culture. The communicative ability important for participation in academic, professional, and social settings comes with practice, practice along with critical and self-critical analysis of language use. Talking about communication involves talking about grammar, yes, and more. Knowledge of language includes knowledge of grammar, syntax, vocabulary, modes of discourse, print and nonprint genres, and rhetorical strategies, the use of language to influence others. Learner metalinguistic and metacognitive awareness begins with awareness of self and of the ways in which one can mean.

There are linguistic rules and there are social rules. Language and language learning are also powerful forces for social change, for breaking rules. In a time of social conflict and disputed values, teachers are challenged to challenge learners to look, to discover, and to reflect. With the ability to interpret the context in which they find themselves, and the courage to express their own meanings, they will be better able to take their place in a multilingual, multicultural world of diversity.

At the same time, language teachers are challenged to speak their own truths, express their own meanings. We come to teaching with our own life experiences, our own goals, our own interpretations. Together we share a commitment to reflection and negotiation. We are teachers because we believe in enabling, in empowering those who will shape the future. As language teachers who understand communication, we are challenged not only to learn and to enable others. We are also challenged to take an active role in the government of our society and nations. We are challenged to identify those who hold power and endeavor to influence them in an enlightened and politically sophisticated way. Education for responsible world citizenship is the solution to our most pressing human problems. The language teaching profession must exert leadership in our global society, not only in the teaching of language, and education in general, but also as good citizens in a changing and globally interdependent world.

REFERENCES

Baker, Houston. 1992. MLA Newsletter 24, 1.3.

Clark, John. 1972. Foreign language testing: Theory and practice. Philadelphia: Center for Curriculum Development.

Comenius, J.A. 1665. Janua Linguarum. Amsterdam.

Gilligan, Carol. 1982. In a different voice. Cambridge: Harvard University Press.

Halliday, M.A.K. 1977. Language as social semiotic: The social interpretation of language and meaning. Baltimore: University Park Press.

Howatt, A.P.R. 1984. A history of English language teaching. Oxford: Oxford University Press.

Jesperson, Otto. 1904. How to teach a foreign language. London: Swan Sonnenschein and Co.

Kingston, Maxine Hong. 1989. China men. New York: Vintage International [Originally published by Alfred A. Knopf, New York, 1980].

Petersen, N.M. 1870. Sprogkundskab i norden. Collected works. Copenhagen, Denmark.

Savignon, Sandra J. 1972. Communicative competence: An experiment in foreign language teaching. Philadelphia: Center for Curriculum Development.

Savignon, Sandra J. 1983. Communicative competence: Theory and classroom practice. Reading, MA: Addison-Wesley.

Tannen, Deborah. 1990. You just don't understand: Women and men in conversation. New York: William Morrow.

The social meaning IN language curriculum, OF language curriculum, and THROUGH language curriculum

James Dean Brown
University of Hawai'i at Manoa

Introduction. Language CURRICULUM has been defined in many ways. Consider the Richards, Platt, and Weber (1985:70) definition of curriculum: 'An educational programme which states: (a) the educational purpose of the programme (the ends); (b) the content, teaching procedures and learning experiences which will be necessary to achieve this purpose (the means); (c) some means for assessing whether or not the educational ends have been achieved'. Notice how the definition, like most others, concentrates on the ends and means of curriculum, that is, the components necessary for delivering instruction and evaluating the success or failure of the curriculum.

The definition of CURRICULUM DEVELOPMENT from the same source (70–71) also focuses on the components of curriculum: 'the study and development of the goals, content, implementation, and evaluation of an educational system. In language teaching, curriculum development (also called syllabus design) includes: (a) the study of the purposes for which a learner needs a language (needs analysis); (b) the setting of objectives, and the development of a syllabus, teaching methods, and materials; (c) the evaluation of the effects of these procedures on the learner's language ability'.

Even in my own work on curriculum (for instance, Brown 1989; Brown and Pennington 1991; Pennington and Brown 1991), a main focus has been on the elements of curriculum design. For instance, Brown (1989) concentrates on the following curriculum components: needs analysis, instructional objectives, tests, materials, teaching, and evaluation. The relationships among these six curriculum elements are shown in Figure 1.

After much reading and considerable work on actual curriculum projects in Los Angeles, the People' Republic of China, Saudi Arabia, and Hawaii, it is clear to me that, while definitions of language curriculum and curriculum design abound, most such definitions miss several key points: (1) language curriculum development is a process of innovation; (2) curriculum development involves people working together and thus is a political process; and (3) various ways of thinking about SOCIAL MEANING can provide a focus for solving some of the political problems that arise in curriculum development.

Figure 1. Curriculum process model (Brown 1989).

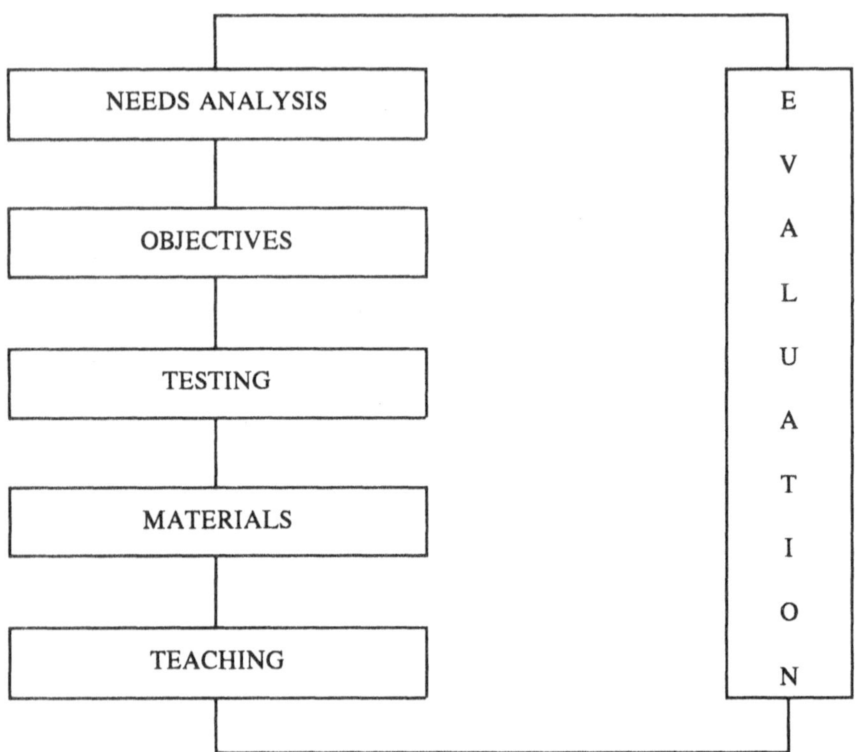

Curriculum development as innovation. Whenever curriculum development is initiated, the process inevitably involves either an entirely new language program or changes in an existing program. Naturally, such changes involve innovation, but innovation is not necessarily a straightforward proposition; there are different approaches to innovation, all of which should be considered. White (1988) devotes an entire chapter to issues of managing and evaluating curriculum. In the process, he describes three models of innovation:

The research and development model. 'Typically, such R and D projects have devoted themselves to the production of materials or the development of new methods, and the package, conventionally in the form of published materials, is disseminated to the mass audience who are the intended users of the innovation.' The author gives the Threshold Level materials of the Council of Europe as an example (White 1988:121–22).

The problem solving model. 'An expression of progressivism and the approach to curriculum development advocated by Stenhouse, who takes the view that all teachers should assume some responsibility for researching their classroom work and that this is an important part of the teacher's professionalism' (White 1988:121). 'Such an approach means that innovations are likely to be highly appropriate to the context in which they occur, but there is the danger that a head teacher and staff can impose their own values on the school' (White 1988:124).

The social interaction model. This model 'highlights the influence and importance of social relations in the transmission and adoption of innovation' (White 1988:125).

Curriculum development as a political process. Thinking similar to that expressed in White's third social interaction model of innovation led me to the realization that curriculum is fundamentally a political process. The remainder of this paper will explore the political nature of curriculum development based on the proposition that all curriculum, regardless of focus, is political in nature.

Any successful political movement or process, at least in an open, democratic society, must have a purpose, must provide leadership, must furnish political structures within which it will operate, must take into account the views of different interested constituencies, must build consensus within and among those constituencies, must furnish a means for resolution of conflict, and must provide for adaptation to ongoing change. Table 1 presents these characteristics as the political features of curriculum development because the unfolding of new curriculum is necessarily a political process, which will in turn have all of the attributes of such a process. In fact, it seems to me that some form of these characteristics and structures will tend to evolve in any curriculum—though the evolution may tend to be of a hodgepodge nature if the processes are not planned and controlled. Thus it is to a curriculum developer's advantage to build these political attributes into the curriculum from the outset.

Table 1. Political features of curriculum development.

Provide purpose
Supply leadership
Control resources
Furnish political structures
Account for different constituencies
Build consensus
Resolve conflict
Adapt to change

In addition, it is important to realize that, like differences in the politics at different levels of government, there are differences in the political processes in language curricula developed for different levels. Laws developed for the international level will be different from those designed for the national level, and those developed at the state or province level will be different from laws developed at the city or ward level. Similarly, there are different levels of curriculum development, as shown in Table 2. Some language curriculum development (for instance, *Threshold Level English* [van Ek and Alexander 1980] developed by the Council of Europe) is done at an international level. Other curriculum development efforts (for example, the English teaching guidelines of the Mombusho, or Ministry of Education, in Japan) are clearly at the national level. If a state board of education develops a language curriculum, it will be different from that developed by a county or local school board. At each of these levels and more (as shown in Table 2, the political characteristics will take different forms, but will nonetheless be present in one shape or other.

Table 2. Levels of curriculum development.

Classroom level
Small program level
Large program level
Multi-program level
County system level
State or provincial system level
National level
International level

The level of language curriculum that will be of most concern in this paper is the locally developed curriculum within a single language program. It is with this type of curriculum that I have had the most experience, and with this type of curriculum development that many, many EFL/ESL teachers are concerned whether they are working in higher education intensive programs, adult education, refugee programs, or vocational training. Ultimately, all curriculum development must probably be finished at the local level. Consider what would happen if the Threshold materials developed for the international level were adopted for a local curriculum. To make the most effective use of those materials, it would no doubt be necessary to change, adapt, flesh out, and fit them to the local conditions, goals, and needs.

Curriculum development and three types of social meaning. In response to the views expressed above, the central thesis of this paper is that there are three very different views of the phrase 'social meaning' that can help to focus our thinking about the innovative political activities involved in language curriculum development: (1) the social meaning which is part of the linguistic system that we teach in the classroom; (2) the social meaning of what teachers, students, administrators, and others do in the curriculum development process; and (3) the social meaning that is projected through the curriculum to affect the lives of the students.

Social meaning in curriculum. The social meaning which is part of the linguistic system that we teach in the classroom is often discussed in terms of what the students need to learn. However, students' needs may be perceived in different ways depending on who is asked, and, indeed, groups other than the students within a language program may have needs which must also be met in the curriculum development process. There are three main constituencies which are of prime importance in language programs: students, teachers, and administrators. Of course, there may be many other potential constituencies (as shown in Table 3, but these others may not be as immediately relevant within most local language programs as the students, teachers, and administrators, nor will they be as directly affected by the curriculum development process.

Table 3. Potential constituencies in curriculum development.

Students
Teachers
Administrators
Parents
Future employers
Future professors
Higher institutional authorities
Government agencies
The public
And others ...

Over the years, a number of different points of view have developed in applied linguistics about what should be going on the language classroom. The two primary issues that may bring students, teachers, administrators, and curriculum developers into conflict are: (1) differing views of the theoretical approach to what students need to learn; and (2) dissimilar ideas on the sequencing of the teaching and materials.

Theoretical approaches. In most cases, I suspect that the participants in a language program begin with preconceptions about the 'correct' approach to students' needs, though they themselves may not realize it. Such preconceptions and assumptions about what should happen in the classroom will be referred to here as APPROACHES. For years, language teachers have drawn on other disciplines in formulating their ideas about what and how their students need to learn. Psychology, linguistics, and education have thus influenced teachers' views of students' needs. More recently, there has been work within applied linguistics (especially second language acquisition research) to draw on, as well. Examples of some of the more influential approaches over the years are shown in Table 4. Remember, the term APPROACH is used here as a way of defining what and how students need to learn.

Sequencing. Regardless of the approaches, or belief systems, that are adopted, is it still necessary to plan and organize that which should be presented and/or learned in order: first, second, third, and so forth? McKay (1978:11) used the term SYLLABUS in a special way that seems to apply here:

> A syllabus provides a focus for what should be studied, along with a rationale for how that content should be selected and ordered. Currently, the literature reflects three major types of syllabuses: structural, situational, and notional.

Table 4. Language teaching approaches (adapted from Brown 1990).

Approaches	Ways of Defining Learner's Needs
Classical approach	Humanism: students need to read the classics.
Grammar-translation approach	Students need to learn with economy of time and effort.
Direct approach	Students need to learn communication so they should use only L2 in class.
Audiolingual approach	Students need operant conditioning and behavior modification to learn language.
Communicative approach	Students must be able to express their intentions, that is, they must learn the meanings which are important to them.

With McKay's article as a starting point, Table 5 defines seven syllabuses, which are simply different ways of organizing the teaching of language. The list provided in Table 5 is far from definitive and could never be a final set of all possible syllabuses for two reasons: (1) because the relative importance of different syllabuses varies over time; and (2) because new types of syllabuses are constantly being created.

With reference to the first point, the relative importance of different organizing principles seems to ebb and flow within the field. For instance, tasks or problem-solving syllabuses may gain consensus in today's language teaching and replace functions as the dominant way of organizing language teaching. Or perhaps topics will become dominant if teaching language through content increases in significance.

As for the second point, language teaching is a dynamic field, and new ways of organizing teaching and materials will no doubt surface in the near future. For instance, in a very recent article, Long and Crookes (1992) distinguish between what they label procedural syllabuses, process syllabuses, and task-based syllabuses, with the first two types of syllabuses posited as precursors of the task-based syllabuses in their argument. Since their first two types of syllabuses are not yet widely used, they are not included in my list. However, someday they may be. The main point to keep in mind is that syllabuses (ways of organizing teaching and materials) are quite different from the approaches (ways of defining learners' needs) discussed above.

Table 5. Language teaching syllabi (adapted from Brown 1990).

Syllabi	Ways of organizing teaching and materials.
Structural	Grammatical and phonological structures are the organizing principles—sequenced from easy to difficult or frequent to less frequent.
Situational	Situations (such as at the bank, at the supermarket, at a restaurant, and so forth) form the organizing principle—sequenced by the likelihood students will encounter them.
Topical	Topics or themes (such as health, food, clothing, and so forth) form the organizing principle—sequenced by the likelihood that students will encounter them.
Functional	Functions (such as identifying, reporting, correcting, describing, and so forth) are the organizing principle—sequenced by some sense of chronology or usefulness of each function.
Notional	Conceptual categories called notions (such as duration, quantity, location, and so forth) are the basis of organization—sequenced by some sense of chronology or usefulness of each notion.
Skills	Skills (such as listening for gist, listening for main ideas, listening for inferences, scanning a reading passage for specific information, and so forth)—sequenced by some sense of chronology or usefulness for each skill.
Task	Task- or activity-based categories (such as drawing maps, following directions, following instructions, and so forth) serve as the basis for organization—sequenced by some sense of chronology or usefulness of notions.

Different views of students' needs. All participants in a language program have ideas about what the students need to learn. Even completely untrained teachers will try to recreate the activities that they experienced when they were taught a language. In a sense, they are mimicking what they think good language teaching should be. Similarly, students will have preconceptions about what they think good language teaching should be—probably modeled on the teaching that they had in their home countries. Thus students may tend to favor the kinds of language teaching that they have become accustomed to. For instance, they may favor traditional grammar translation approaches that are organized around structural or situational syllabuses.

However, for trained language teachers, administrators, and curriculum developers, the teaching may tend to be more theoretically motivated. For example, they may favor communicative approaches organized along the lines of notional, functional, or task-based syllabuses. Such differences in teachers' and students' views of what constitutes good language teaching are potential points of conflict, and may be at the very heart of many of the problems that arise in ESL curricula. Conflict may also arise in EFL settings where the teachers from the outside world have 'more progressive' views than the students with regard to what the students need to learn.

Given that decisions about appropriate approaches and syllabuses may often be points of conflict, the process of needs analysis no longer seems as straightforward and uncontroversial as it is often depicted in books on the topic. Which needs should the curriculum meet? The needs as defined by the students' wants and desires? The 'real needs' of the students (as decided by their teachers and the curriculum developers)? Or the needs of the students as defined by their own ministry of education? Clearly, these are political decisions, and there are different constituencies involved even in determining what needs a curriculum should meet.

Social meaning from linguistics. Because of the potential conflicts discussed in the previous section, social meaning (in the linguistic sense of that phrase) can play a central role in deciding what to teach in the language classroom. For instance, it is important to understand that the 'social function of language serves to establish and maintain social relations between people' (Richards et al. 1985:116). The personal bias expressed in this paper is that, if all constituencies can be coaxed into accepting the importance of the social meaning of language, it will be possible to build a consensus about what and how the students need to learn, as well as how that learning should be sequenced.

Once that step is taken, curriculum developers can consider some of the dimensions that the social meaning of language has. In Halliday's terms, we must consider the social semiotic of language: 'It means interpreting language within a sociocultural context, in which the culture itself is interpreted in semiotic terms—as an information system ... ' (Halliday 1978:2). Students, teachers, administrators, and curriculum developers must realize that the language that students will use after leaving the classroom will ultimately take place in a social context. That social context of language was analyzed by Halliday (1978) as involving three factors:

(1) FIELD OF DISCOURSE—What is happening or being talked about in a

particular social context.

(2) TENOR OF DISCOURSE—Who the participants in the exchange are and what their relationships are to each other.

(3) MODE OF DISCOURSE—What part the language plays in the particular social context, for example, what organization is used to convey the meaning, what channel is used, and so forth.

These three factors are important in thinking about the choices that must be made in the types of language and discourse that will be taught in the classroom.

In other words, the social semiotic nature of language must be at least a part of the underlying theoretical and philosophical underpinnings of any present day language curriculum. The social context of language must also be included in thinking about what type of syllabus will be used in organizing the curriculum. Will it be structural? Situational? Topical? Functional? Task-based? Or some combination of the above? Such choices of approach and syllabus should depend in part on considerations of the social meanings that the students will someday need to convey.

One side effect of the theoretical work of applied linguists like Halliday (1978), Wilkins (1976), and Munby (1978) is that present day teaching methods often focus on getting students to express their meanings for social purposes whether organized around functions of the language or tasks or both. Indeed, the thrust of many of the theoretical developments that surround the development of syllabuses from structural to situational to functional to task-based has been social meaning. In other words, it is important for us to empower the students to communicate their social meanings, meanings with which we may disagree, but nonetheless must promote. Focus by teachers, students, administrators, and curriculum developers on such social meanings can help to bring together their disparate views of what the students need to learn.

Social meaning of curriculum. The focus of this section will be on the social meaning of what teachers, students, administrators, and curriculum developers do together and separately in the curriculum development process. As pointed out above, many definitions of curriculum leave out the political nature of curriculum development. A language program is an institution, like any other institution. As a result, curriculum development turns out to be largely a process of managing people rather than a series of products.

The point being made here is that, if adequate political structures are provided, the people will in turn generate products that will be useful in the curriculum. In other words, to be sound, and to accomplish anything with regard to the 'content, teaching procedures and learning experiences' referred to by Richards et al (1985), a curriculum must provide the political structures necessary to coordinate the efforts of all of the individuals in the program. This section will consider some of the different organizational patterns that a language program might adopt, explore why certain patterns might be adopted in different language programs, and examine the logistics of curriculum development.

Different ways to organize institutions. As listed in Table 6, Toffler (1991:187–194) discusses seven different ways that institutions are organized. First, a PULSATING ORGANIZATION is one that expands and contracts on a regular basis to meet changing cyclical demands. The United States Census Bureau is the example that he gives for an organization that is normally at a small maintenance level, but expands dramatically every ten years to conduct the census. Second, a TWO-FACED ORGANIZATION is one which can operate with two different lines of command under different circumstances. The example that the author gives is of a military commando unit in which the command structure is very authoritarian when the unit is in training, but egalitarian when the unit is in combat with each soldier taking equal responsibility for certain aspects of the mission. Third, a CHECKERBOARD ORGANIZATION is one in which two points of view must be represented throughout the institution such that the management is made up of alternating people, who represent the two alternating points of view in the hierarchy. The author cites a Japanese bank in California as an example of how the Japanese and American points of view can be represented by alternating Japanese and Americans in the management. Fourth, a COMMISSAR ORGANIZATION is one in which two main channels are open for the flow of information throughout the organization. An example of this type of structure existed in the Soviet army units, which had separate lines of communication for military officers and political officers (who were responsible for keeping the army subject to the rule of the Communist Party). Fifth, a BURO-BARONIAL ORGANIZATION is one in which, within an overall bureaucratic structure, smaller feudal-like baronies exist with 'lords' who are carefully ranked ruling over people who function very much like serfs. Sixth, in a SKUNKWORKS ORGANIZATION, a group or team of people is given a loosely defined goal or problem to solve, and then supplied the resources that they will need and allowed to work on their own outside of any bureaucratic structures that exist in the institution. Seventh, a SELF-START TEAM is similar to the skunkworks organization, but is self-organized in the sense that a group of people is drawn together (for instance, on a computer network) by a common problem or goal. They then find their own resources, and proceed to work together outside of any other bureaucratic structures in the institution.

Table 6. Organizational structures.

The pulsating organization
The two-faced organization
The checkerboard organization
The commissar organization
The buro-baronial organization
The skunkworks organization
The self-start team

Different structures for different language programs. Some intensive language programs like the Hawai'i English Language Program (HELP) in Summer Sessions at the University of Hawaii at Manoa (UHM) are organized as pulsating programs to serve very large influxes of students during the summer. Though it functions throughout the year, HELP is relatively small during the school year but gears up each summer to handle large contingents of students. Expansion and contraction on a yearly basis are regular features of this organization.

Other institutions in which the administrators are also teachers may benefit from using the two-faced form of organization so that at some times the teacher/administrator can function in a hierarchical relationship with the other teachers and at other times as an equal colleague.

Still other language teaching institutions which involve administrators and teachers from two different countries might benefit from using the checkerboard form of organization.

The commissar type of organization would be most appropriate where an outside administrative or political organization wants to keep an eye on a language program even though the program has its own chain of command. A representative of that outside organization would be sent in to work in the program. While this may seem distasteful at first glance, there are probably situations in which an outside administrative unit does want to keep tabs on a language program in this manner.

As to the buro-baronial organization, Toffler's own words (1991:191) point to how it works in some educational settings:

> The best surviving example of feudal organization today is found in the university, where each department is a barony, and professors are ranked and rule over graduate assistants, who make up the body of the serfs. This feudal holdover is embedded within (and often at war with) the bureaucratic administrative structure of the university.

In all probability, the buro-baronial organization is found in many of the intensive ESL programs that exist in university settings.

In the English Language Institute at UHM, teams of teachers are organized by the skill area and level that they are teaching. These groups can be viewed as a form of skunkworks organization because they are given loosely defined goals and then supplied with the resources that they will need and allowed to work on their own.

There are probably also instances of self-start teams to be found in language programs. Such self-organized groups would be drawn together in a manner similar to the skunkworks groups just described except that they would be united by their own goals or problems rather than by the design of a curriculum developer. Such groups may very well exist in some language programs with or without the knowledge of the administrators.

The central points that I am trying to make here are: (1) that some form of organizational structure is necessary to get people working together on language curriculum; (2) that there are alternative structures that should be considered; and (3) that the existing structure in a given program may not be the best for developing curriculum to meet the goals of the program and should therefore be reconsidered.

It seems clear that in one way or another successful curriculum development must be structured such that the multiple talents of all participants in a program can be marshalled so that, working together, the participants can create innovation and change. In other words, structures must be put in place that will encourage teachers to reflect on what they are doing in the classroom.

No individual teacher can be expected to do an adequate job of analyzing the students' needs, setting goals and objectives, creating (as well as administrating, scoring, and analyzing) tests, developing materials, teaching, and evaluating the results. These elements of curriculum development are too large and, in some cases, too technical to be done well by busy teachers.

The skunkworks organization has turned out to be particularly appropriate at UHM. Teams of teachers are put together to work on curriculum tasks for a few hours per week (in addition to their teaching), and, over the course of three or four years, they have accomplished a great deal for the curriculum as a whole. If this structure is set up as an ongoing process, it can be very successful. However, other forms of organization may prove more appropriate at other institutions.

The logistics of curriculum. Even under the best of circumstances, curriculum development will take time. In fact, if it is viewed as an ongoing process of development and maintenance, a curriculum will never be completely finished. Hence it is important to set up structures that will continue. At some level or other, someone must oversee the logistics of curriculum development using at least the steps shown in Table 7. These steps involve: (1) finding and marshalling resources; (2) setting up structures to help teachers do their job of teaching; (3) providing political structures and leadership that will help the teachers to work together to share their pooled talents and abilities; (4) dispensing the available resources in as equitable a manner as possible; (5) buffering the teachers from external negative forces so that they can get on with curriculum development projects; and (6) representing the curriculum to the outside world.

Table 7. Major logistical considerations in language curriculum development.

Marshall resources
Set up structures for teaching
Get teachers working together
Dispense resources equitably
Buffer teachers from external forces
Represent the organization to outside

In short, sound curriculum development must provide the appropriate organizational structures and safeguards so that those who are closest to the students can help the organization investigate the needs of the students, set institutional goals and objectives, develop materials and tests, teach those materials, and constantly revise all of the elements through continuing program evaluation procedures. It is crucial to provide political structures that will promote the purposes of the curriculum and, at the same time, provide enough freedom for teachers to excel at what they do best—teaching.

Social meaning through curriculum. The last form of social meaning that will be discussed in this paper is that which can be projected through the curriculum to affect the lives of the students. In creating any curriculum, it is inevitable that spoken or written text of the target language will be used. Using target language text usually entails selecting and grading materials so that they will be more palatable and accessible to students. However, such selection and gradation does not occur in a vacuum. In the best of all worlds, we use needs analysis procedures to decide what the students need to learn. Even if these needs are based on data drawn from students, teachers, administrators, and other interested constituencies, the conclusions that needs analysts draw will depend to some degree on their own preconceptions of sound approaches and syllabuses as well as their biases about what the target language is and what its relationships are to the target culture. If the needs analysts believe in the grammar-translation approach and structural syllabuses and are conservative morally, politically, and socially, they will probably find that the students' needs include structures X, Y, and Z, and that appropriate topics for texts are ones like the need for a strong national defense, the righteousness of the anti-abortion movement, patriotism, nationalism, and so forth. If, on the other hand, the needs analysts are believers in the communicative approach and task-based syllabuses, and are 'politically correct,' they might find that the students need functions A, B, and C delivered through a series of graded tasks based on language that is about world peace, a woman's right to choose, internationalism, etc. In other words, it is inescapable that the belief systems of the needs analysts and curriculum designers will cause them to find what they are looking for to some degree.

In developing curriculum, and particularly in delivering the resulting instruction, these types of social meaning are projected, as well. Especially in ESL situations, we may project social meanings of a political, cultural, or moral nature with or without realizing it. Perhaps it is our responsibility as educators to teach students about the world they live in while we teach language. One perceived need in many foreign language curricula is to broaden students' perspectives culturally (that is, beyond their own culture, ethnocentricity, and so forth). It may be that we are duty bound to explain moral, cultural, and political values with which the students are not familiar or comfortable in order to prepare them to rationally consider, evaluate, and accept or reject such views wherever they may find them.

In higher education intensive programs ESL programs in the United States, it may be common for students from relatively conservative societies to be confronted with politically correct thought (as the correct answer) which is totally alien to them, and to most Americans, as well. Topics may vary from women's issues, to democratic values, to openness in interpersonal relations, to environmental issues, to anti-war sentiments, and so forth. In other situations, students may be confronted with quite different sets of values from the curriculum and teachers. In a religious school, strong family ties, conservative political views, and even racism may be subtexts in the materials and delivery of the language lessons.

Thus, while particular social meanings can be projected through the curriculum to affect the lives of the students, we must be aware that we are projecting those social meanings and consider carefully whether the views that are being projected (1) are the ones we want to project; (2) are appropriate for a language teaching situation; (3) are balanced in approach; and (4) are tolerant of the students' points of view. Perhaps, if we help students develop the skills necessary to deal with social meanings of various types for the rest of their lives, we will have succeeded, but even that should be considered very carefully in the curriculum development process.

Discussion. Less than a year ago, I finished a five-year term as director of the English Language Institute (ELI) at the University of Hawai'i at Manoa. During that time and in the months since, I have thought a great deal about the various ways in which social meaning, as I am defining them in this paper, came to bear on the successes and failures of our curriculum development efforts.

When I first took over as director, the ELI, like many ESL organizations, basically provided support for teachers, who were left on their own in the classroom. For the most part, the teachers' independence meant that they were required to do their own needs analysis, set their own objectives, adopt, develop, or adapt their own materials, do the teaching, design diagnostic or achievement tests as required, and evaluate the success of their own efforts as best they could. Since most of the teachers did not have the time or training to do all of these tasks well, I felt that my job in developing curriculum was to get the teachers to work together so that collectively they could accomplish all of the tasks listed above in an orderly and professional manner without overburdening any single individual.

Example of social meaning IN a curriculum. One consequence of the fact that teachers were almost exclusively alone in curriculum development at the beginning of my directorship was that all choices of approach and syllabus, were left up to individual teachers. Since then, the collective strengths of the ELI teachers as well as graduate students in the Department of ESL have been marshalled to (1) do a complete sets of needs analyses for each of the eight courses; (2) set objectives for each of the courses; (3) develop, administer, and revise criterion-referenced tests for each course; (4) do regular systematic text adoptions and create modules of supplemental materials; (5) generate support documents for teachers; and (6) create an ongoing evaluation system (including observation forms, student questionnaires, and so forth).

Throughout these processes, many changes occurred in our thinking about what the students needed to learn and how the associated teaching should be structured. At the beginning, some of the teachers used a skills-based syllabus. However, other courses were structured in any way that the individual teachers wanted them to be. Since then, many different points of view have been taken into account, including those of the students, teachers, and administrators, as well as the professors in the mainstream of the university. In the process, by consensus, the approaches and syllabuses used in the ELI courses gradually changed. There are still some traces of the skills-based syllabus to be found in the curriculum, but large portions of what goes on in the classrooms is based on the communicative approach organized around either a functional syllabus or, in some cases, a task-based syllabus. The benefit of coming to these decisions by consensus is that, by and large, as the curriculum has changed so have the teachers, and, perhaps more importantly, as the teachers have changed in consonance with major shifts in the field, so has the curriculum.

I am not saying that there were no problems. However, structures were provided, which brought teachers together to discuss and argue and eventually agree by consensus on the most fundamental issues of language teaching—the institution's basic approach and syllabus.

Example of the social meaning OF a curriculum. Structurally, when I took over as Director of the ELI at UHM, there was a 'curriculum committee' made up primarily of those professors and graduate assistants whose courses had so few students that they were canceled. One of the first things that I did to foster curriculum development was to establish three positions for lead teachers. As in many academic situations, I could not give them any extra money, but I did manage to get them released from half of their teaching load and created the title of 'lead teacher.' These lead teachers were each put in charge of one of the three skills that we teach in our courses at UHM (reading, writing, and listening), each of which is taught at two levels (intermediate and advanced). The lead teachers, in turn, called together the teachers in their particular skill area for regular meetings by level and for the whole skill area. These meetings gradually took on the character of what were called skunkworks groups in the earlier discussion.

The curriculum committee was reconstituted to include the director, assistant director, and the three lead teachers. This curriculum committee decided the policies of the ELI and the areas of focus within the curriculum that would be worked on by the smaller skunkworks groups. The lead teachers would then take on curriculum tasks, which they would accomplish by working directly with the teachers. All ideas and products that the teachers came up with in their separate skill-area committees were in turn discussed and reviewed by the overall curriculum committee in order to provide feedback and coordinate the efforts of the three skill areas.

Over the years, modifications occurred in the structure of this curriculum committee. Two more lead teachers (one for our writing lab and one specifically for our testing program) were added, and faculty resource people from the Department of ESL were recruited to help and guide each of the lead teachers. However, the overall structure and function of the committee has stayed essentially the same. The curriculum committee makes policy and provides direction for ongoing curriculum development, while the individual skill area committees help teachers to work together in actually creating or revising the stuff of the curriculum.

The English Language Institute at UHM, like many other higher education intensive language programs, is located within a university department, and we must ask ourselves if this is not a buro-baronial type of organization. If the answer is yes, we should then ask ourselves if the buro-baronial structure is what we want. However, one saving grace in the ELI is that we have been using skunkworks groups to form teams of teachers who are given loosely defined goals, supplied the necessary resources, and then allowed to work on their own. This form of skunkworks organization (despite its unfortunate name) might be useful in other language programs, as well. In fact, if there is not some provision for such work in a curriculum, self-start teams might form on their own accord based on common goals or problems among the teachers.

Thus several types of organizational structure are combined at UHM: the bureaucratic structures of the university administration, the baronial structure of the department of ESL, and skunkworks groups for each of the three skill areas and sometimes for each level within the skills. The skunkworks groupings interact with the curriculum committee, which sets policy and the general direction of curriculum development.

It is important for us to communicate with each other as teachers and administrators and work together on curriculum. It is only through such cooperation, on an ongoing basis, that sound curriculum processes can be established. It is also essential that students be brought into the process on a regular basis so that they can provide feedback, solutions, and good ideas. At UHM this is done through student representative meetings. All of the participants (even students) must feel that they are involved in the curriculum process.

Example of social meaning THROUGH curriculum. An example of how social meaning can be projected through a curriculum came up in the ELI when one of the lead teachers suggested that we should be warning the students about the dangers of AIDS and educating them about the practice of safe sex. The lead teachers took this idea to the teachers in the various courses, and some of them were uncomfortable with the idea. However, in the end, most of the teachers agreed that this was an issue that should be taught. AIDS materials were found and used as the basis for developing lessons which were then taught in the listening courses in a way that made it simply another type of target language text.

In addition, decisions were made that the best way to arm students to deal with such social issues was to present them with a wide variety of viewpoints and to address those viewpoints as just what they are: views and opinions. The goal was to give students the skills needed to further investigate the issues on their own and to form their own opinions. In other words, it was felt that the students should be taught how to distinguish fact from opinion and encouraged to analyze and synthesize the facts in order to form their own opinions. However, we realized in formulating these ideas that the goals just mentioned are themselves culturally conditioned and ethnocentric because in some cultures resources are not available for such investigations and, in any case, expression of personal opinion is not tolerated, or at least not encouraged.

Conclusion. In this paper, I have clearly broadened the definition of social meaning at least as it relates to language curriculum. First, my experience forced me to think about the social meaning in curriculum. I came to realize the importance of embedding social meaning in the curriculum through adoption of approaches and syllabuses that promote expression of the social meanings important to the students' future language use. Second, I had to act on the social meaning of curriculum. Curriculum can no longer be viewed as a series of products, but must instead be considered an ongoing process of social interactions among students, teachers, administrators, curriculum developers, and others. The structures will differ from organization to organization because of the political realities involved. However, we do have choices and, in any case, some structure or combination of structures must be consciously used by curriculum developers if the social interactions in a program are to work smoothly and productively. Finally, the social meanings that are projected through a curriculum became important. Such social meanings may take the form of political, cultural, moral, or religious viewpoints. The curriculum developer must be aware that such social meanings exist in the classroom and account for them in some way or another so that they are appropriate and acceptable to the students who must assimilate them.

In short, curriculum is much more than a set of documents. Curriculum must be viewed as innovative and political and as the interaction of people who, in a good curriculum, can all come to a consensus about their common goals. Curriculum development cannot be divorced from this series of human activities, a fact that curriculum developers must keep in mind by remembering the importance of social meaning IN curriculum, social meaning OF curriculum, and social meaning THROUGH curriculum. Any curriculum that does not account for these dimensions is bound to fail.

REFERENCES

Brown, James D. 1989. Language program evaluation: A synthesis of existing possibilities. The second language curriculum, ed. by R.K. Johnson, 222–41. Cambridge: Cambridge University Press.

Brown, James D. 1990. Language teaching methods? Paper presented at the XIV.° Simpósio dos Centros de Cultura Brasil-Estados Unidos, Vittoria, Brazil.

Brown, James D., and Martha C. Pennington. 1991. Developing effective evaluation systems for language programs. Building better English language programs: Perspectives on evaluation in ESL, ed. by Martha C. Pennington, 3–18. Washington, DC: NAFSA.

Halliday, M.A.K. 1978. Language as a social semiotic. London: Edward Arnold.

Long, Michael H., and Graham Crookes. 1992. Three approaches to task-based syllabus design. TESOL Quarterly 26, 1.27–56.

McKay, Sandra. 1978. Syllabuses: Structural, situational, notional. TESOL Newsletter 12, 5.11.

Munby, John. 1978. Communicative syllabus design: A sociolinguistic model for defining the content of purpose-specific language programmes. Cambridge: Cambridge University.

Pennington, M.C., and James D. Brown. 1991. Unifying curriculum process and curriculum outcomes: The key to excellence in language education. Building better English language programs: Perspectives on evaluation in ESL, ed. M.C. Pennington, 57–74. Washington, DC: NAFSA.

Richards, Jack C., John Platt, and Heidi. Weber. 1985. Longman dictionary of applied linguistics. London: Longman.

Toffler, Alvin. 1990. Power shift: Knowledge, wealth, and violence at the edge of the 21st century. New York: Bantam.

van Ek, Jan A., and L. G. Alexander. 1980. Threshold level English. Oxford: Pergamon.

White, R.V. 1988. The ELT curriculum: Design, innovation and management. Oxford: Blackwell.

Wilkins, D. A. 1976. Notional syllabuses: A taxonomy and its relevance to foreign language curriculum development. Oxford: Oxford University Press.

How to ask: Question formation in written representations of spoken French

John Moran
Georgetown University

1 Introduction. In discussing the development of interrogative forms in French, Aurélien Sauvageot (1962:111) makes the following comment: 'Le mécanisme de l'interrogation est l'un des secteurs de notre langue où les choses ne vont pas pour le mieux dans la meilleur des mondes.' This Voltairean observation is particularly appropriate for the study presented here. This is a preliminary exploration of the types of interrogatives in written representations of spoken French. A growing body of research in the field (Terry 1970, Roulet 1974, Walz 1986, Joseph 1988) has found that the interrogative system in French is in a state of flux. Subject–auxiliary inversion, interrogative intonation with traditionally declarative word order, and the insertion of the phrase *est-ce que* 'is it that?' appear to be used by French speakers to signal questions with different rates of frequency and in different contexts. An examination of this realm of French is crucial not only for a more thorough understanding of the language and syntactic patterns in general, but also for a more appropriate treatment of French in foreign language courses. Time and time again, critics of textbook grammar presentations have found that the three main possibilities of question formation in French are simply presented, but not explained in view of actual usage (Walz 1986, Joseph 1988, Di Vito 1991a). This situation needs to be rectified if we desire effective courses which produce competent language users.

2 The data. The data for this study consist of written representations of the spoken language. While examining written sources allows one to compile a far greater amount of data in a much shorter time, one needs to remember that the written form of a language generally lags behind the spoken form with regard to change. With this consideration in mind, I examined the quoted dialogue portions of four detective novels: *Solution au Cimetière, La Nuit de Saint-Germain-des-Prés, and 120, Rue de la Gare* by Léo Malet and *L'Evadé* by

George Simenon.[1] These detective novels were chosen not only for their high frequency of quoted dialogue (questions contained within the narrative portions of the novels were not considered), but also because the authors represent characters from all walks of life (e.g. lawyers, detectives, bartenders, wealthy bourgeoisie, everyday citizens) in a wide variety of settings (rural and city) and in a great number of subsettings such as cafés and homes. It is assumed that the written representations of spoken language in these novels provide at least partial insight into trends in actual spoken language use.

The types of question counted were yes–no questions (Y/N–Q) and questions containing an interrogative word (WH–Q). Three ways of forming these questions were examined: the use of intonation (e.g. *Il est malade?* 'He is sick?'), the use of subject–verb inversion (S/V inversion) (e.g. *Est-il malade?* 'Is he sick?'), and the use of the interrogative phrase *est-ce que* (e.g. *Est-ce qu'il est malade?* 'Is it that he is sick?'). A total of 744 questions were recorded, 51% (382) formed with intonation, 42% (309) formed with subject–verb inversion, and 7% (55) formed with the use of *est-ce que*.

The following question types were not counted for this study:

1. Questions consisting of an incomplete phrase (i.e. lacking a subject and/or a verb):

   Pour qui le mille-feuille? Et l'andouillette? [Simenon:176]
   'Who gets the mille-feuille? And the andouillette?'

   Où cela? [Malet 3:5]
   'Where's that?'

2. Questions formed by adding a particle such as *hein* or *non* or a phrase such as *voulez-vous* or *n'est-ce pas* to the end of a declarative or imperative sentence:

   Ça t'intéresse quand même, ce crime, hein? [Malet 2:782]
   'This interests you any way, this crime, huh?'

   Ne me faites pas rigoler, voulez-vous? [Malet 3:15]
   'Don't make me laugh, o.k.?'

---

[1] Examples cited from the four texts will be referenced in the following manner:

Solution au Cimetière: Malet 1
La Nuit de Saint-Germain-des-Prés: Malet 2
120, Rue de la Gare: Malet 3
L'Evadé: Simenon

Ça lui a fichu un coup, n'est-ce pas? [Malet 1:250][2]
'That really threw him for a loop, didn't it?'

3. Questions of the form *si* 'how about' + subject + verb in the imperfect tense:

   Si je lui racontais tout, comme à une camarade? [Simenon:132]
   'How about I tell him everything, like a pal?'

4. Questions containing *qu'est-ce qui* 'what is it who' or subject *qui* 'who':

   Qu'est-ce qui lui est arrivé? [Malet 2:739]
   'What happened to him?'

   Qui est là? [Malet 3:70]
   'Who's there?'

Question types (2), (3), and (4) are syntactically 'fixed'—there is no other way to formulate them—and question type (1), since it lacks a subject and/or a verb, cannot display inversion or be used with *est-ce que*.

3 WH-Questions (WH-Qs). The vast majority of WH-Qs—75% (181 examples out of 243)—were formed by the use of subject-verb inversion. The use of *est-ce que* accounted for another 19% (47 examples), while only 6% (15 examples) were formed with intonation. The interrogative word itself appears to be the cause of such a high percentage of examples containing S/V inversion. In a WH-Q the interrogative word is the most important element in the sentence; it conveys to the hearer the nature of the information desired by the speaker. Consequently, one would expect the interrogative word to receive the most stress or emphasis. Terry (1970:101-102), in describing the occurrence of written WH-Qs in popular ('boulevard') French plays, comments:

> Because interrogation by intonation change cannot be used for a question which requires an answer other than yes or no, since the only means of characterizing this form is by the interrogative intonation pattern, and since, by effective dislocation, only one portion of the sentence can be empha-

---

[2] Diller discusses the problem with treating sentences such as *Il est mignon, n'est-ce pas?* and *Danish is beautiful, isn't it?* She comments, 'Ces phrases sont, même partiellement, des phrases interrogatives, bien qu'elles ne soient pas toujours considerées comme des questions' (Diller 1984:41).

There is a sense, although minimal, of 'interrogativeness' to these types of examples yet, as mentioned in the body of the paper, they are invariable. For example, *Il est mignon, n'est-ce pas?* cannot be realized as **Est-il mignon, n'est-ce pas?* or **Il est mignon, ce n'est pas?*

sized, it is evident that the two remaining modes of interrogation (inversion and *est-ce que*) are the forms which most easily can place the stress on one particular element in the sentence.

Such an observation certainly holds for the data examined here, in which 96% of the WH–Qs are formed by means of either S/V inversion or *est-ce que*.[3]

The 47 examples with *est-ce que* provide interesting information as well. 94% of the examples are *qu'est-ce que* 'what is it that', the remaining 6% being divided between *où est-ce que* 'where is it that' (4%) and *qui est-ce que* 'who is it that' (2%). The preponderance of examples with qu'*est-ce que* has to do with the nature of the interrogative word *que*. *Que* cannot function in some circumstances like other interrogative words such as *combien* and *où*. Terry (1970:102) explains: '*Que* is a tonically weak word which cannot bear the stress of interrogation. For this reason, the inclusion of *est-ce que* moves the stress from *que* to the whole expression.' Other interrogative words can bear the stress, and thus can stand 'unsupported' with an inverted subject and verb; they are rarely found in combination with *est-ce que* (in these data, *quel(le)* 'which', *pourquoi* 'why', *comment* 'how', *combien* 'how much', and *quand* 'when' never occurred with *est-ce que*).

There is an interesting similarity among the intonation and *est-ce que* examples (i.e. all those examples which do not follow the interrogative 'norm' for WH–Qs). Many of these questions are produced during dramatically marked scenes, situations of great emotion—surprise, fear, frustration—as can be seen in the following examples from the data:

1. -Police? sursauta-t-elle. Non, personne de la police est venu. Pourquoi qu'elle viendrait la police? On est honnête ... [Malet 2:781]
   'Police?', she started. 'No, no one from the police has come. Why would the police come? We're honest ...'

2. -Vous le savez bien.
   'You know full well.'

   Il sursauta:
   'He started.'

[3] It should be mentioned here that the high percentage of WH-Qs formed with inversion could at least be in part the result of the type of data examined, that is, written spoken French. Researchers examining actual spoken data have found that interrogative intonation seems to be preferred across the board, along with *est-ce que*, in informal conversational settings (Sauvageot 1962, Grundstrom 1973, Walz 1986, Joseph 1988, Di Vito 1991b). Sauvageot (1962:106) goes so far as to say 'On sait que la langue parlée répugne à employer ces constructions: "Que vous a-t-il écrit?" "Comment vous portez-vous?"'

Comm...comment...je le sais bien? [Malet 2:835]
'How ... how ... would I know?'

3. -Ce n'est donc pas toi qui l'as buté?
'Then it wasn't you that ran up against him?'

-Foutre non! s'exclama-t-il, sincèrement indigné. Où est-ce que vous prenez ça? [Malet 2:805]
'Hell no!', he exclaimed, truly indignant. 'Where did you hear that?

4. -Fan de garce! jura-t-il, avec une pointe d'accent méridional. Ce vieux frappe comme une mule, c'est pas des moeurs, ca. Et vous? Qui est-ce que vous êtes? [Malet 2:804]
'Damn!', he swore, with a southern accent. 'This old one hits like a mule, that's not right. And you? Who are you?

5. (spoken by a character who has just regained consciousness after having been unconscious for thirty hours)
-Il y a combien d'heures que ça m'est arrivé? [Malet 2:810]
'How many hours ago did this happen to me?'

6. -Et voilà, conclut-il brusquement. Pas d'autres questions? J'y répondrai, tu sais. Comme j'ai répondu au commissaire Faroux et à ses hommmes. Kif-kif. Contente-toi de ça, mon pote. Si je dois me dédire...Et pourquoi je me dédirais? Je me le demande... [Malet 2:781]
'And that's it', he concluded brusquely. 'No more questions? I'll answer them, you know. Like I answered commissioner Faroux and his men. Kif-kif. Be happy with that, my friend. If I must recant ... and why would I recant? I wonder ...'

7. -Qu'est-ce que ça peut te foutre? aboya-t-il. [Malet 2:841]
'What the hell do you care?', he barked.

A consideration of written data has the advantage of allowing one to examine the language in which the author couches the dialogue to find insights into the emotional states of the characters. In the above examples we find phrases such as *sursauta-t-elle* 'she started' in (1), *conclut-il brusquement* 'he concluded brusquely' in (6), *jura-t-il* 'he swore' in example (4), *s'exclama-t-il* 'he exclaimed' in (3), and *aboya-t-il* 'he barked' in (7), all of which indicate some type of emotional intensity on the part of the speaker. Dramatic context is clearly a factor in the selection of the form of the interrogative phrase. Other researchers (Terry 1970; Di Vito 1991a, 1991b) have emphasized this importance of the speaker's emotional or mental state as a factor in the syntactic form of the question. In the data for this study the characters were likely to use the *est-ce que* or intonation types of WH–Qs (those forms which are not the norm) when expressing strong emotion.

4 Yes–No questions (Y/N–Qs). For Y/N–Qs the distribution of syntactic forms is quite different from the distribution for WH–Qs. Nearly three fourths (73%, 367 of 503 examples) of the Y/N–Qs in the data are formed with intonation. Of the examples, 25% (128) are formed by means of S/V inversion, and only 2% (8) have *est-ce que*.[4]

Grundstrom (1973:20), in discussing the frequency of the use of intonation for signaling a Y/N–Q, remarks 'Se servir de la mélodie de phrase pour poser une question est non seulement une possibilité, mais c'est le moyen le plus couramment utilisé dans la langue parlée.' The explanation for the high frequency of the use of intonation to form this type of question cannot be a phonological one involving stress placement, as we saw above for WH–Qs, for two main reasons: (1) there is normally no one element which is more important, and thus receives more stress, than any other element in a Y/N–Q and (2) Y/N–Qs can have myriad forms (i.e. they can contain an infinite number of lexical combinations), whereas WH–Qs all contain at least one item from a closed set of interrogative words, one of which is unable to bear tonic stress (*que*).

Previous research (Di Vito 1991a) has noted that in spoken French, the more formal the setting, the higher the frequency of cases of S/V inversion. Equating the occurrence of *vous* with more formal settings and *tu* with less formal settings, one might expect to find that the intonation examples contain more occurrences of *tu* and the examples showing S/V inversion contain more examples of *vous*; however, this is not the case in these data.

Once again, the explanation lies in the dramatic context of the utterance (or rather, the written representation of the utterance). Unlike the WH–Qs, however, there is an added consideration in determining the interrogative form—the semantic nature of the verb. When characters speak, displaying strong emotions, the form of the question tends to be the less frequent form for that category, not the norm; however, for Y/N–Qs there seem to be two norms operating at the same time. The syntactic form of the interrogative phrase depends in a large part on whether the verb is stative or dynamic. While among all verbs in Y/N–Qs there is a general preference for the use of intonation, this preference is much weaker for the stative verbs. These verbs are the only verbs which occur in inverted Y/N–Qs with any noticeable frequency. Virtually 50% of all the occurrences of *croire* 'to believe', *vouloir* 'to want to', *pouvoir* 'to be

---

[4] This extremely small, virtually negligible, number of Y/N-Qs formed with *est-ce que* is interesting when one considers the comment found in many introductory French language textbooks that question formation with *est-ce que* is informal and common.

It is also interesting to note that the data from this study closely parallel those from Terry's (1970) study on interrogative forms. Out of all the Y/N-Qs he found, 3% were formed through the use of *est-ce que*, 11% were realized by way of inversion, and the remaining 86% used intonation to signal the interrogative form.

able to', *savoir* 'to know (something)', *connaître* 'to know (someone)', and *comprendre* 'to understand' in Y/N–Qs are found in structures exhibiting S/V inversion, while dynamic verbs such as *venir* 'to come', *donner* 'to give', *s'enlever* 'to come out/off', *danser* 'to dance', and *fouiller* 'to go through' are almost always found in examples of questions formed with intonation.

Taking these two norms into consideration, we arrive at the accompanying schematic for the syntactic structures one is likely to find in 'marked' situations (e.g. when speakers are exhibiting strong emotions). The following examples from the data provide evidence for the division presented in this study:

	unmarked contexts	marked contexts
dynamic verbs	SV	VS
stative verbs	VS	SV

Dynamic verbs in Y/N–Qs formed with S/V inversion

8. -Votre assaillant était-il français?
   'Was your assailant French?'

   -Et sa grande-mère faisait-elle du vélo? Excusez-moi, mais j'ai omis de lui demander. [Malet 3:52]
   'And does his grandmother go biking? Excuse me, but I forgot to ask him.'

Note that the use of S/V inversion in example (8) shows the speaker's frustration with having to sit through a detailed interrogation. It also seems to indicate that he feels that the questions are of ridiculously minute detail.

Terry (1970:104) remarks that 'inversion ... has a very weak interrogative intensity ... it is ... inversion that is chosen when there is a relatively weak curiosity attached to the evoked response.' This observation seems somewhat contradictory here, for inversion, especially with dynamic verbs, often indicates strong emotional feeling. There are examples in the data, however, in which one finds inversion where one would expect to find intonation, and many of these examples occur during interrogation sequences, when detailed questions are being asked (although one would be hard pressed to say that the questioners during an interrogation have a 'relatively weak curiosity' in the answers they are seeking): 'Et les ongles de Paul Servieres. Ne récelaient-ils pas des particules de tissu?' [Malet 1:256].

9. (spoken, with sarcasm, by a character who is seeing her employer (and friend) for the first time in several years; she had thought he might be dead)
   -Venez-vous me chercher pour traquer un escroc septuagénaire? [Malet

3:70]
'Are you coming to get me to track down some seventy-year-old con man?'

10. -Franchement, Montbrison, Colomier vous a-t-il donné l'impression d'avoir une frousse bleue? [Malet 3:30]
'Really, Montbrison, did Colomier give you the impression of being scared stiff?'

Not only does one see in (10) an example of a marked context, the dynamic verb in question is not really used dynamically. There are several examples in the data in which a dynamic verb is used with a non-dynamic meaning, and in these cases the syntactic structure is most often one of inversion:

10a. -En saisissez-vous l'ironie? [Malet 3:113]
'Do you see the irony of it?

10b. -Neuf mille francs de drogue! m'exclamai-je. Le prendriez-vous pour un Cyrano? C'est invraisemblable. [Malet 3:29]
'9,000 francs worth of drugs!', I exclaimed. 'Would you take him for a Cyrano? It's unlikely.'

10c. Faroux, mon vieux, vous est-il déjà arrivé d'appréhender un de vos supérieurs? [Malet 3:117]
'Faroux, my friend, have you already happened to arrest one of your superiors?'

11. -Monsieur Octave, prendrez-vous quelque chose également? [Malet 2:795]
'Mister Octave, will you take something too?

Note in example (11) politeness is presented as a type of marked context.

Stative verbs in Y/N–Qs formed with intonation:

12. -Et tu crois que tu vas toucher à mon argent sans même m'en parler?
'And you think you're going to take my money without even talking to me about it?'

-Ce n'est pas ton argent.
'It's not your money.'

-Ce n'est pas mon argent? Ose répéter que ce n'est pas l'argent de ma dot! [Simenon:97]
'It's not my money? Just try to repeat that it isn't the money from my

dowry!'

13. -Tu ne crois pas que tu deviens fou? [Simenon:101]
'Don't you think you're becoming crazy?'

14. Elle renifla et d'une voix mouillée:
'She sniffled and asked in a soft voice',

-On a voulu ... vous ... vous jeter dans le Rhône? [Malet 3:44]
'Someone wanted to ... to ... throw you in the Rhône?'

15. -J'ai une voiture à la porte.
'I have a car down front.'

-Une voiture ... une voiture de police?
'A car ... a police car?'

-Dame!
'Of course!

-A ma porte? Vous voulez donc me couler définitivement dans l'esprit de ma concièrge? [Malet 3:89]
'At my door? Do you want to ruin me in the eyes of my concierge?'

16. J'attaquai:
'I attacked'

-Alors, petit gars? Tu voulais faire chanter monsieur, paraît-il? Tu n'as pas honte? Par un si beau temps? Tu veux donc qu'il pleuve? [Malet 2:804]
'So, little man? You wanted to blackmail this guy, it seems. Aren't you ashamed? On such a nice day? Do you want it to rain?'

In addition to the use of inversion with dynamic verbs and the use of intonation with stative verbs to show contexts marked by heightened degrees of emotion, the few examples of questions formed with *est-ce que* that the data provide (only 2% of the examples, 8 out of 503 Y/N–Qs) also appear in marked contexts (with both stative and dynamic verbs);

17. -Dites-moi. Ce Verodat, c'est vraiment un parent de ...
'Tell me. This Verodat, he's really a relative of ...'

-Est-ce que je sais? ... [Malet 2:762]
'Do I know? ...'

This question is uttered by a man who is frustrated with the large numbers of questions which he is being asked, none of which he knows the answer to. Questions with *je* as the subject are often asked as rhetorical questions, a type of question to which no response is expected. Terry (1970) mentions that this type of question often has a syntactic structure containing inversion because their is no 'curiosity' about the response. Another example from the data:

17a. -Vous doutiez de son existence?
'You doubted his existence?'

Je haussai les epaules.
'I shrugged my shoulders'

-Est-ce que je sais? ... Qu'attendez de moi, monsieur? [Malet 2:802].
'Do I know? ... What do you want from me, sir?'

18. (said with sarcasm)
-Ne vous tracassez donc pas. Est-ce que mon genre de beauté ne s'accommode pas de l'absence de tels colifichets? [Malet 2:793]
'Don't worry. Doesn't my type of beauty succeed without all these trinkets?

19. J.P.G. hésita à se servir d'une arme qu'il avait en réserve ...
'J.P.G. hesitated to make use of a weapon he had in reserve ...'

-Est-ce que je te parle du capitaine, moi?
'Should I talk to you about the captain?'

-Quel capitaine?
'What captain?'

Elle avait tressailli et son visage était devenu pâle. [Simenon:99]
'She had shuddered and her face became pale.'

20. -Tu as l'air d'oublier que tu as une famille, une femme, des enfants, et que nous sommes sans fortune. J'ai déjà eu assez de peine à obtenir que tu prennes une assurance-vie. Est-ce que la dernière prime est payée, seulement? [Simenon:100]
'You seem to forget that you have a family, a wife, children, and that we have no money. It was hard enough for me to get you to take a life insurance policy. Has the last payment been made at least?'

It is evident, then, that dramatic context plays an important role in the formation of Y/N–Qs as it does in the formation of WH–Qs. With Y/N–Qs, however, there is the additional factor of the semantic qualities of the verb.

5 Discussion. Question formation in French is a complex process; not only does one need to take into consideration the type of question being asked—Y/N–Q or WH–Q—but also the context of the question and, in some cases, the nature of the verb. The two major competing interrogative structures appear to be subject–verb inversion and interrogative (i.e. rising) intonation. Question formation with *est-ce que* accounts for only 7% of the data (55 of 746 examples); speakers, at least as they are represented on the written page, do not seem to resort to this interrogative option very often.

The differences between the syntax of Y/N–Qs and WH–Qs appear to be at least in part phonological. WH–Qs contain an interrogative word which very often bears the stress of the sentence and is often set off through inversion (when the interrogative word is moved to the left-most position in the sentence) or the use of *est-ce que*. Y/N–Qs are more frequently posed by using interrogative intonation and leaving the subject and verb in the order in which they occur in a declarative sentence (note that even though stative verbs occur much more often in inverted structures than do dynamic verbs, stative verbs still occur frequently in intonation questions).

Research done as early as 1926 (De Boer) found evidence of a movement toward a subject–verb (SV) word order in French interrogative formation. Current research (Terry 1970; Grundstrom 1973; Di Vito 1991b) has shown that this trend has continued to develop and gain ground. As with all changes in language, however, the growing preference for SV word order in French questions has gradually appeared more and more frequently. The data for this study suggest that Y/N–Qs have 'led the way' in the progression from inversion to intonation in question formation. Yet even within Y/N–Qs we see a differentiated development, the dynamic verbs now virtually always in questions with SV word order, while the stative verbs appear in questions with both SV and VS word order. The presence of interrogative words has slowed the progression toward SV word order in questions for WH–Qs.

	unmarked contexts	marked contexts
Y/N–Qs	SV	VS
WH–Qs	VS	SV

Not only do the data here reveal what structure tends to be the norm for a given type of question, they also indicate what structure is used to indicate a context marked by strong emotional response. Leaving aside questions formed by the use of *est-ce que* for the moment, it is apparent that in general the norm for WH–Qs (i.e. VS word order) is used for Y/N–Qs in marked contexts while the norm for Y/N–Qs (i.e. SV word order) is used for WH–Qs in marked context, resulting in the accompanying distribution. Y/N–Qs and WH–Qs do have one aspect in common with regard to question formation; for both types of question the use of *est-ce que* is restricted largely to marked contexts.

6 Conclusion. These data suggest current trends in the formation of interrogative structures in spoken French. The SV word order is clearly becoming the norm. These findings not only contribute to a more thorough understanding of the French language and its internal structure and changing regularities, but they also give us valuable information about how to present the language to language learners.

Too many students, faced with only textbook grammar descriptions in the classroom, fail to achieve an acceptable level of fluency in the spoken language. A textbook which presents the three question types discussed here with no mention of their relative frequency is misleading the student. The student who learns interrogatives in this manner will only be dismayed when he or she arrives for his or her long-dreamt-of Junior Year Abroad in Paris to find that syntax does not exist in a vacuum.

The findings of this study and others like it can contribute to a solution to this problem in two major ways: (1) by providing accurate descriptions of how the language is really spoken so that the student does not talk 'like a textbook,' and (2) by showing that an analysis of literary works, when done properly, can contribute greatly not only to the students' knowledge of written French but also their knowledge of spoken French.

REFERENCES

De Boer, C. 1926. L'évolution des formes de l'interrogation en français. Romania 52.307-27.

Diller, Anne-Marie. 1984. La pragmatique des questions et des réponses. Germany: Gunter Narr Verlag Tübingen.

Di Vito, Nadine O. 1991a. Incorporating native speaker norms in second language materials. Applied Linguistics 12, 3.383-96.

Di Vito, Nadine O. 1991b. A French evolution: Toward SV question order. Georgetown University Round Table on Language and Linguistics 1991, ed. by James E. Alatis, 250–59. Washington, DC: Georgetown University Press.

Grundstrom, Allan. 1973. L'intonation des questions en francais standard. Interrogation et intonation: En français standard et en français canadien, ed. by Allan Grundstrom and Peirre Leon, 19-51. Montreal: Didier.

Joseph, John E. 1988. New French: A pedagogical crisis in the making. Modern Language Journal 72, 1.31-6.

Malet, Léo. 1985. Léo Malet: Les enquêtes de Nestor Burma et les nouveaux mystères de Paris. Paris: Robert Laffont.

Roulet, E. 1974. Vers une caractérisation linguistique des normes dans l'enseignement des langues. Linguistic insights in applied linguistics, ed. by S. Pit Corder and E. Roulet, 143-56. Paris: Didier.

Sauvageot, Aurélien. 1962. Français écrit, français parlé. Paris: Librairie Larousse. Simenon, Georges. 1936. L'évadé. Paris: Editions Gallimard.

Terry, Robert M. 1970. Contemporary French interrogative structures. Quebec: Editions Cosmos.

Walz, Joel. 1986. Is oral proficiency possible with today's French textbooks? Modern Language Journal 70, 1.13-20.

Content language learning: Symbiosis in the academe

Diane Musumeci
University of Illinois at Urbana-Champaign

Language, communication, and social meaning: the three are inextricably bound. The realization of the social nature of language is also binding on us as language educators who, in our efforts to teach language, must reflect its essence and convey its integrity to language learners. For this reason, we ought to question how well the methods that we adopt reflect the belief that language is more than the manipulation of morphology and syntax.

The project that I am going to describe began as a simple experiment, based in large part on the overwhelming success of immersion education programs in Canada and the United States (Swain 1991, Swain and Lapkin 1989, Curtain and Pesola 1988, Genesee 1987, Wesche 1984, Harley 1984). Unlike discipline-based approaches to foreign language instruction that restrict themselves to advanced learners (Anderson 1991, Beeman 1991, Baker 1991), the present program is designed for those in the early stages of language learning, the population of beginning or low-intermediate level learners who comprise the vast majority of students enrolled in university foreign language programs. In its evolution over the past seven years, the experiment in Content Language Learning continues to mature, to establish itself, not only as a plausible and viable means to study a foreign language, but as an appropriate and exciting option for foreign language study in the university setting.

The problem. It all started as a problem in the language program. I was a graduate student in Italian and Second Language Acquisition and Teacher Education, a multidisciplinary doctoral program at the University of Illinois at Urbana-Champaign, and a graduate teaching assistant, an enthusiastic and devoted language teacher, proud of my persistent appearance on the 'List of Instructors Ranked as Excellent by Their Students.' The language program in which I taught could best be described as 'traditional': the first year was devoted to the study of grammar; the second entailed grammar review, along with biweekly compositions and a little reading. Upon completion of the initial two-year sequence, students could take a course in Conversation, or Culture, or Introduction to Italian Literature, to be followed by a number of upper-division courses in specific areas of literature: Dante, Petrarch and Boccaccio,

Renaissance Masterpieces, Baroque and Enlightenment, Modern Novel, Modern Poetry. Typical of most language programs at both the secondary school and university levels, enrollment fell off sharply after the first two years; sometimes as few as ten percent of the students who had taken the fourth semester language course continued in the program. The upper division courses were populated mostly by students who had been to Italy for various reasons: family vacations or study abroad for purposes other than learning Italian. In addition, the students who elected to take advanced courses filled the Conversation and Culture courses, not those in literature.

Furthermore, I was confronted with a nagging complaint from the students, expressed on the course evaluations routinely conducted at the end of each semester. Although the evaluations were generally positive—the students consistently praised the fact that I taught in Italian, explained well, and graded fairly—they rarely expressed appreciation for the course content. When asked 'Which aspects of the course were most beneficial to you,' they wrote: 'when you talk about Italy and what it's like,' 'the most interesting part was when you told us about all the dialects,' 'the cultural stuff,' 'your comments about Italy.' In response to 'What do you suggest to improve this course?' they wrote: 'more conversation,' 'don't do the boring exercises in the book,' 'more about Italy,' 'more reading.' A student in second semester summed up his feelings: 'The days we spent all class speaking Italian [were most beneficial]. This was umpteen times better than doing silly exercises from [name of text] ... Also, don't bother with the subjunctive. It took too much time and wasn't really worth it.' The question begged: The students wanted to learn Italian; they wanted the class taught in Italian; they found the compositions helpful and they even wanted more reading. Clearly, the motivation was there, mixed with some frustration. What was missing?

Program assessment. In the fall of 1984, as part of a graduate course in Foundations in Language Teaching, I conducted a survey of the undergraduate students enrolled in all the courses offered in Italian at the University of Illinois at Urbana-Champaign. By means of a questionnaire, students were asked to describe their expectations and motivations for studying Italian, and they were encouraged to select from a list of courses those they would be interested in taking. Two pieces of information emerged: over 80% of the students enrolled in the first two years stated that they intended to travel to Italy within the next three years, and no student was interested in the proposed new courses in literature. Instead, they suggested the following courses: Politics in Italy, Current Issues in Italian Society, Art and Design in Italy, Travel in Italy, Italian for Commerce. What did they want? It seemed they were practically screaming for the opportunity to study Italian in its social context, to delve into Italian culture. Admittedly, I was somewhat taken aback by the intensity of the reactions from these reserved and industrious midwestern undergraduates, but I could not ignore that they articulated a clear answer to my question.

The experiment. Since the fourth semester signaled the end of students' involvement in Italian, I decided that it was a safe place to make some changes: if successful, students might continue; if not, well, the majority would quit anyway. In response to the students' expressed desire to travel in Italy, the fourth semester language course became an experiment in Content Language Learning; the subject matter was Italian Regional Geography. The course was taught entirely in Italian, using the tenets of immersion education. The first half of the course was devoted to general study of the physical geography of Italy: its distinguishing characteristics, the varieties of climate, flora, and fauna. Concurrent with the initial, predominately teacher-centered focus on general aspects of Italian geography, each student selected one region of Italy to research. During the second half of the course, the students presented their research, orally, in class, while the other students asked questions and took notes. The questions for the final examination were drawn from the students' presentations.

The end of the semester course evaluations provided feedback about the transformation of grammar review into subject matter learning. Students' reactions to the course were overwhelmingly positive, for both the format of the course and its content: 'the projects were very helpful because they required you to get in front of the class and actually speak in Italian,' 'listening to everyone speak Italian and trying to speak back,' '[the best part was] learning the culture of Italy and not just the grammar, ' 'now I understand why my grandparents left Basilicata [a region in southern Italy].' One student was especially articulate:

> Rather than answer the questions [on the form], I just want to let you know how much I liked the class. I had the world's worst teacher for 101, and so I had no interest in 102. I went maybe once a week ... maybe. 103 was a little better—I began to learn all the things I should have learned in 101, but I still couldn't get too excited about it. This was the first Italian class that I really enjoyed. I do feel I learned more by listening to you and speaking Italian myself than I have in the past three semesters. Thanks. (Instructional and Curriculum Evaluation Form, Italian 104, Spring 1985)

The course was repeated the next semester with similar results. Two students were not happy with the change in format, and they let me know of their frustrations on the course evaluations: one complained, 'I don't know why I should know more about Italy than I do about the United States' and, the other, 'It's too much to expect students to come to class every day; for other classes you can read the material at home and learn it on your own.'

Although I was pleased that I had 'pulled it off', I was not ready to proclaim the experiment a success until someone other than myself taught the course. As luck would have it, I received a fellowship for the next semester, and another teaching assistant taught what was beginning to be known as the fourth semester 'geography course'. After a brief explanation of the rationale and goals of the course, I gave her copies of my syllabus, grading criteria, exams, and the materials that the students and I had accumulated over the previous two semesters: physical and political maps and puzzles of Italy; pamphlets, posters, and brochures that the students obtained by writing to the Italian regional tourist offices; newspaper and magazine articles from which students had culled information for their presentations; and a list of library resources the class had compiled during the course of individual research. The course, under different direction, underwent a few minor changes. The instructor's interests in architecture and history made their way into the syllabus. She also located copies of a textbook on geography, a somewhat dull and unattractive book used in the Italian middle schools, that proved useful as a reference tool. Under new management, evaluations of the course remained positive and course enrollment continued to flourish.

The repercussions. The success of the experiment started a chain reaction throughout the program. While changes were occurring in the fourth semester, the third semester students had been left reviewing grammar. At the same time, the fourth semester instructor reported that the students wanted to know more than just geography: they were asking for information about politics, mass media, tourism, and industry. Although I had managed to compile an expanding assortment of materials for the geography course, I was not prepared to supply materials on such a wide range of topics, especially since I was not even teaching the third semester. Neither could I expect graduate teaching assistants to procure and prepare course materials on their own. For the third semester course, a compromise solution was reached: at the beginning of each semester, the instructor supplied the students with a list of topics that she or he was willing and able to teach and for which materials were available. From that list, the students could choose the topics that they found most interesting. Thus, the syllabus for third semester was created in tandem, a learners–instructor partnership. The topics included were: the Italian political system, a brief introduction to art history, travel and tourism, tradition and festival, Italian economy.

Enrollment in the entire second year program increased; the percentage of students who continued studying Italian after the first year doubled. Increased enrollments and more sections of the third and fourth semester courses meant more instructors teaching the same courses. The content of the various sections required coordination. At the same time, I noted that the topics for the third semester course tended to repeat: there was very little variation in course content between groups of learners or instructors. Serendipitously, I discovered a textbook. The geography book that we had been using as a reference tool became unavailable, out of print, and the publisher sent a copy of its replacement for us to consider. The new book was perfect: a textbook of Italian social geography, replete with color photographs and a wide assortment of maps, graphs and charts to support clear and concise prose (Loescher 1988). Its pedagogical focus matches that of the course: exercises in the book direct learners to interact with the text, make inferences, and draw conclusions. The academic treatment of facts and concepts is interspersed with perspectives from literary authors, artists and social scientists. Half the chapters are devoted to a study of Italy in general: demography, industry, political system, linguistic situation, folklore and tradition; the second half of the book treats each region individually. The text made it possible to standardize the second year curriculum into a two semester sequence that flowed logically, one from the other. It also relieved new instructors of the burden of finding and creating their own course materials. The topics covered in the third and fourth semester courses can be found in Appendix A.

Concurrently, the effects of change were felt in the first year. As instructors realized the challenges that the second year text presented to learners' reading skills, attention to reading and reading strategies in the first year curriculum accelerated. And as instructors became aware of the motivating power of interesting subject matter, the second semester course began to focus more on the content of classroom activities and quizzes. Although the goal of the first year curriculum was the development of functional language abilities at a personal level, the content of activities gradually began to move students toward socialization into the second language culture. By the latter half of the second semester, additional emphasis was placed on learners' acquisition of 'academic' skills in the second language. Listening comprehension quizzes became mini lectures and note–taking sessions on subjects like *presepi* (Italian Christmas *crèche*) and 'housing in Pompeii,' to smooth the transition from learning vocabulary and facts to understanding concepts of 'folklore' and 'economic sectors.'

The benefits. We have more sections of third and fourth semester Italian than ever before. Students report the following: 'I'm a geography/political science/art history/commerce/engineering major and this makes sense to me; this fits with what I want to do.' Instructors understand what they are supposed to teach. Instructors whose only previous experience in language teaching had focused on grammar were angry and frustrated by early attempts to make their teaching more 'communicative' in the first year courses. Alternately, when they are asked to teach the Content Language Learning courses, they catch on quickly to the idea of teaching the subject matter, to focus on meaning, especially since they concur that the content is valid and important. Surprisingly, they express appreciation of their students; they are impressed by what the students CAN do. They recognize that their students are bright; they are impressed when students make connections between what they are learning in Italian and what they've studied in economics or literature or history. Not all students are talented or interested in parsing sentences, but in the fourth semester course they each give a forty-minute presentation on a region of Italy that they have researched; they question when they do not understand or if they disagree, they answer questions addressed to them, they read a minimum of 250 pages of academic text and they routinely write essays of 200–300 words, all in Italian.

Do more students continue? A few. When the experiment first began, several came to me at the end of the geography course and said, 'this is the first time I've been interested in continuing in Italian.' 'Unfortunately,' many graduate. But they leave the program changed, better prepared sometimes in their respective fields because they have been exposed to another cultural perspective, always better prepared as world citizens. The ones who do remain in the program understand more fully the literature that they're asked to read because they know something of the culture that created it. The advanced level culture course is more in-depth because students have acquired a basis, some background with which to interpret the issues. The modifications that have occurred in the first two years of language instruction have had another effect: students are adamant in their refusal to take courses that are not taught in Italian. Whether they have made the connection between language and culture, or whether, having functioned successfully in Italian, to do otherwise would be seen as regression, they understand that 'something is lost in the translation.'

Caveats. Each learning context is unique. In this paper I have reconstructed the past seven years of changes that forged the language program in place today at one particular university with its specific student population. The vantage point of experience suggests the following be kept in mind before instituting a new curriculum:

- Innovation began with a problem. If what you have works for you, then 'don't fix what ain't broke.' There is no 'best method' that works for all language learners, instructors, and settings.

- The content was selected to address learners' interests and perceived needs. A needs and interests survey was conducted to ensure an objective assessment of learners' motivations and expectations for learning the second language.

- The subject matter must also reflect instructors' interests. No one can be an enthusiastic instructor if she finds the materials boring, banal.

- In addition, the subject matter and materials must meet learners' and instructors' expectations of appropriateness in the academic setting. Learners' personal needs are not always well defined or generalizable, but program needs are: students who wish to pursue advanced study in the second language must be able to read intensively and extensively, to follow a lecture, to write an essay and to take notes. It is also essential that they obtain sufficient background knowledge of the second language culture to interpret what they are hearing and reading.

- Instructional strategies designed to develop specific skills in the second language are incorporated into the content language classroom. For example, a lecture format will develop learners' listening comprehension skills, not their ability to speak or read effectively (Swain 1985). If reading ability and productive language use are intended outcomes of instruction, then classroom practice must focus on their development (Musumeci 1992).

- Testing in the discipline-based curriculum reflects course content and instructional goals. Quizzes and examinations test learners' knowledge of the subject matter. If the focus of instruction includes both comprehension-based and productive skills, the test format elicits both modalities of language use. Sample questions from a recent midterm examination in the third semester course appear in Appendix B.

- Students are informed of the approach and rationale. For most students, Content Language Learning represents a radical departure from any previous experience in language learning, one they have never encountered. Even if they are willing to participate in the innovation, they will benefit from an explanation of the methodology, the learning outcomes it can produce and what will be expected of them. A copy of the letter that accompanies each student's syllabus for the experiment in Content Language Learning is provided in Appendix C.

Conclusion. The experiment in Content Language Learning works because it evolves: from its inception, it has responded to the needs of learners, instructors, and program alike. However, metamorphosis involves risk. What began as a 'simple experiment' has had consequences for the entire language program. Moreover, the more subtle effects of change may be the most far-reaching. Participation in the experiment in Content Language Learning has changed the way students leaving the program view language learning. Those who are now our students will soon be the policy makers in our society; the potential for social change and the role that foreign language education will play in our culture is within their power. When issues concerning foreign language education arise, it is very likely that they will be resolved based on the decision-makers' personal experiences in foreign language learning.

I began with a reference to the social nature of language, and I have attempted to describe an option in foreign language learning consonant with the belief that language as social meaning and communication can exist in symbiosis with the academe, if language professionals are willing to initiate changes that reflect those beliefs.

REFERENCES

Anderson, Keith. 1991. The applied foreign language component in the humanities and the sciences at St. Olaf College. Paper presented at the Consortium for Language Teaching and Learning, Brown University, October 18–20.

Baker, Steven. 1991. The Monterey model: Integrating international policy studies with language education. Paper presented at the Consortium for Language Teaching and Learning, Brown University, October 18–20.

Beeman, William. 1991. An experimental course in Japanese culture and society. Paper presented at the Consortium for Language Teaching and Learning, Brown University, October 18–20.

Curtain, Helena A., and Carol Ann Pesola. 1988. Languages and children—Making the match. Reading, MA: Addison-Wesley.

Genesee, Fred. 1987. Learning through two languages. Rowley, MA: Newbury House.

Harley, Birgit. 1984. How good is their French? Language and Society 12.55–60.

Loescher. 1988. Geografia Loescher: Italia 1. Turin, Italy: Loescher Editore.

Musumeci, Diane. 1992. Second language reading and content area instruction: The role of second language reading in the development of communicative and subject matter competence. Language and content: Discipline-based approaches to language study, ed. by M. Krueger and F. Ryan, 169–80. Lexington, MA: DC Heath.

Swain, Merrill. 1985. Communicative competence: Some roles of comprehensible input and comprehensible output in its development. Input in second language acquisition, ed. by Susan Gass and Carolyn Madden, 235–53. Rowley, MA: Newbury House.

Swain, Merrill. 1991. French immersion and its offshoots: Getting two for one. Foreign language acquisition research and the classroom, ed. by Barbara Freed, 91–103. Lexington, MA: DC Heath.

Swain, Merrill, and Sharon Lapkin. 1989. Canadian Immersion and Adult Second Language Teaching: What's the Connection? The Modern Language Journal 73, ii.150–59.

Wesche, Marjorie B. 1984. A promising experiment at Ottawa University. Language and Society. 12.20–25.

Appendix A. Topics covered in the third and fourth semester Content Language Learning Courses in Italian at the University of Illinois at Urbana–Champaign (Loescher 1988).

Italian 103

- Gli Uomini
  - Le prime tracce della presenza dell'uomo in Italia
  - Da 7 a 60 milioni di persone: la popolazione italiana degli ultimi 2.000 anni
  - La popolazione italiana, oggi
- I Modi di Abitare
  - La campagna
    - Per secoli, il predominio della campagna
    - Le case contadine
  - La città
    - Una nazione con tante città
    - I vari tipi di città
    - Le città italiane, oggi
- Il Lavoro
  - Agricoltura, Allevamento, Pesca
    - Un tempo, solo il lavoro contadino
    - Le trasformazioni dell'agricoltura
    - L'agricoltura italiana, oggi
    - Cereali, patate, pomodori, vite e ulivo, frutta, colture industriali
    - La pesca
  - Industria, Artigianato
    - La nascita dei mestieri
    - La rivoluzione industriale e il nuovo modo di produrre
    - L'industria italiana, oggi

L'energia elettrica
L'artigianato
Settore Terziario
Un settore in travolgente espansione
Strade, Porti, Ferrovie, Linee Aeree
Il primo formarsi di una rete di comunicazioni: la grande importanza del territorio
Lo sviluppo dei trasporti
Le comunicazioni in Italia, oggi
Il Paesaggio dell'Uomo
L'azione dell'uomo sulla natura, e della natura sull'uomo
Le trasformazioni dell'Italia
L'attacco alla natura
Religioni, Tradizioni, Folclore
Un sentimento religioso molto antico. La preminenza della religione cattolica
Tradizioni e folclore
Aspetti della Società Italiana
La suddivisione dello stato in regioni, province, comuni
Come si è formato e come si parla oggi l'italiano
Salute e assistenza medica
Le diverse cucine regionali italiane
Il movimento turistico

Italian 104
La Terra
Il Mare
Il Clima
Montagne, Colline, Pianure
Ghiacciai, Fiumi e Laghi, Acque Sotterranee
La Vegetazione
Gli Animali
Il Paesaggio Naturale
La Raffigurazione della Terra
La Geografia in Italia
Le Regioni d'Italia

Appendix B. Sample test items from midterm examination in third semester Content Language Learning Course in Italian at the University of Illinois at Urbana-Champaign.

Lettura. Questo articolo si trova nella rivista 'BELL'ITALIA' e cerca di rispondere alle domande che un turista potrebbe fare prima di andare a visitare la città di Salerno. Leggilo per rispondere alle seguenti domande.

Le frasi si riferiscono alla storia di Salerno; mettile in ordine cronologico scrivendo il numero corretto nello spazio vuoto prime della frase.

Necropoli di Fratte
Salerno è una città normanna nell'XI secolo
Irna diventa Salerno
Salerno è conquistata dai barbari
Salerno è città sveva e meno importante di Napoli
Salerno diventa città bizantina

Salerno diventa capitale di un principato indipendente

Scegli solo 10 delle seguenti 15 affermazioni e decidi se sono vere o false. Se la frase è falsa, indica il perché.

In Italia oggi le città con più di 100.000 abitanti sono circa 50.
Le case a corte sono abitazioni che troviamo nella pianura del Veneto, Lombardia, Emilia-Romagna, dove l'agricoltura è più ricca.
Con il termine 'Colure industriali' si intendono quei prodotti che vengono trasformati per trarne materia prima per le industrie.

Scegli solo 5 termini fra quelli elencati e scrivi per ciascuno una descrizione chiara e completa. Per illustrare meglio il significato della parola dai anche un esempio.
preistoria, censimento, latifondo, artigianato, settore primario, emigrazione, metropoli

Tema. Descrivi lo sviluppo dell'agricoltura italiana e parla degli aspetti positivi e di quelli negativi. (150 parole)

Appendix C. Letter to the students enrolled in the Content Language Learning Courses in Italian at the University of Illinois at Urbana-Champaign.

D. GOALS AND OBJECTIVES

TO: All students in Italian 103 and 104
FROM:Prof. D. Musumeci, Director of the Italian Language Program, 4019 FLB

Welcome to the second year of Italian studies at the University of Illinois! Italian 103 and 104 are unique language courses because they were designed to serve two purposes: first, to continue to increase your language competence in Italian and, second, to provide you with information about Italians and Italy. Whereas in first year Italian you learned to communicate on a personal level (how to buy a train ticket, order a meal, talk about your family), in the second year courses you will learn about Italy at the societal level (its systems of transportation and communication, agriculture, economy, demography). The instructional approach is called Content Language Learning; i.e. learning language through the study of another subject. In your case, it means learning Italian through the study of the social (103) and physical (104) geography of Italy. The textbook provides much of the subject matter information for the course; through discussion, presentations and additional materials, you, your classmates, and your instructor will bring more insight to the text. All quizzes and exams will test your knowledge of the subject matter. In this way, you will simultaneously learn Italian and the geography of Italy.

If you've completed Italian 101 and 102 at the U of I, you'll notice many similarities with past practices; if you're new to the language program, these courses may be very different from the way you've studied language in the past. One similarity with the first-year courses is that all instruction takes place in Italian. Another is the heavy emphasis on reading. The textbook, written in Italy for Italian students, is 'academic writing,' carefully selected to best expand your current language skills. You probably won't find it easy to read: for example, you will not understand every word, and many of the concepts introduced may be new. Nonetheless, you will be able to get the gist and pick out the most important information. Remember to use the reading strategies that you practiced in 101 and 102, work with the other students, and use your instructor. A difference between this semester and earlier ones is that the successful completion of the second-year program requires more production from the students: more speaking and more writing. It is still your responsibility to let fellow students and the instructor know if you don't understand. Figuring out what the other person or the text is trying to say, by asking and answering questions, plays a major role in learning a language. Don't be afraid to use this strategy often!

At the end of the second year, you will have acquired enough information about Italy to help you understand when Italians speak or when you read what they've written, not simply because you 'know the words', but because you'll share some of the cultural background that is necessary to interpret their meaning.

I wish you an exciting and successful semester.

Buon lavoro e buon divertimento!

A nonhierarchical relationship between grammar and communication Part I: Theoretical and methodological considerations

Diane Larsen-Freeman
School for International Training

Introduction. Marianne Celce-Murcia and I have been asked to speak about grammar and communication—a fitting focus for a Round Table with the overall theme of Language, Communication, and Social Meaning. It is not only thematically appropriate, however; it is also entirely relevant given the current state of the art in the language teaching field. Indeed, perhaps more often than any other question we are asked is one concerning the role of grammar instruction in the language pedagogy of today in which communicative activities have come to occupy so central a position.

In order to address the question of the relationship between grammar and communication in language pedagogy, it is helpful to understand why it is so frequently posed. To do so requires a brief digression into the modern history of language teaching. It was not always the case, of course, that communicative activities in the classroom were the means employed to achieve communicative proficiency in a second language. Indeed, earlier in this century, a very different means was used with the same end in mind. Courses were organized around grammar structures, which were sequenced according to increasing linguistic complexity. Pattern practice and structure drills were teaching techniques designed to inculcate the habits of the target language. Even when the view of language acquisition shifted from one of habit formation to that of rule formation, the focus on grammar was maintained. It was assumed that the ability to use the target language would result from the 'steady accumulation of more and more complex language entities' (Rutherford 1987:5).

It was not surprising that the language teaching field maintained its allegiance to grammar structure aggregation even when the view of the learning process was so radically transformed from habit to rule formation. For despite this very different perception of the acquisition process, the importance accorded grammar in linguistics was, if anything, on the ascendancy. So while teaching techniques may have been more cognitively engaging, created to have students discover the system of rules at work which allowed for the generation and comprehension of novel utterances, the centrality of grammar remained.

Such pre-eminence, of course, was to be dramatically challenged during the 1970s. Arguing for an approach to language teaching in which 'there is no attempt at careful linguistic control of the environment,' Wilkins (1976:2) was among the first to contribute to the revolutionary Communicative Approach through his book *Notional Syllabuses*. Later, of course, it was pointed out by Widdowson that a meaning-based notional–functional syllabus, no less than a structural syllabus, assumed that 'acquisition was a process of gradual accumulation,' even though its units—notions and functions—differed significantly from grammar structures (1990:134). Nevertheless, the idea of making grammar subservient to meaning represented a truly significant departure from the practice of the day. Gone from many materials and classrooms were pattern practice, structure drills, and rule-based exercises; in their stead were tasks of a problem-solving nature designed primarily to promote communicative interaction, and role plays in which sociolinguistic variables could be manipulated to give students abundant practice with learning appropriacy constraints. In the drive to put communication first, grammar was relegated to a supporting role—or in some cases, given no attention in class at all. Rather, learners were thought to learn the language through practicing it as it was used naturally in communication, with grammatical structures thought to be acquired inferentially without deliberate focus, much as children learning a first language do.

It was little wonder the Communicative Approach had the impact it did. Learners having studied a second language via a structure approach were often ill-prepared to use the language they had learned. They could produce accurate and meaningful sentence patterns, but their repertoires were constrained by their lack of awareness of requisite sociolinguistic variation. Unfortunately for practitioners, it was not long before the Communicative Approach revealed a glaring deficiency as well. For while students could now express concepts and do things with language appropriately, they often did so inaccurately. 'It turns out learners do not readily infer knowledge of the language system from communicative activities. The grammar, which they must acquire somehow as a necessary resource for use, proves elusive' (Widdowson 1990:161). Grammatical accuracy was sacrificed for communicative appropriacy. Control of grammatical structures did not emerge on its own, and 'learners acquired a fairly patchy and imperfect repertoire of performance which was not supported by an underlying competence' (Widdowson 1990:161). 'Grammatical knowledge did not always follow as a necessary corollary of communication' (Widdowson 1990:165).

I have pushed descriptions of the structure-based approach and the Communicative Approach to their extremes to make a point. Doubtless most teachers were much more moderate in their implementation of each approach than what has been portrayed here. Still, the historical sketch just completed makes it perfectly understandable why the question should arise about the relationship between grammar and communication. Most educators today would agree on 'the communicative importance of formal accuracy' (Garrett 1991);

what is at issue is how to bring it about, as the two—grammar and communication—are not thought to fit together in obvious ways. It would behoove us at this point to examine the nature of our traditional assumptions regarding grammar and of communication, to see why such incompatibility is assumed. Following this, the terms for a reconciliation will be proposed. This paper will conclude with the pedagogical implications of this proposal.

Assumptions about grammar. One view of grammar is that it is a concatenation of paradigms, structures, and word order rules dictating the form of utterances of a particular language. This view assumes that the meaning of an utterance exists apart from its form. It is not difficult to see how meaningless structures and arbitrary rules are inconsistent with the notion of meaningful communication.

Another perspective on grammar, which is at odds with communication, derives largely from the influential views of Noam Chomsky. The importance Chomsky accorded his notion of 'competence' or 'intrinsic tacit knowledge' in 1965 would indeed heavily influence many linguists' and applied linguists' concept of grammar for some time to come. This knowledge could be characterized by rules of grammar and was to be distinguished from performance, or the actual use of language in a concrete situation (Chomsky 1965). While the former was a mental state, the latter involved a process. Indeed, according to Chomsky, one could in theory have that cognitive structure we call knowledge of English fully developed with no capacity to use it (Chomsky 1975). The linguist's generative grammar is an effort to capture this declarative knowledge and to make it explicit (Chomsky 1981). Not only is grammar viewed as a static concept or knowledge, it is a description of the knowledge of an individual idealized native speaker in a homogeneous speech community—it is totally devoid of any context (Chomsky 1965:3). Thus, it had nothing at all to contribute to a discussion of use. Finally, it took as its basic unit of organization, the sentence. Later, Hopper (1988) would refer to Chomskyan grammar as an 'a priori grammar', a 'discrete set of rules which are logically detachable from discourse and precede discourse' (1988:118). 'It was Chomsky's immense achievement to show how natural language can be reduced to a formal system' (Halliday 1978:4). However, it is no wonder that his view of sentence-level grammar as an autonomous, self-contained module, stripped of context and more static than dynamic, should be at variance with subsequent emphasis on communication.

Assumptions about communication. Hymes (1971) receives the credit for isolating from Chomsky's notion of performance certain aspects of language use which can also be explained in terms of underlying knowledge or competence. A speaker 'acquires competence as to when to speak, when not, and as to what to talk about with whom, when, where, in what manner' (Hymes 1972:277). Hymes' notion of communicative competence differed, however, from Chomsky's grammatical competence in that communicative competence was not only dependent upon knowledge but also incorporated the notion of ability. Certainly, as it has been adopted into the language teaching field, communicative competence has come to mean 'a dynamic, rather than static concept' (Savignon 1983:8), the ability to communicate, rather more akin to communicative performance, if we adhere to the original distinction Chomsky made (Taylor 1988:164).

To the work of Hymes, we must also add that of Halliday, whose own notion of a socially constrained meaning potential is similar to Hymes' notion of communicative competence. Significant for contrastive purposes, Halliday's 'orientation is to language as a social rather than individual phenomenon' (1985:xxx). Also noteworthy is that his functional approach is designed to account for how language is used in context (xiii).

Concurrent with the contributions of Hymes and Halliday were those of a number of others within tagmemics, sociolinguistics, and conversational analysis who seriously questioned the study of the syntax of isolated sentences, advocating instead investigation of discourse (e.g. paragraph structure, narrative and conversational structure). Thus, the renewed attention granted discourse also came to play an important role in the evolution of communicative language teaching.

With these brief characterizations of grammar (individual, static, sentential in scope and decontextualized) and communication (social, dynamic, discourse-level and highly context-bound), it is easy to see why there should be confusion regarding how the two fit.

Reconciliation of grammar and communication. While so far in this paper I have called attention to the differences in the traditional views of grammar and communication, I feel a reconciliation between the two is possible, if the features the two share are also acknowledged. For our purposes, it is worth calling attention to four of them. The first of these is scope. While I have already mentioned that grammar is associated with sentence or even subsentence phenomena and communication with discourse-level phenomena, it is worth pointing out that in fact both operate at many different levels of language from single morphemes up through texts. A single English word *cats* can both exhibit the correct grammatical inflection for the plural of a singular (count) common noun and the communicative function of supplying an opinion when one is sought regarding the most popular musical in recent times. Similarly, longer stretches of text reflect both grammatical and communicative features. The first paragraph in a short story can fulfill the communicative function of orienting the reader and drawing the reader into what is about to be related. Use of verb tense inflections in the same paragraph can aid the reader in distinguishing the main story line or foregrounded information from what is supplied as background.

A second shared feature of each is the fact that they both exhibit three dimensions of form, meaning, and function/use (Larsen-Freeman 1991). If we take a communicative unit such as a speech event, for example, a riddle, we easily recognize its form, especially as it is often formulaic in character (e.g.

Why did the chicken cross the road? Why does the fireman wear red suspenders? or *How many x does it take to y?*) Its meaning resides in the words which comprise the question and its punchline. Its function or use is to amuse, or in the case of the latter, to cast aspersions on a particular group in a jocular manner. A grammar structure, too, of course, has a form—this is the dimension that is usually associated with grammar. So we might speak of the passive voice in English being formed with the verb *be* and the passive participle. But grammar structures also have meaning and use. The meaning of the passive is one of conferring focus on an object or consequence of an action (as opposed to the canonical active-voice agent) and it is used in cases where the agent is unknown, unimportant, redundant, obvious, etc. Likewise, a grammar structure such as an embedded yes–no question (*I wonder if you could tell me the time*) can be described in terms of its form (presence of complementizer if, lack of subject–auxiliary inversion, past form of modal), its meaning (here a need for information regarding the time), and its social use (as opposed to linguistic discourse use) as a polite request.

The third shared feature of grammar and communication has to do with the fact that although grammar has been conceived of as a state and communication as a process, they both in fact have static and dynamic characteristics. There are rules of grammar, just as there are communication conventions. One has intuitions about grammaticality and appropriateness. Thus, there is declarative knowledge or 'competence' underlying both. They both also, however, concern performance or the ability to do something and thus have a dynamic quality. With communication, this procedural knowledge has been presumed. But it is no less true of grammar. Having grammatical competence with no ability to draw on it may be theoretically possible (cf. earlier quote by Chomsky), but it is pragmatically useless. When we speak, write, listen, read, we access our knowledge of grammar to achieve accurate and meaningful production and comprehension.[1]

Language learning then 'involves getting to know something and being able to do something with that knowledge. Language learning has two sides to it: knowing and doing (competence and performance)' (Widdowson 1990:157). This is true for both grammar and communication. One needs to know the systemic properties of grammar and communication, as well as how to do grammar ('grammaring'?) and communicating.

The final, and perhaps most controversial, point of the four is that we believe it follows that grammar and communication are in a non-hierarchical relation. Others would not concur: they would assign grammar a 'discourse-processing' role (Givon 1979), and call it 'a DEPENDENT functionally-

---

[1] And following Halliday, grammar in this sense might be better considered as lexico-grammar because we now recognize (through the work of Bolinger 1976, Becker 1981, Pawley and Snyder 1983) that a great deal of our linguistic knowledge is comprosed of 'chunks of more or less ready-made lexico-syntactic units.' Becker aptly refers to the accessing of and use of such chunks as 'pushing old language into the present.' (in Tannen 1981:2).

motivated entity (1979:82) or point to its 'being subservient to lexis' (Widdowson in Rutherford and Sharwood Smith, 1988:154). We think not. Grammar and communication shape each other. While clearly there is an initial communicative intent, it is not the case that a form is selected before the communication is initiated, nor is it the case that a speaker/writer starts with a total message in mind. The processing does not happen in a linear fashion. Speakers do not choose words, then arrange them in order, then add sounds and then articulate the sounds. The two, the message and the code, interact and ideas take shape in the moment. We can get a glimpse of the complementary (as opposed to the hierarchical) nature of the two when we point out that sometimes an utterance is articulated (i.e. given form) and then withdrawn with a *NO, that's not what I mean*, before the listener ever responds. Thus, the lexico-grammar interacts with communication to help shape the ultimate meaning in keeping with the context.

Applications to pedagogy. In sum, there are at least four features which grammar and communication share:

- scope (They both apply to all levels of language. We can have communicative texts which are simple words; conversely grammar can make salient relevant discourse phenomena.)
- three dimensions of form, meaning, and use
- static and dynamic properties
- a non-hierarchical relationship

It would admittedly be easier for those responsible for language pedagogy to see the complementarity of grammar and communication if there existed more dynamic models of grammar (Halliday 1985) and more complete descriptions of communication rules. But their absence is no justification for excluding grammar from instruction, as has sometimes been the case with zealous practitioners of the Communicative or Natural Approach. As Garrett (1991:81) has put it:

> To separate communicative meaning from grammar, to argue that it is possible to 'use' language meaningfully without grammar, is to define 'grammar' so narrowly as to distort the concept beyond all recognition.

Instead, acknowledging that there are at least four common features to grammar and communication can provide a rationale for a means to integrate grammar and communication. Several have made suggestions for how to do so (see Rea Dickens and Woods 1988, Gatbonton and Segalowitz 1988, Widdowson 1990, Larsen-Freeman 1993).

My own approach for integrating grammar and communication calls for an initial phase in which students engage in a communicative task. The task is designed so that the need for certain grammatical structures is likely to arise. The students' attention at this moment, however, is upon completing the task, not consciously directed to the forms. Thus, the structures are to be used within a meaningful context. If the students can't access the structures, they will become aware of the need to acquire them. If they can access them partially, the teacher can assess what difficulties they are experiencing. If the students are able to accomplish the task satisfactorily using the necessary structures, there will be no further need for grammar instruction.

In the case of students' demonstrating partial access, the teacher will need to determine where the students' challenge lies—in the form, the meaning or the use of the particular structure. In a second phase, students can work their way through focused exercises having to do with the dimension of language with which they are experiencing difficulty. These exercises operate at different levels of language.

The final phase is to ask students to once again take part in communicative activities. Through these, it is expected that students will have further opportunity to practice grammar and communication in tandem.

It should be noted that these three phases do not constitute a comprehensive approach to language teaching. What they do is to offer a means of integrating grammar with communication, building upon their commonalities. It is hoped that by doing so, the complementarity of grammar and communication can be appreciated in a way that leaves no room in future pedagogy for either to be excluded again.

REFERENCES

Becker, Alton. 1981. On Emerson on language. Georgetown University Round Table on Languages and Linguistics 1981, ed. by Deborah Tannen, 1-11. Washington, DC: Georgetown University Press.

Bolinger, Dwight. 1976. Meaning and memory. Forum Linguisticum 1, 1.

Chomsky, Noam. 1965. Aspects of the theory of syntax. Cambridge, MA: MIT Press.

Chomsky, Noam. 1975. Reflections on language. New York: Pantheon Books.

Chomsky, Noam. 1981. Interview with John Maddox. Scientifically Speaking. BBC Radio 3.

Garrett, Nina. 1991. Theoretical and pedagogical problems of separating 'grammar' from 'communication'. Foreign language acquisition research and the classroom, ed. by Barbara Freed, 74-87. Lexington, MA: D.C. Heath.

Gatbonton, Elizabeth, and Norman Segalowitz. 1988. Creative automatization: Principles for promoting fluency within a communicative framework. TESOL Quarterly 22, 3.473-492.

Givon, Talmy. 1979. From discourse to syntax: Grammar as a processing strategy. Syntax and semantics, discourse and syntax, ed. by Talmy Givon, 81-109. New York: Academic Press.

Halliday, M.A.K. 1978. Language as social semiotic. London: Edward Arnold.

Halliday, M.A.K. 1985. An introduction to functional grammar. London: Edward Arnold.

Hopper, Paul. 1988. Emergent grammar and the a priori grammar postulate. Linguistics in context: Connecting observations and understanding, ed. by Deborah Tannen, 117-34. Norwood, NJ: Ablex Publishing Company.

Hymes, Dell. 1971. Competence and performance in linguistic theory. Language acquisition: models and methods, ed. by Renina Huxley and Elisabeth Ingram, 3-28. New York: Academic Press.

Hymes, Dell. 1972. On communicative competence. Sociolinguistics, ed. by J. Pride and J. Holmes, 296-93. Harmondsworth: Penguin.

Larsen-Freeman, Diane. 1991. Teaching grammar. Teaching English as a second or foreign language, 2nd edn., ed. by Marianne Celce-Murcia, 279-96. New York: Newbury House.

Larsen-Freeman, Diane. (Series Director) 1993. Grammar dimensions: Form, meaning, use. Boston: Heinle and Heinle.

Pawley, Andrew, and Frances Snyder. 1983. Two puzzles for linguistic theory: Native-like selection and native-like fluency. Language and communication, ed. by Jack Richards and Richard Schmidt, 191–225. London: Longman.

Rea Dickens, Pauline, and Edward Woods. 1988. Some criteria for the development of communicative grammar tasks. TESOL Quarterly 22, 4.623-46.

Rutherford, William. 1987. Second language grammar: Learning and teaching. London: Longman.

Rutherford, William, and Michael Sharwood Smith. (eds) 1988. Grammar and second language teaching. New York: Newbury House Publishers.

Savignon, Sandra J. 1983. Communicative competence: Theory and classroom practice. Reading, MA: Addison-Wesley.

Tannen, Deborah (ed.) 1981. Georgetown University Round Table on Languages and Linguistics 1981. Washington, DC: Georgetown University Press.

Taylor, David. 1988. The meaning and use of the term 'competence' in linguistics and applied linguistics. Applied Linguistics 9, 2.148-68.

Widdowson, Henry G. 1988. Grammar and nonsense, and learning. Grammar and second language teaching, ed. by William Rutherford and Michael Sharwood Smith, 146–55. New York: Newbury House Publishers.

Widdowson, Henry G. 1990. Aspects of language teaching. Oxford: Oxford University Press.

Wilkins, David. 1976. Notional syllabuses. Oxford: Oxford University Press.

A nonhierarchical relationship between grammar and communication Part II: Insights from discourse analysis

Marianne Celce-Murcia
University of California, Los Angeles

A transitional introduction. In the preceding paper, which addresses the same topic, Diane Larsen-Freeman has provided theoretical and methodological grounds for reconciling grammar and communication. She describes four similarities between grammar and communciation that I shall summarize briefly here:

1. Both grammar and communication operate at different levels of language including word, utterance, and extended discourse;
2. Both can be characterized in terms of their form, meaning, and function;
3. Both can be viewed as static, declarative knowledge (or COMPETENCE), on the one hand, or as dynamic, procedural knowledge (or PERFORMANCE), on the other;
4. The relationship is nonhierarchical in that grammar and communication interact to shape each other.

We agree that these points of commonality provide a basis for reconciling and integrating grammar and communication in language learning and language teaching.

The particular perspective that I shall explore in my half of this plenary is that authentic discourse (or authentic text, if you like) provides appropriate content and context for resolution of the pedagogical dilemma Diane Larsen-Freeman has articulated since it allows us to teach both grammar and communication without being forced to choose one to the exclusion of the other.

Background. The relationship of discourse to grammar – or of discourse to communication – has not always been clear-cut. With reference to grammar and discourse, early work by Harris (1952) proposed that discourse is a product of morphological and syntactic rules, that is, that grammar provides the building blocks for describing the structure of discourse. Twenty-seven years later, in a complete reversal, Givón (1979) claimed that syntax is a low-level processing mechanism for discourse, that is, that discourse drives – and provides the raison d'etre for – grammar. While Givón's perspective is in tune with much of today's thinking in Communicative Language Teaching, we argue instead that the relationship between grammar and discourse is nonhierarchical, that grammar and discourse are complementary, and that they shape and influence each other in important ways.

This complementarity is articulated by functional linguists representing both North American and European perspectives. The North American functionalists such as Thompson (1985) and her students (e.g. Chen 1986 and Fox 1987) maintain that we need to look at discourse to fully understand grammar. European functionalists such as Halliday (1985) argue that we need to base discourse analysis on grammar. These two functionalist perspectives – that is, that discourse analysis illuminates our understanding of grammar and that grammar is an integral part of discourse analysis – are complementary and represent two sides of the same coin. In this paper we will view grammar as representing primarily the microlevel of discourse; however, there are cases where lexico-grammatical frames interact with macrolevel features and serve as routines for generating discourse episodes such as in the examples to be discussed in set (3).

The relationship between discourse and communication seems somewhat less problematic. In theoretical models of communication (e.g. Osgood and Sebeok 1954), discourse (or text) is equivalent to the verbalized message/utterance, which may consist of a word, a phrase, a sentence, or a multisentence sequence. While such models of communication also mention the addresser/encoder, the addressee/decoder, the code, and the channel, there is little discussion of social and contextual factors.

For more detailed social and contextual information about messages, we turn to ethnographers of communication such as Hymes (1972a, 1972b), who show us that the message is a speech act (e.g. directive, request, compliment) embedded in a speech activity such as a conversation, lecture, joke, etc., which occurs as part of a speech situation. Such messages also may belong to a genre (e.g. poem, proverb, personal letter, commercial, editorial), and they have a describable key (e.g. formal or informal, ironic, comic, serious, solemn). The speech situation (setting or scene) influences the topic, verbal behavior, and expectations of the participants such that characteristic language as well as characteristic social interaction tend to accompany any given speech situation such as a funeral, a trial, a committee meeting, a cocktail party, etc. Furthermore, in specific situations, the participants will use a variety of speech (dialect, register, jargon, etc.) that reflects their social relationships, and their attitudes toward each other and the message content. Finally, messages (or speech acts) have purposes or goals, on the one hand, and outcomes or consequences, on the other. The most general of these properties of messages can be considered macrolevel properties of discourse, while the more specific language-related properties may well manifest themselves at the microlevel in the speaker's choice of specific words or grammatical devices.

Thus discourse is the level at which grammar and communication intersect. The microlevel of discourse typically consists of the lexis and grammar used, while the macrolevel typically includes the communicative intent and the socio-cultural context in which the message occurs.

Examples of grammar and communication at work in discourse. At the most basic message level, the set of examples in (1) demonstrates that grammar – which in English consists of word order, inflections, and function words – is necessary for semantic precision in communication:

(1a) Word order: MIKE HIT BOB. / BOB HIT MIKE.
(1b) Function words: (from a billboard advertisement by a Los Angeles legal clinic): SEVEN DAY DIVORCE.
'divorce in seven days'(?), 'divorce for seven days'(?)
(2c) Inflections: JOHN LIVES IN OMAHA./ JOHN LIVED IN OMAHA.

In other words, the wrong word order, the wrong function word, or the wrong inflection (or a missing function word or inflection) may be a source of ambiguity or miscommunication in a message. This need for precision, in fact, is undoubtedly the reason why early humans went beyond compiling a lexicon and invented grammar in the first place: grammar was and is necessary for efficient communication.

At a level already more sensitive to discourse context, the second set of examples shows us how grammar is used to manage information as part of the communication process:[1]

(2a) After looking for weeks to find the perfect gift for her boyfriend, MARCIA FINALLY BOUGHT HIM A CD
(# ... Marcia finally bought a CD for him)
(2b) Mrs. Weiss didn't know what to do with the teddy bear she had won in the raffle. Her husband suggested that SHE GIVE IT TO THE LITTLE GIRL NEXT DOOR.
(# ... she give the girl next door ((*it/the bear))

These examples show that the speaker's knowledge of what is new

---

[1] In addition to the asterisk (*), the traditional indication of ungrammaticality, I add the pound symbol (#) to indicate an inappropriate discourse sequence, a convention I borrow from Gary (1974).

information versus what is given information often determines constituent order in clauses that can undergo dative alternation in English. In (2a), *him* comes before *a CD* [a compact disc] because *him* refers to Marcia's boyfriend, who has already been mentioned and is thus old information, whereas *a CD* comes last because it is new information. This is a general pragmatic constituent-ordering principle in English and many other languages: old information tends to precede new information and new information tends to occur toward the end of the message unit or utterance. The segment in parentheses in (2a) is grammatically well formed but pragmatically less appropriate given the preceding context. Similarly, in (2b), the old information, which in this case is the direct object *it*, referring to the previously mentioned teddy bear, comes before the indirect object (*the little girl next door*), which is the new information. Furthermore, the pragmatically inappropriate segment in parentheses in (2b) is well formed only if the full lexical noun phrase *the bear* is used. This is because, in addition to the pragmatic conventions already mentioned regarding the sequencing of old and new information, American English grammar does not permit unstressed *it* to occur as the direct object when the indirect object precedes and is a lexical noun. Thus we can see that rules of form, meaning, and function interact in complicated ways even in apparently straight forward messages.

The third set of examples shows us how the English tense–aspect system helps to establish coherence in longer stretches of discourse such as oral narrative. Segment (3a) was produced by a gas-meter reader discussing his encounters with dogs:

(3a) Almost every time you go into a house, they jump on you and sniff you and if you do 300 homes a day, it gets aggravating. I'VE BEEN BIT once already by a German Shepherd. And that was something. It was really scary. It was an outside meter the woman had. I read the gas meter and was walking back out and heard a woman yell. The first thing I thought of was he might go for my throat, like the movies ... (Terkel 1974:366)

Segment (3b) comes from a stewardess talking about how she copes with the inherently dangerous nature of her job:

(3b) What if I die today? I have too much to do. I can't die today. I use it as a joke. I'VE HAD emergencies where I'VE HAD to evacuate the aircraft. I was coming back from Las Vegas and being a lively stewardess. I stayed up all night, gambled. We had a full load of passengers. The captain tells me we're going to have an emergency landing in Chicago because we lost a pin out of the nose gear ... So I had to keep this in me for two more hours ... (Terkel 1974:80)

The research of Suh (1992) shows how both of these oral accounts follow a similar pattern. The speaker begins by discussing some job-related topic in the habitual present, then makes a transition and introduces a specific experience with the present perfect tense, then elaborates on the specific event using the past tense interspersed with occasional use of the past progressive for ongoing activities or occasional use of the historical present to highlight important segments; specifically, the stewardess uses the historical present to report the captain's message in (3b). This is one of the most typical functions of the historical present, according to Hymes (1992).

Suh's (1992) analysis shows us that the ever-problematic present perfect tense, among other things, is used in oral narrative to make a smooth temporal transition between habitually occurring current events and noteworthy specific past events that all relate to the same general topic. Texts like the two above show us that grammar and communication both serve to shape discourse; they suggest that facts about grammar such as the use of the present perfect that are so elusive at the sentence level begin to make much better sense and are easier to teach and learn if appropriate texts are used at some point in the learning process. Furthermore such texts can also be used to raise learner awareness of–and to focus learner attention on–salient forms of the lexico-grammar.[2]

The fourth set of examples come from transcribed conversations used at the University of California Los Angeles by Professor Emanuel Schegloff and his students for purposes of conversation analysis (CA). I have edited the CA notation slightly to facilitate reader comprehension because my focus is on the function of the wh-clefts in conversation, a topic which has been studied in great detail by Kim (1992).

The segment in (4a) comes from a radio talk show. Speaker A is the talk-show host, and speaker B is the caller (Kim 1992:50–51):

(4a) A: The papers, I read.
B: Yes.
A: have stated uh that the current feelings would apply to those people in that special group we were talking about. Blind, etcetra.
B: Yes.
A: That it-Those would not change. So you would still be eligible. It wouldn't change, your eligibility.
→ B: Well. What I know is that they gave me a letter an' they never sent me my card, hh-my Medicare card.

[2] 'Lexico-grammar' is a term I borrow from Halliday (1985), which I have come to appreciate because it suggests that lexis and grammar are a continuum, with lexis generally encoding more conventionalized messages and grammar more creative messages. Also, it allows for the possiblility that what is encoded lexically in one language may be encoded grammatically in another.

The segment in (4b) comes from a group therapy session; Ken (K) and Louise (L) are two of the teenagers in the group (i.e. the ones who happen to be talking in this segment) and Dan (D) is the therapist (Kim 1992:138):

(4b) K: My father's forty five, or forty three I think uh forty three, an' he'll go over to my grandmother's house, and insteada my grandmother offering him a drink, a beer, she'll say Wouldju-
L: 'Wanna glassa milk?' Hehhh
K: No 'Wouldju like a little bitta honey?'
L: Heh. ha ha!
K: 'Wouldju like some crackles?'
L: ehh ha ha ha ha
K: 'Wouldja like a peanut butter 'n jelly sandwich?'
→ D: So in a way, what you're saying is-is, 'you'll never get through that.'
K: heh
L: ehhehh

In segment (4a) the caller uses the wh-cleft to indirectly disagree with the talk-show host (note the *well*, which precedes the cleft and signals some upcoming disagreement). The caller draws on what she knows from her own experience, which is that she herself has never received a Medicare card. She uses a wh-cleft to redirect the conversation and make her point, which she had not been able to do while giving all her background information, mainly because the talk-show host kept chiming in with everything he knew about Medicare eligibility.

In segment (4b) the general topic at this point in the therapy session is how to deal with the fact that parents tend to treat teenagers as if they were still little children. Ken elaborates on this topic by using his father and grandmother as an even more exaggerated example of this phenomenon; he role-plays his grandmother treating his father as if his father were still a boy. Note that Ken does not want Louise to role-play his grandmother even though Louise has a good idea of what is going to happen and indicates she would like to be part of the role-play. Louise backs off and is content to listen to Ken's role-play and to provide positive feedback in the form of laughter at appropriate intervals. After the third such role-playing turn by Ken, the therapist Dan uses a wh-cleft in an attempt to sum up the gist of Ken's contribution and to get the therapy session back on track. After Dan's use of the cleft, Ken and Louise continue laughing over Ken's performance. However, in the next turn, someone else offers a new perspective on the topic, and we can assume that Dan's intervention has been successful in terms of moving the therapy session forward.

In both of these cases we see how a speaker uses a wh-cleft to intervene in a conversation that is not evolving according to the speaker's agenda. By using the cleft, the speaker attempts to redirect the ongoing communication along lines closer to his or her desired agenda. The two most common ways of doing this with a wh-cleft are through an appeal to the speaker's own cognitive knowledge or emotional state as in (4a) or through metalinguistic statements about the gist or intent of someone's contribution (one's own or someone else's) as in (4b).

Pedagogical implications. The pedagogical implications of the previous examples and of my earlier discussion of grammar and communication are that authentic discourse or text is a useful element for optimal language teaching; that is, when learners have reached intermediate level, discourse supplies the appropriate content and context for analyzing and learning the lexico-grammar of the target language. The communicative activities and tasks that the learner is expected to master in a language course should be adequately presented and modeled at the level of discourse or text. Ideally, these discourse samples will be elicited from suitable 'model' users of the target language.

The discourse or text can then be used to illustrate verbal performance given the content and context of the task. It can be used to guide practice, to raise awareness of macrolevel and microlevel features of text, and to provide a baseline against which learners can compare their own performance given the same task or similar tasks. In the early stages of a unit the texts can be used for listening or reading comprehension; at a later stage they might be used for text dictation/transcription or text reconstruction; in the final stages learners should have the opportunity to create original parallel texts that are personally meaningful to them and to compare the results of their efforts with an appropriate model.[3]

Such activities, when used in combination with a variety of other freer communicative activities, will help ensure that lexico-grammar is not neglected when the learning objective is communication and that communication is more precise and effective because the messages and utterances (i.e. the discourse) have been shaped by accurate and effective use of lexico-grammar.[4]

Finally, inspired by Wenden's (1991) work on learner strategies for learner autonomy, I'd like to suggest that teaching learners the rudiments of

---

[3] After giving this paper, I was asked by several people to explain exactly how I use such texts in a language classroom. First I use four to five parallel texts, not just two as I do for illustration in this paper. Second, I put students in pairs or small groups with the texts and with guiding questions so that they can analyze the macrostructure and the microstructure of the texts. Third, we discuss their findings and adjust them as needed. Fourth, the students have an opportunity to write individual and/or group texts on similar topics of interest to them. Finally, these student texts are shared and discussed to see if the essential features of the example texts have been appropriately integrated. I have discussed elsewhere (Celce-Murcia 1990) the usefulness of training ESL/EFL students to do discourse analysis.

[4] This proposal is in keeping with recent suggestions by Widdowson (1990). See also Widdowson (1992).

discourse analysis and the role of lexico-grammar in communication[5] empowers learners to ultimately better plan, monitor, and evaluate their language use, which in turn gives them the strategies they will need to continue developing their second or foreign language skills on their own.

REFERENCES

Celce-Murcia, Marianne. 1990. Teaching discourse analysis to ESL students. Paper presented at the 1990 TESOL Convention, New York.

Chen, Ping. 1986. Discourse and particle movement in English. Studies in language 10, 1.79-95.

Fox, Barbara. 1987. The noun phrase accessibility hierarchy reinterpreted. Language 63, 4.856-70.

Gary, E. Norman. 1974. A discourse analysis of certain root transformations in English. Unpublished Ph.D. qualifying paper in Linguistics, University of California, Los Angeles. Reproduced by the Indiana University Linguistics Club.

Givón, Talmy. 1979. On understanding grammar. New York: Academic Press.

Halliday, M.A.K. 1985. An introduction to functional grammar. London: Edward Arnold.

Harris, Zelig S. 1952. Discourse analysis. Language 28.1-30.

Hymes, Dell. 1972. On communicative competence. Sociolinguistics, ed. by John B. Pride and J. Holmes, 269-93. Harmondsworth, England: Penguin Books.

Hymes, Dell. 1972a. Models of the interaction of language and social life. Directions in sociolinguistics: The ethnography of communication, ed. by John J. Gumperz and Dell Hymes, 35-71. New York: Holt, Rinehart, and Winston.

Hymes, Dell. 1992. Inequality in language: Taking for granted. Georgetown University Round Table on Languages and Linguistics 1992, ed. by James E. Alatis. Washington, DC: Georgetown University Press.

Kim, Kyu-Hyun. 1992. Wh-clefts and left dislocation in English conversation with reference to topicality in Korean. Unpublished Ph.D. dissertation in Applied Linguistics, University of California, Los Angeles.

Osgood, Charles E. and Thomas A. Sebeok (eds.) 1954. Psycholinguistics: A survey of theory and research problems. Journal of Abnormal and Social Psychology 49 (supplement).

Suh, Kyung-Hee. 1992. Discourse functions of the English tense-aspect-modality system. Unpublished Ph.D. dissertation in Applied Linguistics, University of California Los Angeles.

Terkel, Studs. 1974. Working. New York: Ballantine Books.

Thompson, Sandra A. 1985. Grammar and written discourse: Initial vs. final purpose clauses in English. Text 5.1 and 2.56-84.

Wenden, Anita. 1991. Learner strategies for learner autonomy. New York: Prentice-Hall International.

Widdowson, H.G. 1990. Aspects of Language Teaching. Oxford: Oxford University Press.

Widdowson, H.G. 1992. Perspectives on communicative language teaching: Syllabus design and methodology. Georgetown University Round Table on Languages and Linguistics 1992. ed. by James E. Alatis. Washington, DC: Georgetown University Press.

---

[5] I believe that this can be done quickly, using minimal jargon, if students are presented with good, clear example texts.

Proficiency and accuracy: Enemies or allies?

Rebecca M. Valette
Boston College

As language teachers, our goal is to help our students become proficient in the language under study. Ideally, this means that we want our students to attain (or to be on the way toward attaining) an ILR rating of 3 or the corresponding ACTFL rating of Superior. Language at that level is characterized by a relatively high degree of accuracy both in terms of communicative competence and control of language: grammar, lexicon, phonology.

As our students begin to express themselves in the new language, they tend to speak (or write) an interlanguage, that is, an imperfect version of the target language. There are, however, not one, but many varieties of interlanguage which seem to fall into two categories:

- Limited but relatively accurate language that is flawed primarily because of its lacunae: lexical items, structures, patterns, etc., that have not yet been learned and/or internalized;

- Inaccurate language that exhibits faulty pronunciation and contains inappropriate lexical items, wrong syntax, incorrect patterns, etc.

In the latter type of interlanguage, the errors may be DISCRETE and symptomatic of the students' effort to express themselves at a level somewhat beyond their linguistic reach. On the other hand, the errors may be RECURRENT and, over time, risk becoming quasi-permanent or fossilized features of the interlanguage.

Second language teachers face the challenge of how to develop their students' proficiency, that is, their ability to communicate in the second language, while promoting accuracy and avoiding the danger of fossilization. Foreign language teachers in the United States find themselves in a somewhat different situation from that of their English Second Language colleagues, for whereas ESL students in the United States may readily be immersed in the English language and are strongly motivated to communicate, even if it be only for survival purposes, students of French, German, Spanish, and the lesser-taught languages rarely have the occasion to use their language outside of class unless they make a special effort to do so.

Certain foreign language teachers, in their effort to promote oral proficiency, have adopted a 'communication-first' position, namely a conviction that students in the classroom must be encouraged to communicate creatively in the new language and that accuracy of expression will naturally evolve as students receive more comprehensible input and have the opportunity to negotiate meaning with one another. It is the aim of this paper to demonstrate that a concern for accuracy and accurate language input must be present from the outset of instruction if the aim of the course is to develop truly proficient L2 speakers.

A. The claims of the 'communication-first' proponents. First let us look at some of the major claims of those who promote a 'communication-first' approach to second-language proficiency.

Claim 1. Traditional grammar-driven or grammar-based programs have failed to develop language proficiency. While it is true that generations of adult Americans have expressed dissatisfaction with their foreign language studies (hence the lament: 'I had X years of French and I can't speak a word!'), the failure of traditional language programs to build proficiency after a limited classroom experience should be traced not to their emphasis on accurate initial command of grammar and vocabulary, but rather to the students' lack of exposure to authentic spoken language in the form of comprehensible input. As Carroll (1967) concluded in his study of American undergraduate and graduate majors, those traditional language students who subsequently had the opportunity to come face to face with the spoken language through study or residence abroad were able to develop a high level of language proficiency. Twenty years ago at the University of Giessen, Edward Sittler encouraged his traditionally trained English majors to listen extensively to authentic English-language recordings in a free, unstructured environment, a system he called Audio-Immersion (Sittler and Valette 1987). As a result of these heavy doses of accurate comprehensible input, the students in his experiment were able to make significant improvements in their language proficiency.

Many of the adults in this country who speak a second language at the Superior level on the ACTFL scale (or levels 3/4 on the ILR scale) are precisely the products of an initial grammar-based traditional program followed by an immersion experience in which they had the opportunity to communicate and negotiate meaning in an authentic linguistic environment which provided accurate comprehensible input.

Claim 2. Large doses of comprehensible input promote the development of real language proficiency. In the natural approach, as described by Terrell (1977), students are exposed to large quantities of comprehensible input, usually in the form of teacher talk. In its idealized format such an approach might have one second language learner interact regularly with one or two native informants, talking about a variety of subjects of interest. Terrell (1990) carried out such an experiment in which an adult learner engaged in approximately

100–150+ hours of input-interaction with native speakers of Spanish. At the end of the study, Terrell (1990:203–204) concluded:

> Clearly, R [the learner] has spoken more Spanish than an average foreign language student after one year of formal study; and neither his comprehension nor his speech is even close to that of a normal first year student of Spanish. On the other hand, there are some positive sides to R's Spanish. His confidence and ability to maintain conversation are impressive. (Indeed, so impressive that fossilization appears to be setting in!)

It is interesting to note that the fossilized errors in R's speech were acquired not from the speech of the native speaker interlocutors, but rather from the input provided by his own attempts at communication and negotiating meaning. Clearly one's own speech is a form of comprehensible input, and if the inaccuracies in that speech are left uncorrected, those inaccuracies may become part of one's interlanguage.

Claim 3. By participating in content-based immersion programs, students will automatically acquire second-language proficiency. It has been widely believed in the United States and Canada that English-speaking children in French early immersion programs will automatically acquire second-language proficiency as they progress through the curriculum. There are, however, three different types of immersion programs which have each produced different linguistic results.

a. Bilingual schools which begin at the preschool or kindergarten level and offer a French or international baccalauréate degree as well as a high school diploma. English-speaking children who enter such a program acquire French naturally through various games and comprehension-based activities. There may be a couple of native French children in the class, who do provide a certain amount of accurate peer language, and of course the students have the advantage of listening to native teachers. Once the students enter first grade, they are introduced to formal accuracy-based language instruction as well as content-based instruction in other subject areas. As a result of an on going focus on correct language usage, the students who go through the program attain a high level of proficiency.

b. The French early immersion programs in Canada typically begin full immersion in first grade and end up with a limited number of immersion courses at the high school level (see Wesche 1992). Usually all the students in the class are English speakers, and the teacher, who is the main source of authentic comprehensible input, may be either a native or a near-native speaker. Although language arts are part of the curriculum, the attention to correct usage is not rigorous. Rather, the emphasis is on teaching content via the second language. The result is that students completing the program attain rather high levels of listening and reading comprehension, but that their speech contains significant grammatical and lexical errors. According to several research studies summarized by Hammerly (1991:3–5), these basic language errors are already present in the speech of first- and second-graders, and the students' level of accuracy does not seem to progress over time. Since most of the comprehensible input these students receive is from one another, it is not surprising that they tend to acquire and fossilize the mistakes they hear in one another's speech. The minority of students who do attain higher levels of proficiency, according to Wesche, are those who have had the opportunity to interact with native French speakers outside of class, and who, consequently, have had the opportunity to benefit from more accurate input.

c. In an American immersion program in Linguaville (a fictitious name: teachers in the school system wish to remain anonymous), the original philosophy was that the children's French should not be corrected at all, even on written worksheets. Accuracy would develop over time. Although the program offered extensive opportunities for interpersonal communication and negotiation of meaning, the children were interacting with their peers and quickly developed an interlanguage all their own, with a heavy English base: for example, **C'est joli intéressant!* 'That's pretty interesting'. Similarly, their written language was characterized by a simplified, idiosyncratic spelling system. By age 14, their French interlanguage was so fossilized that it proved highly resistant to the 'repair' efforts of the secondary school language teachers.

Claim 4. In a communication-based language curriculum, accuracy will improve over time. In her discussion of writing proficiency at the Novice, Intermediate, and Advanced levels, Omaggio (1986:226–34) points out that the Novice examples are limited but quite accurate, that the Intermediate examples very inaccurate and probably not readily comprehensible to speakers, and that the Advanced examples are extensive and accurate. It would be tempting to consider this an indication that there is a natural continuum from very inaccurate Intermediate interlanguage to a much more accurate interlanguage at the Advanced level. However, since most of the college students in our intermediate courses drop out of the language sequence, it is much more logical to conclude that those who reach the Advanced level are those whose writing at the Intermediate level exhibited accurate but limited interlanguage, rather than highly inaccurate interlanguage. The following question would make an interesting topic for a longitudinal research project: to what extent does the nature of the interlanguage at the Intermediate level enhance or inhibit the student's chances of reaching the Advanced level?

B. The role of accurate input in building language proficiency and preventing fossilization. Clearly the nature of the COMPREHENSIBLE INPUT that students receive plays a dominant role in determining the quality of their L2 output or interlanguage. This comprehensible input can be of four types:

- Culturally and linguistically accurate recorded input: from films, videos, songs, radio programs, tapes, etc.);

- Linguistically accurate spoken input: from native or near-native teachers and other native speakers;

- Input of varying degrees of accuracy (or inaccuracy): from nonnative teachers and peers;

- The learner's own output, which is perceived as input.

In order for students to develop real language proficiency, that is, the ability to express themselves fluently and accurately, it is essential that their second-language learning experience maximize the quantity of accurate comprehensible input they receive and minimize the quantity of inaccurate input. Conversely, to the extent that students process large amounts of inaccurate input (from their peers or by listening to themselves), they will tend to acquire an inaccurate interlanguage whose features, over time, run the danger of becoming fossilized.

It is time that we stop viewing PROFICIENCY and ACCURACY as enemies, but rather recognize that fluent but inaccurate speech is not a sign of proficiency but rather a sign of an interlanguage in danger of fossilization. In order to foster true proficiency, teachers must focus their attention on accuracy, promoting accuracy of comprehension and accuracy of expression, and especially providing students with large quantities of accurate comprehensible input.

REFERENCES

Carroll, John B. 1967. Foreign language proficiency levels attained by language majors near graduation from college. Foreign Language Annals 1.131-51.

Hammerly, Hector. 1991. Fluency and Accuracy: Toward balance in language teaching and learning. Clevedon, England: Multilingual Matters Ltd.

Omaggio, Alice C. 1986. Teaching language in context: Proficiency-oriented instruction. Boston: Heinle and Heinle.

Sittler, Edward V. and Rebecca M. Valette. 1987. Audio-Immersion: A new vocation for the language laboratory. Canadian Modern Language Review 44.134-45.

Terrell, Tracy D. 1977. A natural approach to the acquisition and learning of a language. Modern Language Journal 61.325-37.

Terrell, Tracy D. 1990. Natural vs. classroom input: Advantages and disadvantages for beginning language students. Georgetown University Round Table on Languages and Linguistics 1990, ed. by James E. Alatis, 193-206. Washington, DC: Georgetown University Press.

Valette, Rebecca M. 1990. Fossils or forests? The challenge of teaching for proficiency in the secondary schools. Georgetown University Round Table on Languages and Linguistics 1990, ed. by James E. Alatis, 235-44. Washington, DC: Georgetown University Press.

Valette, Rebecca M. 1991. Proficiency and the prevention of fossilization—An editorial. Modern Language Journal 75.325-28.

Wesche, Marjorie. 1992. French immersion graduates at university and beyond: What difference has it made? Georgetown University Round Table on Languages and Linguistics 1992, ed. by James E. Alatis. Washington, DC: Georgetown University Press.

Internationalization of the university: Where are the foreign languages?

Wilga M. Rivers
Professor emerita, Harvard University

Abstract. Internationalization is an 'in' word. Japan now wishes to 'internationalize' by bringing in large numbers of 'guest' workers from the poorer countries of Southeast Asia, clearly an economic interpretation. Every self-respecting college is at present talking about 'internationalizing' its campus. This often reduces to the fact that more international students must be attracted to help defray rising institutional costs, again an economically motivated decision. Sometimes implementation involves sending more students abroad to study; less often it leads to serious consideration of the need for more internationally oriented courses in the curriculum. What meaning or meanings can we give to 'internationalization' that has any kind of social or cultural reality on a campus? Beyond curriculum tinkering, what kinds of attitude changes are involved? Do we need to develop a new vocabulary for discussing this trend and illuminating its essence? Various aspects of 'internationalization' as presently proposed are analyzed, implications for foreign language teachers are drawn, and suggestions for implementation in educational settings are outlined.

Everywhere one hears of internationalization—of curricula, of campuses, of international business. In Japan, one is told that the nation is conscious of its need to 'internationalize'. On further investigation, one finds the term seems to refer to a project to bring in some 100,000 guest workers from the poorer, less-developed nations of Southeast Asia to perform tasks the Japanese do not now wish to perform themselves, all this with very little reference to integrating these new workers into the social or linguistic scene in their host nation. An equally economic interpretation of the term applies when one hears of internationalizing the campus of some small, financially strapped college, which hopes to balance its budget by inviting in, or enticing in, a large number of fee-paying overseas students, with no clearly articulated plan for integrating these newcomers into the life of the campus, or its surrounding community, and learning from their presence. Still others hope to 'internationalize' the student body by sending whole segments of it to study in other countries (often English-speaking and

Western European in culture) in American enclaves where the students are effectively insulated, or insulate themselves, from the suspect influence of local ideas and mores. Some hope to 'internationalize' the curriculum by providing a smorgasbord of options, such as Medieval Literature of Outer Mongolia, the Marital Habits of Peewee Tribes under Colonialist and Noncolonialist Regimes, or Astrological Beliefs of Extraterrestrials, from among which students may select one to fulfill a requirement in Understanding the World We Live In. Yet others build a new International Center, staff it with an International Affairs Officer, and leave it at that. The spirit is willing, but the implementation is weak.

One problem with all this is that the term 'internationalization' does not have a very clear denotation, although it seems to have quite a lot of connotation. Does it refer to internationalization of the university or college (in the sense of setting up branch campuses abroad); internationalization of the curriculum; internationalization of campus life; intercultural education for American students (developing crosscultural understanding); international cooperation (working collectively on international problems, like global warming, pollution of the air and water, the drug trade, proliferation of armaments or nuclear waste, the curbing of international terrorism, or the saving of endangered species); or international assistance to developing or emerging nations? Much of this action comes under the broader heading of international education, although we hear the terms international studies, international affairs, area studies, internationalization across the curriculum, peace studies, study abroad, international exchange, international internships, development education, global education (and globalization), international perspective, and the international dimension. (One needs very little imagination to recognize the need for other languages in all of these areas.) Arum maintains that 'the fuzziness seems to have served everyone's purposes, allowing everyone to do his or her own thing, without interference from others' (1987:6).

It is clear that we need a framework within which to discuss this very important subject, so that we may recognize where each other's contributions fit into the picture and avoid arguing at cross-purposes. Clarification would be helpful for our students as well. Rosenau (cited in Trahan 1988:34) speaks of the 'intellectual perplexity' of students who find themselves confronted by 'not a discipline, but rather a conglomerate of foci, preoccupations, skills, and disciplines'. In an attempt at rationalization, Arum (1987:8) suggests the use of INTERNATIONAL EDUCATION as the superordinate term, drawing under its wings the three areas: INTERNATIONAL CONTENT OF CURRICULA, INTERNATIONAL MOVEMENT OF SCHOLARS AND STUDENTS concerned with training and research, and arrangements engaging United States education abroad in TECHNICAL ASSISTANCE AND EDUCATIONAL COOPERATION programs (this would include agricultural, economic, industrial, and educational advising, and such service experiences as the Peace Corps and much English as a Second Language activity). I shall restrict my remarks to the first two of these areas, while adding a further important category: the INTERNATIONALIZATION OF CAMPUS LIFE, that is, promoting international attitudes and extracurricular crosscultural experiences, which may include outreach to the surrounding community. It is so much easier to love Extraterrestrials in the abstract: it is so much more exciting and intriguing to learn about them and their exotic ways when they are distant from us than it is to love and appreciate the Extraterrestrial who lives next door or shares our office. Yet this is what we must learn to do in our interdependent, constantly changing world. The campus gives us a concrete place to start. In all of these areas what we are seeking to develop is what the American Council on Education (1984) has called INTERNATIONAL COMPETENCE.

Possibly we still need a rationale for developing international competence, since there are so many areas of knowledge fighting for their share of time and effort on the campus. We have heard so often of the global village—the fact that the world is getting so much smaller all the time as we become more interdependent and join larger and larger area groupings; that cultures everywhere seem to be becoming homogenized into one great global culture, especially for youth, under the worldwide influence of pop, sports, and television culture; that soon we will all be watching and listening to the same thing at the touch of a button, especially as English, it is generally believed, is becoming everyone's language and we have nothing foreign to understand anymore. Into this chorus, it is interesting to hear an occasional small voice making itself heard that strikes a different note. One such is the voice of President Keohane of Wellesley College, a director of IBM, who believes that technological advances in communications equipment and computer programs that can translate material rapidly into other languages may actually distance us from each other in important ways. They may give us 'only the electronic illusion of being in touch' (Boston *Globe*, January 12, 1992:22), computer bulletin boards and electronic mail notwithstanding. We may think we are on the same wavelength, when we are actually coming from very different presuppositions and assumptions. Recent events have demonstrated also the opposite overt trend: the tendency to break apart and declare differences. We still need much sensitization in our centrifugal centripetal world.

Where is the foreign language profession in all of this? In 1978 foreign languages were forced into a shotgun marriage with international studies, when President Carter set up his Presidential Commission. Both the foreign language and the international studies professions were somewhat startled, and both have been forging ahead, each in its own way, since that time. It seems almost as though, having accepted a marriage of convenience to satisfy others, they have set up separate households. I doubt if they even have breakfast together. Except for certain rather lonely watchdogs who have tried to keep us alert to movement in either household, each of the parties has seemed to remain fairly oblivious to the thinking and action of the other.

One has only to read the literature on international studies or international business to be struck by the fact that there is a loud cry to the foreign languages to come out and play. One reads such statements as these: 'Any plans for the improvement of international studies as a whole must be centrally concerned with foreign language teaching' (Lambert 1989:49), and 'Business needs people who understand foreign languages and cultures—who, through learning at least one language, have changed their mindset, have lost the 'we'–'they' syndrome, who are alert to cultural differences' (A. Micou in U. Mass *Training* 1984:88). Yet where are the foreign languages? They remain hidden away in departments that are rapturously following the evolutions and convolutions of Derrida, Christeva, or Chomsky; they remain in thrall to earlier liaisons. Richard Lambert (1989:148) puts it well when he states that 'reform movements in international studies [subsuming foreign languages] are like a tide surge fragmenting on the rocks of school, departmental, faculty, and course autonomy. What starts as a unified force quickly disintegrates and loses its power as it flows through the established channels.' The 'established channels' for foreign languages are foreign language and literature departments, even in the case of many of the so-called 'critical' or less commonly taught languages.

Academia is moving on, however. There is a constant flow of reports and recommendations for the development of international competence in colleges and universities, in general education and core curricula, in schools of business and departments of politics and government, all of which call for the development of a 'usable competence' in foreign languages (something that cannot be achieved in the ubiquitous 'basic skills' sequences). What reply is coming out of the average foreign language and literature department? In many cases a deafening silence, as these departments scramble for students in order to produce more experts on Cervantes, Goethe, and Dante, rather than on Monnet, the OAS, or Mitsubishi's role in the Japanese economy.

In 1984, and again in 1989, the American Council on Education (ACE) practically shouted at us with two discussion documents: *What we don't know can hurt us* and *What we can't say can hurt us*, both of which called on foreign languages to look beyond their traditional borders and reach out to help all students develop international competence. The 1989 statement was even subtitled *A call for foreign language competence by the year 2000*. Yet how many of our departments read and discussed these books? How many high school foreign language chairs called these books to the attention of their principals, school boards, or local communities?

What was the ACE, and other influential bodies like the American Association of State Colleges and Universities (1984), calling us to? To take up our rightful role as language experts in the education of all students and all future citizens, not just liberal arts students, but those in engineering, science, law, medicine, business, or agriculture as well. Foreign languages belong everywhere. The 1989 ACE report asks us to provide continuity in language learning throughout the educational process; to give students a base on which to build higher-level proficiency; to stress language competence as a vital educational outcome, a normal part of the education of every American as the key to cultural competence, integrating language instruction with other studies and programs; to work for institutional initiatives that will facilitate the process of language learning (that is, the learning of any language, not just the one we ourselves love) for students, but also for faculty, helping those in whatever discipline who already possess competence in another language to maintain it, so that we may increase the possibility of the use of foreign languages in many areas of study. We have friends in unexpected places. Are we availing ourselves of the friendly support they offer us?

We have friends too in the legislature (the Panettas, the Simons, the Bradleys, the Dodds, the Borens, among others). There is reason to rejoice over the passing of the Neighborhood Schools Improvement Act (1992), which includes foreign languages among the core subjects in the National Education Goals of the President's America 2000 program. Title V, Educator Recruitment, Retention and Development, of the Higher Education Act, as amended in 1992, also includes foreign language as a core area for teacher education; this amendment provides demonstration grants for critical languages and area studies that enable consortia to operate programs, develop materials, and train teachers at the elementary and secondary levels, and funds for the development of foreign language and culture instructional materials. The Foreign Language Assistance Act (1988) also supports critical languages, with provisions for states to substitute the more commonly taught languages in case of necessity. Rep. Leon Panetta's Global Education Opportunities Act (introduced in 1992) provides for inservice training, institutes, and materials development for elementary and secondary school foreign language teaching, matching grants for states to establish language development initiatives and assist businesses and professions in gaining international competence, and demonstration grants for distance learning and for consortia in critical languages and area studies; this act also encourages study-abroad initiatives (see Panetta 1992a, 1992b). The National Security Education Act (NSEA), passed and funded in 1991, provides funds for language instruction at colleges and universities and fellowships for graduate students, as well as money for study-abroad programs. When funding is not forthcoming, our friends in the legislature try again. Doors are being opened for us. We cannot allow these opportunities to pass us by, because we are reluctant to take up our true position as central to a modern education.

For these aims to be achieved, however, the language program must become autonomous, with its own goals and directions. It cannot remain a handmaid, preparing a few students to undertake studies in literary theory, nor should it spend endless repetitive hours on elementary language studies, which students soon, and happily, forget. The real work of the autonomous language program is developing courses at all levels for students with many different objectives, with particular emphasis on advanced level opportunities where true international and linguistic competence becomes an attainable goal (Rivers 1992:vii).

Lambert (1989) found, in a survey of internationally oriented courses in different types of institutions, that half of those offered were foreign language courses. 'In many cases,' he says, 'they are the only internationally oriented courses taken by many students'; consequently, 'many college administrators think of foreign language courses as coterminous with international studies' (p.48). 'This situation,' he continues, 'is the result of historic accumulation, not specific planning.' (p.49). It would seem, then, that foreign language courses are already well placed to move on in a planned provision of what the university or college and its students need.

Without turning this into another dissertation on internationalization of universities and curricula (see Backman 1984 for an exhaustive account; Smith 1990 lists eight elements in an emerging consensus), we may note in passing that all agree that, for a successful international education program, there needs to be a commitment on the part of the university through its administration to a global perspective and preferably a mission statement, to strengthen the hand of international education advocates. International education is frequently spearheaded by a central office for international programs, although there are a number of other models that are decentralized (Backman 1984 describes 17 models, each with a different history, approach, and focus). Whatever the structure, we find the four main strands listed earlier. We will now examine these to see what role foreign languages can play in their development.

Internationalization of the curriculum. Such an influential body as the American Association of State Colleges and Universities has come out with a very clear statement on this subject, asserting that 'International education is a fundamental part of general and professional studies. It is the preparation for social, political, and economic realities that humans experience in a culturally diverse and competitive, interdependent world' (AASCU 1984). The American Assembly of Collegiate Schools of Business (AACSB) has mandated the cultivation of an international dimension in an attempt 'to internationalize the entire discipline root and branch' (Goodwin and Nacht 1991:20). Of late, schools of mining and engineering (like the Colorado School of Mines) have realized that new technologies are being developed far from traditional centers in the United States and Europe and that it is imperative for their graduates to understand the politics, economics, and cultures of countries about which they knew very little before. Internationalization of the curriculum has become an urgent priority for many fields under the academic umbrella.

Expanding the curriculum or permeating it to encompass a global perspective is a campus-wide responsibility. In some institutions this has led to the establishment of a separate international studies major; in others, a minor or concentration within the majors of traditional departments. In some cases, the international major coalesces into a dual major with such departments as government, business, or economics, which gives the student a solid grounding in the traditional discipline, while encouraging a parallel international purview of the principal areas of the discipline. In order to reach the bulk of the students, international content is being included across the curriculum in all kinds of courses.

The foreign language response. Lambert observes that 'foreign-language departments whose base is most often in the humanities, frequently do not play as central a role as they might in [initiatives to introduce ... an international dimension to undergraduate education]. Foreign-language study is an important part of international studies. Moreover, colleagues engaged in international studies can be important allies within the college and university community in the promotion of foreign-language instruction' (1992:281).

(i) Foreign language departments can act as the purveyor of the international perspective through language study geared toward the needs of the major discipline, broadening this with knowledge of the historical and contemporary culture of the speakers of a particular language area and the way they approach the discipline or act in a professional context, so that the graduate of the program is better prepared to operate within that culture or in association with its culture bearers (whether as a health professional, technical adviser, business representative, archaeologist, anthropologist, educator, or whatever). The foreign language collaboration sometimes takes the form of a dual major with the professional field or, alternatively, a minor in the language with a major in the professional field. The German Department at Stanford University has taken this route with double majors with Economics, International Relations, Political Science, History, and Engineering (Rivers 1992:35).

(ii) The foreign language faculty may assist a professor of the discipline who teaches in English by providing tutorial sections where language material related to the topic or culturally determined aspects of professional behavior are elucidated and discussed. This approach of FOREIGN LANGUAGE ACROSS THE CURRICULUM has been implemented successfully at Earlham College (Jurasek 1988) and St. Olaf College (Allen et al. 1992) among others.

Where foreign language instructors have expertise in the discipline, they can use content from the discipline in advanced-level (sometimes upper-intermediate) courses where students learn to feel at ease in dealing with the content entirely in the language. This has been the approach in foreign language departments for many years in teaching language through literature, history, civilization and contemporary culture, the study of political and social institutions, or scientific material. These traditional content areas are now being expanded to courses for health professionals, law enforcement personnel, or hotel management, where career-related material is introduced and discussed in the language, and students act on it in ways that simulate the real situations in which they might have to use the language later. Courses in language for business are now widespread, often preparing students for overseas certificates or diplomas (Frommer 1992). In these, the case study method is more and more frequently being used (Dow and Ryan 1987). Any subject matter is possible material for language courses, provided that it is dealt with in the language and serves as a basis for classroom discussion and participation

It must be emphasized, however, that the foreign language instructor should be, or should become, well versed in the field being taught through the language. This is not an area for amateurs, if the courses taught in the language are to be responsible, reputable, and acceptable to the major discipline departments. We must remember that we still have to persuade other disciplines and professional departments, overloaded with requirements for their majors, to make room for credits from outside their department.

Lambert (1992) urges foreign-language departments to work closely with instructors of core and general education courses with an international dimension to encourage the inclusion of reading (and, if possible, discussion) in another language as an incentive for students to use the language they have been studying for the language requirement. This can be achieved by offering leaders for sections conducted in the foreign language on related foreign language material. This is what St. Olaf College has called the Applied Foreign Language Component (Allen et al. 1992). In some colleges and universities, foreign language faculty have been able to create courses acceptable for the foreign cultures or international studies segment of the institution's core or required general education program.

(iii) If internationalization of the curriculum is to provide students with more than an outsider's monocultural view of the affairs, perspectives, and achievements of other national or cultural groups, students will need to be able to read fluently in another language, understand it when it is spoken, and speak it well enough to be understood, so that authentic documents (written or audiovisual) may be analyzed, persons involved with the area under study interviewed, and short investigative trips made, when necessary, to areas where further information or documentation can be unearthed. Hence the call from across the campus for ADVANCED PROFICIENCY in a language. Foreign language departments must begin to take much more seriously their responsibility to develop a progressive series of advanced language courses, varied in content and focus, and with clearly indicated placement levels, that will encourage students to develop further their control of the language at the level at which they are proficient. A recent survey at Harvard found that entering students who had reached a level where they felt comfortable using the language were much more likely to continue with that language above the requirement level than those who were still having difficulties upon entrance. For this reason, as attention turns again to improving the teaching of languages in secondary and elementary schools, it is time for colleges and universities, particularly those that value an international perspective, to make clear to high schools their preference in admissions for students who have already mastered the basics of a language and are advancing toward some usable competence. In Australia, where the need to develop greater international competence in the population is being taken seriously, a number of universities now give bonus credit in the admissions process to students demonstrating that they have attained an advanced level of foreign language competence in high school.

Unfortunately, when students who have become enthusiastic about languages at secondary school come to college, they only too frequently find that there is little to interest them beyond the intermediate level. Proper provision should be made for those who have studied four or more years in high school, sometimes since elementary school, to continue at an appropriate level in college. Advanced language courses can be calibrated to different levels on a placement test, as a guide to students, and can provide a diversity of subject matters, literary, cultural, or professional, so that the students' interests and future needs are met. Rivers (1992:21–33) describes in detail seventeen possible courses at the advanced level, which have an international perspective as well as the goal of developing advanced competence. With ample provision of courses geared to varied interests, students retain their excitement and continue to burnish their control of the language as a valuable element in their international competence.

(iv) As language, literature, and culture specialists, we need not be diffident about the contributions we can make as humanists to international education. Engerman and Marden (1992:19) consider that 'many of the basic needs for international understanding are integral to a liberal arts education: the understanding of parochialism, the openness to change, the acquisition of effective communication skills and the ability to see ideas in their full complexity.' Once students have a level of competence that makes them comfortable working in the language, we can introduce them to so many great thinkers, writers, playwrights, film producers, philosophers, artists, and musicians—poets and peasants—encouraging them to discuss situations, problems, and solutions, ethical and practical, that have universal dimensions.

(v) The kinds of contributions we are discussing require foreign language instructors (Language Teaching and Culture Specialists or LTCSs) to network, to develop crosscampus and crossdisciplinary associations in order to learn more about the concerns of other departments and schools—where they are directing their energies and the new developments taking place in their fields. Where entrenched faculty members are uninterested in new liaisons and do not recognize the need for a broader outlook on the language work of the department, we may have to work around them (in the true sense of 'circumvent'). Confrontation arouses hostilities; circumvention frequently goes unobserved until the moment of the fait accompli. We admire chess masters; we need to learn from them.

If none of the initiatives listed seems possible in the department at the moment, language instructors in the basic courses, which are taken by so many undergraduates, should at least ensure that after the obligatory two, three, or four semesters of elementary language study students will have acquired some international perspective, not just the ability to manipulate verbs and adjectives.

(vi) Another contribution foreign languages can make to international studies is sharing its expertise in teaching and discussion techniques. Foreign languages is an area that has devoted much time and energy to preparing its instructors to conduct lively and participatory classes geared to students' needs and interests. It is true that many departments have ignored this trend, which is now becoming mainstream. More and more departments, however, are recognizing the need to train graduate teaching assistants to conduct communicative, interactive classes, and more and more departments are advertising for LTCSs to give leadership in these endeavors. A five-year assessment of Harvard undergraduate education came up with the 'unexpected finding' that 'foreign languages and literatures [taught fully in the language] are the most widely appreciated courses' on campus (Light 1992:11, 69). In fact, 'classes in foreign languages receive the highest rating [in undergraduate student evaluations] of all groups of courses at Harvard College,' and 94 percent of alumni in the survey urged students to take courses in foreign languages and literatures even if they officially tested out of the requirement (1992:70, 75). Light attributes this 'strong enthusiasm' to the way language 'classes are structured to maximize personal engagement and collegial interaction,' with constant feedback on progress (1992:75–76). Students reported that, despite heavy workloads, their interest in the subject matter remained high (p. 71).

Involving well-trained and motivated foreign language instructors in team teaching in general education courses with an international focus and in specialized courses with a strong foreign language component offered in other departments can export some of this enthusiasm and involvement to what Lambert has described as being, in too many places, 'a melange of unrelated internationally focused courses' (1992:282); it will also ensure that students continue to build up their ability to use the language for professional purposes.

(vii) There still remains the question of faculty rewards. Will LTCSs who serve the campus through a broader view of their task be promoted and tenured, or will they be driving further nails into their academic coffins? In some institutions we already have enlightened senior faculty who have realized the necessity in a modern college or university of recognizing less traditional contributions to scholarship as worthy of consideration. Younger people are rising through the ranks who have broader viewpoints and are branching out into interdisciplinarity in their own fields of research, so the hope is in the future. It is up to the LTCSs to demonstrate their scholarly and applied leadership in their publications and original materials development, as well as in their excellent teaching and supervision.

If present hopes for a change of attitude toward LTCSs are not soon realized and the university moves on leaving the language and literature departments behind, we may find ourselves facing a trend toward the establishment of Departments or Centers of Languages and Intercultural Studies, the direction taken by Warren Wilson College in North Carolina among others (Backman 1984:180).

International movement of scholars and students. Study and residence abroad is no longer the privileged province of foreign language departments, comparative literature scholars, and affluent students from private four-year colleges on a socially requisite visit to Europe. Throughout academe and the wider community of politics, business, and social concerns, people are realizing that young Americans must 'be there', go out to meet their competitors and future collaborators, and begin to understand their mindset, their values, their behavior patterns, and their languages. This usually includes living in families or in close contact with local students in residences or dormitories. As the Report of the National Task Force on Undergraduate Education Abroad (Burn and Smuckler 1990) puts it: 'Study abroad is one of the most effective means to achieve international education for undergraduates and the internationalization of colleges and universities ... It is the internationalization of the undergraduate experience which can have the greatest impact on American society in terms of life long interests and values,' this despite acknowledged deficiencies in some study-abroad programs in the past. Overseas travel is now being expanded more and more to include internships and exchanges in working contexts.

Burn (1991) and Karelis (1991) both point out that the United States is being upstaged by Europe in the area of mobility of students. The problem of transferable credits, such a bugbear for United States students, is being addressed by the European Credit Transfer System, for instance. With programs like ERASMUS (the Action Scheme for the Mobility of University Students) that permits students to continue their studies in different parts of Europe, COMETT (the Community Program for Cooperation between Universities and Enterprises regarding Training and Technology), TEMPUS (Trans-European Mobility Program for University Students, with particular attention to Central and Eastern Europe), and NIT (New Information Technology), Europe is on the move, ensuring that its young people know each other, have a shared educational experience, and can work together within a common frame of reference. Europe plans to spend $190 million over three years on exchanges of students and professors. The United States federal government, as of 1993, has allocated $150 million for the David L. Boren Program (under the NSEA), which supports a variety of language-related activities, including study abroad. The NSEA emphasizes languages critical to United States interests, which is interpreted as referring particularly to such less commonly taught languages as Japanese, Chinese, Arabic, and Korean. Important as these languages are for the future, Karelis (1991) points out that the national interest cannot ignore the new Europe. 'We're in the middle of the wrong debate on Eurocentrism,' he observes. 'College faculty members ought to be talking less about how much of the worthwhile art and literature of the past came from Europe and more about the centrality of the European Community to the world economic order of the next century.' The European Community, he predicts, 'will effectively be writing the rules of trade for the 21st century ... Before 2010 today's undergraduates will probably be looking at a 20-member EC, including many East European nations with few historic ties to the United States.' Europeans are preparing for this eventuality. In one recently established three-year business school program, students will spend one year in France, one year in Germany, and one year in the United Kingdom, using French, German, and English in succession for their studies (The training ... U. Mass. 1985:155).

There will continue to be debate on where United States students should study, but it is clear that they must begin to take seriously areas other than the United Kingdom, to which the majority of non-language majors go at present—that is, areas where they cannot continue to live in a monolingual cocoon. Foreign language departments similarly must become much more aware of their responsibility to develop programs to prepare these students to be able to interact to some degree of sophistication with their counterparts in the country of their choice. One major problem in the past has been inadequate linguistic and cultural preparation of students for the experience of studying alongside native speakers, living within their families, or interacting in the workplace. Some significant control of a language on arrival ensures more progress during the stay and helps students to go beyond superficial impressions of the target culture, which often confirm the stereotypes of those less well prepared; this is also essential if United States students are to study in the new language in any effective way. A few semesters of prior study at the elementary and lower intermediate level are by no means sufficient preparation to ensure solid progress in the language, especially if one also expects them to acquire some specifically discipline-related language. Foreign language departments, in collaboration with the various disciplines the students represent, will do well to study carefully the linguistic and interactional needs of their students, in order to develop learning materials that will adequately prepare them for what they will encounter at the destination point.

Nor should we forget the needs of faculty on exchanges and sabbaticals. More and more colleges are seeking to internationalize the faculty's thinking, as an important influence on that of the students (Goodwin and Nacht 1991). Wheaton College in Massachusetts, for instance, sends its faculty abroad for prearranged short-term internship experiences, preferably in countries about which they know very little. The University of Washington has institutionalized faculty exchanges of social scientists with Western European universities to establish a balance with their already existing Pacific Rim and Russian orientation. This type of experience is no longer confined to large research universities and private colleges, whose faculty are able to draw considerable support from government and private funding. Bunker Hill Community College, also in Massachusetts, leads a consortium of community colleges that encourages faculty to engage in overseas development assistance and exchanges. Goodwin and Nacht (1991:99) found, in this instance, that 'the time overseas had become an intense learning experience for those involved ... For those faculty who had never been abroad before the impact was dizzying.' And this impact is carried over to the students they teach. The foreign language departments have a role to play here too in helping faculty members prepare to gain the most they can from their overseas experience, while profiting from the contacts these colleagues are able to make while abroad. One result of such exchanges has frequently been an influx of overseas students from the areas visited.

The many problems associated with the question of who will be able to profit from an undergraduate study-abroad experience are thoroughly discussed elsewhere. Burn and Smuckler (1990) list major inhibitory factors, ranging from rigidity in home institution curricular requirements to financial regulations that do not permit the use of scholarship and student support funds while abroad. There is considerable concern that overseas study opportunities should be available to as diverse a student population as possible. More work is needed to solve such problems, and foreign language faculty should support, and even lead, their colleagues in other fields in devising measures to overcome factors that make study abroad unaffordable for many (both financially and professionally).

What do students do when they finally settle in to their study-abroad location? Too many observers of the overseas scene lament the American students' tendency to retreat into enclaves, within which they interact almost exclusively with other English-speaking students. There is work to be done in rectifying this situation. The problem is not only the low level of language competence, discussed above, but also the special classes for American students that have to be created as a result. Only a few language majors are usually able to integrate fully into local university courses; the rest are taught by their own home institution instructors, or in a simplified version of the language by specially recruited native speakers.

Thought should be given to structuring the overseas experience, so that, apart from living with native speakers (which may or may not be serendipitous), students are prepared to carry out some independent or group research project that entails, for its accomplishment, considerable linguistic interaction with the target-language population. Students often need some incentive of this kind to force them out into the wider society. Indiana University, for instance, in its Business School exchange program with Tilburg University in the Netherlands, requires a for-credit independent research project of importance to a United States or European business institution on an economic or political issue (The training ..., U. Mass. 1985:135). Many others could be cited. In setting up such projects, gender differences will need to be kept in mind in societies where men and women do not have the same open access to all aspects of the cultural and social environment. (Those interested in research on United States students abroad are referred to Weaver, ed. 1989.)

The question of maintenance programs for returnees should also be addressed in a practical way. As Lambert (1989:79) puts it, unfortunately, 'attrition begins as they step on the plane home.' If students are to retain a usable level of competence, efforts should be made to persuade the disciplines they represent to include foreign-language readings and discussion sections in courses, as at Earlham and St. Olaf (see above). Some institutions have worked out ways of using the returnees' skills in peer teaching. In the Dartmouth College Intensive Language Model, those who have studied abroad may serve as Apprentice Teachers (ATs) for undergraduate language students, and the German Department at Brown University welcomes the collaboration of returnees with their faculty. Prokasy (1990:18) wonders why language departments do not treat the study-abroad period as an integral part of the curriculum for majors, even to the extent of teaching some of the upper-level courses at the site of the program and providing newly devised courses for returnees that will challenge their freshly developed proficiency, enabling them to reach even higher levels of expression in speech and writing.

Many other decisions will have to be made (e.g. Who organizes the program? For what length of time? Where will it be located? Who pays the expenses? Who acts as resident director, under what conditions? What student support services must be provided? Will the program take the form of an exchange, with the home campus welcoming students at a later date from the target language country? Will the program be a solo undertaking or will neighboring institutions be involved?). The answers to questions such as these will depend on the specific needs of the local students, the enthusiasm and involvement of the language faculty, the liaisons they have been able to establish with other disciplines and professional schools on the campus, and the expectations of these collaborators.

In 1990–91, 407,500 students from overseas studied on American campuses. The largest percentage of these were studying business and management, closely followed by engineering, then mathematics and computer science. Only 70,727 United States students studied abroad in 1989–90, the majority being students in the liberal arts, social sciences, and foreign languages. Of these students, 77 percent studied in Europe (most in the United Kingdom), only 9 percent studied in Latin America, and the remaining 10 percent were scattered through Asia, the Middle East, Africa, and Oceania (*Chronicle of Higher Education*, Oct. 23, 1991:A39, 41). It is time to redress these imbalances.

Internationalization of campus life. It has frequently been observed that college students learn as much from each other as they do from the structured curriculum—from discussions of diverse viewpoints, observation of each other's ways, and assessment of each other's values and political and religious ideas. With large numbers of overseas students on our campuses (in some places as high as 18 percent of the student body and commonly from 5 to 7 percent) as well as local students of diverse ethnic backgrounds, undergraduates now have an excellent opportunity to get to know the world without leaving home. Because of their natural tendency to 'hang out' with their own kind, however, many will not seek this kind of experience without a little prodding. This enrichment of student life can be advanced by some careful planning, often by the campus Office of International Affairs (if there is one), but also by the foreign language departments.

Ohio University prides itself on its commitment to 'international community' and to 'education for interdependence.' In 1991, it welcomed about 1,350 international students from more than 100 countries to a campus of 18,000 students. It also conducts more than 50 active programs with nations in Europe, Africa, Latin America, and Southeast and East Asia, and has study-abroad programs in Austria, Ecuador, France, and Mexico. In one week, it celebrated Kwanzaa (an African 'first-fruits' celebration), received a visit from Namibia's education minister, and organized a panel discussion among Arabs and Jews on the Middle East peace talks, a kaffeeklatsch of women from around the world to exchange traditional recipes, and a planning meeting for an Indonesian festival on campus. Despite these efforts, some American students reported that they had had little more than casual contact with foreign students personally, and some of the foreign students felt that most overseas students did not 'assimilate very well despite all the university programs intended to help them to do so.' 'What do you talk about?' a Korean student wondered. 'The guys are always talking about sports, and we don't follow baseball and football that much.' As the university's president, Charles Ping, observed: 'People everywhere don't easily accept difference.' At Ohio, he felt that on the whole they were ahead of the game (*Chronicle of Higher Education*, Nov. 20, 1991:A43–45). I do not intend here to downplay Ohio University's noteworthy efforts to develop understanding and appreciation of other cultures and the problems and achievements of other nations. I merely wish to emphasize the point that changing the attitudes of undergraduates is not an easy task and cannot be left to chance. (For a detailed account of Ohio University's program, see Backman 1984:83–102.)

The Oregon State System of Higher Education has tackled this problem of internationalization of its campuses and the surrounding communities head on with a well-structured International Cultural Service Program (ICSP). Under this program, the Oregon state universities are empowered to utilize a number of their foreign students (300 across the state) as an educational resource, to give Americans at all levels of instruction a better understanding of international affairs. The ICSP enables Oregon state universities to enroll foreign students with a demonstrated need for financial assistance at in-state tuition rates, on the undertaking that they will provide an educational service to the state. Applicants submit a plan outlining what they feel they can contribute to the state of Oregon in 80 hours per year (about 3 hours per week) of cultural and educational service. The educational services rendered at Oregon State University (OSU) at Corvallis (by 37 students from 26 countries) included, during 1990–91, giving slide presentations; sharing music, handicrafts, and folk stories; speaking on issues of development; contrasting modern and traditional lifestyles; and teaching or tutoring a foreign language. The students work with elementary and high school students, undergraduates at the university and in community college classes, and talk to youth groups and civic and service organizations (ICSP at OSU, 1990–91 Annual Report). A COOP grant (NAFSA Cooperative Grant Program) supports a state coordinator. 'The ICSP insures that international students have a rich experience while in Oregon and as "cultural ambassadors" make an important contribution to the mid-Willamette Valley.' Binghamton University used international graduate students from different disciplines as Language Resource Specialists in Language Across the Curriculum courses, also under a COOP grant (ERIC/CLL 1993). Other COOP grant projects are described in COOP (1990).

Overseas students are involved in campus life in many other ways. They participate in Campus Awareness weeks or international days, festivals, film series, or concerts. They are adopted into host families who include them in all their family activities. They help as counselors in summer youth camps. They live cheek by jowl with young Americans in residences, dormitories, and international houses. They eat with them in cafeterias, often from international menus set up to provide variety. All of these normal activities provide many opportunities for international students to mix and make friends with young Americans and with students from nations other than their own, whose viewpoints they also need to understand.

What more can the foreign language department do? They can adopt as their own students who speak the language they teach, from no matter which country they come. First of all, they can set up buddy relationships between American learners of the language and native speakers arriving on campus, so that the language learners can help the newcomers orient themselves to the campus, the university, and American life. These relationships sometimes lead to weekly exchanges of services, the American student and the overseas student exchanging one hour per week in each of their languages, or alternatively setting up regular phone conversations. This is also a valuable way to link up returnees from study abroad programs who need opportunities for language maintenance. As part of their language study, students can be sent across campus to interview foreign students in business, engineering, or agriculture on life in their country, their early education, family traditions, ambitions for the future, and so on, for presentations in a later language class. (Many of these students can be located through our close allies in the English as a Second Language Department.)

Organizers of language tables in residence halls and language houses should make a special effort each year to invite newly arrived native speakers to join them on a regular basis. Foreign students can be recruited to take part in broadcasts on the campus radio or television program, to help with voice-overs on documentaries, to record interesting materials on their country for the language laboratory or assist with the staging of plays in the language. Departments can involve them in pre-departure orientations for students or faculty preparing for exchanges or study abroad, and bring them into class to elucidate cultural readings or enliven discussions of cultural and political frames of reference. Byrnes (1990) observes that many international studies programs in this country reveal a North American perspective; she suggests that foreign language departments target crosscultural awareness as an educational goal. Here is an opportunity for native speakers, fresh from their homeland, to give an authentic cultural perspective on matters under discussion and to elucidate the presupposed and implied meanings of texts. Overseas students may also be recruited as teaching assistants, should they prove to have a good interactive style with American undergraduates and be willing to accept guidance and some training. Departments should explore more fully Sister City arrangements in their area, involving students from the countries in which these are situated, to help plan celebrations of their culture or set up exhibitions and displays of the special cultural achievements of Sister City artists, musicians, or artisans.

Once one has begun brainstorming along these lines, there is no end to the possibilities for involving foreign students in close working and friendship relationships with young Americans, who cannot but profit from the constant exposure to other viewpoints.

One pitfall that foreign language departments need to avoid is the development of a bichauvinism; instead of the student being convinced that American ways and ideas are always right and proper, the student now believes that only Americans and Germans (or Americans and the French, or Americans and Hispanics) have a corner on culture and right thinking. To avoid this eventuality, foreign language departments should encourage their students to become international in outlook, to participate in international activities on campus, and make friends with foreign students, many of whom, although not native speakers, are also looking for opportunities to practice the language they learned in school.

Two important areas of internationalization of universities that cannot be overlooked are TECHNICAL ASSISTANCE AND EDUCATIONAL COOPERATION programs and the ESTABLISHING OF BRANCH CAMPUSES of American universities in other countries (and of overseas universities in the United States).

The first of these areas has commonly taken the form of consultant and support services with foreign institutions. American agricultural universities began in the 1950s to work 'collaboratively with less developed countries in solving problems of hunger and inadequate agricultural production' under the aegis of American government development assistance plans (Backman 1984:1); Backman sees this endeavor as a significant factor in the development of international activities in American universities in that it required faculty to develop international competence in communication and the understanding of other cultural approaches. 'A very significant, even though unintended, side effect of these contracts has been to internationalize and deprovincialize the institutions,' say Goodwin and Nacht. 'It is truly remarkable,' they found, 'to visit one of the major land-grant universities today and find a cosmopolitan faculty and administration, often surpassing in sophistication the older and more liberal arts-oriented sister institutions in the state. We met professors of range science and irrigation engineering who seemed substantially more self-confident about and conscious of the world than their presumably more internationalist historian and linguistic brethren down the road' (1991:17).

The second area, establishing of branch campuses, represents a rapidly expanding aspect of international university life, as more and more institutions take their expertise (and sometimes their students) to other countries. The contribution they can make in this way to genuine international understanding will be dependent, however, on the nature of their motives: Is the establishment of the daughter campus an educational or a commercial undertaking? for instance. Is it a blatant attempt to balance the budget of the parent institution, transplanting holus-bolus the established curriculum, or is care taken to ensure that the education offered is carefully designed to meet the needs and objectives of the local clientele?

Both of these areas would require a separate essay to be dealt with adequately; each is clearly facilitated, when a strong language and culture component, related to the area of location, is incorporated in initial planning. Foreign language and culture specialists should be ready and available to help colleagues across campus and the administrators responsible for the enterprise to ensure that this is so.

Representative Panetta (1992a) calls our attention to the fact that 'human existence' is at 'a historical crossroads ... We must seize the moment,' he warns us, 'and begin now to develop the knowledge and understanding necessary to cope with ... current global complexities ... The greatest danger we face is the quiet crisis of ... global incompetence and lack of international understanding.' Oscar Arias Sanchez, Costa Rica's Nobel Peace Prize winning President, observed at Indiana University in 1990 that 'today, every human being contributes to the fate of ... his [or her] fellow beings. No leader of our era,' he maintains, 'can ignore the obligation of knowing what is occurring in every part of the world, of knowing the other one of his [or her] fellow beings. No leader of our era can ignore the obligation of knowing what is occurring in every part of the world, of knowing the thoughts, actions, and aspirations of all cultures and all nations' (Ehrlich 1992:9). This is a tall order, but our future young American leaders can begin to develop this kind of understanding and knowledge, with our help, in the microcosm of the campus.

REFERENCES

Allen, Wendy, Keith Anderson, and Leon Narvaez. 1992. Foreign languages across the curriculum: The applied foreign language component. Foreign Language Annals 25, 1.11-9.

Allison, Mary. 1986. A review of proposals to strengthen foreign language and international education. Foreign Language Annals 19.533-36.

American Association of State Colleges and Universities. 1984. Guidelines: Incorporating an international dimension in colleges and universities. Washington, DC: AASCU.

American Council on Education. 1989. What we can't say can hurt us: A call for foreign language competence by the year 2000. Washington, DC: ACE.

American Council on Education. 1984. What we don't know can hurt us: The shortfall in international competence. Washington, DC: ACE.

Arum, Stephen. 1987. International education: What is it? A taxonomy of international education of American universities. New York: Council on International Educational Exchange. Occasional Papers No. 23 Forum Series.

Backman, Earl L. 1984. Approaches to international education. New York: American Council on Education/Macmillan.

Bartlett, Thomas A. (chair) 1988. Educating for global competence: The report of the Advisory Council for International Educational Exchange. New York: CIEE.

Burn, Barbara B. 1991. The unfulfilled promise of exchanges. Chronicle of Higher Education, Sept. 11, A52.

Burn, Barbara B., Jerry S. Carlson, John Useem, and David Yachimowicz. 1990. Study abroad: The experience of American undergraduates. Westport, CN: Greeenwood Press.

Burn, Barbara B., and Ralph H. Smuckler (co-chairs) 1990. A national mandate for education abroad: Getting on with the task. Report of the National Task Force on Undergraduate Education Abroad. Washington, DC: NAFSA: Association of International Educators.

Byrnes, Heidi. 1990. Foreign language departments and the cultural component of an international studies program. ADFL Bulletin 22, 1.10-5.

COOP (Cooperative Grants Program). 1990. Model International Student Involvement Programs. Washington, DC: NAFSA Association of Internal Educators.

Dow, Anne R., and Joseph T. Ryan, Jr. 1987. Preparing students for professional interaction. Interactive language teaching, ed. by Wilga M. Rivers, 194–210. Cambridge: Cambridge University Press.

Educational programs planned by the EEC. 1991. ACTFL Newsletter, Fall, 8–9.

Ehrlich, Thomas. 1992. Our university in the state: One world. Bloomington, IN: Office of the President, Indiana University.

Engerman, David C., and Parker G. Marden. 1992. In the international interest: The contributions of America's International Liberal Arts Colleges. Beloit, WI: International Liberal Arts Colleges.

ERIC/CLL News Bulletin. 1993. Binghamton University's Languages Across the Curriculum Initiative 16, 2.1, 6–8.

Frommer, Judith G. 1992. Languages for career support. Teaching languages in college: curriculum and content, ed. by Wilga M. Rivers, 91–115. Lincolnwood, IL: NTC.

Frye, Robert, and Thomas J. Garza. 1992. Authentic contact with native speech at home and abroad. Teaching languages in college: Curriculum and content, ed. by Wilga M. Rivers, 225–43. Lincolnwood, IL: NTC.

Goodwin, Craufurd D., and Michael Nacht. 1988. Abroad and beyond: Patterns in an overseas education. Cambridge: Cambridge University Press.

Goodwin, Craufurd D., and Michael Nacht. 1991. Missing the boat: The failure to internationalize American higher education. Cambridge: Cambridge University Press.

Harari, Maurice. 1981. Internationalizing the curriculum and the campus: Guidelines for AASCU institutions. Washington, DC: American Association of State Colleges and Universities.

Hoopes, David. 1991. Guide to international education in the United States. 2nd ed. Detroit: Gale Research.

International competence: A key to America's future. 1989. A plan of action of the Coalition for the Advancement of Foreign Languages and International Studies. Washington, DC: CAFLIS.

Jurasek, Richard. 1988. Integrating foreign languages into the college curriculum. Modern Language Journal 72.52–8.

Karelis, Charles H. 1991. The new Europe: Replace U.S. indifference with collaboration. Chronicle of Higher Education, October 16, 1991, B1–2.

Lambert, Richard D. 1986. Points of leverage: An agenda for a National Foundation for International Studies. New York: Social Science Research Council.

Lambert, Richard D. 1989. International studies and the undergraduate. Washington, DC: American Council on Education.

Lambert, Richard D. 1992. Languages and International studies. Teaching languages in college: Curriculum and content, ed. by Wilga M. Rivers, 281–94. Lincolnwood, IL: NTC.

Light, Richard J. 1992. Harvard Assessment Seminars. Second Report. Explorations with students and faculty about teaching, learning, and student life. Cambridge, MA: Harvard University Graduate School of Education and Kennedy School of Government.

National Governors' Association. 1987. Educating Americans for tomorrow's world: State initiatives in international education. Washington, DC: NGA.

National Governors' Association. 1989. America in transition: The international frontier. Washington, DC: NGA.

Nehr, Lee C. 1987. The internationalization of the curriculum. Journal of International Business Studies, Spring issue, 83–90.

Panetta, Leon. 1992a. National Foreign Language Week. Congressional Record, March 10, 1992.

Panetta, Leon. 1992b. The quiet crisis of global competence. ACTFL Newsletter, Winter.3–4, 11, 15.

President's Commission on Foreign Language and International Studies. 1979. Strength through wisdom: A critique of US capability. Washington, DC: Government Printing Office.

Prokasy, William F. 1990. International studies: Internal administrative issues. ADFL Bulletin 22, 1.16–9.

Rivers, Wilga M. (ed.) 1987. Interactive language teaching. Cambridge: Cambridge University Press.

Rivers, Wilga M. (ed.) 1992. Teaching languages in college: Curriculum and content. Lincolnwood, IL: NTC.

Simon, Paul. 1980. The tongue-tied American: Confronting the foreign language crisis. New York: Continuum.

Smith, Roch C. 1990. Internationalizing the campus: A national agenda. ADFL Bulletin 22, 1.4–9.

The training of, and U.S. business' needs for, international specialists. 1985. Conference Proceedings. Amherst, MA: University of Massachusetts (with the support of the Business and International Education Program of the U.S. Department of Education and NCFLIS).

Trahan, Elizabeth W. 1988. Comparative literature and international studies: or quo vadis? ADFL Bulletin 19, 2.33–8.

Weaver, Henry D. 1989. Research on U.S. students abroad. A bibliography with abstracts. Washington, DC: CIEE/IIE/NAFSA.

English in Europe: Language pragmatics or language policy?

Margie Berns
Purdue University

Introduction. Throughout Europe language policies characterize English as a foreign language. This classification has implications for the way English is taught in schools and reflects assumptions about the pragmatics of English learning and use by Europeans and the social meaning of English in Europe. This view also reflects assumptions about the possibilities available to Europeans for contact with native speakers and exposure to texts spoken or written in English. English has also been identified as a means of international communication, as an international language. This characterization is similarly related to assumptions about the uses of English and has implications for language pedagogy and learning. But is the policy characterization of the roles of English in Europe accurate? Does it correspond to the social reality of English on the continent? If yes, is it appropriate for a post 1992 unified and integrated Europe? And what are the implications for language policy on language teaching? What approach most appropriately responds to the needs of European learners of English in 1992 and beyond?

This paper explores the policy and practice of English in the European Community (hereafter EC) and raises some questions that bear consideration with respect to policy and pedagogy of English as an EC language. Two general aspects of the situation will be covered: (1) consideration of the appropriateness of identifying English as a foreign and international language and (2) an examination and interpretation of the social meaning of English and its role as a language of communication in the European context.

The European Community and language policy. Serving as a framework for economic unity, the European community evolved from the Common Market, which resulted from the signing of the Treaty of Rome in 1957 by France, Belgium, Holland, Italy, Luxembourg, and West Germany. Its goal is the movement of goods and people across the borders of the member countries, which now number twelve (Belgium, Denmark, France, Germany, Great Britain, Greece, Ireland, Italy, Luxembourg, the Netherlands, Portugal, and Spain) and have a combined population of approximately 340 million.

Community activities in education focus on policies affecting labor and student mobility as in its support of the European Community Action Scheme for Mobility of University Students (ERASMUS). The $230 million program, a first step in the free exchange of scholarly credentials among European Member countries, makes it possible for students from universities and technical colleges to attend schools in other member countries for up to six months. Sixteen thousand students participated in 1987. However, providing funds for exchange did not prove sufficient for insuring the effectiveness of the program. In 1989 the Community allocated additional funds for a language teaching program, called LINGUA, which is to support member states' efforts to improve foreign language learning and teaching competence and ultimately ERASMUS exchange students' success (Commission of the European Communities 1991b:5). The goals of the teaching are proficiency as well as communicative competence. Learners are to get to know the culture, customs, and aspirations of the native speakers of the language and to develop communicative skills in interacting with them (Commission of the European Communities 1991a:2).

A recent document published by the EC summarizes the Community's position on language:

> The Community regards language as an expression of the identity of people. It is the key to understanding their culture, customs and aspirations. Language is a cohesive force in a community and just as science and technology have come to pervade every aspect of human living, so the questions of languages pervades all the ambitions, intentions and policies of the European Community (Commission of the European Communities 1991a:1).

In keeping with this view, all official EC policies support the use and maintenance of the major languages of the community (Danish, Dutch, English, French, German, Greek, Italian, Portuguese, and Spanish). One idea behind this support is not to privilege any language of the Community, but to encourage the unique features of each member state. The language strategy associated with LINGUA, for example, is one of diversification of languages offered. Rather than promote one or two of the priority languages, all official languages of the Community should be taught, including Irish and Letzeburgesch.

The EC goes to considerable expense to implement its language policy, spending large sums annually for translations of documents and correspondence and the services of interpreters for meetings and other official functions. Tugendhat (1988), EC commissioner from 1977 to 1985, provides illustrations of sensitivity to linguistic equality among community members. The Community's language rules put Dutch, Danish, and Greek, for example, on equal footing with English and French. Although it does not work out like that in practice, representatives from the countries in which these languages are spoken value this equality, even if it exists only in theory. In spite of competence in

English or French, ministers and officials from non-English or non-French speaking countries will insist on conducting business in their own language in the Council of Ministers, regardless of the cost and complication involved in providing simultaneous interpretation. They also use their own language in written communication and expect a reply in it.

The EC's ideal position on language equality is difficult to maintain even within the language practices of Community officials, who have been criticized as being poor examples of the diversity the policy espouses (Zapp 1979). In informal settings among Community officials, Tugendhat (1988) reports, everyone, regardless of language background, makes a big effort to use French or English, the EC's working languages, and those who cannot use either language are accompanied by interpreters. Conversations in these settings are described as 'free and intimate' (158–159). Even with respect to English and French, it is difficult to be consistent with policy. For example, use of French in particular has become less common in the European Parliament and Commission, especially in departments concerned with financial and technology-related issues, and is being pushed aside by use of English (van Els and Extra 1987).

It is not only among EC officials that English is dominant. Several studies show that English plays a significant role in many domains, among them business, tourism, science, technology, the media, advertising, and entertainment (see e.g. Berns 1988, 1990; Denison 1981, Flaitz 1988). This role is not limited to that of lexical borrowings. English also is the lingua franca of communication between citizens of Europe in professional and personal interaction, used by Dutch and Italians with one another to get things done as well as to express ideas, thoughts, and feelings that are uniquely European and represent European ways of doing, thinking, and being. Thus, Europeans are not restricted to French, German, or Portuguese for the expression of who they are and what they value. They can express their social meaning in English as well as any American, Briton, Canadian, New Zealander, or South African.

English in the educational system. Insight into the status of English can be gained by considering its place in the educational system. The Community recommends that schools teach not less than two languages, and various EC countries have declared their intent to make at least two foreign languages available to all citizens. Such national policies it is believed would contribute to a more unified Europe and give some attention to the so-called 'small' languages, for example, Dutch and Danish. Additionally, these language proposals address the fear that English will possibly be the only foreign language that a majority of Europeans would ever learn (van Els and Extra 1987:108).

While these policies provide for learning of languages other than English, English is one of the two languages chosen or required in most if not all EC countries. Already in the 1983–84 school year, 87% of European school-age children chose to study English as their first foreign language. In a number of secondary school systems in Europe, English is a compulsory subject. In 1979, in what was at that time West Germany, approximately 98% of school-age learners, in vocational as well as general education tracks, learned English. In France, English clearly has a monopoly position, even in schools where pupils and parents have free choice among languages: 81% learn English as the first foreign language in school; 16% learn German, 3% Spanish, and another .5% learn Italian or Russian. In the Netherlands and France, English is a compulsory foreign language in elementary school. And many university students throughout Europe want to study in an English-speaking country, with the United States an especially popular site for preparation in the fields of business, tourism, communications, engineering, and advertising (Hopkins 1991). It is interesting to contrast this interest for learning additional languages on the continent with the situation in Great Britain, where more than three-fourths of secondary school pupils drop foreign languages as a subject within 2 to 3 years of taking it up (van Els and Extra 1987:112).

Attitudes toward English. The enthusiasm for enrolling in English classes does not imply acceptance of the role and dominance of English by all Europeans. Many fear that the spread of English, which shows no sign of abating, will lead to an erosion of a unique European identity and the encroachment of a different set of values, primarily those of the United States. The values associated with ways of 'doing business' by regional American telephone companies are an example. *The Wall Street Journal* reports that these companies, due to limited expansion opportunities at home, have expanded their markets into Europe. This possibility has not been possible for most public telephone companies in Europe because they tend to see going in and competing as an ungentlemanly thing to do. However, with the success of the American companies, this attitude seems to be changing, reports a communications industry consultant (Simison 1991:R5).

French politicians and intellectuals in particular have been vocal about the hegemony of English and the increasing pervasiveness of American culture. Reactions have ranged from limiting (at the urging of the French) the amount of American programming that could be shown in EC countries to French refusal to sponsor or finance conferences where French is not the conference language and the passage of a law by the French National Assembly forbidding the use of foreign (i.e. English) expressions in business, the media, or government documents and publications. While such fears and reactions are understandable, they have had little if any influence upon the spread of English or interest in American culture among Europeans.

Europe as a linguistic region: English as a foreign language (EFL) and/or English as an international language(EIL). Before looking more closely at the question of 'EFL or EIL', some characterization of the European Community as a region of English-language use is needed to establish a starting point for a description of English as an EC language. It has been customary to think of the twelve member countries separately, as individual states with separate languages and cultures. However, with the implementation of the economic integration of the Community scheduled for the end of 1992, twelve western European countries will begin to move toward the Community's declared objective of full union. As such, the EC increasingly will be perceived as an interdependent unit and, it is expected, more attention will be given to the notion of a European culture and identity as well (see Wistrich 1991, Chapter 6, for discussion of the notion of a European culture). This unity has implications for the way the EC and the role of English within it are viewed sociolinguistically.

Due to considerable similarity in patterns of use of English, exposure to English, and national language policies among EC member states, it is possible, in my view, to talk about the Community as a unit, as one would about multilingual countries, such as India (and many EC policies and practices encourage such an interpretation). One important difference in the EC is the membership of two states, Great Britain and Ireland, which have English, the dominant language of Community communication, as their official, native language. In EC policy, Great Britain and Ireland are equal partners of the other ten. In terms of Kachru's (1985) concentric circle model, the EC can be described as a federation of inner circle and expanding circle countries. The inner circle countries, Great Britain and Ireland, are associated with native varieties of English and are thus norm-providing for countries outside this circle. Expanding circle countries depend upon the inner circle for norms and classroom models; however, expanding circle countries see uses of English increasing. The combination of expanding with inner circle countries in one region is a challenge when drawing up a sociolinguistic description or profile of English in Europe. Precisely how to describe the role of English in the EC?

English as a foreign language (EFL) generally refers to a setting where English is not one of the vernaculars of the country or region in which it is taught. It is taught with reference to a speech community outside national or territorial boundaries. It is usually learned primarily through formal instruction with lack of environmental support, that is, it cannot be 'picked up' outside the classroom. However, if we consider the twelve member states of the EC as a unit, it is difficult to apply the classification 'FL' to English because it is one of the vernaculars of a member state. The referent speech community of Great Britain is not outside the boundaries of the Community, but inside. Is it appropriate to continue to speak of English as being learned for 'external purposes', as a foreign language, when Great Britain and Ireland are now internal to the EC?

The lack or presence of environmental support is also a criterion given for determining whether or not a language is taught as a foreign language. Already prior to unification, some EC countries, such as Germany, had been exposed to a great deal of English through media and contact with English speakers, both native and nonnative. What is the potential influence for richer environmental support when an inner circle country and expanding circle countries are united? Will it still be possible to speak of English strictly as an FL? Might there even be the possibility of English becoming recognized as a second language?

The notion that English is learned and used only as an international language is also called into question if Europe is regarded as a unit. Europeans do use English for communication outside the boundaries of the twelve EC member states; they communicate for example with Africans, Asians, or North Americans who do not speak Spanish, or French, or Danish or any other of the continental EC languages. In this sense English is an international language.

International language is often contrasted with INTRAnational language, with the latter referring to the use and learning of English for wider communication within a country, particularly for educational, commercial, and political purposes. While the united Europe is not a nation and it is not completely accurate to speak of English in this context as an intranational language, English is a language of communication with Europe, as an intra-European language. Its function as a language of wider communication for educational, commercial and political purposes is well established beyond Europe. This function is strengthened through the EC in a number of ways. One is by the policies of the EC concerning the use of English as an official EC language. Another is the use of English within the EC for the educational purposes of exchange programs, such as ERASMUS, whose participants study in member states where English is the medium of instruction, for example, in Great Britain or in some universities in Greece.

Pedagogical implications. What does this mean for English language teaching in the EC? How to interpret this information for pedagogical concerns? In my view, language policy and practice with respect to English are in conflict in Europe. Such mismatches are of course common wherever agencies, institutions, or government offices are involved in regulating human activity. This particular mismatch is of consequence however because it has an impact on the success of communication within EC member states, of their educational programs, and the ultimate success of the unification of Europe.

Officially English is a foreign language and is equal to the eight other languages. The social reality is that English is not equal. It dominates. And this status is not likely to change soon. EC policy seeks to diminish the impact of English and to discourage its spread as the lingua franca. Public school English class enrollments do not support these efforts. English is to be taught for the purpose of increasing knowledge about the culture, customs, and beliefs of the native speakers. But nonnative English-speaking continental Europeans are using English to express their culture, customs, and beliefs to one another, to represent meanings that are uniquely European.

This sociolinguistic description of English in Europe and the social meaning it highlights have particular relevance for the language teaching profession's task of curriculum design. Language teaching itself has a social meaning which influences not only what language is taught, but also the ends to which it is taught. Traditionally a didactic approach has been taken to curriculum design and language instruction in Europe. This approach is based on the assumptions (a) that everyone learns English in order to interact with native speakers of an inner circle country, especially England or the United States, (b) that English is inextricably linked to the culture of England or the United States, and (c) that learning English means dealing with the realities of England or the United States or with British or American ways of doing, thinking, or being. One of the problems with this approach is that it puts a misplaced emphasis on native-like 'mastery' and methodological matters, while ignoring three sociolinguistic issues: (1) which communicative competence learners are to develop, (2) the degree of international mutual intelligibility they are to achieve, and (3) the appropriate mode of language they are to approximate. (See Berns 1992 for discussion of these sociolinguistic issues.)

Since a didactic approach does not match the realities of English language learning and use in Europe, a pragmatic approach seems more appropriate. Such an approach responds to current demands for using and learning English as an international and intra-European language. Most importantly it acknowledges that English is not only the language of Americans, Britons, New Zealanders, Australians, or Canadians, but also that it is a language of Europeans. The context of the language presented in materials cannot be restricted to native-speaker settings. Learners also can expect to be prepared to be users of English for their own purposes, which may or may not include interacting with native speakers. A shift from a didactic to pragmatic approach means breaking away from viewing English as the language of the so-called native speaker and preparing learners throughout the EC for use of English as their language too.

A number of teaching initiatives of a pragmatic nature, implemented in schools in various EC member and non-member countries over the past 15 years, illustrate the feasibility of this approach. Many successful projects are associated with the Council of Europe's 'School Interaction Network' (Bergentoft 1988). These experiments are based on or stimulated by the Council of Europe approach to language teaching, which is a broadly interpreted form of communicative language teaching. This interpretation is consistent with a pragmatic approach to pedagogy in its insistence upon teaching which varies in design according to the context of the learning and teaching. A non-dogmatic approach to methodology allows teachers to develop their own methodology and thus be responsive to the needs and objectives of their learners and their teaching as appropriate to their particular setting.

A pluralistic approach which allows for communicative methodologies is not the only feature of initiatives inspired by the Council of Europe; another important aspect is learner autonomy, or independence. It is related to the communicative needs of learners, development of their self-awareness and self-reliance, and the establishment of an atmosphere of cooperation between learner and teacher. In schools where learner autonomy is stressed, the language is not regarded as a system to be learned, but as a language to be used. The goal is to equip learners with the tools and give them opportunities to express themselves about themselves or about other areas of experience. A variety of sequenced classroom tasks, for example, learning of language structure and form, development of discourse skills, or use of media, organizational, and management skills are a means to achieving this communicative goal. Leguetke and Thomas (1991) provide a comprehensive description of such tasks and the theoretical framework underlying their development and use in the classroom.

Conclusion. The most appropriate response to the needs of learners begins with an examination of the social meaning of English in Europe. English is a language of Europeans, and it is clearly more than a foreign or international language; its role does not compare to that of other foreign languages such as Danish or Dutch, for example. The language policy of the EC is motivated by concern for linguistic equality among member-state languages: any other policy could result in serious language conflicts. Nevertheless, a policy that insists upon limited roles for English, although it may make good politics, raises concern about the policy's effect upon English language teaching and the adoption of a pedagogical approach that will most effectively lead to increased communication among EC member states.

Concern over the mismatch among policy, practice, and patterns of language use have been the focus of this discussion. It is hoped that by raising questions about the official positions and the actual roles of English in the EC and by providing a brief description of these roles that a basis has been established for further investigation of English in the European context. From this point it should be possible to gain increased understanding of the nature of English in Europe and appreciation of its status as a language of Europe. Ultimately, this knowledge will benefit learners by contributing to a pedagogy that is responsive to English as a language that serves Europeans as a means of communication and of expression of their social meaning.

REFERENCES

Bergentoft, Rune. 1988. Consolidated report on the school interaction network. Strasbourg: Council of Europe.

Berns, Margie. 1988. The cultural and linguistic context of English in West Germany. World Englishes 7.37–49.

Berns, Margie. 1990. Contexts of competence: Social and cultural considerations in communicative language teaching. New York: Plenum.

Berns, Margie. 1992. Sociolinguistics and the teaching of English in Europe beyond the 1990s. World Englishes 11.3–14.

Commission of the European Communities. 1991a. The LINGUA programme in 1990: A report presented by the Commission in accordance with Art. 12 of Council Decision 89/489/EEC establishing the LINGUA programme. Brussels.

Commission of the European Communities. 1991b. Education and training. Brussels.

Denison, Norman. 1981. English in Europe, with particular reference to the German-speaking area. Europaeische Mehrsprachigkeit, ed. by W. Poeckl, 2–18. Tubingen: Max Niemeyer.

Flaitz, Jeffra. 1988. Ideology of English: French perceptions of English as a world language. Berlin: Mouton de Gruyter.

Hopkins, John D. 1991. Educational mobility in the New Europe: The professionalization of international education. International Educator 1, 2.38–9.

Kachru, Braj. 1985. Standards, codification, and sociolinguistic realism: The English language in the outer circle. English in the world: Teaching and learning the language and literatures, ed. by Randolph Quirk and Henry G. Widdowson, 11–30. Cambridge: Cambridge University

Press.
Leguetke, Michael, and Howard Thomas. 1991. Process and experience in the language classroom. London: Longman.
Simison, Robert. 1991. Babes in Europeland. The Wall Street Journal, October 4, R5.
Tugendhat, Christopher. 1988. Making sense of Europe. New York: Columbia University Press.
van Els, Theo J. M., and Guus Extra. 1987. Foreign and second language teaching in Western Europe: A comparative overview of needs, objectives and policies. Sociolinguistica 1.100–25.
Wistrich, Ernest. 1991. After 1992: The United States of Europe. London: Routledge.
Zapp, Franz-Josef. 1979. Foreign language policy in Europe. Brussels: European Cooperation Fund.

French immersion graduates at university and beyond: What difference has it made?

Marjorie Bingham Wesche
University of Ottawa

French immersion programs have had a major impact on Canadian education over the past two decades, with implications not only for the individuals who have learned a large part of their school curriculum through their second language, but also for our understanding of how languages are learned and how they should be taught, and even for relations between Canada's anglophone and francophone communities. Referred to as 'possibly the most-studied phenomenon in the history of Canadian education' (Fortier 1990), the immersion experience has informed us about how to effectively teach language via school subject matter, the value of intensive second language exposure, outcomes for different starting ages, and both the potential and the limitations of the classroom as a context for second language acquisition (Genesee 1987, Ouellet 1990, Parkin et al. 1987, Bibeau 1991). While the issue of the influence of school language learning on the development of attitudes toward target language speakers and their culture and on the uses graduates make of the language have been less studied, their importance is apparent in Canada and elsewhere. As increasing numbers of former immersion students become young adults, it is vital to explore long-term attitudinal as well as proficiency outcomes of their experience.

Increasing numbers of graduates from Canadian French immersion programs are reaching university age and beyond. Some of these individuals have spent as much as 14 years in bilingual programs and received up to 40% of their elementary and secondary schooling through the medium of their second language, French. What difference has participation in immersion schooling made in their lives? What kind of first and second language abilities do these young adults have? What are their attitudes toward French and its use, and how much do they actually use French in their daily lives? If they do not use it very often, do they lose these hard-won second language skills? Is the answer different for those living in bilingual communities? Are the interethnic attitudes of former immersion students different from the attitudes of peers whose schooling was mainly in English, and if so, can the differences be attributed to the immersion experience? How do they view French immersion schooling? Will they send their own children to such programs? These and other questions have been addressed over the past six years in a study of two cohorts of Ottawa-area French immersion graduates. While the main first cohort results have been reported elsewhere (Wesche et al. 1986, Wesche 1988, Wesche et al. 1990), the findings of the entire study are reported upon here for the first time.

The French immersion movement began in 1965 as a one-class kindergarten experiment in St. Lambert, Quebec (Lambert and Tucker 1972). It currently involves over 290,000 English-language school children and adolescents throughout Canada (Fortier 1991).[1] There are now more anglophone children enrolled in immersion programs than there are francophone children in French language schools outside Quebec. The immersion approach is also gaining popularity in the United States, where over sixty programs now exist for different foreign languages (Center for Applied Linguistics 1991), and in a number of other countries (Endt 1992).

Immersion programs vary greatly, with different starting points and different proportions of school instruction in the first and second language, but all observe the principles of an initial 'intensive dose' of instruction, use of the second language as the instructional medium, and teachers who are native or highly proficient speakers. The period of intensive exposure, in which from half to all instruction is through the L2, usually lasts up to five years in early-entry immersion or from one to three years in late-entry immersion. For children remaining in bilingual programs it is then followed by years in which from a third to a half of instruction is through the second language. While the emphasis is on experiential language learning through use of the second language, there is also inevitably some code-focused language teaching, generally in language arts periods, as well. Canadian-style French immersion should not be confused with 'submersion' or other kinds of bilingual education for minority language children. Immersion programs are characterized by a volunteer clientele of children whose first language—in this case English—is that of the majority community, where both languages are socially valued. Indeed, parental and community demand for effective French second language instruction has been a major factor in the initiation and spread of French immersion programs throughout Canada. English language development and maintenance of an anglophone cultural identity remain primary objectives of such programs, as does mastery of the same school curriculum as is taught in the regular English stream.

French immersion has had the greatest impact in Ontario, where almost half the school boards offer programs, some 7% of the English language school population is enrolled in some form of French immersion, and where, in Ottawa and the surrounding national capital region, the majority of English language children now experience French immersion instruction at some point during their school years. Rationales for such programs range from parental calls for

[1]The significance of this number becomes clearer when one considers that a similar percentage in the United States would be over three million majority-language children.

educational enrichment and better preparation for bilingual careers in government and business, to the belief that a growing pool of bilingual anglophones with better understanding of the francophone cultural reality in Canada can help strengthen national unity (cf. Calvé 1991).

The study. The present research represents the largest and most comprehensive postsecondary follow-up research to date on former immersion students, and the only longitudinal and replicated study. (For related studies of senior secondary and postgraduation immersion students, see Shapson 1985; De Vries 1986; Hart and Lapkin 1989; Hart, Lapkin, and Swain 1991; Husim and Bruce 1991). It focuses on the experience of that relatively small proportion of students who have completed an elementary school immersion program plus a bilingual high school program (with approximately one-third of their credits in French). Currently there are some 600 to 700 such bilingual high school graduates each year from Ottawa-area programs. This is a small proportion of the anglophone students in the region who have had some immersion experience during their school careers, but given their characteristics, these students represent an important subgroup. Studies here and elsewhere show that 85% to 90% are university bound (McGillivray and Pawley 1985; Hart and Lapkin 1989; Hart, Lapkin, and Swain 1989; Husim and Bruce 1991; Lapkin and Hart 1991; Saskatoon Board of Education 1992).

The present study follows two cohorts of immersion graduates through three years of university studies after graduation from grade 13 (i.e. through their bachelor degree program) in unilingual and bilingual universities. French proficiency data from first-year francophone students allows comparison with native speaker norms. Substudies provide details on the first and second language writing skills of these students at university entry (Vignola and Wesche 1991), and on the interethnic attitudes and language-use patterns of such graduates six years out of high school (MacFarlane 1992).

The replication study with a second cohort has turned out to be important, suggesting to us that the much-studied 1971 Ottawa-area kindergarten immersion cohort which was prominent in the research literature in the 1970s and early 1980s, was not entirely typical of later groups in the same programs (cf. Swain and Lapkin 1981, Parkin et al. 1987).

Research questions. The questions dealt with in the study can be summarized as follows.

1. **What can these students do in French at the end of high school? What can they do at the end of undergraduate studies?** How far do 3,500 to 7,000 hours of exposure to French in school take students in developing the ability to use French for different purposes? How do their skills compare with those of francophone university students? Do they maintain or improve their skills during university studies? After university graduation?

2. **How well can they write in French at the end of high school? Has their English development, as reflected in writing ability, been affected by schooling largely through another language?** Are English compositions written by these students distinguishable from those by English stream students, and if so, in what ways? Do their French compositions differ from those written by francophone students? If so, in what ways? Can interlingual transfer effects be identified?

3. **Does an early (kindergarten) versus a later (grade 6-7) starting age make a long-term difference?** Are the group differences reported in the literature for younger students—generally favoring early-entry immersion students over late-entry students on oral production skills and self-confidence—also found among these immersion graduates?

4. **How do they feel about using French in their daily lives?** How self-confident (or anxious) are they in using French in and out of the university classroom and workplace? Do they have a strong desire to use it, and to continue to improve their skills? Do they believe that it will be useful to them in the future? Why or why not?

5. **What do they actually DO in French?** How frequently do they seek out or take advantage of opportunities to use French in their studies, their social life and work life? Does a bilingual university or community make a difference? Are there changes after university graduation?

6. **Has immersion made a difference in their ethnolinguistic attitudes?** Do they perceive their attitudes toward francophone Canadians, English/French relations in Canada, and Quebec nationalism as differing from those of English stream graduates? If different, can their attitudes be attributed to the immersion experience? Can specific aspects of their immersion experience (e.g. out-of-class contact with francophones) be related to the proficiency and attitudes of these immersion graduates years after they leave high school?

7. **What are their attitudes toward immersion schooling and toward specific program features?** How do they assess their own immersion experience? Would they send their own children to such a program? If so, which entry age would they prefer? Would they suggest changes in immersion?

Subjects. The subjects were 1985 and 1988 graduates of bilingual high schools in the national capital region attending nearby universities (see Table 1). All had completed a full sequence of early-entry or late-entry immersion before entering high school (see Table 2). In early-entry immersion students receive all school instruction in French from kindergarten until grade 2 or 3, at which point one period per day of English language arts is introduced, with a half-and-half program from grades 6 to 8. The late-entry students receive 20 to 40 minutes

Table 1. Proportion of school day in French: Ottawa Board of Education and Carleton Board of Education immersion programs.

Grade	Ottawa Board of Education		Carleton Board of Education		Grade	Bilingual High School
	Early Immersion	Late Immersion	Early Immersion	Late Immersion	9	33.3
K	100	10	100	10	10	33.3
1	100	10	100	10	11	33.3
2	80	10	80	10	12	33.3
3	80	10	80	10	13	33.3
4	80	10	80	10		
5	80	10	80	10		
6	50	100	50	10		
7	50	50	50	80		
8	50	50	50	80		

Approximate hours of school French exposure, kindergarten through grade 13:
Early entry immersion: 6,500–7,000
Late entry immersion: 3,000–3,500

of 'Core French' each day starting in kindergarten. They enter late immersion in grade 6 or 7, where they receive intensive exposure to French for two or three years, at least one of which is 80% to 100% in French. This is followed by high school (grades 9 through Ontario Academic Credit year, formerly grade 13) where these students take approximately one-third of their coursework through the medium of French.

The graduates chosen for the study were those attending four nearby universities with differing sociolinguistic characteristics. These include the bilingual University of Ottawa, which attracts the largest number, with a mixed anglophone and francophone student body and a wide range of undergraduate and graduate programs in French and English; Carleton University, an English language university also in Ottawa; the English language Queen's University in mainly English-speaking Kingston, and McGill University, an English language institution with some French programs, in mainly French-speaking Montreal.

Methodology. Graduating bilingual high school students were located with the help of the Ottawa and Carleton Boards of Education in the spring of 1985 and 1988, and information was collected on their future plans and family addresses. Some of the initial proficiency testing was carried out at this time. Those attending the four universities of interest the following fall were contacted at university entry. All who were willing and able to participate in the study were convoked for further testing. (See Wesche et al. 1986 and Wesche et al. 1990 for details). The 1985 cohort included 81 graduates who completed the

Table 2. Subjects.

University	1985 cohort		1988 cohort	
	1st Year University	3rd Year University (1988)	1st Year University	3rd Year University (1991)
Ottawa	34	24	72	38
Carleton	28	16	51	25
Queen's	14	8	20	9
McGill	5	-	11	6
Total N's	81 (33 early entry, 48 late entry	48* (19 early entry, 29 late entry)	154 (97 early entry, 57 late entry)	78** (51 early entry, 27 late entry)

* 21 of these students completed the 1991 follow-up questionnaire and 13 were interviewed

** 39 of these students took part in the L1 and L2 writing study

tests in 1985, 48 of whom were retested at the end of their third year university studies in the spring of 1988, and 21 of whom participated in a 1991 Post-University study. Of the 1988 replication cohort's original 154 subjects, 78 were retested in 1991. Eighty unilingual francophone first-year university students at the University of Ottawa were also given four of the French proficiency tests, to establish francophone norms.

Tests and questionnaires. Instruments were either specifically developed for the project or came from batteries developed for high school and university students at advanced levels of French proficiency by the University of Ottawa's Second Language Institute, the Ottawa Board of Education Research Centre, the University of Western Ontario Research Group, and the Modern Language Centre of the Ontario Institute for Studies in Education (cf. Clément et al. 1978; Wesche et al. 1986; Hart et al. 1989). They are listed below and described in Appendices A and B.[2]

[2] Most of these instruments are now available to researchers and school boards from the MLC Scoring Service, Modern Language Centre, The Ontario Institute for Studies in Education, 252 Bloor Street West, Toronto, Ontario M5S 1V6, Canada. The Post-University Questionnaire questions are specified in the text and in Tables 9 and 10.

French Proficiency Tests:
- Listening Comprehension
- Listening Dictation
- Reading Comprehension
- Cloze
- Oral Interview
- Elicited Imitation (sentence repetition)
- Self-Assessment of French proficiency
- French (L2) and English (L1) essays (1988 substudy)

French Language Attitudes and Use Questionnaire.

Attitudes:
- Anxiety in Using French
- Desire to Use French
- Reasons for learning French

French Use:
- Frequency of French Use
- Expected Future Use
- Specific French language uses (media, books, films, courses, work, other)
- Perceived difficulty of university study activities in French (1991)

Post-University Questionnaire (1991 substudy): French language use, interethnic attitudes, attitudes toward immersion program and features

The French proficiency measures are all based on texts selected from radio broadcasts, newspapers, magazines, brochures, and textbooks. The tasks are difficult, requiring the ability to use French to understand, and in some cases to reconstruct, informationally dense material intended for adult native speakers, or to use the language in conversation or composition.

The individually administered Oral Interview involves three different tasks with varying degrees of scripting and support documents, each scored by the interviewer according to a descriptive scale. An Elicited Imitation group measure in which students repeat recorded sentences from a radio broadcast was added to the battery in 1988. Scored for exact and semantically equivalent repetition, as well as syntactic and phonological features, it provides a relatively precise measure of both listening comprehension and oral production grammar (cf. Appendix A).

The Self-Assessment asks students to rate their proficiency in daily life activities in French using a 'can do' scale of 1 to 5 (from 'almost never' to 'almost always'). The version used as a placement test at the University of Ottawa was administered in 1985 (LeBlanc and Painchaud 1985). Involving only receptive language activities, it showed a ceiling effect for these students. A revised version with only the more difficult receptive activities plus writing and speaking items was used in 1988 and 1991. Examples:

'Over the phone I can understand some basic information in French, such as the name of the caller and the number where he can be reached.' (1985 and 1988 versions)

'I can read an editorial in French and determine the areas of agreement and disagreement between the author's views and mine.' (1985 and 1988 versions)

'I can write a lengthy research paper in French on a topic related to my field.' (1988 version only).

Correlations with other measures indicate that the Self-Assessment score reflects a combination of student proficiency and self-confidence in using French (Wesche et al. 1986).

The French Language Attitudes and Use Questionnaire is a self-report measure assessing students' attitudes regarding French study and use, their current French use patterns, and projected future use of French (see Appendix B). The attitudes on which students are questioned included Anxiety when speaking French, Desire to use and improve French skills, Reasons for learning French, Frequency of current use of French in different contexts, and intended Future use. Specific estimates of French use include the number of leisure books read, movies and videos seen, and hours of television watched in an average month, as well as information on university courses taken by the student in French and other uses.

Third-year students in 1991 answered additional questions on their linguistic and social background and Perceived Difficulty of Academic French Use (after Hart and Lapkin 1990). A brief Post-University Questionnaire on French proficiency and use, and on attitudes toward francophones, their culture and on immersion was used with a subsample of 1985 graduates in 1991, followed by a structured telephone interview.

Findings. Proficiency. A summary of the French proficiency scores of the 1985 and 1988 cohorts in first-year university and of a group of first-year francophone students at the University of Ottawa is presented in Table 3. There were no significant differences between the two cohorts at university entry on listening, reading, or oral tests, but as might be expected, both showed significant differences on most measures from the francophone students.

Both cohorts performed very well on listening and reading measures (Listening Comprehension, Listening Dictation, Reading Comprehension, and Cloze), indicating high levels of functional proficiency in the skills measured. The immersion students achieved an average of approximately 72% correct overall on the listening and reading tests, as compared with 86% for the francophone comparison group. The 1985 cohort scored slightly but significantly below francophone norms on the Listening Comprehension test: the 1988 cohort performed similarly to the native speakers on both the Listening Comprehension and Reading Comprehension tests. These tests are measures of global compre-

Table 3. French Proficiency of Immersion Graduates and Francophones in First Year University.

French Proficiency Measures	Maximum Possible Score	French Immersion Graduates 1985 Cohort (N = 81)		French Immersion Graduates 1988 Cohort (N = 80)		Francophone Students (N = 80)	
Listening						M	S.D.
Comprehension	14	10.0	2.3	10.5	2.0	11.4*	2.0
Dictation	28	--	--	22.5	2.8	26.8°	2.8
Reading							
Comprehension	19	13.0	3.0	12.8	2.4	14.4	3.0
Cloze	35	26.5	5.2	23.6	4.7	29.2*°	4.2
Oral		M	S.D.	M	S.D.	No immersion students could pass for native speakers, although some were judged 'near native'	
Interview	15	11.1	2.1	10.8	1.2		

* Significant difference ($p < .005$) between 1985 cohort and francophones in first year.
° Significant difference ($p < .01$) between 1988 cohort and francophones in first year.

There were no significant differences between the 1985 and 1988 cohorts at university entry.

hension, where the focus is on understanding different levels of meaning of authentic recorded or written texts; for example, the main idea, the speaker's or author's attitude, or specific details. These results correspond to other studies which have shown immersion students of different ages to have highly developed receptive skills in a school situation—indeed, exactly the skills they need to do what is required of them in school through their second language (cf. Swain and Lapkin, 1986, Genesee 1987). The immersion graduates are not quite so successful when faced with tasks requiring them to go beyond global comprehension of meaning to more precise semantic and syntactic analysis and reconstruction. Thus on the Listening Dictation test, which asks students to remember or reconstruct every word they hear, they perform well although they fall short of native-speaker performance. Likewise their performance on the fixed-ratio, open-format Cloze test, in which they must insert semantically and grammatically appropriate words, is clearly below that of native speakers. Again, these findings are similar to those from studies with younger children in immersion programs. (See for example Swain and Lapkin 1986, Swain 1988, Harley 1989, 1992a, and 1992b.)

The same pattern of highly functional but nonnative skills emerges on the oral and writing tasks. Both cohorts have Oral Interview scores averaging between 3.5 and 3.8 of 5 for each task, for a total average around 11 of 15 possible points (15 by definition representing an educated francophone). These results reflect a very high level of speaking skill, with fluency and the ability to express desired meanings. But when scoring focuses on exact pronunciation, vocabulary precision and range, grammatical accuracy, and idiomatic usage, these students can generally be identified as second language speakers (see also Lapkin and Carroll 1987). Striking individual variation is also found among the immersion graduates on the oral tests. While the lowest-scoring students generally appear capable of carrying on daily life and university coursework in French, even if at some disadvantage from native speakers, a few, perhaps 15%, exhibit near-native skills, and most are somewhere between. Elicited imitation results fit a similar pattern, with high scores on semantically 'equivalent' repetition of sentences, indicating full understanding of the prompt and the ability to reconstruct its meaning. 'Exact' repetition scores are relatively low, however. (In our experience native speakers can generally provide exact repetitions). It is not clear whether the lesser ability of the immersion graduates to do this reflects inadequate attention on their part to formal structure and lexical choice in the prompts as they do the test, or is rather due to gaps in their internalized language knowledge, making online retention and native-like reconstruction of the sentences more difficult. Interesting current classroom research on these issues seeks to sort out the kinds of experiences or pedagogical intervention needed to improve immersion students' production accuracy (Harley 1987, 1993; Swain 1988; Lyster 1990; Day and Shapson 1991).

First and second language writing. The results of the L1 and L2 writing substudy provide further support for this general picture. Compositions written in French (L2) and English (L1) by 39 students from the 1988 cohort were compared with L1 compositions written by unilingual control groups in each language, as well as with compositions in both languages by a small group of bilingual students from English-speaking homes who had attended francophone schools (Vignola and Wesche 1991). The task required a summary of a newspaper article plus a supported personal opinion. Criteria included GLOBAL ratings on nativeness of writing, and analytical ratings of CONTENT coverage (information, details and examples), rhetorical ORGANIZATION (inclusion of introduction, thesis, supplementary paragraphs, conclusion), GRAMMAR (accuracy, clarity of sentence-level meaning), VOCABULARY (variety, appropriateness) and MECHANICS (spelling, punctuation, capitalization). The results (reported in Table 4) indicate a similar pattern of highly functional skills in French, reflecting nativelike performance on CONTENT coverage and essay ORGANIZATION. These students can communicate sophisticated ideas in French without difficulty but in a nonnative fashion. They do less well in their L2 than their L1, and they fall short of unilingual native speaker performance on grammatical and lexical knowledge.

A group of seven anglophone graduates of francophone schools scored higher than the immersion students on their French essays in all categories except MECHANICS, and not significantly different from the francophone students in any category.

Table 4. English (L1) and French (L2) writing skills of French immersion graduates in first year university.

Essay Scores	Immersion: Early entry (E) vs. Late entry (L) Programs (E:N = 20 L:N = 19)		Immersion: (N = 39) L1 (English) vs. L2 (French) Essays	Immersion (I) vs. Unilingual Anglophone (A) or Francophone (F) Controls: English and French Essays	
	English essay	French essay		English essay A: (N=20)	French essay N:(N=20)
Global Rating	n.s.	n.s.	L1 > L2	n.s.	F > I
Content	n.s.	n.s.	n.s.	n.s.	n.s.
Organization	n.s.	n.s.	n.s.	n.s.	n.s.
Grammar	n.s.	n.s.	L1 > L2	n.s.	F > I
Vocabulary	n.s.	n.s.	L1 > L2	n.s.	F > I
Mechanics	n.s.	n.s.	L1 > L2	n.s.	n.s.

With respect to the GRAMMAR scoring category, errors are concentrated in the verb system (choice, auxiliary use, tense, and agreement). They are also found in gender and in the use of pronouns, prepositions, and articles (see Harley 1989, 1992, forthcoming for related studies with immersion students). VOCABULARY use in the L2 compositions is less rich, nuanced, or idiomatic than in the L1 compositions. There is a tendency to overuse generic verbs (e.g. *faire, aller*). Interestingly, there were no significant differences in scores on sentence MECHANICS between the immersion students and francophones on the French essay, although the immersion students were judged better in this category on their L1. Whether the difficulty experienced by both groups and the nonsignificant differences in French can be attributed to the complexities of accent markings and capitalization, or is a statistical artifact given the students' heterogeneity of performance in this category, is not clear. The seven anglophone students who had attended francophone schools were not significantly different from the francophone norms in any category, suggesting the importance of learners' linguistic environment in the development of vocabulary and grammatical knowledge. There were no significant differences of any kind between the three anglophone groups on the English essays, nor were raters able to find any evidence of specific influences of French on English writing (although many examples were identified in the other direction). It appears from these data that CONTENT and ORGANIZATION categories tap knowledge that largely transfers between the two languages (at least in the Canadian context, for highly educated speakers such as these. GRAMMAR and VOCABULARY knowledge, however, must be relearned in the second language, even though the same, individually variable cognitive abilities underlie development in both languages (indicated by high L1 and L2 correlations within these categories).

Self-Assessment results from the 1985 cohort revealed a very high degree of confidence in carrying out functional listening and reading tasks in French in an academic environment. Results for the 1988 cohort on the more difficult Self-Assessment including production skills confirmed this picture for receptive skills, but showed that students lacked confidence in the accuracy of their production skills, with writing and speaking items receiving the lowest ratings. Overall, an average of 75% of the items on the revised (all skills) scale were given maximum ratings (i.e. can 'almost always' do it), as opposed to 90% in 1985 on the easier (receptive skills only) version.

French language maintenance during university studies. Whatever the shortcomings, it must be emphasized that these students possess impressive, highly functional second language skills. And evidence from the third-year testing indicates that these skills are well established and not easily lost, even if they are seldom used (see Table 5). A summary of the comparative scores from university entry and end of third-year testing of each cohort is found in Table 5. (See Appendix C for descriptive statistics.) While the 1985 cohort showed slightly higher scores on Listening Comprehension after three years, scores were lower on the Cloze test, and Oral Interview scores remained stable. Students in the larger and more typical 1988 cohort showed no significant changes on either of the listening tests, either the oral test or the Self Assessment, while they gained significantly on both Reading Comprehension and Cloze performance. (It is possible that these latter gains involve some transfer from intensive L1 reading during university studies.)

Early versus late entry immersion outcomes. The issue of long-term differences between early and later starting immersion students has important implications for the educational system, and also relates to the second language acquisition issue of an optimal age for language acquisition. The question is posed in these data in the following way: To what extent do students who begin intensive school instruction through the medium of French at age 11 or 12 and who may have only half the total hours of instructional exposure to French catch up with those who began French Immersion at age 4 or 5? (It must be remembered that most students in the late-entry program will have had have 20 to 40 minutes per day of core French instruction through elementary school.)

Previous research on immersion students still in school has suggested a trend for early entry immersion students to perform better than late entry immersion students, particularly in oral skills, and to exhibit greater confidence in their French language skills (cf. Swain and Lapkin 1986, Genesee et al. 1989). However, these results are not consistent in all programs. For example, a recent

Table 5. French language maintenance of immersion graduates during university studies, 1985 and 1988 cohorts in first and third year university.

French Proficiency Measures	Test Results: 1985 cohort° (N = 48)	1988 cohort° (N = 78)
	First Year / Third Year	First Year / Third Year
Listening		
Comprehension	1 < 3*	n.s.
Dictation	—	n.s.
Reading		
Comprehension	—	1 < 3*
Cloze	1 > 3***	1 < 3***
Oral		
Interview	n.s. (N = 27)	n.s. (N = 12)
Elicited Imitation	—	n.s. (N = 48)
Self-Assessment		
Total Score	—	n.s.

° There were no significant differences between the scores of the subgroups for each cohort and the larger (first year) samples from which they were drawn, nor between the two cohorts in third-year studies.

* $p < .05$

*** $p < .005$

study of grade 12 students in Calgary showed no statistically significant differences between early and late immersion students for any skill area (Hart et al. 1989). It has also been noted in the literature (particularly by Pawley 1986) that differences are generally not found in written skills, and that during the high school years there is a gradual convergence of the performance of late immersion students in bilingual high school programs with that of early immersion students in the same programs.

Limited support for the tendency for early immersion students to outperform late immersion students was found in our 1985 cohort results at university entry (Table 6). There were relatively small but significant differences favoring early immersion students on the Listening Comprehension and Oral Interview, and on the Self-Assessment, although there were no significant differences on Reading Comprehension or Cloze scores. Early entry students also reported somewhat greater Frequency of French use. Thus it appeared that the early starters had an advantage in face-to-face French use and readiness to use it orally, although not in what one might call 'academic language skills'. The differences in Oral Interview scores had disappeared by the 1988 retesting of the lead cohort, while a small, significant difference persisted on the Listening Comprehension score and on the Self-Assessment.

Table 6. French proficiency of early-entry vs. late-entry immersion graduates in first year university.*

French Proficiency Measures	Early (E) vs. Late (L) Entry Program Graduates	
	1985 cohort (E:N = 33) (L:N = 48)	1988 cohort (E:N = 97) (L:N = 57)
Listening		
Comprehension	E > L	n.s.
Dictation	—	n.s.
Reading		
Comprehension	n.s.	n.s.
Cloze	n.s.	n.s.
Oral		
Elicited Imitation	—	n.s.
Interview	E > L (n = 58)	n.s. (n = 31)
Writing		
Essay	—	n.s.
Self-Assessment	E > L	n.s.*

* The same pattern was found for each cohort in third year university with the exception of E/L Oral Interview differences for the 1985 cohort which disappeared by 1988, and the Self-Assessment, which favored the 1988 cohort early immersion students.

The 1988 replication cohort reveals a different picture, however. Comparisons made between early and late entry immersion students in this larger and more typical sample were made for every test and self-report in the battery. No significant differences were found between the two groups on any variables, including the Dictation, Elicited Imitation, and Essay tests, which had not been given in 1985, nor on the revised Self Assessment, attitudinal, or language use measures. Again, there was a striking range of French proficiency between the weakest and strongest candidates, particularly on production skills. Also striking is that oral and written production, while very serviceable for most graduates, was clearly nonnative. In an attempt to verify whether scholastic ability measures might favor the 1988 late immersion students and explain their ability to catch up, we compared the early and late entry subgroups on grade 10 Differential Aptitude Test verbal reasoning scores. There were no significant differences. Whatever initial differences there may have been in the entry populations, the graduates of early entry and late entry immersion sequences attending university could not be distinguished from one another.

The pattern suggested by our findings and other studies of the Ottawa programs (e.g. Pawley 1986) is that clear differences exist in production skills between the early and late entry groups as many enter common programs in grade 9. The differences lessen as they progress through high school, and by first year university the groups are indistinguishable. Teachers corroborate the statistical findings, saying that they cannot pick out individuals from the two programs by the later high school years. They also note that in grade 9, the early immersion students may coast somewhat, while the academically oriented late immersion students, aware of their inferior oral skills, strive to catch up. Thus for the able, academically successful, motivated students of French who remain in this multi-year program, and given a situation in which many students from the two groups have been together in bilingual high school courses, there is no evidence of a lasting group advantage of an earlier start to intensive instruction. In our view, the most likely explanation of the different patterns for the two cohorts is that the 1985 'lead' early immersion cohort may have had some special characteristics. Given that this is the largest and oldest sample looked at anywhere to date, and that we looked diligently for differences, it is difficult to discount the replication findings. At the same time, they should not lead anyone to the conclusion that early immersion should be abandoned in favor of late immersion. Established early immersion programs tend to take in a far larger proportion of the school population than late programs, which are known to be academically demanding and which appear to attract only students with previous success in Core French and academic study. For example, in the Ottawa Board of Education the proportion of entrants to early immersion in recent years has been between 35% and 45% of the senior kindergarten population, while the late immersion program has attracted between 8% and 12% of the grade 6 population (Ottawa Board of Education 1991).

Attitudes. Scores on the attitude measures were very similar for both cohorts in first year university (Table 7). They indicated relatively low Anxiety when using French (although the individual variation on this scale is striking). Students reported a strong Desire to use French now and in the future, and relatively strong, multiple Reasons for learning French, including better job and travel possibilities, the inherent interest in learning the language and in getting to know French speakers, and the importance for Canadian national unity of citizens who know both languages. All reasons were given similar, relatively high rankings.

Table 7. French language attitudes and uses reported by French immersion graduates in first year university: Changes by third year university.°

	Maximum Possible Score	1985 (N = 81)		1988 (N = 78)	
		M	SD	M	SD
Attitudes toward French					
Anxiety in using•	40	29.7*	6.0	29.4	5.9
Desire to use	36	20.9	2.7	19.8	2.9
Reasons for learning	20	16.4	2.9	15.9	2.8
French use patterns					
Frequency of use	20	10.3*	2.5	10.3	2.9
Expected future use	9	6.5	1.2	6.2	1.4

° There were no significant differences between the 1985 and 1988 cohorts at university entry.

• A high score indicates low anxiety.

* There was a significant change at $p < .05$ when the 1985 cohort was retested in 1988 (third-year university) toward higher anxiety and lower use frequency. The 1988 cohort showed no significant changes between first- and third-year university.

French use. The average actual frequency of French use for both cohorts during first-year studies can only be described as low, indicating that students use French occasionally, in a variety of situations at the university, downtown, at work, and on trips (Table 7). There is a tendency to use it receptively (e.g. for reading, television) and in less personal, more instrumental situations (e.g. at work, travelling). (The continuation of this pattern was confirmed in the 1991 post-university study of a subgroup of the 1985 cohort.) This finding somewhat echoes Genesee's (1987) characterization of 'reactive' (when addressed) French use by immersion students out of class, rather than an 'active' search for opportunities to use it. Still, the students varied considerably in the frequency and specific contexts of their French use, and a small minority of them reported using it frequently and in many aspects of their lives.

Overall, the groups at English language universities (Carleton, Queens) reported that they used French less in first-year university, on average, than they did during grade 13, while the University of Ottawa groups reported about the same French use as in grade 13. Expected Future Use of French was somewhat greater than present use for all groups, however. (A score of 6 indicates expected 'same' future use). The specific measures of French use again indicated that there was relatively little current use of French by these students outside of the classes some were taking in French. French television was the most popular use, reported by 60%, who watched from 1 to 25 hours per month, averaging 4 hours. Some 36% reported occasional French movies, averaging 1 film per month. Even fewer—only 16%—reported reading French leisure books; these averaged one book per month. Only 30% reported significant other out-of-class uses, ranging from 2 to 62 hours per month, and averaging 13 hours for those reporting other uses. These in most cases involved work or social relationships, and in the University of Ottawa group, some campus activities. However, only on the measure of current courses taken in French were University of Ottawa students significantly different from the others, with both cohorts reporting an average of .8 of a full-year course per year versus .4 for Carleton (overall .5) in first-year university. The low averages are perhaps surprising, but the differences are not, given that at the University of Ottawa all courses for francophones are open to proficient second language speakers (and vice versa), so that students can essentially choose the extent to which they wish to carry out their studies and campus life in both languages.

The attitude and language use measures were remarkable for their stability through the university years, with significant changes found only for the 1985 cohort (slightly higher Anxiety and lower Frequency of use when retested in third year). Overall, a positive, low-anxiety self-evaluation of French proficiency persisted, as did a high desire to use and improve French, high expectations of future French use, and low current use of French. University of Ottawa students continued to report approximately twice as many courses in French as the Carleton and Queens students over the three years. A separate archival verification of courses taken by members of the 1985 cohort at the University of Ottawa showed that over 80% of students took courses in French, averaging eight one-semester courses each. Of these, some 28% were courses for second language speakers and 72% were directed at francophone students, 12% of these in Lettres françaises and 60% in a variety of disciplines, the most popular being biology (Wesche 1988). Self-report data for the 1988 cohort in 1991 on courses taken in the four universities showed the following results. For each of the first two years, just under 30% of this cohort reported taking courses in French, with 24% reporting courses during the third year. The total cohort averaged 7 half-courses over the three years. Since the majority were again mainly in nonlanguage courses for francophones, it is clear that University of Ottawa students continued to take more than their share.

While no evidence could be found of a differential influence of the university linguistic environment on gains in French ability or in French language use other than coursework, there was some evidence that the more proficient students in French tended to choose the University of Ottawa, and to a lesser extent, McGill. Thus 1988 cohort members at the University of Ottawa scored higher on Dictation, Reading Comprehension, and Oral Interview tests than did those at Carleton upon entry in 1988, and again in 1991.[3]

When these immersion graduates are questioned as to why they do not take more courses in French, the main reasons given are incompatibility with their degree program or schedule, and concern about lower marks (Wesche 1988). The reason for the latter concern is illustrated in Table 8, which shows 1988 cohort responses to questions on the difficulties they experienced in taking university courses in French. A majority of these students report some disadvantage vis-à-vis francophone peers in academic coursework in French, particularly with writing and speaking activities—taking notes at lectures, writing essays and course papers, and speaking in class—as more difficult than understanding lectures and doing course readings. Nonetheless, most students who do take courses in French report carrying out their course activities exclusively in French, even where there is an alternative (e.g. note-taking in English, using English textbooks). And with the exception of speaking, over a quarter of the students indicate that their French is 'about the same' as that of native speakers.

Post-university substudy: 1985 Cohort in 1991. Twenty-one members of the 1985 cohort who had been tested in first- and third-year university were located and agreed to fill out a questionnaire about their current French language use and attitudes. It was possible to carry out telephone interviews with 13 of these (see MacFarlane 1992 for further details). Most have full-time jobs, while a few are pursuing graduate studies. The majority live in the Ottawa area. This subsample of 21 showed no significant differences from the full 1985 sample on any French proficiency scores, attitude, or language-use measures taken during first-year university; nonetheless the sample is small, and possibly atypical given that its respondents from early immersion programs were members of the lead cohort (mentioned earlier). Thus these results must be taken as suggestive and not generalizable.

Proficiency. Twenty-eight percent of the respondents rated their French speaking ability as 'better' or 'much better' than it had been at high school graduation, while fully half felt that it was worse. However, telephone interviews clarified that almost all respondents felt their listening and reading skills were stable, and in some cases improved. Writing skills were also reported by some to have declined, but were also viewed as less important than they had been in school.

---

[3]Not enough subjects were tested on the Oral Interview from the two groups in 1991 for statistical analysis. There were not enough subjects in either the McGill or Queens groups in either cohort to carry out statistical comparisons for these institutions.

French language use. The frequency and types of French language use reported by these subjects were similar to the findings for both cohorts during their university studies.

- Most of the subjects reported seldom using French (80% marking 2 on a 1 to 5 'never' to 'always' scale to indicate how often they used French).
- The most frequent French use contexts reported were travelling, at work, and socially. Only four (of twenty-one) subjects reported using French from half the time to always at work.
- The most frequent uses were reading and watching television, that is, receptive skills. Two of the twenty-one reported that they listened to French language radio about half the time.
- When asked with whom they used French, subjects reported its use mainly with customers, coworkers, and friends. Some used French with relatives, and only two reported ever using French with neighbors.
- Only two subjects reported having had the experience of 'living' temporarily in French during the preceding three years, one on a trip to France and one on an exchange program.

These results might seem surprising, given the consistent findings in this and other secondary and post-secondary studies indicating that students expected high levels of future use of French, and many expected to use French in their careers. On the other hand, they are an extension of the low levels of actual out-of-class use seen in immersion studies at all levels, as well as in this follow-up study. Perhaps the question to ask is why it was ever thought that students who learned another language in an essentially school-bound context within their own ethnic group would on their own initiative transfer their knowledge to out-of-class uses after graduation. Nonetheless, it is important to remember that some of these former immersion students use their French a great deal, and that all of them can if called upon to do so.

Interethnic attitudes. While French proficiency outcomes of immersion programs have received considerable research attention, little is known about the effect of such programs on graduates' attitudes toward francophone Canadians and their culture. Hopes for improved French-English relations and national unity have often been cited as reasons for establishing immersion programs, and many parents and students also express this as one reason for taking part in them (Wesche et al. 1986, Bibeau 1991, Calvé 1991). Such hopes reflect a widespread assumption that second language proficiency brings with it better understanding of the target culture and more sympathy toward its members. But is this necessarily so? Can we in fact expect interethnic sensitivity and positive attitudes to develop incidently as language skills are improved, or does such development require certain kinds of experiences? If it requires certain experiences, presumably positive, what are they?

With the notable exception of work by Lambert (cf. 1987) and Genesee (1981, 1987) with immersion children in the Montreal area, we know very little about this issue. Discussions with young graduates of immersion programs (not in the current study) suggest that they believe that the immersion experience has led to their having more positive attitudes toward Canadian francophones and their culture. Several kinds of experiences were mentioned as important. Well-liked francophone teachers in elementary immersion were cited. Memorable lessons were also cited when francophone teachers had objected to elements of the English school curriculum they were required to teach in French, and gave their own interpretation. These incidents impressed the students and made them aware of the different interpretations of Canadian history learned by the two groups. Another type of experience available to immersion students was having good enough French skills to be able to understand in depth the literary works they read in French in high school. Insofar as these reflected the French Canadian experience they were seen as valuable for interethnic understanding. Finally, contact with francophones other than teachers was considered important. This came about through occasional resource persons from the community, school outings, family trips to Quebec, and, in a few cases, class trips or exchanges. Somewhat surprising was the minimal acquaintance of these graduates with Quebec media, given that most French-language newspapers and magazines are readily available in Ottawa, and radio and television channels are available throughout the country. Also, the lack of established social relations with francophones in French from the area was notable—given that some 30% of Ottawa's population of 700,000 has French as a first language.

The questionnaire responses of the 1985 cohort in 1991 offer a more general picture which seems to fit the above observations. Table 9 presents the interethnic attitude data reported by these students: (1) a comparison of their attitudes with those of English program graduates, and (2) the perceived effect of immersion on their attitudes.

Most subjects considered their attitudes toward francophones and francophone communities, English-French relations, and French language use to be more positive than those of their English program counterparts. This was not true of their reported attitudes toward Quebec nationalism, however, where most felt that their attitudes were either the same or more negative (52% 'same' and 24% 'more' or 'much more' negative). A subsequent analysis indicated that high satisfaction with immersion was correlated with more negative attitudes toward Quebec nationalism.

A large majority (74-84%) felt that immersion had to some extent influenced their attitudes toward francophones and francophone communities, Quebec nationalism, and English-French relations, and 58% reported some influence on their attitudes toward French language use. Still, many reported in the interviews that family and other influences had also played an important role.

Attitudes toward French immersion. The responses of these young adults to questions on immersion program features and attitudes toward French

Table 8. Perceived difficulty of university study in French vs. English, 1988 cohort in third year university (n = 78).

How well were you prepared in high school (bilingual program) for taking courses in French afterwards?	Very well	Fairly well	Fairly poorly	Very poorly
	36%	55%	9%	—
How difficult has it been to take courses in French compared to English?	**About the same**	**Somewhat more difficult**	**Much more difficult**	**Can't do it**
	25%	21%	52%	2%
Compared to English, how difficult is it for you to do the following in French?	**About the same**	**Somewhat more difficult**	**Much more difficult**	**Can't do it**
Listening to and understanding lectures	42%	54%	4%	—
Doing required reading for courses	32%	55%	14%*	—
Speaking in class or seminars	10%	36%	53%	1%
Taking notes at lectures or seminars	37%	16%	46%	1%
Writing essays and course papers	9%	39%	51%	1%
How often in your French courses do you do each of the following?	**Never**	**Sometimes**	**About half the time**	**Most of the time/ always**
Take lectures or seminar notes in English	72%	22%	—	5%
Do required reading in English translation	71%	19%	5%	5%
Write essays or course papers in English, then translate	79%	14%	7%	—
How good is your French compared to that of a native speaker from Northern Ontario, Quebec or a French-speaking country?	**About the same**	**Somewhat worse**	**Much worse**	**Don't know**
Listening	36%	8%	51%	5%
Reading	33%	13%	51%	3%
Speaking	14%	42%	42%	1%
Writing	27%	28%	44%	1%

* Total is greater than 100% due to rounding.

immersion are presented in Table 10. Most graduates reported a high level of satisfaction with their immersion experience, 81% reporting that they were either 'very' or 'completely' satisfied. The most frequently reported influences on their adult lives were better job opportunities and functional French skills; many also reported greater openness to other cultures. This high level of satisfaction with the immersion experience is most forcefully communicated by the fact that 19 of 20 responding would send their own children to immersion programs. (One preferred a francophone school and one said it depended on the

Table 9. Interethnic attitudes: 1985 graduates in 1991.

N = 19	Maximum Possible Rating	How do you think your attitudes differ from those of students you know who completed a regular English program? Scale: 1 = much more negative 3 = the same 5 = much more positive		Do you feel your attitudes are different than they might have been because of your immersion experience? Scale: 1 = not at all 3 = moderately 5 = completely	
		M	S.D.	M	S.D.
Attitudes toward:					
Francophones	5	4.0	1.0	2.6	1.3
Francophone communities	5	3.9	.9	2.5	1.2
English/French relations	5	3.9	.8	2.7	1.2
French language use	5	4.2	1.0	3.1	1.2
Quebec Nationalism	5	2.7	.7	2.0	.7

child.) The overwhelming preference for early immersion is striking, considering that the majority of these graduates took late immersion programs. (It may be relevant that this was the 1985 cohort in which a few differences in proficiency favoring early immersion were found.)

While 58% of the subjects reported that French use outside the immersion classroom had NOT been a feature of their program, nor had contact with francophones (67%), most felt that both use outside of class (76%) and contact (90%) could be an integral part of the program. When asked to specify how more use outside the classroom could be encouraged, subjects suggested exchanges, more emphasis on French media, more field trips, and less emphasis on accuracy. Suggestions for achieving contact with francophones included exchanges (suggested by 10 of 21), francophone monitors in the classroom, organized out-of-school activities with francophone peers such as sports events,

Table 10. Attitudes toward French immersion program features: 1985 graduates in 1991.

	N	Yes %	No %	Other
Was this an important feature of your French immersion program?				
French use outside of class	19	8 42%	11 58%	
Contact with francophones	21	7 33%	14 67%	
Could such a goal be achieved by immersion programs?				
French use outside of class	17	13 76%	4 24%	
Contact with francophones	21	19 90%	2 10%	
Desire to enrol own child in French Immersion	20	19 95%	1* 5%*	
If so, in which program?	19			Early 13 Middle 5 Late 1

* This subject preferred a francophone school.

workshops, and swapping classes for a week with students from a francophone school. More emphasis on francophone Canadian cultural content was suggested by several subjects. Finally one subject reported feeling that contact was a non-issue because the primary role of immersion was to provide better job opportunities. This was an isolated view, however. Interestingly, little mention was made of bringing in resource persons from the community or integrating French media use into the classroom—although such activities would be relatively easy to build into most Canadian programs.

The potential importance of the activities suggested above is indicated by correlations between events at different points in these subjects' experience.[4] Reports by graduates in 1991 that their school immersion programs had featured French use outside of class were correlated with more positive current attitudes toward French use as well as high levels of current reported French use for reading and at work. Those who reported that their immersion programs had

[4] All tetrachloric correlations reported had magnitudes between .4 and .6, at $p < .05$.

featured Contact with francophones were the ones who tended in their young adult lives to use French on social occasions, to attend French plays, to use French with neighbors, and to take opportunities to live in French. Correlations also showed that the reported immersion program feature of Early Contact with francophones was likewise significantly related to scores on French proficiency measures, and to Confidence in using French reported at high school graduation in 1985 and again in 1988. Both early Contact with francophones and the 1985 and 1988 proficiency measures predicted reported French use in 1991 for the 'integrative' purposes previously noted. These links suggest that early experiences which bring learners into contact with members of the other cultural group and with French language use outside the classroom may have long-term positive effects, and thus might indeed have an eventual influence on interethnic relations in Canada. (Evidently, considerable further research on these issues in different contexts is needed to confirm and extend these preliminary findings.)

Discussion. Given the earlier results reported for the Ottawa-area study and related research, many of the outcomes of this substudy are not surprising. These include the findings of continued low French use by most graduates; receptive L2 skill maintenance in spite of infrequent use; the fact that most use their French in relatively impersonal circumstances (with customers and coworkers and when travelling); and finally, the heartening existence of a minority who use French frequently including in their personal lives, and who have excellent speaking and writing as well as receptive skills. The almost unanimous desire of the graduates to send their own children to immersion programs is also striking, confirming findings at earlier stages of this and other programs (Wesche et al. 1990, Husim and Bruce 1991, Halsall and Clarke 1992, Saskatoon Board of Education 1992).

New and encouraging findings are those reporting positive attitudes toward francophones and their culture and toward French-English relations in Canada, as well as the perceived influence of immersion on these attitudes. It must be noted, however, that while immersion is seen as having some effect, many graduates report that their positive attitudes are even more directly related to those of their families.

The attitudes expressed toward Quebec nationalism were at first puzzling. Telephone interviews clarified that many individuals feel that they have quite positive attitudes toward Canadian francophones and their culture and that they have made a personal effort toward national unity. They see Quebec nationalists as not reciprocating, either individually or collectively, and as not sharing their vision of a bilingual, bicultural country. They tend to show little sympathy for the alternative nationalist view.

Perhaps most interesting from the standpoint of interethnic relations is the indication that early French use and, particularly, contact with francophones outside the classroom is related to the development of higher French proficiency and ultimately to greater and more integrative use of French in daily life.

Conclusion. What lessons can we draw from the French immersion experience based on this six-year study of Ottawa-area graduates? I believe the following conclusions are warranted for this context and others with similar program features:

- High levels of functional L2 ability can be achieved by language-majority children through L2-medium schools.
- Immersion L2 skills acquired through communicative use over many years are robust and are maintained for long periods, even in the absence of frequent use. This is particularly true of receptive skills.
- Even among the strongest students, immersion schooling alone does not develop native-like L2 users except on global comprehension skills involving 'school' language. Gaps are most apparent in grammar, vocabulary range and precision, and familiarity with varied discourse domains. Graduates can, however, 'manage' in their L2 in most situations, including post-secondary study in French. The native-like L2 skills of anglophone graduates of francophone schools suggests that lack of interaction with native peers is an important factor in the nonnative immersion outcomes.
- An intensive L2 dose and use of the L2 as an instructional medium are essential features of immersion; an early start is not. Graduates nonetheless tend to favor as early a start as possible. A major advantage of early-entry programs is that they attract a larger proportion and broader range of children.
- Overall, immersion graduates show very high levels of satisfaction with their immersion experience.
- The individual differences in proficiency, attitudes, and French use among immersion graduates are quite striking, indicating that—as with other school outcomes—instructed exposure is not the only variable.
- It appears to be unrealistic to expect graduates to seek personal and cultural contact with the L2 group on the basis of an essentially school-bound program. This and the preceding point suggest that there may be things which we cannot achieve in school, or at least, which will not be learned 'incidentally'.
- Evidence suggests that out-of-class activity in the L2 and contact with native speakers during immersion study are linked both to proficiency development and to greater use of the language in later life, and that early contact is particularly linked to a more integrative orientation toward speakers of the L2, their culture, and L2 use.

So far, outcomes of the immersion phenomenon in Canada can only be described for individuals, school systems, and to some degree for second language pedagogy, where the verdict is one of clear success. It is not yet possible to see immersion's broader socio-political implications. One is, however, tempted to speculate that, if the immersion language learning experience remains essentially school-bound and contact of most graduates with francophones and their culture remains infrequent, these may—with notable exceptions—be more limited than had been expected. More hopefully, this research suggests ways to overcome these limitations.

Acknowledgements. I wish to express my appreciation to the many individuals who have contributed to this project over the past seven years, including the various groups of subjects. Funding, material, and logistical support was received from the Language Acquisition Development Program of the Secretary of State, the Ontario Ministry of Education, the Ottawa Board of Education (OBE), the Carleton Board of Education (CBE), and the University of Ottawa. Henry Edwards and Roger Lalonde were instrumental in the project's conception, and the original research team included Frances Morrison, Doreen Ready, and Catherine Pawley. Research officers with major responsibilities included Pierre Couture, Joseph Dicks, Alina MacFarlane, Jacqueline Murray, Kimberly Nöels, Michele Thibodeau, and Marie-Josée Vignola. The test and questionnaire battery drew on work from the OBE Research Centre, the University of Ottawa Second Language Institute, the Western Ontario Language Research Group, and the Modern Language Centre at the Ontario Institute for Studies in Education. Christiane Hamm, Suzanne Fortier, Jacques Rebuffot, Juliette Kealey, Sinclair Robinson and the University of Ottawa Institutional Research Office helped organize data collection at the participating universities, and a number of student assistants, teachers, and technical staff provided further assistance in this, in test scoring, and in data entry. A special thanks to Sharon Lapkin, Doug Hart, and Joan Howard of OISE for their ongoing collaboration on instrument development and use. The office staff at the Second Language Institute under Diane Daoust provided excellent administrative support throughout the project, and Doreen Ready helped with all aspects of data handling and analysis. Finally, I am grateful to Beatrice Magyar for her fine graphics and word processing contributions.

REFERENCES

Bibeau, Gilles. 1991. L'immersion:...de la coupe aux lèvres. Études de Linguistique Appliquée 82.127-38.

Calvé, Pierre. 1991. Vingt-cinq ans d'immersion au Canada: 1965-1990. Études de Linguistique Appliquée 82.7-23.

Center for Applied Linguistics. 1991. List of total and partial immersion programs in U.S. elementary schools. Washington, DC: CAL.

Clément, Richard, Patrick Smythe and Robert C. Gardner. 1978. Échelles d'attitudes et de motivation reliées à l'apprentissage de l'anglais, langue seconde. The Canadian Modern Language Review 34, 4.688-94.

Day, Elaine, and Stan Shapson. 1991. Integrating formal and functional approaches to Language teaching in French immerson: An experimental study. Language Learning 41, 1.25–58.

De Vries, John. 1986. Ottawa's French immersion graduates. Final report to the Office of the Commissioner of Official Languages. Ottawa: Carleton University.

Endt, Ernst. 1992. Immersion und Bilingualer Unterricht: Eine Bibliographie. Eichstätt/Kiel: EKIB.

Fortier, d'Iberville. 1990. Commissioner of official languages annual report 1989. Ottawa: Minister of Supply and Services Canada.

Fortier, d'Iberville. 1991. Commissioner of official languages annual report 1990. Ottawa: Minister of Supply and Services Canada.

Genesee, Fred. 1981. Bilingualism and biliteracy: A study of cross-cultural contact in a bilingual community. The Social Psychology of Reading, ed. by J. Edwards, 147–71. Silver Spring, MD: Institute of Modern Languages.

Genesee, Fred. 1987. Learning through two languages. Rowley, MA: Newbury House.

Genesee, Fred, Naoms Holobow, Wallace E. Lambert, and Louise Chartrand. 1989. Three elementary school alternatives for learning through a second language. The Modern Language Journal 73, 3.250-63.

Halsall, Nancy, and L. Clarke. 1992. Secondary school French immersion study. Ottawa: Carleton Board of Education.

Harley, Birgit. 1987. Second language proficiency and classroom treatment in early French immersion. Development of Bilingual Proficiency: Final Report, ed. by J.P.B. Allen, Jim Cummins, Birgit Harley, and Merrill Swain. Toronto: Modern Language Centre, Ontario Institute for Studies in Education.

Harley, Birgit. 1989. Transfer in the written compositions of French immersion students. Transfer in Language Production, ed. by H. W. Dechert and M. Raupach, 3–19. Norwood, NJ: Ablex.

Harley, Birgit. 1992. Aspects of the oral second language proficiency of early immersion, late immersion and extended French students at Grade 10. Comprehension-Based Second Language Teaching/L'enseignement des langues secondes axé sur la compréhension, ed. by Robert Courchêne, Joan Isabelle Glidden, Jennifer St. John, and Christian Therien, 371–88. Ottawa: University of Ottawa Press.

Harley, Birgit. 1993. Instructional strategies and SLA in early French immersion. Studies in Second Language Acquisition 15.245–59.

Harley, Birgit. (forthcoming) Patterns of second language development in French immersion. Journal of French Language Studies.

Hart, Doug, and Sharon Lapkin. 1989. French immersion at the secondary/postsecondary interface. Report to the Ontario Ministry of Colleges and Universities. Toronto: Modern Language Center, Ontario Institute for Studies in Education.

Hart, Doug, and Sharon Lapkin. 1990. French immersion at the secondary/postsecondary interface: Final report to the Ontario Ministry of Colleges and Universities. Toronto: Modern Language Center, Ontario Institute for Studies in Education.

Hart, Doug, and Sharon Lapkin. 1991. French immersion at the secondary/postsecondary interface: Toward a national study. Final report to the Secretary of State. Toronto: Modern Language Centre, Ontario Institute for Studies in Education.

Hart, Doug, Sharon Lapkin, and Merrill Swain. 1989. Evaluation of continuing bilingual and late immersion programs at the secondary level. Final report to the Calgary Board of Education. Toronto: Modern Language Center, Ontario Institute for Studies in Education.

Husim, R., and R. Bruce. 1991. A survey of graduates from a Saskatchewan French immersion high school. The Canadian Modern Language Review 48, 1.135–42.

Lalonde, Roger. 1990. But can they speak French? They sure can but... Le Journal de l'Immersion Journal 13, 2.6-10.

Lambert, Wallace E. 1987. The effects of bilingual and bicultural experiences on children's attitudes and social perspectives. Childhood Bilingualism: Aspects of Linguistic, Cognitive, and Social Development, ed. by P. Homel, M. Palij, and D. Aaronson, 197–201. Hillsdale, NJ: Laurence Erlbaum.

Lambert, Wallace E., and G. Richard Tucker. 1972. The bilingual education of children: The St.Lambert Experiment. Rowley, MA: Newbury House.

Lapkin, Sharon, and Suzanne Carroll. 1987. The role of vocabulary in the development of communicative ability: Some comments. Proceedings from the Symposium on the Evaluation of Foreign Language Proficiency. Bloomington: Indiana University.

LeBlanc, Raymond. (forthcoming) Les programmes d'immersion et l'habileté à communiquer. Études de Linguistique Appliquée.

LeBlanc, Raymond, and Gisèle Painchaud. 1985. Self-assessment as a second language placement test. TESOL Quarterly 19, 4.673-87.

Lyster, Roi. 1990. The role of analytic language teaching in French immersion programs. The Canadian Modern Language Review 47, 1.159–76.

MacFarlane, Alina. 1992. The socio-cultural outcomes of French immersion education. Ph.D. Qualifying Paper, University of Ottawa.

McGillvray, W.R., and Catherine Pawley. 1985. Grade 13 student survey 1985. Unpublished questionnaire, Ottawa Board of Education.

McVey, Marietta, Rosemary Bonyun, Joseph Dicks, and L. Groulx. 1991. Performance of OBE students in grade 8 middle immersion, second cohort, 1990-91. Research paper 91-03. Ottawa:

Ottawa Board of Education.

Ottawa Board of Education. 1991. Review of French as a second language enrollments. Report to the Education Committee. Ottawa: Internal Report.

Ouellet, M. 1990. Synthèse historique de l'immersion française au Canada suivie d'une bibliographie sélective et analytique. Québec: Centre international de recherche sur le bilinguisme, l'Université Laval.

Parkin, Michael, Frances Morrison, and G. Watkin. 1987. French Immersion Research Relevant to Decisions in Ontario. Toronto: Ontario Ministry of Education.

Pawley, Catherine. 1986. What is the French Proficiency of Immersion Students Really Like? Research Report 86-07. Ottawa: Ottawa Board of Education.

Saskatoon Board of Education. 1992. French immersion program review. Saskatoon.

Shapson, Stan. 1985. Post-secondary bilingual education: Identifying and adapting to the shift in second-language demands. The Canadian Modern Language Review 41, 5.827-34.

Swain, Merrill. 1988. Manipulating and complementing content teaching to maximize second language learning. TESL Canada Journal 6, 1.68-83.

Swain, Merrill, and Sharon Lapkin. 1981. Bilingual education in Ontario: A decade of research. Toronto: Ministry of Education of Ontario.

Swain, Merrill, and Sharon Lapkin. 1986. Immersion French in secondary schools: 'The goods' and 'the bads'. Contact 5, 3.2-9.

Vignola, Marie-Josée, and Marjorie Wesche. 1991. Le savoir-écrire en langue maternelle et en langue seconde chez les diplômés d'immersion française. Études de linguistique appliquée 82.94-115.

Wesche, Marjorie, Frances Morrison, Catherine Pawley, and Doreen Ready. 1986. Post-secondary follow-up of former French immersion students in the Ottawa area: A pilot study. Final report to the Secretary of State, Canada.

Wesche, Marjorie. 1988. Les diplômés de l'immersion: Implications dans le domaine de l'enseignement du francais. L'universite de demain: Implications dans le domaine de l'enseignement du français, ed. by C. Dans Elkabas and C. Besnard, 215-29. Toronto: Canadian Scholars' Press. [Reprinted 1989 Canadian Journal of Education. 19, 3]

Wesche, Marjorie, Frances Morrison, Doreen Ready, and Catherine Pawley. 1990. French immersion: Post-secondary consequences for individuals and universities. Canadian Modern Language Review 46, 3.430-51.

Appendix A. French Proficiency Tests*

Test	Description
Listening	
®Listening comprehension	A listening comprehension test which measures the understanding of spoken French in an academic context. It consists of three tape recorded passages. Students listen twice to each passage, which is followed by several content questions. They read the answer options in their test booklet, choosing the one that corresponds best to each question.
Listening dictation	A dictation test of the accuracy and completeness of listening comprehension of a passage from an introductory university textbook. Read three times, the second time in varied length segments meant to challenge short-term memory and require reconstruction. It is scored for the number of meaning units recorded in correct sequence.
Reading	
®Reading comprehension (revised version used in 1988 and 1991)	A reading comprehension test which measures the understanding of written French in an academic context. It consists of three reading passages, students read the selections in their test booklet and answer the multiple choice questions following each one.
®Cloze	A cloze test which provides a general measure of second language proficiency, including reading comprehension. It consists of a prose passage, based on an authentic text, in which selected words have been deleted to be filled in by students.
Oral	
Oral interview (administered to subsamples in 1985/88; 1988/91)	An individually administered interview involving three tasks: (1) description of a sequence of drawings; (2) discussion of tourist brochures from two locales; and (3) a simulated job interview for a summer tourism related job in one of the locales. Each is scored by the interviewer on a scale of 1 to 5, based on performance descriptions.
Elicited imitation (administered in 1988, 1988/91)	A sentence repetition task based on a French language radio broadcast for an adolescent audience. Students first listen to the extended text, then listen to and repeat the individual sentences of varying length which compose it. Scoring is for accuracy of repetition and various oral grammar points.

Writing (administered to subsample, 1988)	
French (L2) essay English (L1) essay	Compositions were written (on separate occasions) in the two languages based on dated newspaper articles reporting results of a poll which in each case included a simple statistical table. Students were asked to give their personal opinion as well as to predict results if the poll were to be repeated today, writing approximately 150 words and at least three paragraphs. Scoring by two judges was global and analytical using a grid with the following criteria: content, organization, grammar, vocabulary, and mechanics.

* Unless specified otherwise, tests were administered to all subjects in 1985/88 and 1988/91. With the exception of the elicited imitation test, developed by the Modern Language Centre (MLC), OISE, these tests were developed by the Second Language Institute, University of Ottawa, in collaboration with the Research Centre of the Ottawa Board of Education. Tests marked with a ® are currently available as the *Senior French Proficiency Test Package for French Immersion* from the MLC, which provides a scoring service. A technical manual is available.[5] See Wesche et al. 1990, Vignola and Wesche 1991.

[5]Most of these instruments are now available to researchers and school boards from the MLC Scoring Service, Modern Language Centre, The Ontario Institute for Studies in Education, 252 Bloor Street West, Rotonto, Ontario M5S-1V6, Canada.

Appendix B. Self-report measures of proficiency, attitudes and French language use.

Questionnaire	Description
Self-Assessment of French Proficiency (revised version used in 1988 and 1991)	The original (1985) self-assessment presented 60 statements about receptive French use ability with which the student indicated level of agreement on a 1 to 5 scale ('never' to 'always'), e.g. 'Over the phone I can understand some basic information in French, such as the name of the caller and the number where he can be reached.' 'I can read an editorial in French and determine the areas of agreement and disagreement between the author's views and more.' Since the original questionnaire showed a strong ceiling effect for these students the revised version replaced the 32 easiest items with 12 more difficult items, including writing and speaking (e.g. 'There is no difference in my reading speed whether the text is in French or in my native language.').
French Language Attitudes and Use	
Anxiety When Using French	A series of 10 questions for which the student indicates on a scale of 1 to 4 how nervous, anxious, or confident he/she would be using French in a given situation. The maximum score possible is 40, indicating very low anxiety.
Desire to Use French	A series of nine questions which the student marks on a scale of 1 to 3 to indicate intensity of motivation (i.e. from 'would never speak it' to 'would speak French most of the time, using English if necessary.' The maximum of 27 points indicates a very high level of desire to use French.

Reasons for Learning French	The perceived importance of five common Reasons for Learning French are marked on a scale of 1 to 4, providing a possible maximum of 20. The proposed reasons are: a. Learning French will help me to improve my job possibilities. b. Knowing French will make it easier for me to travel in French-speaking areas. c. It is interesting to know more than one language. d. In Canada, people who know the two official languages can contribute to national unity. e. Knowing the French language makes it easier to get to know people who are French speaking. A score of 15 would indicate that overall, the reasons are moderately important to the student.
Frequency of Current French Use	This scale is based on a series of five situations such as: 'Talking with francophones in the community' or 'At University between classes or at lunch.' Students respond on a 1 to 4 scale to indicate the frequency of their use of French for each one. The maximum score is 20, with 10 indicating that a student uses French sometimes in a variety of situations.
Expected Future Use of French	This is a measure of the student's intention to use French in the future at studies, at work, and socially. It also includes three questions and uses a scale of 1 to 3 on each. A score of 6 indicates that the student expects to use French in the future about the same amount as at present.
Specific Current Use Measures	These include measures of current French use in academic, social, leisure and work situations.
Academic French Use (1988 cohort in 1991 only)	The 1991 questionnaire included specific questions on perceived difficulties when using French in university studies (adapted from Hart and Lapkin 1990).
1991 Post-University Questionnaire on French Use, Ethnolinguistic Attitudes and Attitudes toward Immersion (administered to subsample of 1985 cohort in 1991)	This questionnaire was designed for graduates who had finished their undergraduate educations. Its purpose was to explore the ethnolinguistic attitudes of students and the influence on them of the immersion experience. Telephone interviews followed.

Appendix C. French Proficiency Tests: Descriptive Statistics for Cohorts and Subsamples, 1985, 1988, 1991

French Proficiency Measures	Max	1985 Cohort						1988 Cohort					
		1985 Full Sample (N = 81)		1985/88 Subsample (N = 48)				1988 Full Sample (N = 154)		1988/91 Subsample (N = 78)			
		M	S.D.	M	S.D.	M	S.D.	M	S.D.	M	S.D.	M	S.D.
Listening													
Comprehension	14	10.0	2.3	10.2	2.5	10.9	2.0	10.5	2.0	10.1	2.2	10.5	2.0
Dictation	28	--	--	--	--	22.9	2.8	22.5	2.8	22.7	2.7	22.9	2.7
Reading													
Comprehension	19	13.0*	3.0*	13.4*	3.2*	13.8**	2.7**	12.8	2.4	12.9	3.2	13.7	3.1
Cloze	35	26.5	5.2	26.5	5.2	24.8	5.4	23.6	4.7	23.9	4.7	25.5	4.1
Oral													
Interview	15	11.1[1]	2.1[1]	11.1[2]	2.1[2]	11.1[2]	1.5[2]	10.8[3]	1.2[3]	10.8[4]	1.1[4]	10.3[4]	1.5[4]
Elicited Imitation													
Exact										6.4	3.1	6.0	3.7
Equivalent										12.5[5]	1.7[5]	12.8[5]	2.2[5]
Self-Assessment													
1985 Version	300	268.4	29.3	--	--	--	--	--	--	--	--	--	--
1988 Version	200	--	--	--	--	--	--	148.3	27.7	148.5[6]	28.0[6]	151.9[6]	25.9[6]

* 1985 Version **1988 Version

[1] N = 58 [2] N = 27 [3] N = 31 [4] N = 12 [5] N = 23 [6] N = 48

EAP oral communication curriculum: Spoken discourse, meaning, and 'communicative pronunciation'

Joan Morley
The University of Michigan

English for Academic Purposes (EAP), a subgenre of English for Specific Purposes (ESP), is a growing specialty area within the field of English as a second language. EAP instruction in institutions of higher education has flourished over the last several years, both in numbers of programs and in linguistic sophistication. In a plenary paper presented at the 1991 Georgetown University Round Table, 'Perspectives on English for Academic Purposes' (Morley 1991a), the advanced EAP program currently under development at the University of Michigan English Language Institute was discussed in detail.[1] In this paper one portion of the Michigan program, specifically, the academically oriented oral communication curriculum, will be reviewed with special attention to three key elements: spoken discourse, meaning, and 'communicative pronunciation'.

1 Introduction. Second language research and instruction that concerns itself with oral communication in English for Specific Purposes needs to have a broad-based focus on spoken discourse within specific social contexts—in the case of EAP, the wide-ranging academic and preprofessional contexts in which students are situated in their various disciplines across the campus. Furthermore, put simply, attention must be given to both WHAT is said and HOW it is said. The latter, the 'how', utilizes a variety of linguistic, paralinguistic, and extra-linguistic components that are brought together here within a notion of

[1] Founded in 1941 by Charles C. Fries, the English Language Institute originated the first intensive English language research and training program of its kind in the world. In April 1987, the ELI phased out its intensive course for non-university students except by special arrangements or in the special-topic summer programs. Today ELI faculty and staff members are involved in carrying out a mission of language research and the development of a full curriculum of courses in English for Academic Purposes and related services for enrolled nonnative speakers at the University of Michigan.

'COMMUNICATIVE PRONUNCIATION'.

Pronunciation with a capital P signifies that pronunciation is AN INTEGRAL PART OF COMMUNICATION, NOT A SEPARATE COMPONENT SET ASIDE FROM THE *CONTENT* OF THE SPOKEN DISCOURSE AND THE *INTENT* OF THE SPOKEN DISCOURSE. That is, the term is intended to cover an expanded definition that considers the domain of pronunciation as one that deals not only with sound segments and their combinations, but also one that gives high priority attention to other important components and how they are used to communicate meaning, including: suprasegmentals (e.g. both basic sentence-level features of stress-rhythm-intonation (SRI), and more complex contextually marked features of SRI); vocal qualities (and other paralinguistic features); elements of 'body language' used in oral communication (e.g. facial gestures, eye contact, arm and hand gestures, body stance, posturing, use of space, and other extralinguistic features).

2 Program development: English for Academic Purposes.

2.1 Introductory comments. The University of Michigan English Language Institute is an academic unit within the College of Literature, Science, and the Arts (LSA), an independent credit-granting program since 1986. The EAP program is designed for advanced-level university-enrolled nonnative speakers of English (NNSs); students enroll for EAP courses along with classes in their degree program. The Michigan EAP student clientele is at the upper end of the continuum in higher education given that over 86% of the international student population of nearly 2,500 on campus is at the graduate and professional degree level, with the majority enrolled in doctoral programs.

While the primary emphasis of the curriculum is on English for (Advanced) Academic Purposes, additional attention to English for CAREER AND PROFESSIONAL Purposes is integrated into course syllabi, as needs arise. Indeed, although the major focus is on the language demands of academia, more and more it has become necessary to incorporate professionally oriented language goals into the curriculum as many ELI students play multiple roles and have special needs.

First and foremost, of course, they are enrolled graduate students working toward master's degrees, doctoral degrees, or professional degrees in programs across the university. Second, a significant number serve as graduate student teaching assistants (GSTAs) and/or research assistants (RAs) in university departments. In fact, in fall 1990, out of nearly 1,800 TAs, 409 (close to 22%) were nonnative speakers. Third, in addition to being students and serving as 'teachers', many are already practicing professionals engaged in preparing field-specific publications and field-specific presentations. Indeed, in a growing number of departments in both LSA and the College of Engineering, demands for both a respectable publications portfolio and oral presentations at conferences, have become virtually a part of the degree requirements. Furthermore, some 'students' are on leave from academic, government, or business positions in their home countries, a not unusual situation in research-oriented American graduate schools. Finally, in addition to the 650–700 regularly enrolled students who register for EAP courses per year, courtesy participation in some of the program's courses, speaking clinic, and writing laboratory is extended to international faculty members, post-doctoral students, and visiting scholars, as scheduling permits.

2.2 Student needs. The challenge since the beginning of program development has been threefold: (a) to identify the needs of this particular segment of the higher education population by administering appropriate competency/diagnostic tests, (b) to design specialized courses to meet these needs, and (c) to undertake relevant research in both areas, research relating to issues of discourse analysis, language use, language learning processes, and effective instructional formats.

Question: What are the needs of this particular group of NNS students? That is, what makes them a specialized population? As the program has developed, one outstanding fact has emerged: MANY OF THESE STUDENTS, WHILE THEY MAY VERY WELL BE ABLE TO 'SURVIVE' LINGUISTICALLY IN THE UNIVERSITY, ARE SERIOUSLY DISADVANTAGED AS FAR AS THEIR CHANCES TO 'SUCCEED' IN THE MILIEU OF SOPHISTICATED LANGUAGE DEMANDS REQUIRED OF FULLY PARTICIPATING MEMBERS OF THEIR ACADEMIC/PROFESSIONAL COMMUNITY, THE FACT THAT THEY HAVE 'PASSED' THE TOEFL WITH SCORES OF 560 OR MORE NOTWITHSTANDING. They are students upon whom greater and greater second language demands are made, but for whom only general-purpose language attention has been provided in many American universities until relatively recently.

Looking at peer institutions across the United States it becomes clear that this is a growing problem, all the more so because at the same time it is well-documented that there is an ever-increasing ascendancy of English as the world's international language of scholarship and research (Swales 1989, 1991). English is today the dominant language in science and technology, medicine, and health care fields, commerce, business and industry, and more. It appears that it will soon be the case, if indeed it is not already largely true, that the student graduating from an English-speaking university with a master's degree or doctorate who does not have a sophisticated field-specific (as well as general-utility) command of both spoken and written English may not be fully prepared to meet the challenges of his or her profession in tomorrow's world.

In point of fact, English-language expertise is becoming a priority academic/professional requirement whether international higher education graduates choose to return to their home countries or whether they choose to stay in the United States—and more and more students are doing just that today, moving into American business and industry and university teaching positions. It is no longer 'enough' to equip international graduate students (or undergraduates for that matter) with general English skills with which to SURVIVE when the need is for a high level of academic and career-specific facility with English, one that will enable them to SUCCEED, both during their campus careers and beyond.

Clearly, there is a pressing need for the development of specialized EAP curricula. Courses need to be pedagogically sound (in scope, sequence, learning tasks, learner outcomes), and linguistically principled with special attention to discourse analysis (forms and functions of written and spoken academic discourse). EAP courses need to be developed to extend, complement, or replace traditional general-purpose ESL classes and existing general university composition and speech-communication courses intended largely for native speakers (NSs).

2.3 Evaluation. In meeting the EAP needs of these L2 learners, the first step must be identification of those students in need and assessment of the nature of their language deficits. At the present time, even though students have achieved a preadmission score of at least 560 on the TOEFL or an equivalent score on the MELAB, the ELI is charged with on-campus reassessment, administering the Academic English Evaluation (AEE) to most newly arrived University of Michigan international students, both graduates and undergraduates. The AEE assesses both linguistic and communicative language competency, and on the basis of the test scores and an oral interview, students are counseled into sequences of courses to meet their needs. Courses are required or optional as indicated by the student's performance levels. It has been surprising to find that 75% of all students who take the AEE appear to have insufficient language skills to handle the rigorous language demands of advanced university work. These findings suggest, PREADMISSION PROFICIENCY SCORES NOTWITHSTANDING, that there are many students entering the university who have language limitations. Some have relatively minor problems, to be sure, but a number have severe limitations, which place them at a disadvantage at the survival level, let alone at the success level.

In ongoing review of the ELI testing program, it has become increasingly clear that a more specialized test for international GRADUATE students is needed. Research and observation over the past several years has shown that the communicative skills expected of the graduate student population differ significantly from expectations for undergraduates (Dobson 1992, Kunnan 1992). At present the ELI Testing Division has begun research and development of the Graduate Test of Academic Skills in English (GTASE). The goal is to develop an instrument that will give ELI faculty, departmental faculty, academic counselors, and admissions personnel useful information on the strengths and weaknesses of students' communicative abilities for academic decision-making.

2.4 Curriculum development. During the past fifty years, as perspectives on language learning and language teaching have changed significantly, the ELI's teaching and research have reflected those changes. This was especially evident as ELI phased out its general-purpose intensive program for nonmatriculated students and turned attention to its new mission of research and development of a range of EAP courses for nonnative speakers enrolled at the

University. From the beginning the goal has been to design courses to help students enhance their language skills in order to become effective, fully participating members of the academic/professional community. From the outset attention was given to taking into account the most recent developments in knowledge of academic discourse per se and applied discourse analysis, learner styles and strategies, and teaching formats, especially task-based instruction.

Over thirty courses and several special programs and services are now in place. (See Appendix A.) The balance of the coursework is contained in four major categories:

- Two courses in integrated communication skills (for conditionally admitted students)
- Ten courses in written communication
- Eleven courses in oral communication
- Six courses for ITA training

Most course offerings are at the 300 level and carry undergraduate (UG) credit; courses at levels 400, 500, and 600 carry graduate (GR) credit. Note that although graduate students get both grades and undergraduate credit for 300-level courses, the UG credit does not count in their grade point average (GPA), as it does for undergraduates.

3 EAP oral communication curriculum: Some principles and practices. The eleven courses that make up the current oral communication portion of the Michigan EAP program have been developed to meet the needs of the largely graduate-level student clientele—needs as perceived by the learners themselves, and by ELI faculty, department faculty, academic counselors, and admissions personnel.

3.1 Language functions. Course content focuses on various functions of English in the academic milieu, both those that are general-academic subgenre areas and those that are field-specific genre areas. The overall purpose of the scope and sequence of the oral communication courses is TO FACILITATE DEVELOPMENT OF A VARIETY OF LEARNER COMPETENCIES IN USING SPOKEN DISCOURSE, BOTH *RECEPTIVELY* AND *PRODUCTIVELY.* Overall, it is also assumed that each separate 'aural/oral' class, even though it is listed under one of four curricular subgroups (i.e. basic courses, listening courses, speaking courses, pronunciation courses) in fact cannot but feature a reciprocal listener/speaker role by the very nature of oral communication. Moreover, work in other portions of the curriculum (i.e. written communication courses, ITA courses, integrated skills curriculum, etc.) also feature listening and speaking in development of class activities and tasks.

3.2 Instruction and practice. In general, the purpose of the course offerings is to provide a variety of instructed speaking and listening experiences.

Courses have two goals, instruction and practice, each with a dual focus.

- Instruction – Featuring a focus on the forms and functions of rhetorical markers and organizational patterns of spoken discourse, and a focus on presentational and/or comprehension techniques and strategies
- Practice opportunities – Featuring tasks that focus on deconstructing texts (Webb 1990) (i.e. analyzing samples of spoken texts for their distinctive features) and tasks that focus on production and comprehension.

3.3 Developmental versus rehabilitative goals. Coursework, while primarily 'developmental' in nature, also includes 'rehabilitative' components as necessary. DEVELOPMENTAL is defined as continuing growth and expansion of spoken L2 skills. Class activities are structured to enable learners to experiment, gain confidence, develop style, to expand, elaborate, enrich their (often impoverished) linguistic repertoire. Students participate in a variety of communicative activities that involve a range of EAP language functions and are linked to the content areas of their graduate studies. Developmental second language instruction can be considered on a par with continuing development of one's first language skills. REHABILITATIVE is defined as implementing measures focused on eliminating distracting error patterns, repairing pronunciation and/or grammatical breakdown (Imber and Parker 1993), and attending to similar needs that will move learners toward the development of LINGUISTIC COMPETENCE. (See Canale and Swain discussion in section 3.5.)

3.4 Discourse functions. Brown and Yule (1983) suggest dividing language functions into two major divisions: language for transactional purposes and language for interactional purposes—areas that correspond to Halliday's categories 'ideational' and 'interpersonal' (Halliday 1970). TRANSACTIONAL DISCOURSE refers to the language used to convey factual or propositional information; the focus is on content and is message-oriented. The primary concern is with 'getting things done in the real world', with a premium on language clarity and precision. Some transactional language uses are instructing, giving directions, explaining, describing, ordering, inquiring, requesting, relating, checking on correctness of details, and verifying understanding. INTERACTIONAL DISCOURSE refers to the language used to express social relationships and personal attitudes; the focus is on person, is listener-oriented. The primary concern is with the establishment and maintenance of cordial social relationships. Vagueness and indirectness are tolerated, as role relationships are negotiated, and there is a premium on establishing speaker/listener solidarity, and turn taking in a conversation. Some features of interactional language use are talking about 'safe' topics (such as weather, the physical setting, etc.), much shifting of topics with a great deal of agreement on them, expressing opinions, maintaining 'face' and respecting 'face', identifying with the concerns of the other person, and, in general, 'being nice' to the other person and a little less careful about detail.

At first it would seem that transactional discourse is the one most important in EAP oral communication in higher education. Indeed, the premium IS on clarity and precision of language use in intellectual language transactions/exchanges, whether the L2 learner is playing the role of 'student' in classroom, laboratory, or office encounters with professors and fellow graduate students, or the role of 'teacher' in teaching assistant or research assistant instructional encounters with undergraduate or graduate students. A closer look, however, quickly reveals that BOTH transactional and interactional discourse functions are essential for the successful use of English for Academic Purposes. Indeed transactional discourse (academic 'business-type talk') and interactional discourse (rapport-building 'small talk') are intricately interwoven in academic contexts involving student–professor and student–student interactions; they mingle and meld so that the lines are not clear ones. The upshot is that it is necessary to include attention to BOTH kinds of discourse functions/forms of expression in EAP oral communication courses.

3.5 Communicative competences. As noted earlier, the purpose of the courses in the oral communication curriculum is to facilitate the development of various L2 learner competencies in the use of both receptive and productive spoken discourse. Overall, the competence framework posed by Canale and Swain (1980) is a useful model in planning different dimensions of oral communication coursework and in measuring outcomes. Following Hymes (1972) in focusing on a conceptualization of communicative competence alongside linguistic competence, Canale and Swain proposed a specific competences model that brings together a number of viewpoints in one linguistically oriented and pedagogically useful framework.

- Linguistic competence—Focus on sentence-level language with attention to form (i.e. the grammar, the phonology, the lexicon of the L2).
- Discourse competence—Focus on discourse above the level of the sentence (i.e. language organization, rhetorical markers, ways of showing relationships in extended oral and written texts).
- Sociolinguistic competence—Focus on manipulating language as appropriate to a specific context (i.e. situation, participants, roles, shared knowledge).
- Strategic competence—Focus on compensating for weaknesses in any of the other three competence areas (i.e. manipulating language as necessary to cope with breakdowns in communication, to repair miscommunication).

Obviously these four competencies do not develop or operate independently, and all are essential for the L2 learner's successful participation in EAP contexts.

4 Course descriptions. The eleven courses in the UM EAP oral communication curriculum can be divided in four groups: basic communication courses, listening courses, speaking courses, pronunciation courses.

4.1 Basic courses. *Language and Communication I and II* (ELI 330 and 331 on the list in the in Appendix A) are intended for low intermediate students and their development of interpersonal communication skills. These courses focus on a pregenre academic discourse level (as well as on general-purpose English) working with development of language skills that are generalizable—applicable to the various specific fields of individual students. Included are two-way interactions, group interaction, student–professor consultations, student–student negotiations.

4.2 Listening courses. *Lecture Comprehension* (ELI 332) and *Interactive Listening and Communication* (ELI 333), are intermediate courses; they feature different goals and different formats. ELI 332 focuses on lecture-listening, critical thinking, and notetaking skills; it includes subject matter comprehension, paralinguistic cues in academic interactions, and cross-cultural differences. ELI 333 stresses interactive communication in the academic context; it includes attention to listening strategies in seminar-style class sessions, communication strategies in presenting topics for group discussion, and interactive strategies in follow-up question-and-comment sessions.

4.3 Speaking courses. Two of the four speaking courses have a pregenre focus. ELI 334, *Speaking in Academic Contexts*, is designed to provide practice for students who have had little previous experience in speaking English and listening to spoken English. It includes attention to academic discussions and organizing and giving oral presentations, with special attention to defining, summarizing, paraphrasing. ELI 434, *Discussion and Oral Argumentation*, focuses on advanced seminar-style presentations that feature oral argumentation, and interactive challenge-and-defense discussions. Instruction includes two areas of study: (1) organizational patterns of spoken language and selection of appropriate discourse markers, (2) effective use of 'communicative pronunciation' (i.e. linguistic, paralinguistic, and extralinguistic features). (See the *Dual Focus Chart* in Appendix B. Linguistic elements are found under the *microfocus* listing; paralinguistic and extralinguistic features are found in the *macrofocus* listing.)

Two advanced-level speaking courses are genre-based. ELI 392, *Interviewing*, and ELI 601, *Speaking in Research Contexts* focus on tasks in field-specific academic and professional contexts and appropriate language forms for specific language functions.

4.4 Pronunciation courses. Each of three pronunciation courses is concerned with 'communicative pronunciation'. Each has a mix of 'rehabilitative' microfocus (i.e. discrete points of pronunciation) toward developing linguistic competence, and 'developmental' macrofocus (i.e. a variety of elements of oral communicability) toward developing discourse, sociolinguistic, and strategic competencies. (See the *Dual Focus Chart* in Appendix B.)

ELI 336, *Pronunciation I,* is a basic course with a systematic review of the discrete elements of English pronunciation—vowel sounds, consonant sounds, and base features of stress, rhythm, and intonation. It is a course for students with serious intelligibility problems, probably at levels one and two on the intelligibility chart. (See the *Speech Intelligibility Index* in Appendix C.) It focuses more on rehabilitative work than on developmental work. Coursework includes three components each week: two class sessions; one small group tutorial with individualized video filming and critiquing; independent self/pair study with self-access audio and video facilities for listening/viewing and recording. ELI 337, *Pronunciation II*, provides more in-class individualization of instruction (with a focus on stress, rhythm, and intonation) and continued small group tutorials and self-access assignments. Developmental work is interwoven with rehabilitative attention in a ratio of perhaps 50-50. ELI 338, *Voice and Articulation*, is an advanced course with a primary focus on developmental instruction and general elements of oral communicability, combined with an individualized focus on rehabilitative intervention, as needed. ELI 338 is for students with less serious, but still distracting, intelligibility/communicability problems and is considered an intermediate/advanced course.

4.5 Speech/pronunciation instructional practice modes. Three practice modes that provide speech/pronunciation practice activities suited to the needs of the students are used in coursework. In REHABILITATIVE work a primary focus is on IMITATIVE SPEECH PRACTICE combined with REHEARSED SPEECH PRACTICE. In DEVELOPMENTAL work, however, most activities focus on EXTEMPORANEOUS SPEECH PRACTICE and REHEARSED SPEECH PRACTICE. The intent of each of these three practice modes is as follows:

- Imitative speech practice—for controlled production of selected sounds or base stress, rhythm, and intonation features.
- Rehearsed speech practice—for stabilization of altered speech patterns through the use of relatively 'fixed' texts (both oral reading scripts and preplanned talks), out-of-class rehearsals, both in-class rehearsals and presentations, and private one-on-one individual work sessions with the teacher.
- Extemporaneous speech practice—for integration of modified speech patterns into naturally occurring creative speech in both partially planned and unplanned talks (monologues), panel discussions, and audience interaction in a question-and-answer format (dialogues).

These practice modes move from DEPENDENT PRACTICE (with a model given), to GUIDED PRACTICE (with self-initiated rehearsed speech), to INDEPENDENT PRACTICE (with the content self-selected and developed by the students and linked to their individual personal academic fields (Morley 1992).

5 Learner problems in spoken discourse. Question: Which students need these oral communication courses in general and the pronunciation courses in particular? What are the 'problems' (e.g. the 'miscommunication' or ineffective communication difficulties) that disadvantage many L2 English speakers? What are the elements of verbal communication that, in the words of Bolinger (1986), does not communicate WHAT the speaker wants WHEN the speaker wants?

In general, four categories of 'problems' can be observed:

- Complete breakdown in communication—Speech patterns result in complete breakdown in communication. Verbal patternings are such that they preclude any functional oral communication; the most serious breakdown is at the microfocus level. (See ratings one and two on the *Speech Intelligibility Index* in Appendix C.)
- Ineffectual performance—Speech patterns result in basically ineffectual performance in either a student role or a teaching assistant role. Speakers are judged to lack credibility, are judged not to inspire confidence in either their knowledge of the content or in their PERSONA; breakdowns are usually a combination of microfocus features and macrofocus features.
- Negative judgments about personal qualities—Speech patterns result in negative judgments made about personality traits and 'foreignerism' stereotyping. Beebe (1978) reports that native speakers describe pronunciation errors as sounding ' ... "comical," "cute," "incompetent," "not serious," "effeminate," or "childish".' When they hear connected speech from a nonnative speaker who has pronunciation problems, they report feeling uncomfortable (even though they can understand what is being said) because they are afraid they will not understand.
- Pejorative stereotyping—Speech patterns result in a problem related to the previous one, negative judgments. That is, nonnative speakers often are assigned to a variety of undesirable socioeconomic categories based on pronunciation. The research of Lambert (1967) in Montreal and Labov (1972) in New York demonstrates that listeners will judge speakers they have never seen or met before as to their personality, intelligence, ethnic group, race, social status—even their height—simply from listening to the way they pronounce a few words.

6 Spoken discourse, meaning, and 'communicative pronunciation'. This section of the paper will examine two areas that are important to EAP research and the continued development of effective oral communication curriculum: (1) linguistic analyses of features of English discourse phonology and (2) current developments in 'communicative pronunciation' instruction in second language.

6.1 Analyzing spoken discourse. Over the last fifty years many linguists have specialized in studying the English system of what has been variously called 'suprasegmentals' or 'prosodics' or 'stress-rhythm-intonation' (among other terminologies), and analyzing how these patterns encode 'meaning' in spoken discourse. Early on, one area of focus has been the search for a 'basic unit of talk' to talk about. And in the literature, both earlier and later, from Pike (1945, 1982) to Bolinger (1964, 1989) there has been a clear convergence on some kind of INTONATION UNIT, although there is no agreement on its shape and its dynamics.

Goldsmith (1982) began a review of *The Structure of Intonational Meaning* by Ladd (1980) with the following neat turn of phrase ' ... intonation is the Golden Triangle of linguistics ... it rests at the spot where syntax, phonology, and semantics uneasily come together ... '. It might be added that intonation is the place where phonology, syntax, semantics, and PRAGMATICS, come together.

In the introduction to *Intonation and Its Parts*, Bolinger (1986) comments, 'That intonation is different from most of the other channels of communication studied by linguists, is indicated by the wide divergence of views on how to go about the study of it,' adding that ' ... in phonology we take our divisions, largely, where we find them: the language itself defines contrasts of voicing that distinguish *tip* from *dip* and *pan* from *ban*—a high level of agreement on these distinctions is attainable—but nothing so ready to hand is found in intonation. More than elsewhere, structure has to be *imposed*.' He comments further that 'We try our best to follow natural fault lines, but they are fluid and the way is easily lost. Fortunately a certain consensus seems to be emerging among linguists that one can look at such simple values as high and low or up and down, and that melodic shapes can be grouped around certain forms associated with the prominent syllable of an utterance, rather generally termed pitch accents.'

Relating conceptualization and intonation, Chafe (1985) introduced a notion of 'one new concept per intonation unit'. He likens his term 'intonational units' to the terms 'information units', Halliday (1967), 'information blocks', Grimes (1975), and 'idea units', Kroll (1977). He ties his delineation of intonation units to two things: the notion of the expression of a single 'focus of consciousness', plus the psychological notion of short-term memory. He employs conceptualizations in marking off intonation units and identifies three distinctions, 'new' information, 'old' information, and 'accessible' information. In addition, he uses the term 'nonconceptual embellishments' to indicate units that provide information on connectivity, on the degree of some property, or on the epistemic background.

These are only a few of the provocative perspectives on intonation that are to be found in the literature on discourse and intonation. In designing EAP oral communication courses that focus on spoken discourse, intonation patternings, and encoding of meaning, it is important to recognize that specialized expertise will be required of both those who design courses and those who teach them. Training programs for second language professionals will need to take responsibility for sophisticated preparation for these tasks. In the meantime, for in-service study, a rich (indeed somewhat overwhelming) resource of linguistic and applied linguistic information on intonation and discourse is available for EAP oral communication curriculum designers to study.

6.2 Current directions in pronunciation instruction. There are some new and potentially fruitful directions in pronunciation teaching theory and pedagogy today and a new sense of excitement about the learning and teaching of pronunciation in the field of L2 instruction. A specific concern that has triggered renewed focus on pronunciation has been the urgent needs of several groups of adult and near-adult learners (Wong 1985, Morley 1988) who are seriously disadvantaged without effective second language oral skills, including intelligible communicative speech patterns.

The excitement has been in the challenging work of expanding the horizons of pronunciation learning and teaching, redefining basic concepts—philosophy, learner goals, instructional objectives, roles of learner and teacher (Morley 1991b)—and constructing communicative approaches featuring creative classroom and self-study instructional activities and procedures.

In retrospect, looking at traditional procedures for teaching pronunciation, it appears that the primary focus was on the competence area that Canale and Swain (1980) designate LINGUISTIC COMPETENCE. In contrast, current directions are moving toward practices that also take into account the areas of DISCOURSE COMPETENCE, SOCIOLINGUISTIC COMPETENCE, and STRATEGIC COMPETENCE. Yule (1990) in a review of three teacher resource books on pronunciation (Kenworthy 1987, Wong 1987, Morley 1987), noted that if the class is called 'pronunciation' class, one may expect to find a focus on 'getting the sounds correct' exercises; however, if a class is called 'Spoken English' class then one may expect to find a focus on 'getting the message across' activities.

Today it appears that classes that COMBINE these two goals are being developed in a number of programs, that is 'Spoken English' class is also partly 'pronunciation' class and 'pronunciation' class is also partly 'Spoken English' class. In the case of the Michigan EAP oral communication curriculum, an attempt is being made to design a program of coursework that encompasses both concepts, and gives attention to all four areas of communicative competence. The terms *rehabilitative* and *microfocus* have been used to describe work with discrete points of pronunciation (i.e. vowel sounds, consonant sounds, and base features of stress, rhythm, and intonation). The terms *developmental* and *macrofocus* have been used to describe work with a variety of elements of oral communicability (i.e. paralinguistic and extralinguistic components, expansion of grammatical and lexical repertoire, and related features that characterize effective oral communication).

A recent state-of-the-art discussion of some of the changes in the pronunciation component of teaching English to speakers of other languages (Morley 1991b) reviewed current directions in shifts in instructional focus over the last several years, including the following emerging trends:

- A focus that views the proper place of pronunciation in the L2 curriculum as an integral part of communication, not as a separate component set aside from the mainstream; in short, a growing trend toward communicative approaches to pronunciation teaching.

- A redirection of priorities within the sound system to a focus on the critical importance of suprasegmentals and how they are used to communicate meaning in spoken discourse, as well as the importance of vowel and consonant sounds (segmentals) and their combinations.
- A focus on an expanded concept of what constitutes the domain of pronunciation, one that incorporates attention to: (a) segmentals, (b) suprasegmentals, (c) voice quality features, articulatory settings, and other paralinguistic areas, and (d) elements of body language used in oral communication (i.e. extralinguistic features).
- A focus on revised expectations in both learner involvement and teacher involvement with an emphasis on the development of learner speech-awareness, self-awareness, and self-monitoring strategies guided by a speech/pronunciation teacher-facilitator.
- A focus on meaningful practice and speech activity experiences suited to the communication styles and needs of learners' real-life contexts.
- A renewed focus on the link between listening comprehension and speech/pronunciation (i.e. 'How you *hear* English is closely connected with how you *speak* English.' Gilbert 1984:3).
- A focus on a range of important sound/spelling relationships and specific instruction in guiding students to use English orthography as a key tool in predicting pronunciation patterns (Dickerson 1989; in press).
- A focus on individualization in the speech/pronunciation class, specifically, a focus on the uniqueness of each ESL learner; each has created his or her own personal pattern of spoken English which is unlike that of anyone else, the product of a variety of influences; instruction needs to guide each learner in his or her unique DEVELOPMENT of effective communication, while at the same time attending to REHABILITATIVE interventions, as necessary.

7 Future directions.

7.1 A focus on 'communicative' approaches and competency goals. It appears that we are on the threshold of some fundamental changes in the ways we go about the teaching of pronunciation—that these will involve looking at both a MICROFOCUS LEVEL and a MACROFOCUS LEVEL; that these will strive to combine goals of DEVELOPMENTAL WORK with goals of REHABILITATIVE WORK (and vice versa); that instructional measures will provide attention to the development of all four competences: LINGUISTIC, DISCOURSE, SOCIOLINGUISTIC, STRATEGIC. It appears that new directions are and will continue to be 'communicative' approaches of the kind that Celce-Murcia (1983, 1987) and others have advocated for some time—that notions such as 'discourse pronunciation' and 'intonation approach to teaching pronunciation', and 'communicative pronunciation' will be explored and clarified.

7.2 A focus on the centrality of intonation and discourse context. Continuing development of Michigan EAP oral communication courses will emphasize 'Pronunciation' with a capital 'P'; will give attention to learners' development of linguistic, discourse, sociolinguistic, and strategic competences in spoken English; will feature instructional goals that integrate linguistic, paralinguistic, and extralinguistic features of spoken discourse toward learners' communicative competencies.

Past experiences bear out a point of view expressed in *Discourse Intonation and Language Teaching* (Brazil et al. 1980), that is, it is doubtful that above some rehabilitative motivation, THERE IS LITTLE MERIT IN MASSIVE DRILLING THROUGH STRESS AND/OR INTONATION EXERCISES WHICH ARE AT SENTENCE LEVEL AND DECONTEXTUALIZED. Candlin (1980:xi) notes that: 'In essence the argument hinges on the inseparability of the meaning of intonation from discoursal context. It would therefore support those materials within a genuinely communicative curriculum which resists a view of language learning as the serial accumulation of sets of formal and functional items, particularly when the forms and the functions are implausibly linked together out of context'. Candlin also comments that the emphasis needs to be '... placed on the use of intonational signals to indicate such discoursally significant information as awareness by speaker of common ground, speakers' choice of presenting information as known or unknown to the hearer, speaker's assessment of the relative information load carried by particular elements in the utterance, role-relationships between speaker and hearer, degrees of solidarity and apartness and so on.'

8 Final comments. In reflecting on the issues involved in a consideration of SPOKEN DISCOURSE, MEANING, and 'COMMUNICATIVE PRONUNCIATION', it becomes clear that future directions in attention to the pronunciation component of communicative competence are challenging ones, with promising territories to be explored.

REFERENCES

Beebe, Leslie. 1978. Teaching pronunciation: Why we should be. IDIOM. 9.119–22.

Bolinger, Dwight. 1964. Around the edge of language: Intonation. Harvard Educational Review. 34.282–93.

Bolinger, Dwight. 1986. Intonation and its parts. Stanford: Stanford University Press.

Bolinger, Dwight. 1989. Intonation and its uses: Melody in grammar and discourse. Stanford: Stanford University Press.

Brazil, David, Malcolm Coulthard, and Catherine Johns. 1980. Discourse intonation and language teaching. London: Longman.

Brown, Gillian, and George Yule. 1983. Discourse analysis. Cambridge: Cambridge.

Canale, Michael, and Merrill Swain. 1980. Theoretical bases of communicative approaches to second language teaching and testing. Applied Linguistics 1.1–47.

Candlin, Christopher. 1980. Preface. Discourse intonation and language teaching, ed. by Brazil et al., ix–xi. London: Longman.

Celce-Murcia, Marianne. 1983. Activities for teaching pronunciation communicatively. CATESOL News. 10–11.

Celce-Murcia, Marianne. 1987. Teaching pronunciation as communication. Current perspectives on pronunciation, ed. by Joan Morley, 1–12. Washington, DC: TESOL.

Chafe, Wallace. 1985. How we know things about language: A plea for Catholicism. Georgetown University Round Table on Languages and Linguistics 1985, ed. by Deborah Tannen and James E. Alatis, 214-25. Washington DC: Georgetown University Press.

Dickerson, Wayne. 1989. Stress in the speech stream: The rhythm of spoken English. Urbana and Chicago: University of Illinois Press.

Dickerson, Wayne. In press. Empowering learners with predictive tools. Perspectives on pronunciation learning and teaching, ed. by Joan Morley.

Dobson, Barbara. 1992. Works in progress: GTASE. English language institute testing newsletter. Spring 1992. 2.

Gilbert, Judy. 1984. Clear speech. New York: Cambridge University Press.

Goldsmith, John. 1982. Review of D.R. Ladd, Jr., The structure of intonational meaning: Evidence from English. Language 58, 2.422–24.

Grimes, John. 1975. The thread of discourse. The Hague: Mouton.

Halliday, M.A.K. 1967. Notes on transitivity and theme. Journal of Linguistics 3.177–274.

Halliday, M.A.K. 1970. Language structure and language function. New horizons in linguistics, ed. by John Lyons, 140–65. Harmondsworth, UK: Penguin.

Hymes, Dell. 1972. On communicative competence. Sociolinguistics, ed. by J. Pride and A. Holmes, 269–93. Harmondsworth, UK: Penguin.

Imber, Brenda, and Maria Parker. 1993. Integrated lessons: Pronunciation and grammar. Ann Arbor: University of Michigan Press.

Kenworthy, Joanne. 1987. Teaching English pronunciation. Harlow: Longman.

Kroll, Barbara. 1977. Combining ideas in written and spoken English: A look at subordination and coordination. Discourse across time and space, ed. by E. O. Kennan and T. L. Bennett, 69–108. Southern California occasional papers in linguistics. 5.

Kunnan, Anthony. 1992. New test for graduate students. MITESOL messages 18, 2.8.

Labov, William. 1972. Sociolinguistic patterns. Philadelphia: University of Pennsylvania Press.

Ladd, D. Robert. 1980. The structure of intonational meaning: Evidence from English. Bloomington: Indiana University Press.

Lambert, Wallace. 1967. A social psychology of bilingualism. Journal of social issues. 23, 2.91–109.

Morley, Joan. 1987. Current perspectives on pronunciation: Practices anchored in theory. Washington, DC: TESOL.

Morley, Joan. 1988. How many language do you speak? Perspectives on pronunciation-speech-communication in EFL/ESL. Nagoya Gakuin University Roundtable on Linguistics and Literature Journal 19.1–35. Nagoya, Japan: Nagoya Gakuin University Press.

Morley, Joan. 1991a. Perspectives on English for academic purposes. Georgetown University Round Table on Languages and Linguistics, 1991. ed. by James E. Alatis, 143–66. Washington, DC: Georgetown University Press.

Morley, Joan. 1991b. The pronunciation component in teaching English to speakers of other languages. TESOL Quarterly 5, 3.481–520.

Morley, Joan. 1992. Intensive consonant pronunciation practice. Ann Arbor: University of Michigan Press.

Morley, Joan. In press. Perspectives on pronunciation learning and teaching.

Pike, Kenneth. 1945. The intonation of American English. Ann Arbor: University of Michigan Press.

Pike, Kenneth. 1982. Linguistic concepts: An introduction to tagmemics. Lincoln: University of Nebraska Press.

Swales, John. 1989. English as the international language of research. American lectures: New listening materials, ed. by Joan Morley, 68–73. Fudan, PRC: University of Fudan Press.

Swales, John. 1991. International graduate students in anglophone research worlds. Rackham reports. 1990–1991 Issue.72–88.

Webb, Carolyn. 1990. Academic language development for tertiary-level students. Network. 26.1–5.

Wong, Rita. 1985. Does pronunciation teaching have a place in the communicative classroom? Georgetown University Round Table on Languages and Linguistics 1985, ed. by Deborah Tannen and James E. Alatis, 226–36. Washington, DC: Georgetown University Press.

Wong, Rita. 1987. Teaching pronunciation: Focus on English rhythm and intonation. Englewood Cliffs, NJ: Prentice-Hall.

Yule, George. 1990. Review of J. Kenworthy, Teaching English pronunciation; J. Morley, Current perspectives on pronunciation: Practices anchored in theory; R. Wong, Teaching pronunciation: English rhythm and stress. System 18.107–11.

Appendix A. EAP courses* and special programs for international students: English Language Institute, The University of Michigan.

110 Integrated Academic Skills.

Written communication:

300 Writing and grammar in academic contexts.
310 Reading and vocabulary.
312 Grammar I.
313 Academic grammar II.
320 Academic writing I.
321 Academic writing II.
322 Term paper writing.
410 (1) Critical reading and writing. (**GR/UG)
520 (2) Research papers and thesis writing. (**GR)
600 (2) Dissertation prospectus and dissertation writing. (**GR)

Special spring courses:

342 Oral academic skills.
343 Written academic skills.
344 Pronunciation skills.

ITA courses:

380 Introduction to ITA work.
381 ITA presenting skills.
383 ITA interacting skills.
392 ITA interactions with undergraduates.
584 (1) ITA seminar and practicum. (**GR)
993 (1) College teaching in the U.S.: Pedagogy, culture, and language. (**GR)

112 Integrated Academic Skills.

Oral communication:

330 Language and communication I.
331 Language and communication II.
332 Lecture comprehension.
333 Interactive-listening and communication.
334 Academic speaking.
336 Pronunciation I.
337 Pronunciation II.
338 Voice and articulation.
392 Interviewing.
434 (1) Discussion and oral argumentation. (**GR/UG)
601 (2) Speaking in research contexts. (**GR)

Business courses:

393 MBA writing for nonnative speakers.
394 Oral communication in business for nonnative speakers.

Tutorial services:

Speaking clinic.
Writing laboratory.

Advanced intensive summer program:

English for business and management studies (6½ weeks)
English for academic purposes (6½ weeks).

* These one-credit and two-credit courses are open to graduate and undergraduate students who are enrolled at the University of Michigan.

** GR = Graduate credit; UG = Undergraduate credit.

Appendix B. Dual focus: Speech production and speech performance in spoken English.

Speech Production [A focus on specific elements of pronunciation[2]] PRONUNCIATION: 'MICRO FOCUS'	**Speech Performance** [A focus on general elements of oral communicability[3]] ORAL COMMUNICATION: 'MACRO FOCUS'
Clarity and precision in articulation of consonant and vowel sounds	Overall clarity of contextualized speech; both sounds and suprasegmentals
Consonant combinations both within and across word boundaries; elisions, assimilations, etc.	Effective use of vocal qualities, rate, and rhythm for discourse-level communication
Neutral vowel use; reductions, contractions, etc.	Overall fluency and ongoing planning and structuring of speech as it proceeds
Syllable structure and linking words across word boundaries; phrase groups and pause points	General speech intelligibility level
Sentence-level features of stress, rhythm, and intonation	General communicative command and control of grammar
Features of rate, volume, and vocal qualities	General communicative command of vocabulary words/phrases
	Overall use of appropriate and expressive nonverbal behaviors

[2] A focus on DISCRETE POINT FEATURES: vowels, consonants, and base features of stress, rhythm, and intonation.
[3] A focus on GLOBAL PATTERNS of 'communicability' in spoken English.

Appendix C. Speech intelligibility index: Evaluation of student communicability.

LEVEL	DESCRIPTION	IMPACT ON COMMUNICATION
1	Speech is basically unintelligible; only an occasional word/phrase can be recognized.	Accent preludes functional oral communication.
2	Speech is largely unintelligible; great listener effort is required; constant repetitions and verifications are required.	Accent causes severe interference with oral communication.

Communicative Threshold A

3	Speech is reasonably intelligible, but significant listener effort is required due to speaker's pronunciation/ grammatical errors which impede communication and cause listener distraction; ongoing need for repetitions and verifications.	Accent causes frequent interference with communication through the combined effect of the individual features of mispronunciation and the global impact of the variant speech pattern.
4	Speech is largely intelligible; while sound and prosodic variances from NS norm are obvious, listeners can understand if they concentrate on the message.	Accent causes interference primarily at the distraction level; listener's attention is often diverted away from the content to focus instead on the novelty of the speech pattern.

Communicative Threshold B

5	Speech is fully intelligible; occasional sound and prosodic variances from NS norm are present but not seriously distracting to listener.	Accent causes little interference; speech is fully functional for effective communication.
6	Speech is 'near-native'; only minimal features of divergence from NS can be detected; near-native sound and prosodic patterning.	Accent is virtually nonexistent.

Notes on speech evaluation

1. Elicit a speech sample of several minutes. The sample should be sustained impromptu speech, not just answers to simple questions or rehearsed biographical comments. The sample should be spontaneous speech on a topic such as: (a) what the student wants to be doing in five years; (b) what makes the student's life interesting; (c) what makes a happy family.
2. Try to listen to the speech sample as if you were an untrained language listener. Err on the conservative side with consideration of the 'lay' listeners whom the student will meet.
3. In a few descriptor phrases, summarize the student's strengths and weaknesses in three areas: (a) use of vowel and consonant sound segments, their combinations, reductions, contractions, elisions, assimilations, etc.; (b) use of features of stress, rhythm, and intonation, and vocal quality features of rate, volume, etc.; (c) features of general 'communicability'. (Use Appendix B as a reference.) Comment on how each of these factors impacts communicative intelligibility, and assign a level number as Speech Intelligibility Level (SIL), using [+] and [-] notations as necessary. Monitor student progress through periodic SIL reevaluation.

Teaching language and culture: A view from the schools

Myriam Met
Montgomery County (Maryland) Public Schools

In the day-to-day life of schools, curriculum developers and teachers continually make decisions about curriculum, instruction, and assessment. These decisions determine what students will learn, how they will learn it, when they will learn it, and how teachers will know what students have learned. For foreign language practitioners in the schools, nowhere are these decisions more difficult than in the area of culturally appropriate communication. We practitioners must determine what we should teach students about the social meanings and uses of language, which strategies and approaches are most likely to enable students to use language in culturally appropriate ways, and how we will know whether students are able to perform effectively.[1]

Proficiency, culture, and language teaching. In the last decades communicative language teaching and the proficiency movement have delineated a more salient and significant role for culture, a role which encompasses and surpasses its previous function. For most veteran teachers, trained in the 1960s and '70s, culture had been the 'fifth' skill (after listening, speaking, reading, and writing). Culture in the curriculum was primarily focused on elements of the civilization of the target language—elements such as history, geography, aesthetic expression in literature and the arts, or surface elements such as the three F's (food, festivals, and famous people). The rise of communicative approaches, including the proficiency movement, has brought a broader view of culture, one in which culture provides the 'playing field' for language rather than serving as an appendage to language.

In the trisection of function, content/context, and accuracy, accuracy is defined more broadly than the traditional grammatical accuracy. Rather, accuracy encompasses appropriateness of language use (Galloway 1987). Thus, just as students' effectiveness as communicators improves with the grammatical

---

[1] My thanks to Heidi Byrnes for her valuable insights and advice regarding the content of this paper. Responsibility for opinions expressed and/or errors made in the paper is, of course, mine.

precision of their messages, so too does it improve to the extent to which students use language in ways which are culturally appropriate and the extent to which students understand the social meanings of language. If students are to successfully interpret, express, and negotiate meaning, they must understand the cultural context within which communication takes place. In this view, language use involves 'the negotiation of subjective meanings' (Kramsch 1988:67). This means more than simply knowing when to use *tú* or *usted*; it means that students must know what you may say to whom, when, and how. It also means that students must understand that even when there may appear to be a one-to-one correspondence between words in their native and target languages, there may not be a similar correspondence between the cultural referents for these words. Thus, students should understand that when a French person says 'On my way home I'm going to stop and buy a loaf of bread' the real-life experiences associated with that statement (how one will get home, the kind of shop the purchase is made in, the kind of bread one buys) may be very different from those in suburban United States. (See Galloway (1992) for further examples in an excellent discussion of how the meanings of such terms as *family*, *work*, and *leisure time* may have similar or decidedly different cultural meanings in the United States and elsewhere.)

While the emphasis on communicative goals has done much to heighten awareness of the role that cultural appropriateness plays in communication, there has not been a corresponding breadth of development in identifying just what students need to learn, how, and when in order to enhance the cultural aspect of language use; nor has there been significant progress in identifying how it can be assessed. Kramsch (1989:10) has argued that we need to develop

> an intercultural approach to the teaching of linguaculture at all levels and in all aspects of the curriculum. This approach takes discourse as the integrating moment where culture is viewed, not merely as behaviors to be acquired or facts to be learned, but as a world view to be discovered in the language itself and in the interaction of interlocutors that use that language.

In the absence of such a clearly defined approach, the intercultural component of language teaching in the schools has changed little from the 1970s. Instructional practices are marked by eclecticism or, frequently, an absence of attention to the cultural dimension of language development.

In schools, curriculum defines what students should learn (the content of the curriculum), describes instructional methods (how the content should be taught), and suggests how learning should be assessed. The foreign language curriculum addresses these questions as they relate to language and culture. But whether at the district level or in the classroom, foreign language curriculum decision-makers are confronted with serious challenges when addressing these questions. The professional literature suggests that effective teaching rests on the ability to make good instructional decisions (Berliner 1981, Costa and Garmston 1985, Jackson 1968). Good decisions depend upon repertoire and the knowledge to select appropriately from within one's repertoire. Repertoire is the array of research-based and theoretically sound instructional strategies available to teachers to help students achieve instructional objectives. Selecting appropriately requires knowing how these strategies differentially interact with variables (such as learner characteristics) in the instructional setting. Significantly, at a time when effective teaching is increasingly defined as the ability to make good instructional decisions, foreign language teachers are challenged to make these decisions in an area where they feel least secure about their repertoire, knowledge base, and skills. In the following sections of this paper, I will examine the factors that affect and constrain instructional decisions and suggest an agenda for future work in this area.

The challenge of instructional decision-making

What should students learn about culturally appropriate communication? The proficiency guidelines have highlighted an important role for accuracy—both grammatical accuracy and cultural authenticity—in communication. (Allen 1985, ACTFL 1982, ACTFL 1986) However, while recent work on defining and developing proficiency has provided useful insights for informed decision-making related to grammatical accuracy, analogous insights related to cultural accuracy are less abundant. Although the proficiency guidelines help describe the role of linguistic accuracy of various stages of development, little of similar usefulness is available to describe cultural appropriateness.

There is a growing body of information from researchers in sociolinguistics and intercultural communication, fields which have rapidly expanded in recent decades. Most teachers, and teacher trainers, completed their professional preparation before much of this body of research findings was available. Thus, although there is more known today than ever before about how cross-cultural knowledge contributes to effective communication, it is questionable whether much of this information has found its way into the classroom. Further, even where the information is widely known, defining what students should learn remains a most perplexing decision.

There are several reasons for this. One is that although the field of linguistics provides ever increasing insights into sociocultural aspects of language use, it remains to be determined how this information can be best utilized in designing curriculum. Because the knowledge bases related to intercultural communication and effective foreign language pedagogy have developed separately (Damen 1987) foreign language educators have yet to define the criteria which govern decisions about what is essential for students to know. Certainly, not all of what is known can or should be taught in foreign language classrooms, particularly at novice or intermediate levels of instruction, so deciding WHAT to teach students is critical in instructional decision-making.

Crawford-Lange and Lange (1984:148) have addressed this question by proposing an interesting model in which culture is ' ... the driver of the curricular program.' In contrast, only two of the ten goals proposed by Lafayette

(1988) for the teaching of culture in foreign language classrooms even tangentially link language with culture. Even the examples provided of curriculum objectives and activities for the teaching of culture lack a focus on appropriate intercultural communication. Moorjani and Field (1988) provide seven useful criteria necessary for students' successful intercultural communication, but they provide only a single example of how these might find expression in classroom instruction.

We have yet to identify what rules of intercultural communication should be taught or what topics should be covered (Kramsch 1988). Perhaps the primary criterion should be the extent to which a given aspect of cultural performance enhances or impedes communication. The effects on native speakers of learners' cultural appropriateness need to be more carefully described, just as the effects of specific grammatical errors on communication have been analyzed. Studies in the 1970s addressed the question of the effect of students' grammatical errors on communicative effectiveness, examining which errors interfere most or least with effective communication, including acceptance by native speakers (Hendrickson 1978, Hanzeli 1975, Burt 1971, Burt and Kiparsky 1972). It has been suggested that where student lack of skill in morphology or syntax do little to impede communication, instruction in such skills might better be postponed, receiving attention later in the instruction cycle. Conversely, those which affect communication the most would be taught early. In comparison, analogous research in the area of cross-cultural appropriateness is far more limited. Determining which cultural elements most frequently enhance or impede communication might better inform curriculum decisions about what students should learn and when.

Another difficulty in making decisions about what to select from the growing body of information on native speakers' reactions is that much of this information changes almost as rapidly as modern societies themselves change. For example, while many were comfortable with traditionally clear definitions of who might be addressed using the formal or informal forms, today such clear definitions are blurred not only by long-standing diversity in actual usage by native speakers but also by accelerating change at most levels of society. Every foreign language educator who has been in recent contact with native speakers can provide evidence of how these distinctions have become much less rigidly defined in the last decade. Similarly, lexical choice, and often, related notions of high and low status language use, are changing rapidly. What was proper yesterday may today be old-fashioned or have changed meaning.

Decisions about WHAT students need to learn to be effective intercultural communicators are also affected by trends common across curriculum areas and within the foreign language field. These trends may both enhance and constrain the effectiveness of foreign language instruction. For example, cooperative learning has been shown to increase student achievement in many subjects, including foreign languages. It places great importance on explicitly teaching students social skills. Students in cooperative settings learn the language needed to paraphrase (to indicate that one has listened to others), to praise the contributions of others in achieving group goals, and to analyze the effectiveness with which the group has functioned. While such verbal interactions legitimately further the goals of cooperative learning, it is unclear whether these interactions would be culturally authentic or appropriate were students to interact with native-speaking peers. Since the limited research on cooperative learning in foreign language settings has yet to address this question (see, for example, Long and Porter 1985 or Nerenz and Knop 1982), teachers making classroom-level decisions about how cooperative learning should be implemented in foreign language classrooms have little support or guidance. Thus, while instructional decisions are supported by one body of research (that which supports the role of pair and group work in the development of language proficiency) it is entirely possible that these same decisions may undermine the attainment of other instructional goals.

Decisions about WHAT students should learn interact with the selection of tasks to prepare students for authentic language use. What should students be taught about authentic language use, particularly younger learners or students of languages with complex rules of social interaction, such as Japanese? Makino (1988) has described how even the simple function of expressing thanks in Japanese is governed by complex rules of social interaction and by cultural values. While she advocates integrating the social dimensions of language use with early language instruction for postsecondary learners, what should be taught to precollegiate students may be less obvious. For example, should children and early adolescents be taught the forms of address appropriate to peers or to adults? If classroom activities involve extensive use of pair and group work, authentic language use would imply that students would employ appropriate language for peers. If students are to be prepared for real-world language use, they will most likely encounter adults. But classroom tasks which simulate child–adult interactions are unlikely to be meaningful, purposeful, or authentic.

WHAT students should learn may be determined by the circumstances in which learners will be expected to function in the language and the extent to which culturally appropriate language performance is required. It has long been suggested that one can't learn another language without learning about the culture of those who speak it. Yet, immersion students have highly developed communicative abilities but frequently have minimal understanding of the cultural aspects of interpersonal communication. For other, older students whose ultimate accomplishment may be to be a polite tourist, the depth of cultural understanding needed may be far less than the lofty goals of foreign language education have long implied. These examples may suggest that cultural appropriateness may not play a major role in communicative effectiveness in some circumstances. In other circumstances, such as living or working in a culturally authentic setting, such appropriateness will be essential to establishing and maintaining effective interpersonal relationships. When deciding what to teach, however, teachers have no way to foresee which of their students will use their foreign language skills, and for which purposes.

It is clear, then, from the above discussion, that in instructional decision-making, 'it is difficult to say what counts and what does not count, to determine what should be included and what should not be included' (Patrikis 1988:22).

How should cultural proficiency be taught? For many foreign language teachers, deciding how to teach the relationship between language and culture is almost as perplexing as knowing what to teach. 'Most language teachers ... acknowledge that language and culture are interrelated [but] there is a general dearth of appropriate techniques to teach language-culture, except through often trivial activities.' (Fantini 1991:115)

Across disciplines, one major trend impacting how curriculum is delivered is constructivism. Constructivism

> is a theory of learning which emphasizes the importance of the learner's active construction of knowledge and the interplay between new knowledge and the learner's prior knowledge ... The key tenet of constuctivist theory ... is that people learn by actively constructing knowledge, weighing new information against their previous understanding, thinking about and working through discrepancies ... and coming to a new understanding. (O'Neil 1992:4)

Constructivism underlies major curriculum reforms in reading/language arts, mathematics, and science. It has clear implications for foreign language instruction.

The transmission model of teaching and learning, characterized by the lecture method or reading about culture, is antithetical to constructivist theory and to the ways in which learners best acquire new skills and concepts. Moreover, it does little to prepare students to handle problems of intercultural communication when they arise. Alternative approaches consistent with constructivist theory are needed to form the foundation of instructional practices related to the teaching of culture. Students need to experience culture; they need to extrapolate from and build upon those experiences to develop an internalized representation of how one interacts linguistically in the target culture.

Constructivist notions already characterize some constructs in the foreign language of literature. Crawford-Lange and Lange's model (1984) presents a process for integrating the teaching of language with culture in eight stages, which, if properly implemented, could be consistent with constructivist theory. Pesola (1991) strongly advocates cultural experiences (both real and simulated) as a means of allowing students to develop cultural perspectives beyond their own (see Curtain and Pesola (1988) for a description of some of these classroom experiences). The notion of interlanguage (the manifestation of the learner's evolving internalization of how the language works) is also consistent with constructivist theory. Kramsch (1988:65) has termed a similar construct INTERCULTURE. This construct for describing, defining, developing, and advancing the learner's internalization of how the target language works socioculturally must also undergird teachers' instructional decisions. As

Galloway (1992:95) reminds us, 'Cultural proficiency, like language proficiency, is a long-term developmental process. Just as legitimate and necessary as learners' individualized stages of interim grammars are their formations of interim cultures'.

Teachers need a repertoire which will enable students to perform their cross-cultural proficiency. The proficiency guidelines provide a performance-based model of learner development: proficiency is defined as what students can DO with language, rather than what they KNOW ABOUT it. Thus, culturally effective communication is also performance-based, and the goal of instruction is to produce students who can interact effectively in encounters with native speakers in culturally authentic and appropriate ways. Yet, much of what is done in culture instruction develops knowledge about culture rather than ability to use that knowledge. If effective teachers (i.e. those who make sound instructional decisions) are those who select from their repertoire those approaches and strategies which enable students to achieve instructional goals, then teachers concerned with how to develop students' intercultural communication skills must have a repertoire of strategies for achieving those student skills. And teachers must know which of those strategies are most appropriate to given cross-cultural language outcomes, learner characteristics, and instructional situations. However, it is not easy to identify which tasks are most likely to result in students' ability to perform.

Textbooks provide little guidance in this area. This is of particular concern because, as Kramsch (1988) observes, for better or for worse, the text is central to most courses in the first years of language instruction. Her review of textbooks reveals that they provide few opportunities for students to synthesize from their native culture and the target culture a new perspective on culture and communication. The extensive instructional materials developed for use in schools pay remarkably little attention to performance of cultural knowledge. Few opportunities are provided for students to put cultural information to use in communication (beyond, of course the obligatory activities in which students discriminate between appropriate use of formal or informal forms of address). Thus, while activities may abound for performance of linguistic knowledge, minimal parallels exist for performance of cultural knowledge. For example, students are rarely engaged in tasks which require them to differentiate levels of politeness or differentiate the social status expressed between two native speakers of the language such as in this example from an ESL text.

Example 1

A: Hey, where are you going with that?
B: Upstairs.
A: I'll take it up. Leave it here.
B: I can't. I have to hand it over personally.
A: You can hand it over personally to me.
B: No good. I was told to go upstairs.

Example 2

A: Excuse me...
B: Yes?
A: I'm sorry, but I can't allow you to go up with that, sir.
B: It's all right, I'm delivering it personally.
A: New regulations, sir. I'm sorry.
B: Look, it is my personal responsibility to hand this over.
A: I understand, sir, but I have to check all incoming parcels.
B: This is not a 'parcel'!

(Maley and Duff 1978:62)

Foreign language texts rarely provide practice in inferring information about the interlocutors based on how they talk to one another (as in the case of the ESL example). As a result, because foreign language students have little practice in interpreting levels of politeness at the comprehension level, they are unlikely to be able to knowingly express such distinctions themselves.

HOW to develop students' intercultural skills may require that teachers choose among a repertoire of classroom communicative tasks which involve competing priorities. Proficiency-oriented classrooms are characterized by communicative tasks which have meaning and purpose for learners. Earlier we observed that decisions about WHAT students should learn interact with the selection of authentic classroom tasks. If authentic tasks are those which students might actually encounter when using the target language, authenticity may mean both authentic to the communicative interests and needs of learners and/or authentic to the target culture. Is it more appropriate that tasks be authentic to the learner or that they be authentic to the target culture? Kramsch (1988) describes the dilemma of choosing between topics likely to be of interest to American students or those topics likely to be discussed by peers in the target culture. Paradoxically, this dilemma may have been reinforced by the proficiency movement. Proficiency activities include personalized language tasks, in which students engage extensively in describing themselves or in expressing personal preferences. These may be highly motivating real-life tasks (i.e. authentic to students) but they may also be culturally inappropriate. While American teenagers and young adults may find themselves and their interests fascinating topics for discussion, young people elsewhere may find such self-reference socially improper; in other societies people are more likely to discuss ideas rather than themselves. Similarly, role-playing a real estate agent is hardly an authentic task for a ninth grader, since 14 year olds will probably not have many opportunities to try to sell their home to anyone. However, a more authentic task, showing your home to a visiting foreign student, may be fraught with cultural danger. Some foreign students in the United States have reported feeling angry when given a tour of an American home (Rhodes, personal communication). These students think Americans are bragging, particularly because homes in the United States are frequently larger and filled with more material possessions than those in other cultures.

As we have seen, the very nature of classroom tasks such as those described above may induce students to develop culturally unacceptable interactive behaviors. Clearly, HOW we prepare students for intercultural communication may be an even greater challenge than WHAT we teach them.

> While knowledge is unstable, the skills and strategies learners develop to process new phenomena can equip them with an enduring system for lifelong learning. How students learn thus assumes a significance equal to or greater than what students learn. (Galloway 1992:97)

When should culturally appropriate communication skills be taught? Decisions about WHEN intercultural communication skills should be taught depend upon the readiness of learners to acquire skills and concepts; they also require that teachers reflect upon the sequence of learning objectives. Each of these is examined below.

At what point are learners most ready to understand aspects of intercultural communication and use this understanding in their linguistic performance? Certainly cognitive maturity plays a role. Piaget (1969) has suggested that the maturing child moves from the stage of Concrete Operations to the stage of Formal Operations, a level of cognitive development in which abstract learning is more readily achieved. Although the majority of the population reaches the stage of Formal Operations in early adolescence, there is some evidence to suggest that even by age 18 a substantial portion of the population still functions more effectively at the level of concrete operations. Obviously, instructional decisions regarding what is taught about culturally appropriate communication, how, and when, will depend upon the maturity of the learner. Future research will need to address the question of which aspects of intercultural communication are cognitively accessible to learners, and it will need to take into account variations in the cognitive maturity of secondary and postsecondary students. Too often, findings from studies at the postsecondary level are extrapolated and applied to secondary schools. Yet real and substantial differences between 12 year olds, 16 year olds, and 20 year olds will affect the generalizablity of research findings.

Teachers and curriculum developers must decide when cultural appropriateness should be a focus of instruction. Phillips (personal communication) has reported that appropriate sociocultural language use begins to appear at the more advanced levels of proficiency. It has yet to be determined whether that is cause or effect: does the ability develop late because it is only taught at advanced levels of instruction or is a given level of linguistic proficiency a prerequisite for sociocultural language performance? Numerous attempts to define and describe a hierarchy of proficiency levels have been made in the last decade (ACTFL 1982, Allen 1985, Nostrand 1991). None of these has as yet received wide acceptance by the profession. Yet, if there are indeed levels of cultural proficiency there are clear implications for curricular scope and sequence. And, if as in linguistic proficiency, development is nonlinear, and curriculum must be recursive, instructional decisions need to be informed by research about how sociocultural language proficiency is developed and refined through a recycling of curriculum objectives and instruction.

Lastly, decisions about scope and sequence relate to time. It is an unfortunate fact that many students in secondary schools study foreign languages for only two years. Given our limited access to students, what should our instructional priorities be? What elements of intercultural communication are essential for students to learn? Confronted with limited time (classes which meet for fifty minutes five times a week), teachers must also decide how instructional time should be allocated. What proportion of available class time should be given to the teaching of culture, as opposed to the development of survival language skills, to skill getting, or to skill using? For teachers committed to content-based instruction, decisions about how culturally appropriate language use can best be integrated, and how time should be allocated to content and/or to culture, can also be difficult. And, given the time to be devoted to the development of cultural proficiency, what is the place of more traditional aspects of culture?

How can we assess students? For all teachers of all subjects at all grade levels, classroom assessment provides important data for instructional decision-making. It provides information to the teacher about the effectiveness of his/her instruction. This information enables teachers to continually improve both instruction and the quality of instructional decisions. Classroom assessment also provides information about learners. It indicates which learners have achieved the instructional objectives, and to what degree. For some learners, assessment reveals areas in need of remediation. In the aggregate, assessment data inform instructional decisions about when it is appropriate to move on to new objectives or units of study and when to continue with current objectives. In sum, assessment is a critical element in the decision loop of planning, delivering, and evaluating instruction.

In the real life of classrooms, foreign language teachers struggle to find out what their students know and how well they can perform. Designing performance-based assessments of students' language proficiency is challenging; designing assessments which also account for students' ability to communicate effectively in cross-cultural settings is even more so. Nationally, performance-based assessment is only now coming into the educational mainstream in all disciplines (Berk 1986, Stiggins 1987). Unfortunately, reliable models for classroom assessment of student foreign language performance do not abound.

The ACTFL Proficiency Guidelines are of limited usefulness. First, the guidelines are not intended for classroom use. The guidelines describe learners in relatively broad ranges of performance, ranges which cannot be spanned through short-term instruction. Indeed the levels of performance bear little relationship with hours or years of instruction in school settings. Thus, while the

ACTFL guidelines may be used to describe the level of proficiency a student has acquired after a substantial period of instruction, they do little to measure the smaller increments of learning which classroom teachers are most likely to assess. Further, while the ACTFL guidelines can provide models of communicative tasks students may be asked to perform, they are far less useful in informing classroom assessment of culturally appropriate communicative skills. In sum, even when teachers have made sound instructional decisions about what to teach, how, and when, they may have difficulty in evaluating how well students have learned.

An agenda for the future. Throughout this paper I have attempted to describe the critical needs of instructional decision-makers. To be effective, teachers need the tools with which to make sound decisions. Among these tools are pedagogical knowledge drawn from theory and research, and instructional materials which provide concrete vehicles for developing student skills.

The need for research. The links between research on intercultural communication and foreign language pedagogy must be strengthened. In Europe, the Durham Project, an international project centered at the University of Durham, England, has undertaken empirical research on the relationship between language and culture in foreign language teaching.[2] One outcome has been an attempt to connect theory and research to curriculum design. The Durham Project has also endeavored to identify and meet the training needs of teachers. We need to build upon such work here.

Promising efforts are underway in the United States as well. The American Association of Teachers of French has undertaken a major project to develop guidelines for the development of cultural competence. These guidelines will address the areas of what students should learn, will provide a hierarchy of competence levels, and will offer practical classroom applications of the levels of competence through 'telling examples.' Additionally, the project will suggest assessments to accompany the cultural competencies. Another project, supported by the National Endowment for the Humanities, is developing a curricular framework for the teaching of culture in grades K–8, tying the objectives and their implementation to the cognitive maturity of students in those grades.[3]

Theory and research are needed to inform pedagogy about what students

---

[2] Four volumes report the work of the Durham Project. All are published by Multilingual Matters (Clevedon, England). The four volumes are:

Cultural Studies in Foreign Language Education (Michael Byram)

Mediating Language and Cultures (Dieter Buttjes and Michael Byram, editors)

Investigating Cultural Studies in Foreign Language Teaching (Michael Byram and Veronica Esarte-Sarries)

Cultural Studies and Language Learning (Michael Byram, Veronica Esarte-Sarries, and Susan Taylor).

[3] For further information, contact the author.

should learn. I have argued that too little of the professional literature and research is accessible to inform day-to-day decisions, and that as a result, intercultural communication is an aspect of the development of student proficiency which gets the least quality attention. While we may have a relatively clear picture of levels of proficiency, that is, what students should know and be able to do with language, the degree of cultural authenticity which students should be expected to develop remains far fuzzier.

If what students should be able to do is unclear, even more so is how we can effectively enable them to do it. Effective instructional decision-making depends upon repertoire and the knowledge needed to select from within one's repertoire the specific strategy most appropriate to a given learning objective and learner. As a profession we need to identify research-based strategies and approaches which develop the cross-cultural communication skills our students need. And, because variables in the instructional setting, in the learner, and in teachers themselves differentially interact with the effectiveness of particular strategies, research also needs to identify the variables which render given strategies most effective. In other words, research needs to inform an expanded instructional repertoire and the appropriate selection of strategies from within that repertoire.

Closely linked with the identification of desired student outcomes and how best to achieve these outcomes is evaluation. Classroom practitioners need to be able to identify the desired behaviors when they see them, and in ways consistent with the constraints of in-class performance. If student learning depends on a continuous cycle of planning, delivering, and assessing instruction, we will have to find ways of finding out what students know and are able to do.

Effecting change through training and resources. Research on effecting change indicates that change is most likely to occur when those who are expected to change share a vision of what is to be, and when they have the skills and resources needed to make change work. The professional literature and the leadership of foreign language education have provided a vision of how students can acquire effective intercultural communication skills. It is a vision shared by many in the schools. But, change will not take place unless teachers are empowered with the skills and resources needed. It is a sad fact that opportunities for professional growth are limited. The average foreign language teacher receives minimal subject-specific inservice training (Wolf and Riordan 1991). When training is available, it usually is focused on redirecting teaching behaviors from traditional grammar-based tasks to more communicative tasks. Far too little of this training incorporates a focus on the cultural dimension of communicative effectiveness. Few teachers are able to attend professional meetings regularly. Burdened by large class sizes and numerous daily preparations, still fewer teachers have the time to even begin to read the overwhelming volume of literature which appears almost monthly.

The foreign language literature reveals that our profession knows more today than ever before about effective teaching. Yet too little of what is known finds its way into classroom practice. Informal surveys of veteran foreign language teachers often reveal that culture is an area where they feel least prepared. Nonnatives are concerned that their knowledge level is neither broad nor deep enough to meet the demands of a sophisticated culture curriculum; worse yet, many teachers fear that inadequate knowledge will result in the teaching of inaccuracies or stereotypes. Even native speakers often express concerns that their knowledge is more implicit than explicit, or is limited to their personal experiences. Native speakers from one area or region may be unfamiliar with, or have differing views of, the culture of the larger society.

Teachers are rightfully concerned. There is an extraordinary amount that they need to know. Some teachers who have graduated from teacher preparation programs have had limited opportunities to acquire cultural knowledge. Other teachers may have had a thorough grounding in these topics, but as veteran teachers, may not have had opportunities to update their knowledge.

> Our new syllabi, curricula, and textbooks have redefined teacher and learner roles. Learner-centered instruction, in the case of culture learning, means roles for teachers that may range from counselor, to participant observer to resident pragmatic anthropologist to mediator to fellow learner. Taken together, these represent the range of skills expected of the modern teacher. (Damen 1987:327)

If foreign language programs in the schools are to successfully develop knowledge of other cultures and intercultural communication skills, teachers will need far more support than is currently available to them. Increasing opportunities for the professional development of classroom teachers must be a professional priority.

Teachers also need quality instructional resources. A cursory review of the most widely used basal textbook programs reveals minimal attention paid to culturally appropriate language use beyond the issue of 'formal' and 'informal' forms of address. This lack of attention may send a strong signal that the cultural dimensions of language use are not of real significance. In this regard, the value of authentic texts cannot be underestimated.

> Efforts to promote cross-cultural understanding must begin by recognition of the role of culture in the use of language for communication. Language as a codifying instrument for the negotiation of meaning is referenced to its cultural context ... The process of constructing another frame of reference will require texts ... that allow learners to engage in their own process of discovery in the other culture, through the language of the culture communicating with its own. Authentic texts, as total communicative events, provide such opportunities. Approached authentically ... such texts afford learners the true-to-life challenges that are inherent in cross-cultural encounters. (Galloway 1992:97–98)

In sum, if we are to improve what students learn, both contrived and authentic instructional materials must allow us to practice what we preach.

Conclusion. The foreign language profession can derive significant value from addressing the concerns raised in this paper. Within our own profession these benefits are obvious: we will be better able to achieve the proficiency goals which have driven professional efforts in the last decade. Yet there is a benefit to foreign language educators which goes well beyond our internal agenda. There is a fortuitous confluence of our own goals for the teaching of culture and the goal of multiculturalism in the broader educational community. Articulated by almost every school and school district, the goal of multicultural education is to help students recognize, accept, and value diversity.

It is a goal toward which we can make a unique contribution. 'Education always implies change, but foreign language education implies social change.' (Kramsch 1988:85) We can help students to recognize and accept linguistic and cultural diversity within the target culture. We can also help students extend this acceptance to the linguistic and cultural diversity which increasingly characterizes the United States. Given the strong emphasis being placed on multicultural education by almost every major school district in America, foreign language educators enjoy a window of opportunity. We can carve out a significant role for foreign language instruction in the achievement of the goals of schooling while advancing the goals we have set for ourselves.

It is time to do both.

REFERENCES

American Council on the Teaching of Foreign Languages. 1982. ACTFL Provisional Proficiency Guidelines. Hastings-on-Hudson, NY: ACTFL.

American Council on the Teaching of Foreign Languages. 1986. Proficiency Guidelines. Hastings-on-Hudson, NY:ACTFL.

Allen, W.W. 1985. Toward cultural proficiency. Proficiency, curriculum, articulation: the ties that bind, ed. by Alice Omaggio, 137–166. Middlebury, VT: Northeast Conference on Teaching Foreign Languages.

Berk, R.A. (ed.) 1986. Performance assessment: Methods and applications. Baltimore: The Johns Hopkins University Press.

Berliner, David. 1981. 'Viewing the Teacher as a Manager of Decisions.' Impact on Instructional Improvement. XVI.17–25 [Summer].

Brown, John Seely, Collins Allan, and Paul Duguid. 1989. Situated cognition and the culture of learning. Educational Researcher 18, 1.32–42.

Burt, Marina K. 1971. Goof Analysis in English as a Second Language. Paper presented at Harvard University. EDRS ED 061 838.

Burt, Marina K., and Carol Kiparsky. 1972. The Gooficon: A Repair Manual for English. Rowley, MA: Newbury House.

Buttjes, Dieter, and Michael Byram. 1990. Mediating Languages and Cultures. Clevedon, England: Multilingual Matters.

Byram, Michael, and Veronica Esarte-Sarries. 1991. Investigating Cultural Studies in Foreign Language Teaching. Clevedon, England: Multilingual Matters.

Byrnes, Heidi. 1991. Reflections on the development of cross-cultural communicative competence in the foreign language classroom. Foreign language acquisition research and the classroom, ed. by B.F. Freed. Lexington, MA: D.C. Heath.

Costa, Art, and R. Garmston. 1985. Supervision for intelligent teaching. Educational Leadership. 42, 5.70–80.

Curtain, Helena, and Carol Ann Pesola. 1988. Languages and children: Making the match. Reading, MA: Addison-Wesley Publishing Co.

Crawford-Lange, L., and Dale L. Lange. 1984. Doing the unthinkable in the second-language classroom: A process for the integration of language and culture. Teaching for Proficiency, the organizing principle, ed. by Theodore V. Higgs, 139–77. Lincolnwood, IL: National Textbook Co.

Damen, Louise. 1987. Culture learning: The fifth dimension in the language classroom. Reading, MA: Addison-Wesley Publishing Co.

Fantini, Alvino E. 1991. Bilingualism: Exploring language and culture. Language, Culture, and Cognition: A Collection of Studies in First and Second Language Acquisition, ed. by Lilliam Malavé and Georges Duquette. Clevedon, England: Multilingual Matters.

Galloway, Vicki. 1992. Toward a cultural reading of authentic texts. Languages for a Multicultural World in Transition, ed. by Heidi Byrnes, 87–121. Middlebury, VT: Northeast Conference on Teaching Foreign Languages.

Galloway, Vicki. 1987. From defining to developing proficiency: A look at the decisions. Defining and Developing Proficiency: Guidelines, Implementations, and Concepts, ed. by Heidi Byrnes and Michael Canale, 25–73. Lincolnwood, IL: National Textbook Company.

Hanzeli, Victor E. 1975. Learner's language: Implications of recent research for foreign language instruction. Modern Language Journal 59.426–32.

Hendrickson, James M. 1978. Error correction in foreign language teaching: Recent theory, research and practice. An Historical Perspective of Learner Errors. Modern Language Journal 62.387–98.

Jackson, Phillip. 1968. Life in classrooms. New York: Holt, Rinehart, and Winston.

Johnson, David W., and Roger T. Johnson. 1989. Cooperation and competition: Theory and research. Edina, MN: Interaction Book Company.

Kramsch, Claire J. 1988. The cultural discourse of foreign language textbooks. Towards a New Integration of Language and Culture, ed. by Alan J. Singerman. Middlebury, VT: Northeast Conference on Teaching Foreign Languages.

Kramsch, Claire J. 1989. New directions in the teaching of language and culture. Washington, DC: National Foreign Language Center.

Lafayette, Robert C. 1988. Integrating the teaching of culture into the foreign language classroom. Towards a New Integration of Language and Culture, ed. by Alan J. Singerman. Middlebury, VT: Northeast Conference on Teaching Foreign Languages.

Long, Michael H., and Patricia A. Porter. 1985. Group work, interlanguage talk,and second language acquisition. TESOL Quarterly 19, 2.207–27.

Makino, Seiichi. 1988. Integrating language and culture through video: A case study from the teaching of Japanese. Towards a New Integration of Language and Culture, ed. by Alan J. Singerman. Middlebury, VT: Northeast Conference on Teaching Foreign Languages.

Maley, Alan, and Alan Duff. 1978. Variations on a theme. Cambridge: Cambridge University Press.

Moorjani, Angela, and Thomas T. Field. 1988. Semiotic and sociolinguistic paths to understanding culture. Towards a New Integration of Language and Culture, ed. by Alan J. Singerman. Middlebury, Vermont: Northeast Conference on Teaching Foreign Languages.

Nerenz, Ann, and Constance Knop. 1982. The effect of group size on students' opportunity to learn in the second language classroom. ESL and the Foreign Language Teacher, ed. by Alan Garfinkel, 47–60. Skokie, IL: National Textbook Company.

Nostrand, Howard. 1991. Basic intercultural education needs breadth and depth: The role of a second culture. Critical Issues in Foreign Language Instruction, ed. by Ellen Silber. New York: Garland Publishing Company.

Nostrand, Howard. 1974. Empathy for a second culture: Motivations and techniques. Responding to new realities, ed. by G.A. Jarvis, 131–159. ACTFL Foreign Language Series (5). Skokie, IL: National Textbook Company.

O'Neil, John. 1992. Wanted: Deep Understanding. ASCD Update 34, 3. Alexandria, VA: Association for Supervision and Curriculum Development.

Patrikis, Peter. 1988. Language and culture at the crossroads. Towards a New Integration of Language and Culture, ed. by Alan J. Singerman. Middlebury, VT: Northeast Conference on Teaching Foreign Languages.

Pesola, Carol Ann. 1991. Culture in the elementary school foreign language classroom. Foreign Language Annals 24, 4.331–46.

Piaget, Jean, and Barbel Inhelder. 1969. The psychology of the child. New York: Basic Books.

Resnick, Lauren B. 1989. Knowing, learning, and instruction: Essays in honor of Robert Glaser. Hillsdale, NJ: Lawrence Erlbaum Associates, Publishers.

Robinson, Gail. 1985. Crosscultural understanding: Processes and approaches for foreign language, English as a second language, and bilingual educators. New York: Pergamon Press.

Robinson, Gail. 1981. Issues in second language and cross-cultural education. Boston: Heinle and Heinle.

Stiggins, R.J. 1987. Design and development of performance assessments. Educational Measurement: Issues and Practice 6, 3.33–42.

Weber, Sandra, and Claudette Tardif. 1991. Culture and meaning in French immersion kindergarten. Language, Culture, and Cognition: A Collection of Studies in First and Second Language Acquisition, ed. by Lilliam Malavé and Georges Duquette. Clevedon, England: Multilingual Matters.

Wolf, W.C. Jr., and Kathleen M. Riordan. 1991. Foreign language teachers: Demographic characteristics, inservice training needs, and attitudes toward teaching. Foreign Language Annals 24, 6.471–78.

Principles and parameters in language and society

Charles A. Ferguson
Stanford University, Professor emeritus

1. Structuralism to transformational grammar (TG). During the period between World War I and World War II, and for a decade or so after World War II, a form of structuralism was the dominant, though by no means the only, approach to linguistics. This approach, for which the Swiss linguist de Saussure is often cited as the founder, made a number of critical assumptions about the nature of human language and the best way to study it. Some of these assumptions were:

- Speech is primary, writing secondary (though different structuralist 'schools' held different attitudes toward the study of written language and especially the language of literature).

- Every language is a unified, structured whole, at any point in time, such that everything in it holds together; a change in any part may have repercussions throughout the language.

- Language consists of arbitrary signs (vocabulary items, grammatical constructions, speech sounds), such that there is no 'natural' connection between the shape of the sounds and the meanings they bear (some linguists emphasizing the view that meaning resides in relationships among signs rather than in the signs themselves).

- Members of a speech community share an abstract system, langue, which is the proper object of linguistic research; actual language in use, parole, is not necessarily systematic and therefore is of interest primarily only as it gives clues to langue.

- Synchronic structure (i.e. structure in place at a given point in time) is primary; diachronic changes (over time) are best understood as successive synchronic stages; innovations spread geographically and socially, and dialect variation may be evidence of changes in process.

Such structuralist assumptions represented a reaction against certain earlier assumptions held, not necessarily all at the same time, by various linguists. Earlier assumptions gave primacy to written language, analyzed patterns atomistically, found essential connections between signs and their senses, did not distinguish between an abstract structure and variable implementation, and gave primacy to diachronic change over synchronic structure as more explanatory.

Looking back at this period it is easy to see some glaring omissions and problems in the consensus of assumptions. One glaring omission was the relative lack of attention paid to characteristics of human language in general, that is, universal aspects of language as opposed to the characteristics of particular languages. Partly this was a reaction against earlier attempts at a 'universal grammar' that was too closely tied to the structure of Classical and modern European languages and could not easily be extended to include the many kinds of linguistic structure found in other languages. Partly, also, it represented a valuable insight that every language or language variety is organized in a way that is uniquely different from all other languages or varieties.

One glaring problem was the failure to integrate the aims, methods, and findings of the study of synchronic structure, dialect variation, and diachronic change. It was not clear how the phenomena of dialect and individual variation could be included in the tight, cohesive structure of a language, and it was not clear how the tight structure of a language could change through time. In spite of the fact that Saussure in his famous posthumous *Cours* and Bloomfield in his highly influential book *Language* deal with all three types of linguistic analysis, their presentations in effect leave synchronic structure, dialectology, and diachrony as separate disciplines. And both men would have agreed that it is impossible in principle to study linguistic change in process.

Another weakness, not obvious from the theoretical assumptions themselves, but clear in practice, was the relatively low priority given to the study of syntax. Linguists placed a heavy emphasis on phonetics and phonology, that is, the ways speech sounds are produced and perceived and the ways they constitute linguistic systems, and on morphology, that is, the way words may have smaller constituent elements and have alternant forms under various conditions. Saussure himself distinguished between associative or paradigmatic relations in language, which are relations between elements that can replace each other, and syntagmatic relations between elements that may combine in sequence. He recognized such relations at the level of sounds, words, and groups of words, but he never arrived clearly at the notion of the sentence as a basic unit of syntax. Bloomfield, on the other hand, treated the sentence as fundamental, in fact as the largest unit of linguistic description. Thus there were different points of view within the structuralist enterprise, sometimes individual and sometimes clustered into 'schools' of linguistics.

One tremendous achievement of this period, although the process began before and continued later, was the accumulation of grammars and dictionaries of different languages. The description of hundreds of languages of Asia, Africa, Oceania, and the Americas extended enormously the data base for linguistic analysis, making possible for the first time not only comparative–historical study and classification of many language 'families' but also the statement of inductive cross-language generalizations and the testing of explicit theories of language.

The dominance of the structuralist consensus was challenged in the late 1950s and early 1960s by a new viewpoint that shared some of the assumptions but disagreed sharply with others. It offered a revision of the aims of linguistic research and initiated a whole new style of doing linguistics. Although some of the new linguistics was foreshadowed by other developments, for example, in the philosophy of science, the 'revolution' that took place was chiefly the work of one man, the American linguist Noam Chomsky. It was his little monograph, *Syntactic Structures* (1957), his teaching at the Massachusetts Institute of Technology, and his public presentations elsewhere on the American scene that spread the new ideas quite rapidly in the United States, and it was his powerful presence at the Ninth International Congress of Linguists, held in Cambridge, Massachusetts, in 1962, that spread his views to Europe and the rest of the world.

Chomsky's position was avowedly rationalist as opposed to the essentially empiricist tradition of most structuralists. He conceived of grammars rather than languages as the focus of linguistics, held that the chief goal of linguistics was to produce a theory of universal grammar with explanatory power rather than simply descriptions of languages. He felt that the linguists' grammar of a particular language should also be regarded as a theory. In opposition to much of American structuralism he was avowedly 'mentalistic' rather than behavioristic and thought that human language results from the exercise of a specific faculty of language, a unique cognitive capacity, almost to be regarded as a special cognitive 'organ'.

Chomsky tacitly accepted the primacy of speech, the structuredness of language, and the primacy of synchrony, but he shifted the abstract system of language from the socially shared LANGUE to the individual speaker's COMPETENCE (vs. actual PERFORMANCE, comparable to PAROLE). He put syntax at the center of grammar. Like many structuralists of the time, he regarded the sentence as the fundamental unit of syntax. One of the striking features of the new form of grammar writing was the assumption of an underlying level of 'deep structure' that was connected with the possible grammatical sentences of the grammar by a series of transformational rules. Chomsky's view of language responded directly to two weaknesses of the structuralist consensus (no universal grammar, poor development of syntax), but, like many structuralists, he left untouched the fundamental problem of how individual competences come to be conventionalized, that is, shared by members of a community. Over the next 25 years, the new transformational–generative model (TG) was repeatedly modified in response to outside challenges and theory-internal problems and took the form of a succession of models, culminating early in the 1980s with the government-binding theory (GB) of principles and parameters (Chomsky 1981a, 1981b), which seems to have won the day and is the dominant model of linguistic theory in the United States and is popular in many parts of the world.

The first purpose of the present paper is to sketch out the nature of the TG break with structuralism (done in the preceding paragraphs) and the nature of the changes from TG to GB (to be done in the following paragraphs). The second purpose of the paper is to investigate the possibility of extending aspects of the GB model to the much larger symbolic system of human culture. Like its core component, human language (read 'grammar' from the Chomskyan perspective), culture can be viewed as a set of individual competences, somehow conventionalized, that is, shared by members of a speech community to some criterial degree, and transmitted from generation to generation but constantly undergoing change.

2. Transformational grammar (TG) to government and binding (GB). To trace the development from the early form of generative grammar (TG) to the present dominant form of generative grammar (GB) is no easy task. However, Newmeyer (1986) provides an insightful and informative history of the development, and Wasow (1985) offers a thoughtful sketch comparing the development of GB with the development of two competing syntactic theories, as a postscript to Sells' lectures comparing the three theories in some detail (Sells 1985). In the brief sketch to be presented here, a few issues are identified for which it is relatively easy to specify the positions taken by the structuralist consensus, early transformational-generative grammar, and the current government-binding model. Although the sketch offered here lacks significant detail and probably misses important issues, I hope it gives the flavor of the changes and some indication of their sources, both external and internal.

Levels. One doctrine of the American brand of structuralism was that each level of the total grammar of a language was independent of all the others, and the various levels constituted a hierarchy from lowest to highest: phonology or 'phonemics', morphophonemics, morphology, syntax; some linguists added a level of 'discourse'. American structuralists felt that in writing a grammar it was not legitimate to draw on information from a higher level than one was describing. Thus, one could not use syntactic information in writing a description of the phonology. This separation of levels was viewed not merely as a 'discovery procedure' but as a fundamental characteristic of the structure of languages, and to accuse a linguist of 'mixing levels' was a serious accusation of misbehavior, a scholarly crime or perhaps a sin against the canons of scientific analysis. American Structuralism: no mixing of levels.

The new TG took the position that the doctrine of separation of levels was misguided, that grammar is a unified total structure in which valid generalizations may cut across traditional levels, and insofar as there is a hierarchy of levels it is the reverse: the syntax is basic and the phonology is derivative, and there is, for example, no line between morphophonemics and phonology, which belong together. 'There remains little motivation for any objection to mixing of levels, and there is no difficulty in avoiding circularity in the definition of interdependent levels' (Chomsky 1957:57). TG: mixing levels is okay.

The GB model assumes the modularity of language in at least two senses. First, language (i.e. grammatical competence) is itself an autonomous module of one's cognitive competence, and in writing a grammar one must acknowledge the interaction between grammar and other modules but not, for example, draw directly on concepts of general (nonlinguistic) cognition. Also, each language/grammar is composed of several autonomous modules, which do not draw on one another's content. These modules are not congruent with the earlier levels: they are not primarily syntax, morphology, etc., although some linguists are still concerned with how legitimate it is to draw, for example, from syntactic knowledge in formulating phonological statements (e.g. Selkirk 1984). GB: mixing levels (modules) is selective and may be important as representing a parameter setting.

Heads. In 1963, Joseph Greenberg published an article on word order that had considerable influence on research in the TG tradition. Although Greenberg (1963) did not share Chomskyan goals and methods, the cross-linguistic generalizations to which it called attention struck many linguists as generalizations worth stating in TG terms, and some felt that his generalizations should somehow 'fall out' from or be explained by TG principles. Greenberg (1963) corrected and elaborated on such earlier typologists as Pater Schmidt (cf. Schmidt 1926). Greenberg's generalizations (often referred to as 'language universals') suggested that (a) grammatical constructions at many levels consist of a 'head' and a modifying or limiting element or 'satellite', and (b) in any given language the satellites tend to be in the same position with regard to their head (i.e. preceding or following). For example, in a language with normal 'basic' word order in simple, declarative, affirmative main clauses of Subject, Object, Verb, adjectives normally precede nouns, relative clauses normally precede their 'antecedents', and postpositions are normal rather than prepositions. American Structuralism: 'heads' and 'modifiers' were widely accepted concepts in constituent analysis, but they were not as pervasive in syntactic analysis as in the Greenberg 'universals', and the cross-linguistic generalizations were not recognized. The new TG made no explicit use of such concepts as 'head' and 'satellite' and did not acknowledge generalizations of the Greenberg type. The GB model has 'head' as a fundamental and central concept, and the Greenberg generalizations are essentially accepted in the important Projection Principle and the whole X-bar module of the grammar.

Case. In 1968 Charles Fillmore published a paper *The case for case* (Fillmore 1968), in which he suggested an alternative version of TG in which the notion of deep structure was recast so that certain sorts of noun phrases could be expressed directly and the structuring of sentences according to which they could be said to be 'subjects' or 'objects' would be taken care of by the transformational apparatus of the grammar (paraphrased from Fillmore 1971: 35–36). Fillmore's proposal was that the propositional core of a simple sentence consists of a predication construction with one or more 'arguments' each related to it in a semantic function called a Case. These deep structure Cases are selected from a small, universal repertoire of case-roles (such as Agent, Experiencer, etc.) and are 'spelled out' in particular ways in any given language. This special deep structure closer to a semantic interpretation proved to be very appealing: many linguists were apparently attracted to it because it resonated with the case morphology and case 'uses' of traditional grammar; others adopted it in one form or another because they found it more satisfying than the alternatives then available such as Generative Semantics, which had no purely syntactic deep structure, or the Extended Standard Theory of Chomsky, which had 'traces', that is, null elements in positions from which elements had been moved or deleted by transformational rules.

The present GB model has incorporated both halves of the Fillmore Case Grammar: each argument has only one thematic role (Θ-role) or Case and vice-versa, and Case is assigned by various devices such as by way of 'agreement' (AGR), an abstract element part of another abstract element 'inflection' (INFL), and also including default assignments. We might offer a simplified summary as follows. American Structuralism: overt morphological cases were recognized along with morpheme alternants and various 'uses', but universal semantic cases were rejected. TG: no cases of any kind. GB: Θ-Theory and Case Theory, which incorporate the basic ideas of Fillmorean Case Grammar, are regarded as more or less independent subsystems or modules in the grammar, although GB has been no more successful than the various Case Grammar models in specifying a principled universal list of cases that would win widespread approval.

Typology. In the period of the structuralist consensus, very few linguists were interested in universal characteristics of human language: they were so much impressed by the enormous structural variation between languages and the fact that a human child born in any speech community grows up acquiring the structure of the ambient language that they neglected almost completely the very considerable commonality in structure shared by all human languages. Insofar as they gave thought to the commonality, they tended to take the empiricist position that any linguistic generalization must be, as Bloomfield put it, an 'inductive generalization' and to look for cross-linguistic generalizations that created 'types' of languages. While typological approaches to linguistic theory construction were not unknown, they gained a new prominence with a series of works including Greenberg (1963), Uspensky (1965), Comrie (1981), Mallinson and Blake (1981), and most recently Croft (1990). TG showed no interest in a typological approach, preferring intensive study of individual languages (grammars) for (dis)confirmation of theory rather than comparisons across languages for ideas contributing to theory. GB has turned strongly in favor of a typological approach. In Newmeyer's (1986:199) words:

What many have found most appealing about GB is that it incorporates a program of comparative syntax, that is, it provides a theoretical foundation for linguistic typology. In the GB view, what appear on the surface to be major structural differences across languages result from each language setting slightly different values ('parameters') for each of the various grammatical subsystems.

Semantics. A widespread view of American structuralists was that semantics was not to be treated as a part of either a general theory of language or the writing of the grammar of a particular language. For structuralists who felt that the primary purpose of language was the communication of meanings, this lack of a treatment of semantics was regrettable, but no serious attempts at an empirically based, 'scientific' theory of meaning were made.

It must be noted that the chief reason given was that it would be too difficult to do, partly because of the Bloomfieldian assumption that any systematic treatment of semantics would require a theoretical understanding not only of the whole universe, since human languages can talk about anything at all, but also of all the concepts that human beings could ever possibly encode in languages, even if they had no counterparts in the real world.

Chomsky continued this exclusion of semantics from linguistic theory, although apparently not for the same kinds of reasons. He had concluded that grammar is 'essentially autonomous and independent of meaning' (Chomsky 1957:17, as cited in Newmeyer 1986:27) and that any assumption that syntax is based somehow on semantics is demonstrably false. He apparently had a view of semantics something like that of the so-called 'ordinary language' philosophers of the time, although he never spelled this out explicitly. Chomsky's exclusion of semantics as such and his confusion about just what a semantic theory might include have persisted to the present time, and although GB posits a 'logical form' (LF) level that serves as the basis for semantic representation, it makes no serious contribution to an understanding of semantic interpretation in general or to the construction of a semantic theory. Other generative models often include some version of 'model-theoretic semantics' in the tradition of the logician Montague (cf. Montague 1974) and find Chomsky's treatment of semantics a defect in GB.

3. Government and binding (GB) to society. Linguists of various periods and various intellectual perspectives have tended to be proud of the theoretical basis of their discipline, generally proud of what they see as its obvious superiority to the theoretical bases of other disciplines, particularly of other social sciences and humanistic studies. They sometimes go so far as to claim that the theoretical insights of other fields are either historically derived from the findings and conclusions of linguistics or would benefit from being related to them in some way. This kind of ethnocentric loyalty to one's own discipline is probably a familiar phenomenon in the sociology of knowledge, but somewhat more unusual is the occasional view from outside linguistics that the research methods or the intellectual organization of linguistics does have a special value and that its claims to superiority have some validity.

In the nineteenth century a number of linguists, for example, noted the similarity between the diachronic regularities of linguistic classification and the diachronic regularities of biological classification and maintained that the discovery of the former preceded the discovery of the latter and that the linguistic principles contributed to the development of the biological ones (cf. Schleicher 1863).

During the period of the structural consensus a number of psychologists (e.g. J. B. Carroll) and anthropologists (e.g. C. Kluckhohn, A. Kroeber, W. LaBarre) expressed their admiration for linguistics and seemed to hope that their respective types of social science could eventually be as successful as linguistics. Occasionally a nonlinguist has attempted to extend linguistic theory beyond language, as when Levi-Strauss extended linguistic structuralism to culture. Sometimes, perhaps less surprisingly, a linguist has done something like this. The most notable is Ken Pike's valiant attempt at *Language in relation to a unified theory of human behavior* (Pike 1954).

These various attempts from inside and outside of linguistics have invariably had profound effects on their proponents and some of their disciples, but they have not, on the whole, been as successful as their proponents felt they should be. To be sure, we have all benefited indirectly from these efforts as well as from the work of comprehensive thinkers such as Halliday and Hymes, whom we have been fortunate to hear in person at this Round Table.

I would like, however, to refer to an almost forgotten effort relating linguistic theory to culture. I have chosen this example not because I think it is in some sense 'correct'—the linguistic theory involved is now totally out of fashion and the cultural theory, while in some respects quite influential, is not recognized as one of the great theoretical options of contemporary anthropology. But the method of attack that was used was—to my mind—an excellent way to go about the construction of a general theory.

In the 1950s, George Trager, a prominent American structuralist linguist of the time, and Ned Hall, an anthropologist of very varied cultural experiences, both keen observers of many aspects of human behavior, were employed at the Foreign Service Institute. They both had certain responsibilities for the training of Americans who were going abroad to bring 'technical assistance' to the so-called 'developing countries', forerunners of the later United States Peace Corps. At an early point in their association Trager and Hall began to spend a lot of time together 'immersed in the whole question of the nature of culture and the relationship of language to culture' (Hall 1992:209).

They started with the conviction that culture was a complex of different symbolic systems that interacted with one another, and that language was one—probably the most basic one—of those systems. Since they were convinced that language was one of the cultural systems, they used several characteristics of language as criteria for identifying other systems. The three criteria they adopted were that the putative system should have a biological basis, should be connected with all other cultural systems, and yet should be recognized as independently learnable. Let us use some of Hall's (1992:213) own words, taken from his step-by-step account of how they proceeded, as recorded in his recent autobiography.

1. There should be no break in the evolutionary chain connecting humans with their mammalian ancestors. For example, all animals, including amoebas, organize space in such a way as to prevent overcrowding.
2. The system should be reflected in ALL other cultural systems. All languages, even though they may not have a word for time, have built-in ways of dealing with time, for example, while all cultural events occur in space as well as time.
3. And, paradoxically, just as another language can be both learned and studied independently of other cultural systems, all such core systems should also be independent.

Trager and Hall met almost every afternoon for about a year and hammered away at their 'culture machine' as people at the Foreign Service Institute jokingly referred to it, and indeed in 1953 a version of their model of human culture as a system of cultural systems was issued by the American Council of Learned Societies.

The existence of GB, the widespread familiarity with its basic features, and in fact some of the very features of the model all suggest to me that a cooperative venture of the Hall–Trager kind might be very productive at this time. After all, if we thought of the whole of human culture (or any single culture) as a total symbolic system and language as a subsystem, we would expect fundamental similarities in any theoretical model. Both are characterized by individual competencies that somehow—we hardly understand how—are conventionalized, that is, shared by members of a speech community (or discourse community) with an extensive variability in form; and both are transmitted somehow—we hardly understand how—from one generation to the next, while at the same time the very shared system is in the process of change.

Now let us note several features of the GB model that would seem to welcome a cooperative venture. First, as already noted, GB assumes grammar as a linguistic system interacting with other cognitive systems. Second, grammar consists of a set of general principles that constrain sentence formation (e.g. under various specified conditions Movement CANNOT take place), and this kind of approach may prove useful in characterizing the other cultural systems. Third, GB proposes a set of parameters which can have various settings that, in effect, typologize grammars and allow—even encourage—empirical exploration of possible parameters, possible settings, and possible interactions among all of them. This strikes me as a fine approach to constructing a model of any cultural system and even an overall system of some kind.

My point of view should not be interpreted as assuming that GB is in some important sense 'correct'. We can be reasonably sure that the successor to GB

25 years from now will be at least as different from GB as GB is from TG and TG was from the model of American structuralism. What I am recommending is that some scholars who have thorough familiarity with GB should work together with some social scientists who have a great interest in language and society to produce some kind of overall model whose insights will well repay their joint efforts. And I would hope that a larger model that resulted from their efforts would not be forgotten as easily and quickly as the Hall–Trager model was.

Of course, there is an important caveat here. It is at least possible that the notion of a set of relatively independent but still somewhat interactive cultural systems is not a useful overall model and some quite different approach might be more productive, such as those represented here by Halliday, Hymes, Fishman, Labov, Pike, and others. The only way to find out is by trying them. At least I would hope that someone will make the effort to build a bridge between the formal theorists of the GB type and the people interested in 'Language, Communication, and Social Meaning'.

REFERENCES

Bloomfield, Leonard. 1933. Language. New York: Holt, Rinehart and Winston.

Chomsky, Noam. 1957. Syntactic structures. The Hague: Mouton.

Chomsky, Noam. 1965. Aspects of the theory of syntax. Cambridge, MA: MIT Press.

Chomsky, Noam. 1981a. Lectures on government and binding. Dordrecht: Foris.

Chomsky, Noam. 1981b. Principles and parameters in syntactic theory. Explanations in linguistics, ed. by N. Hornstein and David Lightfoot. London: Longman.

Comrie, Bernard. 1981. Language universals and linguistic typology. Chicago: University of Chicago Press.

Croft, William. 1990. Typology and universals. Cambridge: Cambridge University Press.

Fillmore, Charles J. 1968. The case for case. Universals in linguistic theory, ed. by E. Bach and Robert T. Harms, 1–88. New York: Holt, Rinehart and Winston.

Fillmore, Charles J. 1971. Some problems for case grammar. Georgetown University Round Table on Languages and Linguistics 1971, ed. by Richard J. O'Brien, S.J., 35–56. Washington, DC: Georgetown University Press.

Greenberg, Joseph H. 1963. Some universals of grammar with particular reference to the order of meaningful elements. Universals of language, ed. by Joseph H. Greenberg, 58–90. Cambridge, MA: MIT Press.

Hall, Edward T. 1992. An anthropology of everyday life: An autobiography. New York: Doubleday.

Hall, Edward T., and George L. Trager. 1953. The analysis of culture. Washington, DC: American Council of Learned Societies.

Mallinson, Graham, and Barry Blake. 1981. Language typology. Amsterdam: North–Holland.

Montague, Richard. 1974. Formal philosophy: Selected papers of Richard Montague, ed. by R. Thomason. New Haven: Yale University Press.

Newmeyer, Frederick. 1986. Linguistic theory in America. 2nd edn. San Diego, CA: Academic Press.

Pike, Kenneth L. 1954. Language in relation to a unified theory of human behavior. Glendale, CA: Summer Institute of Linguistics.

Saussure, Ferdinand de. 1949. Cours de linguistique generale. Publie par C. Bally, A. Sechehaye, and A. Riedlinger. 4th edn. Paris: Payot.

Schleicher, August. 1863. Die Darwinsche Theorie und die Sprachwissenschaft. Berlin.

Selkirk, Elisabeth. 1984. Phonology and syntax: The relation between sound and structure.

Cambridge, MA: MIT Press.

Sells, Peter. 1985. Lectures on contemporary syntactic theories: An introduction to government-binding theory, generalized phrase structure grammar, and lexical-functional grammar (CSLI Lecture Notes 3). Stanford, CA: Center for the Study of Language and Information, Stanford University.

Uspensky, B.A. 1965. Strukturnaja tipologija jazykov. Moscow: Nauka.

Wasow, T. 1985. Postscript. P. Sells, Lectures on contemporary syntactic theories. Stanford, CA: CSLI, Stanford University.

Ethnolinguistic democracy: Varieties, degrees and limits

Joshua A. Fishman
Yeshiva University and Stanford University

With the entry or re-entry of several Eastern European nationalities onto the stage of history as independent polities, the notion of ethnolinguistic democracy deserves to be pondered once again. This is so not only because their (re)entry has implications for any consideration given this matter, in previous times, by such agencies as the European (Economic) Community, but because Eastern Europe in particular has long been the European heartland of the co-occurrence among languages, peoples, and religions and the elevation of this co-occurrence to the level of Weltanschauung.

The centrality of language in ethnoreligious identity (and, therefore, in ethnomoral thought) has been a constant and long-recorded feature of eastern Mediterranean and Eastern European societies since our earliest records of them. The biblical Book of Esther, for example, expresses this view both at the level of collectivities and at the level of individuals. When the King of the Medes and the Persians sent messages to the various provinces and peoples of his Empire, we are told that these messages were sent 'into every province according to the writing thereof and to every people after their language' (Ch. 1, v. 22). However, the purpose of this diglossic arrangement—provinces having their interethnic written varieties but peoples having their own vernaculars—was distinctly a moral one, namely, 'so that every man should bear rule in his own house'. Presumably, these formulations are an early (perhaps the earliest) attempt to define a modus operandi in the realm of ethnolinguistic democracy, namely, one that is based on the view that people and peoples are not treated honorably unless their own languages are utilized, particularly in speech and to some extent in writing as well.

However, in those far distant times, communications upwards to heads of states were not necessarily informed by concerns for reciprocity. The Good Book does not tell us of how Ahasuerus' subjects, or even those acting on behalf of an entire region of his empire, expected to address him, whether orally or in writing. However, from what we know from other sources about the usage of those times it seems probable that such communications were conducted in the language of the central authorities of the empire. In our day and age, indeed, ever since the early nineteenth century, there have been some, particularly among the spokespersons for regional and immigrant collectivities, who have viewed the latter usage as undemocratic because, just as all people should be considered equal before the law, so all languages should somehow be considered equal as well. Of course, individuals, communities, and polities are not all equal in power, but in a moral universe, these spokespersons have claimed, they should each be equally entitled to use their own language if they are so inclined, rather than necessarily expected to constantly show deference to some language associated with greater power. This then will be our first working definition of 'complete ethnolinguistic democracy': the right of both parties in an interaction to USE THEIR OWN LANGUAGES and to RECEIVE IN THEIR OWN LANGUAGES in return, regardless of the power or size differentials that differentiate between them.

A two-dimensional frame of reference for discussing ethnocultural democracy. Let us look more carefully at the two dimensions that are already implicit in our discussion thus far. On the one hand there is the consideration of the extent to which any party's (particularly the weaker party's) preferred language is operative in any interaction. If, through the provision of translators, one's own preferred language[1] can be operative both in encoding messages sent and in decoding messages received, then obviously the two parties to the interaction are totally equalized linguistically. Neither one has to accommodate to the other and neither one has to shoulder the burden of acquiring proficiency, whether active or passive, in the other's language (such bilingual proficiency typically being asymmetrical and a reflection of power differentials, such that the situationally weaker party is far more often bilingual than the stronger). At the opposite end of this dimension, past the end of the horizontal dimension in Table 1, are those interactions where neither party is able to use its own language and where both have become bilingual but not in the native language of the other. Although complete reciprocity nominally also exists in the latter case, BOTH parties being required to use a language not their own, this pattern really falls far short of complete ethnolinguistic equality. Unless the languages involved are International (Artificial) Auxiliary Languages (a case to which we will return later), they are inevitably (a) someone's mother tongue, (b) more accessible to some parties than to others, or (c) both of the above, and the aforementioned 'someones' have a definite advantage in the ensuing interactions. Even when

[1] Perhaps reference should be made here to 'native' language or 'mother tongue', because these expressions are so traditional and expected in connection with ETHNOlinguistic concerns. More technically, however, what is being referred to is often the preferred language of ethnolinguistic identity and/or state functioning. The latter may not be the mother tongue at all for some segments of the population and at various stages of the total process of ethnolinguistic consciousness-raising, relinguification and re-ethnification. In former publications I have used the expression 'ethnic mother tongue' in this same extended sense, as distinguished from 'actual mother tongue'.

both parties freely set aside their mother tongues for the sake of a parsimonious interaction, such self-denial can neither be considered ETHNOlinguistically responsive nor ethno-identity supportive, no matter how commendable from the point of view of parsimony per se (as claimed, e.g., by Turi 1992).

Midpoint on this first dimension (let us call it 'degree of preferred language involvement'), between complete preferred language implementation and complete preferred language implementation substitution, there are nonreciprocal arrangements whereby one party both sends and receives in its preferred tongue and the other either only receives or only sends. This is often a power-dominated interaction, as in our example, above, from the Empire of the Medes and the Persians. However, this pattern is still more ethnolinguistically democratic than the even more restrictive ones just mentioned above, because the weaker party can at least send OR receive messages in its own self-affirming code. When the latter option is removed, then we are left with a situation which is outside of the limits of ethnolinguistic democracy.

The above three operative modes along the dimension of PREFERRED LANGUAGE IMPLEMENTATION BY THE WEAKER PARTY intersect with another dimension which deals with the MAGNITUDE OF SCALE pertaining to the interacting parties. This dimension is usually expressed in terms of political power and demographic numbers. At the top of this dimension there is the sovereign state, followed, in order of decreasing scale, by culturally autonomous regions, immigrant enclaves or neighborhoods and, finally, by discrete individuals. The intersection between these two dimensions minimally produces a 3 times 4 table such as that shown in Table 1.

Table 1. Interaction between degree of preferred language implementation and scale of political power.

	Preferred Language Implementation		
Scale	**1. Full**	**2. Partial**	**3. Restricted**
A. Between States	A1	A2	A3
B. Between States and Regions (Ss/Rs)	B1	B2	B3
C. Between Ss/Rs and Immigrant Neighborhoods	C1	C2	C3
D. Between Ss/Rs and 'other ethnic' individuals	D1	D2	D3

Obviously, the above table can easily be extended by introducing refinements on both of its dimensions, but I propose to leave it as it now stands for the purposes of the following discussion of examples of different degrees and varieties of ethnolinguistic democracy and differing interpretations of when a limit is purportedly reached beyond which a certain advocated degree of ethnolinguistic democracy 'can no longer be afforded'. At this point a third consideration will be introduced, namely, the linguistic complexity (or the number of languages involved) in actual or potential interactions.

Example 1. Complete ethnolinguistic democracy at the interpolity level (Cell A1). As one might expect, the 12 members of the European (Economic) Community (hereafter EC) do not conduct themselves according to the usage of the 'ethnic layer cake' empires of Eastern Antiquity. For the deliberations of the EC Parliament in Strasbourg, a Parliament whose representatives are selected by means of formal elections conducted in each of the member countries, each of the nine state-building languages of the current twelve members are fully equal. Between these nine language there are necessarily 9 times 8 or 72 directions of translation, because not only can all representatives ADDRESS the Parliament in their own state language, but they can all hear the discussion in reply to any intervention in their own state language[2] as well. This arrangement guarantees that the representatives of the roughly two million Danish speakers do not need to be less secure or any more linguistically versatile than the representatives from England, France, or Germany. Granted that not every one of the above-mentioned 72 directions of translation is equally common, and granted that in committee work or in documentary efforts (published or unpublished) a much smaller subset of languages is generally involved, the 'principle of complete multilingualism' (this being the EC's designation of its own ORGANIZATIONAL operational pattern, rather than a characterization of the abilities of its INDIVIDUAL delegates) remains dear to the heart of the initial 12 members of the EC, as we will see in connection with our discussion of cell B2, below.

Nevertheless, the future of the 'principle of complete multilingualism' may well be a rather problematic one for the EC, even at the organizational level. With the Language Service already one of its largest budgetary items, how will the EC cope with the very probable expansion of its membership in the very near future? Sweden[3] is certainly assured of early membership and Norway and Finland are almost in the same category. Membership for Hungary and

---

[2] Ireland has two official languages (Irish and English), but thus far, it has only asked that one of them (English) be recognized at the EC. Similarly, Luxembourg has requested no recognition for Letzebergesch, implementing its EC membership entirely via French and German. Belgium's participation is effectuated via French and Netherlandish. The above three instances of states duplicating languages that would be represented at the EC even without the membership of these particular states, results in the above-mentioned totals of 12 member states but only 9 recognized languages in the EC as of April 1992.

[3] A Swedish linguist recently proposed that Sweden offer to forgo the use of Swedish at the EC, when its membership is approved, in order to lighten the translation burdens of the organization and in view of the fact that its representatives will certainly all be fluent in either English, Danish, German, or French (Suzanne Romaine, personal communication). This suggestion was met with an avalanche of rejection from a large and very vocal segment of Swedish society, and it seems very unlikely that a newly admitted Sweden will now make any such unilateral self-denying gesture.

Czechoslovakia (or separately for Bohemia–Moravia [Czechia] and Slovakia) is already under discussion. If the six state languages of these five (or six) additional prospective members are also to be treated as equal 'in principle' with the current nine, that would result in 210 directions of translation among the 15 languages of 18 (or 19) members. If all of the other pre-perestroika European states are ultimately admitted, that is, even barring separate memberships for all of the recently independent subdivisions of the former Soviet and Yugoslav federations, the application of the principle of 'complete multilingualism' would result in 420 directions of translation for official, parliamentary communication among 21 languages of 24 (or 25) members of a first approximation to an all-European EC.[4] If all of the former Yugoslav and Soviet entities achieve separate membership, as now seems eminently possible within the next few years, that would result in 812 directions of translation among 29 languages of 33 (or 34) members![5] Clearly, sooner or later, some theory of limits must be invoked at the EC, but it is very difficult for sovereign states to agree to limit themselves, particularly when any such limitation not only contravenes a prior moral order but provides advantages to some members of the organization and denies them to others.[6]

Example 2. Partial ethnolinguistic democracy in interactions between states and regions (Cell B2). The EC adopted its 'principle of complete multilingualism' on December 11, 1990, that is, relatively late in its own history and substantially later than the principle itself had begun to be implemented in its own operations (based as these operations were upon earlier, somewhat similar, principles and conventions). This principle was then newly defended and justified on the grounds that it was required in the light of 'the respect which is owed the dignity of all languages which reflect and express the cultures of the

---

[4] The number 21 is arrived at by adding to the previous 15 languages, the following six: Serbocroatian (considered as one language rather than as two), Russian, Polish, Romanian, Bulgarian, and Albanian.

[5] The number 29 is arrived at by adding to the previous 21 the following eight languages of ten new member states: Slovenian, Croatian, Macedonian, Estonian, Latvian, Lithuanian, Moldavian, and Ukrainian. Serbia and Bosnia–Herzegovina are assumed to both opt for Serbian, while Croatian and Moldavian are considered to be different from Serbian and Romanian, respectively. Adding Armenian, Azerbaijani, and Georgian to the above list (assuming that their new polities seek a European rather than a trans-Caucasus affiliation) would bring the grand total to 32 languages and 992(!) directions of translation among 36 (or 37) European states. The addition of Austria and Switzerland would not increase the total number of languages. The further addition of Turkey and Iceland would result in 34 languages and 1,122 directions of translation among 34 languages for 40 or 41 states.

[6] Throughout this discussion I have ignored the problems of translation per se (e.g. costs, fidelity, translation-based miscommunication, etc.). The costs or 'lost savings' attributable to ethnolinguistic democracy, as contrasted to the costs of (mis)communicating via a shared second language such as Esperanto, have yet to be fully or accurately determined. Every human value, including ethnolinguistic democracy or parsimony, creates some problems as well as exacerbating and/or solving others.

different peoples who make up the European Community' (Argemi 1991, Reding 1990). However, some of 'the different peoples who make up the European Community' are also and even more basically members of sub-state ethno-regional entities. These sub-state entities commonly have sub-state languages of their own. Do not these sub-state languages deserve some EC respect and recognition too? This very question was brought to a head by the newly autonomous Catalans in Spain, some six million strong, who brought a petition to the EC in 1987 signed by fully 100,000 individuals, requesting some sort of official standing in the EC for their language, a language of long-standing humanistic accomplishment and a language recognized as regionally co-official in Spain and spoken natively by more individuals than is the state language of Denmark. It was precisely the Catalan petition which finally moved the EC to proclaim that all European languages (by clear implication, even regional ones) deserved recognition so that 'the people of Europe not come to regard European institutions as being out of touch with and foreign to them' but, rather, that they 'look upon them as important elements playing a part in the daily lives of the citizens' (Agemi 1991). In other words, the EC also implicitly applied its principle to the non-state-building peoples of the EC, rather than to the state-building peoples alone, precisely by reaffirming it in connection with the petition of a sub-state entity on behalf of its preferred language.

Nevertheless, it is noteworthy that even after the above truly sympathetic resolution, revealing as it does so much understanding of the ethnolinguistic sensitivities of regional language groups face to face with state languages in the New Europe, the EC still did NOT grant Catalan equal status within its parliamentary deliberations. In essence, that is in strictly operational organizational terms, the EC merely encouraged Catalan[7] to continue seeking some sort of other recognition, one that stops short of that now being implemented in connection with the nine current state-building languages. What might that 'other recognition' amount to? Well, it might very well be one which is reminiscent of a status that was operative in the ancient Empire of the Medes and the Persians, namely, the right to receive communications from the 'center', or (as is more likely today) TO SEND COMMUNICATIONS TO THE 'CENTER', in the language associated with regional identity and culture. The principle of ethnolinguistic democracy need not operate only and exclusively at the level of 'complete multilingualism' via insisting that all languages be literally equally important and privileged for ALL functions. When the number of languages becomes 'too great'

---

[7] By implication, other indigenous regional languages, such as Irish, Scots Gaelic, and Welsh in the United Kingdom; Basque and Galician in Spain; Breton, Occitan, and Alsatian in France; Frisian in the Netherlands; Sorbian in Germany; Friulian and Ladin in Italy; Romansch in Switzerland; and Nynorsk and Sami in Norway; etc., might also consider themselves 'encouraged' by the same resolution. These 'Lesser Used Languages' are all within the purview of the EC's purely consultative 'Bureau of Lesser Used Languages' (Jacoby 1991). The 'etc.' above applies to Aromanian, Asturian, Greenlandic, Sicilian, Stellingwerfsk, Valdostian, and other even smaller indigenous sub-state languages of Europe.

(granted, a very judgmental definitional matter indeed), some consideration of proportionality between languages may ultimately be appealed to and implemented. Some notion of limits must ultimately be appended to the notion of 'complete (organizational) multilingualism', very much as notions of limits have existed in all theories of democracy and individual rights from the very earliest times (Fishman, in press). Cell B2 represents attempts to cope with this issue in a constructive way.

Just WHERE AND WHEN THE LIMITS OF DEMOCRATIC RIGHTS SHOULD BE DRAWN, be they ethnolinguistic, econotechnical or political, can well be viewed as a dilemma within the democratic ethos itself. Limits can obviously be set in self-serving ways, and those who wield greater power are particularly likely to have a disproportionate say in the establishments of such limits for others. Establishments are more likely to limit others than to limit themselves. Establishments tend to appeal to or to implement any notion of limits primarily for the purpose of preserving and furthering their own power, rather than because some natural limit has truly been reached, on the one hand, or in order to engage in magnanimous power-sharing, on the other hand. Of course, the foregoing observations apply to NATIONAL establishments every bit as much as, and even more so, than they apply to INTERNATIONAL establishments such as the EC.

Example 3. Restricted ethnolinguistic democracy: A problem of immigrant enclaves (Cell C3). Living, as we do, in a period of American history when our central and local government authorities often communicate with (and even receive communications from) Hispanics, Amerindians, and various Asians in languages other than the main language of the state, we seldom pause to reflect how unusual such a convention is in historical and international perspective. Immigrant languages[8] are, generally, low languages on the totem pole and whatever recognition is given to them by the authorities is, generally, of a voluntary kind, that is, not protected or required by law, and is therefore easily withdrawn or annulled at the whim of the authorities. It is not unusual throughout the world today to find that the most essential government services, such as police protection, fire protection, health care provision, legal proceedings in courts of law, elementary and secondary education (even if only for stipulated transitional periods), job training and retraining, and even citizenship training per se, are simply not available in other than the official, state-building languages. Western Europe, Australia, Canada, and the United States, although notable differences exist between them as to the extent of (and their statutory provisions for) ethnolinguistic democracy involving immigrant

---

[8] IMMIGRANT languages are distinguished from MIGRANT languages in the following remarks. Thus, neither English in Puerto Rico nor Russian in the Ukraine during the period of Soviet rule are considered immigrant languages within the meaning of the term as used in this paper. Of course, a given language may switch in status from being immigrant-derived to being an indigenous state or regional language after a judgmentally 'sufficient' number of years has elapsed, viz. English in Ireland.

groups, are clearly unusual in this respect, even unusual in the perspective of the entire course of the history of those countries themselves. These countries (and a very few others elsewhere) constitute examples of the degree to which some notions of ethnolinguistic democracy have permeated Western standards of morality since the end of World War II, even if imperfectly so. The efforts of English Only/English Official protagonists in the United States (and of conservative groups, parties, and movements in Canada, Australia, and Western Europe) may be viewed as seeking to return these few exceptional countries to their status quo ante, that is, to move them from some point close to cell C2 ('partial ethnolinguistic democracy') to some point closer to C3 ('restricted ethnolinguistic democracy').

It should also be noted that immigrant groups are even more rarely assisted in any language-in-culture stabilization efforts that might tend to help them consolidate socioculturally over the long term. Such consolidation would, in essence, change immigrant groups from transient minorities (expected to trans-ethnify and translinguify in the direction of the mainstream) into indigenized regional minorities such as the Tamils in Sri Lanka, the Jews in pre–World War II Eastern Europe, and the Rusyns in Voyvodina. It is precisely the nativistic and ethnocentric fear of just such rare long-term developments that makes all but RESTRICTED ethnolinguistic democracy for immigrants the worldwide rule rather than the exception we have noted it to be in the few countries noted initially.

Example 4. Ethnolinguistic rights for individuals: the territoriality and personality principles (Cells D1–D3). The appeal to 'reasonable limits' along the dimension of scale deals not only with the NUMBER OF LANGUAGES involved, as is the case with our EC examples, but also with the NUMBER OF INDIVIDUALS involved. Often, even members of territorial (i.e. indigenous regional) minorities will be treated as foreign immigrants (or even worse) when encountered outside of their legally defined regions. This is the case with Francophones or Italophones in German-speaking Switzerland, or of Walloons in the Flemish-speaking parts of Belgium. In both of these instances a rather pure and unadulterated territoriality principle is invoked, and no ethnolinguistic democracy is accorded to such individuals outside of their 'proper' areas. Such neglect is essentially an example of cell D3 in operation. A more liberal policy has been encountered in India, where a 'sufficient' number of speakers of 'scheduled languages' can expect some government accommodation and consideration, even outside of the linguistic states with which their languages are normally associated. Hispanics in the United States who are relocating in secondary settlement areas are also sometimes accommodated somewhat, merely because their more massive presence elsewhere within reach has resulted in Spanish-related personnel and materials being 'tappable' in a pinch. A single Hispanic family in upper Maine may be in a much better situation than a single Hmong family in the identical location, but generally, what is involved when some such isolates are accommodated is the implementation of a much more restrictive arrangement which is much closer to cell D3 ('restricted ethnolinguistic democracy') than to cell D2 ('partial ethnolinguistic democracy').

Rare as examples of cell D2 are, examples of cell D1 are even rarer. It should come as no surprise that the co-occurrence of full ethnolinguistic democracy and isolated individuals not speaking the dominant state-building language should be an obvious non-starter. The appearance of such individuals (particularly if they have no locally recognized territorial affiliations in an appropriate and nearby region) quickly galvanizes authorities to invoke a theory of limits and to provide, at best, only the most restricted type of emergency assistance. Furthermore, even such assistance as is provided tends to foster an image (with respect to those whose language is exceptionally recognized) of welfare recipients rather than that of co-equals and potential neighbors, friends, and co-citizens.

Parsimony and ethnolinguistic democracy. Ethnolinguistic democracy obviously involves a complex constellation of values which exact a price in time, effort, and resources. But there are no cost-free values. In terms of pure parsimony, it always appears to be easier, simpler, and cheaper to use just one or a very few major languages, regardless of individual or small group ethnolinguistic sensitivities. The movements for one or another international auxiliary language are examples of the triumph of parsimony (or of a theory of limits) over the claims of ethnolinguistic democracy. Similarly, the operational policies of the United Nations or of the Council of Europe are also of this kind (both pertaining to cell A3),[9] since they favor a very small subset of major, Western European languages, languages that are assumed to be 'languages of wider communication' and, accordingly, presumably free of any 'original sin', that is, of 'ethnic contamination'.

That such decontamination is purely perspectival and situational is obvious from the efforts by adherents of French, in particular, and of Spanish, Italian, and German to some extent as well, to keep English from being recognized as the primus (or prima?) enter pares that it has actually become in some EC operations. Thus parsimony of resources or the appeal to limits, as a tactic utilized in order to avoid the purportedly excessive costs engendered by TOO MANY SMALL LANGUAGES. This tactic itself runs into the counter-parsimony interests of those who are concerned with their own loss of status due to the selection of TOO FEW 'SUPER (i.e. SUPER-POWER) LANGUAGES'. The latter counter-parsimony efforts are engaged in by polities that are ready, nay eager, to invoke the notion of limits against the sub-state languages in their own political orbit, while being extremely loathe to have the notion of limits applied above themselves, so to speak, at the level of supra-state organizations and activities. Although ethnolinguistic goals and claims are frequently and widely derided as self-seeking, it is often overlooked that the appeals to limits and to

---

[9] Neither of these organizations aims at a degree of sociocultural integration nor sponsors popular elections to elect the 'representatives' that are involved in them as does the EC.

parsimony in linguistic affairs are similarly inspired by self-interest and pack a considerably stronger wallop as well, being associated with the ethnolinguistic interests of the mightiest powers on the world arena. Because of their power, the linguistic Big Brothers deflect discussion of the costs to human creativity that would be occasioned by their restrictions of ethnolinguistic democracy under super-power tutelage. Seemingly, what is sauce for the goose is not sauce for the goslings in ethnolinguistic affairs.

Summary and conclusions. I have tried to stress just a few major considerations throughout this presentation. Ethnolinguistic democracy is far from being an open and shut affair. There are different varieties, degrees, and even dimensions of ethnolinguistic democracy, and the entire notion is very perspectival in nature, even more so than most other value-laden societal phenomena, all of which tend to have a subjective component. Most STATES are prone to strive for more ethnolinguistic democracy AT THEIR OWN LEVEL, that is, in inter-polity affairs, or at the level above their own, that is, in supra-polity organizations. Conversely, they tend to be resistant to notions of ethnolinguistic democracy at the intra-state or sub-state level, due to their mistaken association of intra-polity linguistic heterogeneity with civil strife, on the one hand, and with decreased per capital gross national product, on the other hand (Fishman 1991). As a result of this mistaken association of intra-polity linguistic heterogeneity only with NEGATIVE CONSEQUENCES, states (and their creations: inter-state associations) are often, curiously enough, increasingly loathe to permit sub-state entities to enjoy full ethnolinguistic democracy, the further removed these entities are from already-recognized political and cultural self-regulation.

This means, in an era in which intranational and international migrations are both at an all time high, that sub-state ethnolinguistic democracy is particularly in danger of being restricted. Similarly, as the Eastern European events of the past year reveal, it also means that regions and groups striving toward the attainment of greater ethnolinguistic democracy may increasingly opt for regional autonomy and even political independence in order to attain ethnolinguistic security. However, if and when their independence is attained, the new polities that arise often tend to recapitulate the same types of negative ethnolinguistic approaches vis-à-vis their own minorities that were directed toward them, prior to their own attainment of self-regulation. All in all, ETHNOLINGUISTIC DEMOCRACY TENDS TO BE PURSUED AND ADVOCATED UPWARD AND DENIED AND DENIGRATED DOWNWARD ON THE DIMENSION OF POWER AND SCALE.

In view of the foregoing circular developmental patterns, the reaffirmation of the 'principle of complete multilingualism' by the European Community is particularly noteworthy, most particularly so as it pertains to and was brought about by a concern for sub-state languages. Although the European Community will necessarily need to move from 'complete' toward 'partial ethnolinguistic democracy', and to do so not only at the sub-state level but even at the interstate level (thereby tending to equalize the treatment that most state-building and all regional languages will receive in its operation), its legacy of championing the 'dignity of all languages' and recognizing the need to make sure that people NOT come to regard the institutions that govern them 'as being out of touch with and foreign to them', will remain noteworthy landmarks in supporting the strivings of little languages and peoples all over the world. If the European Community can hold the line for 'moderate' or 'partial' ethnolinguistic democracy, the benefits of that line will redound to the good of all of multicultural and multilingual humanity.

Western Europe was the original home from which political democracy, enlightenment rationalism, and ethnolinguistic romanticism (Fishman 1972, Penrose and May 1991) spread throughout the world. There is now reason to hope that the European Community's stance with respect to 'complete ethnolinguistic democracy', and its predictable future stance on behalf of more moderate ethnolinguistic democracy, will enable this value cluster too to have more of a worldwide currency than it otherwise might. In a sense, a Western European debt may be being paid off in this connection. Europe (and Western Europe in particular) initially became more hostile to sub-state linguistic heterogeneity as its econotechnical and econopolitical development progressed. Perhaps Western Europe's more recent POSTmodern ability to compromise in this regard will be a harbinger of a greater willingness to do the same in Eastern Europe, in Africa, in Asia, and, who knows, even in the Americas as well. Ojalá! We must not let the recent multiplication of recognized state languages turn into a route for indigenous sub-state and foreign-derived immigrant tongues. The former does not have to be at the expense of the latter when partial ethnolinguistic democracy is seriously considered and honestly implemented.[10]

REFERENCES

Argemi, Aureli. 1991. European recognition for Catalan. Contact: Bulletin of the European Bureau for Lesser Used Languages 8, 1.6.

Coulmas, Florian. (ed.) 1991. A language policy for the European Community: Prospects and quandaries. Berlin: Mouton de Gruyter.

Fishman, Joshua A. 1991. An inter-polity perspective on the relationship between linguistic heterogeneity, civil strife and per capita gross national product. International Journal of Applied Linguistics 1.5–18.

Fishman, Joshua A. 1972. Language and Nationalism. Rowley, MA: Newbury Press. [Reprinted in 1989. Language and Ethnicity in Minority Ethnolinguistic Perspective. Clevedon: Multilingual Matters, 105–75 and 269–367.]

Fishman, Joshua A. (in press) On the limits of ethnolinguistic democracy. Linguistic human rights, ed. by Tove Skutnab-Kongas and Robert Phillips.

Haarmann, Harald. 1991. Monolingualism vs. selective multilingualism: On the future alternatives

[10] Further evidence of the EC's continuing interest in regional and/or minority languages in Europe, with the goal of preparing and adopting a 'European Charter for Regional or Minority Languages', is available in the reports of March 26 [CAHLR (92) 5] and April1 [CAHLR (92) 6], 1992, of its Ad Hoc Committee of Experts on Regional or Minority Languages in Europe. I am indebted to Dr. Donall O Riagain, Secretary General of the EC-affiliated European Bureau for Lesser Used Languages, for providing me with copies of all of the above.

for Europe as it integrates in the 1990s. Sociolinguistica 5.7–23.

Haselhuber, Jakob. 1991. Erste Ergebnisse einer empirischen Untersuchung zur Sprachsituation in der EG-Komission (February 1960). Sociolinguistica 5.37–50.

Jacoby, Lucien. 1991. European Community Activity in Favor of Lesser Used Languages and Cultures, 1983–1989. Baile Atha Cliath: Wilwerwitz, European Bureau for Lesser Used Languages.

Leitner, Gerhard. 1991. Europe 1992: A language perspective. Language Problems and Language Planning 5.282–96.

Penrose, Jan, and Joe May. 1991. Herder's concept of Nation and its relevance to contemporary ethnic nationalism. Canadian Review of Studies in Nationalism 18.179–86.

Reding, V. 1990. Report drawn up on behalf of the Committee on Petitions. Strasburg, European Parliament; Session Documents: DOC-EN/RR/87761.

Turi, G. 1992. The right to language; the value of Esperanto. The New Party 26, 7.11.

A brief update on my interest in relating language to philosophy

Kenneth L. Pike
Summer Institute of Linguistics and
The University of Texas at Arlington

My interest in philosophy was an 'accident' of my relating the study of unwritten languages to the need to teach others to make such studies. One could not study an unwritten language for even a few hours without the need for some discovery of the presence and partial meaning of some 'words' in that language. The meaning of the words, in turn, had to have some relation to observable actions (e.g. 'pointing') and cultural behavior (e.g. eating), when no 'dictionary' had ever been made for that language. And the interpretation of behavior required some information about, or guesses concerning, the intentions of the people involved in that behavior. Discovery of intended deception, as well as the integrity of surface purpose, had to be included. The contrast between cheating and integrity implied the universal presence of some kind of local standards—with these relations of morality. And underlying such implicit or explicit facts was often an unstated conviction of the local people involved about their ultimate mechanistic or religious sources for the validation of such convictions. This integration of needs has forced me, over time, to a HOLISTIC philosophy, rather than one searching for or concentrating on logical consistency within a limited 'scientific' area.

In 1935 I was instructed by the founder of our institute (The Summer Institute of Linguistics) to learn an Indian language of Mexico without studying Spanish first—lest the latter interfere with my best learning of the former. In 1936 I taught others in the institute to do the same—inventing the 'monolingual demonstration' for that purpose. Much later, the philosophers Quine and Ullian (1978:28) called the 'observation sentences' (obtaining a linguistic response from pointing or acting in such a situation) elements 'at the bottom edge of language ... It is ultimately through them that language gets its meaning, its bearing on reality ... [and] they convey the basic evidence for all belief, all scientific theory'.

When I was first teaching phonetics in 1936, my students were headed either for Mexico or for Guatemala, and the number of sounds needed for that group was relatively small. A few years later, however, students were headed for a large variety of languages, in various countries, and the number of sounds which they needed to learn was much larger—and included sounds I had not myself heard. I tried, therefore, to invent all the kinds of sounds that I could, with a 'phonetic experiment' involving all kinds of movements of the tongue, lips, and throat. This material grew into my dissertation, published in 1943. Philosophically, however, it resulted in a holistic view of the possibility of human sounds—a small part of a total study of human behavioral capacity in general, underlying my later philosophical world. (I felt like one climbing a mountain: at first, looking backward, one saw only a small distance into the valley; later, at the top, one could see in all directions!)

When I tried to write a manual for people learning to make alphabets for preliterate cultures (final publication in 1947) I was astonished to get a letter from Czechoslovakia telling me that they were delighted to get my book, after the materialistic material coming from the Yale school! I had not realized, philosophically, that I was not writing like a behaviorist. I deduced that my explicit reliance, in that book, on 'native reaction' as a crucial ingredient in judgment (of phonemic sameness or difference), rather than observation on outward behavior alone, placed me philosophically in a camp far away from my knowledge of myself. And there I have remained ever since—with a double reliance philosophically on body plus mind, as well as on physical event plus mental relevance.

I wearied of studying phonology, and in 1949 I asked myself if there were phonemic theoretical components which might be applicable to grammar. So I went through the phonemics book and focused on contrast, variation, and distribution (or on feature mode, manifestation mode, and distribution mode), finding all of them in grammar. But when, that year, I asked myself: 'What is a language like English distributed into?' I was troubled. Not into itself. Not into another language. But into culture! That was an extraordinary moment. From then on, I tried to apply all my general principles to anthropology, nonverbal behavior, breakfast scenes, football games, church services, science fiction, dreams, etc. Philosophically, my horizon had in fact expanded (without my knowing that it was related so basically to philosophy) to include the analysis of all human behavior. With the unexpected encouragement of the philosopher Abraham Kaplan, however, I wrote up the material, which then appeared in three volumes 1954, 1955, and 1960, with a second edition in 1967. But philosophy, as such, is listed in the index only in the 1967 volume, even though some philosophers are referred to in the earlier volumes and bibliographies. Of these, Sinclair (1951) had the greatest impact on me, via his discussion of epistemology; he forced me to look at the ultimate difficulties or impossibility of proving a starting point. And Frank (1957:33) encouraged me by insisting that 'men have had to accept succeeding theories because they yielded practical results'— which allowed me to continue to be happy with the combination of theoretical fun-guessing plus useful applicability.

I continued for a number of years trying to write general statements about these principles, which resulted in my *Linguistic Concepts* book in 1982. Yet, during that process, in 1975 I was at a workshop in Irian Jaya, with the philosopher–linguist Professor John Ver Haar. On the plane leaving there, I was able to discuss these principles with him. He said—I seem to recall—'You sound like a phenomenologist!' I did not know what that was. He sent me some of his materials. And later at the University of Texas at Arlington, Professors Lenore Langsdorf and Harry Reeder, both phenomenologists, encouraged me to go ahead with my starting philosophical inquiries. They also asked me to speak to the university philosophical club. At the end, Langsdorf said: 'You sound like Immanuel Kant.' Oh? I checked, and agreed with Kant that we do not know 'the thing-in-itself.' I felt that as observers we are involved in creating our world view. I linked it, as a linguist, with the fact that in giving names to things, we 'sort' or 'classify' them into manageable items, classes, or events; and without such classification we could not have discussions such as this one. (A shepherd dog can do much that I cannot attain to—but the dog cannot argue this point with us.) Here, again, my linguistic biography was tying into my growing epistemological commitments. Names and philosophy join together.

This tie continued, as I worked further on emics and etics (terms which I had created years before from phonemics and phonetics) for social analysis and linguistic explanation. In Spain, in 1985, philosophers asked me to talk to them, because they had become interested in the emic–etic discussions of the cultural materialist Marvin Harris. In the paper which I wrote for them (Pike 1987) I gave the best summary I could of my philosophy to date. I wanted philosophy linked to my linguistic experience, including a relation to my monolingual demonstrations; linked to the relation to language and other behavioral structures of particular cultures, versus to innate human characteristics; to the observer as part of the data; to language as hierarchical and as patterned in interlocking hierarchies of phonology, grammar, and reference; to contrasts and likenesses between different cultural world views; and the relation of such matters to the four-cell tagmemic structure posited in tagmemic theory (e.g. Pike and Pike [1977] 1982, and 1983). An extensive discussion with Harris has since appeared (Headland, Pike, and Harris 1990), with my emphasis more on the emic structure arrived at synchronically, and Harris having a focus more on a diachronic orientation with culture crucially influenced by infrastructural situations. Philosophically the difference of starting points as materialistic-diachronic cultural representation versus my search for emic synchronic structures by way of etic crude and changeable preliminary data can both be useful, even though quite different in procedure and descriptive endings.

In relation to *Language, Communication, and Social Meaning* (the topic of this Round Table), a potentially important philosophical topic surfaces there: I claim that a culture may be heavily in danger of deteriorating via greed—as the source of social entropy. But I also claim that society has not disintegrated, because there is an anti-entropy present—seen in the intent not to harm one's neighbor, but with positive effort to help him. (See Headland, Pike, and Harris 1990:423–44, 28, 72, 8.) A comparable item in linguistic change (pp. 42, 196) would be fusion of sounds in rapid speech, as leading to entropy, but with analogical extension of patterns as anti-entropy (with the plural of *foot* becoming *foot-s*, for example).

Of importance in understanding the current philosophical implications of tagmemics is to note that three patterned hierarchies, interlocking with each other, are posited: phonological, grammatical, and referential. The phonology includes the structure from phoneme, to syllable, to rhythm group, to breath group, and up to phonological sentences or paragraphs or texts (e.g. poetic forms). The grammar includes structures from affixes, to words, to phrases, to clauses, sentences, paragraphs, and structured texts; the grammatical form is the structure of the sequence in which the text is TOLD. The referential structure is that of the sequence or structures in which something HAPPENS—or the n-dimensional structures of a society and its activities. No one structure is totally independent of the others: no phonology is emic unless it is manifesting words; no grammar is relevant if it includes no meaning of phrases or cultural background; no reference material is accessible if it is not formed into patterns of brain activity as heard through words and sounds, or seen through gestures or other physical actions. The sentence 'John came home and then went to the movies' is heard in its sounds and syllables; it represents the referential sequence of John coming home followed by his going to the movies. But the grammatical focus in English can express the same referential materials in *John went to the movies after he came home*. Many native speakers of Papua New Guinea cannot do that—they have no word for *after*—so they must say something like *Coming home, John went to the movies*—accomplishing the same communication. (The theory of the referential material has been heavily developed by Evelyn Pike, in Pike and Pike [1977] 1982, and 1983.) The approach through the three hierarchies leaves room for different kinds of meanings in phonology (e.g. angry voice), as well as in grammar (e.g. active versus passive focus), and in reference (e.g. the different meanings of words, or different plots of two stories). Note, further, that this (Pikean) tagmemic belief differs philosophically—as well as linguistically—from those linguistic theories which claim that three areas are present, but with different definitions from these tagmemic ones—e.g. they may claim the presence of phonology without meaning, grammar also without meaning as such, and meaning as a separate structure.

In relation to the three hierarchies, our tagmemics has developed four universally necessary components for each unit at each tagmemic level of each hierarchy. This, too, relates to philosophy, in that it affirms universals of human nature. Specifically, it says, for example, that a subject of a sentence has a place (SLOT) in a structure, of the sentence; that it has a manifesting member of a CLASS of units (here, say, of a class of noun phrases); a relevance or purpose or reason or cause or intent of the item in that subject slot (called ROLE, in this terminology); and a background pattern controlling some aspect of the material, or controlled by such a larger pattern (COHESION, as a plural subject controls a plural predicate). Further, there can be changes under grammatical attention: If a place itself comes under attention (e.g. as the subject of a larger sentence, as in *Subjects must be related to predicates*), then this 'class' member must itself be found in a slot in a higher or different statement (e.g. in relation to human characteristics, or abstractions of some kind). Thus one has a 'kaleidoscope' of bits of structure that can shift to different places under attention, but only with resultant concomitant shifts which preserve the human universally present (whether implicit or explicit) new slot, role, and cohesion (background).

This has been shown, for poetry, in Pike 1988 (edited by Deborah Tannen of Georgetown University); one poem is told in several different ways, preserving the referential background (social and human function and relevance) but changing grammatically the focus of the component under attention. Here, again, autonomy of one part, or of one hierarchy, or of one tagmemic component, is not possible. Always the others are vacuums waiting to be filled by replaceable bits from the implicit background, if one is changed. My most recent handling of a small poem to represent this poetic form is to appear in a volume in the proceedings of the 12th National Symposium for Developing English Language Teaching, in Cairo, Egypt (presented Feb. 26, 1992). The starting poem, *Poems are Windows*, gives an underlying matrix (cohesion) of persons as 'I' versus 'You', and poems as windows versus feelings, and contrasted with the experience of seeing versus the aim of the hearer. In the second poem, the focus changes to the need to understand pain in others. In the third, focus is on 'Help' for others. The fourth puts time in focus, 'Now.' The fifth fuses person to background, via soul bound to word. In the sixth, the horizon is turned upside down—which changes the basic referential thrust, by abandoning interest in others:

<table>
<tr>
<td>Poem 1
POEMS ARE
WINDOWS
Through which one looks
Via eyes
Of feeling soul
On other's toil.</td>
<td>Poem 2
PERSONS SHOULD
FEEL
Pain in others
Where sympathy
In words
Blunts the thorn—
or scorn.</td>
<td>Poem 3
HELP
Your aching friend
By aesthetic bandaids
Of poetic patches
Pasted on hurting
soul.</td>
</tr>
<tr>
<td>Poem 4
NOW
You've helped me,
After times of strain
From isolation.</td>
<td>Poem 5
PERSONS AS
POEMS
Tie together
Both soul and words
To patch the pain
Of people alone.</td>
<td>Poem 6
LEAVE 'EM
ALONE!
Let them die
In lone despair.
Why care
For them, not us?</td>
</tr>
</table>

But such multiple relations of patterns within patterns—of interlocking hierarchies, and with the four components at each level also interlocking kaleidoscopically—have led me to another philosophical conviction: Truth is not a set of randomly related bits or sections of knowledge; rather a truth is A SET

OF PATTERNS WITHIN PATTERNS, hierarchically upwards and downwards, and crosswise between them at various levels. EXPLANATION IS THE DESCRIPTION OF THESE PATTERN INTERACTIONS. And, at the top, we reach the limit of our beliefs and knowledge, and can go no further, scientifically. But before reaching that point, the need for studying role, purpose, intent, and naming by person, before social and personal knowledge can be reached suggest the reason for my conviction that PERSON IS ABOVE LOGIC, in the philosophical search for social truth. Recent study of 'snowflakes' in 'chaos' theory (Gleick 1987) gives objective support for the need for pattern beyond simple atoms. Older studies of gestalt (Koffka 1935) pushed me in that direction in the fifties.

But this leads to a further philosophical question—the most recent one I have been struggling with: How can different views of linguistic theory be reconciled with one another? If more than one can not be consistent and true, which shall we choose? And how can we enjoy watching the historical process of theories in change, as they are modified or replaced from time to time? In Egypt, at the University of Cairo in March, I tried a metaphor to help me live with such questions. Consider a HELIX, as a structure with an outside shape like that of a screw, with its 'thread' coiling around a cylinder. Think of all of knowledge and reality as composing the total cylinder plus the thread winding around it upwards. Consider the total to be reality (with the top of the cylinder and screw part not visible to us). Then we can think of the winding thread as modeling changing linguistic (or philosophical) theory. At one moment the thread is on one side of the cylinder; at another moment it is on the opposite side of the cylinder, apparently 'in contradiction' to the other. Yet, be patient! presently we shall be back on the other side, seeing again things which had been seen from that view before. The fact of the thread being in different positions would be the changing of theory. The apparent opposites would represent states of the discipline, in temporary disagreement. The continued rise of the thread would imply hope for getting closer to the reality as a whole. This, it seems to me, helps me understand how rival theories can be different, but each be partially true, and yet none of them complete.

So let's keep on! Keep encouraging colleagues who have different vantage points—and hope to see soon how the views merge over time.

REFERENCES

Frank, Phillip. 1957. Philosophy of science: The link between science and philosophy. Englewood Cliffs, NJ: Prentice-Hall.

Gleick, James. 1987. Chaos: Making a new science. New York: Penguin Books.

Headland, Thomas N., Kenneth L. Pike, and Marvin Harris. (eds.) 1990. Emics ands etics: The insider/outsider debate. Newbury Park: Sage Publications.

Koffka, K. 1935. Principles of gestalt psychology. New York: Harcourt, Brace and Co.

Pike, Kenneth L. 1954, 1955, 1960. 1st edn. Language in relation to a unified theory of the structure of human behavior. Glendale, CA: Summer Institute of Linguistics. [1967. 2nd edn. The Hague: Mouton and Co.]

Pike, Kenneth L. 1982. Linguistic concepts. Lincoln, NE: University of Nebraska Press.

Pike, Kenneth L. 1987. The Relation of Language to the world. International Journal of Dravidian

Linguistics 16, 1.77–98.

Pike, Kenneth L. 1988. Bridging language learning, language analysis, and poetry, via experimental syntax. Linguistics in context: Connecting observation and understanding, ed. by Deborah Tannen, 221–245. Norwood, NJ: Ablex.

Pike, Kenneth L. 1991. A revolutionary 'helix' in linguistic history: As seen over half a century by one who has lived it. Cairo Studies in English [special Issue], 21–26. Giza, Egypt: Department of English Language and Literature.

Pike, Kenneth L. In press. Poetry seen as kaleidoscopic with relation to multiple viewpoints. Proceedings of the 12th national symposium for developing English language teaching [Egyptian TEFL]. Cairo, Egypt.

Pike, Kenneth L., and Evelyn G. Pike. [1977] 1982. 2nd edn. Grammatical analysis. Dallas: Summer Institute of Linguistics and the University of Texas at Arlington.

Pike, Kenneth L., and Evelyn G. Pike. 1983. Text and Tagmeme. Norwood, NJ: Ablex.

Quine, W. V., and J.S. Ullian. [1970] 1978. The web of belief. 2nd edn. New York: Random House.

Sinclair, Angus. 1951. The conditions of knowing. London: Routledge and Kegan Paul.

Communication, community, and the problem of appropriate use

H. G. Widdowson
University of London

The three noun phrases of the title of this year's Round Table can be said to trace a sequence of thought and practice in linguistics and language pedagogy over the past thirty years. In the minds of some people the sequence seems to be a natural and necessary order of development, the working out of an instinctive, innate sense of the intrinsic nature of language, an emergent truth. You cannot analyse language on its own in dissociation from its use as communication. You cannot talk about communication without considering social meaning. Language is communication is social meaning. The concepts arrange themselves in implicational progression and the scope of linguistics and language pedagogy widens accordingly. But as it does so, the factors, features, perspectives, or what have you, become increasingly difficult to manage: the more comprehensive the range of phenomena we seek to account for, the more difficult does it become to comprehend the account. There are times when one longs for the simplifying assumptions and simpler certainties of yesteryear, when the wood was so much easier to discern.

Is this longing then just a craven reluctance to face up to the truth of things? I do not think so. Truth is anyway, we have been led to believe, socially constructed, the figment of the collective imagination of different discourse communities, a cultural variable. In accepting the progression of thought as progress we have simply been acculturated into a currently dominant ideology. So we do not necessarily progress in the sense of improve when we become progressive in our ideas. And to subscribe to a wider definition of what language study and language teaching is all about is necessarily, if somewhat paradoxically, to constrain our thinking.

In this paper I want to try to break away a little from such constraint and question some of the assumptions of current thinking about language teaching and learning, including some I have made myself. In particular I am concerned with those assumptions, often taken as self-evident truths, about the relationship among language, communication, and social meaning.

Let me begin by describing what seems to be the pedagogic position which is in current intellectual favour as the most enlightened, the most consistent with research findings and theoretical developments in the field as follows. It is not enough for language learners to acquire linguistic competence, a knowledge of grammar and lexis which enables them to compose and comprehend correct sentential forms. They must also acquire communicative competence. This will enable them to handle language, both as producers and receivers, as appropriate to actual contexts of use, to manage communicative functions fluently THROUGH language and not just to manipulate accurately the forms which are IN language. Unless one takes this as the objective of instruction, learners will achieve only a partial or diminished competence which does not correspond with full or complete native-speaker mastery, which is the real purpose of learning. And the most effective means towards this achievement is through an experience of authentic language use in the classroom.

What we have here is a set of ideas constituting a pedagogic position (variously, and vaguely, referred to as an approach, a model, or a paradigm) to the definition of the ends and means of language teaching: what learners ought to achieve as an objective and what they ought to do in order to achieve it. There is reference, therefore, to two contexts: the context of language learning on the one hand and the context of language use on the other. Now clearly there must be some relationship between the two: learning must be a preparation for using. But what is that relationship? The assumption in this approach is that there must be a close correspondence between them, even, wherever possible, an exact coincidence. If learners are to acquire communicative competence to be deployed in contexts of use, then it is that which they must experience in contexts of learning. Authentic learning depends on authentic use. And authentic use is communicative behaviour which is pragmatically appropriate to different cultural contexts, that is to say behaviour which has appropriate social meaning.

Such a position would seem to be based on impeccable reasoning. It has face validity and powerful adherents. But I think that in certain crucial respects it is mistaken: flawed in conception, and damaging in its practical effects. I want to argue that it is a mistake to try to fashion contexts of instruction to replicate conditions of use, and, further and more boldly, that teaching appropriate social behaviour is inappropriate as the objective of a language course. My belief is that there has been too much loose talk about culture and authenticity and appropriate use, and above all of communicative competence.

Above all of communicative competence. So let me begin with that. Ever since Dell Hymes proposed the concept as in some sense in opposition to Chomsky's it has been problematic. A number of people have had a try at analyzing it into constituent components (most notably Canale and Swain 1980, Canale 1983, Bachman 1990), and in consequence we have had a bewildering proliferation of competences proposed: pragmatic, sociolinguistic, sociocultural, discoursal, strategic, textual, illocutionary, and so on—competences dividing and subdividing like some strange and primitive amoebic form of conceptual life. But such componential analysis of what the term might denote has, I believe, left the central problem untouched. It is that, as I have suggested before (Widdowson

1989), Hymes does not only extend the denotation of the term competence, but he changes its sense. For Chomsky competence is a matter of knowledge. For Hymes it is a matter of knowledge AND ability. To be competent in this sense is not only to know the communicative potential of a language (its meaning potential in Halliday's phrase) but also to know how to act upon this knowledge, to actualize this potential as behaviour in contexts of use. Now as Chomsky (1980:53) himself has pointed out in reference to first language acquisition, a child may have 'internalized the requisite mental structure, but for some reason lacked the capacity to use it'. This distinction between knowledge and behaviour is indeed the very basis of his competence/performance distinction, and the main force in his attack against the behaviourists. You cannot simply infer knowledge directly from the evidence of behaviour. Cognition is one thing; the capacity to access it, the ability to control it, is another (cf. also Bialystok and Sharwood Smith 1985). Knowledge of language will be variably activated according to different contextual conditions. You may not be able, or you may not find it necessary, or desirable, to act upon what you know on particular occasions.

And this point applies, of course, not only to language but to social behaviour in general. There is always bound to be some disparity between the private world known only to ourselves and the image we project for public view. The recent general election in Britain provides a striking illustration of this. The result came as a surprise. It was unexpected because the opinion polls had, up to the last moment, been confidently predicting that the Labour Party would gain a higher percentage of the votes than the Conservatives. In the event the opposite happened. The swing to the right in the actual election was the reverse of the swing to the left recorded by the opinion polls. Why then the disparity? How could conclusions based on such a mass of empirical evidence be so completely wrong? One explanation is that hundreds of thousands of people changed their minds at the last moment. This seems unlikely. It is more reasonable to suppose that they did not actually speak their minds when asked for their opinion.

There are two sets of contextual conditions here, and they are likely to elicit different patterns of behaviour. When in the context of a questionnaire interview, people are asked to give public expression to what they think, they are naturally under social pressure to project a favourable image of themselves; and this, in many cases, may well not be consistent with being seen as supporting the Conservative Party. In the very different context of the polling booth, however, they are free of such constraint: they can express their private selves in secret. They can now act on what they really think. They can vote Conservative and nobody will ever know. Thus vowing that they would ne'er consent, they consented. It is, one might say, the Galileo phenomenon: you protect yourself by telling people not what you think, but what you think it is convenient or safe for them to hear. 'And yet it moves.' So people do not always say what is in their minds. That is a social fact, a fact indeed about social meaning. But people do not always know what is in their minds either. That is a psychological fact. There are all manner of ideas, impressions, mental images lurking in the neural networks which have never been (perhaps never will be) excited or made verbally explicit in response to any SOCIAL requirement, but which may nevertheless be apprehended by the individual. All meaning is NOT social meaning. But the point at issue for my present argument is that what is consciously or unconsciously known is distinct from what is actually MADE known.

No doubt I am labouring the point. This distinction is clear. Why state the obvious? But clear and obvious or not, one finds the distinction persistently disregarded. Over and over again in the second language acquisition (SLA) literature, for example (it would be invidious to single out particular instances), a certain stage in acquisition, or state of interlanguage, is adduced on the evidence of what subjects do with language, on what they say or write in response to different kinds of contextual prompting. What this shows is the ability to control access, or the disposition to exercise such control, but it does not show what is there available for access under different conditions. One can make essentially the same point about descriptions of language as corpus data: the language which is attested as actual behaviour does not cover availability or disponibilité - the language which is known, and so in principle available, disponible, but which may not be drawn upon, at the disposal of users who may not themselves, for all kinds of reason, be disposed to use it (cf. Widdowson 1991). The issue here concerns language use, but one can make a similar point about language learning. Indeed such a point has been made, most recently by Larsen-Freeman and Long. In their excellent survey of SLA research they make reference to the Contrastive Analysis Hypothesis (CAH) and review the reasons for its rejection. Larsen-Freeman and Long (1991:56) conclude by saying:

> Perhaps the most fatal flaw of CAH, as pointed out by Long and Sato (1984), was the dubious assumption that one could depend solely upon an analysis of a LINGUISTIC PRODUCT to yield meaningful insight into a PSYCHOLINGUISTIC PROCESS i.e. second language learning.

But a good deal of the SLA research which these authors so comprehensively review assumes in like behaviourist manner that the linguistic products of subjects in controlled performance can be reliably used as a source of insight into the psycholinguistic processes of knowledge acquisition. The fatal flaw now seems to be overlooked. And yet we find the same confusion PASSIM between what people know and what, for all kinds of reasons, they reveal of their knowledge. Behaviourism casts a very long shadow.

For all kinds of reason? What kinds? Pragmatic kinds. And here's the rub. When learners reveal what we might call inadequacies, non-conformities, 'errors' or 'infelicities' of behaviour in respect to native-speaker norms (another problematic concept to which I shall return), how can we tell whether this reveals restricted knowledge or restricted access. We can, of course, set learners elicitation tasks which require them to demonstrate what they know, but then we might say (and researchers have said) that this knowledge does not really count, it is learnt not acquired, a graft which has not taken. So when these learners are required to use it more 'naturally' it is not there any more. But then we are back where we started. It may be there, but they may simply fail to call it up. Why should they so fail?

One answer to that is that they are using their knowledge with the same pragmatic tactics as does any natural language user. The pragmatic use of language (as Sperber and Wilson (1986) among others have pointed out) operates on a least effort principle. People are not usually profligate with their language: they use it economically and expediently to the extent that it is necessary to key into context. That much and no more. This is the point of the Gricean Cooperative Principle, of course. So if language learners are encouraged to use the second language naturally, they will take whatever short cuts they can in the interests of pragmatic expediency. In such circumstances they are unlikely to display what they know. On the other hand, as I have argued, if they do display what they know, their knowledge is likely to be discounted. Catch 22. By certain SLA rules, it seems, the language learner just cannot win.

With reference to the pedagogic position I outlined, the objective of language teaching is to guide the learner to an acquisition of communicative competence. So what does this mean: a knowledge of the communicative potential in the language or an ability to actualize this potential as behaviour appropriate to the occasion, or both? Presumably both, but it is generally communicative ability which is given primacy. Hence the emphasis on authenticity. But the authentic language of recorded use is a record of communicative performance, warts and all, incomplete, elliptical, pragmatically expedient, dependent on context, and unreliable as evidence of communicative competence. How then are learners to infer communicative competence from it?

It is an appealing idea that we should deal with authentic data and, in one way or another, instruct learners in the appropriate socio-cultural use of the language they are learning. But it raises a number of very tricky questions. I have just mentioned one: namely that the communicative data will often of its very pragmatic nature be uninformative. Let me give one particular example of what I mean. There is a school of thought in pedagogic lexicography which insists that all examples illustrating the meanings of particular lexical entries in a dictionary should be authentic, that is to say drawn from a corpus of actually attested use. As a result, many of the cited instances provide no illustration of meaning at all, precisely because they so effectively illustrate use. For in use the word works indexically to key in with and complement a context of shared knowledge which does not need to be spelled out. Naturally occurring utterances will not generally therefore provide a gloss of any particular word within it. To do this you need to contrive a sentence.

There is, then, the problem of uninformative data, of what Chomsky, in reference to grammatical competence, has referred to as the poverty of the stimulus. But there are other problems too. Let us suppose (as has indeed been proposed) that we can solve the data limitation or poverty problem by treating the raw material of performance in some way, so that it is no longer strictly speaking authentic but 'modified' authentic. What we do in this case is to adjust language use in the interests of language learning. I will return to this issue presently. But meanwhile there is another difficulty to confront. It has to do with the selection of the source of this raw material of use.

If we seek to teach by reference to authentic language data, real English in the sense that it is attested native speaker behaviour, perhaps modified but not originally designed for instruction, then where do we get this language from? From native speakers, of course. But who are these people? Native speakers of any kind, and perhaps especially of English, are a heterogeneous collection. They belong to all kinds of community and conform to all manner of different socio-cultural and linguistic norms of appropriacy as far as language is concerned. So which native speakers are to be favoured as the providers of the authentic data? Real English, real uses of English, but whose reality? One answer might be: that which the learners are likely to encounter and be called upon to conform to. But how do we know? There are, of course, occasions when we can be specific about what is required in reference to target discourse communities and their genres, when we can determine objectives in reference to a needs analysis as in the case of programmes in English, or any other language, for specific purposes. But the point of a general English course, presumably, is that it is designed to develop a more general capacity for use, to prepare learners to cope with communicative situations which CANNOT be specified in advance.

And of course, whatever social community is decided upon, by whatever criteria of relevance, it is not just a matter of recording occurrences of its language but also the sociocultural contextual concomitants of the utterance concerned. A particular word or phrase or extended stretch of language can perhaps be said to be authentic as a form by virtue of its occurrence alone, but its communicative function can only be authenticated by the reference to the circumstances of its occurrence. Only then can its indexical value be established: what it means to the users, its social meaning, in terms of reference, force, and effect.

The recording of authentic data is then a complex business. It involves, to use Jenny Thomas's distinction (Thomas 1983), both sociopragmatic and pragmalinguistic aspects of language use (two more kinds of competence to set alongside the others!). Beginnings have been made in this most daunting ethnographic enterprise. One example is the work of Nessa Wolfson (cf. Wolfson 1983) on rules of speaking (work so sadly cut short); another example is the research on cross-cultural speech act realization patterns (CCSARP) (Blum-Kulka and Olshtain 1984). Descriptive work of this kind is seen as a prerequisite for effective teaching of appropriate use. This is how Wolfson (1986:119) puts it:

> If true communication is to take place among people who come from different cultural backgrounds, and if interference is to be minimized in second language learning, then we must have cross-cultural comparisons of rules of speaking.

If learners are to engage in true communication (in real English, we might add) then we need to base our teaching on the ethnographic analysis of actual use. Gabriele Kasper (1989:42) makes much the same point in speaking of the learner's need 'to develop and use pragmatic knowledge'. She goes on:

> The learner's task is not very different from that of the pragmaticist: She has to discover the contextual (situational) and co-textual (linguistic) constraints governing SA (Speech Act) selection and modes of realization in the target language and culture. In Hymes' (1971) terms, she has to discover what is possible, feasible, appropriate and done in carrying out SAs in L2.

One can readily recognize that these are things which language learners have to discover, at some point and in some measure at least, in order to communicate effectively in a particular social community, but if we are to wait until they are described before we can direct the discovery by some sort of informed pedagogic guidance, we are likely to have to wait a long time. The descriptive work done to date, interesting though it is, is tiny: a few speech acts, a few conventions of interaction. And even here the sociocultural categories are crudely conceived: we are told, for example, that the Americans follow one formula in telephone conversations, the French another. ALL Americans, ALL French people, of whatever sex, ethnic background, social class? The Germans apologize in one way the English in another. Which Germans? Which English? You can make general statements about how apologies in German and in English are different, but these should not be confused with the much more particular statements needed to describe how different Germans and English people apologize. The appropriate use of language in particular contexts calls for a much more sensitive tuning in to sociocultural variation. One could argue, indeed, that neglect of the fine tuning on a mistaken assumption of cultural homogeneity is more likely to lead to pragmatic failure than is a complete ignorance of sociocultural factors. A foreigner who realizes the speech act of request perfectly in accordance with the middle-class norms of acceptable behaviour in southern England, but does so, let us say, in a working-class pub in Manchester, is likely to get a rude reply. A little learning is (or can be) a dangerous thing.

So how much learning is necessary? It seems clear that even if we had the ethnographic information available for us to be more specific about patterns of appropriate behaviour, it does not follow at all that we should require learners to conform to them in the interests of authenticity. Quite the contrary in fact. For to do so is to induce a commitment to the norms of a particular community. And in so doing, of course, they bid for membership of that community. Quite apart from the fact that learners may not wish to assume such a social identity, the community itself may resent the claim to membership and close ranks against the imposter. There are advantages in retaining the status of stranger.

It seems clear that we do not want to confine learners to very specific patterns of behaviour appropriate to particular communities, even if we had descriptions to refer to, but to provide them with a more general capacity to communicate. In other words, it is not a matter of learning authentic use but learning FROM authentic use, detaching it from the contexts in which it is specifically appropriate. For authentic language to be effective for learning, it has in this sense to be deauthenticated as use, generalized from the particular contextual conditions of its appropriacy. Only in this way can it be reauthenticated, so to speak, as use in other contexts. Now people naturally do, in fact, learn FROM particulars, recognize them as INSTANCES of something more general—that is what learning means: inferring beyond the data. We all know that intake does not equal input, that is to say that conceptual knowledge is an abstraction from contextual behaviour.

Learners who are confronted with actually occurring language data in the form of written text or transcriptions of speech are already detached anyway, at one remove from immediate participation. They are not the intended receivers but onlookers, eavesdroppers, witnesses to other people's behaviour. What they experience therefore is a secondhand and simulated reality in another language. And this detachment can be seen as an advantage from the point of view of learning. Naturally the language behaviour to which they are witness has to be such as to engage their interest; and authentic language may, IF THE LEARNERS RECOGNIZE IT AS SUCH (a crucial condition), have a face validity which may in turn have a motivating effect. But then its justification, it seems to me, is not that it simulates use but that it stimulates learning.

I referred earlier to loose talk about authenticity and appropriate use. My argument, in essence, is that it is a mistake to try to transfer these features of communication and social meaning into the classroom. The authenticity does not survive the transfer; and appropriate use, even if it could be specified, is not appropriate for learning. Learners acquire a restricted competence if they do indeed learn to conform to particular patterns of socio-cultural behaviour. The argument against a pedagogic investment in linguistic competence is that it does not yield much in the way of actual communicative return. It is too abstract and general. But a communicative competence which is confined to particular conditions of appropriacy does not yield much in the way of generalized ability to communicate either. It is too actual and particular. Of course, learners are not likely to be confined. As always they will be busy converting input into intake and generalizing beyond the data. But then why insist on authentic data in the first place if learners are going to deauthenticate it by generalization anyway? And would it not be pedagogically preferable to give them some guidance on generalization rather than to leave them to their own devices?

There is a curious contradiction in current pedagogic thinking in this respect. On the one hand there is this emphasis on authenticity and appropriate use, which requires learners to conform to certain exo-normative social conventions, to achieve social meanings which are not their own. Authenticity implies submission. On the other hand there is an emphasis on autonomy, which allows learners the freedom to take the initiative and to develop endo-normative patterns of behaviour consistent with their own socio-cultural conventions.

Autonomy implies assertion. Thus considerations of what goals learners have eventually to achieve submissively in terms of use, conflict with considerations of what they need to do assertively in the process of learning.

And here, I think, we come to the heart of the matter, the central problem of language pedagogy, as indeed in so many other things, namely the relationship between the ends and the means, the eventual goal and the mediating process of learning. What kind of investment do we need in the process in order to achieve the right kinds of return in the form of an appropriate payoff?

All learning involves the acquisition of knowledge, the abstraction of generalities from particulars. Let us call this the inferring of concepts from contexts. The application of learning to the concerns of practical life involves the reverse process, the enactment of behaviour whereby we make sense by relating particulars to generalities. Let us call this the referring of contexts to concepts. Now if we consider the position that I outlined at the beginning, it is clear that the emphasis is on contexts: the assumption is that conceptual inference will happen as a natural consequence. This contrasts very clearly with a structural orientation to language teaching where the emphasis is on concepts. The assumption here is that once linguistic competence is in place, once the conceptual knowledge of the abstract properties of the language itself are acquired, then they will be available for use as required. In the first position learners are left to conceptualize from contextual particulars, in the second position learners are left to contexualize from conceptual generalities. It is, as I have said, the first position which is currently in favour and the second is generally discredited. But there seems to be no very good reason to suppose that learners are any better at the conceptual inference required by the first position than at the contextual reference required by the second. Learners may not readily acquire the ability to communicate by acquiring linguistic knowledge. But they apparently do not readily acquire the necessary linguistic knowledge by communicative activity either (cf. for example Harley and Swain 1984, Lightbown and Spada 1990, Spada 1986, and Wesche 1992 on the shortcomings of the Canadian Immersion Program in this respect).

So where do we go from here? As I have suggested elsewhere (Widdowson 1990), it is possible to conceive of an approach to teaching which engages the learners in communicative activities which are purposeful without being replications of authentic conditions of use in the native speaker community. Indeed such attempts at replication may, in representing an unfamiliar social reality, actually prevent engagement. What I have in mind are task-based, problem solving activities of the kind proposed in, for example, Prabhu (1987) and Tarone and Yule (1989). Such activities are designed more in reference to things that go on in other parts of the school curriculum than to naturally occurring communicative events in the social life of the native speaker community. In that respect they have a socio-cultural character of their own and they are designed to be context creating, not context conforming. This means that they can be contrived to bring linguistic features to conscious awareness, make them noticeable (cf. Schmidt 1990) because they are necessary for the task outcome. There can be a focus on form not as an end in itself but as a means to a more sharply defined focus on meaning. In brief, tasks of this kind require learners to realize the communicative potential of the language as a generalizable resource for the negotiation of meaning. This is the basic pedagogic investment for the development of proficiency.

This does not mean that in addition learners cannot be, should not be, sensitized to specific socio-cultural differences, have their consciousness raised about particular pragmatic subtleties and problems of appropriate use, and be exposed to actually attested native speaker data for that purpose. But it seems to me that this development of language and culture awareness can, and should, run parallel to, but apart from, a course which is designed to develop practical ability in a language. Learners may indeed draw on this awareness in the development of their proficiency, just as they may draw on the ambient language they are exposed to. But this is an incidental benefit. And, of course, such awareness has an independent EDUCATIONAL justification, quite apart from its pedagogic utility. But that is a different matter. My discussion in this paper has to do with the design of instruction for the investment of basic language proficiency, with conditions which need to be contrived by teachers to activate the language learning process.

These conditions are set up in classrooms, which constitute contexts of their own, contexts of instruction, which create their own communities. They are enabling conditions which activate learning rather than replicate use, and they are designed to instruct learners in the general parameters of social meaning which are encoded in the lexico-grammar—ideational parameters like time, space, causation, for example, and interpersonal parameters which are defined in reference to the co-operative and territorial imperatives (cf. Widdowson 1990, chapters 5 through 7). How these general parameters are contextually set on communicative occasions for particular communities, how the cultural niceties and subtleties are regulated by fine tuning, are matters which, in my view, and in most cases at least, we waste time in trying to teach: they are best left to be learned, as and when and IF required in whatever contexts of use the learners will subsequently encounter. What learners subsequently do with their competence, which community they feel disposed to associate with, the extent to which they wish to conform to other socio-cultural conventions—all that is their affair. Our business is not to determine their options but to provide them with the opportunity to decide their own.

And our business is also to be realistic about what can be achieved. In this respect I think we need to recognize that in the vast majority of English language teaching situations in the world, the context of instruction is much more likely to be influenced by the conventions of communication and social meaning in the L1 community rather than those of the L2 community, however these might be defined. For appropriate pedagogy requires that it be located in the socio-cultural matrix of the learners' own world.

In conclusion, and in brief: given the range and variability of English as an international language, given the different socio-economic and socio-cultural circumstances in which the language is taught, given the harsh realities of so many language classrooms, I do not think we should talk too loosely, or glibly, about the need for authenticity of data, the teaching of social meaning, and conformity to the norms of appropriate use.

REFERENCES

Bachman, Lyle F. 1990. Fundamental considerations in language testing. Oxford: Oxford University Press.

Bialystok, Ellen, and Michael Sharwood Smith. 1985. Interlanguage is not a state of mind: An evaluation of the concept for second-language acquisition. Applied Linguistics 6, 2.102-17.

Blum-Kulka, Shoshana, and Elite Olshtain. 1984. Requests and apologies: A cross-cultural study of speech act realization patterns (CCSARP). Applied Linguistics 5, 3.196-213.

Canale, Michael. 1983. From communicative competence to communicative language pedagogy. Language and Communication, ed. by Jack C. Richards and Richard W. Schmidt, 2–27. London: Longman.

Canale, Michael, and Merrill Swain. 1980. Theoretical bases of communicative approaches to second language teaching and testing. Applied Linguistics 1, 1.1-47.

Chomsky, Noam. 1980. Rules and Representations. Oxford: Basil Blackwell.

Harley, Birgit, and Merrill Swain. 1984. The interlanguage of immersion students and its implications for second language learning. Interlanguage, ed. by Alan Davies, C. Criper, and A.P.R. Howatt, 291–311. Edinburgh: Edinburgh University Press.

Kasper, Gabriele. 1989. Variation in interlanguage speech act realization. Variation in second language acquisition, ed. by Susan Gass, Carolyn Madden, Dennis Preston, and Larry Selinker, 37–58. Clevedon and Philadelphia: Multilingual Matters.

Larsen-Freeman, Diane, and Michael H. Long. 1991. Introduction to second language acquisition research. London: Longman.

Lightbown, Patsy M., and Nina Spada. 1990. Focus-on-form and corrective feedback in communicative language teaching: Effects on second language learning. Studies in Second Language Acquisition 12, 4.429–48.

Prabhu, N. S. 1987. Second language pedagogy. Oxford: Oxford University Press.

Richards, Jack C., and Richard W. Schmidt. 1983. Language and communication. London: Longman.

Schmidt, Richard W. 1990. The role of consciousness in second language learning. Applied Linguistics 11, 2.129-58.

Spada, Nina. 1986. The interaction between type of contact and type of instruction: Some effects on the L2 proficiency of adult learners. Studies in Second Language Acquisition 8.181-200.

Sperber, Dan, and Deirdre Wilson. 1986. Relevance: Communication and cognition. Oxford: Basil Blackwell.

Tarone, Elaine, and George Yule. 1989. Focus on the language learner. Oxford: Oxford University Press.

Thomas, Jenny. 1983. Cross-cultural pragmatic failure. Applied Linguistics 5, 3.226-35.

Wesche, Majorie Bingham. 1992. French immersion graduates at university and beyond: What difference has it made? Georgetown University Round Table on Languages and Linguistics 1992, ed. by James E. Alatis. Washington, DC: Georgetown University Press.

Widdowson, H. G. 1989. Knowledge of language and ability for use. Applied Linguistics 10, 2.128-137.

Widdowson, H. G. 1990. Aspects of language teaching. Oxford: Oxford University Press.

Wolfson, Nessa. 1983. Rules of speaking. Language and communication, ed. by Jack C. Richards and Richard W. Schmidt, 61–87. London: Longman.

Wolfson, Nessa. 1986. Compliments in cross-cultural perspective. Culture Bound. Bridging the cultural gap in language teaching, ed. by Joyce Merrill Valdes, 112–20. Cambridge: Cambridge University Press.

Discourse community and the evaluation of written text

John M. Swales
The University of Michigan

There are some perceptions about texts in the modern world that are now quite widely shared. One is that texts are socially situated—or to rephrase in accordance with this year's theme, language, written communication, and social meaning are functionally interlinked, however much a particular analyst for whatever purpose may be able to tease out a separate strand. The perception that we may need a more eclectic approach than provided for by cognitive research on the one hand, or process welfare on the other, may partly explain the sudden interest among those who study socially situated writing in Anthony Giddens' Structuration Theory (Giddens 1984). Apparently, this theory has been reverberating through the field of sociology for several years. Its sudden appeal to writing scholars (Bazerman 1992, Berkenkotter and Huckin 1992, Miller 1992) lies in the realisation that texts in general and documentation in particular can be added to Giddens' mid-level structures which both enable and constrain social praxis and mediate between institution and individual mind.

A consequent and similarly shared perception is that texts in the modern world are increasingly typified and labelled. No longer is it the case that 'Choughs, water-rugs and demi-wolves are clept all by the name of dogs.' Further, these typifications are no longer the inevitable outcomes of slow historical evolution. Increasingly, they seem textual responses to rapidly changing social need, technological innovation, and even prescription and design (Witte 1992). Thus we have new genres associated with the answerphone, new phenomena such as 'flaming' in electronic mail, and deliberate innovations such as the doctoral dissertation as a student's collected works rather than the traditional synoptic monograph. Thus, it may no longer be any more fanciful to talk about generic engineering than it now is to talk of genetic engineering. Indeed in my professional lifetime perhaps the most significant of these engineered changes has been the attack on sexist language. I was brought up in an epoch when, using the epigram of John Bright, one of the great forgotten pioneers of English as a second language (ESL), 'In English grammar man embraces woman'. To this day, I remember the dislocation I felt some twenty years ago when I first read an article engineered to show that in English grammar woman could embrace man.

A third perception is particularly common among those who have fallen under the spell of Bakhtin (particularly, Bakhtin 1986). We see what we can learn when, in Bakhtin's terminology, genres are 'reaccentuated', when we offer versions of our generic repertoire for parody, humor, irony, and verbal play. Within any discourse community there is I suspect more of this going on than is admitted in our linguistic and discoursal accounts or is brought to light in our pedagogic materials. We have somehow lost the influence of Goffman, skewered perhaps for all time by Geertz's (1983:25) summative one-liner 'For Goffman, life is just a bowl of strategies.' In the meantime we have gone on to the serious businesses of the felicity and sincerity conditions of promises, to the unpacking of information structure, and to the troubles of communication among cultures, ethnic groups, generations, and the like. And yet while the search for gender-neutral language is rightly serious, the spoof is not simply a trivial exercise in ridicule. Parodies and caricatures reveal the concerns, conventions, and obsessions of discourse communities in ways that are useful for experts and novices alike. By making fun of our texts we see what they are. Here are two brief abstracts targeted at us; they reached me anonymously, but I believe them to be written by Michael Swan, that scourge of our pretensions.

Interlanguage in MA Students

> Utterances of Applied Linguistics students can be sited along a continuum running from pure L1 forms (e.g. 'We have to teach them to understand English') to pure TL forms (e.g. 'Our prime pedagogic task is to encourage strategies which will enhance the learner's capacity to attend to the pragmatic communicative semiotic macrocontext'). The paper offers a choice of five models to account for non-systematic variability in the data, treating L1, IL and TL as hierarchically independent semipermeable systems in each case.

Coming Clean on Cohesion

> If you refer more than once to a person, thing, or event, the second mention can be made either by using the same words as before (iteration), other content words (synonymy), grammatical substitutes (anaphora), or no words at all (ellipsis). All of these are cohesive devices. This has led some critics of the theory to ask what would not count as a cohesive device. The answer is nothing. Everything is cohesive. Life itself is a cohesive device.

These two abstracts both enlighten and (I hope) entertain. The first takes second language acquisition (SLA) theory and neatly applies it to our efforts at discourse community formation in language teacher education. The second takes an overarching concept in discourse analysis and extends that concept to life itself. They shift the footing by legitimate exaggeration so that we see ourselves as others may see us.

My third and final example of genre reaccentuation takes us back to the dissertation, seen of course by many as an ultimate rite of passage into academic discourse communities. This example is not, in fact, a parody since it is taken from a successful dissertation. Indeed, perhaps it is more than that, since it was published as exactly written by the University of Chicago Press, and has got to be talked about even at the Georgetown University Round Table on Languages and Linguistics 1992. I refer to Ashmore (1989) on the vexed topic of reflexivity in the sociology of knowledge.

The dissertation is itself a Bakhtinian reaccentuation of a more serious kind since it attempts to rewrite the rules of what a dissertation can be. On the macrolevel, it opens with a literature review cast in the form of an introductory lecture by the candidate with noisy interjections by the adviser. Chapter Two is an alphabetic Encyclopedia on the topic of reflexivity, the first entry being very conveniently ASHMORE, wherein we find a summary of the dissertation. The final chapter is cast in the guise of a mock transcript of the oral defence. There is reaccentuation on the microlevel as well. The beginning of the endnotes to the volume give something of the flavor (Ashmore 1989:227):

> NOTES
>
> Chapter One
>
> 1. Welcome to the Notes. I hope you will visit this section of the text regularly. Quite a lot will be going on here and it would be a shame to miss it all. But to get to the business of this particular note: May I ask you by which route you have arrived at Chapter One, note 1? If you are a 'notephile' you were probably guided here directly by the note number in the text on page 15—and quite right too. However, you might also have come to be reading this by way of the reference to Mulkay 1984b which would have led you to the bibliography, where the text in question would turn out to have the strange title '15 August 1984, Dear Malcolm' and to be located in this very text (Ashmore 1989) at this very point (page 227, note 1). And here it is:
>
> .....

I have argued so far that it is valuable to consider written texts as (1) socially situated, (2) typically specified as to genre, and (3) open to revealing reaccentuation. The fourth and final characteristic I would like to mention is that texts are locally evaluated; that is to say, they are judged in terms of the expectations, norms, and agendas of their target discourse communities. This last presents those of us who are concerned with teaching and evaluating the writing of nonnative speakers (NNS) with a problem. We are asked, as professionals, to evaluate such texts on behalf of other discourse communities such as employers, academic departments, admissions officers, and so on. But if the premise of socially constructed texts holds, it holds just as much for us as it does for others. We are presented with a 'tu quoque' rejoinder since we ourselves have a socially constructed vision of what good and bad NNS writing is (and of how the former might be fostered and the latter eroded).

Consider, by way of illustration, the vexed issue of topic difficulty. Hamp-Lyons and Prochnow (1991) investigated topic difficulty in the composition section of the Michigan English Language Assessment Battery (MELAB). Professionals were asked to rate MELAB topics for difficulty, and they consistently rated topics requiring personal writing as easier than those requiring public writing, and topics requiring description as easier than those requiring argumentation. So easy topics were like the following:

> When you go to a party, do you usually talk a lot, or do you prefer to listen? What does this show about your personality?

And the hardest:

> What is your opinion of mercenary soldiers (those who are hired to fight for a country other than their own)? Discuss.

So far so good. However, when the scores of a large batch of 8500 scripts were aligned with the type of prompt, an unexpected reversal occurred. The adjudged more difficult topics scored somewhat higher than those adjudged by the expert raters to be easier.

There are several possible explanations for this puzzle that may occur to the reader. We could suggest that the composition readers were somehow compensating in their scoring for their perceived difficulty of the topic (although there is little evidence of this). Or we could say that the candidates are self-selecting, the weaker ones choosing personal, descriptive topics. However, I do not think in general test-takers have much of a track record in making good judgements about task difficulty. Alternatively, it could be a teaching effect in that students are better prepared for public argumentation. But again there must be some doubt about this when empowering the individual voice remains such a rallying cry across much of the composition territory. Or it could be that it is the students, not their instructors, who are overachieving by rising to the challenge of more cognitively demanding and abstract topics. Whichever way we go, Hamp-Lyons and Prochnow have presented us with a serious difficulty about difficulty.

In *Georgetown University Round Table on Languages and Linguistics 1990* there is a very interesting paper by Henry Widdowson on paradigms and epistemes as controlling modes of thought. Widdowson (1990:39) suggests that '... all discourses of theory, including those of linguistics, are ideologically loaded, cultural constructs designed to establish control and a sense of security.' We can see here, I suggest, ESL writing getting into the wrong paradigm. ESL writing, for sociological reasons that I will not go into, seems to have adopted some of the belief systems central to first language (L1) writing and its development. Among these are private before public, narrative before description, description before exposition. Indeed, it is precisely this progression that is fleshed out in the vast majority of textbooks designed to teach ESL writing. But, as Hamp-Lyons and Prochnow discovered, this evaluative and judgemental scheme fits ill with certain large ESL populations, however much it may be appropriate of NNS immigrants in the school system. It certainly does not fit the 25% of international graduate students who enter my university highly literate in their first language but who have never written anything longer in English than the 20-line statement on their graduate application form, if they even wrote that. For them, as I expect for us, the mercenary question is much easier, at least partly because we have a schema available to moderate our response—it meets our educated expectations of what a sample of our writing might be about.

Now I am not saying that we do not know a lot about evaluating ESL writing; indeed the recent volume edited by Hamp-Lyons (1991) hugely demonstrates how much we do know. After all, we are the best at seeing the general flow of NNS writing beneath the eddies of deviant article usage and the like. But I do suggest that for those many of us who work in postsecondary institutions (either in foreign language (FL) or ESL) we may be insufficiently aware of how we continue to be a captured discourse community. We have borrowed rather too easily a majoritarian account of writing development which does not fit the situation of many of our students.

To round off this discussion, I would like to turn away from our role as evaluators of ESL texts on behalf of the external world in order to consider our role as mediators of ESL texts to be evaluated by that external world itself. In so doing, we move in discourse community terms from insider to outsider, from expert in evaluating product to expert in facilitating process. And in so doing we meet a more widely recognised set of difficulties than the ones I have discussed so far. For as long as I have been in this business, a significant number of ESL/EFL writing instructors have argued that whenever we try to help our students write like physicists or sociologists or lawyers we may not know what we do. Whenever we second guess the exigencies and expectations of other discourse communities we are likely to fall into error; or if not always that, at least to enhance the prospect of hubris or to retreat into a trivializing concern with minor repairs. A fairly recent locus for these concerns was the 1988 *TESOL Quarterly* article by Ruth Spack and the attendant Forum discussion (Spack 1988, Braine 1988, Johns 1988). Here is the penultimate paragraph of Spack's (1988:708) final response:

> I am uneasy with the practice of asking teachers who have a weak grasp of other disciplines to teach, supervise, or evaluate the writing of those

> disciplines. This is a practice that needs reexamination, regardless of student level or interest. Yes, students need to learn 'to determine the important problems in a discipline the appropriate methods of argumentation, and the data that are accepted in support of an argument'. But they will learn most efficiently and accurately from those faculty members who have fully grasped the concepts and conventions. To suggest that an ESL/EFL instructor can unlock the door to an entire academic universe of discourse is to overlook the complexity and diversity among and within disciplines.

While I would be the last to claim that an ESL writing instructor like myself 'can unlock the door to the entire academic universe', yet I seem to teach a successful course—at least as measured by student evaluations—in 'Prospectus and Dissertation Writing' for nonnative speakers (Morley 1992). If the fifteen or so participants in my class do not quite represent the entire academic universe, over the last five years I have had representatives from a great proportion of it. It seems to me that part of the solution lies in refiguring the instructor role to take account of Spack's concerns.

To start with, it is worth reminding ourselves that there is much useful discussion of instructor role in the Writing Center literature (e.g. Wallace and Simpson 1991), none more valuable than in Stephen North's influential article (1984:438) wherein he says ' ... in a writing center the object is to make sure that writers, and not necessarily their texts, are what gets changed by instruction.' This noble aim is, of course, one incessantly suborned by the pressures to assist in making a particular text fit for submission, publication, or defense. Nevertheless it does serve as a guiding light. It sets the course up in my mind as a one-window opportunity for senior graduates to enlarge the envelope of their rhetorical space—to get them out from under their parochial concerns with their own texts.

The trick of the matter is to turn disciplinary disparity into socio-rhetorical community (Swales 1990). This is not as impetuous as it might sound. For one thing, my students are typically senior graduates three or four years into their doctoral programs. As a group they are largely ready for rhetorical consciousness-raising. For another, those who do not work as members of lab teams often come to class with the loneliness of long-distance dissertation writers. Whatever else may happen, the weekly two-hour class becomes a social occasion for sharing the academic news, for reporting on triumph or disaster, and for surprising fellow participants with the idiosyncracies of individual positions and programs. The weekly 'block party' ethos evinces sympathy rather than Schadenfreude and suggests that the carpet is not always greener in the department down the corridor.

All this helps us to see our texts as socially situated; as one of my Chinese students wrote in a marvellous pairing of adjectives, our approaches are both 'complicitous and contestatory'. I can also provide some particular help with the typification of texts, and not only with the 'open' genres of academic work (the research article, the published abstract, the long lines of previous dissertations in departmental libraries), but also with the more out-of-sight genres that orchestrate the processes of application, request, review, report, and recommendation. As waystages I tell many stories of the academic game, give personal perspectives as editor and reviewer, share edited examples of correspondence, and continually ask them to evaluate and pass judgements on texts.

I also work hard to give them responsibility for their own texts since, as I have argued, texts are locally evaluated. I encourage them to investigate the perceptions of their primary readers. How do advisers and other key players line up on active or passive, on much or little metadiscourse (Crismore 1990), or on certain methodological issues? In consultancy, I increasingly expect them to arrive with an agenda for our individual meeting so that they learn to be good critics of their own work. In the final class session each student showcases a paragraph of their own work, explaining why they chose it and how it got to be worth showcasing. After two hours of this, I remain amazed that I have been listening to insights provided by nonnative speakers of English.

And increasingly I turn to reaccentuation. This semester I have for the second time given some attention to recommendations and references since my students may be involved in these as when asked to contribute to promotion or teaching award files. I feel I am getting somewhere with my attempts to integrate them into the academy when towards the end of the semester all can spontaneously laugh at such ambiguous recommendations as the following:

> I urge you to waste no time in offering this candidate a position.
> I am glad to say that this applicant is a former colleague of mine.
> You will be lucky if you can get this person to work for you.

Kramsch (1992) rightly emphasizes the crucial role of the instructor in establishing the 'conversational floor', thus influencing the nature of the consequent discourse. She shows how one particular text led four different instructors to the floors of vocabulary lesson, topic discussion, logical argumentation, and cross-cultural communication. The most typical floor in ELI 600 is not the cross-disciplinary dissimilarity problematized by Spack, but the forward challenge shared by all participants. All of us in 600 have to turn presentations into papers (and vice versa), be 'complicitous and contestatory' in our handling of prior scholarship, develop networks, strive for recognition, and negotiate with committee members. The floor is designed to cover this wider rhetorical space.

REFERENCES

Ashmore, Malcolm. 1989. The reflexive thesis: Wrighting the sociology of scientific knowledge. Chicago: University of Chicago Press.

Bakhtin, M. M. 1986. Speech genres and other late essays. Austin: University of Texas Press.

Bazerman, Charles. 1992 (April). The generic performance of ownership: The patent claim and grant. Paper presented at the Rethinking Genre Colloquium, Carleton University, Ottawa.

Berkenkotter, Carol, and Tom Huckin. 1992 (April). Rethinking genre from a sociocognitive perspective. Paper presented at the Rethinking Genre Colloquium, Carleton University,

Ottawa.

Braine, George. 1988. A reader reacts ... TESOL Quarterly 22.700-02.

Crismore, Avon. 1990. Metadiscourse and discourse processes: Interactions and issues. Discourse Processes 13.191-205.

Geertz, Clifford. 1984. Local knowledge. New York: Basic Books.

Giddens, A. 1984. The constitution of society: Outline of the theory of structuration. Cambridge: Polity Press.

Hamp-Lyons, Liz (ed.) 1991. Assessing second language writing in academic contexts. Norwood, NJ: Ablex Publishing.

Hamp-Lyons, Liz, and Sheila Prochnow. 1991. The difficulties of difficulty. Current developments in language testing, ed. by S. Anivan. Singapore: SEAMEO: RELC.

Johns, Ann. 1988. Another reader reacts ... TESOL Quarterly 22.705-07.

Kramsch, Claire. 1992. The dialogic emergence of culture in the language classroom. Georgetown University Round Table on Languages and Linguistics 1992, ed. by James E. Alatis. Washington, DC: Georgetown University Press.

Miller, Carolyn. 1992 (April). Rhetorical community: The cultural basis of genre. Paper presented at the Rethinking Genre Colloquium, Carleton University, Ottawa.

Morley, Joan. 1992. Spoken discourse, meaning, and communicative 'pronunciation'. Georgetown University Round Table on Languages and Linguistics 1992, ed. by James E. Alatis. Washington, DC: Georgetown University Press.

North, Steven. 1984. The idea of a writing center. College English 46.433-46.

Spack, Ruth. 1988. The author responds to Johns ... TESOL Quarterly 22.707-08.

Swales, John M. 1990. Genre analysis: English in academic and research settings. Cambridge: Cambridge University Press.

Wallace, Ray, and Jeanne Simpson (eds.) 1991. The writing center: New directions. New York: Garland.

Widdowson, H. G. 1990. Discourses of enquiry and conditions of relevance. Georgetown University Round Table on Languages and Linguistics 1990, ed. by James E. Alatis, 37-46. Washington, DC: Georgetown University Press.

Witte, Steven. 1992. Context, text and intertext: Toward a constructionist semiotic of writing. Written Communication 9.237-308.

Second culture acquisition: A tentative step in determining hierarchies

Nadine O'Connor Di Vito
University of Chicago

1 Introduction. Many researchers now believe that it is primarily through meaningful interaction that language learners make, test, and confirm hypotheses about target language structures and their use, and that engagement in meaningful interaction is essential to the acquisition process (Ellis 1984, Kramsch 1986, Prabhu 1987, Rivers 1986, Swain 1985). Not surprisingly, this new perspective of foreign language acquisition has spread to the development of pedagogical materials, which now boast an increasing number of exercises whose purpose is to engage the learner in communicative exchanges.

There is also a growing body of research indicating that typical textbook exercises, even those that are communicative and personally meaningful, do not always reflect native speaker norms (Bland 1988, Di Vito 1991a, 1991b, 1992; Herschensohn 1988, Holmes 1988, Scotton and Bernsten 1988, Walz 1989); therefore, we might hope that future textbook editions not only stress communicative exercises in the classroom but also more consistently model those exercises on actual target language patterns.

However, EVEN WITH appropriate target language models AND interactive, communicative exercises, we should not expect native-like mastery of the target language to develop spontaneously. Let us consider, for example, students participating in extended study-abroad programs. We can assume that the language these students hear reflects native speaker norms and that the interactions they have with native speakers are, at least on some level, communicatively meaningful. Nevertheless, while many students do improve their linguistic fluency and their knowledge of vocabulary and idiomatic expressions on study-abroad programs, few of them successfully develop native-like mastery or anything resembling native communicative competence.

2 Language as a reflection of cultural norms. If one accepts the claim of numerous sociolinguists and ethnolinguists that language is inseparable from culture (Brown 1987, Hymes 1974, Lado 1957, Sankoff 1980, Sapir 1921, among many others), we might begin to understand why native-like mastery is seemingly so elusive. For if language is inseparable from culture, then language acquisition is impossible without culture acquisition. Language learners may succeed in being able to express linguistically their thoughts and desires, and they may also understand the semantic meaning of the language produced by native speakers of the target language. But even with this linguistic success on both the production and comprehension levels, it is difficult to say how much communication is really taking place if the language learner does not share the sociocultural values and beliefs which underlie native speaker norms of communication. More and more studies are indicating, in fact, that communication difficulties can and do arise because the participants in an interaction are behaving according to different sociocultural norms (Beebe, Takahashi, and Uliss-Weltz 1990, Manes 1983, Ohlstain and Cohen 1983, Thomas 1984, Yamada 1990).

Obviously, if we hope to guide learners to acquire native-like mastery of another language, we cannot ignore the issue of culture acquisition, nor can we afford to postpone dealing with this issue until the advanced language levels. First, even those target language structures generally taught at the beginning language level are used by native speakers according to culture-specific norms. And second, if 'postponing cross-cultural concept development until the superior level is tantamount to building American cultural stereotypes right into our student's language proficiency' (Kramsch 1986:368), the acquisition of target cultural norms must be viewed as essential to each and every step of the language acquisition process.

3 The acquisition of a cultural norm. Of course, it is one thing to claim that culture and language are inseparable, and that language acquisition is impossible without culture acquisition, and another to define, specifically, what acquiring the norms of another culture might mean. For this, we must have some notion of the term 'culture'. Goodenough has written that 'culture consists of standards for deciding what is, standards for deciding what can be, standards for deciding how one feels about it, standards for deciding what to do about it, and standards for deciding how to go about doing it' (1981:62 [1963:258–59]). Many current researchers of language and culture have followed the same path as Goodenough in describing the nature of culture as a set of standards or shared norms. The 'communicative style' of a culture is described by Clancy as arising from 'shared beliefs about people, what they are like, and how they should relate to one another' (1990:33). Nostrand describes culture as a 'ground of meaning' which includes values, ways of thinking and 'certain prevalent assumptions about human nature and society' (1989:50), while Brown views culture as the 'context within which we exist, think, feel, and relate to others' (1987:122).

These and other currently accepted notions of culture include shared norms of characterizing, interpreting, and evaluating (Robinson 1988). Therefore, when talking about the acquisition of the behavioral norms of another culture, we mean not only the acquisition of knowledge concerning the range of behavior appropriate in specific contexts and the range of contexts appropriate for a specific behavior but also the acquisition of those shared values and beliefs which determine how one should characterize, interpret, and evaluate that context-specific behavior.

Before examining the process of acquiring a behavioral norm, we must note an important distinction between the acquisition of a behavior and the acquisition of a behavioral norm. Just as members of a particular speech community share norms of characterizing, understanding, and evaluating speech but do not necessarily speak exactly alike (Labov 1972), membership in a culture does not necessarily entail that an individual conform to a particular pattern of behavior, only that the individual share in the group's norms of characterizing, understanding, and evaluating that pattern.

Therefore, although a particular member of American culture may personally dislike the taste of coffee, s/he would typically know HOW coffee is prepared and served within American culture (e.g. much less concentrated than the way European coffee is made and, unlike Turkish coffee, with as few grounds as possible in the bottom of the cup); s/he would share knowledge concerning WHEN coffee may be drunk (e.g. during some classes and lectures as well as before, during, or after a meal), and s/he would share knowledge concerning HOW MUCH coffee is appropriate to drink at a sitting (e.g. unlimited cups are the norm rather than the exception in restaurants, and a full cup of coffee with cream, after a formal dinner, would certainly be unremarkable in a group sharing general, American cultural norms). So while culture acquisition may not necessarily entail the adoption of new or different behavior, it does entail the adoption of new norms of viewing such behavior, as well as an understanding of the social repercussions of employing or of not employing such behavior.

4 Establishing a cultural importance hierarchy for behavioral norms. Of course, certain norms are more significant than others with respect to how one is evaluated within a culture. For example, researchers have indicted that people within Japanese culture place a positive value on using various types of circumlocutions and indirect negative expressions to voice disagreement, and that people who avoid linguistically direct confrontation are considered more polite and better educated than people who use direct negatives—who, in turn, can be viewed as aggressive, disrespectful, or rude for such behavior (Condon 1984, Robinson 1988). Slurping soup broth, on the other hand, may indicate within Japanese culture that the person slurping thinks the soup is very good, and so like indirect negatives, can have positive value; however, someone who slurps is not thought of as someone who is smarter, more polite, or in any way better than someone who does not slurp.

Therefore, even though both behaviors may be associated with Japanese culture and may have positive value in Japanese culture, one might propose that acquiring Japanese behavioral norms of indirectness is more important than acquiring norms for slurping soup. Whether one does or does not slurp will not impact on how one is perceived by members of the culture; at worst, the non-slurper has one less means of offering a compliment to his or her host than the slurper. On the other hand, one's conformity to Japanese behavioral norms for indirectness will impact on how polite or aggressive s/he will be perceived within Japanese culture. It follows, therefore, that one could hypothesize a HIERARCHY OF IMPORTANCE for the acquisition of various target behavioral norms (cf. Figure 1) based on the degree to which certain behavior will reflect on the individual as well as the degree to which these personal traits are viewed as important within the culture.

Figure 1. Hierarchy of cultural importance for Japanese behavioral norms.

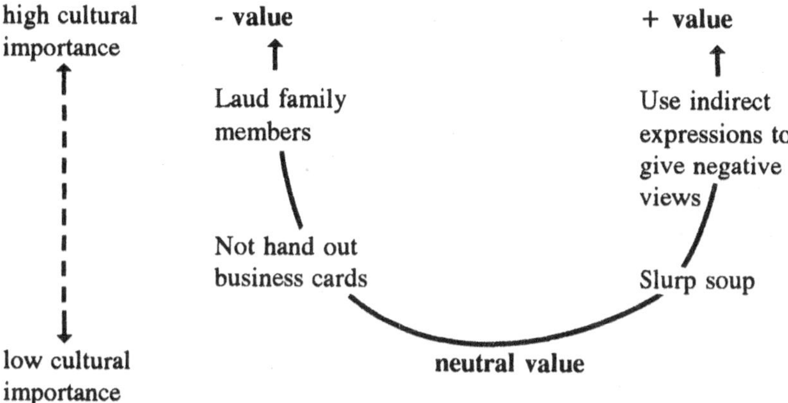

However, while one behavioral norm may be more significant than another to how one is perceived within a culture (e.g. how polite, smart, kind, aggressive, and so on), this cultural importance may have little or nothing to do with one's predisposition to acquiring that norm. Therefore, before using cultural importance as the deciding factor in selecting and ordering behavioral norms in the foreign language classroom, we must take into consideration the ease or difficulty with which learners will acquire these new norms.

5 Issues in establishing an acquisitional hierarchy for behavioral norms. One's attitude toward new behavioral norms is greatly determined, I believe, by the degree and type of compatibility of those new norms with one's existing norms. Depending on the cultural groups in question, certain behavioral norms may be completely different in each group, but other norms may be the same or particular aspects of norms may be shared (cf. Figure 2).

For example, with respect to coffee-drinking behavior, having a big cup of coffee for breakfast would fall within both French and American general norms, while having that breakfast coffee arrive in a bowl would fall within French but not American norms, and having a large cup of coffee at lunch or dinner would fall within American but not French norms (cf. Figure 3).

Figure 2. Possible cultural overlapping of behavioral norms.

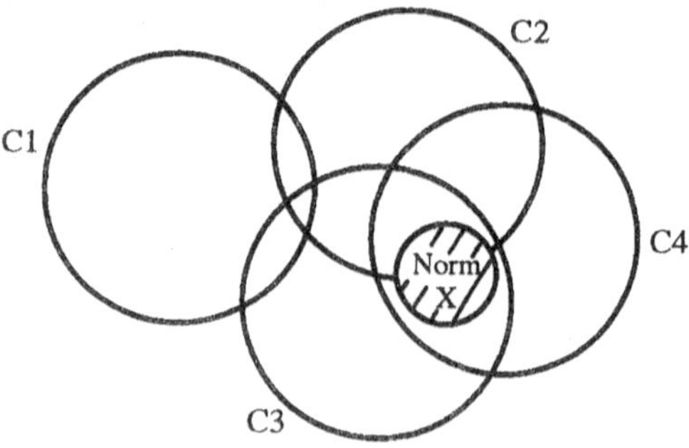

With respect to Norm X:
a. Norm is the SAME in Culture 3 (C3) and Culture 4 (C4)
b. SOME ASPECTS OF THE NORM ARE THE SAME in C4/C3 and C2
c. C4/C3 norm is DIFFERENT from all C1 norms

Figure 3. Relationship between coffee-drinking norms within French and American cultures.

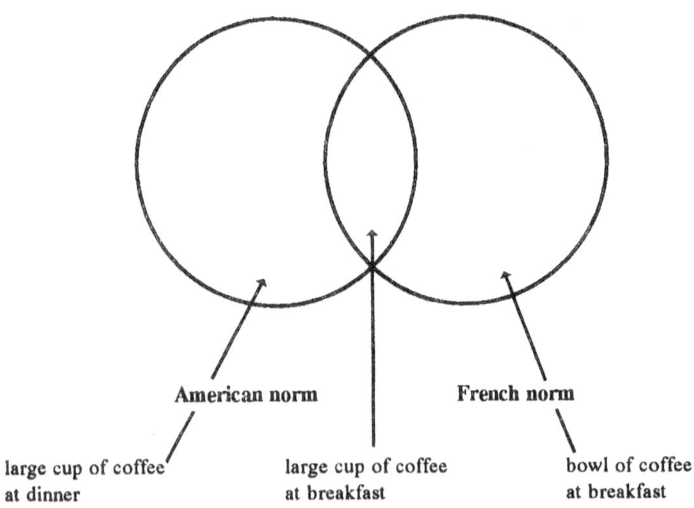

6 Cultural value conflicts and the acquisition of new behavioral norms. Given the fact that past experiences and knowledge influence the way we perceive and process new knowledge and experiences, we will expect that, at various acquisitional stages, learners will use their existing behavioral norms to help them to understand and acquire target behavioral norms. Numerous studies have indicated the many ways in which one's native language influences the acquisition of target language syntactic patterns (Fathman and LoCoco 1989), semantic interpretations (Harley 1989, Seliger 1989), and discourse functions (Bartelt 1989, Richards and Sukwiwat 1985, Flashner 1989). There is also a growing body of research indicating that one's cultural background also influences one's interpretation and use of the target language (Beebe, Takahashi, and Uliss-Weltz 1990; Manes 1983, Ohlstain and Cohen 1983, Thomas 1984, Yamada 1990, Zuengler 1989).

Such behavioral transfer strategies can be helpful in acquiring norms which are the same in both cultures. However, these strategies may result in communication difficulties and even acquisitional roadblocks if the norms in question reflect conflicting values in the two cultures. Listed in Figure 4 are some examples of acceptable target behavioral norms which have been noted as disagreeable to members of American culture in various published research studies, personal interviews with American students living in France, and personal analyses of Japanese behavioral norms submitted by Japanese teachers of English as class papers during the Georgetown University 1991 summer program in Tokyo, Japan.

Figure 4. Behavior which has negative value within American culture but positive or neutral value in other cultures (CULTURAL VALUE CONFLICTS).

Behavior with positive/neutral value within Japanese culture

- Slurp soup broth
- Use indirect expressions to voice disagreement
- Demean oneself or one's family members in public
- Offer little defense/justification for accused wrongdoing

Behavior with positive/neutral value within French culture

- Drink breakfast coffee directly from a bowl
- Maintain constant eye contact when talking to someone
- 'Break' administrative rules (e.g. skip ahead in lines, bypass channels of command, etc.)

In all of these examples, the behavior which may be considered typical, certainly acceptable, and, in some cases, greatly encouraged within either French or Japanese culture IS ASSOCIATED WITH SOCIALLY UNACCEPTABLE BEHAVIOR WITHIN AMERICAN CULTURE. For example, it is considered poor manners to put bowls or dishes to one's lips and to make noise while eating and drinking. Americans are taught to avoid indirect or passive expressions because they lack oratorical strength and can be viewed as inarticulate or ambiguous. Self-degradation or the degradation of one's family members may be viewed as lack of strength, self-confidence, or loyalty. Allowing an accusation to go unchallenged would be considered tantamount to admitting guilt within American culture, and the failure to offer an excuse may be seen as overly proud, insensitive, or arrogant. Constant eye contact is seen as staring which is, of course, considered to be bad manners. And while no one likes to wait in line a long time, people who achieve their goals by 'breaking the rules' would more likely be viewed as dishonest than clever within American culture.

Of course, the difficulty in overcoming negative associations in order to acquire new behavioral norms depends on:

1. The strength of the negative association with that behavior in the learner's culture (e.g. how arrogant or how impolite would one be considered for exhibiting such behavior); and
2. The relative importance of that negative trait within the learner's culture (e.g. is being impolite better or worse than being inarticulate, insensitive, or arrogant?).

Also, it goes without saying that the degree to which the learner publicly and privately shares these cultural norms will affect the learner's predisposition to acquiring new norms. In other words, the strength of one's personal experience with a culture's norms and personal identification with that specific culture will influence one's attitude toward new norms of behavior.

Of course, if the target culture behavior is not associated with any negative personal traits in the learner's culture, we would expect little acquisitional difficulty. And, in fact, we can think of many examples where new behavioral norms are easily acquired. Most Americans successfully acquire the norm of driving on the left side of the road in Britain, of exchanging business cards in Japan, of punching their train tickets before boarding in France, and of enjoying afternoon 'tapas' in Spanish bars, despite the fact that these behavioral norms would all be considered obviously different from norms within American culture. Therefore, DIFFERENCE is not necessarily synonymous with DIFFICULTY. While all sorts of norms may be perceived as 'different' by the learner, only those that are in conflict with existing norms will be problematic.

7 Differences in behavioral range as important to the perception of new cultural norms. We may, in fact, hypothesize that the perception of a difference in norm is actually a necessary first step in the process of acquiring a new norm and that, all other things being equal, target behavioral norms which are perceived to be similar to one's existing behavioral norms but which, in fact, reflect different underlying cultural values will be more difficult to acquire than norms easily perceived as different.

Foreign language acquisition studies have indicated that one's ability to acquire a linguistic rule in the target language which is different from a similar rule in one's native language depends on the learner's ability to perceive that the rule is, in fact, different. Researchers have suggested that the degree to which the language learner perceives differences between the target language and native language will influence his or her interlanguage development, and that target linguistic structures which are erroneously perceived by the learner to be the same as those in the native language may be more difficult to acquire than linguistic structures which learners perceive as clearly different (Corder 1978, Jordens and Kellerman 1981, Kellerman 1983, Myhill 1982). Thus, it would seem logical to propose that the perceptual salience of norm differences also influences one's ability to recognize and acquire target behavioral norms.

What makes it difficult for a learner to perceive differences in norms? Let us examine behavior which seemed perfectly acceptable to American students living in France until their French hosts voiced objections to it (cf. Figure 5).[1]

Figure 5. Student behavior considered objectionable to French.

- Bought fruit and ate it for breakfast (instead of eating bread like the other family members)
- Spent 20 minutes or more in the shower
- Spent 20 minutes or more on the phone
- Had a cup of hot chocolate after dinner

In all of these cases, the range of acceptable behavior is in some way greater in the American behavioral norm than in the French norm (cf. Figure 6).

Figure 6. Differences in the degree of individual variation (behavioral range) for a norm in two cultures.

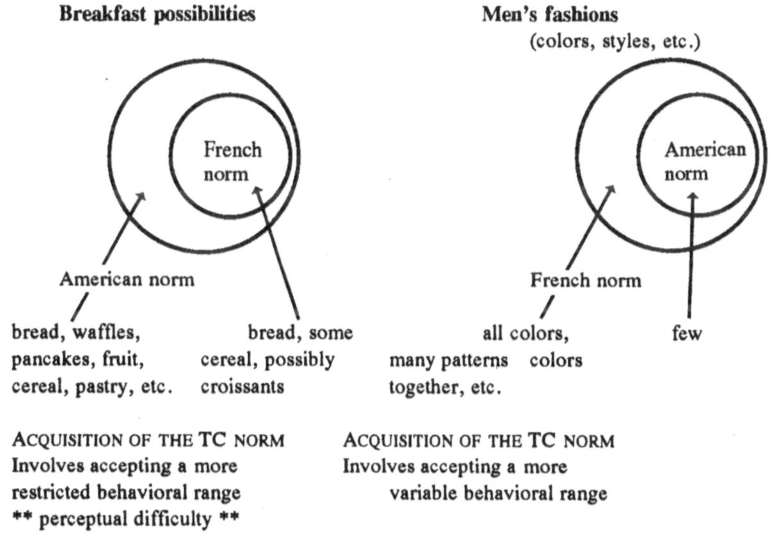

[1] These incidents took place while I was director of the Georgetown University summer program in Tours (1988, 1989) and while I was collecting data for my dissertation from American students studying in Bordeaux between 1983 and 1984.

Americans eat all sorts of things for breakfast, spend variable amounts of time in the shower or on the phone, and can consume a variety of types and quantities of beverages after dinner. Thus, expecting the French norm to allow similar variation in behavior, we might predict that American students would either view the target culture norm as restrictive or would not perceive the more limited boundaries of behavior acceptable within French culture (especially where the behavior involved is typically not a group activity, such as taking a shower or talking on the phone).

In fact, in all of the cases cited here, it was only through a student–host confrontation that the students had any idea that their behavior was at all unacceptable, and were completely shocked to be accused of being rude, impolite, selfish, or unsociable by their French hosts. Upon learning the cause of ill feeling toward them, some students willingly agreed to modify their own behavior, while others felt that their French hosts should 'lighten up' and not have so many rigid rules of behavior.

When the behavioral range is greater in the target culture (TC) than in the learner's culture (LC), as in the case of the color and style of men's fashions in France (TC) and in the U.S. (LC), the potential perceptual difficulty is reversed (cf. Figure 6). Nonnative-like learner behavior may be relatively overlooked because of great individual variation in the target culture (Ohlstain and Cohen 1983); however, the learner may view that target culture behavior which is outside the range of his or her own cultural norm as inappropriate or in bad taste. The acquisitional difficulty of acquiring a target cultural norm will depend, thus, on the degree and type of difference in behavioral range in the two cultures as well as on the type of value associated with the behavioral range.

8 Acquisitional implications for differences in contextual range. The acquisitional difficulty of a new behavioral norm will also be affected by the ways in which (and the degree to which) the CONTEXTUAL range appropriate for a specific behavior overlaps in the two cultures. Let us take, for example, KISSING and SMILING. Numerous studies have indicated that American stereotypes of French people include both 'sexy' and 'romantic' as well as 'cold', 'hostile', and 'closed'. On the other hand, stereotypes of Americans by French people include both 'friendly' and 'warm' as well as 'superficial' and 'insincere'. Such seemingly conflicting cultural generalizations become much more understandable when one examines the contextual ranges of behaviors such as KISSING and SMILING within French and American cultures.

In both French and American cultures, KISSING and SMILING are behaviors with positive value; therefore, attribution of cultural communication difficulties to value conflicts does not appear warranted. However, comparison of the contextual ranges of these behaviors within French and American cultures yields interesting results. The contextual range where SMILING is generally appropriate is greater within American culture, while the contextual range where KISSING is generally appropriate is greater within French culture (cf. Figure 7). One could hypothesize that extending the contextual range of a behavior (as an American would have to do to acquire French norms of KISSING) would be difficult because it would entail 'cheapening' its significance, while reducing the contextual range of a behavior (as an American would have to do to acquire French norms of SMILING) would also be difficult because it would entail refraining from exhibiting behavior which one associates with 'being a nice person'.

Figure 7. Differences in the CONTEXTUAL RANGE of (similarly valued) behavior in two cultures.

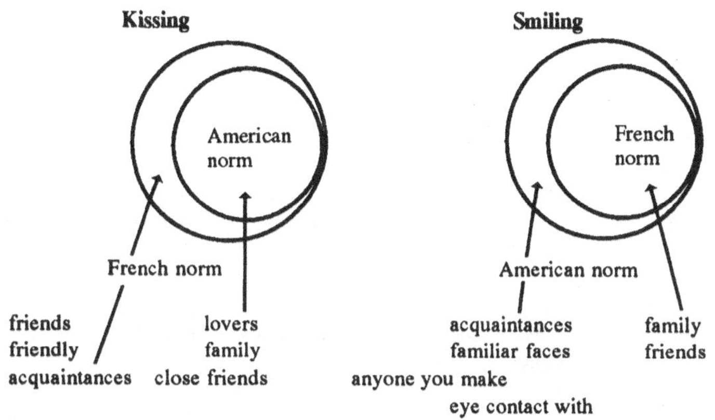

ACQUISITION OF THE TC NORM
Involves accepting a more
expanded contextual range

ACQUISITION OF THE TC NORM
Involves accepting a
reduced contextual range

In summary, we have examined the interaction between the ways two cultures value certain behavior, and consider certain behavioral ranges or contextual ranges appropriate. Robinson (1988) and others have suggested that essential to culture acquisition is the building of empathic bridges between the learner's culture and the target culture. In this paper, I have proposed a procedure for comparing behavioral norms which can be used to both explain and predict varying degrees and types of difficulty one will have in developing such intercultural empathy. In order to facilitate culture acquisition, we must first know which behavioral norms are important to share in order to be accepted by members of the target culture, and then understand where and why learners will need guidance in recognizing and accepting these new cultural norms. I have proposed here that by examining the behavioral and contextual ranges and the values associated with these ranges both within and across cultures, we should eventually be able to define hierarchies of cultural importance and of acquisitional difficulty. Together, I feel that these hierarchies will allow us to establish principled guidelines for facilitating culture acquisition without which, I fear, our efforts to promote language acquisition are and will continue to be necessarily limited.

REFERENCES

Bartelt, H. Guillermo. 1989. A formal analysis of discourse transfer processes in Apachean English interlanguage. Transfer in language production, ed. by Hans W. Dechert and Manfred Raupach, 99–114. Norwood, NJ: Ablex.

Beebe, Leslie M., Tomoko Takahashi, and Robin Uliss-Weltz. 1990. Pragmatic transfer in ESL refusals. Developing communicative competence in a second language, ed. by Robin C. Scarcella, Elaine S. Andersen, and Stephen D. Krashen, 55–74. New York: Newbury House.

Bland, S. K. 1988. The present progressive in discourse: Grammar versus usage revisited. TESOL Quarterly 22, 1.53–68.

Brown, H. Douglas. 1987. Principles of language learning and teaching. 2nd ed. Englewood Cliffs, NJ: Prentice-Hall.

Clancy, Patricia. 1990. Acquiring communicative style in Japanese. Developing communicative competence in a second language, ed. by Robin C. Scarcella, Elaine S. Andersen, and Stephen D. Krashen, 27–40. New York: Newbury House.

Condon, John C. 1984. With respect to the Japanese: A guide for Americans. Yarmouth, ME: Intercultural Press.

Corder, S. Pit. 1978. Language-learner language. Understanding second and foreign language learning: Issues and approaches, ed. by Jack C. Richards, 71–93. Rowley, MA: Newbury House.

Di Vito, Nadine O'Connor. 1991a. Incorporating native speaker norms in second language materials. Applied Linguistics 12, 4.383–96.

Di Vito, Nadine O'Connor. 1991b. Looking at and towards the future in French textbooks. Georgetown University Round Table on Languages and Linguistics 1991, ed. by James E. Alatis, 250–59. Washington, DC: Georgetown University Press.

Di Vito, Nadine O'Connor. 1992. 'Present' concerns about French language teaching. Modern Language Journal 76, 1.50–57.

Ellis, Rod. 1984. Can syntax be taught? A study of the effects of formal instruction on the acquisition of WH questions by children. Applied Linguistics 5, 2.138–55.

Fathman, Ann K., and Veronica LoCoco. 1989. Word order contrasts and production in three target languages. Transfer in language production, ed. by Hans W. Dechert and Manfred Raupach, 159–70. Norwood, NJ: Ablex.

Flashner, Vanessa E. 1989. Transfer of aspect in the English oral narratives of native Russian speakers. Transfer in language production, ed. by Hans W. Dechert and Manfred Raupach, 71–98. Norwood, NJ: Ablex.

Goodenough, Ward H. 1981. Culture, language, and society. 2nd ed. Menlo Park, CA: Benjamin Cummings. [reprinted from Ward H. Goodenough. 1963. Cooperation in change. New York: Russell Sage Foundation.]

Harley, Birgit. 1989. Transfer in the written compositions of French immersion students. Transfer in language production, ed. by Hans W. Dechert and Manfred Raupach, 3–20. Norwood, NJ: Ablex.

Herschensohn, Julia. 1988. Linguistic accuracy of textbook grammar. Modern Language Journal 72, 4.409–13.

Holmes, Janet. 1988. Doubt and certainty in ESL textbooks. Applied Linguistics 9, 1.21–44.

Hymes, Dell. 1974. Foundations of sociolinguistics. Philadelphia: University of Pennsylvania Press.

Jordens, Peter, and Eric Kellerman. 1981. Investigations into the 'transfer strategy' in second language learning. Actes du 5ième congrès de l'association internationale de linguistique appliquée, ed. by Jean Guy Savard and Lorne Laforge, 195–215. Quebec: University of Laval.

Kellerman, Eric. 1983. Now you see it, now you don't. Language transfer in language learning, ed. by Susan M. Gass and Larry Selinker, 112–34. Rowley, MA: Newbury House.

Kramsch, Claire. 1986. From language proficiency to interactional competence. Modern Language Journal 70, 4.366–72.

Labov, William. 1972. Sociolinguistic patterns. Philadelphia: University of Pennsylvania Press.

Lado, Robert. 1957. Linguistics across cultures. Ann Arbor: University of Michigan Press.

Manes, Joan. 1983. Compliments: A mirror of cultural values. Sociolinguistics and Language Acquisition, ed. by Nessa Wolfson and Elliot Judd, 96–102. Rowley, MA: Newbury House.

Myhill, John. 1982. The acquisition of complex sentences: A cross-linguistic study. Studies in Second Language Acquisition 4, 2.193–200.

Nostrand, Howard Lee. 1989. Authentic texts and cultural authenticity: An editorial. Modern Language Journal 73, 1.49–52.

Ohlstain, Elite, and Andrew D. Cohen. 1983. Apology: A speech-act set. Sociolinguistics and Language Acquisition, ed. by Nessa Wolfson and Elliot Judd, 18–36. Rowley, MA: Newbury House.

Prabhu, N.S. 1987. Second language pedagogy. Oxford: Oxford University Press.

Richards, Jack C., and Mayuri Sukwiwat. 1985. Cross-cultural aspects of conversational competence. The context of language teaching, ed. by Jack C. Richards, 129–43. New York: Cambridge University Press.

Rivers, Wilga M. 1986. Comprehension and production in interactive language teaching. Modern Language Journal 70, 1.1–7.

Robinson, Gail L. Nemetz. 1988. Crosscultural understanding. New York: Prentice Hall.

Sankoff, Gillian. 1980. A quantitative paradigm for the study of communicative competence. The social life of language, ed. by Gillian Sankoff, 47–80. Philadelphia: University of Pennsylvania Press.

Sapir, Edward. 1921. Language. New York: Harcourt, Brace, Jovanovitch.

Scotton, Carol Myers, and Janice Bernsten. 1988. Natural conversations as a model for textbook dialogue. Applied Linguistics 9, 4.372–84.

Seliger, Herbert W. 1989. Semantic transfer constraints on the production of English passive by Hebrew–English bilinguals. Transfer in language production, ed. by Hans W. Dechert and Manfred Raupach, 21–34. Norwood, NJ: Ablex.

Swain, Merrill. 1985. Communicative competence: Some roles of comprehensible input and comprehensible output in its development. Input in Second Language Acquisition, ed. by Susan M. Gass and Carolyn G. Madden, 235–53. Rowley, MA: Newbury House.

Thomas, Jenny. 1984. Cross-cultural discourse as 'unequal encounter': Towards a pragmatic analysis. Applied Linguistics 5, 3.226–35.

Walz, Joel. 1989. Context and contextualized language practice in foreign language teaching. Modern Language Journal 73, 2.160–69.

Wolfson, Nessa, Lynne D'Amico-Reisner, and Lisa Huber. 1983. How to arrange for social commitments in American English: The invitation. Sociolinguistics and language acquisition, ed. by Nessa Wolfson and Elliot Judd, 116–28. Rowley, MA: Newbury House.

Yamada, Haru. 1990. Topic shifts in American and Japanese business conversations. The Georgetown Journal of Languages and Linguistics 1, 2.249–56.

Zuengler, Jane. 1989. Identity and IL development and use. Applied Linguistics 10, 1.80–96.

Information flow in written advertising

Peter H. Fries[*]
Central Michigan University and Hangzhou University

Both native English speaking and nonnative English speaking students have difficulty ordering the words in their sentences. Should one, for example, place an adverbial such as *yesterday* at the end of its sentence and produce *John left early yesterday* or should one place the adverbial at the beginning of the sentence and produce *Yesterday John left early*? The question of the ordering of constituents concerns what Systemic linguists call the 'textual metafunction of language'. In Systemic grammar, the textual metafunction includes two types of structures: thematic structure and information structure. Looking at how these two structures organize the language of a text focuses on the role of the text as message. This paper constitutes part of a project to explore the nature of both thematic structure and information structure with the view that comparing the two will provide insight into the functioning of each one.

To begin, I should point out that Systemic grammar provides a multifunctional view of language. Each major function (or metafunction) imposes its own structure on the language. Figure 1 presents a representative analysis of a spoken clause complex.

Each heavy horizontal line separates a metafunction. Figure 1 illustrates: (a) that each metafunction assigns its own structure; (b) that these structures differ in important ways, though they partially overlap; and (c) that thematic structure and information structure form part of a complex of interlocking structures. Let

---

[*] I would like to acknowledge the help and advice of Mary Ann Crawford, who gathered the data, organized it, and provided me with an initial analysis. The following advertisers have generously given permission to use quotations from their copyrighted advertisements: CPC International Inc., for the advertisement for Niagara Professional Finish; Canon USA, for the advertisement for Canon Color Laser; Chesebrough-Ponds, for the advertisement for Cutex 'Strong Nail' Nail Strengthener; Chrysler Motor Corporation, for the advertisement for Jeep Eagle; Corning Incorporated, for the advertisement for Corning PhotoGray Extra Lenses; COSMAIR, Inc., for the advertisement for L'Oreal Avantage and L'Oreal Creme Conditioner; Hyundai Motor America, for the advertisement for Sonata GLS V 616 from Hyundai; James River Corporation, for the advertisement for Brawny Paper Towels; Kraft General Foods for the advertisement for Shake'N Bake; Nissan Motor Corporation in USA, for the advertisement for Nissan; Reynolds Metals Company, for the advertisement for Reynolds Oven Cooking Bags; Sunshine Biscuits Inc., for the advertisement for Sunshine Cookies and Crackers.

Figure 1. The multifunctional structure of a clause complex.

<table>
<tr><th></th><th>//4 If</th><th>he</th><th colspan="2">brings</th><th>the car</th><th>//1 we</th><th>can</th><th>use</th><th>it//</th></tr>
<tr><td rowspan="4">Textual Metafunction</td><td colspan="5">Theme 1</td><td colspan="4">Rheme 1</td></tr>
<tr><td>structural</td><td>topical</td><td colspan="3" rowspan="2">Rheme 2</td><td>topical</td><td colspan="3" rowspan="2">Rheme 3</td></tr>
<tr><td colspan="2">Theme 2</td><td>Theme 3</td></tr>
<tr><td colspan="4">Given →</td><td>New</td><td colspan="3">Given</td><td>New</td></tr>
<tr><td rowspan="2">Interpersonal Metafunction</td><td></td><td>Subject</td><td>Finite</td><td>Predicator</td><td>Complement</td><td>Subject</td><td>Finite</td><td>Predicator</td><td>Complement</td></tr>
<tr><td></td><td colspan="2">Mood</td><td colspan="2">Residue</td><td colspan="2">Mood</td><td colspan="2">Residue</td></tr>
<tr><td rowspan="2">Ideational Metafunction</td><td colspan="5">$_x\beta$</td><td colspan="4">α</td></tr>
<tr><td></td><td>Actor</td><td colspan="2">Material</td><td>Goal</td><td>Actor</td><td colspan="2">Material</td><td>Goal</td></tr>
</table>

us turn to thematic structure first (the top three lines of the analysis in Figure 1). Thematic structure assigns the functions Theme and Rheme. The clause complex has one thematic structure as a whole (Theme 1 and Rheme 1 in the top row of the chart), and each clause itself also has a thematic structure (Theme 2 and Rheme 2 in the first clause, and Theme 3 and Rheme 3 in the second clause). Halliday defines thematic structure primarily for the clause, but he makes it clear that other units such as clause complexes also have thematic structures. (See Fries 1981 and Halliday 1985 for analyses of Themes at the ranks of clause complex and clause.)

Thematic status is signaled in English by initial position in the clause or clause complex. The meaning of Theme is described as the 'point of departure of the message' and as 'that with which the clause is concerned' (Halliday 1985:38). Halliday clearly intends these two wordings to be paraphrases; however, the second wording in particular tends to be associated with the notion of Topic. In my view, Topic is a rather different concept. Indeed Fries (1981) and Downing (1991) explicitly attempt to disassociate the definitions of the notions Theme and Topic.[2] In my view, a better description of the significance of Theme is that the Theme of a clause provides a framework for the interpretation of the clause. The Theme orients the receiver to what is about to be communicated. This orienting function is nicely described in Bäcklund's (1989:297) discussion of initial infinitive clauses. She suggests that initial infinitive clauses can be viewed as reflecting questions posed by an imaginary reader. In her words, ' ... they indicate which potential question the writer has chosen to answer.'

In contrast to thematic structure, information structure is not directly a structure of the clause, but of the information unit. Information units are signaled in the spoken language by the tone group. Each tone group has some section which expresses information which is presented as New information. The tonic foot (the location of the so-called sentence accent) indicates 'the culmination of what is New' (Halliday 1985:275). In addition to information which is presented as New, information units may contain information which is presented as Given, but they do not necessarily do so. New information is information which is presented as 'newsworthy'—as worthy of the listener's attention, while Given information is presented as information which is recoverable in some way. Two points are important here. First, Given[3] and New are functions within language. It is not true that all information which happens to be new (=unfamiliar) to a listener is presented as New, nor is it true that all information which is presented as New is in fact new (=unfamiliar) information for the listener (even taking into account issues concerning differences in the knowledge

---

[2] It is worth noting that, in my view, these attempts to disassociate the definitions of Theme and Topic are quite consistent with Halliday's view of the notion of Theme.

[3] Terms which refer to grammatical functions are capitalized. Terms which are being used informally are written normally.

and beliefs of the speaker and listener). Second, as described above, the functions of New and Given are overtly signaled only in the spoken language. Clearly, written language must present some information as New. One means by which this task is achieved is through the correlation of the tone group with clause structure. A number of linguists (e.g. Chafe 1980:13, 1984:437, 1987:38 and 40, and Halliday 1985:274) have found that in spoken English there is an unmarked association of clause structure with unit of information. Further they find a tendency to place New information toward the end of the information unit. (See, for example, Clark and Haviland (1977:13) and Chafe (1987:37).) As Halliday (1985:276) expresses it, 'The unmarked position for the New is at the end of the information unit.' Indeed many linguists refer to the tendency to place important information toward the end of the clause with the term 'end focus'.

It is often said that writers tend to use this association of placement at the end of the clause with importance to make their written language flow naturally. If this is true, there ought to be a correlation between placement at the end of clauses and information which appears to be the focus of attention. Systemicists therefore have two theoretical constructs, Theme and New. In written English, theme is associated directly with initial position in the clause and functions as orienter to the information which is about to come, while New is associated indirectly with the end of the clause. Information which is presented as New is the focus of attention. It is the newsworthy part of the message. Although systemicists have a term (Theme) which refers to the initial constituent of a clause or clause complex, they do not have a term which refers to the final constituent of a clause or clause complex. As a result, I have coined the term N-Rheme (for New-Rheme) to provide a convenient way of referring to the last constituent of the clause or clause complex.

We can use the descriptions of Theme and N-Rheme as the source of hypotheses to predict the placement of information in written language.

- N-Rhematic information contains the newsworthy information, information which is in focus in that message. As a result the N-Rhemes are likely to contain information which is directly relevant to the goals of the text or text segment.
- Thematic information serves as orienter for the message which is about to come up. As a result it responds to local issues in the text and is less likely to contain meanings which are directly relevant to the goals and purposes of the text or text segment.

Written advertising appeared to be a good place to explore these hypotheses, since much of written advertising is constructed to read as if it were spoken. As a means of exploring these hypotheses, I and a student collected 150 written advertisements from issues of *People*, *Good Housekeeping*, and *U.S. News and World Report* that appeared in September 1990. Four additional advertisements which had attracted our attention were added to the data. We are in the process of analyzing that data. The present paper is a progress report based on the analysis of 63 of these advertisements. We are comparing the information which is found in the Themes with the information which is found in the N-Rhemes of the component clauses and clause complexes to see where information which is directly relevant to the goals of the advertisements is placed.

First, we had to determine what information was 'directly relevant to the goals of the advertisements.'[4] The approach taken in this paper is to make use of the strong, persuasive purpose which underlies all advertising. All advertisements are intended to establish an association with the product in the readers' minds, preferably an association which will lead the readers to purchase the product at some time. Thus, we can regard all advertising as persuasive language, regardless of whatever else it is. (We made sure that this was the case by including in our data only advertisements which, in our view, were overtly attempting to sell some product or service or line of products or services.) How can a copy writer persuade readers to buy a product? Clearly the writer cannot simply say 'Buy Franklin Widgets.' and expect such an advertisement to be successful. The request must be motivated. (Indeed, few advertisements in our data contained such bald requests to purchase. Rather, advertisements requested readers to 'find out more about X' or to 'write for a list of our service centers', etc.) The motivations for the potential purchases were largely achieved by describing some good feature which was inherent in the product or which the writer wished the reader to associate with the product. Sometimes these features would be highlighted in a type of argumentative text in which the advertisement would pose a problem with which the reader could identify, and then the advertisement would demonstrate how the product solves that problem.

Given these purposes of advertising, meanings which relate to the attributes of the product and to the functions which the product performs can all be seen to be important in this context and therefore are likely to be presented as New. Similarly, evaluations of the product as good, and the problem (or in relatively rare cases, other competing products) as bad are also likely to be important and presented as New. Last, since one major goal of the advertisement is to achieve name recognition for the product and for the company, one should expect the names of the products and companies to be repeated and to occur in emphatic

---

[4] Often focal information is identified by noting how topic-like various nominal constituents are (see Givón 1983, Schiffrin 1985, and Thompson 1990 for examples). The approach taken here differs for three reasons. First, other linguists have regularly used the measurement of topicality for purposes which are very similar to mine. I would like to demonstrate that at least one other approach to this issue is valid. Second, I am interested in separating the definitions of Theme and Topic. (Of course there is a general correlation of Theme and topic-like nominals, but that is not my point in this paper.) Third, there was a practical reason. A quick examination of several apparently typical advertisements from our data convinced me that they contained a considerable amount of repetition, and that this repetition would make it difficult to establish a significant difference between the topical status of Thematic nominals and that of N-Rhematic nominals even though impressionistically the topic-like nominals in the N-Rhemes were NOT being used like topics. Rather they were part of the focal information in the advertisements.

positions. In this case, since the goal is simply memorability, we should simply find that the product and company names are regularly placed in important positions. Both the Theme and the N-Rheme positions provide a sort of emphasis. As a result, we should find that product and company names occur in those two positions, but not in the middle of the clause (what I have called the 'other' position). I see no strong reason to predict the occurrence of these names in the N-Rheme as against the Theme.

Table 1 presents the distribution of terms which refer to the product or company, or the features, functions, and evaluations of the products in the complete clauses of our data.

Table 1. Distribution of name of company or product, evaluative terms, descriptions of features, and functions in clauses. (Based on 305 clauses)

Term	Theme	Other	N-Rheme
Company or product name	52 33.8%	25 16.7%	77 50.0%
Evaluative terms	79 22.3%	78 22%	197 55.6%
Product features	15 21.7%	26 37.7%	28 40.6%
Product functions	1 2%	19 → 37%	31 60.8%

As was predicted above, references to the product and company name are found predominantly in either Thematic or N-Rhematic position, and rarely occur in the 'other' position. Product and company names were more frequently placed in the N-Rhemes of their clauses. Evaluative terms and descriptions of functions occur predominantly in the N-Rhemes of the component sentences. The figures for the features are less skewed.

Two bits of information are relevant for interpreting the figures in Table 1. First, the numbers reporting the mentions of the functions of the products are misleading because locating the descriptions of the functions in one particular portion of a clause was often problematic. Specifically, in each case where the description of the function begins in the 'other' position, the description continues into the N-Rheme.

A second issue with Table 1 is that it considers only complete clauses in well-formed sentences. Clearly, advertising contains a great many sentence fragments. Since the term 'sentence fragment' carries with it a pejorative association let me use the term 'minor sentence'. A minor sentence is any punctuated sentence which does not contain at least one complete independent clause. Slightly over half the data (54%) consisted of minor sentences. Forty-nine of the 363 minor sentences were present for purely legal purposes (such as copyright notices) and did not contribute to the persuasive function of the advertisements. The remaining 314 minor sentences seemed to form part of the persuasive apparatus of the advertisements. Of these, most (182) had a clear grammatical or rhetorical relation to some part of the linguistic context. For example, a series of minor sentences might relate to the previous linguistic context by forming part of an extending nominal group complex as in Text 1.

Text 1. Advertisement for Sonata GLS V616.

7. Standard equipment includes the largest V6 of any import in its class.
8. A smooth, 4-speed automatic transmission with overdrive.
9. Air conditioning.
10. And enough power on tap to outrun a Ford Taurus L, Lexus ES250 or even a BMW 735i from zero to sixty.*

Similarly, in Text 2, a rhetorical relation holds between sentences 1 and 2.

Text 2. Advertisement for Cutex 'Strong Nail' Nail Strengthener.

1. Only one nail strengthener has Knox® Gelatine.
2. Cutex Strong Nail®

The first sentence of Text 2 contains the focusing adjunct *only*. The word *only* has a clear association with negation. Since sentence 1 does not tell us which product contains this feature, it creates what might be termed an information 'vacuum' and it is to be expected that some later sentence will provide the correct information. Indeed, we find the answer in the minor sentence that follows.[5]

Occasionally a minor sentence itself encodes a relation between text segments. Punctuation unit 3 of Text 3 provides an example.

Text 3. Advertisement for Sunshine cookies and crackers.

2. Everyone loves Sunshine.
3. And for lots of good reasons.
4. Like great taste.
5. And the fact that just about every cookie and cracker Sunshine makes contains no cholesterol and is low in sodium.

Here the minor sentence 3 functions as a Circumstance for Sentence 2 and

---

[5] Winter (1977) finds a strong correlation between denials (which involve negations) and corrections of the information.

expresses a causal relation. Punctuation units 4 and 5 elaborate that causal relation. The result of the structures used in sentences 2 through 5 is that a causal relation is created between sentence 2 and sentences 4 and 5, but this relation is expressed through an elaboration of the Circumstance expressed in minor sentence 3.

Table 2 presents the figures for the distributions of company or product names, and words which describe functions or features of the products, and evaluations within preposed and postposed minor sentences.

Table 2. Distribution of company and product names, features and functions of product, and evaluations in preposed and postposed minor sentences.

	Preposed	Postposed	Total
Number of minor sentences	21 11.54%	162 88.46%	183
Company or product name	14 28.57%	35 71.43%	49
Product features	3 3.06%	95 96.94%	98
Product functions	2 6.25%	30 93.75%	32
Evaluations	14 7.61%	170 92.39%	184

Far more minor sentences are postposed than preposed. This in itself indicates that initial parts of sentences (Themes) function quite differently than do the ends of sentences (N-Rhemes). (See also Chafe (1984) for figures demonstrating that preposed and postposed adverbial clauses are both pronounced differently in spoken English and punctuated differently in written English.) Further, Table 2 indicates that preposed and postposed minor sentences contain different sorts of information. Fourteen of 21 (66%) preposed minor sentences mention the product name or the company name, while only 35 of 162 (21.60%) postposed minor sentences mention the product name or the company name. In contrast, only three features are mentioned in the 21 preposed minor sentences, and all three mentions are located in one example. That is, 20 preposed minor sentences do not mention any product feature at all. On the other hand, 68 of 162 (41.98%) of the postposed minor sentences mention product features. Since some of these postposed minor sentences mention more than one feature of the product, a total of 95 mentions of product features are found in postposed minor clauses. Terms which refer to the functions of the products and the evaluations of the products show similar distributions.

Further, not only do the preposed and postposed minor sentences seem to contain different sorts of information, they seem to present this information in different ways. Most frequently, the preposed minor sentence poses a topic, which is then used in the later punctuation unit (usually a complete grammatical sentence). Sometimes the topic introduced in the first punctuation unit is 'reentered' into the follow-up sentence by a pronoun. Text 4 provides an example.

Text 4. Advertisement for the Sonata GLS V616 from Hyundai.

16. The surprising Sonata GLS V6 from Hyundai.
17. It makes everyone feel good inside.

Most frequently, preposed minor sentences of this sort consist of the name of the product (often accompanied by the name of the company).

A second sort of preposed minor sentence occurs when the initial punctuation unit enters into a grammatical relation with the following punctuation unit. The resulting construction will be some sort of grammatical construction of English. For example, the resulting construction may be a clause, a nominal group, or a clause which evades the choice of mood.[6] Text 5 illustrates an instance in which the preposed minor sentence expresses a carrier which has the attribute expressed by the following minor sentence.

Text 5. Advertisement for Shake'N Bake.

3. Shake'N Bake
4. No MSG.
5. Naturally seasoned.

Texts 4 and 5 are typical in that the preposed minor sentence functions as topic—the expression of topic is, of course, one of the uses of Theme. (Compare the effect of these preposed minor sentences with that of the postposed minor sentence in Text 2.)

One further way in which the information placed in initial position can be shown to differ from information placed in final position is to examine how meanings of similar sorts are used in the different positions. Since advertisements are intended to be persuasive texts, we can expect that relations such as cause, reason, and purpose or goal will be prominent. (Leech 1966 also reports this.) It is easy to express causes, reasons, purposes, and goals first in the clause or clause complex or last in the clause or clause complex. Let me consider the expression of purpose/goal first.

The advertisements which form the basis for this paper contain 17 instances

---

[6] See Halliday 1985:374f.

of explicit expressions of purpose or goal. These expressions have been achieved either through the use of an infinitive clause or through the use of *for*. Further, they may either precede or follow the expression of the action. Texts 6a and 6b illustrate the expression of purpose using an infinitive clause, and Texts 7a and 7b illustrate the expression of purpose through the use of *for*.

Texts 6a and 6b. Sentences with infinitive clauses of purpose.

6a. **Infinitive clause is preposed:** Advertisement for Canon Color Laser.

> 7. TO FIND OUT MORE, make it your business to call 1-800-OK-CANON or write us at Canon USA Inc. [address given]

6b. **Infinitive clause is postposed:** Advertisement for Nissan.

> 21. The VG30ET uses the latest computer technology TO ACHIEVE ITS EXTRAORDINARY PERFORMANCE AND PRECISION.

Texts 7a and 7b. Sentences with the preposition *for* expressing purpose.

7a. **Prepositional phrase is preposed:** Advertisement for Reynolds Oven Cooking Bags.

> 4. FOR FREE RECIPES, write the Reynolds Wrap Kitchens [address given].

7b. **Prepositional phrase is postposed:** Advertisement for Niagara Professional Starch.

> 6. And don't forget Niagara original spray starch FOR A CLASSIC WELL DRESSED LOOK.
> 7. And Niagara Sizing to give permanent press and cotton blend fabrics body without stiffness.

Texts 6a and 7a involve preposed expressions of purpose, while Texts 6b and 7b involve postposed expressions of purpose. Table 3 provides the distributions of these four different situations.

Of the 12 preposed expressions of purpose, 11 motivate an action (such as *call* or *write*) on the part of the reader which is connected with the major purpose of the advertisement. Texts 6a and 7a are typical examples. It is obvious that getting the reader to act with respect to the product is a major focus of attention in these sentences. The sole example of a preposed expression of purpose which does not precede an action such as *call* or *write* on the part of the reader occurs in Text 8. Here the main clause introduces the product itself.

Table 3. Distribution of preposed and postposed expressions of purpose.

	Preposed	Postposed	Total
Infinitive clauses	5	14	19
for	7	16	23
Total	12	30	42

Text 8. Advertisement for L'Oreal.

7. The day you color your hair, you love the color, the feeling.
8. And TO KEEP IT, now there's Colorvive Technicare

Here, the preposed infinitive clause poses a goal which is closely associated with the ideas expressed in the previous sentence, while the main clause introduces the product as a means to achieve that goal. Again, the introduction of the product is the main focus of the sentence and of the advertisement. These preposed expressions of purpose anticipate and answer the question 'Why should I act?'—they orient readers to the main message they are about to encounter.

The postposed expressions of purpose are much more varied and, when they occur, tend to express information which is more important to the persuasive function of the advertisement. Texts 6b and 7b are typical in this regard. In Text 6b, the postposed infinitive clause expresses very strong positive evaluations of the product and its performance, notions which are intimately connected with the persuasive goal of the advertisements as a whole. Similarly the final prepositional phrase of sentence 6 of Text 7b describes a major function of spray starch as well as evaluating that function positively. (Compare these meanings with the meanings expressed in preposed prepositional phrases introduced by *for*.) While the verbal group *don't forget* expresses a command to the reader, it does not involve the reader in acting to contact the company as do commands such as *send*, *call*, and *write*. Again, the meanings which are more critical to the persuasive function of the advertisement are placed at the end of the construction.

It is worth noting that sentences which contribute less directly to the persuasive function of the advertisement sometimes do contain expressions of purpose which follow requests for the reader to act. Text 9 illustrates this situation.

Text 9. Advertisement for Jeep/Eagle.

11. 7/70: Limited warranty.
12. See Dealer for details.
17. Limited time offer.
18. See dealer FOR DETAILS.

Sentences 11–18 are found in small type at the bottom of the page, and they provide support for the body of the advertisement. I suspect that the writers assumed that most readers would not read this portion of the advertisement. Rather, these sentences describe some of the relevant legal restrictions and tell readers who are particularly interested where they can obtain more information. Thus the commands in sentences 12 and 18 do not function as major requests for action on the part of the reader.

Of the 30 postposed expressions of purpose or goal, 25 are found in the body of the text of the advertisements. Of these 25, only two postposed expressions of purpose are used to motivate the reader to contact the company to gain more information. In both cases, there is already a preposed expression of purpose in the sentence in addition. On the other hand, many of the 25 postposed expressions of purpose which occur in the body of the advertisements contain expressions of features, functions, and evaluations—notions which were predicted to constitute the focus of advertisements. Table 4 reports the mentions of these notions in preposed and postposed expressions of purpose. Clearly, features of the product, functions of the product, and evaluations of the product occur more frequently in postposed expressions of purpose than they do in preposed expressions of purpose.

Let me turn now to the expressions of cause and result. In this discussion I will limit myself to those expressions which involve relations within the clause complex. Several factors affect the expression of these relations and their effect in written language:

1. Is the cause placed first or the effect placed first?
2. Is a subordinating conjunction or a coordinating conjunction used?
3. If a subordinating conjunction is used, is the subordinate clause preposed or postposed?
4. Which conjunction is used (e.g. *because*, *since*, *so*)?
5. How are the clauses punctuated?
    a. Does no punctuation mark separate the clauses?
    b. Are the clauses separated by a comma?
    c. Are the clauses separated by a period?
    d. Are the clauses separated by a period and a paragraph indentation?

Table 5 summarizes the occurrence of the markers of causal relations in my data. Since *so* may occur ONLY in a postposed position, no value is provided in the preposed cell for *so*. Both *because* and *since* MAY occur either preposed or

Table 4. Distribution of mentions of product or company names, features, functions, or evaluations of the product in expressions of purpose.

	Preposed Purpose					Postposed Purpose				
	Total	Product or company name	Features	Functions	Evaluations	Total	Product or company name	Features	Functions	Evaluations
for	7	2	0	0	1	16	1	2	6	6
to	5	1	0	0	2	14	0	3	11	8
Total	12	3	0	0	1	30	1	5	17	14

postposed. However, it is clear that in advertising, the preferred position for clauses introduced by these words is postposed.

Table 5. Distribution of preposed and postposed expressions of cause and result.

	Preposed	Postposed	Total
because	1	9	10
since	1	0	1
so	—	8	8
Total	2	17	19

The punctuation used for these expressions may provide some insight into what is happening here. A summary of the punctuation of postposed expressions of clause and purpose is provided in Table 6.

Table 6. Punctuation of postposed clauses expressing cause and result.

	Separated by				
	no mark	comma	period	period+¶	Total
because	4	1	3	1	9
so	1	3	4	0	8
Total	5	4	7	1	17

Twelve out of 17 examples are separated from the remainder of the clause complex by some punctuation mark. In eight of these examples, the punctuation mark signals a major division (a sentence or paragraph boundary). Since styles of punctuation vary greatly in advertising writing, it is worth looking at these examples in detail. In general, in combinations of clauses, the first clause continues issues which have been established in the previous context, while the second makes a major point of the combination. Since this result differs in part from that of Schiffrin (1985),[7] it bears some discussion. Text 10 illustrates the

[7] In discussing the differences in the uses of Y *because* X and X *so* Y, Schiffrin found that topic continuity with the preceding discourse was an important factor controlling which construction was used. If X had greater topical continuity with the preceding discourse, then X *so* Y was used, while if Y had greater topical continuity with the preceding discourse, then Y *because* X was used. In contrast, she found no significant effect involving topical continuity of the second member of the pair with following discourse. As a result, she challenged Van Dijk's (1977) suggestion that

sort of situation I find when no punctuation mark separates the two clauses.

Text 10. Advertisement for Brawny Paper Towels.

4. Thanks to these new Brawny prints, paper towels have just been elevated to a new form of art that is both beautiful and functional.
6. They're beautiful BECAUSE THERE ARE SEVEN NEW BOLD DESIGNS, SOME FEATURING TWO COLORS.
7. They're functional BECAUSE BRAWNY HAS THE BIGGEST SHEET YOU CAN BUY, SO THEY'RE BIG ENOUGH AND TOUGH ENOUGH FOR EVEN THE MESSIEST SPILLS.

Sentence 4 introduces the notion that Brawny Paper Towels are both beautiful and functional. Each of these evaluations is taken up in a following sentence and justified with *because* clauses. In Sentences 6 and 7, the repetitions (*They're beautiful* and *They're functional*) begin their respective sentences, while the *because* clauses are postposed. Further, notice that these *because* clauses describe relevant features and functions of the product—ideas which we have already said are likely to be important and emphasized in an advertisement. Of the nine examples of postposed *because* clauses, two occur as the last clause of the body of the advertisement and summarize the point of the advertisement. Four more postposed *because* clauses justify evaluations (Text 10 provides two examples) by listing the positive features the product has. Two additional postposed *because* clauses introduce the problems which the product is to solve. It should be clear that postposed *because* clauses typically contain information which is highly important to the effect of the text or text segment in which they occur.[8] This fact is particularly obvious when the *because* clause is not separated by punctuation from the clause which precedes it (as in Text 10 above). In this case, the first clause of the pair introduces minimal new information and the major new information of the entire clause complex is contained in the *because* clause.

The other situation in which the *because* clause clearly introduces important new information is found when the postposed *because* clause begins a new sentence or paragraph. When a postposed *because* clause is given its own

---

sentence-final *because* clauses have a prominent discourse role because they are in final position in the sentence—a position of emphasis. While my data confirm her results with respect to topical continuity with preceding discourse, they do not do so with respect to information prominence in the particular clause and sentence. I believe that the major reason for this difference lies in how we operationalized the notion of discourse prominence and topical continuity. Schiffrin operationalized topic as 'subject noun phrase, or noun phrase in marked focus position within the clause ... ' (1985:293). Subjects are typically Themes and usually contain Given information. As a result, it is highly unlikely that examining the information contained in Subjects will locate prominent information within a clause or clause complex.

[8] Schleppegrell (1992) finds similar results.

sentence, the preceding clause also contains information which is relevant to the purpose of the advertisement, as in Text 11.

Text 11. Advertisement for Corning PhotoGray Extra lenses.

1. Protect your eyes without moving a muscle.
2. With ordinary prescription lenses, your eyes get a workout trying to protect themselves from glare.
3. Yet, despite all this effort, you still can't see as comfortably as you should.
4. Even with sunglasses, there's work to be done.
5. BECAUSE AS THE LIGHT CHANGES, YOU SPEND THE DAY SWITCHING FROM SUNGLASSES TO EYEGLASSES AND BACK AGAIN.
6. Corning PhotoGray Extra prescription lenses protect your eyes without this routine.

Sentences 1–3 present a problem. Sentence 4 poses a possible solution to this problem and evaluates it negatively. Sentence 5 justifies the evaluation by specifying exactly what the issue is. That issue, of course, functions as a new problem. Sentence 6 introduces Corning PhotoGray lenses, which solve that second problem. Both sentences 4 and 5 (which together express one *X because Y* relation) contain information which is essential to describing the problem which the product being advertised is supposed to solve.

Clauses related by *so* exhibit similar tendencies to those related by *because,* although there seem to be some differences as well. Constructions with *so* resemble constructions with *because* in that the second clause regularly contains information which is seen to be important to the entire text or to the text segment in which the construction occurs. In every example of a construction which involves X *so* Y in my data, the Y clause contains some description of a problem to be solved by the product, a function of the product, or an evaluation of the product. The first part of the *X so Y* combination, however, seems to be more important to the text than the corresponding portion of the *Y because X* combination. The first part of the *X so Y* combination can range over several sentences. Indeed, in two of my examples, it is difficult to determine exactly how much of the previous text to include within the X portion. In addition, the first part of the *X so Y* combination regularly mentions meanings which are important to the persuasive function of the advertisement. Finally, in none of the examples I have analyzed so far does the *X* part of the *X so Y* combination merely repeat information from the previous context in a way that is at all similar to the situation in Text 10.

Let me end by summarizing. Early in this paper I referred to the importance of the persuasive function of advertising, and on the basis of that function I predicted that references to product features, product functions, and evaluations of the product would typically be given focal attention. Further, I predicted that the names of products or of companies would be prominent, but not necessarily focal. Using the definitions of Theme and New, and using the indirect correlation of New with the end of the clause and sentence, I predicted that those notions which were given focal attention would tend to be found at the ends of the clauses and sentences (the N-Rhemes) in written advertising. The general results confirm that Themes and N-Rhemes are being used in different ways, while the more detailed examinations of the expressions of clause, reason, purpose, and goal confirm the orienting function of Thematic information.

REFERENCES

Bäcklund, Ingegerd. 1989. To sum up: Initial infinitives as cues to the reader. Proceedings from the Fourth Nordic conference for English studies, Helsingør, May 11–13, 1989, ed. by Graham Caie, Kirsten Haastrup, Arnt Lykke Jakobsen, Jørgen Erik Nielsen, Jørgen Sevaldsen, Henrik Specht, and Arne Zettersten, 289–302. Department of English, University of Copenhagen.

Chafe, Wallace L. 1980. The deployment of consciousness in the production of a narrative. The pear stories: Cognitive, cultural, and linguistic aspects of narrative production, ed. by Wallace L. Chafe, 9–50. Norwood, NJ: Ablex.

Chafe, Wallace L. 1984. How people use adverbial clauses. Proceedings of the tenth annual meeting of the Berkeley Linguistics Society, 437–49. Berkeley: Berkeley Linguistics Society.

Chafe, Wallace L. 1987. Cognitive constraints on information flow. Coherence and grounding in discourse, ed. by R.S. Tomlin, 21–51. Amsterdam: John Benjamins.

Clark, Herbert H., and Susan Haviland. 1977. Comprehension and the Given-New contract. Discourse production and comprehension, ed. by Roy O. Freedle, 1–40. Norwood, NJ: Ablex.

Downing, Angela. 1991. An alternative approach to theme: A systemic functional perspective. Word 42.119–44.

Fries, Peter H. 1981. On the status of theme in English: Arguments from discourse. Forum Linguisticum 6, 1.1–38.

Fries, Peter H. (in press) Patterns of information in initial position in English. Discourse and meaning in society: Functional perspectives, ed. by Peter H. Fries and Michael Gregory. Norwood, NJ: Ablex.

Givón, T. 1983. Topic continuity in discourse: A quantitative cross-language study. Amsterdam: John Benjamins.

Halliday, M.A.K. 1985. Introduction to functional grammar. London: Edward Arnold.

Leech, Geoffrey. 1966. English in advertising: A linguistic study of advertising in Great Britain. London: Longmans.

Schiffrin, Deborah. 1985. Multiple constraints on discourse options: A quantitative analysis of causal sequences. Discourse Processes 8, 3.281–303.

Schiffrin, Deborah. 1987. Discourse markers. Cambridge: Cambridge University Press.

Schleppegrell, Mary J. 1992. Subordination and linguistic complexity. Discourse Processes 15, 1.117–31.

Thompson, Sandra A. 1990. Information flow and dative shift in English discourse. Development and diversity: Language variation across time and space, ed. by Jerold Edmondson, Crawford Feagin, and Peter Mülhäusler, 239–53. Dallas: Summer Institute of Linguistics and University of Texas at Arlington.

Van Dijk, Theo. 1977. Text and context. London: Longman.

Winter, Eugene. 1977. Replacement as a function of repetition: A study of some of its principal features in the clause relations of contemporary English. Ann Arbor: UMI.

When and how old age is relevant in discourse of the elderly: A case study of Georgia O'Keeffe

Elif Tolga Rosenfeld*
Georgetown University

1 Introduction. Research on the discourse of the elderly has thus far tended to focus on either the discourse of the elderly who are cognitively impaired or on discourse produced in contexts in which old age is at issue. For example, studies focus on intergenerational talk and talk within caretaking institutions. In both types of talk, age difference is often viewed as causing a problem in communication. While these studies have contributed to our knowledge of the problems faced by the elderly in communicating, there is still little research which focuses on elderly discourse in which 'problems' do not seem to arise. The implicit assumption is that discourse of the elderly in which there is no obvious problem, nor any obvious avoidance of a problem, is the same as the discourse of younger people. Thus, while these studies often seek to avoid viewing aging as a process of decrement, they support a decrement perspective by primarily focusing on problematic discourse specific to the elderly segment of the population.

In analyzing the discourse of Georgia O'Keeffe, as presented in the 1977 WNET–13 movie *Georgia O'Keeffe*, produced by Perry Miller Adato, a movie celebrating her 90th birthday, I have found that although there are no apparent breakdowns in communication, her discourse, nonetheless, is distinctly that of an elderly woman. Specifically analyzing prosodic, discourse, and paralinguistic features of her discourse I have found linguistic evidence to support the claim that her old age is but one characteristic of her identity. Further, this characteristic varies in the extent to which it is relevant and whether it is positively or negatively valued, within the different identities she presents through her discourse.

While sociolinguistics, for the most part, has ignored the discourse of the elderly, it has become a significant issue in other fields, most notably psycholo-

* I would like to thank Heidi Hamilton for her comments and suggestions, as well as her encouragement, while I was developing this paper. I take full responsibility, however, for the content of this paper.

gy and health care. While sociolinguists can benefit from the theoretical foundation other scholars have developed, they have been late in contributing to the theory of language upon which this preliminary work has been based. The task for the sociolinguist is thus twofold.

First, the literature must be reviewed so that we immediately build upon work already done, rather than take steps backwards, before going forward, by discovering anew the problems which seem to arise in any study of the elderly. Such a review of the literature leads to an understanding, for example, of the complexity of the question: What is old age? Is it a biological characteristic based merely on chronology, or is it a social characteristic based on a person's role in society?

Once the linguist is aware of the problems encountered by previous researchers, the second task is to analyze the discourse of the elderly from a sociolinguistic perspective. In my analysis of O'Keeffe's discourse, I build upon communication accommodation theory (CAT) (cf. Giles et al. 1987). CAT is a theory of interactive communication which has been used to account for style shifting in talk. In my analysis of the data, I further expand CAT, drawing on the work of Goffman (1981) and Tannen and Wallat (1983). Similar to the work of Tannen and Wallat I identify the different registers (speech styles) O'Keeffe uses and identify shifts in the activity being engaged in at the time of talk, what Goffman (1981) identifies as shifts in 'footings'. That is, I identify the activity O'Keeffe is engaged in at the time of talk for each register. I then identify O'Keeffe's different roles reflected in her talk within each register. Having identified the registers as well as the footings and roles associated with each, I then analyze the discourse to determine whether or not age is relevant as part of her role, and further, whether it is valued as being negative or positive. I have identified four footings which correspond with four different registers (or speech styles) which, in turn, reflect four different roles (or identities) that O'Keeffe presents through her discourse.

In what follows I present my analysis of O'Keeffe's discourse, discussing background literature (2), focusing on the issue of 'age' as a variable in social science (2.1), previous work concerning discourse and aging (2.2), and my theoretical approach based on Goffman's (1981) theory of footing and Tannen and Wallat's (1983) research (2.3); the data (3); and my analysis of the data (4), identifying the different registers used by O'Keeffe (4.1), and analyzing the relevance of age based on these registers (4.2). Ultimately I argue that being elderly has a different qualitative and quantitative impact on O'Keeffe's role in the interaction depending on the context of the particular moment of interaction. Being elderly can be more or less salient or not, and it can be valued more or less positively or negatively. Thus my analysis supports the claim that the diversity found in the elderly as a group can also be found within a single elderly person.

2 Literature. In the following, I first review some of the issues which the label 'old age' raises. Next, I review previous research which has focused on discourse of the elderly. Finally, I review Goffman's theory of footing and Tannen and Wallat's analysis of shifts in footing as shifts in register.

2.1 Old age. Research of the elderly population has led to the realization that 'age' is itself a vague term, indicating both chronological and social age. This research also shows that there is a significant difference between the way the elderly view their lives and the way the rest of society does. I discuss each of these in turn.

2.1.1 Chronological age and social age. Eckert (1984:219) suggests that the label 'age' does not adequately describe age as an independent variable in any research in which age differences are compared to behavior differences. She claims age can and should be broken down into two categories, chronological age and social age, arguing that 'insofar as individuals' linguistic behavior is part of a strategy associated with social roles, it is the roles that each individual plays that correlate with linguistic variation' (1984:224). Thus, in researching social old age Eckert (1984:230) claims that one is discovering sociolinguistic behaviors which 'might not correlate with linguistic differences' between the chronologically old and young, 'but rather the roles and linguistic needs associated with' old age as a life stage.

Although Eckert is specifically addressing sociolinguistic variation studies of sound change, this distinction seems relevant for any linguistic study of the discourse of the elderly. Thus, in my analysis, although O'Keeffe is chronologically 89 years old, I consider this to be only a rough indicator of the social roles that might be reflected in her discourse.

2.1.2 Emic and etic understandings of old age. Anthropologists use the term ETIC to describe the observations of a group of people from the perspective of someone outside the group. This contrasts with an EMIC description made by someone within the group. For example, the action described as the killing of an animal from an etic perspective might be described as a sacred ritual of offering a sacrifice to the gods from an emic perspective. It is important to keep in mind, however, that any description based on a certain group's perspective is emic. Someone outside of one group still belongs to some other group, and in describing the action they might give an outsider's description that is not etic to the group being described, but rather emic to a group other than that being described. For example, the etic description of killing an animal might be described by ingroup members as a ritual sacrificing and by, for example, animal rights activists outside the group as the killing of an animal for entertainment. 'For entertainment' is an evaluative phrase, reflecting a perspective which is emic to an animal rights group.

Eckert (1984:229) notes that the 'elderly, being the farthest from the experience of young and middle-aged researchers, comprise the age group that is most subject to stereotyping in linguistics as well as other research.' Thus, as researchers we are not within the group we are describing and our descriptions run the risk of being outsiders' (emic) descriptions, rather than emic descriptions of how aging is experienced by the elderly.

In analyzing child behavior, adult researchers face a similar problem. The difference, however, is that, although at the time of research they are not within the group, they once were. Further, childhood is thought of as a positive stage in the life span, in which one develops into an adult. Old age, however, is something which has not been experienced *yet*, and which is generally viewed in American society as a time of decrement. Sankar (1984:251), for example, cites a Harris poll in claiming that:

> Americans believe that the main causes of the disabilities associated with old age is age itself. For Americans old age is seen as a kind of disease, a terminal illness that uniformly begins in the sixties.

Thus, our 'own anxieties about the inevitability of death are associated with old age as a disease—a disease whose only outcome is ultimately death' (Sankar 1984:262). The belief that the process of decrement begins due to chronological old age is also supported, as Sankar (1984:261) points out, by social legislation which has fixed 65 as a marker of old age. Further, as Ward (1984:228) notes, in modern societies the aged receive a low status due to our work ethic as well as intellectual and moral segregation of the old and young.

The belief that the aging process is an inevitable process of decrement is often reflected not only in the public at large, but also in the work of gerontology. Ward (1984) discusses the conflict between outsiders' and insiders' emic views of old age as a paradox in the gerontological literature. That is, while it is found that old age has a marginal and stigmatized status in our society, it is also found that this status does not seem to significantly affect the daily lives and self-evaluation of the elderly themselves (1984:227).

Ward (1984:230) claims that 'our models and methods still lead us to expect that age will have a central significance and to look for its effects in our research of the elderly.' That is, our emic view of old age as a negative and salient characteristic of elderly people influences our research. Ward (1984:230) urges us to 'strive to understand lives *as they are lived*,' in other words, to gain an insider's emic perspective.

It is important to note that while the decrement paradigm for research is clearly a faulty one, the extreme opposite to this, an anti-ageist paradigm, is equally faulty. To claim that any research supporting the idea of decrement is ageist is clearly misguided since there is obvious decrement associated with aging. Thus, in agreement with Coupland and Coupland (1990), I suggest that one should not select either of these outsiders' emic research perspectives, but rather seek to understand decrement as *part* of the aging process.

Ultimately Ward suggests that age is a social fact which represents one characteristic of the many possessed by an elderly individual. Thus, as researchers we must seek to identify the contexts in which age is relevant. Further, one must discover how, in these contexts, age is valued. Rather than assuming that whenever age is salient it will be negatively valued, Ward (1984:230) claims that 'under some conditions being old may be both salient and positive, as when later life is linked with such favorable qualities as wisdom.'

There are at least two research methods which might lead to an insiders' emic understanding of the elderly. One, which has traditionally been used by anthropologists, is to use an ingroup informant. For example, Sankar (1984:259) notes that although doctors seem to have difficulties in distinguishing illness due to specific diseases and illness due to old age, her elderly informants 'could be clear and concise concerning the distinction between their complaints due to old age and those due to illness.' Thus, the physical condition of the elderly is viewed differently by the doctors and the elderly.

A second method for gaining an insiders' emic description of the experience of aging is discourse analysis. Although an outsiders' emic analysis of discourse of the elderly is equally possible, an insiders' emic description can be achieved by grounding one's analysis on the discourse itself as much as possible and at the same time being aware of researcher bias. In my analysis of the O'Keeffe data I analyze the discourse which reflects how O'Keeffe, herself, manages her identity as an elderly woman.

2.2 Discourse and aging. The literature on discourse and aging falls into two categories. The first reflects the view that linguistic ability is a set of cognitive abilities; the second reflects the view that linguistic communication is a feature of social interaction. Since my analysis is based on an interactional sociolinguistic perspective, in what follows I briefly review the former category, and then discuss the literature which falls into the latter.

2.2.1 Language as a cognitive ability. Due to the relatively high incidence of cognitive impairment in the elderly segment of the population, as opposed to younger segments, researchers who are interested in understanding the processes of human cognition and cognitive impairment have conducted research focusing on the linguistic abilities of the elderly. While their focus tends to be that of impaired linguistic ability, 'normal' elderly tend to be used in their research insofar as they represent a control group for experiments.

Within this perspective, language is viewed as a set of cognitive skills of which the individual human being is capable. Researchers, such as Obler and Albert (1985), use tests such as the Boston Naming Test and the Wechsler Adult Intelligence Scale. These tests involve researcher and subject interviews in which the researcher elicits subject responses to controlled questions and tasks which are designed to test specific skills, such as naming pictures and giving definitions.

Such data is then analyzed, for example, in terms of theories of memory organization and processes, or information processing theory (Bayles and Kaszniak 1987). While this research has contributed to our understanding of cognitive functioning and cognitive impairment, it has been less successful in describing the way language abilities of the elderly, and especially the healthy elderly, affect communication in everyday living. Thus, Bayles and Kaszniak (1987:133), studying linguistic processing in normal aging, write that 'In the opinion of these authors, age effects on processing capacities do not handicap individuals in normal everyday communication.'

One of the reasons why this approach may not inform our understanding of language use in 'normal everyday communication' may be the definition of language used by these researchers. For example, Bayles and Kaszniak (1987:47) define communication as 'the sharing of information by means of a symbol system; it is linguistic when words are used and nonlinguistic when other symbol systems, such as mathematical notation, are used.' They further define speech as the 'motor production of sounds', the language system as the 'system by which sounds are paired with meaning' and communication as the 'cognitive process of sharing ideas through language' (1987:48).[2] This theory of language does not include the concept of communication as a process which involves not only the linguistic symbols but also the particular context in which the interaction takes place. Language is viewed as the cognitive abilities of a human being, rather than as a feature of everyday interaction for social beings.

2.2.2 Language as part of social interaction. The second category of research concerning discourse and aging reflects a shift by researchers in their theory of language toward a more social interactive theory. Much of the literature explicitly criticizes the way in which language has been treated previously in this area. For example Coupland and Coupland (1990:460–461) write that 'much existing work is arguably reminiscent of the early eras in other sociolinguistic domains where a variety of contrastive, decontextualized, non-interactional designs were dominant.' They go on to claim that there is a need for an interactive perspective. Similarly, Shadden (1988:12) notes the lack of an interactional approach to analyzing language by which we might more fully understand how the elderly use language in their lives, when she writes:

---

[2] This view of language reflects what Reddy (1979) identified as 'the conduit metaphor'. Analyzing the metaphors we use to describe communication, Reddy points out that they correspond with a general underlying metaphor of communication as a system whereby one individual uses language to encode an idea and sends the idea to another individual who then decodes the language to receive the original idea of the speaker. Thus it is as if language is used to wrap up the actual ideas of speakers and send them through a conduit to hearers who can then unwrap the language and receive the idea. Bayles' definition of communication as 'the cognitive process of sharing ideas through language' cited above, clearly reflects this conduit metaphor.

Reddy (1979) notes that the conduit metaphor is deeply embedded in the English language, to the extent that it is difficult, if not impossible, to avoid using terms which reflect it. There is, however, a difference between using the language while strongly advocating the view reflected by the metaphor, and using the language to articulate a theory of communication in which the intersubjective element of communication and the significance of the particular context of the interaction are included.

> Unfortunately, as one pages through the gerontological literature seeking references to communication processes and disorders, it is far too easy to become distracted by theories and isolated facts—and to lose perspective on the daily reality of communication with and by older persons.

These researchers note the lack of any sociolinguistic research of discourse and aging, and have begun to develop their own sociolinguistic approach. Thus, Coupland, Coupland, Giles, and Henwood (1988:5) note that 'since there is currently no clear-cut agenda for a sociolinguistics of aging, there is much to be gained from particularistic analyses of elderly talk in context'.

Although the theory of language has begun to move closer to that of the interactional sociolinguist, many researchers are burdened with a research methodology which makes it difficult to conduct experiments which will allow them to analyze natural discourse so as to further develop such a theory. For example, in an effort to study narrative discourse style in the elderly, Obler (1980:75) writes that:

> Early attempts to elicit and analyze spontaneous discourse showed that the wide range of individual variation in narrative styles, when combined with the freedom of conversation, made it extremely difficult for us to draw conclusions about changes in narrative style across age groups. As a result we turned to more directed discourse tasks by which we could elicit narrative discourse units that would be comparable across subjects.

Thus, although the shift in communication theory requires the study of natural everyday discourse, the research methodology of fields other than interactional sociolinguistics requires a theory driven approach, with the collection of data being controlled so as to clearly relate to the theory. This conflict between the communication theory and the research methodology has influenced the research in two ways.

First, the conflicting needs for natural discourse and experimental control over the data have often been accommodated by eliciting discourse which is produced in a clearly experimental situation which is meant to approximate a real-world context. Thus, the discourse produced is at best quasi-natural, if not unnatural. For example, Stover and Haynes (1989:140), analyze topic manipulation and cohesive adequacy in conversations of normal adults between the ages of 30 and 90. They address the theoretical and methodological conflict, stating that they:

> feel that the conversational task engaged in by the subjects was as close to natural discourse as possible for an experimental context and that results can be generally extended to conversation in non-experimental situations.

Some researchers have, however, made clear efforts to shift not only their theory of language, but their methodology for data collection as well. For example, in their study of the social functioning of disclosing chronological age in context, Coupland, Coupland, and Giles (1989:132) set up participants in 20 young–old dyads, 10 young–young dyads and 10 old–old dyads. They asked that the people 'get to know one another', and tape recorded the following eight minutes of conversation. Thus, they exerted less control on the context of talk.

The second way in which methodology has inhibited researchers from analyzing discourse from a fully interactive sociolinguistic framework is due to the 'theory driven' approach to discourse analysis, as opposed to a more 'data driven' approach. That is, researchers seem to collect and analyze discourse based on their theoretical interest in the issue of aging. The result is that the research question raised by Ward (1984) is not being addressed. Focusing on discourse in which age is assumed to be salient, (i.e. intergenerational talk or talk between caregivers and care receivers), researchers are not moving toward a better understanding of when and how age is salient in the everyday lives of elderly people. Boden and Bielby (1986:73) address this issue, claiming that age is a 'socially accomplished category' and suggesting that

> Research on naturally-occurring interaction—i.e. studies that are unmediated by analysts' constructs and the problems inherent in retrospective accounts—is an important enterprise in understanding the experience of older persons.

2.2.3 Findings relevant to the present analysis. While my analysis represents an extension of the preliminary interactive theory of communication reflected in the literature on communication accommodation theory, it also draws on two specific findings in the literature. First, Coupland and Coupland (1990:454), reviewing the literature, refer to the work of Ramig (1983) in which it has been shown by matched-guise tasks that the elderly voice is 'regularly discriminable from younger voices', to the extent that subjects were able to correctly identify the elderly voice based on single prolonged vowels. Ramig (1983) claims that the regular change in voice is due to degenerative changes in the larynx. Coupland and Coupland (1990:454) further claim that 'voice quality ... has the potential to act as a social marker of elderly speech.' Thus, in my analysis of O'Keeffe's discourse, although I identify subtle shifts in her register, her voice is always clearly identifiable as that of an elderly woman.

Second, Coupland, Coupland, Giles, and Henwood (1988) study the functions of disclosing chronological age in discourse of the elderly. They identify disjunctive disclosing of chronological age as instances when telling one's old age reflects either 'favorable self evaluation' or 'perceived incongruence between chronological age and contextual age' (1988:137). The O'Keeffe film was made to celebrate O'Keeffe's 90th birthday. Although she does not disclose her chronological age in the discourse, there are instances in the discourse when a disjunctive sense of O'Keeffe's age is clearly expressed.

The research which has focused on an interactive perspective of communication has led to the development of communication accommodation theory (cf.

Giles et al. 1987; Coupland et al. 1990). Communication accommodation is defined by Shadden (1988:35) as referring to 'modifications in speech style designed to expedite the transmission of a message and to signal willingness to engage in communication interactions.' Thus, breakdowns in intergenerational talk have been identified as being due to problems in accommodation strategies, where, for example, either the elderly or the younger participants over- or underaccommodate to each other's speech style. One example of accommodation is the use of baby talk (BT) by younger interlocutors with elderly people. It can be a case of overaccommodation when perceived as demeaning by the elderly individual. Caporeal (1981), however, has shown that not using baby talk can be seen as underaccommodation in some contexts in which BT is perceived as nurturing, and thus, when care-takers do not use it they are perceived as not being nurturing.

Using the term 'register' rather than 'speech style', I focus on the relative (qualitative) variation in the use of certain prosodic, discourse, and paralinguistic features of O'Keeffe's speech in my analysis of the data. The five prosodic features are as follows. (1) pitch: relative differences in (overall) pitch, (2) tempo: the rate of speech production, (3) intonational range: extent to which contrastive pitch is used (wider or narrower range), (4) function of intonation: whether contrastive pitch is functioning primarily grammatically, (e.g. to distinguish between questions and statements), emphatically (to emphasize a single word) or to express emotion, (e.g. surprise), (cf. Crystal 1969)[3]. (5) Loudness: used for emphasis. Further I identify, as a discourse feature, what Tannen (1989) calls 'constructed dialogue'. This term refers to what is commonly thought of as reported speech. The basic difference in terminology which is relevant to the present analysis is that constructed dialogue allows the quoted speech to represent previous thoughts that were not necessarily uttered. Finally, I identify laughter, as a paralinguistic feature of the discourse.[4]

O'Keeffe's use of these features varies throughout the discourse. Identifying distinct registers is not a matter of a discrete 'use' or 'absence of use' of the features, but rather the different degrees of use within each register. I identify the registers based on the distinctive (relative) use of certain features with each register.

---

[3] I describe the function of intonation as primarily grammatical, emphatic, or attitudinal, rather than only serving certain functions to indicate my agreement with Crystal's (1969:272) suggestion that when describing tonal contrasts one must speak of scales of contrastivity. He writes '... it seems impossible to pronounce any utterance in such a way that it will be interpreted as carrying no attitude whatever—even the most "objectively" pronounced utterances will be labelled "cold", "unworried", "matter-of-fact", "precise", etc.' Thus, in distinguishing between different registers I identify in my data, I describe the types of tonal contrast (grammatical, emphatic, or attitudinal) which are used 'more' than others.

[4] Such an analysis a speaker's style, or register, has been established in interactional sociolinguistics (cf.Tannen 1984).

2.3 Goffman's theory of footing. Goffman (1981:126) identifies as changes in footing, cases in which the tone of discourse changes along with 'an alteration in the social capacities in which the persons present claim to be active'. Goffman (1981:128) summarizes this phenomenon as follows:

1. Participant's alignment, or set, or stance, or posture, or projected self is somehow at issue.

2. The projection can be held across a strip of behavior that is less long than a grammatical sentence, or longer, so sentence grammar won't help us all that much, although it seems clear that a cognitive unit of some kind is involved, minimally, perhaps, a 'phonemic clause'. Prosodic, not syntactic, segments are implied.

3. A continuum must be considered, from gross changes in stance to the most subtle shifts in tone that can be perceived.

4. For speakers, code switching is usually involved, and if not this then at least the sound markers that linguists study: pitch, volume, rhythm, stress, tonal quality.

5. The bracketing of a 'higher level' phase or episode of interaction is commonly involved, the new footing having a liminal role, serving as a buffer between two more substantially sustained episodes.

Tannen and Wallat (1983:205) examine a pediatric interview, identifying the way in which the pediatrician, in communicating with the child, mother, and a video camera/crew (recording the interview for use in training students) is 'addressing three audiences, each of which is involved in at least three "frames" associated with distinct footings [Goffman 1979] marked by use of identifiable linguistic registers.' My analysis of the data is similar to Tannen and Wallat's insofar as I identify four registers which are associated with four different footings.

The term 'frame' however, refers to 'the definition of what is going on, without which no message could be interpreted' (Tannen and Wallat 1983:207). The notion of frame thus involves the recognition of the frame by participants in the interaction (as in smooth communication), or the lack of such a joint understanding of what is going on in the interaction (as in problematic communication). In my study, the data are excerpts from a movie which is clearly focused on O'Keeffe talking about herself, since it is an interview of her. The overall activity, or the frame, is 'participating in an interview'. While this does not mean that there is no further, subtler, shift in interactive frame throughout the interviewing, I do not analyze the frames in my data for two reasons.

First, the excerpts in the movie represent chunks of the discourse of the interview when, for the most part, O'Keeffe is dominant in the interaction. As a result there is not enough evidence in the data to support theories concerning the reactions or participation of interlocutors other than O'Keeffe. Second, the goal of my analysis is to identify the way in which age is part of O'Keeffe's identity. Rather than focusing on people's reaction to how age is manifested in O'Keeffe's discourse, I wish to further understand how age is part of the identity O'Keeffe presents in her discourse.

In the data I analyze, it is possible to identify a hierarchy of levels of activities. The higher level activity throughout the excerpts in the movie is 'interviewing'. Based on my analysis of the different registers used in the data, I have identified four different footings, three of which are associated with the 'interviewing' activity, and one of which results in what Goffman (1981:128) describes as a 'bracketing' of the interviewing activity.

Goffman (1981:128) goes on to claim that 'a change in footing implies a change in the alignment we take up to ourselves and the others present as expressed in the way we manage the production or reception of an utterance.' Thus I also identify the different roles which correspond with the different footings.

The notion of role, as I use it here, is based on Goffman's (1981) analysis of the notion of speaker as 'production format'. The production format is made up of three elements. The animator is the person who produces the utterance; the author is the person who has determined what those utterances are to be; and the principal is the person 'whose position is established by the words that are spoken, someone whose beliefs have been told, someone committed to what the words say'. Goffman (1981:144) goes on to describe the principal, suggesting that:

> one deals in this case not so much with body or mind as with a person active in some particular social identity or role, some special capacity as a member of a group, office, category, relationship, association, or whatever, some socially based source of self-identification.

In my analysis I focus on the way in which the principal of O'Keeffe's production format changes, referring to the principal of her talk as her role. I have found that with each shift in register, and footing, there is a corresponding shift in role. Further, in each role the value and relevance of age varies. That is, in the different roles her age seems to be either valued (negatively or positively) or not valued, and seems to vary in the extent to which it is salient to her overall identity.[5]

---

[5] Applying Goffman's notion of footing, Tannen and Wallat (1983) identify three different footings in pediatric interviews. Each footing corresponds with a different register. In analyzing O'Keeffe's discourse, I have found that she uses four different registers which correspond with four different footings.

3 The data. The film, produced by Perry Miller Adato for WNET–13 NY, celebrating Georgia O'Keeffe's 90th birthday was broadcast on WETA–26 DC in 1977. She was 89 at the time of filming. The movie is a collection of excerpts of O'Keeffe talking with the interviewer and her assistant, Juan Hamilton, at her ranch in New Mexico. Interwoven with O'Keeffe's discourse are (1) images of her art work, (2) photographs of her, places she lived, and people involved in her life, (3) interviews with art critics, and (4) letters O'Keeffe wrote at earlier points in her life, read by a woman other than O'Keeffe. Thus, the film is, in a sense, a collage.

The movie celebrates O'Keeffe. One can assume that the excerpts from O'Keeffe's discourse which were included in the movie were selected by adults who produced the film. It is important to remember, then, that there may have been communication breakdowns during the interviews, but that these segments would obviously have been 'edited out' of the final film. As a result my analysis of O'Keeffe's discourse focuses on understanding the discourse of an elderly woman which has been favorably evaluated by the editors.

4 Data analysis. In what follows I first identify the four registers which O'Keeffe uses in the data, based on, as mentioned previously, the relative use of the following prosodic, discourse, and paralinguistic features: pitch, tempo, intonational range, function of intonation, loudness, constructed dialogue, and laughter. In identifying the registers I also identify four different footings and four different roles which correspond with these registers. Second, I analyze the content of the discourse in each of these registers (and footings), focusing on the references to O'Keeffe's age. This analysis contributes to my identification of O'Keeffe's roles, allowing a determination of whether old age is reflected in the discourse as a salient characteristic of her identity in each role. Further, in those cases in which old age is salient, the way in which it is valued is identified. That is, old age can either be evaluated or not, and if evaluated it can be evaluated either negatively or positively.

4.1 Four registers, four footings ... four roles. In the following excerpt O'Keeffe shifts back and forth in her register between reporting and narrating[6]. She is describing her paintings of animal bones. She says:

(1)

reporting	1	At first I painted the horse's head.....
	2	And then I got this cow's head.

[6] The transcription of the data follows the conventions which are further described in Tannen (1989:202). The discourse is divided into intonation units. Sentence final falling intonation is represented by a period (.); final rising intonation is represented by a question mark (?); pauses are represented by repeated periods (...), the number of which indicates roughly the length of pause.

narrating 3 And I had the cow's head painted against the blue
4 and I thought
5 "Well I have to do something else about that."
reporting 6 And that was at the time that
7 the men were all talking about
8 the great American..novel,
9 the great American play,
10 the great American..
11 oh it was the great American everything.
narrating 12 And I thought they didn't know anything about America
13 mo-a lot of them had never been across the Hudson.
14 So I thought
15 "I'll make my picture..a red white and blue (laughs)
16 I'll make it an American painting
17 for these people that don't go across the Hudson"
reporting 18 And this was my painting.
19 I put a red stripe down either side..
20 it entertained me
21 but I don't think anybody else caught on to it
22 for quite a while

In lines 1 and 2, O'Keeffe begins describing the paintings using a relatively flat intonation, emphasizing *horses* and *cows* by using contrasting (higher) pitch and a louder voice, and ending both lines with falling intonation. In line 3 there is a shift in register. Her voice has a subtle shift to a higher pitch than it has in lines 1 and 2. In line 3 she emphasizes the word *blue* by using a pitch which contrasts with her overall pitch more than the contrast in pitch when she utters *horses* and *cows* in lines 1 and 2. In fact, overall in lines 3–5 she uses a wider intonational range than she does in 1–2. Then, in line 5, *Well I'll have to do something else about that*, O'Keeffe utters constructed internal dialogue: she vocalizes her thoughts behind the painting.

In lines 1 and 2 O'Keeffe's speech is characterized by a relatively lower pitch and narrower intonational range, functioning to emphasize words or signal the end of the utterance with utterance-final falling intonation. I have labelled this register 'reporting', based on the content of her talk. Here she is describing her artwork itself, her artistic career: first she painted the horse's head, and then the cow's head. Thus, the footing, is 'doing an interview on her artistic career'. In this footing her role is that of an interviewee describing her career.

The register used in lines 3–5 I have labelled her 'narrating' register[7]. This

[7] The term 'narrating' is being used as a general term, referring to the anecdotal nature of the talk uttered in this register. It is not being used to refer to the structural concept of narrative as presented in Labov (1972). The question naturally arises, however, as to what the relationship between the 'narrating register' and the structural concept of narrative may be. Due to both the scope of the present study as well as the amount of relevant data for further research on this issue,

register is characterized by a relatively higher pitch, use of a relatively wider intonational range, and the use of constructed dialogue. The content of her talk in this case is describing her personal experience in developing her painting. That is, in line 3 she refers to an original version of the painting of the cow's head, and then communicates her decision to redo this painting by vocalizing her thoughts (at that time) in line 5, *Well I'll have to do something else about that.* Here she is giving information about the personal life and experience behind the paintings described in lines 1 and 2. Thus, the footing is 'telling personal stories about her art work'. Her role in this footing is that of narrator of these personal anecdotes.

In line 6 there is a register shift back to 'reporting'. Her voice assumes a lower pitch, emphasizing the utterance-final *novel* and *play* (lines 7 and 8), indicating, with loudness as well as a slight rise in intonation, that the clauses are part of a list. In lines 1 and 2 O'Keeffe reports on her artwork. In lines 6 through 11 she is describing the historical context in which these paintings were painted. Thus, the 'reporting' register is used to describe her career and to describe the historical context of her career.

In line 12, again there is a shift back to the 'narrating' register. Her voice not only assumes a higher pitch, but again she uses a relatively wide intonational range. In line 12 her pitch gradually rises until *about*, when it falls and then rises to a pitch relatively higher than the pitch preceding *about*. Then, in pronouncing *America* she uses a lower pitch. In line 13 the intonational contour is similar to line 12, with a slight rising in pitch, culminating with the first syllable in *Hudson* being the highest pitch while the second syllable is uttered with a lower pitch. Unlike the reporting register, where changes in pitch are used only to either emphasis certain words, or mark grammatical functions (such as the end of a sentence, or an element in a list), in lines 12 and 13 the wider intonational range seems to express her amazement or disbelief that these people who were so concerned with America did not even know about America.

O'Keeffe also uses constructed dialogue in lines 15–17 to describe her reasons for painting the cow's head the way she ultimately did, *I'll make my picture a red white and blue/ I'll make it an American painting/ for these people who don't go across the Hudson.*' Thus, again, the narrating register corresponds with talk about her personal experience behind the painting.

Finally, in lines 18–22, she switches back to the reporting register. She is describing the final version of the painting. Notice that in lines 18–22, although she is describing her views of the painting, she does not switch to the narrating register. I suggest that this is because she is not talking about her personal experience in producing the painting, but rather, she is factually describing the way the painting was understood by the public. She claims in lines 20–21 that she does not think *anybody else caught on to it for quite a while*, that is, people

---

I have not explored this relationship.

did not understand the significance of the color scheme, until later.

In the following excerpt O'Keeffe talks about her artistic process on an abstract level. Here she uses the narrating register, as well as two other registers, which I have labelled 'teaching' and 'interacting'.

(2)

teaching	1	...I s- can see shapes.
	2	It's as if my mind creates shapes
	3	that I don't know about.
interacting	4	I can't say it any other way (laughing)
teaching	5	that I get this shape in my head.
narrating	6	and sometimes I know what it comes from
	7	and sometimes I don't
teaching	8	and I think...with myself...
	9	that there are few shapes
	10	that I have repeated
narrating	11	a number of times during my life
	12	and I haven't known I was repeating them
	13	until after I had done it.

Lines 1 through 3 are spoken with a slower tempo than the utterances spoken in the other three registers. She also articulates each word very clearly, to the extent that it seems as if her voice is putting emphasis on every word. In lines 1 through 3 O'Keeffe is describing the artistic process. I have labelled the register she uses her 'teaching' register, since the characteristics of the register, slowness of speech and careful articulation, both function to make the discourse more easily understood. It is as if she is teaching her audience, explaining to them something which may be difficult to understand. Thus, the register helps ease language comprehension. The footing when this register is used is 'teaching the young what she has learned', while her role in this footing is that of a wise woman.

In line 4 O'Keeffe switches to what I have labelled her 'interacting' register, that is the register she uses when managing the social interaction at the time of speaking. In line 4, this register is reflected in her significantly faster rate of speech production, less careful articulation, and laughter. In line 4 O'Keeffe breaks from her description of her artistic process to comment on this description. She recognizes that what she has said, about visualizing shapes, may not be easily comprehended by her interlocutor when she says *I can't say it any other way*, laughing. While her description of her artistic process is not firmly grounded in the time and situation of talk, this utterance in line 4 is clearly more grounded in the immediate social context of talk. Thus, the footing here is 'managing the social interaction at the time of talk'. This footing represents a shift in activity (i.e. frame), from 'doing an interview' to 'interacting'. Thus, it is a 'bracketing' of the interview frame.

In the footings described as 'doing an interview about an artist's career', 'telling personal stories behind the art work' and 'imparting wisdom', O'Keeffe's role (the principal of her talk) can be identified clearly as 'interviewee', 'storyteller' and 'teacher'. For the footing described as 'managing the social situation at the time of interaction', however, O'Keeffe's role is not as clearly identifiable as one identity. Rather, since this footing involves interaction, her role is more clearly dependent on the immediate context of talk and her interlocutors' contributions. As a result O'Keeffe's interactive register seems to describe her everyday conversational style, (cf. Tannen 1984).

Although the interacting register is used for longer segments at other points in the interview, it is important to recognize that a footing can be held momentarily, as it is here. While this shift is clearly reflected as a register shift, it only lasts for one line in the transcript.

Again, the shift back to her teaching register in line 5 only lasts for one line. Although it is short, there is a clear shift in register. Her speech in line 5 is again relatively slow and she articulates each word carefully. Then in lines 6 and 7 she shifts to the narrating register. Although she does not use the fast speech of the 'interacting' register, she is no longer using the slow rate of speech of the 'teaching' register. This median rate of speech is characteristic of both the 'reporting' and 'narrating' register. What distinguishes lines 6 and 7 as narrating, and not reporting, is the higher pitch and the fact that she uses a wider intonational range.

In lines 8 through 10, the shift to the teaching register is again marked by a slower rate of speech production and careful articulation. Finally, in lines 11 through 13, O'Keeffe uses the narrating register.

The four registers, four footings, and four roles which represent the principal of O'Keeffe's discourse are summarized in Figure 1. While none of the features listed for each register are present in all four registers, there is some overlap between them. The features which distinguish the register from all other registers appear in bold. Note that the narrating register does not have a single distinctive feature, but rather the co-occurrence of the features of this register are unique.

4.2 When and how is old age salient? Having identified these four registers as corresponding to four different footings and roles, the question remains: When and how is age relevant? That is, to what extent and how is O'Keeffe's identity as 'old' associated with her role, or identity, reflected in the discourse? Analyzing the data in terms of the content of the discourse, I have identified the different ways in which 'old age' seems to emerge in O'Keeffe's discourse. Each of these, again, corresponds with the different registers and footings.

When O'Keeffe is 'doing an interview on her career as an artist', using the 'reporting' register, her age does not seem to be very salient. Although she is talking about past events, her age does not emerge in the discourse. The only time her age does becomes relevant is when she is reporting on the historical

Figure 1. Four registers, activities and roles.

Register	Characteristics of register	Activity	Role
reporting	**narrower intonational range**; intonation used to signal grammatical relation or emphasis	doing an interview about her artistic career	interviewee
narrating	wider intonational range; relatively higher pitch; intonation used to signal grammatical relation or emphasis and to express emotion; laughter; constructed dialogue	telling the personal stories behind her artwork	storyteller
teaching	**relatively slower rate of speech production**; very clear articulation	teaching the young what she has learned (imparting wisdom)	teacher
interacting	wider intonational range; intonation functions to signal grammatical relations and emphasis, or to express emotion; relatively higher pitch; **faster rate of speech**; laughter	managing the social situation at the time of the interaction	participant in interaction (dependent on immediate context of talk)

context, as in excerpt (1), which is reproduced here as excerpt (3). Here O'Keeffe is describing the cultural context which made her want to use a red, white, and blue theme in her painting of the cow's head:

(3)

1 And that was at the time the men were all talking about
2 the great American..novel,
3 the great American play,
4 the great American..
5 oh it was the great American everything.

In describing the spirit of America at the time she painted the picture, she is describing a time which the reporter and the public audience may not remember. She is describing something in the past which she experienced but which, due to their younger ages, her audience did not. Thus, she has to describe a cultural context which her age allows her to have experienced. Here her 'old age' does not seem to reflect either a particularly negative or positive value.

When O'Keeffe is 'telling personal stories behind her art work' her age becomes more salient. In the following excerpt she describes what her daily painting schedule used to be when she would go out into the desert and paint in New Mexico:

(4)

1 I don't go out like that now
2 but I used to get right up in the morning
3 and start out and stay out all day.
4 I'd start off around seven
5 and not get back until around five.

In lines 1 and 2 O'Keeffe explicitly contrasts what she used to be able to do (physically) and what she can now do: *I DON'T go out like that NOW/ but I USED to get right up in the morning'*. Since her ability to get up and 'stay out all day' does not involve a particular physical ability, but rather physical endurance, the contrast is between the physical vigor of youth and the frailty of age. Although age is more relevant here than in excerpt (3), the issue of her old age is still not central to the discourse. She goes on to talk about what she used to do when she painted in the desert. Thus, it seems that although her age is mentioned, her activities as an younger artist seem to be more salient than her age at the time of the discourse. It should be noted, however, that this subtle reference to physical weakness due to old age reflects the fact that old age is being negatively valued in this context.

Another way in which O'Keeffe's age becomes salient while she is 'telling personal stories behind her art work', is in excerpt (2), repeated as excerpt (5):

(5)

1 and I think...with myself...
2 that there are few shapes
3 that I have repeated
4 a number of times during my life
5 and I haven't known I was repeating them
6 until after I had done it.

As mentioned previously, O'Keeffe uses the 'teaching' register in lines 1–3, and then switches to the narrating register in lines 4–6. In lines 4–6 her old age is implied by the fact that she is describes a pattern over her life time. Thus, while her old age is not mentioned directly, the fact that she is looking back on her life with the hindsight of her age makes the fact of her old age salient. Further, whereas it was negatively valued in the previous excerpt as causing frailty, here it positively valued as it provides her with a lifetime of experience which she can look back on and use to understand her own artistic process more clearly. In summary, then, in the footing 'telling personal stories', age is somewhat salient but can be valued either positively OR negatively.

When O'Keeffe is 'imparting wisdom', her old age does not seem to be mentioned in the content of the discourse. For example, in the above excerpt, in lines 1–3, while using the teaching register, O'Keeffe does not mention her age. Although there is neither direct reference to her age in the content of the discourse, nor is it reflected in the features of her register, because of our stereotype of elderly wisdom, age is nonetheless salient to her identity as one who is imparting wisdom.[8]

Old age is clearly salient when O'Keeffe uses the 'interacting' register. For example, in the following excerpt Juan and O'Keeffe are in her studio, and Juan mentions O'Keeffe's health:

(6)

1	Juan:	Georgia you know everybody's not the way you are
2		they don't take care of themselves as well as you do
3	O'Keeffe:	That's because they don't try to live to be a hundred

[8] While one might expect that her wisdom would be clearly connected with her old age, so that her old age would become positively valued and salient in the content of her discourse, this does not seem to be the case. It is interesting to note, however, that while the slowness and clarity of her teaching register can be interpreted as functioning to make what she is saying more easily comprehended, an alternate interpretation is possible. A slowing down of speech has been found to be typical of the aging voice. Although this is often accompanied by problems in articulation, it is possible that the linguistic characteristics of this teaching register signal two different identities. The clarity of articulation signals that she is teaching, while the slowness of production signals that what she is teaching is the wisdom of old age.

Although there is no explicit disclosing of chronological age, it seems clear that what Coupland, Coupland, Giles, and Henwood (1989) identify as disjunctive age is the view of O'Keeffe's age presented here. Juan initiates the topic in lines 1 and 2 by claiming that O'Keeffe is not like everybody else in that she takes good care of herself. O'Keeffe responds, in line 3, 'that's because they don't try to live to be a hundred'. The discourse reflects an image of O'Keeffe as being in better health than most people, due to the fact that she takes particularly good care of herself. Her chronological age here is contrasted with her social age: She is healthier than most people her age.

Another example of the disjunctive view of O'Keeffe's age which is made evident in the 'interacting' register is the following. O'Keeffe is leaning on Juan's arms as they make their way across a rocky patch of ground in the desert:

(7)

1	O'Keeffe:	Don't break your leg or anything like that Juan
2		It'd be awful hard for me (laughing) to carry you
3	Juan:	Oh!
4		Well, you'd just have to work at it!
		(O'Keeffe laughs)
5		Look over there there's no there's no
		(O'Keeffe slips)
6		over there there's no stone
7		then we get into the good stuff

In lines 1–2 O'Keeffe jokes about her frailty, claiming that Juan should not hurt himself because she would not be able to carry him.[9] Juan responds to this in lines 3–4 by telling O'Keeffe she would 'just have to work at it!'. O'Keeffe's positive response to this is made evident by her laughter. Then, while Juan is uttering lines 5–6, O'Keeffe slips on the rocks, but since she is leaning on Juan's arm, he manages to keep her standing and help her to regain her balance. There is no mention of the fact that she has slipped.

In the excerpt in which O'Keeffe is narrating the story of how she used to spend her days painting, analyzed in excerpt 4, the reference to her frailty due to old age is directly indicated. In the above excerpt, O'Keeffe makes reference to the same negatively valued characteristic of old age, in a very indirect way: she jokingly warns Juan to be careful, and then mentions her frailty insofar as she would be unable to carry him. The idea of O'Keeffe's chronological age and social age being disjunctive, due to her efforts, was analyzed in the previous

[9] In fact, due to O'Keeffe's size, one might argue that she never could have carried Juan. The idea of her carrying him now, thus can be seen as hyperbole. Used in this joking context, her disjunctive age is further emphasized.

excerpt, in O'Keeffe's explanation of her efforts to try to live to be one hundred. Here, Juan expresses this same idea, that her disjunctive age is due to her efforts, when, in line 4 he says that she would just have to work at carrying him. The implication is that if she works at it she will be able to do it. That is, if she wishes to, she can overcome the negatively valued effects of old age.

Particularly interesting, however, is the fact that right after they joke about Juan hurting himself, she slips on the rocks. Neither Juan nor O'Keeffe draw any attention to this incident. Juan, in fact, seems to be diverting attention away from the incident by continuing his talk as if nothing had happened. Thus, while her old age is mentioned in talking about the past, and contrasting what she could do then with her present frailty, the issue of her age seems more salient in this instance. It seems plausible that, when she is using the 'interacting' register, the discourse and activity are firmly set in the present time and negatively valued effects of old age are very salient, and very negative. Both Juan and O'Keeffe make efforts to avoid recognizing these effects explicitly, although they are mentioned indirectly.

At other points in the discourse when O'Keeffe uses this 'interacting' register, however, her age seems to be positively valued, and salient. In the following excerpt Juan and O'Keeffe are riding in a car.

(8)

1	Juan:	How do you like being one of the roots of Abstract American Art?
2	O'Keeffe:	Well, I must be one of the old roots.

Line 2 is the most direct reference O'Keeffe makes to her age. Whereas the salient characteristic of old age in the previous excerpt is her frailty, here her old age is positively valued: she is among the artists considered to have started an entire movement in American Art. Thus, here, she makes a more direct reference to her age, within the present context, in a positively valued way. In summary then, within the footing 'managing the social interaction at the time of talk' age is very salient and can be valued either positively or negatively.

Figure 2 is an extension of the chart from figure 1, incorporating the analysis of the saliency of old age and the evaluation of old age (as positive, negative, both positive and negative, or neither positive nor negative) to the previous chart which summarized the four registers, four footings, and four roles identified in O'Keeffe's discourse.

5 Conclusion. Previous research on discourse and aging includes the development of communication accommodation theory (CAT) which allows researchers to analyze the way in which the elderly communicate with others from an interactive perspective, similar to that of Tannen and Wallat (1983). In my analysis I have tried to move away from the research question 'how do people manage interactions when one of the participants is elderly', and toward

Figure 2. Registers, activities, roles: the relevance and evaluation of old age.

Register	Characteristics of register	Activity	Role	Relevance of old age	Evaluation of old age
reporting	narrower intonational range; intonation used to signal grammatical relation or emphasis	doing an interview about her artistic career	interviewee	not very relevant	neither positive nor negative
narrating	wider intonational range; relatively higher pitch; intonation used to signal grammatical relation or emphasis and to express emotion; laughter; constructed dialogue	telling the personal stories behind her artwork	storyteller	somewhat relevant	negative or positive
teaching	relatively slower rate of speech production; very clear articulation	teaching the young what she has learned (imparting wisdom)	teacher	relevant	positive
interacting	wider intonational range; intonation functions to signal grammatical relations and emphasis, or to express emotion; relatively higher pitch; faster rate of speech	managing the social situation at the time of interaction	participant in interaction (dependent on immediate context of talk)	very relevant	negative or positive

'to what extent is age relevant at all, and how is it valued, by the elderly themselves'. To do so, I have analyzed O'Keeffe's discourse identifying shifts in register use and focusing on her role when using the register, and the way in which her identity as old is a part of her role. I have demonstrated that the analysis of speech style in elderly discourse is a valuable research methodology, not only for intergenerational talk where age is salient, but for talk in other contexts as well. Equipped with an analytical tool which can be used to examine the everyday discourse of the elderly, it then becomes possible to begin to answer Ward's (1984) question: When and how is age salient in the everyday lives of elderly people?

I have demonstrated that it is possible to identify subtle differences in O'Keeffe's register based on certain linguistic and paralinguistic features of her discourse. The use of these different registers can then be analyzed as corresponding with different footings: the registers are used when a certain type of activity is being engaged in. In turn, the roles of the speaker correspond with the different footings. In analyzing the content of the discourse it is then possible to determine where age is salient in the discourse, and whether it is valued positively, negatively, both, or not at all. I have demonstrated that in my data the salience and value of old age vary depending on the specific role in which O'Keeffe is at the time of talk: it might not be salient, it may be salient but not valued, salient and negatively valued, salient and positively valued, or salient and both positively and negatively valued.

While many researchers recognize the heterogeneity of the elderly population as a whole, as well as a diversity in the variety of behaviors a single elderly person may exhibit, the response is often to increase the number of subjects used in the study and thus be able to generalize about normative elderly behavior. In this case study of Georgia O'Keeffe's discourse I have demonstrated that the diverse ways in which she speaks correspond with diverse ways in which old age is part of her identity. Age can be experienced in a variety of ways for each individual, and to try to eliminate this individual variation in research will ultimately inhibit researchers from understanding how the elderly experience old age in their everyday lives.

REFERENCES

Bayles, Kathryn, and Alfred W. Kaszniak. 1987. Boston: Little, Brown and Company.

Boden, Deirdre, and Denise Bielby. 1986. The way it was: Topical organization in elderly conversation. Language and Communication 6.73–89.

Caporeal, Linnda R. 1981. The paralanguage of caregiving: Baby talk to the institutionalized aged. Journal of Personality and Social Psychology 40.876–84.

Cohen, Donna, and Suzanne Wu. 1980. Language and cognition during aging. Annual Review of Gerontology and Geriatrics 1.71–96.

Coupland, Nikolas, and Justine Coupland. 1990. Language and later life. Handbook of Language and Social Psychology, ed. by Howard Giles and William P. Robinson, 451–68. Chichester, England: John Wiley and Sons Ltd.

Coupland, Nikolas, Justine Coupland, and Howard Giles. 1989. Telling age in later life: Identity and face implications. Text 9.129–51.

Coupland, Nikolas, Justine Coupland, Howard Giles, and Karen Henwood. 1988. Accommodating the elderly: Invoking and extending a theory. Language in Society 17.1–41.

Coupland, Nikolas, Karen Grainger, and Justine Coupland. 1988. Politeness in context: intergenerational issues (Review Article). Language in society 17.253–62.

Coupland, Nikolas, Karen Henwood, Justine Coupland, and Howard Giles. 1990. Accommodating troubles-talk: The management of elderly self disclosure. Reception and response: Hearer creativity and the analysis of spoken and written texts, ed. by Graham McGregor and R.S. White, 112–44. London: Routledge.

Craig, Grace J. 1989. Human development. Englewood Cliffs, NJ: Prentice Hall.

Crystal, David. 1969. Prosodic systems and intonation in English. Cambridge: Cambridge University Press.

de Santi, Susan, Loraine Obler, Helene Sabo-Abramson, and Joan Goldberger. 1990. Discourse abilities and deficits in multilingual dementia. Discourse ability and brain damage: Theoretical and empirical perspectives, ed. by Yves Joanette and Hiram H. Brownell, 224–35. New York and Berlin: Springer Verlag.

Eckert, Penelope. 1984. Age and linguistic change. Age and Anthropological Theory, ed. by David I. Kertzer and Jennie Keith, 219–33. Ithaca: Cornell.

Erickson, Erik H. 1963. Childhood and Society. New York: W.W. Norton and Co.

Giles, Howard, Anthony Mulac, James J. Bradac, and Patricia Johnson. 1987. Speech accommodation theory: The first decade and beyond. Communication Yearbook 10: An annual review published for the International Communication Association, ed. by Margaret L. McLaughlin, 13–48. Newbury Park, CA: Sage Publications.

Goffman, Erving. 1967. On face work. Interaction Ritual, 5–45. New York: Pantheon Books.

Goffman, Erving. 1981. Footing. Forms of Talk, 124–59. Philadelphia: University of Pennsylvania Press.

Hutchinson, John, and Mary Jensen. 1980. A pragmatic evaluation of discourse communication in normal and senile elderly in a nursing home. Language and Communication in the Elderly, ed. by Loraine K. Obler and Martin Albert, 59–73. Lexington: Lexington Books.

Kausler, Donald. 1988. Cognition and aging. Communication Behavior and Aging, ed. by Barbara Shadden, 79–106. Baltimore: Williams and Wilkins.

Labov, William. 1972. The transformation of experience in narrative syntax. Language in the inner city, 354–396. Philadelphia: University of Pennsylvania Press.

Lubinski, Rosemary. 1988. A model for intervention: Communication skills, effectiveness, and opportunity. Communication Behavior and Aging, ed. by Barbara Shadden, 294–308. Baltimore: Williams and Wilkins.

Obler, Loraine. 1980. Narrative discourse style in the elderly. Language and Communication in the Elderly, ed. by Loraine K. Obler and Martin Albert, 75–90. Lexington: Lexington Books.

Obler, Loraine K., and Martin Albert. 1981. Language and aging: A neurobehavioral analysis. Speech, Language, and Hearing: The Aging Process, ed. by D. Beasley and G.A. Davis, 107–21. New York: Brune and Stratton.

Obler, Loraine K., and Martin Albert. 1985. Language skills across adulthood. Handbook of the Psychology of Aging. 2nd ed., ed. by James E. Birren and K. Warner Schaie, 463–73. New York: Ban Nostrand Reinhold Company Inc.

Östör, Akos. 1984. Chronology, category, and ritual. Age and Anthropological Theory, ed. by David I. Kertzer and Jennie Keith, 281–304. Ithaca: Cornell.

Reddy, Michael J. 1979. The conduit metaphor—case of frame conflict in our language about language. Metaphor and Thought, ed. by Andrew Ortony, 284–324. Cambridge: Cambridge University Press.

Robinson, Roxana. 1989. Georgia O'Keeffe: A life. New York: Harper and Row.

Ryan, Ellen B., Howard Giles, Giampiero Bartolucci, and Karen Henwood. 1986. Psycholinguistic and social psychological components of communication by and with the elderly. Language and Communication 6.1–24.

Sankar, Andrea. 1984. 'It's just old age': Old age as a diagnosis in American and Chinese medicine.

Age and Anthropological Theory, ed. by David I. Kertzer and Jennie Keith, 250–80. Ithaca: Cornell.

Shadden, Barbara. 1988. Communication Behavior and Aging. Baltimore: Williams and Wilkins.

Smithers, Janice. 1977. Institutional dimensions of senility. Urban Life 6.251–276.

Stover, Susan, and William Haynes. 1989. Topic manipulation and cohesive adequacy in conversations of normal adults between the ages of 30 and 90. Clinical Linguistics and Phonetics 3.137–49.

Tannen, Deborah. 1984. Conversational style: Analyzing talk among friends. Norwood, NJ: Ablex.

Tannen, Deborah. 1989. Talking voices: Repetition, dialogue, and imagery in conversational discourse. [Studies in Interactional Sociolinguistics 6] Cambridge University Press: Cambridge.

Tannen, Deborah, and Cynthia Wallat. 1983. Doctor/mother/child communication: Linguistic analysis of a pediatric interaction. The Social Organization of Doctor-Patient Communication, ed. by Sue Fisher and Alexandra Dundas Todd, 203–19. Washington, DC: Center for Applied Linguistics.

Ward, Russell. 1984. The marginality and salience of being old: When is age relevant? The Gerontologist 24.227–32.

WNET–13 movie. 1977. 'Georgia O'Keeffe'. Produced by Perry Miller Adato.

Social meaning and creativity in Indian English speech acts

Yamuna Kachru
University of Illinois at Urbana-Champaign

This paper has three aims: theoretical, descriptive, and pedagogical. To achieve the first, a framework is suggested for research on conversational interactions in nativized varieties of English. The framework is based on what has been termed 'socially realistic' linguistics (see, e.g. Halliday 1978, Hymes 1974, B. Kachru 1981, 1986). Subsequently, a partial description of data from Indian English texts is provided to illustrate the major theoretical points. The emphasis is on looking at the text 'as actualized meaning potential' (Halliday 1978), showing that not only the interpretation, but also the identification of an intended speech act depends upon the socio-cultural meaning of the locutionary act. This discussion also illustrates the linguistic processes of creativity used to structure speech acts in Indian English. Finally, the implications of such studies for teaching and understanding World Englishes in appropriate sociolinguistic and literary contexts is discussed briefly.

Introduction. I would like to begin this paper with an anecdote. A short time ago, a colleague of ours at a major midwestern university, a scholar from the non-western world, was appointed head of an academic unit. As usual, a great deal of faculty input was sought in making the appointment. At the completion of the process, one of the faculty members of the concerned department, an American scholar, met the wife of the newly appointed head, and congratulated her on her husband's appointment. According to the faculty member, the wife replied, 'Thank you for having him.' The faculty member was puzzled by her response and asked me, 'Why did she say that? Does she think we did a favor by supporting him?' I was startled by this question, and mumbled something about the nature of responses to compliments—explicit or implicit—and the sociocultural values of humility and modesty in such situations in some of the Asian and African cultures I am familiar with. I was not sure if I should go into any further explanations, since this person had lived and taught in several different cultures across Europe and Asia.

The incident I have just narrated is nothing new; the ESL literature is full of instances of miscommunication between the native and nonnative speakers of

English. It is not important that the person in this case was an American; similar miscommunication may occur between any two interlocutors. Such incidents, however, make it clear that the conventional ESL approach to the whole situation of native–nonnative communication is uninsightful from the point of view of users of world varieties of English, whatever pedagogical goals it may serve in the American or British academic settings. And I address this vital issue within the theoretical paradigm of what has been appropriately termed 'socially realistic linguistics' (see, e.g. Halliday 1978, Hymes 1974, B. Kachru 1981, 1983, 1986). However, it is appropriate to take a brief look at the status of research in the area of cross-cultural verbal interaction before proceeding with the major concern of this study.

Cross-cultural speech act research. Recent research on verbal interaction in general and speech acts in particular has raised serious questions about the universal applicability of several theoretical notions of pragmatics (Levinson 1983, Green 1989). For instance, Wierzbicka (1985a, 1985b) claims that speech genres and speech acts are not comparable across cultures and suggests a semantic metalanguage for cross-cultural comparison of speech acts.[1] Matsumoto (1988, 1989) questions the adequacy of the theoretical notions of conversational implicature as proposed by Grice (1975), and 'face' as postulated by Brown and Levinson (1978, 1987) to account for the politeness phenomena in Japanese conversational interactions. Blum-Kulka (1990 in Blum-Kulka and Kasper 1990) argues for incorporating speech event (Hymes 1974) as a determinant variable in assigning politeness values in speech act analyses. Schegloff (1988) points out that speech act theoretic analysis has no way of handling temporality and sequentiality of utterances in actual conversation. Wetzel (1988) suggests that the term 'power' as discussed in the context of linguistic behavior in Western cultures (e.g. in Brown and Gilman 1960) is culturally bound and demonstrates that it has no equivalent in Japanese.

Furthermore, cross-cultural speech act research so far has utilized only a limited range of variables, for example, the variables of social distance and dominance (Blum-Kulka et al. 1989), and as Rose (1991) points out, even these are not well defined. It is clear that a more complete set of variables, for example, the set proposed in Hymes (1974), or the set of variables entailed by the notion of register (Halliday 1978), is likely to be more useful in speech act research. The simplistic categorization of societies in terms of vertical vs. horizontal and individualistic vs. group-oriented for the purposes of speech act research, as though these labels apply in all domains of a community's life, are clearly inadequate.

A deeper understanding of individual self vs. familial/group self and positive

---

[1] It is interesting to note that the same arguments can be made on the basis of data from varieties of English, certainly the indigenized varieties used in Africa, South Asia, Southeast Asia, and other parts of the world.

vs. negative face in different domains in both Western and Eastern cultures is necessary before one could argue about the universality of any proposed universal. Recent psychoanalytical and social scientific literature suggests that it is impossible to clearly demarcate the notion 'self' in terms of 'individual' or 'group-oriented' on the one hand, and societies as either 'vertical' or 'horizontal' on the other. For instance, Roland (1988:6) has the following to say in the context of both India and Japan: 'I am now convinced that we must speak of three overarching or superordinate organizations of the self: the familial self, the individualized self, and the spiritual self, as well as an expanding self. Each forms a total organization of the self in Eastern and Western (particularly Northern European/ American) societies, respectively, with varying suborganizations.' It is clear from the very perceptive discussion of the similarities and differences between Western and Eastern structures of self in Roland (1988:8) that in both India and Japan, the familial self predominates whereas 'the individual self is the predominant inner psychological organization of the Americans.'

In addition, it must be remembered that it is not necessary that caste structure in India be seen essentially as horizontal, as opposed to the vertical class structure in, for example, the Western industrialized societies. Not only are the different castes arranged in a hierarchy, even subcastes within a caste are arranged in hierarchies. Also, although the caste system appears to be inflexible, it is actually surprisingly flexible in that rank within the hierarchies is negotiable under certain circumstances.[2]

The data. The data for this study come from several works of Indian English fiction published in the last four decades. Insofar as conversations in literary works have to 'ring true' to be convincing, creative literature can be a valuable source of data for research on speech acts, politeness, conversation analysis, and contextualization in general (see, e.g. Adegbija 1988, Brown and Gilman 1989, B. Kachru 1983). Such data are certainly as 'authentic' as those elicited by questionnaire or role-play type instruments, which are common in cross-cultural speech act research. I am not suggesting that data from imaginative literature is all that one needs for such research, only that they are as valuable a source as any other for gaining insight into speech acts.

Analysis. The passage in (1) is taken from a novel by R.K. Narayan (*The World of Nagaraj* 1990). It occurs in the textual context of the protagonist, Nagaraj, conversing with a pundit who has been suggested to him as a possible teacher of Sanskrit. The protagonist has been warned that the pundit does not accept just anyone as a pupil, hence he has to be very persuasive to make

---

[2] For a comprehensive discussion of caste, see Karve (1961); for excellent case studies of caste and social change in India by both Indian and Western social scientists, see Singer (1959), Srinivas (1966) and Mandelbaum (1970).

himself acceptable.

1. Nagaraj said, 'I have not had the good fortune to learn Sanskrit—only English and Tamil.'
The pundit said, 'I am not surprised. Sanskrit is not a bazaar language. It [sic] is known as "Deva Basha". Do you know what it means?'
"'Language of gods",' translated Nagaraj promptly, feeling proud of his answer.
'At least you know this much; I am glad. Are you aware Sanskrit can not be picked up at any wayside shop? YOU MUST HAVE PERFORMED MERITORIOUS DEEDS IN SEVERAL BIRTHS TO BE BLESSED WITH A TONGUE THAT COULD SPELL THE SANSKRIT ALPHABET.'
'Ah, what wisdom, perhaps one's ears too must be blessed to hear the Sanskrit sound,' added Nagaraj, much to the delight of the pundit. More wrinkles appeared on his face as his smile broadened. Nagaraj added to the pleasure of this dialogue by saying, 'GOD CREATES A SCHOLAR LIKE YOUR GOOD SELF TO KINDLE THE FLAME OF KNOWLEDGE IN AN IGNORAMUS LIKE ME.'
'Ah, do not degrade yourself,' said the pundit. 'You talk like a poet, no wonder you want to engage yourself in kavya.' [Narayan 1990:95–96]

This piece of text provides several insights. Note, for example, the following. Nagaraj is obviously attempting to please the pundit by showing appropriate veneration for 'the language of the gods'. The first capitalized part of the exchange is uttered by the pundit with a purpose: to impress upon Nagaraj that he must be a 'deserving candidate' (*supātra*) to become the recipient of the knowledge of the language. The concept of *supātra* is very important in several contexts of the Hindu way of life, for example, in giving alms, giving donations, giving one's daughter away in marriage, and so on. That is to say, in the context of any kind of giving, the focus is not only on the giver or what is to be given, but also on who the deserving recipient is. Giving of oneself or one's possessions to the deserving counts as a meritorious deed; giving to the undeserving is futile. The recipients, in turn, must have performed meritorious deeds in order to have the status of the deserving in their current lives. Thus, the belief system regarding the cyclicity of life is built into the notion of what counts as giving.

The second capitalized utterance may seem like Nagaraj's attempt at flattering the pundit, but that perhaps is not the intended interpretation. The Indian notion of *maryādā* (or *adab* or *lihāz*, to use the Urdu terms) demands a rhetorical style in addressing a person of superior status that sounds hyperbolic in contemporary native varieties of English. Note that expressions such as 'your good self' are common in spoken Indian (or, South Asian) English. If one is not anglicized, one asks *What is your good name?* or *Where does your good self reside?* instead of asking *What is your name?* or *Where do you live?* The latter do not sound polite enough to the South Asian ear.

Now, it is worth looking at the total passage to discover the purpose of the six turns or three sets of exchanges between the two participants. The first turn is a hint, requesting the pundit to agree to teach Nagaraj Sanskrit. The pundit does not reply directly to the intended request; instead, he makes a series of assertions and asks an information question which is intended to challenge Nagaraj to prove himself to be deserving of the knowledge he seeks. Nagaraj, in turn, comes up with an answer to the question and the challenge. This prompts the pundit to utter an assertion and ask a yes–no question and make a further assertion. The first assertion is a guarded compliment, the latter two, the question and the second assertion, make up a more generous and direct compliment. Nagaraj reciprocates by indirectly accepting the compliment and paying a generous, but correct, direct compliment to the pundit. This is done not only to please the pundit, but to keep the 'pleasures of the dialogue' going.[3] Finally, the pundit utters a command which is an indirect compliment, follows it up with a direct compliment, and brings the dialogue back to the starting point by referring to Nagaraj's desire to learn Sanskrit in order to read Sanskrit literary works (*kāvya*).

Taken as a whole, the passage under discussion illustrates the speech act of requesting and a response to it. This overall interpretation is not possible unless the text is contextualized within the sociocultural context of South Asia. For instance, the interpretation of the speech acts of asserting, questioning, etc. as requesting, challenging, complimenting, etc. depends upon the specific context of the interaction, especially the interlocutors, their mutual relationship, and their roles as a seeker of favor and one possessing the power to bestow the favor. A lack of familiarity with the notion of a deserving recipient may block the interpretation of the assertions and the questions in the pundit's utterances as challenges or compliments. A change in the nature of the participants—for instance, two friends discussing their education—could lead to the interpretation of the information question in the pundit's first turn as a genuine request for information. Textually speaking, it is the second capitalized part of the exchanges that make it possible to interpret the preceding exchanges as they have been interpreted here.

Furthermore, the strategies for making the initial request (a hint instead of the more common indirect speech act) and issuing the challenge in response (again, by hint) do not support the claims of cross-cultural speech act research (Blum-Kulka et al. 1989) which claims that indirect speech acts are the most favored strategy for making requests while hints are the least favored.

---

[3] Western scholars working on Indian society and culture have characterized 'the widespread tendency of Indians to use language as a form of incantation and exuberant rhetorical flourish' as representing a 'culture of sound' (Lannoy 1971:176, 275).

What kinds of issues does this short text raise? It is obvious from the discussion so far that cross-cultural speech act research is impossible if based on the limited framework of classical theory of speech acts within pragmatics (as discussed, e.g. in Austin 1962, Searle 1969, 1979). The next point I wish to make is that Indian English utilizes certain speech genres (in the sense of Wierzbicka 1985b) unique to it. The next two examples that come from a collection of short stories by Raja Rao exemplify one such speech genre:

2a. 'Hé , brother, what is it all about?'
'Nothing. I think it's about the quarrel between Ramaji and Subbaji. You know about the Cornerstone?'
'But, ON MY MOTHER'S SOUL, I thought they were going to the court?' [Rao 1978:17]

2b. '... And Ramu,' she cried desperately, 'I have enough of quarrelling all the time. IN THE NAME OF OUR HOLY MOTHER can't you leave me alone!' [Rao 1978:88]

Describing the speech genre 'from the inside' (Wierzbicka 1985b), the capitalized parts of the two excerpts exemplify what would be labelled in Hindi–Urdu *saugandh* or *qasam khānā*, which may be loosely translated as 'swearing'. [4] Swearing is used to perform various speech acts in Indian languages, including Indian English. It may be used, for example, to persuade, challenge, promise, or entreat. In the first excerpt here, the purpose of the swearing is to persuade the hearer(s) that the speaker genuinely believed what he was saying, and in the second, it is to entreat. The entreaty is strengthened by an appeal to one's mother; no one would dare ignore a request accompanied by the name of one's or anyone else's mother. Note that one may swear not only by some sacred object or by a deity, but also by someone whom one holds dear, such as a relative or friend or one's own self. The *holy mother* in (2b) does not refer to any deity, it refers to the biological female parent of the character who is addressing these remarks to her brother, Ramu.

The following text from a novel by Khushwant Singh (1959) illustrates the same phenomenon, that is, blessing as a speech genre in Indian English. The verbal interaction cited here takes place in a Sikh family. The son and daughter-in-law are taking leave of the mother before retiring for the night. The first exchange occurs between the daughter-in-law and the mother-in-law, and the second between the son and the mother.

---

[4] According to *The Compact Edition of the Oxford English Dictionary Vol. II* (1971:3189), the word 'swear' has, among others, the following two meanings: 'To make a solemn declaration or statement with an appeal to God or a superhuman being, or to some sacred object, in confirmation of what is said', and 'to affirm, assert or declare something by an oath'. Although these meanings do not capture the sense of *saugandh* or *qasam*, I am using 'swearing' as a convenient label. A detailed analysis of the speech genre of *saugandh* or *qasam khānā* is beyond the scope of this paper.

3. ... She bent her head to receive her mother-in-law's blessing. '*Sat Sri Akal.*'
'*Sat Sri Akal,*' replied Sabhrai lightly touching Champak's shoulder.
'*Sat Sri Akal,*' said Sher Singh.
'Live in plenty, Live a long age,' replied Sabhrai taking her son's hand and kissing it.
'Sleep well.' [Singh 1959:16]

The expression *sat sri akal* 'God is truth' is the formulaic greeting Sikhs use to greet each other at meeting as well as at parting. It is also customary for elders (in the family or in the relevant group) to respond to a greeting by a 'blessing' such as *live long*, etc.[5] Hence, in the context of the two exchanges in the above example, a reader familiar with the South Asian context is likely to interpret the interaction in a certain way. The fact that the daughter-in-law's greeting draws a formulaic response whereas the son's greeting draws an elaborate set of 'blessings' is significant. Given the relationship among the participants and the occasion, the interpretation is that the mother-in-law is cool to her daughter-in-law.[6] Note that this interpretation is not based on conversational implicature (Grice 1975), either conventional or special, since it is customary to respond to formulaic greeting with a formulaic greeting in Indian as well as in most other cultures. The interpretation in this case is calculated on the basis of domain (family), setting (home), mutual relationship of participants (mother/son/daughter-in-law), occasion (leave taking for the night) AND the linguistic context (i.e. the two sets of exchanges). In the absence of any one of these contextual clues, the implicature that one participant is cool to another participant will not arise. Note that the speech acts of 'greeting' and 'blessing' are part of the overall speech act of 'leave-taking'; thus the greeting functions as a presequence (Schegloff 1988) for blessing and the two together are interpreted as leave-taking in the context of the interaction (for a detailed discussion of the functions of blessing in Indian English speech acts, see Y. Kachru (1991).

Conclusion. The above brief analyses prove the point that speech act theory by itself is not adequate to account for the negotiation of meaning taking place between speakers and addressees/hearers. In order to account for the socially realistic use of the English language in India (B. Kachru 1981), a richer theory

---

[5] 'Relevant group' may comprise village elders, elders in the extended family, caste elders, one's teachers, friends of elders in one's family, and occasionally, one's peers, or even strangers older than oneself, but never someone younger than oneself. Thus, 'blessings' in the Indian context are not comparable to formulaic blessings as in 'God bless you' in native varieties of English.

[6] In fact, the reader's interpretation turns out to match the writer's intentions. The following occurs on page 169: 'Sabhrai, who had never particularly cared for Champak, ...'

incorporating the notions of speech acts, conversation analysis, sociolinguistics, and ethnography of communication is needed to study the illocutionary force and perlocutionary effect of locutionary acts (Y. Kachru 1991). The claim is not that users of other varieties of English have no interpretation for the Indian English utterances. As Nelson (1991) points out, the utterances are more often than not intelligible, comprehensible, and interpretable, and yet there is an underlying 'otherness' in the discourse. In the words of Bharati Mukherjee (1985:140), 'That slight undetectable error, call it an accent, isn't part of language at all. I speak Hindu. No matter what language I speak it will come out slightly foreign, no matter how perfectly I mouth it. There's a whole world of us now, speaking Hindu.' What Mukherjee calls 'error' is referred to as 'otherness' in Nelson (1991). This otherness may lead either to a misinterpretation, or a poor interpretation. This otherness shows up in the empirical study carried out in India in Sridhar (1991). The claim is that an awareness of the sociocultural variables incorporated in the more comprehensive theory suggested here would lead to a richer interpretation.

An additional point worth making is that literary sources can provide valuable data for identifying culture-specific speech act effects, for example, the role of blessing or swearing in South Asia. These data are perfectly authentic in that they were not specifically produced for speech act research. They were reproduced in writing because in the judgment of the authors, they simulated actual conversations in real-life situations. To the extent that data collected in role-play situations are considered valid for speech act research, these data should be a welcome addition to the range of data available for research on cross-cultural verbal interactions.

Paradigms of research that look at an indigenized variety of English as a language with its own 'complex network of meaning potential' (Halliday 1978) have important implications for ESL instructional as well as teacher education programs. If the ultimate goal of such programs is to encourage global bilingualism in English, a great deal of sensitivity toward what learners bring to the task of learning an additional language has to be developed. At present, there is a wide gap between the theoretical conceptualization of how children are socialized through language (for example, in Halliday 1975, Hasan 1988, Hasan and Cloran 1990, Heath 1983, Ochs 1982) and the pedagogical attempts in ESL programs to teach even adult learners the idealized communicative competence of a monolingual speaker of English. A more realistic, and perhaps more effective, pedagogical strategy would be to respect the social meanings learners bring to the language learning task and extend their range with those of the target language. This would be possible only if, as D'souza (1988) suggests, monolingual speakers of English realize the need for a wider awareness of the different meaning potentials of different varieties of English. Perhaps the time has come for the ESL teacher education programs to take a leading role in this venture and give it some priority on their agenda for theoretical and pedagogical research. In my view, understanding and responding to the issues raised here is vital for research on communicative competence in world varieties of English and applications of such research for pedagogical purposes.

REFERENCES

Adegbija, Efurosibna. 1988. Toward a speech-act approach to Nigerian literature in English. Language and Style 21, 3.259–69.

Austin, J.L. 1962. How to do things with words. Oxford: Clarendon Press.

Blum-Kulka, S., and G. Kasper (eds.) 1990. Politeness. Special issue of Journal of Pragmatics 14, 2.

Blum-Kulka, S., J. House, and G. Kasper (eds.). 1989. Cross-cultural pragmatics: Requests and apologies. Norwood, NJ: Ablex.

Brown, Penelope, and Stephen C. Levinson. 1978. Universals in Language Usage: Politeness phenomena. Questions and politeness: Strategies in social interaction, ed. by Esther M. Goody, 56–289. Cambridge: Cambridge University Press.

Brown, Penelope, and Stephen C. Levinson. 1987. Politeness: Some universals in language usage. Cambridge: Cambridge University Press.

Brown, R.W., and A. Gilman. 1960. The pronouns of power and solidarity. Style in language, ed. by T. Sebeok, 253–76. Cambridge: M.I.T. Press.

Brown, R.W., and A. Gilman. 1989. Politeness theory and Shakespeare's four major tragedies. Language in Society 18.159–212.

D'souza, Jean. 1988. Interactional strategies in South Asian languages: Their implications for teaching English internationally. World Englishes 7, 2.159–71.

Green, Georgia M. 1989. Pragmatics and natural langauge understanding. Hillsdale, NJ: Erlbaum Associates.

Grice, H.P. 1975. Logic and conversation. Syntax and semantics 3: Speech acts, ed. by P.Cole and J.L. Morgan, 41–58. New York: Academic Press.

Hasan, Ruqaiya. 1988. Language in the process of socialization: Home and school. Language and socialization: Home and school, ed. by L. Gerot, J. Oldenburg and T. van Leeuwen, 36–95. Sydney: Macquarie University.

Hasan, Ruqaiya, and C. Cloran. 1990. Semantic variation: A sociolinguistic interpretation of everyday talk between mothers and children. Learning, keeping and using language: Selected papers from the 8th World Congress of Applied Linguistics, ed. by M.A.K. Halliday, J. Gibbons and H. Nichols, 67–100. Philadelphia: John Benjamins.

Halliday, M.A.K. 1975. Learning how to mean: Explorations in the development of language. London: Edward Arnold.

Halliday, M.A.K. 1978. Language as social semiotic. Baltimore: University Park Press.

Heath, Shirley B. 1983. Ways with words: Language, life and work in communities and classsroom. Cambridge: Cambridge University Press.

Hymes, Dell. 1974. Foundations in sociolinguistics: An ethnographic approach. Philadelphia: University of Pennsylvania Press.

Kachru, Braj B. 1981. Socially realistic linguistics: The Firthian tradition. International Journal of the Sociology of Language 31.65–89. [also published in in Studies in the Linguistic Sciences 10, 1.85–111.]

Kachru, Braj B. 1983. The Indianization of English: The English language in India. Delhi: Oxford University Press.

Kachru, Braj B. 1986. The alchemy of English: The spread, functions and models of non-native Englishes. Oxford: Pergamon Press. [Reprinted 1990. Urbana: University of Illinois Press.]

Kachru, Braj B. 1987. The bilingual's creativity: Discoursal and stylistic strategies in contact literatures. Discourse Across Cultures: Strategies in World Englishes, ed. by L. Smith, 125–40. New York: Prentice Hall.

Kachru, Yamuna. 1991. Speech act in world Englishes: Toward a framework for cross-cultural research. World Englishes 10, 3.299–306.

Karve, Irawati. 1961. Hindu society—An interpretation. Poona: Deccan College Postgraduate and Research Institute.

Lannoy, Richard. 1971. The speaking tree: A study of Indian culture and society. New York: Oxford University Press.

Levinson, Stephen C. 1983. Pragmatics. Cambridge: Cambridge University Press.

Mandelbaum, David G. 1970. Society in India, Volumes I and II. Berkeley and Los Angeles, CA: University of California Press.

Matsumoto, Yoshiko. 1988. Reexamination of the universality of face: Politeness phenomena in Japanese. Journal of Pragmatics 12.403–26.

Matsumoto, Yoshiko. 1989. Politeness and conversational universals: Observations from Japanese. Multilingua 8: 207–21.

Mukherjee, Bharati. 1985 [1990] Darkness. Canada [India]: Penguin Books.

Narayan, R.K. 1990. The world of Nagaraj. London: Heinemann.

Nelson, Cecil. 1991. New Englishes, new discourses, new speech acts. World Englishes 10, 3.317–23.

Ochs, Elinor. 1982. Talking to children in Western Samoa. Language in Society 2.77–104.

Rao, Raja. 1978. The policeman and the rose. Delhi: Oxford University Press.

Roland, Alan. 1988. In search of self in India and Japan: Toward a cross-cultural psychology. Princeton: Princeton University Press.

Rose, Kenneth. 1991. Speech acts and questionnaires: The effect of hearer response. Linguistics Seminar, University of Illinois at Urbana-Champaign, February 7. (Unpublished ms.)

Schegloff, Emanuel A. 1988. Presequences and indirection: Applying speech act theory to ordinary conversation. Journal of Pragmatics 12.55–62.

Searle, John R. 1969. Speech acts. Cambridge: Cambridge University Press.

Searle, John R. 1979. Expression and meaning. Cambridge: Cambridge University Press.

Singer, Milton (ed.) 1959. Traditional India: Structure and change. Philadelphia: The American Folklore Society.

Singh, Khushwant. 1959. I shall not hear the nightingale. London: John Calder.

Srinivas, M.N. 1966. Social change in modern India. Berkeley and Los Angeles: University of California Press.

Sridhar, Kamal K. 1991. Speech acts in an indigenized variety: Sociocultural values and language variation. English around the world: Sociolinguistic perspectives, ed. by Jenny Cheshire, 308–18. Cambridge University Press.

Wetzel, Patricia J. 1988. Are 'powerless' communication strategies the Japanese norm? Language in Society 17, 4.555–64.

Wierzbicka, Anna. 1985a. Different cultures, different languages, different speech acts: Polish vs. English. Journal of Pragmatics 9.145–78.

Wierzbicka, Anna. 1985b. A semantic metalanguage for a cross-cultural comparison of speech acts and speech genres. Language in Society 14.491–514.

Formulaic opposition markers in Chinese conflict talk

Sai-hua Kuo[*]
Georgetown University and National Tsing Hua University

1 Introduction. Goffman's (1967, 1971) study of face-to-face communication has pointed out that in adult conversation, speakers tend to show deference to the other party, and they also have a watchful concern that potential discord does not become overt in the interaction. Brown and Levinson (1978/1987) also consider showing disagreement a face-threatening speech act that therefore should be mollified either by indirect delivery or by prior concessions.

While adult speakers tend to avoid or minimize conflict to maintain ritual equilibrium, direct and aggravated argumentative strategies are frequently found in children's disputes. Boggs (1978) observes that part-Hawaiian children frequently resort to the forceful use of *Not!* as an outright contradiction by one speaker of another, and this verbal response is the most ubiquitous component of the 'contradicting routine', a speech activity that is 'composed of rather standardized sets of utterances that are typically linked in certain sequences to accomplish particular functions within an encompassing dialogue' (Boggs 1978:325).

Goodwin's (1983) study of aggravated disagreement in American urban black children's conversation notes that the use of opposition markers such as *yes*, *no*, and their equivalents, as well as tokens of disbelief such as *Ah*, brackets the entire utterance as polar in relation to what it precedes.

On the other hand, as Schiffrin (1984) has pointed out, there are cultural differences in both the overall predisposition to open disagreement and the use of argument for interactional ends. Her study of Jewish argument finds that speakers may disagree with one another in ways that suggest their use of argumentative forms of talk for sociability, and therefore argument can be valued as a sign of involvement and intimacy.

---

[*] This paper is based on the fourth chapter of my dissertation (Kuo 1992). Part of the paper was presented at the Annual Meeting of the American Association for Applied Linguistics, Seattle, WA, February 28 - March 2, 1992. I would like to thank Deborah Tannen and William Hannas for their comments and suggestions.

Tannen's (1990) study of gender differences in conversational styles observes that men and women have quite different perceptions of verbal opposition. While women tend to avoid conflict as a threat to rapport and affiliation, men consider conflict the necessary means by which status is negotiated and intimacy is reinforced. Therefore, women's attempt to avoid conflict can actually spark it with men for whom conflict is valued as a way of creating involvement with others.

This paper examines formulaic opposition markers as disagreement strategies in Chinese conflict talk. My analysis of casual conversations among adult Chinese friends shows that when verbal conflict arises, disputants frequently confront their opponents and phrase their disagreement in direct and forceful ways. Among those aggravated disagreement strategies found in my data, formulaic opposition markers, which tend to occur in turn-initial position and are generally delivered in an emphatic tone, unequivocally signal the upcoming unit as a contrasting action.

In this paper, Section 2 describes the data on which my analysis is based. Section 3 gives examples from my data to illustrate how the speakers use formulaic opposition markers to disagree with their interlocutors. Section 4 discusses the theoretical significance and sociolinguistic interpretations of this argumentative strategy. Section 5 summarizes and concludes the paper.

2 Data. This analysis of Chinese conflict talk is based on data collected in 1989 and 1990 in both Taiwan and the United States. In all, more than twenty hours of multi-person casual conversations with three to five participants were tape-recorded. I participated in all the analyzed conversations that took place in sociable events. The other participants are my friends, ranging in age from 32 to 40. All of us are well-educated native Chinese speakers who were born and raised in Taiwan. Although code-switching (to English) may be found in those conversations recorded in the United States, the data are overwhelmingly in Mandarin.

I chose to be a participant, sometimes an active one, instead of a mere detached observer in the conversations mainly because as all the other participants are my friends and they know that I am by no means a reticent person, it would be extremely odd if I did not participate in the conversations. In other words, I believe that my involvement in the ongoing activities made the situation more natural and the other participants more comfortable in the presence of the tape recorder, and therefore minimized the effect of the 'observer's paradox' (Labov 1972), a problem that keeps sociolinguists from obtaining spontaneous speech from their informants. Thus, this method of data collection, on the one hand, provided me with natural language used by people in their everyday life; on the other hand, my familiarity and relationship with other participants better enabled me to grasp and interpret the individual, cultural, and social meaning constructed in the talk.

This is a well-established method of data collection used by many discourse analysts. For instance, Tannen's (1984) analysis of conversational style is based on a Thanksgiving conversation in which she was a participant. Although Schiffrin's (1984) study of Jewish argument is based on data collected during sociolinguistic interviews, her sharing of ethnic identity with her informants, and above all, her participation in their talk, enabled her to mitigate the salience of the interview format and to obtain relatively natural data as well as insightful analysis.

3 Analysis. In addition to the negators *bu* 'not', *bu shi* 'not to be', and *bu dui* 'not right', various formulaic expressions that indicate outright contradiction of a prior talk are found in my data. Section 3.1 illustrates and discusses the opposition markers *suanle ba* and *luanjiang*, Section 3.2 discusses and illustrates the opposition marker *nali*, and Section 3.3 illustrates and discusses the opposition markers *buyiding* and *bujiande*.

3.1 The opposition markers *suanle ba* and *luanjiang*. The most direct and aggravated turn-initial opposition markers found in my data are those that not only mark the upcoming unit as a disagreement but also negatively evaluate the prior talk made by one's opponent.

Example (1) is taken from a three-hour conversation I had with three of my best friends, Cheng, Yang, and Shen, in the summer of 1990 when I was in Taiwan.[1] In this dispute, Yang and Shen have different opinions about whether Americans are 'loose', that is, whether or not Americans take sex and marriage seriously. Whereas Shen, who has been living in the United States for more than ten years, says that Americans are not as loose as Chinese think and some of them are very serious about relationships, Yang insists that Americans are looser than Chinese, although she has only been to the States twice for sightseeing. The intensity of the argument is characterized by their sustained nonalignment with each other's position, particularly the aggravated disagreement strategies they use. Both of them use formulaic opposition markers to refute their opponent's position.

Prior to (1), Shen explained to us that her purpose in wearing several rings was to show her American boss that she was married so that he would not dare take advantage of her.

---

[1] The transcription conventions used here are taken from Tannen (1984).

Symbol	Meaning
.	Sentence-final falling intonation
..	Noticeable pause or break in rhythm
...	Half second pause, as measured by stop watch (an extra dot is added for each half second of pause)
Underline	Emphatic stress
?	Rising intonation
,	Phrase-final intonation
Brackets	Second utterance latched onto first without perceptible pause
→	Point of analysis

Example (1)[2]

1 Shen: Meiguo henduo xiaojie dou zhe yangzi,
America many young-lady all this way

2 baohu ziji ma!
protect self PRT

→ 3 Yang: Suanle ba!
forget PRT

4 Meiguo..zheme xuyao baohu ziji ma?
America this need protect self PRT

....

8 Cheng: Meiguoren dui hunyin shi bu shi haishi
American to marriage is not is still

man zhongshi?
very take-seriously

9 Shen: Dangran zhongshi!
of-course take-seriously

10 bu shi hen kaifang, buhui suibian o!
not is very open not loose PRT

→ 11 Yang: Wo cai bu juede ne! luanjiang!
I just not feel PRT wild-talk

....

33 Yang: Wo kan Meiguoren hai shi bijiao suibian yidian
I see American still is more loose a-little

→ 34 Shen: Luanjiang!
wild-talk

---

[2] The following abbreviations are used to specify grammatical information about Mandarin utterances:

Abbreviation	Grammatical function
ASP	Aspect marker
CL	Classifier
INT	Interjection
NOM	Nominalizer *de*
POS	Possessive marker *de*
PRT	Particle (e.g. *a, ne, ma, ba, le*)

Free translation:

	1	Shen:	In America many single women do this
	2		to protect themselves.
→	3	Yang:	Oh, come on!
	4		The U.S...is it this necessary to protect oneself?
			....
	8	Cheng:	Do Americans still take marriage seriously?
	9	Shen:	Of course they do!
	10		They're not very open, not loose!
→	11	Yang:	I don't think so! Nonsense!
			....
	33	Yang:	I still think Americans are a little looser.
→	34	Shen:	Nonsense!

When Shen says in lines 1 and 2 *Meiguo henduo xiaojie dou zhe yangzi, baohu ziji ma* 'In America many single women do this [wear wedding rings] to protect themselves!', Yang in the following turn expresses her disagreement with Shen's statement. She initiates her disagreement in line 3 by the formulaic expression *Suanle ba* 'Oh, come on!' which indicates that she does not believe what Shen has said, and her following question in line 4 *Meiguo..zheme xuyao baohu ziji ma* 'The U.S...is it this necessary to protect oneself?' challenges Shen's prior statement and implies her opposing position, that is, it is not necessary for single women to protect themselves in the United States.

Her view about Americans becomes even clearer when in line 11 she says *Wo cai bu juede ne, luanjiang* 'I don't think so! Nonsense!' to contradict Shen's prior statement in lines 9 and 10 saying that Americans do consider marriage important and they are not very open or loose. Yang shows her disagreement in a most direct and aggravated way. She explicitly expresses that she does not think Americans are really like what Shen has said. Moreover, the formulaic disagreement expression *luanjiang* 'nonsense', literally 'talking wildly, speaking foolishly', is a 'metalinguistic evaluation' (Schiffrin 1980) that refers to Shen's prior talk and denounces it as not making sense.

In the following turns, Shen tries very hard to explain to Yang that some Americans are very serious; both Cheng and I agree with and support Shen. However, Yang still insists on her initial position by saying *Wo hai shi juede Meiguoren bijiao suibian yidian* 'I still think Americans are a little looser' in line 33, although this time the hedge *yidian* 'a little' in her statement softens her opposition. Shen at this moment, maybe somewhat losing her patience, also refutes Yang directly by using *luanjiang*, the formulaic opposition expression Yang has used before. This argument finally ends when we start talking about AIDS.

Yang's tendency to use formulaic opposing terms to refute or negatively evaluate her opponent's prior statement is most obvious in an argument in which she and I have a dispute over a plastic surgeon who appeared on a TV talk show. While Yang maintains that the surgeon spent big money to get on the program to promote himself, I insist that he was invited because of his good looks and eloquence. In this argument, we repeatedly disagree with each other's position, and the disagreement lasts for ten turns. Yang frequently uses aggravated disagreement strategies, particularly formulaic opposition markers, to contradict me. Example (2) illustrates this point.

Example (2)

→ 1 Yang: Aiyo! jiemu nenme hao a!
INT program that good PRT

2 suibian keyi zhao yisheng a? ⌝
randomly can find doctor PRT

3 Kuo: ⌞Zhao yige
find one

zhangde bucuo de,
grow not-bad NOM

4 zai neige jiemu bijiao hao.
in that program more good

→ 5 Yang: <u>Guiche!</u> shei yao zhao bucuo
ghost-prevaricating who want find not-bad

6 de, you jige bucuo de, piaoliang
NOM have how-many not-bad NOM handsome

→ 7 yisheng a? <u>luanjiang</u>
doctor PRT wild-talk

8 Kuo: Suoyi jiu qu zhaodao ta ma!
so just to find him PRT

Free translation:

→ 1 Yang: Aiyo! Was the program that kind
2 to pick out a doctor randomly⌝
3 Kuo: ⌞They picked out someone
who's good-looking,
4 it's better to do this in that kind of program.
→ 5 Yang: Baloney! Who's going to pick out good-looking ones?
→ 6 How many good-looking, handsome doctors are there,

anyway?
→ 7 Nonsense!
→ 8 Kuo: That's why they invited him!

In lines 1 and 2 Yang refutes my prior talk about why the plastic surgeon was invited by the talk show. Her *Aiyo!* in line 1 is a token of disbelief indicating that what I said is unbelievable to her. At the same time, this interjection also implies the following question is a challenge, a way to display disagreement, rather than a request for information.

In lines 3 and 4, I justify my position by explaining to Yang that since that program was talking about plastic surgery, namely, how one can become better-looking, it would be more convincing if the expert himself is not bad looking. However, this justification is again refuted by Yang in a most aggravated way. In line 5, the turn-initial formulaic opposition marker *Guiche* 'Baloney' (literally, 'ghost prevaricating') is a metalinguistic evaluation by which she denounces my prior talk as rubbish or something that a sensible human being would never say. The turn-final *luanjiang* 'nonsense' (literally, 'wild talk'), which is preceded by two questions, further intensifies her negative evaluation and outright contradiction. Bracketed by two formulaic opposition expressions, this turn illustrates Yang's most aggravated disagreement strategies.

3.2 The opposition marker *nali*. Literally, *nali* means 'where'. *nali*, *nali* is most used as a reply to a compliment, and it is translated as 'not at all' in that context. In Chinese society, it has traditionally been considered proper and matter of course to reject any compliment received, no matter how much truth there is to it. Many people still regard *xiexie* 'thank you' as an immodest reply to a compliment, since that would amount to agreeing that the compliment was justified. Thus *nali* has become a formulaic opposition marker that is always followed by a disagreement.

Example (3) is taken from a conversation recorded during a dinner party in which several Georgetown graduate students got together to celebrate the Chinese New Year. Prior to the argument, Li and Liang have been saying that compared with Chinese, Americans are much less modest, and they tend to simply say 'Thank you' as a compliment response.

Example (3)

1 Li: Buguo wo juede tamen zixin
but I feel their self-confidence

nengli bi women hao. ⌉
ability compare we good

2 Liang: ⌊Dui, tamen bijiao you
right they more have

zixin.
self-confidence

→ 3 Fang: Nali! cha! cha!
not-at-all less less

4 Li: Cha?
less

5 Liang: Bu dui! wo pongdao de dou hen you
not right I meet NOM all very have

zixin na!
self-confidence PRT

6 Fang: Wo pongdao name duo ren,
I meet that many person

7 wo dou juede tamen zixin nengli
I all feel their self-confidence ability

hen cha.
very little

Free translation:

1 Li: But I think they have more self-confidence than we do⌐
2 Liang: └Right.
They're more confident.
→ 3 Fang: Not at all! Less! Less!
4 Li: Less?
5 Liang: No. All those people I've met are very confident!
6 Fang: I've met many of them,
7 and I think they have little confidence in themselves.

Li's statement in line 1 saying that Americans have more self-confidence than Chinese do is echoed by Liang in the following turn. Fang, however, holds a different view and maintains that Americans are less confident. The turn-initial *nali* 'not at all' in line 3 unambiguously displays her strong disagreement. When Liang refutes Fang directly in line 5, saying that Fang is wrong and those Americans she has met are very confident, Fang in lines 6 and 7 also insists that many Americans have little confidence in themselves.

3.3 The opposition markers *buyiding* and *bujiande*. The opposition markers *buyiding* and *bujiande*, both translated into English as 'not necessarily', are two other frequently used turn-initial opposition markers that are followed by disagreement components. Although explicitly signalling the whole turn as a contradiction, these two expressions are less aggravated than other formulaic opposition markers in that they do not disagree with the prior statement completely; they just indicate it is not absolutely true. In addition, the statement in the same turn or subsequent turns by the same speaker is likely to be a specific example to support or justify one's disagreement.

The marker *buyiding* is found in the following dispute (Example 4) between my friend Zhao, an electrical engineer, and myself. Before the dispute, we were talking about the ethnic problem in Taiwan; that is, the conflict between mainlanders and Taiwanese. In the dispute, I hold the view that being able to speak the language of other ethnic groups may lead to a better understanding of their cultures. However, Zhao disagrees, and he initiates his disagreement by using *buyiding*.

Example (4)

1 Kuo: Ni dui bieren de xiangfa hui bijiao
you to others POS thinking will more

rongyi liaojie.
easy understand

→ 2 Zhao: Ah, buyiding!
Ah not-necessarily

3 Kuo: Buyiding ma?
not-necessarily PRT

4 Zhao: Wo xue Taiyu ye shi cong xiao xue de.
I learn Taiwanese also is from small learn PRT

Free translation:

1 Kuo: It'll be easier for you to understand other people's way of thinking.
→ 2 Zhao: Ah, not necessarily!
3 Kuo: Not necessarily?
4 Zhao: I learned Taiwanese from the time I was young.

Being a 'mainlander'—that is, my parents came to Taiwan in 1949—and having grown up in a neighborhood where everyone was a mainlander, I hardly had any contact with Taiwanese in my childhood and therefore cannot speak their language. Based on my personal experience, I believe that if mainlanders can speak Taiwanese, they may be better able to understand the Taiwanese culture. I expected that Zhao, who shares my mainlander identity, would agree with my point. Therefore, his explicit disagreement in line 2 *Ah, buyiding* 'Ah, not necessarily!' is a sheer surprise to me. In the subsequent turns in this conversation, Zhao supports and elaborates his point by telling us that even though he can speak Taiwanese and grew up in a Taiwanese neighborhood, he does not think that he understands the Taiwanese way of thinking better than I do. His *Ah, buyiding* in line 2, therefore, indicates that my point is not completely true; at least, it does not apply to his case.

The opposition marker *bujiande* 'not necessarily', like *buyiding*, is a turn-initial opposition component that characterizes the whole turn as a disagreement in a less aggravated way. Example (5) is from a conversation in which Zheng and his female colleague Li argue whether the American high school educational system is better or more flexible than that of Taiwan. Both of them are engineers in a research institute in Taiwan. Prior to the following segment, Li asked Zheng whether it was true that he planned to go to study in the United States for his doctoral degree, as she had heard other colleagues talk about this. When hearing Zheng say that he would go and leave his wife and children in Taiwan, Li suggests that he take them with him, because as everybody in Taiwan knows, students there suffer from unbelievable pressure from studies. However, Zheng disagrees and believes fierce competition is everywhere.

Example (5)

1 Li: Keshi zhishao tamen you tanxing a!
but at-least they have flexibility PRT

→ 2 Zheng: Bujiande!
not-necessarily

3 zai xiang neige Xigu neige difang o,
in like um Silicon-Valley that place PRT

....

10 na ta neige Xigu neige Huaren a
and he um Silicon-Valley um Chinese PRT

11 ye shi pingming yao qu shenqing
also is try-hard want go apply-for

zhe zhong sili xuexiao a!
this kind private school PRT

12 Li: Wo juede haoxiang you Zhongguoren de
I feel seem have Chinese NOM

difang dou shi zhe yang.
place all is this way

Free translation:

1	Li:	But at least theirs are more flexible!
→ 2	Zheng:	Not necessarily!
3		Places like Silicon Valley....
		....
10		Then those Chinese who live in Silicon Valley,
11		also do their best to get into private schools.
12	Li:	I think..it seems that wherever there are Chinese, the situation is like this.

When Li argues that at least the American high school educational system is more flexible, Zheng in line 2 initiates his oppositional move by saying *bujiande* 'not necessarily!', which is followed by a specific example to support his point that Li's prior talk is not completely true. His example illustrates how the Chinese tradition of emphasizing education has forced parents to do their best to send their children to good schools, and therefore Chinese children in the United States tend to suffer from the same pressure and competition. Li seems to accept this and the dispute ends.

To sum up, the formulaic opposition markers found in my analysis of informal conflict talk can be further categorized into three groups according to the directness and aggravation of the illocutionary force they convey:

(1) *Luanjiang* 'wild talk' and *guiche* 'ghost prevaricating' are types of meta-talk functioning as evaluative brackets, negatively evaluating the prior talk made by one's opponent as 'nonsense' or 'rubbish'. Therefore, they mark the disagreement in a most direct and aggravated way.

(2) *Suanle ba* 'come on' and *nali* 'not at all' simply display contradiction and an opposing position.

(3) *Buyiding / bujiande* 'not necessarily', although they also characterize the whole turn as a disagreement to the prior statement, are semantically least aggravated. They do not negate the prior statement completely; they just claim it is not necessarily true and tend to be followed by an example to justify the disagreement.

4 Sociolinguistic interpretation. The Chinese have always been depicted as reticent, emotionally restrained, and harmony-oriented. In Chinese society, a submissive, obedient, and conforming individual is the model for all, and nonconformity and argumentativeness are seen as negative qualities. For instance, more than 2,000 years ago, Mencius had to defend himself when he was criticized as being argumentative, 'I am not fond of disputing, but I am compelled to do it' (Mencius, Book IV, Part II, Chapter 9).

The fact that the Chinese prize harmony in social relationships may even be evidenced linguistically. Young's (1982) analysis of formal speech encounters involving Chinese speakers of English finds that the information structure of Chinese discourse strategies could be related to the Chinese preference for harmonious interpersonal relationships. Chinese tend to employ topic–comment structure to unravel and build up information before arriving at the important message. This strategy, she argues, effectively prevents a polarization of positions and a resulting conflict among the participants, although it appears evasive and vague to most Westerners.

It has also been found, however, that the formality of a situation and the participants' relationships seem to be the most important constraints governing Chinese people's communicative behaviors. Both Benedict (1943) and La Barre (1946a, 1946b) point out that the field of Chinese interpersonal behavior can be divided into an 'outer world' with strangers and an 'inner world' with intimates. The social content in each 'world' is qualitatively different. Generally speaking, Chinese tend to exercise 'defensive' politeness and show a great measure of reserve in the 'outer world'. The formality of Chinese public manners also emphasizes styles of verbal behavior that would reflect modesty, restraint, and cooperation.

On the other hand, Chinese are by no means reticent and constrained in the 'inner world'. In fact, any casual observer of the Chinese in their natural, intimate social contexts can see immediately that Chinese enjoy talking and talking boisterously and with great mirth. Therefore, for Chinese people, an informal and private gathering like chatting among friends presents a 'back region' (Goffman 1959) in which interactants who are of relatively equal power and status communicate freely without suppressing their spontaneous feelings and paying too much attention to impression management.

Therefore, the overt and nonmitigated linguistic strategies I found in informal Chinese conflict talk, which is contrary to Young's analysis of formal speech activities, confirms that the Chinese display quite different communicative behaviors in various social contexts. In other words, the occurrence of direct and aggravated disagreement strategies, such as formulaic opposition markers, characterizes not only the intensity but also the informality of the conflict talk among Chinese friends.

However, we may still ask, if seeking agreement or avoiding disagreement, as Brown and Levinson (1987) have claimed, are positive politeness strategies designed specifically to facilitate interaction in discourse types such as ordinary conversation, why do the speakers in my corpus tend to use aggravated linguistic devices, such as formulaic opposition markers, to directly convey disagreements or opposition in social gatherings whose interactive goal is to establish or enhance rapport and solidarity?

My first explanation, following Simmel (1908/1955), is that conflict is not exclusively disruptive and disintegrative. Rather, as Simmel has observed, conflict can be a sign of closeness and stable relationship. Simmel's functionalist view of conflict is further expounded by Schiffrin's (1984) study of 'sociable argument'. Schiffrin points out that talk that is argumentative in form may have sociable functions for members of some ethnic groups, in her example, lower-middle-class Jewish Americans of East European background. Sociable argument, defined as a 'speech activity in which a polarizing form has a ratificatory meaning' (Schiffrin 1984:331), is characteristic of Eastern European Jewish culture. In sociable arguments, speakers repeatedly disagree and remain oppositional to each other. However, they do so in a nonserious way, and their competitive verbal exchanges in this nonserious interactional form actually display their solidarity and protect their intimacy.

My analysis also shows that high degrees of positive affect among Chinese friends may increase the likelihood of dispute, particularly the use of explicit and nonmitigated disagreement strategies. For instance, Yang and I have been best friends since our high school days. Our argument over the plastic surgeon, in which she uses formulaic opposition markers to denounce my position as 'nonsense' or 'rubbish', like many others in that conversation and those we had in the preceding twenty years, neither jeopardizes our friendship nor hinders the process of the ongoing activity. Both of us, however, are more restrained when we talk with those to whom we do not feel close.

In this sense, the overtly competitive and argumentative behavior among Chinese friends, as evidenced by their frequent use of formulaic opposition markers and other aggravated disagreement strategies, can also be explained by Bateson's notion of frame, particularly his distinction between message and metamessage. Bateson (1972:188) claims that 'a frame is metacommunicative', that is, it conveys information about how the communication is meant, including the relationship among speakers, their attitudes toward one another, and what they are saying and doing. Tannen (1984:23) also points out that while message simply refers to the information conveyed by the meanings of words, metamessage is a 'superordinate message about how the communication is intended', and therefore it helps speakers know how to interpret what others are saying by identifying the activity that is going on. Further, Tannen notes that although indirectness may avoid confrontation in a situation where social distance is maintained and formal politeness is required, directness, which seems to break the formal rules of politeness, can send a metamessage of camaraderie when intimacy and informality are expected.

In a sociable argument, a direct or overt challenge or contradiction carries the information that the speaker does not agree with his or her interlocutor's position. This is the message conveyed by the meaning of the speaker's words. However, in the meantime, the metamessage signals that within such a context, aggravated disagreement strategies should be interpreted as signs of rapport and involvement. In other words, the relationship communicated is 'we are so close that we don't have to be vague or indirect when we disagree with each other'. Thus, the strategy to express disagreement baldly or directly, just like addressing close friends by their first names, does not signal impoliteness or intention to disempower the recipient and threaten their face wants, it signals in-group solidarity.

On the other hand, this strategic choice may also reflect a speaker's strong desire to present a sincere and independent self in the interactive frame. Most conflicts among Chinese friends' arguments I analyzed are differences of belief and opinion. An opinion, as defined by Schiffrin (1990:244), is 'an individual's internal, evaluative position about a circumstance.' In conducting a conversation, there exists a set of tacit understandings that what is being said is what the speaker believes (Grice 1975), and as a speech act, belief is the sincerity condition for opinions (Atelsek 1981). Schiffrin (1990:245) also claims that in argument, opinions 'free the speaker from a claim to truth, by emphasizing the speaker's claim to sincerity.' In other words, in presenting an opinion, the speaker may not claim the absolute truth of his or her proposition; however, s/he personally believes what is being said and the sincerity of the position cannot be disputed.

Vuchinich (1984:233), following Goffman (1971), has also suggested that oppositional interchanges are interpersonal rituals in which 'respect for self is displayed by marking and enforcing prohibitions associated with interpersonal boundaries.' Therefore, the intense and sustained arguments found in my data may imply that there is a strong affective attachment between a self and the territorial preserves of that self, and through the use of explicit and aggravated argumentative strategies the speakers display their respect for the 'sacred' status they hold and express a relation to other status.

In sum, the argumentative, overtly competitive behavior found among Chinese friends in private, informal gatherings, on the one hand, shows that Chinese speakers who have strong confidence in their relationships consider that open disagreements enhance rather than threaten the solidarity among them, and therefore serve the function of serving their interlocutor's positive face. On the other hand, it may imply that the speakers' need to present an independent and sincere self is a more important concern than their need to maintain nonconfrontation in the interaction.

Finally, this finding conforms to Emihovich's (1986) observation that to argue successfully, one must not only possess structural knowledge of various forms and their function in a specific context, but also a sense of what strategies can be used relative to one's status and the interactive frame. This appropriate use of argumentative strategies and correct assessment of other's intentions are socio-culturally related and should be an essential part of a speaker's 'communicative competence' (Hymes 1972).

5 Summary and concluding remarks. In this paper, I have examined the formulaic opposition markers used in informal Chinese conflict talk. I have found that formulaic opposition markers in my data, ranging from the most aggravated *luanjiang* 'wild talk' and *guiche* 'ghost prevaricating' to the most mitigated *buyiding/bujiande* 'not necessarily', are disagreement strategies that explicitly mark the upcoming unit as a contrasting action.

I argue that the occurrence of these formulaic opposition markers characterizes both the informality and the intensity of the conflict talk among

Chinese friends. Furthermore, the willingness to use this type of direct and aggravated disagreement strategy shows not only the intimate relationship among the speakers but also their strong desire to maintain an sincere and independent self within the interactive frame.

REFERENCES

Atelsek, Jean. 1981. An anatomy of opinions. Language in Society 10.217–225.

Bateson, Gregory. 1972. Steps to an ecology of mind. New York: Ballantine.

Benedict, Ruth. 1943. A note on Chinese culture and personality. Mimeo. Washington, D. C.

Boggs, Stephen T. 1978. The development of verbal disputing in part-Hawaiian children. Language in Society 7.325–344.

Brown, Penelope, and Stephen C. Levinson. 1978/1987. Politeness: Some universals in language usage. Cambridge: Cambridge University Press.

Emihovich, Catherine. 1986. Argument as status assertion: Contextual variation in children's disputes. Language in Society 15.485–500.

Goffman, Erving. 1959. The presentation of self in everyday life. New York: Anchor Books.

Goffman, Erving. 1967. Interaction ritual. Garden City, NY: Doubleday.

Goffman, Erving. 1971. Relation in public: Microstudies of the public order. New York: Harper and Row.

Goodwin, Majorie H. 1983. Aggravated correction and disagreement in children's conversations. Journal of Pragmatics 7.657–677.

Grice, Paul. 1975. Logic and conversation. Syntax and semantics, Vol. 3: Speech acts, ed. by Peter Cole and Jerry Morgan, 411–458. New York: Academic Press.

Hymes, Dell. 1972. On communicative competence. Sociolinguistics, ed. by J. B. Pride and Janet Holmes, 269–293. Harmondsworth: Penguin.

Kuo, Sai-hua. 1992. Conflict and its management in Chinese verbal interactions: Casual conversations and parliamentary interpellations. Ph.D. dissertation, Georgetown University.

La Barre, Weston. 1946a. Some observations on character structure in the Orient: The Chinese. Part one. Psychiatry 9.215–237.

La Barre, Weston. 1946b. Some observations on character structure in the Orient: The Chinese. Part two. Psychiatry 9.375–395.

Labov, William. 1972. Sociolinguistic patterns. Philadelphia: University of Pennsylvania Press.

Schiffrin, Deborah. 1980. Meta-talk: Organizational and evaluative brackets in discourse. Language and social interaction. Special edition of Sociological Inquiry, ed. by Don H. Zimmerman and Candace West. 50.199–236.

Schiffrin, Deborah. 1984. Jewish argument as sociability. Language in Society 13.311–335.

Schiffrin, Deborah. 1990. The management of a co-operative self during argument: The role of opinions and stories. Conflict talk, ed. by Allen D. Grimshaw, 241–259. Cambridge: Cambridge University Press.

Simmel, Georg. 1908/1955. Conflict. Conflict and the web of group affiliation, ed. and trans. by Kurt Wolff, 11–123. New York: Free Press.

Tannen, Deborah. 1984. Conversational style: Analyzing talk among friends. Norwood, NJ: Ablex.

Tannen, Deborah. 1990. You just don't understand: Women and men in conversation. New York: William Morrow.

Vuchinich, Samuel. 1984. Sequencing and social structure in family conflict. Social Psychology Quarterly 47.217–234.

Young, Linda Wailing. 1982. Inscrutability revisited. Language and social identity, ed. by John J. Gumperz, 72–84. Cambridge: Cambridge University Press.

Sociocultural parameters of intelligibility

Cecil L. Nelson
Indiana State University

As a starting point, to be revised very quickly, 'intelligibility' may be taken in a straightforward dictionary-definition sense of 'being understandable or clear; getting meaning or sense across.' Early studies of intelligibility were rather limited in two respects: they focused primarily on phonology/pronunciation features, and they were ethnocentrically based.

For a long time 'good speech' was held to be mostly, if not entirely, a matter of good pronunciation and learned 'habits.' The preface of the textbook *English Pattern Practices* (Lado and Fries 1958:xiii) begins: 'PATTERN PRACTICE forms the most important activity of learning a foreign language. All classes of the English Language Institute devote considerable time to the types of practice that will make the language patterns of English automatic responses.' And, further on, the text refers to 'the principle that to establish new language habits the practice must shift ... TO exercises in which THE ATTENTION CENTERS UPON A VARIETY OF LEXICAL MEANING SUBSTITUTABLE IN THE STRUCTURAL FRAME' (original emphases). Clear emphasis is placed upon the linguistic system and on memorization ('habit').

Catford (1950) added some linguistic and interactional dimensions to the notion of Intelligibility. He defined EFFECTIVENESS (1950:7–8) in terms of 'appropriate response to purpose in speaking,' in accord with the assumption that language is primarily an instrument for eliciting cooperation. His presentation cannot easily differentiate Intelligibility and effectiveness, because evaluation relies on observables of response behavior, which might be 'appropriate' by chance; so 'Intelligibility' for the purposes of the paper includes understanding of the linguistic elements and appropriate response, mirroring clear and purposeful encoding on the part of the user.

Catford also put forward the notion of THRESHOLD OF INTELLIGIBILITY (1950:14), which refers to the degree of exposure to another language or variety which has made one familiar with it, with a proportionate increase in Intelligibility. Catford further refers to relevant objects and elements in the speech situation (1950:13), including 'perceived attitudes' of participants. So, in fact, many elements that have come under more detailed later scrutiny were anticipated in Catford's treatment.

Bansal (1969) is a study of the intelligibility of Indian English which follows the Structuralist paradigm and the criteria of the British phoneticians. His experiments and data involved recognition of words and phrases in the pronunciation of Indian English speakers. Most of his hearer-respondents were first-language English users, and the summary and conclusions of the work are written in terms of increasing the intelligibility of Indian English users TO native speakers. However, with a bit of reflection and examination of some supporting examples, it is easy to see that intelligibility cannot be a 'responsibility' laid solely upon the PRODUCER of an utterance or text. Intelligibility is a function of the COOPERATION of the participants in a situation and must entail taking into account relevant elements of the situation itself.

Studies contained in two volumes of papers resulting from, respectively, ground-breaking conferences at the East–West Center in Honolulu and the University of Illinois, Urbana, in 1978 (Smith 1981 and B. Kachru 1982) clearly indicate the 'discovery' that Intelligibility is a sociolinguistic concept, necessarily including data and considerations of both codes per se and cultures. Neither sort of consideration—linguistic code or culture—is much good without the other. It is not that we have 'gone beyond' the need to pay attention to formal characteristics of codes, but rather that we must try to be more inclusive in our perspectives. Certainly CODE-knowledge must underlie any facility in 'A language' or 'A VARIETY OF a language.' If fewer surprises await us in these domains, it will only be because language, being by definition more limited as a PART of culture, contains fewer variables.

Smith and Rafiqzad (1979), for example, examined cross-variety intelligibility of Englishes by means of cloze passages and arrived at a foundation-shaking finding which perhaps has still not filtered very deeply into the general awareness of researchers and teachers in ESL: that 'the native speaker was ALWAYS found to be among the LEAST intelligible speakers' (1979:375, emphases added). This is contrary to everything that traditional intuition and practice, perhaps especially regarding pedagogy, would have led us to think. (This result was replicated in a separate, later study by Smith [1988]). Language is by definition a matter of form AND function, and studies in both areas will continue to be of rewarding interest.

Further research and resulting refinement of the notions surrounding intelligibility led Larry Smith to a three-level partitioning of intelligibility (in its general sense) into a set of LEVELS of analysis, in ascending complexity in terms of the variables that they comprise, namely Intelligibility, Comprehensibility, and Interpretability, as presented in Smith and Nelson (1985) and in a paper given at the Georgetown Round Table on Languages and Linguistics in 1987 (Smith 1988). For convenience, it may not be out of place to give brief examples and explications of these concepts here.

The INTELLIGIBILITY, or word-level recognizability, of any text is high if it accords with the expectations of a fluent user in its pronunciation, rhythms, and lexicon. The papers in this volume are clearly presented in English, as even elementary-school-age American readers could attest, though they might not comprehend the information or arguments presented.

To the extent that you can understand the INFORMATION of the text, that is, assign referential meanings to its parts and to it as a whole-thus-far, its COMPREHENSIBILITY is also high. A passage such as the following, from Stephen Hawking's *A Brief History of Time* (1988:106), has high INTELLIGIBILITY, but probably low COMPREHENSIBILITY (to non-physicists), at least on a first hearing or reading:

> Because energy cannot be created out of nothing, one of the partners in a particle/antiparticle pair will have positive energy, and the other partner negative energy. The one with negative energy is condemned to be a short-lived virtual particle because real particles always have positive energy in normal situations. It must therefore seek out its partner and annihilate with it.

A physicist would likely find this passage reasonably comprehensible even on one hearing or reading, and even out of context as it is. If the topic, information, and vocabulary are out of one's experience, however, then it is hard to paraphrase the passage (a usual test of COMPREHENSIBILITY or 'understanding'), and even the questions that one might ask a more knowledgeable person about the paragraph would probably have to start at a definitional level, for example, 'What's an ANTIPARTICLE?'

A passage such as the following from Quirk (1990:8) probably has quite high Comprehensibility (as well as Intelligibility) for most readers of this volume, by reason of topic familiarity, lack of technical jargon, absence of non-English elements, and so on:

> No one should underestimate the problem of teaching English in such countries as India and Nigeria, where the English of the teachers themselves inevitably bears the stamp of locally acquired deviation from the standard language.

When you ask, 'What did she mean by that?' you are questioning INTERPRETABILITY. For example, in Bharati Mukherjee's *Jasmine* (1989:49) the mother says to the protagonist: 'Good, they're speaking English. Dida [speaker's mother-in-law] will be less of a problem.' The INTELLIGIBILITY and COMPREHENSIBILITY of this passage are both quite high. What she MEANS BY THAT, however, is that, basically, the mother-in-law does not understand English. And, beyond that, that English is the language of advancement and of a kind of sophistication in which the mother-in-law does not participate; it is a covert language, a 'code,' in the narrower sense, in this context and for these participants. There is, further, the implication (to be interpreted) that the mother-in-law WILL interfere in what is being cooked up if she can—has done so in the past—and that she has some power to do so, whether by simple virtue of being an elder in the family, father's mother, or whatever. At any rate, one must know a lot about a text in order to interpret it to any extent, and a lot about a society in order to interpret the language phenomena encountered in it. As Smith puts it (Smith and Nelson 1985:335):

> Because intelligibility, comprehensibility, and interpretability are not equally weighted in terms of difficulty, they are not interchangeable. Although all three are important to communication, the most serious misunderstandings occur at the level of comprehensibility and interpretability. We think it would be helpful, therefore, for researchers in cross-cultural communication to keep intelligibility, comprehensibility, and interpretability separate and distinct from one another.

Smith's precise analysis of what had been mainly viewed as a monolithic whole provides a framework for the progress of study of Intelligibility, from the simplest segmental elements to the broadest concerns of language in use in a context and across contexts.

We can now comfortably turn to issues to which Intelligibility, Comprehensibility, and Interpretability may be usefully applied, namely the monocentric view that many have taken as the basis of Intelligibility study. In Bansal's Conclusions section (1969:171), for example, one finds the following sorts of characterizations: 'For further DIVERGENCES FROM R.P. see sections 13.4 ... ,' and 'The sentence stress, rhythm and intonation patterns in Indian English are not always in accordance with the NORMAL R.P. PATTERNS ... The location of the intonation nucleus is not always at the place where it would be IN NORMAL ENGLISH' [emphases added]. One cannot but note the directly implicit characterization of IE as 'non-NORMAL'; this is an extremely negative sort of attitude toward a language used by so many millions of people, rather smacking of Selinker's later (1972:217) 'not only can entire [Interlanguage] competences be fossilized in individual learners ... , but also in whole groups of individuals, resulting in the emergence of a new dialect (here Indian English), where fossilized IL competences may be the normal situation.'

In any case, it is clear that Bansal was holding up R.P.—an outside variety, let alone its strict reference solely to PRONUNCIATION—as the standard by which his subjects' English should be judged. It is not trivial to note the monocentricity of such statements in fairly modern times (about twenty-five years ago, now), in a work BY an Indian entitled 'Intelligibility of INDIAN English.'

The notion of 'plural-centricity' of a language (see, e.g. B. Kachru 1992:66), a 'major' language, one that is in practice almost always implicitly presumed to have 'a standard form' founded in 'standard norms,' is not an easy one to digest. The single standard position is adopted forcefully by Quirk (1985, 1988, 1990), when he writes, for example (1985:5), that while

> There are in fact good historical, even good linguistic reasons for reaction against the whole received notion of standards in language ... Nonetheless, understandable as all this is, I hold that the stated or implied orthodoxy of

> regarding the term "standard" as fit only for quotation marks is a TRAHISON DES CLERCS.

The expression means, according to Mr. Brewer's *Dictionary*, 'treason of the intellectuals,' that is, 'The incursion of the intelligentsia, who should be concerned with the pursuit of truth and guided by abstract principle, into the field of partisan politics and propaganda.' Quirk's introduction of 'politics and propaganda' into the discussion is itself a denial that there is any substantive sociolinguistic question to be discussed—which there plainly is. As Graeme Kennedy (1985:7) says in his discussion of Quirk:

> Professor Quirk's paper reflects ... the position Prator [1968] advocated, namely, the desirability of a global standard. However, since the orthodoxy has changed, it might be argued that Professor Quirk articulates a new British heresy. You simply cannot win.

It is probably too much to say that 'the orthodoxy has [or had] changed'; rather, it has become apparent that linguistic 'orthodoxies' of any sort exist to be examined and challenged, and that is sufficient grounds for our investigative enterprise.

Quirk's position had solidified (fossilized?) by the time of the publication of his 1987 Georgetown University Round Table paper 'The Question of Standards in the International Use of English' (1988:236), in which he ignores the distinction of EFL/ESL because, as he wrote, 'I doubt its validity and frequently fail to understand its meaning.' In strongest opposition to such Englishes, according to Quirk (1990:6), (ignoring with him the EFL/ESL distinction for the moment), are INSTITUTIONALIZED national varieties, namely American and British. Just these two varieties, writes Quirk, are 'INSTITUTIONALISED in the sense of being fully described and with defined standards observed by the institutions of state.'

It is apparent to casual observation that both parts of this depiction of 'institutionalization' are flawed: no one can reasonably claim that ANY variety of any known language has been 'fully' described to date, and it is by no means clear that the 'institutions of state' (whatever exactly those may be) observe the standards in any ideal-speaker way. When Quirk quotes Kujore as having written of Standard Nigerian English that 'any such standard is, at best, in process of evolution,' he merely begs the question: all living languages are in process of evolution, so in itself and in principle the 'evolution' of Standard Nigerian—or Indian or Singaporean—English is no different from that of the American or British varieties.

In any case, it is clear that no very limited standard is 'correct' for all times, events, and places. Berns, in the Preface to her book *Contexts of Competence: Social and Cultural Considerations in Communicative Language Teaching*, writes (1990:v) that 'As communicative competence is defined by the social and cultural contexts in which it is used, no single communicative competence can serve as the goal and model for all learners.' An added complication, in these days of open borders and relatively easy long-distance travel, is the appearance of one's communicative competence in an environment other than the one in which it arose, as in the availability in a Midwestern American bookstore of novels set in Pakistan or India, by authors such as Anita Desai, Bapsi Sidhwa, and Raja Rao. Berns (1990:35–36) gives this delightful example of a cross-cultural conversational exchange which, while Intelligible and Comprehensible, required some investigation on her part to make it Interpretable:

> One day [a Zambian fellow-student] greeted me with "Hello, Margie. How are you? Oh, I see you've put on weight," an utterance which ... struck me as inappropriate, since I had not been ill or in any other circumstances which would cause concern over weight loss and subsequent cause for remarking on weight gain ... When I asked what he had meant, my friend explained that he intended nothing more than to express his pleasure at my apparent good health and the prosperity it signified.

Berns arrives at the Interpretation that, 'In the context of a greeting in Zambia, where a healthy, robust appearance is valued more highly than a lean, slender figure, my friend's observation would have been recognized as appropriate to the situation by other Zambians.' The necessity for a long explication of what was intended by the speaker as a simple positive greeting shows, in part, the culture-boundness of greeting rituals, a language function in which literal Comprehension is often less important than the social, communicative Interpretation (cf. English *Good morning*, a sentence-fragment if ever there was one, or Japanese *konnichi wa* 'this day'). But it serves as an example for the broader consideration: participants must be familiar with the culture out of which the language-forms come, if they are to interpret user intent at all accurately.

Even a passage in standard, academic English, supposedly transparent to any educated reader or hearer, is more than likely to harbor social and cultural facets that the users do not see, exactly because those elements are underlying assumptions. In the passage from Quirk (1985) given above, for example, the author uses a phrase in French (NOT Spanish, Russian, Swahili, or Arabic), perhaps to enhance the 'tone' of the assertion, presumably because the author feels that it is a phrase that will be immediately understandable to his audience as a concise way of characterizing those who adopt a particular point of view. He picks French because of its place in the history of English as a historically influential parallel code in the development of an educated class among English speakers, which is such that many English users have at their disposal a stock of French terms and phrases, even though they are not in any substantial sense 'French speakers.' A multilingual writer, say from India, might have mixed a phrase in Sanskrit, Arabic, or Persian. For example, in the Introduction to a volume of papers on South Asia as a sociolinguistic area dedicated to G. Kelley,

Braj Kachru (Kachru et al. 1992:1) writes:

> there is another relationship which marks the contributors to this volume as an extended family of scholars: In the South Asian tradition this relationship may be termed GURU-ŚISYA PARAMPARĀ ['teacher–disciple tradition']. Among the contributors to this volume, the PARAMPARA starts with Murray B. Emeneau ...

If the introduction of code-mixing seems to cloud the point, one can go to other illustrative samples quite easily. The opening line of Berns' book (1990:v), 'The introduction of communicative competence as the goal of second and foreign language teaching has led to recognition of the role of context in language learning and use,' presupposes the familiarity of the reader with the concept of communicative competence, with its contrast to earlier structure-based language-learning approaches and methods, and with its role in defining 'second' vs. 'foreign' language.

The very existence of the burgeoning popular American literature examining the nature of men (as such) and their roles in relationship to women and each other (represented by, for example, *Iron John* and *King, Warrior, Magician, Lover*), probably presupposes and mirrors the existence of an earlier feminist literature focusing on the history and contemporary place of women in American or Western society. And a sample from such a text includes references to 'themes' that are all but omnipresent matters of concern, as represented in all manner of movies, novels, essays, and private conversations; for example, the following text from Moore and Gillette (1990:7):

> We just know we are anxious, on the verge of feeling impotent, helpless, frustrated, put down, unloved and unappreciated, often ashamed of being masculine. We just know that our creativity was attacked, that our initiative was met with hostility, that we were ignored, belittled, and left holding the empty bag of our lost self-esteem. We cave in to a dog-eat-dog world, trying to keep our work and our relationships afloat, losing energy ...

One cannot but notice the 'me-ness' of this orientation, the emphasis on some sorts of personal fulfillment. These are American (or Western?) features of the overall text; one can compare, by contrast, the apparently extensive Japanese literature of NIHONJIN-RON or 'theory of the Japanese' cited by Jared Taylor (1983), which comes out of a deep cultural concern over societal and group identification, often (stereotypically) contrasted with American emphasis on individuality.

In a recent paper, Yamuna Kachru (1991:303) explicates a passage from Singh (1959:61), an exchange between Indian participants. A group of non-Sikhs are seeking a favor from a Sikh named Buta Singh. The interaction ends in this exchange:

> "ACCHAJI NAMASTEY ... Some water or something?" asked Buta Singh mechanically and without waiting for a reply dismissed them: "NAMASTEY."
> "This is like our own home. We would ask for anything we want. SAT SRI AKAL.."

Kachru points out that it is the NON-SIKHS who use the Sikh formulaic leave-taking *Sat Sri Akal* 'God is truth', the Sikh, Buta Singh, uses the Hindu formula *Namastey*. This use of the other's code, according to Kachru, 'is common in the ethnically and religiously pluralistic context of India to show mutual deference, and all the participants are being "correct" by following this convention' (1991:302–303).

The last parts of the exchange, *This is like our own home* and *We would ask for anything we want*, would probably seem overbearing and intrusive to an American, but 'these utterances merely represent a "correct" response to the conventional offer of refreshments' (1991:303). And there is the point: one must be familiar with the context in which the utterances are produced: not merely the immediate conversational context, but the broader sociolinguistic, sociocultural context underlying it. (See also Y. Kachru 1987 for further discussion of cross-cultural discourse.)

Contrast with this the 'big finish' to Quirk's 1985 paper, his strongest and most implication-filled assertion (1985:6):

> The relatively narrow range of purposes for which the nonnative needs to use English (even in ESL countries) is arguably well catered for by a single monochrome standard form that looks as good on paper as it sounds in speech. There are only the most dubious advantages in exposing the learner to a great variety of usage, no part of which he will have time to master properly, little of which he will be called upon to exercise, all of which is embedded in a controversial sociolinguistic matrix he cannot be expected to understand.

World-class New-English authors would certainly disagree. Compare the often-quoted assertion of Chinua Achebe (1965:222)—'If ... you ask: "Can [an African] ever learn to use [English] like a native speaker?" I should say, "I hope not." It is neither necessary, nor desirable ... '—or of Raja Rao (cited by B. Kachru 1988:583–584), who 'has granted the English language a status equal to that of Sanskrit':

> We cannot write like the English. We should not. We cannot write only as Indians. We have grown to look at the large world as part of us. Our method of expression therefore has to be a dialect which will someday prove to be distinctive and colorful as the Irish or the American.

When one is confronted by 'nonnative' English text, it is those of us who are monolingual and monocultural who 'cannot be expected to understand the controversial sociolinguistic matrix' without help from a thoughtful author or conversational partner.

A pragmatic, realistic summation of the facts of World Englishes today has been put succinctly, I believe, by Larry Smith (1988:281):

> Being a native speaker does not seem to be as important [for understanding and being understood] as being fluent in English and familiar with several different national varieties ... [T]he increasing number of varieties of English need not increase the problems of understanding across cultures if users of English develop some familiarity with them.

Users of English in its world context need almost to have multiple personalities, to allow the flexibility to interpret a language used with so much sociocultural cross-over. The traditional 'from MY point of view' attitude can no longer be regarded as adequate to the tasks that English has taken on.

REFERENCES

Achebe, Chinua. 1965. English and the African writer. Transition 4, 18.27–30. [Reprinted in Morning Yet on Creation Day, 1975]

Bansal, R. K. 1969. The Intelligibility of Indian English. Hyderabad, India: Central Institute of English and Foreign Languages.

Berns, Margie. 1990. Contexts of competence: Social and cultural considerations in communicative language teaching. New York: Plenum Press.

Bly, Robert. 1990. Iron John: A book about men. Reading, MA: Addison-Wesley.

Catford, John C. 1950. Intelligibility. English Language Teaching 1.7–15.

Hawking, Stephen W. 1988. A brief history of time: From the big bang to black holes. New York: Bantam Books.

Kachru, Braj B. (ed.) 1982. The other tongue: English across cultures. Urbana: University of Illinois Press.

Kachru, Braj B. 1988. Toward expanding the English canon: Raja Rao's 1938 credo for creativity. World Literature Today (Autumn), 582–86.

Kachru, Braj B. 1991. Liberation linguistics and the Quirk concern. English Today 7.1.3–13.

Kachru, Braj B. 1992. Models for non-native Englishes. The other tongue: English across cultures, ed. by Braj B. Kachru, 48–74. 2nd ed. Urbana: University of Illinois Press.

Kachru, Braj B. (ed.) 1992. The other tongue: English across cultures. 2nd ed. Urbana: University of Illinois Press.

Kachru, Braj B., E. Dimock, and Bh. Krishnamurti (eds.) 1992. Dimensions of sociolinguistics in South Asia: Papers in memory of Gerald Kelley. New Delhi: Oxford University Press and IBH.

Kachru, Yamuna. 1987. Cross-cultural texts, discourse strategies and discourse interpretation. Discourse across cultures: Strategies in world Englishes, 87–100. New York: Prentice Hall.

Kachru, Yamuna. 1991. Speech acts in World Englishes: Toward a framework for research. World Englishes 10, 3.299–306.

Kennedy, Graeme. 1985. Commentator 1. English in the world: Teaching and learning the language and literatures, ed. by Randolph Quirk and H.G. Widdowson, 7–8. Cambridge: Cambridge University Press.

Lado, Robert, and Charles C. Fries. 1958. English pattern practices. Ann Arbor: The University of Michigan Press.

Moore, Robert, and Douglas Gillette. 1990. King, warrior, magician, lover: Rediscovering the archetypes of the mature masculine. San Francisco: HarperCollins.

Mukherjee, Bharati. 1989. Jasmine. New York: Grove Weidendeld.

Quirk, Randolph. 1985. The English language in a global context. English in the world: Teaching and learning the language and literatures, ed. by Randolph Quirk and H.G. Widdowson, 1-6. Cambridge: Cambridge University Press.

Quirk, Randolph. 1988. The question of standards in the international use of English. Georgetown University Round Table on Languages and Linguistics 1987, ed. by Peter Lowenberg, 229-41. Washington, DC: Georgetown University Press.

Quirk, Randolph. 1990. Language varieties and standard language. English Today 6, 1.3-10.

Quirk, Randolph, and H.G. Widdowson (eds.) 1985. English in the world: Teaching and learning the language and literatures. Cambridge: Cambridge University Press.

Selinker, Larry. 1972. Interlanguage. International Review of Applied Linguistics 10.3.209-231.

Smith, Larry E. (ed.) 1981. English for cross-cultural communication. London: Macmillan.

Smith, Larry E. (ed.) 1987. Discourse across cultures: Strategies in world Englishes. New York: Prentice Hall.

Smith, Larry E. 1988. Language spread and issues of intelligibility. Georgetown University Round Table on Languages and Linguistics 1987, ed. by Peter Lowenberg, 250-64. Washington, DC: Georgetown University Press. [reprinted in The other tongue: English across cultures, ed. by Braj B. Kachru, 75-90. 2nd ed. Urbana: University of Illinois Press.]

Smith, Larry E., and Cecil L. Nelson. 1985. International intelligibility of English: Directions and resources. World Englishes 4, 3.333-42.

Smith, Larry E., and Khalilullah Rafiqzad. 1979. Cross-cultural communication: The question of intelligibility. TESOL Quarterly 13, 3.371-80.

Taylor, Jared. 1983. Shadows of the rising sun. New York: William Morrow.

Some new evidence for an old hypothesis

Stephen Krashen
University of Southern California

'The provision of a rich supply of high-interest story books is a much more feasible policy for improving English learning than any pious pronouncements about the urgent need to raise teacher quality ... ' (Mangubhai and Elley 1982).

1 The Reading Hypothesis. According to the Reading Hypothesis, comprehensible input in the form of reading is the source of our ability to read, our writing style, much of our vocabulary and spelling ability, and our more advanced grammatical development (Goodman 1982, Smith 1988a, 1988b; Krashen 1984, 1985a, 1988, 1989a, 1992). Evidence supporting the Reading Hypothesis is consistent with the more general Input Hypothesis, which claims that comprehensible input is the essential environmental ingredient for language acquisition (Krashen 1982, 1985b).

In my interpretation of the research literature, one kind of reading appears to be the most effective: Free voluntary reading—reading because you want to, with no book report and no obligation to finish the book you started.

In recent years, few have argued against the Reading Hypothesis, but the fact that reading is hardly ever encouraged in second and foreign language programs, and the persistent popularity of phonics, spelling workbooks, and vocabulary building exercises in literacy programs indicates that the case for reading has yet to be convincingly made.[1]

---

[1] Explicit arguments have been made against free reading. In an article entitled 'The evil of unlimited freedom in the use of juvenile fiction', Bean (1879), a librarian, claimed that the 'craze for books' among schoolchildren leads to 'inattention, want of application, distaste for study, and unretentive memory' as well as 'utter neglect of home as well as school duties' (Bean 1879:342). Bean does not provide any evidence supporting these assertions, but her view was shared by others at the time. Graff (1979:39), in his discussion of 'the moral basis of literacy,' presents the view of the weekly newspaper, *The Christian Guardian*, in an editorial published on July 31, 1850:

> No part of education ... is of greater importance than the selection of proper books ... No dissipation can be worse than that induced by the perusal of exciting books of fiction ... a species of a monstrous and erroneous nature.

In previous publications, I have reviewed the research supporting the reading hypothesis (see references previously cited). In this paper, I review additional evidence supporting the reading hypothesis, evidence from recent studies as well as evidence from older research that had until now escaped my notice. Evidence for the reading hypothesis can be categorized as follows:

1. Research showing that more reading leads to greater literacy development. These studies can be further subcategorized as in-school and out-of-school studies, the former showing that children who participate in free reading programs in school outperform children doing traditional instruction, and the latter showing that those who report more free reading on their own read better and write better.
2. Research showing problems with alternate approaches to literacy development. Traditional instruction cannot account for literacy development, because the systems to be acquired are forbiddingly complex. Also, evidence exists showing that literacy development can take place without instruction, and that reading alone can account for full literacy development. Output, writing, cannot account for literacy development because people simply do not write enough, and studies show that increasing writing does not result in improved writing.

2 In-school free reading studies. In a recent review of this literature (Krashen 1992), I argued that children who participate in sustained silent reading and self-selected reading programs in school did better than comparison children on tests of vocabulary and reading comprehension as long as the program lasted at least seven months or longer. Short-term programs show mixed results, probably because it takes time for children to find reading material they like.

Elley's Singapore study is a spectacular new addition to this research (Elley 1991). Elley reported on three projects, one lasting one year and two lasting three years, involving over 3,000 elementary school children. Experimental students participated in the REAP (Reading and English Acquisition Program), a combination of Shared Book Experience, Language Experience, and a 'book flood', while comparison students followed a traditional audio-lingual, structured approach to English as a second language. REAP was an easy overall winner in all three studies. REAP students showed superior gains in most comparisons, excelling in reading comprehension, vocabulary, grammar, listening comprehension, and writing. REAP students also made fewer spelling errors in one study, were equivalent to comparisons in another study, and were superior in punctuation in the two studies in which it was measured.

More recently, Wertham (1954) in his book *Seduction of the Innocent* maintained that comic book reading, because of the pictures, was hurting reading development, and that the lurid stories were leading children into lives of crime and other forms of anti-social behavior. Research on comic book reading does not support these accusations (Krashen 1989a).

Elley also reported that teachers and principals were enthusiastic about REAP, but they were concerned that it would not prepare students for standardized tests. As Elley points out, the data show that this worry was unwarranted.[2]

An older first language development study that I had missed in previous surveys is Southgate, Arnold, and Johnson (1981:254), who reported that classes of seven to nine year olds in England that made the greatest progress in reading achievement in one school year were those in which teachers devoted more time to 'uninterrupted private reading and to discussion of books'. (Southgate et al. found a negative correlation between progress in reading achievement and the amount of time teachers spent listening to children read out loud. Interestingly, three-fourths of the children said they preferred to read silently, rather than read aloud to someone else.)

3 The rivals. As noted earlier, instruction and the 'Writing Hypothesis' are the two main rivals of the Reading Hypothesis.

3.1 Instruction. Instruction fails as a major source of literacy development for several reasons—and any one of these reasons is enough to disqualify it. The first is the complexity argument, the argument that language is simply too complex to be taught and learned. A good example of this complexity is vocabulary size. As discussed in earlier papers (e.g. Krashen 1989a), researchers have argued for many years that there are too many words to learn one at time. Seashore and Eckerson (1940) maintained that educated speakers of English know about 156,000 words. As Smith (1985) has pointed out, this could not be the result of 156,000 trips to the dictionary, 156,000 flash cards, or 156,000 fill-in-the-blank exercises.

Estimates of vocabulary size made since Seashore and Eckerson's study have been lower. Lorge and Chall (1963) argued that Seashore and Eckerson committed certain methodological errors, and concluded that the total number of words known by educated English speakers could be as low as 39,000. This is still a large number of words. More recent estimates of adult vocabulary size are still lower. Two studies estimate that adults know about 17,000 words (Goulden, Nation, and Read 1991; D'Anna, Zechmeister, and Hall 1991). Put crudely, vocabulary size estimation is done as follows: Investigators test subjects on a sample of words taken from a dictionary. If subjects get 50% of the words right in the sample, it is assumed they know 50% of the words in the dictionary.

---

[2] Elley (1991:403) notes an additional concern in his review of the research:

> In several of these studies teachers, principals, and parents expressed concern that children were merely enjoying themselves, rather than learning. Indeed, a few teachers dropped out for such reasons. The assumption that language learning must be hard work is strong in many cultures. Nevertheless, that recreational reading produced such regular gains in acquisition suggests that it is a misconception.

Goulden et al. and D'Anna et al. excluded many categories of words from their samples of potentially known words. Goulden et al. excluded proper words (such as names), compound words, and derived words, while D'Anna et al. excluded slang, foreign words, hyphenated words (e.g. *free-lance*), capitalized words, words 'identified as old use', names of letters (e.g. *alpha*), and 'multi-word entries' (e.g. *video cassette*). Because of these restrictions, the potential vocabulary size of their subjects, the pool of words sampled from, was only 58,000 in Goulden et al. and only about 27,000 words in d'Anna et al. (Goulden, Nation, and Read estimated that had they included proper and compound words with meanings unrelated to other base words, their pool would have been 110,000 words.)[3]

Thus, recent studies claiming to show that adults know fewer words use narrow definitions of what a word can be and seriously underestimate vocabulary size. Even if we use Chall and Lorge's estimate of 39,000 words, it is clear that people know many more words than they learn in individual word study.[4]

A second argument against instruction is the finding that aspects of literacy can be developed without instruction. In previous publications, I have reviewed 'read and test' studies in which subjects encounter new words in meaningful texts and are tested on their meanings or spellings. Since subjects are not told to focus on the unfamiliar words, and do not expect a test, such studies probe incidental learning, or acquisition. Nagy, Herman, and Anderson (1985) is a very important study of this kind, since they concluded that the small amount of vocabulary knowledge students gain from even a single exposure to an unfamiliar word in context is enough, given an adequate amount of reading, to account for observed growth in vocabulary.

An unusual modified read-and-test study confirms what every experienced

---

[3] In addition, D'Anna et al. further underestimated true vocabulary size by using the Oxford American Dictionary, which does not include many scientific and technical words (p. 113). On the other hand, D'Anna et al. argue that they may have overestimated vocabulary size since they only asked subjects if they recognized the words and did not ask for definitions. Also, some entries in the dictionary were from the same word family (e.g. *impede*, *impediment*), so knowing one word in a family would help subjects with other words. Nevertheless, their severe restrictions on the pool of words made it impossible for subjects to display their true vocabulary size.

[4] It could be argued that vocabulary teaching methods that teach roots and affixes circumvent the problem by giving students knowledge that will enable them to understand large families of words. There are two problems with this argument. First, not all affixes have straightforward and consistent meanings; as White, Power, and White (1989) note, *unassuming* does not mean *not assuming*. Second, those that have straightforward meanings may be rapidly acquired anyway, without deliberate instruction. O'Rourke's results (O'Rourke 1974), show that children gradually acquire the meanings of prefixes and affixes over time. Straightforward prefixes, such as *ante-* ('before') reach the 90% correct level by grade 12. Less obvious affixes, such as *-fy* ('to make') reach only about 20% correct at grade 12. This data is typically used to show that direct instruction is necessary. It can also be interpreted to show the exact opposite; the meanings of transparent affixes, those easy to teach, might be acquired without instruction. Those that are not acquired early are probably far more difficult to teach, since their meanings are more opaque.

elementary school teacher knows: your own spelling deteriorates after you read a pile of student papers. This is powerful evidence that reading effects spelling. Jacoby and Hollingshead (1990) asked college students to read words that were frequently spelled incorrectly; half the words were correctly spelled and half were incorrectly spelled. Subjects did significantly worse on a spelling test on those words they had seen misspelled, even though they had seen them only once.

Jacoby and Hollingshead (1990:356–7) point out that the effect of seeing an incorrectly spelled word just one time on spelling performance was not large. They noted, however, that

> ... much more dramatic results were produced ... by the second author of [the] paper. In the course of collecting the data ... she read the incorrectly spelled words a large number of times. As a result of this extended experience with those incorrect spellings, she reports having lost confidence in her spelling accuracy. She can no longer judge spelling accuracy on the basis of a word 'looking right'. The word might look right because it was one of our incorrectly spelled words ...

Studies by Rice (1897) and Cornman (1902) have also been cited as evidence of spelling development without instruction. Both Rice and Cornman claimed that they found no relationship between spelling proficiency in students grade 4 through 8 and the amount of time devoted to spelling instruction. These claims, however, were based only on visual inspection of the data, as Rice and Cornman did not have the tools for statistical analysis. In Krashen and White (1991), we analyzed Rice's and Cornman's data using statistical procedures. In agreement with Rice and Cornman's interpretation of their data, we found that most correlations between scores on spelling tests and time devoted to spelling instruction were inconsistent and insignificant. In each case, we calculated 'simple correlations' (correlations between spelling scores and time devoted to spelling for each grade level) and 'cumulative correlations' (correlations between spelling scores and total time devoted to spelling, for that grade and for all previous years for which we had data).

Table 1 presents correlations between amount of instruction and scores on one of Rice's measures, the Sentence Test. In the Sentence Test, target words were read by examiners in sentences; i.e. for the target words *running*, *slipped*, *listened*, *speech*, and *believe*, students would hear: *While running, he slipped. I listened to his queer speech but I did not believe any of it.*

Clearly, neither simple nor cumulative correlations between instruction and spelling scores were significant.

Similar results were found for spelling of words in students' own compositions (Rice). For the 'term examination' (Cornman), the standardized spelling test given by the city at the end of the school year, positive cumulative correlations were found between time devoted to instruction and spelling scores, which did not reach significance, and for Rice's column test results (words dictated in isolation), both simple and cumulative correlations were clearly positive. Such findings are consistent with language acquisition theory, since in the latter two tests, subjects were, most likely, more deliberately focused on form.[5]

Table 1. Correlations between scores on Rice's sentence test and amount of time devoted to spelling instruction (Krashen and White 1991).

Grade	Simple	Cumulative
4	-.063	
5	-.266	-.201
6	.287	.290
7	.104	-.240
8	-.065	-.305

Cornman also conducted a study to examine the effects of dropping spelling instruction in two elementary schools for a total of three years. During this time, spelling errors were still corrected, however. Cornman concluded that dropping spelling instruction had no significant effect on spelling, and our re-analysis confirmed that this conclusion was correct. Table 2 presents a sample of these results. The 6/97 group in table 2, tested in June of 1897, serves as a control group, while the 6/98 group, tested in June of 1898, had no spelling instruction for one school year. Application of t-tests for correlated samples showed that there was no significant difference in spelling proficiency between the two groups for the Sentence Test.[6]

Results for other tests were similar; most comparisons did not reveal significant differences between students who had spelling instruction and those who did not, although we found a tendency for instruction to have its greatest effect for the younger children in the sample, consistent with later results (Hamill, Larsen, and McNutt 1977).

The only second language study I know of examining whether spelling can improve without instruction is Haggan (1991:359): Fourth-year English majors at the University of Kuwait made fewer errors in their papers than first-year remedial students, even though 'little emphasis is placed on the explicit systematic teaching of spelling' in the curriculum.[7]

---

[5] Rice, however, questioned the validity of the column test results, reporting that some teachers gave students hints as to the correct spelling of certain words by exaggerating their pronunciation.

[6] Median scores do not show a steady improvement from year to year, since different tests were used at different grade levels.

[7] Haggan (1991:59) also reported that the two groups had somewhat different error 'profiles'. First-year students, for example, made far more errors spelling homophones (*their*, *there*) and errors involving silent *e*, while advanced students made relatively more errors involving consonants, especially sibilants (e.g. *s* instead of *c* in *sentence* and *t* instead of *s* in *controversial* and *conclusion*). Haggan suggests that the greater frequency of this latter kind of error may be due to the advanced students' use of more complex vocabulary.

Table 2. Sentence test results (medians) from Cornman (1902).

Northwest School		
Grade	Comparison Group 6/97	Experimental Group 6/98
3b	57.8	57.7
3a	86.5	70.4
4b	85.8	85.3
4a	75.1	80.7
5b	78.8	79.2
5a	80.6	76.9
6b	72.7	71.7
6a	83.5	77.5
7	86.1	78.7
8	89.8	90.6
Agnew School		
	Comparison Group	**Experimental Group**
Grade	6/97	6/98
3b	66.1	67.7
3a	72.3	73.7
4b	82.5	83.7
4a	76.8	82.0

Experimental group: No spelling instruction for one year. Note: Upper grades tested on 75 words, lower grades on 50 words. Also, test for 3, 4b slightly different from test given to 4a and 5.

3.2 The Writing Hypothesis. The second rival hypothesis to the Reading Hypothesis is the Writing Hypothesis, the claim that we develop literacy through writing.

As indicated earlier, arguments against the Writing hypothesis include evidence showing that increasing writing quantity does not result in better writing style, and that it appears that people simply do not write enough for writing to have any significant impact on literacy, given the complexity of the systems to be acquired (evidence reviewed in Krashen 1991).

Jacoby and Hollingshead (1990) show that output has no effect on spelling accuracy. In their study of spelling discussed earlier, they included one condition in which subjects typed or printed the target word after reading it aloud. These groups did no better on the spelling test than subjects who simply read the target words. Those who typed or printed, however, reproduced correctly spelled words more rapidly on the spelling test, which was typed. Their superiority was slight, however, about 100-200 milliseconds per word.[8]

4 New applications.

4.1 Acquiring the standard. In previous papers, I have discussed how free reading can impact language arts programs, second language acquisition, and foreign language acquisition (e.g. Krashen 1991). Here I consider its possible effect on the acquisition of a second dialect.

Nearly everyone who has written on dialects in education agrees on the necessity of acquiring the standard written dialect. While there is tolerance of some first-dialect influence or 'accent' in speaking (and even total acceptance of some high-prestige dialects), there is agreement that everyone should acquire the written standard. As Whitehead (1951) points out, ' ... to speak with a local accent is not disadvantageous; to write prose with a local accent definitely is' (cited in Finegan 1980).[9]

---

[8] While writing does not directly cause language acquisition, there is good evidence that it can have positive effects of thinking and problem solving. Recent evidence for this includes studies by Langer and Applebee (1987) and Ganguli (1989).

Michalak (1989:44) is an apparent counterexample. College students in a course on foreign policy analysis were given 13 writing assignments (one for every class hour up until the first exam). The assignments included 'preparing lists of questions, writing summaries, diagramming arguments, compiling lists of strengths and weaknesses, analyzing and evaluating'. Michalak reported no difference between experimental and comparison students on an objective and essay examination.

One possible explanation for these results is that the experimental group did too much writing. So much writing was assigned that the students' focus may simply have been on finishing the assignment, rather than solving problems.

[9] My discussion is limited to the linguistic aspects of second dialect acquisition, not other features such as interactional style. In addition, I am assuming that the second dialect acquirer has genuinely not acquired at least some of the forms of the second dialect. In some cases, the second dialect form has been acquired, but is simply not performed, or is only used in certain situations. In this latter case, what appears to be second dialect acquisition may actually be a new willingness to use an already acquired form, or a lowering of the 'output filter' (Krashen 1985a). An example of this are the men of Martha's Vineyard, described by Labov (1972:31), who, after trying life on the mainland, return to and identify with life on the island, and adopt the island accent. As the mother of one of Labov's subjects remarked to him, 'You know, E. didn't always speak that way ... it's only since he came back from college. I guess he wanted to be more like the men on the docks'. My interpretation is that E had 'acquired' the island accent earlier in life, but only felt

It is nearly universally assumed that the written standard needs to be deliberately taught and consciously learned. (But see Labov 1978:30, who suggests that teachers teach only 'a small number of type II rules', which I interpret to be rules that can only be applied when the speaker or writer is consciously Monitoring.)

The arguments presented previously against the possibility of consciously learning a second language as well as aspects of literacy such as spelling and writing style can be applied to the learning of a second dialect: The system is too complex (see, for example, Labov's description of the often subtle and complex grammatical differences between standard English and Black English; Labov 1978), and there is good evidence that pedagogical techniques such as correction do not work (Krashen 1991). Also, there is suggestive evidence that those who have successfully acquired the standard have done so largely through reading. Richard Wright (1966:275), for example, explicitly gave reading the credit:

> I wanted to write and I did not even know the English language. I bought English grammars and found them dull. I felt that I was getting a better sense of the language from novels than from grammars.

Similarly, Malcolm X (1964:179) credits his 'prison studies', with providing him with his speaking style. These prison studies consisted largely of reading:

> Not long ago, an English writer telephoned me from London, asking questions. One was, 'What's your alma mater?' I told him, 'Books.'

Finally, it must be more than coincidence that those groups who are perceived of as not being successful in acquiring the standard are also those who live in print-deprived environments, namely, the poor.[10]

Reading is the missing ingredient in Delpit's discussion of the 'process

---

comfortable using it when he considered himself a member of the island 'club' (see footnote 10).

[10] It is also assumed that acquisition of a second dialect inevitably entails acquisition of the values of the dominant culture. This may not be the case. Smith (1988b) argues that successful language acquisition occurs when acquirers not only obtain comprehensible input, but also when they consider themselves to be potential members of the group that speaks the language. (See also Labov 1972, Gardner and Lambert 1972; Beebe 1985 is a concise review of evidence showing the relationship between group membership and both second dialect and second language acquisition.) For literacy development, acquirers need to consider themselves to be people who read and write. Smith argues that if acquirers feel they can join 'the literacy club,' they will 'read like writers,' and will acquire the conventions of writing as they read.

This view could be interpreted to mean that second dialect acquirers must in fact accept the values of the dominant group. But there is another club to join: the literacy club. Richard Wright, for example, acquired the standard written language because he considered himself to be a reader and writer, not because he accepted the values of the majority group. And the language readers and writers use is the standard.

writing' versus skills controversy. Delpit observed that process writing does not give minority children competence in the forms 'demanded by the mainstream' (Delpit 1986:383), and she recommended teaching of skills in context along with writing.

Delpit's conclusion that process writing will not do the job is consistent with research on writing discussed here and elsewhere (Krashen 1991), and there certainly is a place for limited direct instruction for those conventions of writing that even well-read people may not acquire (Krashen 1984). But most of 'standard English', in my view, can be acquired through reading.

My prediction is that with sufficient reading and an invitation to join what Smith (1988b) calls 'the literacy club' (see footnote 10), we will not need to convince second dialect speakers to study hard in order to acquire the standard in addition to their first dialect. It will simply happen.

4.2 Bilingual education. Free reading in the child's primary language can make successful bilingual programs even better. It has been hypothesized that successful programs have the following characteristics (Krashen and Biber 1988):

1. They provide comprehensible input in the second language, through second language classes and sheltered subject matter teaching.
2. They provide subject matter teaching in the child's first language, which gives children the knowledge that makes English input more comprehensible.
3. They provide for the development of literacy in the first language, which transfers to the second language.

It has also been suggested that an important component of bilingual education is enrichment, continuing the development of the first language. There are practical, cognitive, and affective advantages of advanced first language proficiency.

Free reading can help in every category: Obviously, it is an important source of comprehensible input in English. Also, free reading in the child's primary language is a major source of subject matter information and information about the world. Evidence for the role of reading in increasing knowledge comes from Ravitch and Finn (1987), who found that 17 year olds who read more did better on a test of literature, and those who grew up in a more print-rich environment did better on tests of literature and history.

The research reviewed above and in previous papers indicates that first language reading is the best way to develop first language literacy; in addition, there is every reason to suspect that if a pleasure reading habit is formed in one language, this habit will transfer to the second language.

Finally, free reading may be the best way of insuring continuing development of the primary language. My observations are that those who have an incomplete knowledge of their first language no longer read in that language.

5 Access. The main problem in implementing free reading remains access. Many children in public school simply do not have access to books outside of school. A clear example of this was provided by Feitelson and Goldstein (1986), who reported that Israeli children in schools where children tended to do well had approximately ten times as many children's books in the home as children in neighborhoods where children tend not to do well in school, and 61% of the homes of children in poor-achieving neighborhoods had no books at all.

The access problem extends even to foreign language programs, where often little is available to read other than textbooks and classics.

I have argued that simply providing access to books is the first and most important step toward solving the 'literacy crisis'. Abundant evidence exists showing that providing greater access to books results in more free reading (studies reviewed in Krashen 1987), and research suggests that in some cases, it might be the entire solution.

Table 3. The effect of magazine reading on CTBS Reading test scores (from Rucker 1982).

	Pre	Post	Difference
Rural-remedial			
Experimental	3.48	5.03	1.55
Control	3.74	4.68	.94
Suburban			
Experimental	7.18	9.31	2.13
Control	7.21	8.88	1.67

Experimental group: Received two free magazine subscriptions.

Rucker (1982) provided junior high school students with two free magazine subscriptions related to their interests. A 'rural-remedial' group received the subscriptions for one and a half years and a 'suburban' group received subscriptions for one year. Neither the students, their parents, nor their teachers knew that an experiment was being conducted. Rucker reported that both magazine reading groups gained an additional one half year on the CTBS Reading test over comparison groups (pre- and post-tests given two years apart; see table 3). There were no differences, however, on the CTBS Language test (mechanics, spelling).

A reasonable interpretation of these results is that the magazines not only served as a source of comprehensible input, but that they stimulated more reading. As Rucker (1982:33) pointed out, magazines are the most 'reader interest specific' of all mass media, and 'may thus consequently be the most valuable as stimuli to reading'.

The most obvious source of books is libraries, and for many people it is the only source. Several studies confirm that school children get a substantial percentage of their books from libraries (studies reviewed in Krashen 1987).

The larger the library, and the longer it stays open, the more books are taken out. Houle and Montmarquette (1984) studied school libraries in Quebec and found a clear relationship among library size, library hours, and circulation: For every x percent increase in the number of books (per student) in the library, loans went up about .45x. Thus, if the library increases the number of books by 20%, this will lead to a 9% increase in circulation. As Houle and Montmarquette point out, this is a strong relationship. Increasing library hours x percent was predicted to result in a .83x increase in loans in secondary schools and a .175x increase in elementary schools. Thus, increasing hours a modest 20% would mean 17% more loans in secondary school and 3.5% more loans in elementary school. These figures represent the independent contributions of increasing books and hours. Thus, doing both, increasing both books and hours, would have an additive effect.

If school libraries are an important source of books, and if larger libraries mean more reading, we would expect that a larger library would result in better reading. Such results would be consistent with other research on the relationship between access and reading ability, and have been reported. Elley and Mangubhai (1979; reported in Elley 1984:293) found that the most important predictor of English reading scores among children in the Fiji Islands was the size of the school library:

> Those schools with libraries of more than 400 books produced consistently higher mean scores than those with smaller libraries or none at all ... no school had high scores without a large library.

Similar results have been reported by Gaver (1963) for libraries in the United States.

Elley noted that schools in Fiji and in most Pacific countries had few books, with the typical Fijian school having only about 200 books, and many of these are instructional readers.

The access problem is severe in parts of the United States as well. Kozol (1991) reported that one elementary school he visited in an affluent area in the Bronx had 8,000 books in its school library for 825 children, a ratio of 9.7 books per child. Another school, one in a poor area, had only 700 books for its 1,300 children, a ratio of about one half book per child. Since children in wealthier areas also have far more books available to them at home, it is no wonder that 'the rich get richer'.

Educational reformers and critics are plentiful these days, and they use a variety of approaches. They exhort students to try harder (see discussion in Kozol 1991:81), call for reforms in teacher training, and talk about raising standards. The data, however, clearly show that a large part of the problem of language education can be solved simply by providing good magazines, newspapers, and books, by enriching a print-deprived environment.

6 Will they only read junk? It could be argued that if we encourage free reading, children will only read 'trash' and little literacy development will occur. This is a serious argument; an exclusive diet of light reading will, it appears, not lead to high levels of literacy. Several studies show that the amount of magazine reading reported is not as good a predictor of reading comprehension as the amount of book reading reported (Anderson, Wilson, and Fielding 1988; Nell 1988, Kirsch and Jungblut 1986), nor is magazine reading a good predictor of vocabulary development (Anderson et al.) or spelling (Stanovich and West 1989), and correlations between the amount of magazine reading done and measures of literacy are often very low.

Magazines, comic books, and other forms of 'light reading', however, may be at the right level ('i+1') for less-mature readers, such as junior high school students, and may provide a 'conduit' to more challenging reading. Thus, introducing light reading into an environment where little print has been available may have dramatic effects, as Rucker's study, discussed above, shows (for case histories of comic books serving as conduits, see Krashen 1989b). (In this respect it is interesting to note that Rucker's magazine readers who showed the greatest gains in the suburban group were those who read at or below grade level; above-average readers, it can be assumed, were already pleasure readers and the free magazines did not significantly increase their reading.)

There is, in addition, evidence that most children who do extensive free reading eventually choose what experts have decided are 'good books' (Schoonover 1938), and LaBrant (1958) reported that readers gradually expand their reading interests as they get older. Moveover, several studies show that books children choose on their own are typically harder than the reading that teachers assign (Southgate, Arnold, and Johnson 1981; Bader, Veatch, and Eldridge 1987). Apparently, we can trust readers to select their own pleasure reading.

REFERENCES

Anderson, Richard, Paul Wilson, and Linda Fielding. 1988. Growth in reading and how children spend their time outside of school. Reading Research Quarterly 23.285-303.

Bader, L., J. Veatch, and J. Eldrige. 1987. Trade books or basal readers? Reading Improvement 24.62-7.

Bean, M. 1879. The evil of unlimited freedom in the use of juvenile fiction. The Library Journal 4.341-43.

Beebe, Leslie. 1985. Input: Choosing the right stuff. Input in second language acquisition, ed. by Susan Gass and Carolyn Madden, 404–14. Rowley, MA: Newbury House.

Cornman, Oliver. 1902. Spelling in the elementary school. Boston: Ginn.

D'Anna, Catherine, Eugene Zechmeister, and James Hall. 1991. Toward a meaningful definition of vocabulary size. Journal of Reading Behavior 23.109-22.

Delpit, Lisa. 1986. Skills and other dilemmas of a progressive black educator. Harvard Educational

Review 56.379-85.

Elley, Warwick. 1984. Exploring the reading difficulties of second-language learners in Fiji. Reading in a foreign language, ed. by J. Charles Alderon and A. H. Urquhart, 281–97. London: Longman.

Elley, Warwick. 1991. Acquiring literacy in a second language: The effect of book-based programs. Language Learning 41.375-411.

Feitelson, Dina, and Zahara Goldstein. 1986. Patterns of book ownership and reading to young children in Israeli school-oriented and nonschool-oriented families. The Reading Teacher 39.924-30.

Finegan, Edward. 1980. Attitudes toward English usage: The history of a war of words. New York: Teachers College Press.

Ganguli, A. 1989. Integrating writing in developmental mathematics. College Teaching 37.140-42.

Gaver, Mary. 1963. Effectiveness of centralized library service in elementary schools. New Brunswick, NJ: Rutgers University Press.

Gardner, Robert, and Wallace Lambert. 1972. Attitudes and motivation in second language learning. Rowley, MA: Newbury House.

Goodman, Kenneth. 1982. Language and literacy: The selected writings of Kenneth S. Goodman, ed. by Frederick Gollasch. London: Routledge.

Goulden, Robert, Paul Nation, and John Read. 1991. How large can a receptive vocabulary be? Applied Linguistics 11.341-63.

Graff, Harvey. 1979. The literacy myth. New York: Academic Press.

Haggan, Madeline. 1991. Spelling errors in native Arabic-speaking English majors: A comparison between remedial students and fourth year students. System 19.45–61.

Houle, R., and C. Montmarquette. 1984. An empirical analysis of loans by school libraries. The Alberta Journal of Educational Research 30.104-14.

Jacoby, Larry, and Ann Hollingshead. 1990. Reading student essays may be hazardous to your spelling: Effects of reading incorrectly and correctly spelled words. Canadian Journal of Psychology 44.345-58.

Kirsch, Irwin, and Ann Jungblut. 1986. Literacy: Profiles of America's young adults. Princeton, NJ: Educational Testing Service.

Kozol, J. 1991. Savage inequalities. New York: Crown.

Krashen, Stephen. 1982. Principles and practice in second language acquisition. New York: Prentice Hall.

Krashen, Stephen. 1984. Writing: Research, theory, and applications. Torrance, CA: Laredo.

Krashen, Stephen. 1985a. Inquiries and insights. New York: Prentice Hall.

Krashen, Stephen. 1985b. The input hypothesis: Issues and implications. Torrance, CA: Laredo.

Krashen, Stephen. 1987. Encouraging free reading. Claremont Reading Conference, 51st Yearbook, ed. by Malcolm Douglas, 1–10. Claremont, CA: Claremont Graduate School.

Krashen, Stephen. 1988. Do we learn to read by reading? The relationship between free reading and reading ability. Linguistics in context: Connecting observation and understanding, ed. by Deborah Tannen, 269–98. Norwood, NJ: Ablex.

Krashen, Stephen. 1989a. We acquire vocabulary and spelling by reading: Additional evidence for the Input Hypothesis. Modern Language Journal 73.440-64.

Krashen, Stephen. 1989b. Language teaching technology: A low-tech view. Georgetown University Round Table on Languages and Linguistics 1989. Washington, DC: Georgetown University Press. 393-407.

Krashen, Stephen. 1991. The Input Hypothesis: An update. Georgetown University Round Table on Languages and Linguistics 1991, ed. by James E. Alatis, 409–31. Washington, DC: Georgetown University Press.

Krashen, Stephen, and Douglas Biber. 1988. On course: Bilingual education's success in California. Sacramento: California Association for Bilingual Education.

Krashen, Stephen, and Howard White. 1991. Is spelling acquired or learned? A re-analysis of Rice (1897) and Cornman (1902). ITL: Review of Applied Linguistics 91-92.1-48.

Labov, William. 1972. Sociolinguistic patterns. Philadelphia: University of Pennsylvania Press.

Labov, William. 1978. The study of nonstandard English. Urbana, IL: National Council of Teachers of English.
Labrant, L. 1958. An evaluation of free reading. Research in the three R's, ed. by C. Hunnicutt and W. Iverson, 154–61. New York: Harper and Brothers.
Langer, Judith, and Arthur Applebee. 1987. How writing shapes thinking. Urbana, IL: National Council of Teachers of English.
Lorge, Irving, and Jeannie Chall. 1963. Estimating the size of vocabularies of children and adults: An analysis of methodological issues. Journal of Experimental Education 32.147-57.
Mangubhai, Francis, and Warwick. Elley. 1982. The role of reading in promoting ESL. Language Learning and Communication 1.151-60.
Michalak, Stanley. 1989. Writing more, learning less? College Teaching 37.43-5.
Nagy, William, Patricia Herman, and Ricard Anderson. 1985. Learning words from context. Reading Research Quarterly 20.233-53.
Nell, Victor. 1988. The psychology of reading for pleasure: Needs and gratifications. Reading Research Quarterly 23.6-50.
O'Rourke, J. 1974. Toward a science of vocabulary development. The Hague: Mouton.
Ravitch, Diane, and Chester Finn, Jr. 1987. What do our 17-year-olds know? New York: Harper and Row.
Rice, J. 1897. The futility of the spelling grind. Forum 23.163-72, 409-17.
Rucker, Bryee. 1982. Magazines and teenage reading skills: Two controlled field experiments. Journalism Quarterly 59.28-33.
Schoonover, R. 1938. The case for voluminous reading. English Journal 27.114-18.
Seashore, Robert, and Lois Eckerson. 1940. The measurement of individual differences in general English vocabularies. Journal of Educational Psychology 31.14-38.
Smith, Frank. 1985. Reading without Nonsense. New York: Columbia Teachers College Press.
Smith, Frank. 1988a. Understanding reading. Hillsdale, NJ: Erlbaum.
Smith, Frank. 1988b. Joining the literacy club. Portsmouth, NH: Heinemann.
Southgate, Vera, Helen Arnold, and Sandra Johnson. 1981. Extending beginning reading. London: Heinemann.
Stanovich, Keith, and Richard West. 1989. Exposure to print and orthographic processing. Reading Research Quarterly 24.402-33.
Wertham, Frederick. 1954. The seduction of the innocent. New York: Rinehart.
White, Thomas, Michael Power, and Sheida White. 1989. Morphological analysis: Implications for teaching and understanding vocabulary growth. Reading Research Quarterly 24.283-304.
Wright, Richard. 1966. Black boy. New York: Harper and Row.
X, Malcolm. 1964. The autobiography of Malcolm X. New York: Ballantine Books.

Social meanings for how we teach

Earl W. Stevick
Independent researcher

There is social meaning not only in what we say, but in how we say it; not only in what we teach, but in how we teach it. So I'd like to begin with a brief quotation from a recent article by Alastair Pennycook. Writing about what he calls critical pedagogy and its relation to second language education, Pennycook (1990:309) says that

> all claims to knowledge are 'interested', i.e. [they] reflect the particular concerns of a group or individual and are always thus bound up in the relationships of power.

Pennycook here is of course talking mainly about the overall social setting of second language education, and that is not what I will be talking about today. I'll be talking instead about something much smaller and much more humble—about teaching strategies, and not about society at large. I would nevertheless paraphrase Pennycook, to say that the things that go on inside the classroom are in their own way 'interested', that is, that they reflect the particular concerns of a group or individual, and I would echo Pennycook exactly in my belief that these acts, these events, are always bound up in relationships of power. I would further suggest that the oft-repeated goal of (to use a currently stylish term) empowering students, however far upward or however far outward it may hope to reach, needs to find solid footing in how we treat those same students day by day.

Having made this generalization, let me be more specific: first a little more specific, and then very specific. Here to begin with are two rather distinct sets of conclusions that a student might draw from his or her experience in a foreign language class. I've put them together largely out of some of the things Leo Loveday said in his 1982 book on *The Sociolinguistics of Learning and Using a Non-native Language*. One set of conclusions is the set that Loveday seems to think we should enable our students to reach (numbers refer to pages in Loveday 1982):

- Language is a medium (134) for creating (130) one's own meanings

(141), and for exchanging meanings with other people.

- In this process of creating and exchanging meanings, one discovers oneself (130) more fully.
- The process [of creating and exchanging meanings] also provides opportunities for expressing one's freedom (127) and autonomy (137), and for developing them further.
- At the same time, one also recognizes and affirms the freedom, autonomy and uniqueness of others. (Contrast with 'intolerance' (129), 'judgmental' (125, 134).)
- In the process of learning a language, one should be freed from unnecessary social pressures (145).
- In order to exchange meanings with other people, one needs to know how they will react to various possible ways of using words (125f). That is to say, one must be able to use the 'conventions' of the language and of the culture in question.
- Conformity to norms of correctness is less important than comprehensibility is.
- The teacher is primarily a resource and a facilitator.

In dramatic contrast to this set of conclusions is the set that Loveday believes are too often reached by people who have sat or worked their way through a language course:

- Language must be treated as an object for a long time before it can be treated as a medium.
- Spoken language should not depart too far from written language (e.g. say *pro-ba-bly* and not *probbly*.)
- The most important thing about language as an object is its form. This means that what I say is less important than how correctly I say it.
- Some conventions that affect the form of language are acceptable (e.g. *it doesn't*); all other conventions are entirely unacceptable (e.g. *it don't*). (These conventions are what Loveday calls 'norms.')
- Decisions as to which linguistic and which social conventions become norms are made by a small group of socially powerful people. By enforcing conformity to these norms, this oligarchy—actually, the upper middle class (174)—both expresses and perpetuates its own power at the expense of larger groups of subjugated and despised speakers (175).
- The language of monolinguals is—or at least may be—acceptable by those norms; language that is not consistent with acceptable monolingual usage is not acceptable.
- If I follow unacceptable conventions, I will be unacceptable as a speaker of the second language (L2), and my utterances may be rejected or ignored by competent (i.e. conforming) speakers.
- Conformity to norms is more important than comprehensibility.
- Therefore learning a language is first of all a process of learning to

conform to norms (social as well as linguistic); success in a language course first of all requires the learner to demonstrate his or her willingness and ability to conform.

- The teacher is primarily a judge and corrector (134).
- I will be judged every time I open my mouth.

Here is the same contrast in a nutshell: two quotations from people to whom I had put the question, 'What besides language did you learn from your language class?'

'I learned that it is important for a learner to explore, and not just follow what's given by the teacher.'

'I learned the importance of what the teacher's voice conveys. I also learned anxiety and anger.'

Next I'd like to turn to a very specific example of what I believe is the same issue. So let's look now at a minimal pair of techniques—at two quite different ways of implementing a single format. That format is the pairing of a picture with a dialogue. This format has been with us for centuries, but it's still the object of comment in the literature. In one of last year's issues of *The Modern Language Journal*, for example, Hammadou cites research that seems to indicate that cueing readers about an upcoming topic with a picture aids comprehension more than teaching vocabulary does, and that this is particularly useful for low-proficiency students.

First let's look at a fairly standard audiolingual procedure in seven very familiar steps:

1. The students look briefly at the picture. The purpose is to establish at least a bit of meaning in their heads before bringing in the linguistic forms.
2. The students close their books and listen to the dialogue. This allows and requires them to focus on the linguistic forms.
3. The students repeat the dialogue bit by bit after the teacher, and the teacher corrects their pronunciation. Focus is still very much on form.
4. The students listen again, this time with their books open. Now they are matching audible forms with visible forms. (At the same time they may be picking up a little of the meaning.)
5. The students read the translations provided in a parallel column. Focus here is of course on meaning.
6. The students repeat the dialogue numerous times, both for further polishing of their pronunciation, and in order to commit it to memory. Emphasis is once again on form.
7. The students become able to recite the dialogue correctly and unhesitatingly. The product is linguistic form, although we of course hope that as they practice, students will also have in their heads the meanings that

they picked up in Steps 1 and 5. (I suspect that students for whom audiolingual instruction worked may have played mental videotapes as they drilled the forms. I know I did.)

Now here's an alternative technique (from Frankel and Meyers 1991), also using a picture-dialogue combination, and also in seven steps:

1. Before the students come into contact with the dialogue in any form, they look at the picture and describe it in whatever words or phrases they can supply. They also guess what the people in the picture might be saying to each other. The teacher reflects what the students say, using an interested, appreciative tone and correct language. The students don't repeat after the teacher. Focus is on meaning, which is expressed through linguistic forms that the students themselves already to some extent control.
2. The students listen together to the full text of the dialogue and report what they think they have heard. The teacher writes their contributions on the board, without filling in gaps and without correcting. Focus is on form, but students are unlikely to suggest forms for which they have no meanings.
3. The students listen again, this time with their books open. They now check the forms that they have suggested against the forms on the page. At the same time, they pick up at least a little meaning.
4. The students indicate what they have not understood. The teacher explains or demonstrates meanings.
5. The students work on pronunciation either by conventional imitation-correction, or by using some learner-initiated technique such as The Human Computer™. Focus is on form.
6. The students practice together in dyads, working for greater familiarity and fluency, though not necessarily for absolute memorization.
7. The students take turns acting out the dialogue or some variant of it. Their purpose is to interest or amuse. Focus is on combination of forms and meanings.

Here, as Allwright (1984) put it, classroom interaction is being managed by all present, not just by the teacher. Now what are some of the conclusions that a learner might draw from these two ways of handling the dialogue-plus-picture format? From the first way, he or she might decide (a) that both the meanings and the words necessarily originate with the management, not with me; (b) that both the meanings and the words through which I am to express them are the property of management; (c) that whatever meanings I might contribute would at worst be inaccurate (be semantically wrong), at best would divert class time from the task at hand (be socially wrong), and would in any event eventually be rejected, so why bother? (d) that whatever forms I might contribute from experiences outside of class or from other sources would at worst be linguistically wrong, and at best would again be a distraction from the task at hand (be socially wrong); (e) that I'm expected to use the part of my brain that copies, but not the part that creates; (f) that power—both the power to decide what is to be done and the power to decide whether it has been done acceptably—is in the hands of the teacher; (g) that any initiative is to come from the side with the power; (h) that my conformity should be not only complete, but also quick and unhesitating; (i) that my fellow students at worst are sources of undependable models, and at best are sources of competition for the teacher's time and approval.

The second way of handling dialogue-plus-picture obviously leads toward very different conclusions. Some of those conclusions would likely be (a) that my perceptions, my meanings, and the past experiences on which I base them, are of interest here; (b) that whatever language I already know is going to be valued even if it isn't exactly what is in the book; (c) that initiative from me is welcomed, even needed; (d) that the person with the linguistic and administrative power—the teacher—will respond to my initiatives in ways that help me; (e) that it's all right for me to use the part of my brain that creates; (f) that guessing and approximation are acceptable; (g) that guesses and approximations do not lead me to wrong learning if I am careful to verify and correct them; (h) that I can safely assume some of the responsibility for evaluating my own accuracy; (i) that there is value in working together with other learners at almost every step in this technique.

None of this second set of conclusions can be drawn from the first technique. On the other hand, if the second technique is well executed, the first set of conclusions are unlikely to flow from it. There are of course numerous other ways to combine pictures and sample dialogues. It would be worthwhile to examine each of them to see which of these two sets of conclusions they would lead toward.

And that would be an interesting, perhaps even a profitable, intellectual exercise. In the real world, however, the question is what we should do, which technique we should use, and there is no one clear answer to this question. It depends on which of a number of possible aims we are trying to reach. Let me list just ten of them:

Provide a LINGUISTIC SAMPLE that the students can rely on.
Provide clear OVERALL STRUCTURE for the activity.

The first two desiderata are well served by either of the two techniques I have sketched. The rest however are not:

Provide clear MOMENT-TO-MOMENT STRUCTURE for the activity.
Provide a few CLEAR MODELS for learning.
Work for maximum accuracy in COPYING of models.
Work within FAMILIAR power/status relationships.

These four make for very clear cognitive focus. They are consistent with the larger aims of having the class go smoothly and efficiently, and of preparing students for standardized—or for standardizable—tests. They are well served by the first of my two techniques, but poorly served by the second.

On the other hand, we may have a quite different list of desiderata:

ENRICH THE MEANINGS of the forms being practiced.
Encourage the students to take INITIATIVE.
Reduce the STATUS/POWER differential between teacher and students.
Encourage COOPERATION among the students.

These four are much better served by the second technique than by the first. They are consistent with the larger aim of producing independent, resourceful, and responsible language users outside of the class.

If we had time, we could readily illustrate the same kind of contrasting aims in alternative techniques for activities other than dialogue-plus-picture: for grammar drill, or for the teaching of vocabulary. This single brief example is however sufficient to raise the question that would only be intensified after further illustration. That question is, Which of these larger aims should we choose? And I'm afraid that even after we have exercised our greatest ingenuity, we do have to choose.

This question brings us to a final level of social meaning. Because just as our choice of technique depends on larger aims, so our choice among larger aims is related to—is an expression of—our deeper values. And if these relationships—if these values—are not clearly recognized, then they can give rise to reactions that are expressed not in logical propositions, but in adjectives. If I am mainly interested in smooth, clearly focused and clearly demonstrable learning, then I may use techniques that are in the same family as the first—techniques with traditional distribution of power and responsibility. And then the aspects of my method that I feel are 'responsible' may be described by those whose aim is different as 'dull'. Other pairs of terms are 'orderly'/'lock-step', 'thorough'/'compulsive', 'accurate'/'conformist', and 'discipline'/'drudgery'. The first descriptor in each pair is earnest; the second is an expression of something akin to moral outrage.

If on the other hand my aims are such as to lead me to select the second technique and other techniques that embody nontraditional power relationships, if I am concerned, as Prabhu (1987) would say, to enable the learners, to help them build what Gattegno called 'awareness of awareness' (Stevick 1990, chapter 6) and to let them achieve what Vygotsky (1962) called self-regulation (Foley 1991), then at those points where I say I am 'encouraging spontaneity,' others may charge that I'm just 'creating confusion.' Additional pairs of epithets from this point of view might be 'excitement'/'self-indulgence', 'exploration'/'dilettantism', 'concern for security'/'coddling', 'intuition'/'mysticism', and 'flexible'/'fumbling.' Again, the contrast between earnestness and moral outrage.

And here, unfortunately, is where social meanings, precisely because they and their sources are dimly recognized if they are recognized at all—here is where social meanings can be both distracting and destructive. If what we want to generate is light and not heat, if we intend to make choices that are informed and not just intuitive or ideological, then we need to expend no little effort first in identifying our own values, next in tying those values to an appropriate set of larger aims, and only then devising or rejecting, adopting or adapting techniques.

REFERENCES

Allwright, R. L. 1984. The importance of interaction in classroom language learning. Applied Linguistics 5, 2.156-71.

Foley, Joseph. 1991. A psycholinguistic framework for task-based approaches to language teaching. Applied Linguistics 12, 1.62-75.

Frankel, Irene and Cliff Meyers. 1991. Crossroads 1. New York: Oxford University Press.

Hammadou, Joann. 1991. Interrelationships among prior knowledge, inference, and language proficiency. The Modern Language Journal 75, 1.27-38

Loveday, Leo. 1982. The sociolinguistics of learning and using a non-native language. Oxford: Pergamon.

Pennycook, Alastair. 1990. Critical pedagogy and second language education. System 18, 3.303-14.

Prabhu, N. S. 1987. Language education: Equipping or enabling? Language education in human resource development, ed. by B. K. Das. Singapore: RELC.

Stevick, Earl W. 1990. Humanism in language teaching. Oxford: Oxford University Press.

Vygotsky, L. S. 1962. Thought and language. Cambridge, MA: MIT Press.

Communication with second language learners: What does it reveal about the social and linguistic processes of second language learning?

Teresa Pica*
University of Pennsylvania

Abstract. The purpose of this paper is to examine the role of communication in the cognitive, linguistic, and social processes of second language (L2) learning. In order to do this, the paper will focus on a specific type of communication, negotiation for meaning, in which interlocutors work together to resolve communication breakdowns and achieve mutual understanding. What will be shown is that as learners negotiate with their interlocutors, they work within a social relationship which is conducive to the linguistic and cognitive aspects of the L2 learning process. This is accomplished as learners and interlocutors signal and respond during impasses in communication by repeating, reformulating, and segmenting both their own and each other's utterances. These linguistic adjustments provide learners with opportunities to understand L2 input, manipulate and modify their own output, and attend to relationships between L2 form and meaning. In this way, the social moves and strategies of negotiation can assist the linguistic and cognitive processes of L2 learning.

To illustrate the range and variation with respect to negotiation and the L2 learning process, examples will be drawn from a corpus of informal, experimental, and classroom interaction of English language learners and native speakers across several types of communicative contexts, each of which places learners in a different social role and relationship with an interlocutor. These examples will also be used to explain the inhibiting effects on the L2 learning process when learners' social roles and relationships require them to demonstrate their knowledge of L2 rules or to apply this knowledge to communicative practice, and the enhancing effects on the L2 learning process when learners' roles and relationships motivate them to negotiate over L2 meaning.

---

* This paper was written while the author was Ethel G. Carruth Associate Professor of Education at the University of Pennsylvania Graduate School of Education.

1 Introduction. Objectives and processes of language learning are explicit or implicit to all second language (L2) learning theories and teaching methods, whether communication-oriented, structurally based, or a combination thereof. Among theories and methods that are considered 'traditional', the objectives of L2 learning have focused on units of language such as sound patterns and prescriptive grammar rules and on the learner's need to master and control them, first in isolation and later in meaningful and communicative contexts. This sequence, as Hatch (1978a, 1978b) has noted, reflects the belief that the learning of L2 forms is a first and necessary step toward success with L2 communication.

With respect to L2 learning processes involved in attainment of these objectives, diverse, often competing, views have been held. Some of these views have highlighted activities such as rule formation, inference, and generalization, while others have featured behaviors such as imitation and habit formation. (For critique and discussion, see histories by Howatt 1984, Kelly 1969, Richards 1985, Richards and Rodgers 1986; and Titone 1968, among others).

L2 learning objectives and processes have also been described within a communicative perspective. Here, language is viewed as an instrument of social discourse and a vehicle for conveying message meaning. In its most recent incarnation, the communicative perspective has given a great deal of attention to the objectives of L2 learning. These have been set through specification of notional, functional, and grammatical features of L2 communicative competence and calibrated with respect to media, modalities, and levels of formality and appropriateness. (See, for example, theoretical writings and methodological texts by Brumfit and Johnson 1979; Canale and Swain 1980; Krashen and Terrell 1983; Savignon 1983; Widdowson 1978; and Yalden 1983 as well as the vast array of classroom materials in circulation).

A communicative perspective can also be seen among current theoretical claims about the L2 learning process. Hatch (1978a, 1978b) has argued that L2 structure learning evolves out of the learner's participation in L2 communication. Krashen (1980, 1983, 1985) has held that communication, with its focus on meaning, allows the learner to understand L2 input and thereby access L2 forms which encode that meaning. Long (1980, 1981, 1983, 1985a, 1985b) has emphasized that certain aspects of communication are necessary for L2 learning, for example, that it must involve learners in a mutual exchange of information with their interlocutors and allow them to seek and receive help in understanding unfamiliar L2 input.

These and other theoretical claims have emphasized that the L2 learning process is embedded within the learner's communicative experience. However, compared to the very detailed explication of communication as the objective of L2 learning, considerably less description and explanation have been directed toward communication as the process or activity through which L2 learning takes place. How do the social moves of communication assist L2 learning? How do these moves make the L2 available as data for L2 learning? Answers to these and other questions can serve to illuminate the role played by communication in the L2 learning process.

In order to examine the role that communication might play in the linguistic, social, and cognitive processes of L2 learning, this paper will focus on a specific type of communication, widely referred to as 'negotiation for meaning'. (See, among others, Gass and Varonis 1984, 1985, 1986, 1989; Long 1980, 1981, 1983, 1985a, 1985b; Pica 1987a, 1987b; Varonis and Gass 1982, 1985a, 1985b, and articles in the collection edited by Day 1986). What occurs during negotiation is shown in the following excerpts from communication tasks in which native and nonnative speakers (NSs and NNSs) took turns, one describing a picture for the other to draw or select.[2] Some of their communication went smoothly, with mutual understanding about the pictures. Descriptive information was conveyed successfully and when information was sought, these questions were responded to quickly. At other times, such as those shown in Excerpts 1–3, their communication did not go as smoothly and triggered their negotiation about the meaning of the information being conveyed or sought about the picture. They expressed their lack of understanding with respect to the picture description through a variety of signals. These are shown in *italics*. Their responses to each other's signals are shown in **bold**. These signals and responses characterize the negotiation process.

	Native Speaker (NS)	Nonnative Speaker (NNS)
(1)	... it's a rectangular bench	*rectangular?*
	yeah it's in the shape of a rectangle	
	with um you know a rectangle has	
	two long sides and two short sides	*rectangle?*
	re-rectangle it's it's like a square	
	except you you flatten it out	*square except*
	uh a rectangle is a square	uhuh
	except a square has four equal sides	yes
	a rectangle has two sides	
	that are much longer and two sides	
	that are much shorter	ok
(2)	*the windows have what?*	**closed**
	crossed? I'm not sure	
	what you're saying there	**windows are closed**
	oh the windows are closed oh ok sorry	

[2] Except where indicated, all examples have been drawn from data from Pica, Holliday, Lewis, and Morgenthaler 1989 and Pica, Holliday, Lewis, Berducci, and Newman 1991.

(3)

NNS	NNS
where do you put the three floor house	
three floor	three floor em I put it at the um right and the middle
right and middle	yes close the cir cir the circuit
in across the circle circle	yes
ok	um three floors
three floors	yes

As these selections reveal, and as will be discussed below, what makes negotiation a distinctive kind of experience in L2 communication and learning is that it comes about, not during the even flow of social exchange all too often associated with effective communication, but rather when the flow of communication is on the verge of disruption due to a lack of clarity in message meaning. Such disruption, whether perceived, anticipated, or actual, provides learners and interlocutors with opportunities to seek message clarification or confirmation and to respond accordingly, toward mutual comprehension. It is this work of attempting to reach mutual understanding that characterizes negotiation, and, as will be addressed in this paper, provides a social context for L2 learning.

2 Theoretical background. The term, negotiation, is neither original nor unique to work on L2 learning but has been used in a variety of contexts, including those pertaining to business and politics (See e.g. Pruitt 1981, Putnam and Jones 1982, Rubin and Brown 1975). It has been the focus of very fruitful research in the field of ethnomethodology and conversation analysis, where it is used to refer to the ongoing process by which interlocutors structure their social relationships through interaction as they take turns at talk and communicate meaning to each other. (See, for example, Garfinkel 1967).

Ethnomethodologists' view of negotiation has shed light on communication as not only a social and linguistic OUTCOME of the work of individuals in building a social relationship but also a social and linguistic PROCESS in structuring the relationship. This perspective on negotiation as outcome and process has contributed substantially to L2 research through studies on 'interaction', 'interactional modification', and 'repair' (by, for example, Doughty and Pica 1986, Gass and Varonis 1984, 1985, 1986, 1989; Hatch 1978a, 1978b; Long 1980, 1981, 1983, 1985a, 1985b; Pica 1987a, 1987b; Pica et al. 1986, Pica et al. 1987, Varonis and Gass 1982, 1985a, 1985b; and articles in the collection edited by Day 1986).

Interest in negotiation among L2 researchers grew primarily out of earlier work on the linguistic environment of L2 learning. Much of this work was focused on the social aspects of NS-NNS communication. Through studies on question types, lexical choice, and discourse markers, researchers sought to identify a special register for NS-NNS interaction and to pinpoint what distinguished it from the communication of other interlocutors, for example, native speaker–native speaker (NS–NS). There was interest in how these social features were connected to L2 learning processes, but, it was not until initiatives taken by Hatch and Long, that empirical work was carried out in this area.

The challenge to investigate possible connections between the properties of social discourse and the processes of L2 learning was initiated by Hatch (1978a, 1978b) as she called for a new approach to research on L2 learning. She argued that researchers needed to reverse their assumption that the nature of the learning process was one in which L2 structure learning LED TO the learner's communicative use of L2. Instead, studies should focus on how the learning of L2 structure EVOLVED OUT OF communicative use. Researchers would thus continue to focus on communication between learners and their interlocutors, not only for what it revealed about social aspects of speech to learners, but also for what it might uncover about linguistic and cognitive features of the L2 learning process.

The most seminal work in this area came from Long (1980), who described and quantified features of negotiation, referred as 'interactional modification' in the social discourse of NNSs and their NS interlocutors and compared these features with those generated through NS–NNS discourse. Long identified negotiation as a process which included requests for clarification and confirmation of message meaning and checks on message comprehensibility. He found that negotiation occurred during all human interaction but was far more prevalent during communication with second language learners. Based on his findings, Long identified negotiation as a type of communication most suited to meet L2 learners' needs and requirements in the learning process. Many studies have followed, which have further described negotiation as a social process and connected it to linguistic and cognitive processes of L2 learning.

3 Negotiation as a social, linguistic, and cognitive enterprise in the L2 learning process. As was illustrated in the excerpts above, negotiation begins as one interlocutor signals to the other that the other's message is not clear. Through their signals, they often draw each other's attention to individual words or phrases which impede their access to message meaning. They respond to each other's signals by repeating and reformulating all or part of their initial utterances. Thus, negotiation unites social processes such as signalling and response moves, linguistic processes of repetition, reformulation, and other lexical and syntactic adjustments within these moves, and cognitive processes of attention and comprehension, all of which have been claimed to play a role in successful L2 learning.

3.1 Negotiation Signals. Negotiation signals can take a variety of forms. As shown in (1–3), as well as in (4–11), they can be open requests for clarification such as *What?* in (4) and *I don't understand* in (10). Signals can also be encoded as utterances which linguistically modify or adjust a preceding utterance by repeating, repronouncing, or rewording all or part of it. In (3), for example, which displays negotiation as it takes place between two NNSs, one of them signals to the other by modifying the previous *yes close the cir cir the* *circuit* as the more target-like *in across the circle circle.* Similar modifications appear in both NS and NNS signals of (1) through (11). Such signals serve to seek confirmation of what was perceived to be heard or to indicate its insufficiency with respect to message meaning. Of course, individual negotiation signals can contain both open requests and linguistic adjustments to a previous utterance. This can be seen in the second signal of (2) which contains both *crossed?*, a re-pronunciation of the interlocutor's utterance and the more general signal *I'm not sure what you're saying there.* A similar pattern can be seen in (6), in which the NNS repeats the NS *hinges?* and follows it with *I don't know what that means.*

(4)	NS	NNS
	and is your drawing very neat?	⇒*what?*
	neat I mean all the lines come together it's orderly?	
(5)	are they facing one another	*facing?*
	um are the chairs at opposite ends of the table or-	yeah
(6)	the door has hinges	⇒*hinges? I don't know what that means*
	like hinges hold it together	
(7)		and so dog is um right hand of girl
	the dog is at the right hand of the girl	**yes**
(8)		this country like bik
	big?	**yeah** (Farah 1991)
(9)	I have a piece of toast with a small pat of butter on it	hm hmm
	and above the plate	*what is buvdaplate?*
	above	*above the plate*
	yeah not up—as if you are sitting at the table it would be farther away from you than the plate	hm hmm
(10)	NNS	NNS
		the house has two windows its a rest wall
	hmmm hmmn?	**left window**

hmmm left?	**yeah left side left wall**
left wall	**the house has two windows on the left wall**
its a big two window and a small windows	**on the two window** *you got it no?*
⇒*I don't understand*	**the most east hint is em the house has two ... steps in front of the entrance**
hm hmmm ... ok ...	
(11) ... I put it at the down right	*down right?*
down down and right	*it means means on the three floor house*
behind on the	*under the three floor house?*
under yes under the three floor house	

3.2 Negotiation Responses. In their responses to signals, learners and interlocutors often use the same kinds of linguistic adjustments to modify their own preceding messages that they use when signalling about the other's message. In (2), for example, the NNS re-pronounced his initial *crozed* as *closed* in response to the NNS signal. In (1), the NS described the dimensional attributes of *rectangle* in his response. Such use of descriptors as well as synonyms and examples can also be found in the responses to the signals regarding *neat* in (4), *facing* in (5), *hinges* in (6), and *above* in (9).

Structural adjustments to an initial utterance are also shown in NS responses to NNS signals, particularly in (1), where the NS repeated *square* and *except* about which the NNS had signaled, but segmented it more clearly by using *except* as a conjunction to link two simple sentences, the first of which ended with *a square* as object and the second one, that is, that immediately following *except*, which used this same word *square* as its subject.

In (9), the NS responded to the interlocutor's unsegmented signal *what is buvdaplate?* by extracting *above* from his initial utterance. Finally, in (11), the NNS inserted the conjunction *and* between the words *down* and *right* in response to the NNS query regarding these juxtaposed words.

In sum, then, when learners and their interlocutors negotiate to resolve communication breakdowns, they engage in a social process which often invites, and indeed requires, them to modify their speech linguistically. These linguistic adjustments in turn provide learners with conditions and experiences believed to be crucial for successful L2 learning, that is, through opportunities to comprehend initially unfamiliar L2 input, receive feedback on their own comprehensibility, manipulate and modify their output, and access L2 lexis and structures. The following sections will therefore elaborate these learning experiences, describe the ways in which negotiation brings about them about, and explain how they contribute to the process of L2 learning.

4 Negotiation for L2 input adjusted or modified for comprehension needs. One of the most widely held theoretical claims is that learners' comprehension of L2 input is an essential requirement for L2 learning. It is widely held that in order for learners to be able to internalize L2 rules and structures, they must first understand the meaning of messages encoded therein. Support for this claim has come through evidence that in the absence of comprehensible input, little, if any, L2 learning occurs. (See Krashen 1980, 1985 and Long 1981, 1985 for theoretical arguments and summaries of supportive research).

Research on how learners come to comprehend initially unfamiliar L2 has pointed to the contributions made by negotiation in this process. Specifically, what has been found to be crucial to the comprehension process are repetitions, rephrasings, and other linguistic elaborations to initially unfamiliar L2 input. Such message adjustments are especially abundant in negotiation signals and responses. Thus, negotiation moves serve as vehicles for making L2 input comprehensible to learners, more so than other moves in NS–NNS discourse. This has been documented in studies by Blau (1982), Cervantes (1983), Chaudron (1983, 1985), Johnson (1981), Kelch (1985), Long (1983, 1985a), Gass and Varonis (1985), Pica et al. (1986), Pica et al. (1987), and Varonis and Gass (1982). Further, as revealed in Pica (1991), negotiation signals and responses appear to have a positive effect on comprehension even among those NNSs not directly involved in negotiation. Thus, L2 comprehension is aided through negotiation whether the signals and responses of negotiation are produced by and directed toward specific NNSs or are made in the presence of NNSs who are attending to the L2 input under negotiation but are not themselves directly involved in the negotiation.

5 Negotiation as a source of feedback on production. With regard to the role and importance of feedback in L2 learning, the type of feedback which Schachter labels 'negative input' has received the greatest theoretical prominence. Negative input provides learners both with metalinguistic information about their interlanguage and the L2 variety of their interlocutor as well as with a basis for comparison of the two (See Schachter 1983, 1984, 1986). That such information is available during negotiation has been supported by research (Gass and Varonis 1989, Pica 1987a; Pica 1989 and Pica et al. 1991) and can be seen in the NS signals of (2), (7), and (8) and in the NNS signals of (3) and (11), as well as below in the signals regarding *can* and *cannot* in (12) and those regarding *glasses* in (13).

(12) NS	NNS
	there is a sofa there's a sofa against a wall which I can't see
sofa against the wall which you ⇒can or cannot see?	**cannot**

ok how do you know it's there	... the sofa I can see two legs
⇒*you can see two legs of the sofa?*	**yes**
⇒*I thought you said you couldn't see the sofa*	**I can see I can see but I can see just two legs**
⇒*you can see two legs of the sofa*	**yeah**
ok	

(13) NS	NNS
	next to the notebook there is there is a pen
uh huh	and next to the pen there is a glass
does the glass have anything in it?	
does the glass have anything in it?	
glass? glass?	
oh glasses	**glass**
oh glasses	**glasses glasses**
⇒to say glass make it plural ok	glasses
right ok	

In (12), the NNS was asked to clarify his message regarding the visibility of the sofa to which he had referred. To assist this process, the NS signal offered the NNS both positive and negative versions of the modal *can* as well as the conditional *couldn't*. In (13), the initial signals about *glass* assumed that the NNS was referring to a drinking glass. Once the NS realized that the NNS was referring to eyeglasses, the signal was adjusted through the addition of the plural morpheme *-s* and the statement of the plural rule.

6 Negotiation as a context for modification of output. As revealed throughout the data so far, NNSs were offered different kinds of feedback during the course of negotiation, each of which had a different impact on their follow-up responses. In (2), for example, the NNS was given feedback through the open signals, *the windows have what?* and *I'm not sure what you're saying there*, and responded by re-pronouncing an earlier self-corrected version of *closed* and then inserting it into his new response. In (13), the NS addition of the plural *-s* morpheme to the NNS *glass* prompted the NNS to modify accordingly. Similarly, in (12), the NS choice of *can or cannot* to what appeared to have been an incomprehensible version of the NNS *can't* was followed by the NNS response of a modified version of her original utterance.

This phenomenon of feedback provision and response highlights yet another phenomenon, which Swain (1985) has claimed is also necessary for successful L2 learning. Swain has made the important point that comprehension of L2 input is necessary throughout the acquisition process, but that production of L2 output is also important, especially with regard to learners' ultimate L2 attainment. She argues that it is possible to understand the meaning of an utterance without reliance on or recognition of its morphology or syntax. However, in order to master an L2, learners must be given opportunities to produce 'comprehensible output', that is, to organize and syntactically structure their messages. That negotiation can promote such opportunities for learners is not only seen in the excerpts discussed above, but has been well documented in studies by Pica et al. (1989) and Pica et al. (1991).

What is particularly important is that during negotiation NNSs have opportunities to manipulate both their own lexical and syntactic resources as well as linguistic features in L2 input. For example, in (12), the NNS, in responding to NS signals elaborated her initial utterance, 'there is a sofa against a wall which I can't see' into 'the sofa I can see two legs' and 'I can see I can see, but I can see just two legs.' In these responses, the NNS substituted *two legs* as the object in her original verb *see*, then further modified *two legs* by use of *just*. As this example reveals, NNS output modification through responses to NS signals can involve addition of lexis (e.g. *just*) as well as insertion of new constituents, for example, *two legs*, into the production of L2 structures. And in excerpt (14), the NNS used *switch off* from the NS signal as a substitution for his own *switch on* to modify his original utterance.

(14) NS	NNS
	he forgot to switch on...
to switch off?	**he forgot to switch off**

7 Negotiation as a source of data for L2 development. In addition to evidence for the role of negotiation in assisting L2 comprehension, providing learners with feedback on their production, and offering them opportunities to modify their output—each considered important for successful L2 learning—there is a growing body of support for the role of negotiation in making the L2 accessible as data for building an L2 developmental system. (See, e.g. Gass and Varonis 1989; Holliday 1992, and Pica 1992). At present, research in this area is limited in scope, possibly due to conflicting theoretical positions on the nature of such data. Although all L2 learning theories place some degree of importance on L2 input as a source of data for L2 learning, they differ in their views on the nature and sufficiency of such data and on whether and how the data must be organized for L2 learning to proceed (Compare, for example, Krashen 1985, Schmidt and Frota 1986; and White 1988).

From a nativist theoretical perspective, such as that expressed in Cook 1988, sufficient L2 data would be that which allowed learners to reset the parameters of innate principles of language structure and to recognize restrictions on L2 lexis. Thus, useful L2 data would help learners identify whether complements preceded or followed the verbs and prepositions with which they are used. Such data would indicate to the learner whether the relationship among the subject *he*, the object *car*, and the verb *drive* would be *he a car drives* or *he* *drives a car*. Useful L2 data would also reveal which verbs allowed both prepositional phrase and dative constructions for indirect objects and which verbs allowed only prepositional phrase constructions. In English, for example, such data would reveal *gave* as a verb in the former category (as in *She gave some money to the scholarship fund* and *She gave the scholarship fund some money*) and *donate* in the latter (*She donated some money to the scholarship fund* but not **She donated the scholarship fund some money*).

From a theoretical perspective which assumes a more active language learner (see, e.g. Faerch and Kasper 1987), sufficient L2 data would be that which enabled learners to discover and induce L2 rules and structures through application of their own cognitive processing procedures. The L2 data could be identical to those described above, but the manner through which the learner accessed them would be different. Compared to the nativist structures of principles and parameters, a cognitive perspective would look to processes such as attention, induction, and generalization to explain how the learner could access L2 as data for L2 learning. However, what made these data useful for language learning could very well be the same as that described for the nativist perspective, that is, their encoding of relationships among subject, verb, and object categories.

Working from yet another theoretical perspective on L2 learning, Krashen (1983) has claimed that in order to learn a new form, learners must notice a difference between the new form and whatever forms are in their current level of competence. As Schmidt and Frota (1986) argue, learners need to 'notice the gap'. They must also have the opportunity, or perhaps a number of opportunities, to recognize and confirm the form in L2 input that they can understand. Accordingly, for Krashen and for others such as Long (1985a, 1985b, 1990) and Pica (1991), comprehension of L2 input is a particularly relevant condition for L2 learning, not only because comprehension of L2 meaning is an important skill for building L2 competence, but also because comprehension of L2 meaning appears to allow learners to induce structure from input, to focus on L2 form, and to recognize and confirm the form and its relationship to the encoding of meaning in L2.

Thus, even when L2 meaning is negotiated, but ultimately miscomprehended or misinterpreted by one interlocutor in ways not intended by the other (as demonstrated by Hawkins 1985), theoretically, the miscomprehending learner may still be benefiting from participation in this experience. This is because negotiation for L2 meaning can highlight L2 structural and semantic features that occur as interlocutors work to understand each other. Thus it is the work of negotiation toward mutual comprehension that may be as critical to language learning as the goal of comprehension itself.

Swain (1985), citing work from child language development, has proposed another way in which comprehension of L2 input might provide learners with L2 data, particularly with respect to relationships of form and meaning. She argues that understanding of L2 input frees up the learner's attention so that new L2 forms can be induced. Research on induction of form through comprehension has shown that this can indeed occur if learners are given a sufficient amount of time. Thus, VanPatten (1990) has shown that Spanish L2 learners were not able to induce a number of target forms after listening to four successive exposures to a Spanish passage which contained those forms within a single stretch of time. On the other hand, Doughty (1991) found the opposite results with English L2 learners' exposure to written texts, abundant in relative clauses, given to them over the course of ten days. Here, subjects' comprehension was highly related to their induction of rules for relative clause formation.

Given this theoretical and research context, where does negotiation of meaning fit in with provision of data for L2 learning? As noted above, research has shown that learners' participation in negotiation provides them with important opportunities and experiences for comprehension of L2 input, particularly through the many repetitions and rephrasings that occur therein. Such repetitions and reformulations of L2 input which occur during negotiation might also serve to highlight structural and semantic properties of L2 forms and point out L2 form–function relationships. This can be accomplished especially well when the repetitions and reformulations require that L2 items be extracted or segmented from the utterance in which they had initially appeared, then uttered in isolation or embedded or repositioned into new utterances. In this way, the repetition and modification of L2 input which make it comprehensible might also help to make salient those features such as individual words and forms, relationships between L2 forms and the meanings they encode, and structural relationships into which the L2 forms can enter.

As the excerpts given thus far have shown, such relationships can appear in two distinct aspects of linguistic modification. Lexical relationships can be seen again in (6), through the NS repetition, rephrasing, and elaboration of preceding input, that is, the NS utterance(s) which had triggered the NNS signal. Here the NS added *hold it together* in response to the learner's query about *hinges*.

Presentation of structural relationships to the NNS can also be seen in (6) through segmentation and movement of units in the triggering input. Here the NS extracted *hinges* from his original input in response to the NNS question about it and in so doing, the NS moved it from its original position as object of *has* to subject position in the phrase *hold it together*, which provided its definition.

The preceding analysis of excerpt (6) has been used to illustrate ways in which the linguistic manipulations which occur during negotiation can draw learners' attention to L2 lexical and structural relationships. That such manipulations are common throughout NS–NNS negotiation can be seen in Tables 1 and 2. Summarized there are the results of a quantitative analysis of the signal and response utterances of 20 NSs as they negotiated with their NNS partners on four oral communication tasks, which revolved around the transmission and exchange of information and opinions. Among the utterances included in the analysis were those of excerpt (6) as well as many of the excerpts featured throughout this paper. A total of 1,257 response and signal utterances were analyzed with respect to their lexical and structural modification.

Table 1. Frequencies and proportions of NS utterances of response to NNS signals for twenty NS–NNS dyads on four communication tasks.

Types of NS Utterances of Response:	n NS utterances of response	% NS utterances of response
without Repetition or Modification of original NS input	169	24
with Repetition of original NS input	12	2
with Modification of original NS input	467	67
with Repetition or Modification of NNS Signal	51	8
Total	699	

Types of Modification in NS Utterances of Response to NNS Signals

Types of Modification	n NS modified utterances of response	% NS modified utterances of response
Lexical	227	48
Structural	129	28
Lexical + Structural	111	24
Total	467	

As shown in Table 1, it was found that of a total of 699 NS utterances of response to NNS signals, 467 or 67 percent were modified linguistically. Among these 467 modified utterances, 48 percent contained at least one lexical modification, 28 percent contained one or more structural modifications, and the remainder contained both lexical and structural modifications. A similar pattern was found in NS signal utterances to learners during negotiation. As revealed in Table 2, 79 percent of a total of 558 signal utterances were modified. Forty percent of these 558 modified signal utterances contained at least one lexical modification, 42 percent contained at least one structural modification, and the remainder contained both types of modifications.

This analysis has shed light on the scope and abundance of input manipulation and modification in NS signal and response utterances of negotiation. What remains a provocative, but as yet unanswered, question, however, is exactly how such input modification is used by L2 learners as they are confronted with the formal and functional possibilities of the L2 and search for useful data for L2 learning.

8 The central role of negotiation in L2 learning. What makes negotiation particularly distinctive as a type of communication for L2 learning is that

Table 2. Frequencies and proportions of NS signal utterances to NNSs for twenty Ns–NNs dyads on four communication tasks.

Types of NS Signal Utterances:	n signal utterances	% signal utterances
without Repetition/Modification of original NNS utterance	67	12
with Repetition of original NNS utterance	49	9
with Linguistic Modification of original NNS utterance	442	79
Total	558	

Types of Modification in NS Signal Utterances

Types of Modification	n NS modified signal utterances	% NS modified signal utterances
Lexical	179	40
Structural	184	42
Lexical + Structural	79	18
Total	442	100

whereas the role of communication in general has been disputed with respect to the learning process, a more central place can be seen for negotiation. Thus, as Higgs and Clifford (1982) have argued, too early a focus on communication can lead learners to stabilize an understandable yet nontarget-like variety of L2 and thereby dampen their motivation, or even their ability, for further L2 development. They argue that learners' participation in communication can provide opportunities for L2 practice, but it is practice of what has already been learned that can prevent learners from moving beyond their current developmental levels of comprehension and production. Although negotiation is also a kind of communication, it bears little relationship to the modes of practice to which Higgs and Clifford are so opposed. Communicative practice is focused on L2 use, often at the learner's current level of proficiency. Negotiation, by nature, is focused on mutual comprehension. This requires learners to come to understand new and unfamiliar L2 input, modify their own output toward comprehensibility, and thereby use communication to participate in the L2 learning process.

Further, Sato (1986) has noted that communication enables learners to use their interlocutor as a resource, leading to fluent discourse, but at the same time minimizing their need to adjust their own output toward more target-like production. In her research on two young male L2 learners of English, what this often meant was that to establish and continue references to past time, the boys relied on the use of past tense markers by their interlocutors and the context of the communicative situation in which they shared background knowledge with them. This led to fluent discourse, but had little, if any impact on the learners' own grammatical marking.

In negotiation, on the other hand, the demands for precision are such that learners have been shown to adjust their L2 output both grammatically and lexically, increasingly so in communication tasks which require attention to L2 form and structure. (See, for example, Goldstein and Conrad 1990; and Pica, Porter, Paninos, and Linell in preparation). Thus, in looking at the impact of writing conferences on English L2 students' subsequent written performance, Goldstein and Conrad found that learners wrote qualitatively better drafts after they had negotiated with their teachers the meaning of their compositions as well as their proposed strategies for revision. Compositions improved markedly when revisions regarding composition structure and detail were negotiated rather than simply embedded within a question-and-answer sequence. Pica et al. (in preparation) have found that asking L2 learners to reconstruct a picture narrative by exchanging their own unique portions of details brought about not only negotiation, but negotiation targeted toward learners' adjustments in verb tense and aspect marking; for example, a learner would modify the uninflected verb in *she turn on the stove* to *turned* and *turning* when asked to provide clarity about a story sequence.

Other researchers, such as Schmidt and Frota (1986), have shown, through language learner data, that even when learners communicate successfully in L2, they fail to notice nontarget-like features in their interlanguage unless these are indicated them explicitly. As will be addressed below, negotiation heightens communication in ways which push learners along the course of L2 development and provide them with access to L2 data for their learning. Although not a pervasive characteristic of negotiation, such occurrences are found, as was shown in example (13). There, the NS cited a rule for pluralization in negotiating with the NNS about his production of *glass* and *glasses*. A further example is given in (15), in which the negotiation leads to NS instruction on pronunciation of *flower*. (See Pica 1991 for further discussion and examples).

(15) NS	NNS
	and left tree is a [flo: wer]
is what?	**[flo: wer]**
a what?	**a [flo: wer] [o]**
yeah get the book	**[flow er]**
oh a flaUer	flaUer oh pronunciation is very difficult
	flaUer

flaU:	*eh? flower*
um	*what's [f]?*
[f...o...]	[aU]
you hold your tongue and go [au]	

9 The social sources and forces of negotiation. The multiple contributions that negotiation between learners and interlocutors can make to the L2 learning process have focused researchers' attention on the social contexts conducive to negotiation, ranging from those contexts which make negotiation possible to those which make it highly likely for negotiation to occur. After all, negotiation is not inevitable when learners and interlocutors communicate with each other. Research has shown that whether negotiation is viewed as an outcome of social interaction or as the process through which social interaction is constructed, it is influenced by the negotiators themselves—their roles and relationships, their familiarity with their topic and with each other, and the distribution, transfer, and exchange of information among them.

Frequently, topics and referents are so mutually familiar that learners and interlocutors are confronted with few impasses in their communication over which they can negotiate. Or, as Long (1980, 1983) has shown, what can also happen is that when troublesome topics or unclear referents arise, learners and interlocutors abandon them or switch to new ones. At other times, a topic may be more familiar to one than the other interlocutor. Although this might bode well for negotiation, what can happen when the topic-familiar interlocutor holds other kinds of power and authority over the communication, the other interlocutor may feel reluctant to initiate negotiation for fear of appearing uncooperative or creating further social distance. In a classroom context, an imbalance in familiarity with the topic can create conditions in which learners are reluctant to initiate negotiation as signalling a lack of understanding might suggest a lack of competence or loss of attention on their part. This situation, discussed in detail in Pica (1987b), is illustrated in (16), as the teacher's numerous checks on students' comprehension is followed by silence on their parts.

(16) NS Teacher	NNS students
⇒do you understand all that?	(silence)
⇒you wrote sneezes right?	yes
ok the rest of the words are pretty easy	
if if a person happened to sneeze	
⇒you know do you know what happened means?	(silence)
something happened it occurs it takes place	
so if a person if it happened that a person sneezed?	
⇒do you understand this?	(silence)
nobody's saying anything	yes
hmn you understood it and you got it right	
ok read the next one	

Further limiting the amount of negotiation that can occur during communication is the possibility that when learners interact with NSs familiar with the features of their interlanguage, the NSs have little need to ask them for clarification. This deprives the learners of the kinds of negotiation that can provide feedback on their interlanguage or opportunities for them to modify their production toward comprehensibility. The element of familiarity can make classrooms particularly unfavorable as contexts for negotiation. As discussed in Pica (1987b), the L2 teacher is especially vulnerable in this area and therefore will have to look to other variables which condition negotiation. Fortunately, as research has revealed, there are many such variables.

Some of the things that make negotiation favorable for social purposes, such as to facilitate communication, make negotiation unfavorable for certain processes of L2 learning. As work by Hawkins (1985), noted above, has revealed, learners can negotiate during guessing game type tasks, while at the same time misunderstand the meaning of what was being negotiated. Further, as the data in this paper have shown, negotiation signals are often simple, open questions such as *What?* or *huh?* or statements such as *I don't understand.* Such signals provide an excellent opportunity for the NNS to respond by modifying initially incomprehensible output. However, they carry no explicit information on L2 form and function relationships.

Taken together, what this body of research has suggested is that within the communicative activity of L2 learners, participation in negotiation is not a guaranteed social experience. Further, there is considerable variation in the L2 learning opportunities that negotiation can offer. This latter point is evident in a comparison of (2) and (12) with (7) and (8). In (2) and (12), the signals of the NS were followed by responses of modified output from the NNS. This may have been a function of the NS signal itself, which incorporated words perceived from the NNS as unclear utterance into statements of incomprehension and wh- and or-choice questions. In (12), for example, the NS provided the choice of *can or cannot* to what appeared to be an incomprehensible version of the NNS *can't*. The NNS was able to use this signal as feedback to respond with a modified version of her original utterance. In (2), the NS questions and statements about the incomprehensibility of the NNS *closed* elicited NNS responses of repetition until the NS was able to follow what the NNS had been trying to communicate.

However, the NS signals of (7) and (8), as well as two of the signals of (9), re-coded the NNS utterances with more target-like forms. These utterances needed only to be acknowledged by the NNS in order for the interaction to continue. Thus, in (7), the NS modified both NNS noun phrases in *dog is um right hand of girl* by inserting definite articles. In (8), the NS provided a more target-like pronunciation of the NNS *bik*. Both signals offered the NNSs feedback which was directly focused on their original utterances. Rather than repeat or modify their original utterances, however, the NNSs simply acknowledged the NS signal as encoding the meaning they had intended.

Such negotiation outcomes and signal–response patterns are not unique to these few excerpts from NS–NNS data. Studies by Holliday (1987, 1988), Pica

(1987a), Pica, Holliday, Lewis, and Morgenthaler (1989), and Pica, Lewis, and Holliday (1990), have provided statistical evidence that NNSs are more likely to modify their output to signals posed as open requests for clarification or or-choice questions than to signals formed as model versions of their original utterance. Thus, signals given during negotiation, while always worthwhile as L2 input to the learning process, can vary in the extent to which they provide feedback to language learners.

On a more promising note, however, what has also been revealed, in (10) and (15) for example, is that NS signals which model NNSs initial utterances are often part of a longer negotiation sequence, after an open request fails to elicit an NNS response that allows communication to proceed. In (10), for example, the NNS goes from the initial signal *hmmm hmmm* to subsequent segmentations and repetitions of his NNS interlocutor. In (15), the NS opens up *is what* and *what* into helpful repronunciations for the NNS. (See Sacks, Schegloff, and Jefferson 1974 for similar findings on NS–NS discourse).

One additional note of promise is that the confirmation signal–affirmation response sequence may be typical only when NNSs communicate with NSs. Research currently underway (See Pica et al. in preparation) has revealed a different pattern when NNSs communicate with other NNSs. This can be seen in (17), in which NNS responses of *dark* and *entrance is two steps* were characterized respectively by lexical and syntactic modifications of initial output rather than affirmations of the other's model.

(17) NNS	NNS
roof is very black	*black?*
⇒**dark**	dark yeah hmmn
two stone steps	*yeah steps its a entrance?*
⇒**entrance is two steps**	yeah yeah two steps

Finally, the negotiation that best meets learner needs appears to depend on the learner's L2 developmental level. Results of research to date suggest that negotiation might be most helpful to L2 learning processes at levels beyond the early stages of L2 learning. Although beginning learners do enter into negotiation, they are more likely to do so as input receivers than output providers, probably due to lack of linguistic resources for output modification. This has been revealed in studies by Pica (1987a) and Holliday (1987, 1988), and was illustrated in the signal–response sequences of negotiation in (7) and (8) and in (18). What typically happens when the beginner produces an unclear utterance is that the NS signals by repeating or reformulating the utterance. As was discussed above, such signals operate as models to be confirmed to which the NNS need respond only with a form of *yes*.

Advanced and even intermediate NNSs, on the other hand, often make self-repairs of what they perceive to be a lack of clarity in their production. When negotiation does occur, it is less about clarity and comprehensibility and more about opinion and interpretability.

(18) NS	NNS
	I think on the front is a small stone
on the front?	**⇒yeah oh doors**
in the front of the door?	**⇒yeah**
there is a small step, yes?	**⇒oh yes**

Finally, with respect to the relationship between negotiation and L2 learning over time, only speculations can be made in light of existing research. There is a substantial amount of research to document that negotiation signals have an immediate impact on learner production with respect to clarification of meaning and manipulation of form. However, what has yet to be studied systematically is the extent to which such learner modifications become internalized within the interlanguage system and/or carry over to later use.

10 The social desirability of negotiation. Just as negotiation is not inevitable when learners and interlocutors engage in social interaction, so too is negotiation not always necessary or desirable. Indeed, some of the things that make negotiation favorable for learning L2 form and function make negotiation unfavorable for social purposes. A steady stream of clarification questions, when asked by either interlocutor, can be a source of frustration in attempts to move a conversation forward. And as Aston (1986) has argued, negotiation moves can be an annoyance to NSs within conversational discourse. Further, Porter (1986) has shown that L2 learners often use negotiation moves that are too explicit, direct, and generally sociolinguistically inappropriate in form for the contexts in which they are seeking clarity of input. Thus, both the quantity and quality of negotiation require a bit of fine-tuning. This is an area of concern which can be informed by research on NS–NS interaction

What is often observed during NS–NS interaction is restraint from making requests for clarification, which can impact favorably in the direction of both interlocutors. (See again Sacks, Schegloff, and Jefferson 1974). The interlocutor who needs clarification can often find it only a few turns away. And the interlocutor whose speech is not clear, when given an opportunity to hold the floor and speak at length, can often repair and clarify meaning without having to be told about incomprehensibility as it arises. Certainly the stresses, strains, and expectations of everyday social interaction are such that L2 learners should not be led to assume that negotiation is the only type of communication in which to engage when they are having difficulty understanding message meaning. Too much negotiation may lead to no communication at all.

Still and all, however, negotiation is too precious a commodity in the L2 learning process to be deemed undesirable for the learner. This is where classrooms designed as contexts for negotiation can best serve learner needs to comprehend L2 input, to gain feedback on, and opportunities to, modify production, and to focus attention on L2 relationships of form and meaning. Too often, perhaps, the communicative movement in language teaching has tried so hard to replicate contexts of communication outside the classroom that it has deprived learners of the opportunity to negotiate inside the classroom. Thus, target language behaviors have been equated with L2 learning behaviors. This equation of communication and learning has focused attention on objectives aimed at successful communication and on activities designed to put classroom participants into the social relationship of native and of nonnative speakers rather than that of teachers and learners. In effect, teaching language for communication has placed an emphasis on the learning of target behaviors at the expense of the activation of learning behaviors.

11 Social meaning of negotiation for L2 learners. What is the social meaning of negotiation for L2 learners? If negotiation is seen as the work that learners and interlocutors do to assist the L2 learning process, it is not target language communication that should be emphasized in the classroom, but rather, the language learning processes that can be created therein. Why would learners choose to negotiate? How can we provide conditions under which they would want and need to do so? These questions can best be answered in light of what research has revealed about the conditions under which negotiation can best occur.

First, research has shown that negotiation is favored when there is mutual recognition and concern for each other's objectives among interlocutors. Both participants must be aware of the objectives of their interaction, both their own objectives and those of their interlocutors, and must be willing to work toward mutual attainment. As research has shown, there is more negotiation when learners and their interlocutors are given activities and tasks whose completion depends on the transfer of information from one to the other or the pooling or exchanging of individually held information. Tasks referred to respectively as 'information gap' and 'jig-saw' have been shown to be superior in this regard. As revealed in research on these tasks (by Doughty and Pica 1986, Gass and Varonis 1986, and Pica et al. 1989), even simple assignments such as explaining a picture for a partner to replicate, pooling clues to solve a mystery, or sharing details in order to assemble a picture have been shown to be effective because they require that learners and interlocutors take each others' needs into account at the outset of the communication and to respond to these needs as they arise.

In contrast, more reflective, often socially provocative tasks involving debates, decisions, and problem-solving can, and often do, inspire little negotiation. What often happens is that one L2 learner dominates the debate, makes a decision, or solves the problem while the other less-assertive learners listen, either with tacit or feigned agreement. (See Pica, Kanagy, and Falodun 1993 for a review of these studies; Crookes and Rulon 1985; Doughty and Pica 1986; Duff 1986, Gass and Varonis 1985; Hawkins 1985, Long 1980, Pica 1989;

Rulon and McCreary 1986 for data on some of the actual studies). Such a contrast can be seen in the modest 'plant the garden' task of (19a) and (19b) and the more serious 'adoption' and 'heart transplant' debates of (20a) and (20b). The (a) and (b) versions of these tasks, representing teacher-directed and student group work, are provided to show that even when the teacher participates in a negotiation-oriented activity, others in the class have opportunities to participate in L2 learning processes. Such is not the case, however, in either the teacher-directed or student group debates.

In (19a) and (19b), taken from a low intermediate class of English L2 learners, each participant had sole possession of some of the flowers to be planted according to a master garden plan, hidden from everyone's view. To replicate the master, participants had to exchange information about flower appearance and placement. In (19a), one student was shown taking a turn to describe his flower to the other classroom participants. In (19b) in which four students worked together on the task, the student in column 1 is shown taking a turn to describe the flower; later the student in column 4 took such a turn. Even though this latter student engaged in negotiation only a little during the earlier phase of the task, she took quite a few opportunities to do so during her turn.

(19a)

Student	Other Participants: teacher (T) and students (S)
the flower is a bowl is uh left side on the bottom and has blue color eh dark blue color and the middle of this dark blue color you can see light blue color	S triangles?
	S triangles?
light blue color	S triangle?
triangle	S triangle
and what else do you want to know?	S which position? vertical?
	S is on the left? normal position?
is the normal position up on the left on bottom ... of the board	S *left is in- in the middle ... in the top?*
	S *in the middle down*
	S *left at the bottom?*
no at the bottom	S *at the top or the bottom?*
	S *bottom?*
	S *bottom or top?*
	S *up or down?*
	S *where is it please?*
top	Ss top top

(19b) (from Pica and Doughty 1985)

L2 learner (1)	L2 learner (2)	L2 learner (3)	L2 learner (4)
the stem is yellow and			
it has two	*two leave?*		
one dark green			
the other blue and			
it is on the top	uhuh		
right side	mmm		
	position?		
vertical corner?			
corner?		*normal vertical?*	
ahha normal position			
the other one is			
I don't know			
like uh this how			
you call this		*squir?*	
square? square? just off the corner?			**yeah quadratic**
yes square just on			
the corner			
yes ok			

(later, during the same activity)

L2 learner (1)	L2 learner (2)	L2 learner (3)	L2 learner (4)
			the nother flower is a triangle of violet and two dark green leaves
		two dark green leaves?	yes
	I think you have several violet		
it's light violet?			**yes light violet light violet** there is a blue estem inside the triangle and two dark green leaves
		yeah	right is in the right left side down
um *on the left?*			**left side** is not down the tree but it's beside the tree and the position's horizontal which the leave is going to the left
but is down? is down?			**down ... left down ... beside the tree ... not**

		down the tree it's beside the tree but you don't put this flower beside the tree you put a little bit down beside the tree
		you know what I mean?
ok	**ok**	finished?
yes		

Excerpts (20a) and (20b) were taken from Values Clarification tasks used in a low intermediate class, in which all participants (teacher and students) had access to the same text of information to be used in coming to a consensus. The text used in (20a) described the characteristics of five families to be used for a class decision as to which one family should be allowed to adopt a child. The text in (20b) described the characteristics of five patients to be used by a group of four students in deciding which one patient was most eligible for a heart transplant. Each excerpt is illustrative of question-answer communication, without the need for negotiation.

(20a) NNS Teacher	L2 Learners
all right, which family do you think i-which families are too old to have children?	
which families are right- are old enough or a good age to have children?	number one
all right, so the first one ... what's good about them is they're the right age and also?	the health
the health ... they're in good health.	
all right. who else should we consider? ... all right.	
so family one's strong-strongest points are they're a good age for having children and also their health is-you know good health.	
all right. who else should we consider?	number three
number three (Pica and Doughty 1985)	

(20b)

L2 learner (1)	L2 learner (2)	L2 learner (3)	L2 learner (4)
	I think Carlos Whannon		
Why Carlos			
Whannon?	because he is		
	more young	is very young	
but-		very young	
maybe	he has a lot of life for-		
I think they			
Elena-I think			
he isn't old			
and he isn't			
young	but what? ... I think-		
	I don't know is very		
	difficult but I think is		
	Elena Rodriguez too		
is singer	because she is very young		
but is sing in			
the Metropolitan			
Opera	ok go go to um	look look in your family	
	this- no-		
um no?	*everybody ok?*	**ok**	
the second maybe		ok Elena singer in the	
		Metropolitan Opera	
		divorced two children ok	
	maybe	Franklin Jones	
	Helen Jackson three children		
	and four eight and ten		
maybe	what's that? maybe but I think		
	the most important the two most		
	important is Elena Rodriquez		
	and Carlos Whannon (Pica and Doughty 1985)		

The excerpts seem especially important for language teachers to bear in mind as they structure their classes toward communication. Even the most provocative content cannot promote negotiation if learners do not share in the objectives of the task they are assigned. Further, even beginning learners can be involved in negotiation, as they can be given simple content to work with and still be drawn toward negotiation to complete classroom tasks. It has even been suggested by Clarke (1991) that teachers and learners should negotiate classroom objectives. This may lead to a double dose of negotiation, in both negotiation of objectives and activities to meet these objectives. Investigation is needed into this all important area of classroom life.

Research has also revealed that questions are particularly influential in promoting and impeding negotiation. What studies have shown is that negotiation is promoted by questions which signal lack of understanding on the part of the question poser and impeded by questions which seek to evaluate an expected answer. The former are especially abundant in the circumstances described above, that is, both interlocutors are aware of each other's goals and work toward meeting them, and in so doing, must take into account each others' needs for comprehension. Thus the usual classroom staple of evaluation questions whereby teachers ask learners to display what teachers know already, although still alive and well even in communicative classrooms (See Long and Sato 1983 and Pica and Long 1986), needs to be replaced by signalling questions which seek clarification of what has been said. And there need to be opportunities for both teachers and students to ask such questions. When asked by teachers, these questions provide important feedback to learners on their production and provide them with opportunities to modify their output. When asked by learners, these questions provide them with access toward input they can understand. Such a complementation is revealed in (21):

(21) NS Teacher	L2 Learners
why don't we talk about the words together	
all right start with the first—	
do you know what whales mean?	
what a whale is? anybody know?	*whale?*
whale? W-H- first word is a big animal	
	in in ocean
right yeah	
do you know do you understand that?	*the big?*
the big big big fish the biggest fish	

Third, negotiation can occur in the presence of a need for one interlocutor to transfer information to the other. This information can be distributed and re-distributed in various ways. It can be held initially by one interlocutor or can be differentially distributed, then mutually shared or exchanged. There is less negotiation, however, in typical communication tasks, in which information is accessible to all participants, used in debating an issue or reaching a decision. In such instances, where participants start off knowing what each other already know, there is likely to be shared comprehension to begin with, hence little need to work toward it through negotiation.

Finally, the affective environment conducive to negotiation is one in which face-threatening moves are kept to a minimum. Negotiation occurs in an environment in which displays of incomprehension do not reveal the weaknesses of L2 learners, but rather their strength as workers completing an information transfer task in which they play a pivotal role. In this respect, those tasks which require the transfer and exchange of information are especially important, not because they provide problems to be solved, but because they force interlocutors to take account of listeners' needs, knowledge, and goals, and to make their meanings as explicit as possible, adjusting their language when necessary. In other words, learners must be made to feel that they need to seek help because it is the task which is difficult rather than it is they who are weak.

12 Negotiation and classroom communication. This paper began by addressing the role played by negotiation as an important aspect of communication that serves a role in the process of L2 learning. Given the possibilities that communication brings to L2 learning through negotiation, it is important that approaches to instruction which espouse communication expand their emphasis on target language objectives to serve learners with respect to the L2 learning process. Thus, the paper has ended with a return to classroom issues and the ways in which the communicative classroom might provide an environment for successful L2 learning. Actually, what needs to be done seems quite simple. Learners need to feel like learners, not like the NNSs they are outside the classroom and not like the NSs they will never be, but in accordance with their goals for L2 learning.

Of course, learners also need to be prepared to continue learning outside the classroom, in contexts where they will operate as NNSs. They need to be helped to find socially appropriate ways to learn language through communication, through participation in tasks which are socially appropriate to this goal, and through instruction on both strategies for managing conversations and social skills for getting L2 input. Further, learners need to know when to negotiate and when NOT to negotiate and to be able to strike a balance between signalling a need for clarification and suspending such signalling when necessary. What needs to be emphasized throughout these learning experiences is that negotiation is a collaborative activity, as both learners and their interlocutors modify and adjust their messages in their attempts to manage their L2 communication and sustain the L2 learning process.

REFERENCES

Aston, Guy. 1986. Trouble shooting in interaction with learners: The more the merrier? Applied Linguistics 7.128–43.

Birdsong, David. 1989. Metalinguistic performance and interlinguistic competence. New York: Springer.

Blau, Elaine. 1982. The effect of syntax on readability for ESL students in Puerto Rico. TESOL Quarterly 16.517–28.

Brumfit, Christopher, and Keith Johnson (eds.) 1979. The communicative approach in language teaching. Oxford: Oxford University Press.

Canale, Michael, and Merrill Swain. 1980. Theoretical bases of communicative approaches to second language teaching and testing. Applied Linguistics 1.1–47.

Cervantes, Raul. 1983. 'Say it again, Sam': The effect of repetition on dictation scores. Term paper, University of Hawaii at Manoa. [In Long, Michael H. 1985. Input and second language acquisition theory. Input in Second Language Acquisition, ed. by Susan Gass and Carolyn G. Madden, 377–93. Rowley, MA: Newbury House.]

Chaudron, Craig. 1983. Simplification of input: Topic reinstatements and their effect on L2 learners' recognition and recall. TESOL Quarterly 17.437–58.

Chaudron, Craig. 1985. Intake: On models and methods for discovering learners' processing of input. Studies in Second Language Acquisition 7.1–14.

Clarke, David. 1991. The negotiated syllabus: What it is and how is it likely to work? Applied Linguistics 12.13–28.

Cook, Vivian J. 1988. Chomsky's Universal Grammar: An Introduction. Oxford: Basic Blackwell.

Crookes, Graham. 1986. Task classification: A cross-disciplinary review. The Center for Second Language Classroom Research/Social Science Research Institute, University of Hawaii at Manoa. Technical report No. 4.

Crookes, Graham, and Kathryn Rulon. 1985. Incorporation of corrective feedback in native speaker/nonnative speaker conversation. The Center for Second Language Classroom Research/ Social Science Research Institute, University of Hawaii at Manoa. Technical report No. 3.

Day, Richard R. (ed.) 1986. Talking to learn: Conversation in second language acquisition. Rowley, MA: Newbury House.

Doughty, Catherine. 1991. Second language instruction does make a difference: Evidence from an empirical study of SL relativization. Studies in Second Language Acquisition 13.431–70.

Doughty, Catherine, and Teresa Pica. 1986. Information gap tasks: An aid to second language acquisition? TESOL Quarterly 20.305–25.

Duff, P. 1986. Another look at interlanguage talk: Taking task to task. Talking to learn: Conversation in second language acquisition, ed. by Richard R. Day, 147–81. Rowley, MA: Newbury House.

Farrah, Iffat. 1991. Term paper. University of Pennsylvania.

Faerch, Claus, and Gabriele Kasper. 1987. The role of comprehension in second language acquisition. Applied Linguistics 8.256–74.

Garfinkel, H. 1967. Studies in ethnomethodology. Englewood Cliffs, NJ: Prentice-Hall.

Gass, Susan and Evangeline Varonis. 1984. The effect of familiarity on the comprehensibility of nonnative speech. Language Learning 34.65–89.

Gass, Susan, and Evangeline Varonis. 1985. Task variation and NNS/NNS negotiation of meaning. Input in second language acquisition, ed. by Susan Gass and Carolyn G. Madden, 149–61. Rowley, MA: Newbury House.

Gass, Susan, and Evangeline Varonis. 1986. Sex differences in NNS/NNS interactions. Talking to learn: Conversation in second language acquisition, ed. by Richard R. Day, 327–51. Rowley, MA: Newbury House.

Gass, Susan, and Evangeline Varonis. 1989. Incorporated repairs in NNS discourse. The dynamic interlanguage, ed. by M. Eisenstein. New York: Plenum.

Goldstein, Lynn, and Susan Conrad. 1990. Student input and negotiation of meaning in ESL writing conferences. TESOL Quarterly 24.443–59.

Hatch, Evelyn M. 1978a. Acquisition of syntax in a second language. Understanding second and foreign language learning, ed. by Jack C. Richards, 34–70. Rowley, MA: Newbury House.

Hatch, Evelyn M. 1978b. Discourse analysis and second language acquisition. Second language acquisition: A book of readings, ed. by Evelyn M. Hatch, 401–35. Rowley, MA: Newbury House.

Hawkins, Barbara. 1985. Is 'an appropriate response' always so appropriate? Input in second language acquisition, ed. by Susan Gass and Carolyn G. Madden, 162–80. Rowley, MA: Newbury House.

Higgs, Theodore, and Raymond Clifford. 1982. The push toward communication. Curriculum, competence, and the foreign language teacher, ed. by T. Higgs. Skokie, IL: National Textbook Co.

Holliday, Lloyd. 1992. NS syntactic modifications in NS–NNS negotiation as input data for second language acquisition of syntax. Philadelphia: University of Pennsylvania unpublished Ph.D. dissertation.

Holliday, Lloyd. 1987. NS–NNS negotiations in spoken interaction to eliminate comprehension difficulties. Philadelphia: University of Pennsylvania Ms.

Holliday, Lloyd. 1988. Let them talk: A study of native—nonnative interaction in conversation. Working Papers in Educational Linguistics 4.89–100. Philadelphia: University of Pennsylvania Graduate School of Education.

Howatt, Anthony P.R. 1984. A history of English language teaching. Oxford: Oxford University Press.

Johnson, Patricia. 1981. Effects of reading comprehension on language complexity and cultural background of a text. TESOL Quarterly 15.169–81.

Kelch, Ken. 1985. Modified input as an aid to comprehension. Studies in Second Language Acquisition 7.81–90.

Kelly, L. G. 1969. Twenty-five centuries of language teaching. Rowley, MA: Newbury House.

Krashen, Stephen. 1980. Second language acquisition and second language learning. Oxford: Pergamon Press.

Krashen, Stephen. 1983. Newmark's ignorance hypothesis and current second language acquisition theory. Language Transfer in Language Learning, ed. by Susan Gass and Larry Selinker, 135–56. Rowley, MA: Newbury House.

Krashen, Stephen. 1985. The Input Hypothesis: Issues and implications. London: Longman.

Krashen, Stephen, and Tracy D. Terrell. 1983. The Natural Approach: Language acquisition in the classroom. Oxford: Pergamon.

Long, Michael H. 1980. Input, interaction, and second language acquisition. UCLA. Ph.D. dissertation.

Long, Michael H. 1981. Input, interaction, and second language acquisition. Native Language and Foreign Language Acquisition, ed. by Harris Winitz, 379.259–78. New York: Annals of the New York Academy of Sciences.

Long, Michael H. 1983. Linguistic and conversational adjustments to nonnative speakers. Studies in Second Language Acquisition 5.177–94.

Long, Michael H. 1985a. Input and second language acquisition theory. Input in second language acquisition, ed. by Susan Gass and Carolyn G. Madden, 377–93. Rowley, MA: Newbury House.

Long, Michael H. 1985b. A role for instruction in second language acquisition: Task-based language training. Modelling and assessing second language acquisition, ed. by K. Hyltenstam and M. Pienemann, 77–99. London: Multilingual Matters.

Long, Michael H. 1990. The least a second language acquisition theory needs to explain. University of Hawai'i Working Papers in ESL 9.59–75.

Long, Michael H., and Charlene Sato. 1983. Classroom foreigner talk discourse: Forms and functions of teachers' questions. Classroom oriented research in second language acquisition, ed. by Herbert W. Seliger and Michael H. Long, 268–85. Rowley, MA: Newbury House.

Pica, Teresa. 1987a. Interlanguage adjustments as an outcome of NS–NNS negotiated interaction. Language Learning 38.45–73.

Pica, Teresa. 1987b. Second language acquisition, social interaction, and the classroom. Applied Linguistics 8.1–25.

Pica, Teresa. 1991. Classroom interaction, participation, and comprehension: Redefining relationships. System 19.437–52.

Pica, Teresa. 1992. The textual outcomes of native speaker–nonnative speaker negotiation. Text and context: Cross-disciplinary perspectives on language study, ed. by Claire Kramsch and Sally McConnell-Ginet, 198–237. Lexington, MA: D.C. Heath and Co.

Pica, Teresa, and Catherine Doughty. 1985. Nonnative speaker interaction in the ESL classroom. Input in Second Language Acquisition, ed. by Susan Gass and Carolyn G. Madden, 115–32. Rowley, MA: Newbury House.

Pica, Teresa, Catherine Doughty, and Richard Young. 1986. Making input comprehensible: Do interactional modifications help? ITL Review of Applied Linguistics 72.1–25.

Pica, Teresa, Lloyd Holliday, Nora Lewis, Dom Berducci, and Jeanne Newman. 1991. Language learning through interaction: What role does gender play? Studies in Second Language Acquisition 13, 3.343–76.

Pica, Teresa, Lloyd Holliday, Nora Lewis, and L. Morgenthaler. 1989. Comprehensible output as an outcome of linguistic demands on the learner. Studies in Second Language Acquisition 11.63–90.

Pica, Teresa, Ruth Kanagy, and Sola Falodun. 1993. Choosing and using communication tasks for second language research and instruction. Task-based learning in a second language, ed. by Susan Gass and Graham Crookes, 9–34. London: Multilingual Matters.

Pica, Teresa, Nora Lewis, and Lloyd Holliday. 1990. NS–NNS negotiation: An equal opportunity for speech modification? Paper presented to annual TESOL Convention, San Francisco, March, 1990.

Pica, Teresa, Felicia Lincoln-Porter, Diana Paninos, and Julian Linnell. In preparation. What can second language learners learn from each other? Only their researchers know for sure. University of Pennsylvania.

Pica, Teresa, and Michael H. Long. 1986. The linguistic and conversational performance of experienced and inexperienced teachers. Talking to Learn: Conversation in Second Language Acquisition, ed. by Richard R. Day, 85–98. Rowley, MA: Newbury House.

Pica, Teresa, Richard Young, and Catherine Doughty. 1987. The impact of interaction on comprehension. TESOL Quarterly 21.737–58.

Porter, Patricia. 1986. How learners talk to each other: Input and interaction in task-centered discussions. Talking to learn: Conversation in second language acquisition, ed. by Richard R. Day. Rowley, MA: Newbury House

Pruitt, Dean G. 1981. Negotiation behavior. New York: Academic Press.

Putnam, L. and T. Jones. 1982. The role of communication in bargaining. Human Communication Research 8.262–80.

Richards, Jack C. 1985. The secret life of methods. The context of language teaching, ed. by Jack C. Richards, 32–45. Cambridge: Cambridge University Press.

Richards, Jack C., and T. Rodgers. 1986. Approaches and methods in language teaching. Cambridge: Cambridge University Press.

Rubin, J., and B. Brown. 1975. The social psychology of bargaining and negotiation. New York: Harper and Row.

Rulon, Kathryn, and Jan McCreary. 1986. Negotiation of content: Teacher-fronted and small group interaction. Talking to learn: Conversation in second language acquisition, ed. by Richard R. Day, 182–99. Rowley, MA: Newbury House.

Sacks, H., Emanuel Schegloff, and Gail Jefferson. 1974. A simplest systematics for the organization of turn-taking for conversation. Language 50.694–735.

Sato, Charlene. 1986. Conversation and interlanguage development: Rethinking the connection. Talking to learn: Conversation in second language acquisition, ed. by Richard R. Day, 23–48. Rowley, MA: Newbury House.

Savignon, Sandra. 1983. Communicative competence: Theory and classroom practice. Reading, MA: Addison-Wesley.

Schachter, Jacqueline. 1983. Nutritional needs of language learners. On TESOL '82: Pacific perspectives on language learning and teaching, ed. by Mark A. Clarke and Jean Handscombe, 175–89. Washington, DC: TESOL.

Schachter, Jacqueline. 1984. A universal input condition. Universals and second language acquisition, ed. by W. Rutherford, 167–83. Amsterdam: John Benjamins.

Schachter, Jacqueline. 1986. Three approaches to the study of input. Language Learning 36. 211–26.

Schmidt, Richard, and Sylvia Frota. 1986. Developing basic conversational ability in a second language: A case study of an adult learner of Portuguese. Talking to learn: Conversation in second language acquisition, ed. by Richard R. Day, 237–326. Rowley, MA: Newbury House.

Swain, Merrill. 1985. Communicative competence: Some roles of comprehensible input and comprehensible output in its development. Input in second language acquisition, ed. by Susan Gass and Carolyn G. Madden, 236–44. Rowley, MA: Newbury House.

Titone, Renzo. 1968. Teaching foreign languages: An historical sketch. Washington, DC: Georgetown University Press.

VanPatten, B. 1990. Attending to form and content in the input: An experiment in consciousness. Studies in Second Language Acquisition 12.287–302.

Varonis, Evangeline, and Susan Gass. 1982. The comprehensibility of nonnative speech. Studies in Second Language Acquisition 4.41–52.

Varonis, Evangeline, and Susan Gass. 1985a. Miscommunication in native/nonnative conversation. Language in Society 14.327–43.

Varonis, Evangeline, and Susan Gass. 1985b. Nonnative/nonnative conversations: A model for the negotiation of meaning. Applied Linguistics 6.71–90.

White, L. 1988. Against comprehensible input: The input hypothesis and the development of second language competence. Applied Linguistics 9.89–110.

Widdowson, H. G. 1978. Teaching language as communication. Oxford: Oxford University Press.

Yalden, Janice. 1983. The communicative syllabus: Evolution, design, and implementation. Oxford: Pergamon.

The dialogic emergence of culture in the language classroom

Claire Kramsch
University of California at Berkeley

Despite decades of communicative language teaching, the language classroom is still viewed as the place where students mouth foreign words in predictable, standard contexts of use. The concept of language as social practice is now putting this view into question. Social practice means not only the grammar rules and dictionary definitions of a given speech community, but the ways of speaking of a variety of discourse communities, defined both by the conventions of society and by the participants themselves. Learners are exposed to the French of marketplaces, the German of television debates, and the Spanish used in conversations among friends, as well as to the very special language of American classrooms. But they are also exposed to the language of subcommunities within these larger ones: the language of power, of solidarity, of gender, or of political ideology.

Bizzell (cited in Swales 1990:29) writes: 'A "discourse community" is a group of people who share certain language-using practices.' It is not only a speech community, whose members share the same linguistic code and sociolinguistic practices; it is also an interpretive community, that is, the members share common communicative purposes that are inscribed in the way they use language to convey both conventional and particular meanings. Academic debates, informal conversations, pattern drills, are classes of language-using practices that Swales calls 'genres', but so are verbal challenges to authority, verbal abuse and self-defense, and expressions of solidarity. According to Swales' (1990:45ff) definition, genres are 'communicative events in which language plays both a significant and an indispensable role; ... the principal criterial feature that turns a collection of communicative events into a genre is some shared set of communicative purposes; ... the rationale behind a genre establishes constraints on allowable contributions in terms of their content, positioning and form.' Genres constitute much of what we call culture, that is, 'the staged purposeful social processes through which a culture is realized in a language' (Martin and Rothery 1986:243).

Classrooms are not usually examined from the perspective of genres. Linguists and psycholinguists have focused primarily on the form of utterances and interactional mechanics. For example, Willis Edmondson (1985:162) talks about the different functions that language fulfills in the classroom as so many 'coexisting discourse worlds', but as a linguist he views language either as a structural system or as a medium: 'In the language classroom, the foreign language maybe the content of instruction, the goal of instruction, the medium of instruction, the medium of classroom management, the medium of everyday (nonpedagogic) talk, and the medium for practising target discourse.' Edmondson does not consider the use of language as building a community of practice that has its own cultural ways of speaking, its own struggle over who will speak and who will remain silent, and on who will assign which meanings to which words.

If, by contrast, we view the foreign language classroom from a sociolinguistic perspective, using the contextual categories developed for example by Fowler (1986:88) or Halliday (1978:63), we can view teachers and learners as having to define for themselves, in and through the foreign language, which ways of speaking they will adopt for which activity. For example, when responding to students, teachers have a choice of at least five different conversational floors that each reflect the genre they wish to establish in the classroom. The following examples are in part prefabricated.

1. They can choose to attend to the linguistic or to the pragmatic form of a student's utterance, thus establishing the genre VOCABULARY LESSON:

   S. Die Jugendlichen haben keine goals
   'young people have no goals'
   T. Keine Ziele [writes the word on the board]
   'no ZIELE'

2. They can respond to its informational content, thus choosing the genre DISCUSSION OF A TOPIC:

   S. Sie haben keine goals
   T. Du hast recht, sie wissen nicht, was sie wollen
   'you are right, they don't know what they want'

3. They can react to its value within the ongoing discourse, corresponding to the genre LOGICAL ARGUMENTATION:

   S. Sie haben keine goals
   T. Was hat das mit der Freiheit zu tun?
   'what does that have to do with freedom?'

4. They can point to its cultural or ideological value, foregrounding the genre REFLECTION ON CULTURAL CHARACTERISTICS OF DISCOURSE:

   S. Sie haben keine goals

T. Tja, das ist eine sehr amerikanische Sprechweise
'well, that is a very American way of putting it'

5. They can reflect on the way the utterance orients the speaker toward the topic or toward the other interlocutors, setting up a genre one could call CROSS-CULTURAL COMMUNICATION:

S. Sie haben keine goals
T. Was meinst du genau? bist du derselben Meinung wie X?
'what do you mean by goals? is it the same as what X said?'

Each response can, of course, partake of several genres simultaneously. The choice of conversational floor is determined by the communicative purposes shared by the interlocutors and by the constraints these purposes impose on allowable contributions. Whether they are conscious of it or not, participants in language classrooms choose forms of discourse that are likely to reproduce, resist, or change the genres traditionally found in and out of the classroom. As they negotiate genre and whose definition of genre they will settle for, language learners acquire what we call LANGUAGE AND CULTURE.

Now when we examine the kinds of communicative events that go on in language classrooms, we can rightly ask: Which culture is realized there through language? Which genres get settled for: those of the many NATIVE discourse communities to which teachers and learners belong? Those of the target communities? Those of American educational discourse communities? and How do teachers reconcile conflicting genres?

In order to explore these questions, I observed four German classes at the third semester college-level German taught on the same day by four different graduate student instructors. All four were American native speakers of English, in their mid-twenties, with a near-native command of the German language, but with varying amounts of exposure to the culture of German speech communities.[1] Teacher A is female, the other three are male instructors. My analysis will focus on a frequent activity in foreign language classes: the class discussion of a text, in this case, a so-called 'authentic' text.

My purpose here is not to EVALUATE the quality of the text or of its instruction. Rather, I am interested in DESCRIBING the negotiation that teacher and students engage in as they try to deal with various and often conflicting discourse communities—a kind of genre crossing so to speak. I will identify the gaps between genres as these may offer opportunities for reflecting upon the rhetorical and linguistic choices made by teacher and learners in their joint

[1] I consciously chose four non-German instructors for this study. Young native German graduate students teaching the German language in the United States often have ambivalent feelings about having to be the representatives of 'German culture'; the relationship they establish between their language and their culture is a historically complex one that would warrant a study in itself.

construction of culture. I will argue with John Swales (1990:41) that 'recognizing these gaps is not only valuable in itself, but can have important consequences for [the] cross-cultural awareness and training' of graduate student instructors.

The text. The one and a half page reading in the 1991 intermediate-level German textbook *Youth without a future?* is an extract from the written transcription, ('Jugend ohne Zukunft? *Die Zeit* 33, August 10, 1979) of a live eight-hour-long debate conducted in August 1979 on German television (SWF Baden-Baden) on the state of German youth. An almost all-male panel: a moderator, two vocational school students, a psychiatrist, a Gymnasium student, a journalist, an educator, and a politician each make lengthy statements about the depressing situation of German youth. They describe the fear of a nuclear war, high technology, and unemployment; the concerns about the environment and the Third World; the resulting feelings of powerlessness, frustration, resignation among the young; and the solutions proposed: political activism, grassroots initiatives, and keeping the channels of communication open through public debates. The text is reproduced in the Appendix.

This text can be placed into its proper context using Halliday's three variables: field, tenor, and mode (cf. Halliday 1978). The FIELD refers to the ideas, the information or absence of information contained in the text, and how this information or lack thereof is presented through the choice of words (naming) and grammatical structures (transitivity patterns). The TENOR refers in spoken texts to the status and role relationships among the ratified or unratified participants, eavesdroppers, and bystanders (Goffman 1981) as reflected in the mood of the exchange, the conventions of the genre regulating interpersonal relationships (e.g. turn-taking, topic management, cohesion). In written texts, tenor refers to the relationship between reader and text, the purpose or intended effect on the reader, and the shared knowledge of socio-rhetorical conventions. The MODE relates to the channel of communication, the degree of involvement or detachment elicited by the text in the reader or interlocutor, the influence of prior texts.

Field. August 1979 in the Federal Republic of Germany: stationing of American troops on German soil, public controversy surrounding nuclear plants, environmental concerns. In addition, disillusion with the economic miracle of the 1950s and 1960s in light of the cap on university admissions (NUMERUS CLAUSUS) and rising unemployment, the social market economy (SOZIALE MARKTWIRTSCHAFT) that ensured security of employment provided you got occupational training (BERUFSAUSBILDUNG), or a college education (UNIVERSITÄTSBILDUNG), the economic prosperity (WACHSTUMSGESELLSCHAFT) that promised unlimited growth provided you bought into technological—and nuclear—progress, the democratic institutions (RECHTSSTAAT) that promised political stability provided you accepted the Pax Americana, were all felt to break their promises: unemployment even with vocational training, restrictions in the access to higher education and unemployed academics, pollution, threat of a nuclear holocaust. 1979 was the year of the anti-nuclear movement, the beginning of the Greens, the anti-American demonstrations.

How is this ideational content realized linguistically? The extreme nominalization and high lexical density of the passage, the impersonal syntax, the abundance of passive constructions, embedded clauses, conjunctors (*however*, *therefore*, *furthermore*) as well as the monologic nature of the individual contributions by the panelists, are all evidence of the highly literate register conventionally associated with the genre TELEVISION DEBATE on German public television and with the daily national newspaper *Die Zeit*.

Tenor. The choice of participants is also characteristic of the genre. Like the members of the boards of the various public television stations, these are representatives of the various 'educated' segments of the population with the conventionally appropriate balance of political views (PROPORZ): psychiatrists, educators, politicians, scientists, representatives of youth associations, experts, and, of course, young people themselves. All these participants are listed by status and profession, members of the educational elite are named only by their last name, students from vocational schools and the university-bound high school students remain nameless, if not classless (*Schüler vs. Gymnasiast*). Both as a generational class and as representatives of a given social class they ARE—for the purposes of the moment—only a TOPIC under discussion: 'Youth in Germany'. This nominalized topic is the only thing that counts here: abstract nouns (*die Jugend*) or collective nouns (*die Jugendlichen*) to which are attached several subtopics, also in the form of nouns, for example, hopes, fears, expectations (*Hoffnungen*, *Angst*, *Erwartungen*). Foregrounding the topic itself, not the individual interlocutor, is a characteristic feature of German academic discourse communities (Jäger 1976).

The participants too view themselves and others as representing their social status: for example, the *Schüler* talks of himself as the anonymous member of a generation: *da kann man als Jugendlicher doch keine ideelle Befriedigung finden* (line 12), the high school student too: *ich meine, daß wir Jugendlichen* ... (line 33). The psychiatrist IS his professional status: *Was einen als Psychiater natürlich besonders interessiert* ... (line 17). The educator refers to *unsere Jugend*, and the politician calls the young students present *die Jugendlichen hier*. Only the female student at the end of the passage refers to *wir*, not as the fixed members of a class, but as a group of individual interlocutors, defined by the here-and-now context of the discussion itself: *Allein daß wir hier sitzen und über Lösungsmöglichkeiten diskutieren* (line 55). Her delivery style is markedly different: lexically much less dense, it has a more ornate flavor that invites participation, involvement, action.

Mode. The features of field and tenor mentioned above make for a highly rational discourse mode that elicits from the participants mutual respect for their respective public personae. It is a public type of discourse activity, evocative of prior academic disputes and political debates. It is also the discourse of power, predicated on the viewers' respect for expertise and trust in institutionally sanctioned knowledge and in the display of that knowledge on the institutionally legitimized public media. Nothing out of the ordinary for viewers of SWF Baden-Baden. It is meant to reinforce their confidence in the ability of such familiar discourse types to solve the problems of German society.

In sum: We are dealing here not only with a sample of a German speech community (a reading in an intermediate-level German textbook), but with the common practice of a specific discourse community that shares certain common views of the world: the distinction between public and private spheres, the socially sanctioned forms of transmittal of knowledge and information (BILDUNG, television), status and class in German society, male dominance in speaking rights and privileges. This discourse community agrees on which topics can and need to be talked about on public television, which topics need not be, and indeed should not be talked about.[2] All these features are part of what we generally call German culture. What happens when that text is taught to American students of German in the United States?

Genre crossings. The textbook gives no historical or social background information whatsoever; it does not even mention the date of the television debate. Only the small print in the Acknowledgements section of the textbook reveals the source of this article. Apparently the authors felt that exposing learners to the type of historical facts and events mentioned above could intimidate them and prevent them from talking about themselves. They chose this text because of its perceived relevance to present-day American students. The learners are asked to skim the text 'for its main ideas', not to analyze its details, and to get from it a basic—albeit mainly nominalized—vocabulary with which to organize their own experience, and give IT new meaning. In the pre-reading activities the students are asked to get into groups and 'make up a list of specific problems encountered by young people in the USA'. The post-reading activity 'Diskutieren Sie mit!' invites them to continue the conversation featured in the German text.

In all the classes observed, the instructors attributed the difficulty of teaching the text either to its boring nature or to the lack of social awareness of their students. The problem did not seem to be a lack of vocabulary or grammar, but, rather, the gaps between various socio-rhetorical contexts or discourse communities and their expected behaviors: the community of German television viewers and *Zeit* readers, the schooled community of the American classroom, the everyday communities of the learners outside the classroom. The following excerpts from the four lessons illustrate the attempts by the teachers

---

[2] For example, in January 1979 the American film *Holocaust* was broadcast for the first time on German television, triggering a nationwide debate on recent German history. This topic is not talked about among the 'problems of young people', although it is precisely the time when young people started asking their parents some uncomfortable questions.

to bridge these various gaps.

Teacher A. Teacher A, a female instructor, sees herself as a friendly conversational partner whose role is to make students talk. She believes, like the female student in the German text, that 'talking about the issues is already one way to start solving them.' The German text is therefore less important for her as a text than as a source of vocabulary for high phatic involvement between her and her students. S1 is a male student; S2 is a female student. The following gives a flavor of this dialogue:

T: was sind jetzt die Probleme der heutigen Jugend?
S1: keine Berufe
T: keine Berufe, ja, keine Jobs jetzt, ja, sie haben alle Angst vor den Berufsaussichten. Noch was?
S2: alles kostet sehr viel, die Uni, und die Bücher und die Miete
T: ja, ganz genau, ganz genau, ja, alles kostet sehr viel: Uni, Bücher, Miete, und das alles wird höher, nicht?, das wird immer höher, jedes Jahr. Ja da habe ich auch Angst. Okay. Noch was? Probleme von euch, oder von uns, von der heutigen Jugend, Jugendlichen?

T: What are the problems of today's youth?
S1: No work.
T: No work, yes, no jobs now, yes, they are all afraid of the work situation. What else?
S2: Everything costs a great deal, the university, and the books and the rent.
T: Yes exactly yes everything costs a great deal: the university, books, rent and it is always going up, isn't it? It is always going up, every year. Yes, I am afraid too. Okay. Anything else? Problems you have, we have, today's youth, young people?

The teacher establishes a bond between her and her students through the frequent use of repetitions, backchannel cues, first person singular and plural pronouns, and by a discourse exuberance that signals solidarity and common membership in a student discourse community. This style, however, is challenged by male students in the class. In the following exchange, the responses of S2 use the language learning dialogue as a way of challenging the community the teacher wants to establish. (S2 and S3 are female students; S4 is a male student. T is the female teacher.)

T: ja warum gibt es so viele junge Obdachlose?
S2: viele Jugend WOLLEN ihre Eltern nicht wohnen
T: okay. Viele Jugendliche wollen nicht mit den Eltern wohnen, ja das stimmt, das stimmt. Noch was? Warum können sie denn nicht arbeiten? Und eine Wohnung mieten?

S4: sie sind faul
T: sie sind faul. Okay. (accelerated speech) Das denke ich immer aber ich weiß nicht sie sind nicht alle faul. Ja
S3: (to S4) aber wenn man einmal obdachlos ist man kann nicht ein Beruf bekommen, weil du hast keine Adresse und keine Telefonnummer (T:ja!) und du kannst nicht duschen und so was
S4: sie brauchen keine Beruf sie brauchen nur Arbeit
S3: └Arbeit
S4: sie können bei McDonalds arbeiten
S3: aber du du kannst nicht bei McDonalds arbeiten weil hm McDonalds kannst du nicht anrufen, und du kannst nicht waschen und du bist sehr eh schmutzig (all laugh)
S4: lachen machen (all laugh)
T: okay. (laughs) Ja, das meine ich auch immer, aber sie haben bestimmt Probleme. Ja? Noch was? Ja Okay sehr gut.

T: Well why are there so many young homeless people?
S2: Many youth don't WANT to live.. their parents.
T: Okay. Many young people don't want to live with their parents. Anything else? Why can't they work? And rent an apartment?
S4: They are lazy.
T: They are lazy. Okay. (accelerated speech) That's what I thought too, but I know that they are not lazy. Yes?
S3: (to S4) But when you are homeless you can't get a profession, because you don't have an address and telephone number (T:yes!) and you can't take a shower and all that.
S4: They don't need a profession, all they need is work.
S3: └Work.
S4: They can work at McDonalds.
S3: But you you can't work at McDonalds because you can't call McDonalds and you can't wash and you are very hm dirty (all laugh)
S4: Make [people] laugh (all laugh)
T: Okay. (laughs) Yeah, that's what I always thought too, but they surely have problems. Yes? Anything else? Yes Okay very good.

The negotiation of reference in the foreign language (*Beruf* vs. *Arbeit*) serves as a catalyst for the negotiation of deeper meanings: male/female power relationships, conservative vs. liberal positions on the problem of the homeless, German vs. American ways of speaking about it. If, as mentioned above, a characteristic of genre is some shared set of communicative purposes, and if a genre establishes constraints on allowable contributions, then we can say that in the passage above the teacher is faced with conflicting genres. Her way out is to reinstate her teacher's authority by returning to the safest genre of all: the pure linguistic exercise of language.

Note that she had other options: she could have pointed out, for instance, that the despair and hopelessness of the homeless might be due precisely to the lack of a sense of pride and self-respect that come with having a *Beruf* rather than McDonald's type *Arbeit*. She could have placed the students' utterances in the larger context of American vs. German attitudes toward work. However, she feared that highlighting the gap might impede the students' ability and willingness to talk. Her comment after class reflects that concern:

> C: Could one make it more explicit where each student in the class is coming from?
>
> T: You mean restating the angle that they are coming from? I don't know. I am so happy that they can even say something!

So the teacher tries to reduce the multiplicity of genres at hand, rather than reflect upon them.

> C: Is it something one can talk about?
>
> T: I think you can talk about the way the Germans spent eight hours talking about POLITISCHES ENGAGEMENT, but I feel that that's not quite our level, I mean, we are meant to scan for information and vocabulary.

The genre FRIENDLY CONVERSATION, together with the pedagogic genre INFORMATION-PROCESSING ACTIVITY, have established constraints on what can be considered allowable contributions. The culture that is emerging in this particular class is, curiously, limited by the communicative purposes set by the teacher.

Teacher B. Teacher B, a male instructor, sees himself as a discussion moderator. He views it as his responsibility to raise the students' social awareness and moral understanding of the issues, as evidenced by his frequent use of the second person singular and plural (*Sie*, *ihr*) that clearly establish a distinction between him and the students, by contrast with the *wir* form used by teacher A. His precise questioning, the way he follows up on his students' utterances further realize his role as a moderator (S1 and S2 are Anglo-American males; S3 is a Japanese male, S4 is an Anglo-American female; and S5 is a Lebanese female).

> T: was ist Engagement? Politisch aktiv: engagiert. Sie sind engagiert: was heißt: Politisches Engagement?
>
> S1: man geht aus und schreit
>
> T: ist das wirklich politisches Engagement? Ich finde in diesem Kapitel wird sehr binär gedacht: entweder–oder. Engagiert oder
>
> S2: nicht engagiert
>
> T: apathisch. Das wäre die nächste Frage: bist du engagiert oder apathisch? ich glaube, viele Leute würden 'nein' und 'nein' sagen. Fragt

doch mal einander. (Students in pairs ask each other whether they are ENGAGIERT or not)

T: What is ENGAGEMENT? Politically active: ENGAGIERT. You are ENGAGIERT. What does POLITISCHES ENGAGEMENT mean?
S1: You go out and you shout.
T: Is that really POLITISCHES ENGAGEMENT? I find in this chapter everything is very binary: either/or, ENGAGIERT or
S2: Not ENGAGIERT.
T: Apathetic. That would be the next question: are you ENGAGIERT or apathetic? I believe many people would say 'no' and 'no'. Why don't you ask each other?

The teacher obviously wants the students to experience the multiplicity of points of view that he feels is absent from the German text. However, having led them out of binary thinking, he now has to deal with diversity.

T: (to S3) nun. sind Sie politisch engagiert? was heißt für Sie Engagement?
S3: wählen gehen, die politische Situation wissen, die Zeitung lesen
T: wie kann man die politische Lage verstehen? Sie lesen Zeitung, Sie informieren sich und Sie wählen. Ist das genug?
S1: nein.
T: warum nicht? muß man schreien?
S1: man muß andere Leute überzeugen.
T: möchten SIE andere Leute überzeugen?
S1: (silence)
T: ... ich finde, wenn Raymond [S3] sich informiert und wählt, warum wollen wir mehr? ... Warum ist das ein so großes Problem? Was wollen die Leute vom Leben überhaupt?
S2: Glück.
T: glücklich sein? Ja? Was ist Glück? (silence) Es ist eine schwierige Frage. Was wollen Sie hier?
S4: eine Familie, schöne Kinder
T: schöne Kinder
S5: aber es ist nicht ...
S2: essen und wohnen
T: essen und Obdach: also die Hauptbedingungen des Lebens, meinen Sie nicht? nein?
S5: nein.. diese Dinge sind nötig zu leben aber nicht zu glücklich
T: oder? ohne Essen können Sie doch nichts
S5: ja ja aber für mich also ... nicht Glück
T: └kein kausaler Zusammenhang. Essen kann nicht glücklich machen, aber ohne Essen kann man nicht existieren.
S5: (laughs) ja

T: (to S3) Well are YOU politically involved? What is ENGAGEMENT to you?
S3: To go and vote, to know the political situation, to read the newspaper
T: How can one understand the political situation? You read the newspaper, you get informed and you vote. Is that enough?
S1: No.
T: Why not? Do you have to shout?
S1: You must convince other people.
T: Would YOU want to convince other people?
S1: (silence).
T: I find, if Raymond keeps informed and votes, why do we want more? Why is it such a big problem? What do people want from life anyway?
S2: Happiness.
T: To be happy? Is that it? What is happiness?
Ss: (silence).
T: That's a difficult question. What do YOU want here?
S4: A family, beautiful children.
T: Beautiful children
S5: But it is not..
S2: To eat and to live
T: Food and a roof. So ... the basic *Lebensbedingungen*, don't you think? No?
S5: No ... these things are necessary to live, but not to happy!
T: Aren't they? without food you can't do anything!
S5: Yes yes but for me ... not happiness
T: └No causal relationship. Food can't make you happy, but without food you cannot exist.
S5: (laughs) yes

The teacher has rightly identified one difficulty with the German text: its reductionist binary oppositions: ENGAGEMENT VS. RESIGNATION, the generation of the fifties vs. the generation of the sixties. By personalizing the issues the teacher tries to get the students involved and contemplating alternative solutions. Indeed, the social mix of students in the class provides multiple points of view on the issue of political involvement. However, the teacher is handicapped by his 'me vs. them' attitude, that he expresses in the interview after class:

T: It seems to me people always want to give the 'right' answer, like on a multiple choice test. But what is really ENGAGEMENT? I said: I read the paper and I inform myself and I vote. And in a democracy,who could want more? And people said: That's not enough, you have to go and yell on the street. I don't do that, but they say: 'I can tell you that you're not engaged if you don't do that.' So I wanted to get behind that kind of talk.

Instead of foregrounding and thematizing the diversity of views in the classroom, the teacher chooses to return to the safe genre: QUESTIONS ON THE TEXT and a purely linguistic conversational floor. This makes him fall back precisely into the binary oppositions he wanted to avoid:

T: ja das ist nicht leicht, nicht? also, der Text spricht von diesen zwei verschiedenen Generationen, nicht? In den fünfziger Jahren, was war da los?
'yeah it is not that easy, eh? So, the text mentions these two different generations. In the fifties, how was it?'

In this class the teacher attempted to broaden the cultural context of the classroom, but was not able to deal with the diversity he himself had elicited.

Teacher C. Teacher C, a male instructor, sees himself as providing as much as possible the model of a near-native speaker. His role is to give his students access to the text of the German television debate by adopting a German reader's perspective. This is a difficult endeavor given the lack of contextual knowledge provided by the textbook. Nevertheless this teacher keeps close to the text and tries to explain it from the inside. S1 is a male student; S2 is a female student; T is the male teacher.

T: jetzt gucken wir uns die erste Antwort an und zwar ist das ein Schüler. Wie alt ist ein Schüler?
S1: weniger als 17?
T: also ungefähr bis 17. Also ziemlich jung, nicht, es ist ein sehr kluger Schüler. Okay. Die konkreten Lebensbedingungen, eine Bedingung ist ungefähr 'condition', ja? (reads) 'Die konkreten Lebensbedingungen sind dermaßen repressiv, daß den meisten Jugendlichen gar kein Vorwurf zu machen ist, daß sie sich nicht engagieren. Wenn mir heute in der Klasse gesagt wird: 'Gehen Sie doch auf den Bau!', dann kann man als Jugendlicher doch keine ideelle Befriedigung finden, sondern fühlt sich eigentlich nur unterdrückt.'
S2: aber kann ein Schüler so sprechen?
T: das ist eine gute Frage, nicht?
S2: ich glaube es nicht
T: also ich glaube es auch kaum. Aber das ist ziemlich schwierig, was er da sagt. Was ist mit den konkreten Lebensbedingungen?

T: Now let us look at the first response. It is from a SCHÜLER. How old is a SCHÜLER?
S1: Less than 17?
T: So roughly 17. Fairly young, isn't he? he is a very smart SCHÜLER. Okay. The concrete LEBENSBEDINGUNGEN, a BEDINGUNG is like 'condition' Okay? (reads) 'The concrete living conditions are so

repressive, that one cannot blame most young people for not being politically active. When I am told in class today: 'Why don't you go into the construction business?' as a young person you cannot find any intellectual satisfaction, you just feel oppressed.'

S2: Can a SCHÜLER speak like that?
T: That is a good question isn't it?
S2: I don't believe so.
T: I don't believe it either. It is quite complex what he says there. So what about the concrete living conditions?

The student S2 offers an opportunity to address the very discourse of the German text, but that opportunity is not recognized by the teacher.

C: Was the problem due to the abstract discourse style of the German text?
T: No I don't think so. I think that allows us to pass over very nicely without getting anything right on, but I think the problem is with the students' lack of social awareness.

The teacher seems here to identify with the speakers on the German television panel who complain about the lack of involvement of German youth. He is trying to recreate in the American classroom the discourse community implied in the German text.

T: ich möchte daß wir einander fragen was für Probleme wir sehen, für uns, als Jugendliche, denn Jugendliche, das sind nicht nur Schüler, nicht, er redet hier von Menschen zwischen 15 und 25. Was sind die problematischen konkreten Lebensbedingungen für uns?
S1: die Jugendlichen haben zu viel Freiheit
T: wirklich? was meinst du?
S1: sie haben keine goals
T: ziellosigkeit
S1: weil sie haben keine guidance
T: hm auf Deutsch Führung, na ja, ich verstehe was du meinst. Was machen die Jugendlichen mit ihrer Freiheit?
S2: drogen
T: Drogen. Sind diese Probleme überall in der Gesellschaft? Haben in allen Schichten der Gesellschaft Jugendliche Drogenprobleme?
SS: ja

T: I would like us to ask ourselves what kinds of problems we see for ourselves as young people. What are the problematic concrete living conditions for us?
S1: Young people have too much freedom.
T: Really? what do you mean?
S1: They don't have any 'goals'.

T: ZIELLOSIGKEIT.
S1: Because they don't have any 'guidance'.
T: Hm in German FÜHRUNG, well hm I understand what you mean. What do young people do with their freedom?
S2: Drugs.
T: Drugs. Are these problems everywhere in society? Do young people from all social classes have drug problems?
SS: yes

By contrast with the other teachers, teacher C uses purposely German discourse patterns (*in der Gesellschaft*, *alle Schichten der Gesellschaft*, *für uns als Jugendliche*) and tries to keep the topic-centered style of the German discussion, as evidenced by his high degree of nominal and impersonal constructions. However, since German concepts and American concepts do not overlap, the two communities enter into conflict with one another. For example, a *Schüler* is not just any American *student* but a vocational school student in his teens; the term *Führung* has uncomfortable connotations for a German speaker and does not quite match the American concept *guidance*. The teacher is constantly aware of the clashes between nonequivalent concepts. In the excerpt below, in which the class is discussing employment prospects of young people in the United States, he is faced with the ideological gap between the German concepts *Beruf/Job/Arbeit* on the one hand, and the American concept of *job* on the other.

T: was sind die Chancen, daß Sie den Beruf bekommen, den Sie wollen?
S1: gut
T: gut? ja? was wollen Sie werden?
S1: ich möchte ... ich weiß nicht ... eine Frau
T: dann ist es sicher gut. Eine Frau ist das ein Beruf?
S1: hausfrau (general laughter)
T: was sind die Chancen, daß man Hausfrau werden kann?
S1: wenn man heiratet.
T: wenn man einen reichen Mann heiratet, hat man vielleicht die Wahl.
S1: ja.
T: da muß man sich aber auf reiche Männer beschränken.
S1: aber es gibt
T: ja sicher - wer hat noch - Craig, arbeitest du schon?

T: What are the chances that you get the BERUF that you want?
S1: Good.
T: Good? yes? what do you want to be?
S1: I would like ... I don't know ... a woman
T: Well then it's sure to be good. A woman, is that a BERUF
S1: HAUSFRAU 'housewife/homemaker'.
T: What are the chances that one can become a HAUSFRAU?
S1: When you get married.

T: When you marry a rich man, then you may have a choice.
S1: Yes.
T: But then you have to restrict yourself to rich men.
S1: Yes but there are …
T: Yes, sure. Who else here has a - Craig, do you work already?

A BERUF is the result of vocational, professional or academic training, an occupation legitimized by a societally sanctioned diploma, that ensures quality control, recognized expertise, and the privilege of belonging to a professional organization or trade union. The student challenges the German concept of BERUF by using the American definition of homemaker and its feminist claims to professional occupational status. But this new meaning of the term BERUF is not part of its standard dictionary definition. It is used here in a genre that the male teacher cannot deal with at that time, busy as he is clarifying the German historic distinction between BERUF and JOB. So he chooses a safer example and turns to a male student in the class:

T: Craig arbeitest du schon?
S2: ja
T: was für ein Job?
S2: Merrill Lynch
T: also deine Berufschancen scheinen gut zu sein. Ich bin mir selber nicht so sicher, ich bin ein Germanist, ich studiere deutsche Literatur. Aber ich habe noch keinen Job, nicht? Ich unterrichte noch keine deutsche Literatur
S3: werden Sie kein Deutsch unterrichten?
T: weiß ich nicht, das kann sein, wahrscheinlich auf einer Ebene könnte ich auch mal Deutsch unterrichten aber das ist nicht, was ich machen möchte. Ich möchte irgendwann die Literatur unterrichten und das ist nicht so leicht, also die Berufschancen sind zwar nicht schlecht, aber nicht sicher.
S3: gibt es zu viele Leute?
T: es gibt mehr Leute als es Jobs gibt.

T: Craig do you work already?
S2: Yes.
T: What kind of a job?
S2: With Merrill Lynch
T: So your BERUFSCHANCEN seem quite good. I am not quite sure myself, I am a germanist, I study German literature. But I still don't have a JOB. I still don't teach German literature.
S3: Won't you teach German?
T: I don't know, it is possible, probably on one level I could teach German from time to time, but it is not what I want to do. I would like to teach literature sometime and it is not easy, the BERUFSCHANCEN are

not bad, but not sure.
S3: Are there too many people?
T: There are more people than there are Jobs.

A German *Job* is untrained—generally temporary—labor and the criteria for selection are not diplomas but the ability to 'do the task'. The availability of *Jobs* is up to the vagaries of the market. Students, however, get vocational or professional training to obtain a *Beruf*, not a *Job*. There is therefore in German no word like *Jobchancen* 'chances of getting a job or job opportunities', only *Berufschancen* 'career opportunities'. The American term *job*, by contrast, is much broader. It includes any type of work, both skilled and unskilled, and can refer also to a 'position on the professional market'. By using the term *Job* where a German would have used *Arbeit* or *Stelle*, the teacher shows his solidarity with the American discourse community to which his students belong.

I would like to argue that the distinction and the teacher's confusion between *Beruf* and *Job* is precisely the clash between several discourse communities present in the language classroom. As in teacher A's class, the relationship between 'education' and 'the job market' can be discussed either from the perspective of the German discourse community, (in which case American concepts like *Gelegenheit*, *Job*, *Chancen* will be deceptive), or from within the American discourse community (in which case German concepts like *Beruf*, *Lebensbedingungen* will be in the way).

But it can also be used to problematize existing male definitions of *Beruf* or to question the existing dichotomy between the status of language vs. literature teaching in American academia.

I do not wish to imply in the least that teacher C should have been aware of the multiple discourse genres that were all competing for his attention in the classroom. It is easy to analyze a transcript of the lesson in hindsight. My point is only that the options provided by the totality of the discourse context are much more numerous than teachers usually think.

Teacher D. Teacher D, also a male instructor, sees himself as a facilitator, intent on having his students 'experience the language and the culture.' He instinctively decides to bridge the genre gap by bringing in an article from the *People* section of the *San Francisco Chronicle*, featuring two generations of baby boomers in the United States: those born between 1946 and 1954 and those born between 1955 and 1964.[3] Personalized shots, individual opinions and comments from informants with specific names and ages, the reporting style is chatty and informal. Women here are prominently visible with the appropriate ethnic distribution. The experts are represented in the form of statistics. Teacher D feels that this lively and familiar treatment of the topic should help his students 'experience the problem' and, hence, understand it.

---

[3] Alice Kahn, 'The New Generation Gap', *San Francisco Chronicle*, February 18, 1992.

Through the give and take of classroom dialogue, teacher D first reconstructs with the students the discourse community of the *Chronicle*'s average readers; he then draws on the lexical structures of the German text and embeds them into the American discourse (S1, S3, and S4 are male students; S2 is a female student):

T: diese Frau meint das sei eine Sache von Generationskonflikt innerhalb dieser Generation ... Was fällt euch auf?
S1: die Alter sind idealistisch die Junge hm sind hm exactly the opposite
T: sie sind ja realistisch. Ja was bedeutet das? Man spricht von der älteren Generation als idealistisch, und von der jüngeren Generation als realistisch. Aber was bedeutet realistisch? (long silence)
S2: auf der Universität wir müssen alles kaufen für Macht haben und dann die Eltern später kann ein Haus kaufen haben viel Wert und wenn wir das nicht haben wir müssen mieten eine Wohnung (laughs) statt zu kaufen
T: das ist sehr - sehr gut ich glaub das kommt unter Bildung aber besprich das: Wer ist dann idealistisch/realistisch? (silence)

T: This woman says it is a generational conflict within this generation. What do you notice?
S1: The old are idealistic, the young hm are hm 'exactly the opposite'.
T: They are realistic. Yes, what does that mean? One speaks of the older generation being idealistic and the younger generation being realistic. But what does realistic mean? (long silence).
S2: At the university we must buy everything to get power and then the parents later on can buy a house - much value - and if we don't have that - we must rent an apartment (laughs) instead of buying.
T: That is very - very good I think it falls under education but discuss that: who is then idealistic/realistic? (silence)

By changing the abstract opposition found in the German text, adults vs. youngsters, to an American way of framing the problem, namely the early vs. the late baby boomer generation, or idealistic vs. realistic, teacher D is able to move the students from mere information retrieval to an expression of their own experience. However, he fails to make them reflect upon that experience: S2 answers to his request for a definition of the term *realistic* not by NAMING her experience but by ENACTING it. In an effort to broaden the discussion, the teacher then tries to introduce German ways of talking about the issues.

T: aber dann bringst DU etwas anderes zur Diskussion: ob wir genug Geld haben ob wir ein Haus kaufen, ob wir eine Wohnung haben. Das sind materielle - oder man kann auch gleich von den 'konkreten Lebensbedingungen' (writes *konkrete Lebensbedingungen* on blackboard) sprechen. Lebensbedingungen haben etwas mit dem Lebensstandard zu tun. Lebensbedingungen sind was?

S3: wo man wohnt, was man fährt

T: ach Transportmittel, wie man fährt (writes *wo man wohnt, was man fährt* on blackboard); was noch?

S4: was man arbeitet

T: ach Arbeitsplatz: was für eine Arbeit man hat (writes *was für eine Arbeit* on blackboard). Was noch?

S1: was man verdient

T: (writes *wieviel man verdient* on blackboard) für uns bedeutet das Geld, einerseits. Andererseits, hat es auch mit der Gesundheit zu tun, ob ich gesund bin, ob meine Welt gesund ist oder nicht. Hygiene? Gesundheit? (writes *die Gesundheit* on blackboard).

T: But then YOU are bringing something else in the discussion: Whether we have enough money, whether we buy a house, whether we own an apartment. These are material - or one can speak right away of the *konkrete Lebensbedingungen. Lebensbedingungen* have something to do with standard of living. *Lebensbedingungen*, what is that?

S3: Where one lives, what one drives.

T: Transportation, how one drives (writes on blackboard). What else?

S4: What one works.

T: Workplace: what kind of work one has (writes on blackboard). What else?

S1: What one earns.

T: For us it means money, on the one hand. On the other hand, it has to do with health, whether I am healthy, whether my world is healthy or not. Hygiene? Health?

The teacher tries to bridge the American discourse community of the classroom and the German discourse community of the reading by using the terms *konkrete Lebensbedingungen* taken from the German text. As used by the *Schüler*, however, this term refers not to daily necessities, but to such concepts as the loss of human dignity in the workplace, psychological stress, social class discrimination, as well as environmental pollution and threat of a nuclear war. Note that for a German these conditions are eminently CONCRETE, whereas for the young American reader, they are eminently ABSTRACT. By relating *Lebensbedingungen* to *Lebensstandard*, the teacher is offering a concept that is more accessible to American students, but it deviates somewhat from the original. The list of examples he receives from the students is firmly embedded in their own, more anecdotal, world view: housing, car, job, money. The teacher has to add the item *health* in order to lead the students to the larger issues mentioned in the German text, such as environmental pollution.

In other words, by following his students' experiential lead, teacher D ensures active participation, but he has to abandon his original intention of having the students UNDERSTAND the problem by experiencing it. The voice that emerges through the German language is just the unreflected voice of their own familiar discourse community: personal, concrete, anecdotal. It is worlds apart from the discourse community of the German text and its intended readers/viewers.

The direct conflict between two discourse communities is apparent in the following excerpt, in which the teacher tries once more to get the students to reflect on their experience.

T: warum verdienen die älteren Baby Boomers mehr Geld als wir? weil sie idealistisch sind?
S1: sie haben mehr Gelegenheit
T: (writes *die Gelegenheit* on blackboard) Kannst du das Wort beschreiben? Was bedeutet das: Gelegenheit?
S1: man kann viel machen in der Welt.. hm.. es ist schwer

T: Why do the older baby boomers make more money than we do? because they are idealistic?
S1: They have more GELEGENHEIT?
T: Can you describe the word? what does GELEGENHEIT mean?
S1: One can do a lot in the world .. hm .. it is difficult

The teacher is aware that the term *Gelegenheit* used by the American student in this absolute sense is not only grammatically incorrect, but it corresponds to an American type of public discourse that is totally foreign to Germans. The German language uses the word *opportunity* only with a preposition (i.e. the opportunity to do something) and it refers to a very practical state of affairs. By giving the German word the highly ideological American meaning, the student is echoing prior texts such as *the land of opportunity* and *equal opportunity*, that have no direct equivalents in German. The German approximations, *das Land der unbegrenzten Möglichkeiten* and *Chancengleichheit* focus, unlike their American counterparts, less on the external conditions than on the empowerment of the individual to make use of these conditions. The teacher tries to tackle the problem head-on.

T: Was heißt Gelegenheit? Es ist schwer zu beschreiben, nicht? wir gebrauchen das Wort einfach so hin. Gelegenheit bedeutet hm (louder in a didactic tone) ... Sagen wir, meine Eltern haben sehr viel Geld; WEIL meine Eltern viel GELD HA::ben (American intonation), habe ICH ... viellEICHT (rising intonation) die Gelegenheit, viel zu reisen -als Kind. Ich habe diese Gelegenheit (acc.) Aber ein anderes Kind, dessen Eltern vielleicht nicht so viel Geld haben, hat nicht diese Gelegenheit, soviel um die Welt zu reisen, sagen wir mal. Gibt es da einen Unterschied zwischen mir und dem anderen Kind, dessen Eltern kein Geld haben? und wie sehe ich die Welt? das ist vielleicht ... deswegen brauchen wir nur Gelegenheit zu sagen, vielleicht ist es nicht ein

Unterschied zwischen Generationen.

T: It is difficult to describe, isn't it? we use the word so often. GELEGENHEIT means ... hm ... (Louder in a didactic tone) let's say, my parents have a lot of money. BECAUSE my parents have a lot of money, I have MAYBE the GELEGENHEIT to travel a lot, as a child. I have this GELEGENHEIT. But another child, whose parents may not have as much money, does not have this opportunity, to travel as much, let's say. Is there a difference between me and the other child, whose parents don't have any money? and how do I see the world? That is why maybe we only need the word GELEGENHEIT, maybe it is not a difference between the generations.

I suggest that in this critical moment, the teacher is not dealing with a difficulty in vocabulary, but with a conflict between two world views, two interpretive communities. Caught between his empathy with the students' discourse and his responsibility to give them access to the German discourse community, the teacher hesitates, and settles for a LEXICAL explanation that leaves the DISCOURSE problem intact.

His perceptible relief at having found an example that allows him to use the German word within German grammatical constraints is prosodically and syntactically marked: not only does he recover his normal fluency, a more secure didactic tone of voice and a paradigmatic grammatical intricacy, but we notice the emergence of a distinct, and for him, unusual, American discourse intonation. He is undoubtedly returning to the safe discourse community of the American classroom.

The postobservation conversation with the teacher revealed that he was aware of the difficulty, but like the other teachers, he felt caught between his role as a language teacher and as a teacher of culture.

C: All these meta-aspects of the text—that are so much bearers of culture—would they be worthwhile talking about?

T: I don't know how that would be. It goes kind of against how I consider my job as a facilitator to learn German, and the culture associated with it. Because I go from an experiential ... and I don't know how to get to that. It's hard to decide whether we are going to talk about THAT text, this discussion AS A TEXT, or whether we're going to engage in the discussion itself.

Discussion. Each in their own way, the four instructors tried to engage their students in a discussion of the problems facing young people today in the United States. They were thereby using lexical and grammatical structures that belonged to the ways of speaking of another discourse community, as reflected in the German text. Moreover, they conducted this discussion in a classroom setting that had its own traditional ways of speaking, and that reflected the usual social and cultural diversity of American language classrooms. This diversity enabled other discourse genres to come to the fore, some more gender-related, some more politically flavored.

The teachers hoped that, by having students experience the problem in the foreign language, they would not only learn the linguistic structures needed to describe their experience but they would come to understand that experience in new ways. Since the feelings and events referred to in the German text seemed too distant and abstract, they had their students relate their own concerns in German. However, the words that were used in the text to discuss the topic (*Berufschancen*, *konkrete Lebensbedingungen*, *Gelegenheit*) did not quite fit the students' American experience, because these words have their roots in quite other discourse conventions, born from historical conditions that have produced, for example, different work ethics, different social conditions, different ideologies of opportunity.

At every turn, these instructors were faced with gaps between various discourse genres. In teachers A and B's classes, students brought in the voices of their own family, social, and national discourse communities. Teachers C and D had to grapple with the gap between the world views of German and American discourse communities. In all these cases, the difficulty was not a lexical one, but one of negotiating multiple definitions of the communicative event under the avowed goal of learning the foreign language: German educated ways of speaking about problems, American ways of viewing work opportunities, gendered definitions, political stances.

In the face of conflicting genres, the teachers fell back on building the safe community of the American classroom with its traditionally paradigmatic discourse practices. The negotiation returned from a negotiation of emergent meanings to a navigation around stable worlds of reference.

It is interesting to note that, while the instructors were all extremely aware of the unwieldy language of the German text, they were not convinced of the link between the discourse of the text and its cultural meaning. For most of them, it was just a 'bad' and 'boring' text. Their dislike of the German text was echoed by their frustration with their own classroom text. The communicative roles they saw for themselves—conversational partner, facilitator, moderator, model native speaker—encouraged them to attend above all things to the CONTENT aspects of the lesson, not to its DISCOURSE features. And yet, the difficulties they encountered had to do precisely with those discourse features.

Implications for teacher training. At every turn at talk, the teachers had a choice of levels on which to respond to a student's utterance: they could respond to its propositional content, they could link it to other utterances made by other students, they could address its lexical and grammatical aspects, or its conceptual frame, or its contextual connotations, or its cultural implications. The level on which the teachers chose to respond contributed to defining the discourse community they were creating in the classroom.

The training of foreign language teachers has focused traditionally on the linguistic aspects of language and the pragmatics of classroom management. It has been predicated on the belief that learners should strive to become native speakers of the language. But it is far from certain that they should strive to become the representatives of any given culture. Culture is not a cluster of stable, conventional meanings but, rather, a constant negotiation of genres that emerge within the discourse community of the classroom. You can only understand the culture of that community if you see it both from the inside and the outside, like actors do on the stage and ethnographers in the field.

However, in the same way that as ethnographers cannot at the same time observe, take notes, and understand the phenomena observed, but need time for post-observation analysis and reflection, in the same way we cannot expect language teachers to be participants and observers of their classrooms without training. The hesitation of the four instructors to reflect on the very discourse of both the text in the textbook and the text they were creating in the classroom stems from an uncertainty of what their role as teachers should be and a lack of understanding of language as social practice. It is not due to a lack of good will. The training of language teachers should focus less on instructional strategies and techniques and more on an understanding of discourse processes in the classroom (cf. Kramsch 1993).

As Swales wrote recently (1990), understanding discourse genres can be a source of power and self-respect. The power of speakers in classroom lessons derives from their understanding of the socio-rhetorical situation, that is, the nature of the genre of both language learning texts and classroom discourses. It is these genres that make it clear why a teacher would ask a given question, why a student would make a given comment, why a writer would have written a given text. Being aware of the concept of discourse community can give teachers and learners greater options in the range of things they might say in class and the way they might say them.

REFERENCES

Edmondson, Willis. 1985. Discourse worlds in the classroom and in foreign language learning. Studies in Second Language Acquisition 7.159-68.

Fowler, Roger. 1986. Linguistic criticism. Oxford: Oxford University Press

Goffman, Ervin. 1981. Forms of talk. Philadelphia: University of Pennsylvania Press

Halliday, M.A.K. 1978. Language as social semiotic. London: Edward Arnold.

Jäger, Karl-Heinz. 1976. Zur Argumentation in Texten gesprochener Sprache. Deutschunterricht 28, 4.59-71.

Kramsch, Claire. 1993. Context and culture in language teaching. Oxford: Oxford University Press.

Martin, James R., and Joan Rothery. 1986. What a functional approach to the writing task can show teachers about 'good writing'. Functional approaches to writing: Research perspectives, ed. by Barbara Couture, 241-65. Norwood, NJ: Ablex.

Swales, John M. 1990. Genre analysis. Cambridge: Cambridge University Press.

Walker, R.W., and E. Tschirner, B. Nikolai, G.F. Strasser Assoziationen. 1991. Deutsch für die Mittelstufe. New York: McGraw-Hill, Inc.

APPENDIX

The following text was reprinted with permission by McGraw-Hill.
From Walker et al, 1991:169-70:

Im Studio 1 des Südwestfunks Baden-Baden diskutierten Jugendliche, Vertreter von Jugendorganisationen und Experten aus allen politischen Richtungen, aus Wissenschaft und Verbänden über Situation und Bewußtseinlage der heute 15- bis 25jährigen in der Bundesrepublik.

BOTTLINGER (MODERATOR): Viele Jugendliche stehen der Gesellschaft der Erwachsenen mit Distanz gegenüber, fühlen sich unverstanden, teilweise sogar betrogen. Sie haben wenig Erwartungen und Hoffnungen für die Zunkunft. Manchnmal scheint es fast so, als seien sie Fremde in unserer Gesellschaft.

SCHÜLER: Die konkreten Lebensbedingugnen sind dermaßen repressiv, daß den meisten Jugendlichen gar kein Vorwurf zu machen ist, daß sie sich nicht engagieren. Wenn mir heute in der Klasse gesagt wird: "Gehen Sie doch auf den Bau!", dann kann man als Jugendlicher doch keine ideelle Befriedigung finden, sondern fühlt sich eigentlich nur unterdrückt.

STIERLIN (PSYCHIATER): Diese Frustration, Ohnmacht, Resignation, dieses apolitische Verhalten, diese Wut auch, sind mir sehr vertraut bei vielen Studenten, aber auch von Berufsschülern und Abiturienten, mit denen ich zu tun habe. Was einen als Psychiater natürlich besonders interessiert, ist die Frage nach der Angst, die ja hier aufgeworfen wurde. Es gibt viele objektive Erscheinungen, die uns angst machen können, wenn wir in die Zukunft blicken: die Technologie, die Ansammlung von atomaren Vernichtungswaffen, die Zerstörung einer Umwelt, in der die jungen Leute später leben müssen, nicht wir Alten. Auch die Arbeitsplatzsituation macht den Jungen mehr angst als uns Alten, weil sie ja die Welt betrifft, in der sie leben werden, nicht wir. Aber daneben spielt natürlich auch eine irrationale Angst mit, die tiefer geht.

GYMNASIAST: Ich muß sagen, daß ich die Zukunft unserer Gesellschaft und unserer Welt ziemlich schwarz sehe. Ich sehe vor allem folgende Probleme: Einmal die wahnsinnige Umweltzerstörung. Wenn man sich überlegt, wieviel Land einfach überbaut wird, da schnürt sich mir richtig der Hals zu. Dann die lebensfeindliche Einstellung dieser Wachstumsgesellschaft. Das ist ein großes Problem, das mir außerordentlich angst macht. Dann das Wettrüsten. Es gibt so viel Waffen, daß die Erde x-mal zerstört werden kann. Und schließlich der Unterschied zwischen den Industrienationen und der dritten Welt. Auch da sehe ich ganz, ganz große Probleme—nicht nur das Elend der Leute, die dort leben, sondern auch die Konflikte, die sich daraus ergeben. Ich meine, daß wir Jugendlichen uns dieser Probleme viel stärker annehmen müssen. Deshalb finde ich es sehr wichtig, daß man sich in Bürgerinitiativen zusammenschließt und etwa gegen die Umweltzerstörung angeht.

MATTHIESEN (Journalist und Pädagoge): Wir haben eine sehr schwierige Frage von Herrn Bottlinger gestellt bekommen: Gibt es ein gemeinsames Bewußtsein von 18 Millionen Jugendlichen? Und es scheint fast so, als ob man sagen könnte, dieses gemeinsame Bewußtsein heißt Resignation, Lähmung, Angepaßtheit. Einen ähnlichen Stempel hat auch die Generation der fünfziger und sechziger Jahre getragen. Die skeptische Generation der fünfziger Jahre und die rebellierende, die aufmüpfige, die revoltierende Generation der sechziger Jahre. Vielleicht ist das symptomatisch, daß unserer Jugend heute trotz aller Differenzierung dazu neigt, den Rücken zu beugen, keinen Widerspruch zu riskieren, aus Angst gelähmt ist und in Gefahr ist, in eine große Distanz zum Staat zu geraten.

ZANDER (FAMILIENMINISTERIUM): Ich fand das sehr eindrucksvoll, was hier vor allem die Jugendlichen selbst gesagt haben über ihre Bewußtseinslage. Die Gründe dafür, aus denen heraus sie das sagen, machen mir angst: Sie haben von der dritten Welt, von der Rüstung gesprochen, von der Umwelt und vom Rohstoffmangel. Aber die Frage ist doch, was wir Erwachsenen tun, um mit den Problemen in der Welt fertig zu werden. Meine Antwort wäre: politisches Engagement für Entspannung und Abrüstung. Resignation is die falsch Konsequenz.

SCHÜLERIN: Am Anfang der Diskussion ist von vielen gesagt worden, es sei doch alles unheimlich beschissen und man könne doch überhaupt nichts ändern. Ich glaube, das ist nicht richtig. Allein, daß wir hier sitzen und über Lösungsmöglichkeiten diskutieren, zeigt doch, daß wir etwas ändern können und daß wir versuchen müssen, etwas zu verändern. Und dann noch ein Punkt: Jugend ohne Träume, ohne Ideale und ohne Hoffnungen. Ich glaube, das ist ein falsches Bild von der heutigen Jugend, wenn man sagt, die heutige Jugend hat keine Hoffnungen, hat keine Wünsche und hat keine Träume. Denn die Jugend von heute hat genauso, glaub' ich, wie die Jugennd vergangener Jahre Hoffnungen und Illusionen. Sie sind da. Und sie mal zu wecken, das ist auch eine Aufgabe.

Metaphorical competence in second language acquisition and second language teaching: The neglected dimension

Marcel Danesi
University of Toronto

1 Introduction. In this paper I will use the term second language (SL) to refer to the learning of a language other than the native one in formal classroom environments. The history of second language teaching (SLT) and the research in second language acquisition (SLA)—so defined—have been characterized above all else by a debate between formalists and functionalists, i.e. between those who focus on the development of techniques that aim to foster in the learner a control of linguistic structure (formalists) and those who focus on developing in the learner a functional knowledge of the communicative uses of the second language. Specifically, the thrust in the formalist orientation has been toward the development of so-called LINGUISTIC COMPETENCE, while in the functionalist orientation it has been in the direction of so-called COMMUNICATIVE COMPETENCE. Although it has taken on an increasingly sophisticated terminological guise, this debate is really as old as civilization itself, dating back to the times of the Sumerians in 3500 B.C. (Titone 1968, Kelly 1969)!

Against the backdrop of this debate, contemporary SLT has been operating within the framework of a flexible modus operandi, searching constantly for all kinds of ideas and constructs—COMPREHENSIBLE INPUT, PROFICIENCY, etc.—in a valiant and seemingly endless effort to transform the classroom into an effective learning environment. Much progress has been made in this regard, but some problems continue to loom large. The purpose of this paper is to focus on what is perhaps the most persistent problem plaguing the entire SLT and SLA enterprise. For lack of a better term, I will refer to it as the student's inability to achieve CONCEPTUAL FLUENCY in the SL. I will first specify what I mean by CONCEPTUAL FLUENCY, discussing its relation to what can be called METAPHORICAL COMPETENCE; then I will report on some data I have recently collected on this notion; and, finally, I will draw from the notions of metaphorical competence and conceptual fluency some tentative implications both for SLA research and SLT methodology.

2 Metaphorical Competence and Conceptual Fluency. There is no need to go into the SLA literature here that documents learning outcomes as they correlate with teaching approaches, motivational factors, learning styles, and the like. However, there is one particular pattern of findings that I wish to comment upon briefly here. It would seem that levels of grammatical and communicative proficiency correlate rather well with both pedagogical and learning variables. In a word, we seem to have become rather successful in training SL learners to gain a firm control over grammar and communication—the latter being understood in the usual sense of 'how to do things with the language in specific interactional contexts.' So, the issue of whether grammatical syllabuses and formalistic instructional styles are more or less productive than communicative or functional ones is, in my view, a moot one. As Savignon (1992) has recently suggested, it is perhaps more appropriate, and certainly more useful, to think of the two kinds of syllabus as cooperative and complementary contributors to SLA in the classroom, not as antagonistic or mutually exclusive competitors.

But, despite the great strides made towards enhancing learning outcomes in the classroom since the demise of the audiolingual movement in the sixties, there continues to be something still not quite 'kosher,' so to say, in the actual speech samples produced typically by our SL learners—something that seems to go beyond grammatical and communicative proficiency, i.e. something that cannot be explained in strictly grammatical and/or communicative terms. Both these kinds of knowledge—grammatical and communicative—can be considered to be constituent aspects of VERBAL FLUENCY. While student-produced discourse texts (oral and written) often manifest a high degree of verbal fluency, they invariably seem to lack the conceptual appropriateness that characterizes the corresponding discourse texts of native speakers. To put it another way, students 'speak' with the formal structures of the target language, but they 'think' in terms of their native conceptual system: that is, students typically use target language words and structures as 'carriers' of their own native language concepts. When these coincide with the ways in which concepts are structured in the target language, then the student texts coincide serendipitously with culturally appropriate texts; when they do not, the student texts manifest an asymmetry between language form and conceptual content. What student discourse typically lacks, in other words, is CONCEPTUAL FLUENCY.

My claim is that to be conceptually fluent in a language is to know how that language reflects or encodes its concepts on the basis of metaphorical structuring. This kind of knowledge, like grammatical and communicative knowledge, is by and large unconscious in native speakers. If I were to speak about 'ideas' in English, my mind would automatically scan conceptual domains that typically reveal an A IS B structuring. So, if I were to say something like *I don't get the POINT of your idea*, or *I don't quite see how your idea is PARALLEL to mine*, the conceptual domain enlisted by my mind has the form IDEAS ARE GEOMETRICAL OBJECTS. Of course, my mind can search out other appropriate domains—e.g. *Your ideas are coming to fruition*; or *Your ideas are growing on me* (conceptual domain = IDEAS ARE PLANTS); *Your ideas are well constructed*, or *Your ideas are grounded on a solid foundation* (conceptual domain = IDEAS ARE BUILD-

INGS); etc.—or combine them in various ways. The grammatical forms and categories that are used in actual discourse are consistently linked etiologically to such conceptual domains.

There are two comments that must be made right from the outset vis-à-vis the notion of conceptual fluency. First, whether or not all concepts are structured metaphorically, as Lakoff and Johnson (1980) claim, is a question that is open to research and debate. As SL educators, it is certainly judicious to at least entertain the possibility that a wide range of concepts is metaphorical in structure. Second, even if this were so, it must not be forgotten that there are many aspects of language learning that are not conceptual. These may be perceptual, iconic, indexical, or denotative, for instance. But I believe it is fair to say that advanced language proficiency is attained especially when the learner's verbal fluency coincides with the conceptual fluency demonstrated by a native speaker of the language.

In the last two decades, the plethoric research in cognitive psychology and linguistics on metaphor has made it impossible to assign metaphor to some subordinate category vis-à-vis other semantic systems. In the area of SLA, the current research on metaphor gives us a probable explanation of why student discourse is often so unnatural (Danesi 1986, 1988; Mininni 1986). In 1977 Howard Pollio and his associates showed that the average speaker of English invents in the order of 3,000 metaphors per week (Pollio et al. 1977). Work such as this has clearly showed that metaphor is hardly a discourse ornament or option. Rather, it constitutes, arguably, a fundamental aspect of discourse programming. The 'literalness' of learner discourse, therefore, seems to bear witness to the fact that students have had little or no opportunity to access the metaphorically structured conceptual domains inherent in SL discourse. To put it another way, it can be said that 'metaphorical competence'—to coin an analogous term to grammatical and communicative competence—is almost completely lacking from the discourse programming abilities of SL learners.

Although interest in metaphor is as old as Aristotle, the experimental study of its relation to cognition and communication is a relatively recent phenomenon. Since the seventies attention to metaphor on the part of cognitive scientists has become so intense that it is virtually impossible to skim even the surface of the data their research has generated. As Hoffman (1983:35) put it a decade ago, metaphor has become 'a very hot topic' in the cognitive sciences. What stands out most from this research domain is that metaphor is an intrinsic feature of language and cognition. (See Danesi 1989 and Nuessel 1991 for recent summaries of the relevant findings and theories.)

This line of inquiry has not as yet penetrated the mindset of SL researchers, probably because its general implications for language learning and for discourse programming have not as yet been examined. It is, for SL researchers, still a virtually unknown area of cognitive science. But, in the same way that researchers have gained specific insights from psychological research in the past—e.g. sequencing structures according to a natural acquisition order, putting comprehension before production to comply with a natural learning tendency, etc.—so too, in my view, can concrete insights be gleaned from the work on metaphor for both SLA research and SLT methodology.

The model which has become the basic schema to discuss metaphorical programming in cognitive science is the TOPIC–VEHICLE–GROUND model put forward by Richards in 1936, and then refined by Wheelwright (1954), Black (1962), and Perrine (1971). After Black, this model has come to be known as the 'interactional model.' The TOPIC is what is talked about in the metaphor (also known as the A-REFERENT); the VEHICLE is that part which makes a comment on the topic (the B-REFERENT); the GROUND is the meaning that is generated by the semantic 'interaction' between topic and vehicle. Thus in the metaphor *Time is money*, *time* is the topic, *money* the vehicle, and the meaning—which would obviously require an extensive paraphrase—is the ground.

Research on metaphor has shown many intriguing things about this phenomenon. It has shown, for instance, that literal paraphrases never quite encompass the metaphorical ground, that a large area of conceptualization is embedded in metaphor, that children produce metaphors regularly in order to express a physical resemblance between objects, that huge chunks of discourse are based on metaphorically structured concepts, etc. The catalogue of findings on metaphor has become an extensive one indeed. Suffice it to say here that, when considered cumulatively, the research seems to suggest that at least a portion of the human mind is 'programmed' to think metaphorically.

It is perhaps the work of Lakoff and Johnson in linguistics over the past decade (e.g. Lakoff and Johnson 1980, Lakoff 1987, Johnson 1987) that is the most germane to developing the notion of metaphorical competence (MC) and conceptual fluency for SLA and SLT. The essential claim made by these two scholars is that our most common concepts are forged via metaphor. They show this by simply taking concepts apart and revealing their underlying metaphorical structure. Consider, for example, the following common metaphorical portrayals of health by our culture (Lakoff and Johnson 1980:15 and 50):

1. You're at the PEAK of your health
2. My health is DOWN.
3. You're in TOP shape.
4. My body is in perfect WORKING ORDER.
5. My body is BREAKING DOWN.
6. My health is going DOWN THE DRAIN.
7. His pain WENT AWAY.
8. I'm going to FLUSH OUT my cold.

The first three sentences represent health in terms of an orientation analogy: that is, the state of being healthy is conceptualized as being oriented in an upwards direction, while the opposite state is conceptualized as being oriented in a downwards direction. This is probably because in our culture, as Lakoff and Johnson (1980:15) point out, serious 'illness forces us to lie down physically.'

Sentences (4) and (5) conceptualize health, and its converse, as a machine-like Gestalt. And in the last three sentences, health and its converse are envisaged as being entities within a person. This is why they can *go away*, why they can be *flushed out*, and so on.

It is interesting to note that even before the current wave of fascination with metaphor within cognitive science, the writer Susan Sontag wrote a compelling book in 1978, *Illness as Metaphor*, that has become a classic study of how metaphor shapes our conceptualizations of disease. A decade later, after the advent of AIDS, Sontag (1989) followed this up with a sequel study on the metaphors we commonly use to conceptualize AIDS. The main point made by Sontag in these two brilliant books is that illness is not a metaphor, but that cultures invariably think of diseases in metaphorical ways. Using the example of cancer, Sontag (1978) points out that in the not-too-distant past the very word *cancer* was said to have killed some patients who would not have necessarily succumbed to the malignancy from which they suffered: 'As long as a particular disease is treated as an evil, invincible predator, not just a disease, most people with cancer will indeed be demoralized by learning what disease they have.' Sontag's point that people suffer more from conceptualizing about their disease than from the disease itself is, indeed, a well-taken and instructive one.

The upshot of the work of Lakoff and Johnson and others is that metaphor probably underlies the representation of most of our common concepts, and that it structures the ways in which we perceive, think, and act. In terms of the interactional model of metaphor, it can be said that 'health' is the topic and that its various conceptualizations (as orientation, as an entity, as a machine, etc.) are its vehicular lexicalizations. The end result is a way of thinking and talking about health in English that takes place unconsciously in the domain of metaphor—*'healthiness' is up/'unhealthiness' is down, 'healthiness' is a well-functioning machine/'unhealthiness' is a malfunctioning machine*, etc.

The work of Pollio et al. (1977), and other surveys of the use of metaphor in everyday communicative behavior (e.g. Dundes 1972, Beck 1982, Kővecses 1986, 1988, 1990), have made it obvious that this kind of conceptualization is an intrinsic feature of discourse programming. The implications of this line of research for SLA and SLT are quite clear: the programming of discourse in metaphorical ways is a basic feature of native-speaker competence. It underlies what I have designated conceptual fluency. As a 'competence,' it can be thought about pedagogically in ways that are parallel to the other competencies that SLT has traditionally focused on (grammatical and communicative).

Conceptual fluency can be thought of as a cognitive mapping operation. It is a largely unconscious strategy which maps sensory experience onto the world of conceptualization. As an example of how it might work in discourse programming consider the following hypothetical situation. Let us say that I am practicing the piano. It is a rainy day and I am playing a sad piece of music. Someone walks into the room where I am playing and asks me how I feel. The sad music and the rain outside have put me in a frame of mind that leads me to make a commentary on my mood. Seeing raindrops on a nearby window, I might answer my interlocutor with *I'm feeling* DRIPPY. In the context of the experiential domain in which the utterance was uttered it makes perfect sense. The reason why it makes sense to my interlocutor is because it reflects an underlying metaphorical concept *mood is an environmental state* (*I'm feeling under the weather, I'm in a stormy mood today*, etc.).

In a fundamental sense, therefore, MC is closely linked to the ways in which a culture organizes its world conceptually. It inheres, as Lakoff and Johnson (1980:5) remark, in 'understanding and experiencing one kind of thing in terms of another.' Common concepts, ranging all the way from love to justice, seem typically to be grounded in metaphor, and since communication is based in large part on the same conceptual system that we use in thinking and acting, then language is an important source of evidence of what that system is like. As Winner (1982:253) has aptly put it, the recent experimental literature has made it conspicuously obvious that if 'people were limited to strictly literal language, communication would be severely curtailed, if not terminated.'

3 A research report. What is lacking are sufficient data on the role of metaphor in SLA. The few studies that exist in this domain look at SLA in natural (i.e. bilingual) contexts. Johnson (1989, 1991) and De Cunha (1991) for instance, have shown that access to two metaphorical mapping processes enhances the child's overall metalinguistic competence. No studies on the development of MC in the classroom exist, at least to the best of my knowledge.

In an attempt to gain a better understanding of various issues related to MC and SLA in classroom environments, several pilot studies were undertaken at the University of Toronto in the last two years by a team of researchers under my guidance. The detailed results of two of these studies are reported upon elsewhere (Danesi, forthcoming). Here they will be discussed only in terms of the general patterns that they reveal.

Study 1. Perhaps the most basic question that a consideration of MC raises is to what extent it develops in typical classroom learners. At the end of a course, or program of study, the student is generally capable of applying the grammatical and communicative skills and knowledge gained to new domains and tasks. In general, the learner can compute grammatical and communicative tasks within a predictable range of topics. The question that interests us here is to what extent, if any, do typical classroom learners, at various stages of learning, can comprehend SL metaphors. That was the aim of the first study.

Two groups of students of Italian at the University of Toronto were examined: Group A consisted of 12 nonnative students, 4 from each of the three levels of study offered at the University (elementary, intermediate and advanced). Group B, the comparison group, consisted of 12 students of Italian background who spoke Italian as a native language. In B as well there were 4 students from each level (elementary, intermediate, advanced). Given the limited size of the sample, it was not possible to draw inferences of statistical significance from the results. The idea was not to establish any pattern statistically, but simply to get some indication if typical classroom learners are capable of comprehending metaphor. As a pilot study, therefore, it was intended to provide insights on how to design a more elaborate one on metaphorical comprehension. As such, therefore, it constituted more of a 'probe' than a research study.

The subjects were not informed of the goals of the probe. Each student was given three comprehension tasks separately within the last two weeks of the 1991 academic year. The first task required the students to select the meaning of ten metaphorical statements on a questionnaire from three given cues—one literal, and two metaphorical (of which only one represented the true meaning). The 'literal interpretation' simply took the words in the metaphor at face (literal) value. Thus, in the metaphor *Giovanni è una volpe* 'John is a fox', three options were given for the student to select: 1. *Giovanni reagisce come un animale* ('John reacts like an animal' = literal); 2. *A Giovanni piacciono le galline* ('John likes chickens' = false metaphorical); and *Giovanni è furbo e astuto* ('John is smart and astute' = correct metaphorical). The idea was simply to see if the learners were able to understand metaphorical statements in the SL. The second task was a translation task consisting of 10 metaphorical sentences, 5 from Italian into English and 5 from English into Italian. This task required the learners to decode (Italian to English) and program (English to Italian) statements metaphorically. The third task required the subjects to read two brief texts in the SL, one literal and one metaphorical, and then to paraphrase each text in the SL. The paraphrases were recorded on cassette (See Danesi, forthcoming for a complete summary of the testing materials).

The results on the first task were as follows: Group A achieved, overall, a 57% correct response level, and Group B an 83% level. Most of the correct responses in both groups (92% and 85% respectively) came from students enrolled in the advanced courses. Group A learners tended to interpret and translate SL metaphors literally. Group B performed much better on the tasks, especially at the advanced level.

Both groups performed equally well on the paraphrase task of the literal passage, and equally poorly on the paraphrase task of the metaphorical text. Indeed, an analysis of the interpretation appropriateness of both groups shows that only 4 of 12 in Group A and 6 of 12 in Group B gave acceptable paraphrases.

The translation task, clearly the most difficult one, produced the lowest results. Indeed, overall, of all the possible translations, Group A came up with a 23% acceptability level and Group B a 34% one. This was calculated by taking the total number of sentences translated by all the students into account.

Clearly, in order to test for statistical significance, a much larger sample size is required in a future study. But in the context of a pilot study, these results suggested that MC, even at the level of comprehension, is inadequate in typical classroom learners. The reason for this is not that they are incapable of learning metaphor, but most likely that they have never been exposed in formal ways to the conceptual system of the target language. To be conceptually fluent in the SL the student must be able to convert common experiences into conceptually and linguistically appropriate models. At the present time there seems to be nothing in SLT methodology that takes this into account.

Study 2. A second study was conducted later in 1991 to measure conceptual fluency in students who had completed a minimum of three years of Spanish at the University of Toronto. The sample in this case consisted of a group of 30 third- and fourth-year students of Spanish at the University of Toronto who were separated into two groups of 25 nonnative speakers (A) and 25 native speakers (B). As in the previous study, the native group constituted a comparison group.

The subjects were asked to write a short, in-class essay on one of the following topics: 1. *¿Qué es la amistad?* 'What is friendship?' 2. *El teléfono: la invención que ha revolucionado nuestra sociedad* 'The telephone: The invention that has revolutionized our society' 3. *La presencia de los soldados canadienses en el Golfo* 'The presence of Canadian soldiers in the Gulf'. The essays were collected and examined for the presence of metaphor in terms of conceptual fluency. An index of 'metaphorical density' (MD) was computed for each essay. This simply measured the number of metaphorical sentences in those who wrote on a topic as a percentage of the total number of sentences written. A metaphorical sentence was defined as a token or instantiation of the underlying culturally-appropriate conceptual system: e.g. an orientation metaphor, an entity metaphor, etc. Repeated instantiations of a conceptual metaphor were not counted again, since these can be seen to be simple elaborations. An average metaphorical density (AMD) was then computed for both groups. The results are tabulated as follows:

Group A	Group B
	AMISTAD
MD = 9.4	MD = 32.5
	TELÉFONO
MD = 6.97	MD = 11.7
	SOLDADOS
MD = 7.65	MD = 12.94
	AMD (by year)
3rd = 6.87	3rd = 12.22
4th = 9.42	4th = 13.13

A check of significance between the two means (A and B) showed that the difference is significant at the $p < .05$ level, although the size of the sample does not really permit any inferential generalizations. What can be gleaned from this pilot study, basically, is that vis-à-vis native speakers, students have little access to the conceptual system of the language. This is why their compositions show a high degree of 'literalness'. And when we compared the actual sentences that were tagged as metaphorical in Spanish with corresponding ones in English, we found that they matched: that is, the students tended to use conceptual metaphors that were alike in both languages. This means that they learned virtually no 'new ways' of thinking conceptually after three or four years of study in a classroom.

Follow-up study. These studies suggested that students are not exposed in any systematic fashion to the ways in which metaphor structures concepts in the target language. I therefore checked ten commonly used textbooks in elementary, intermediate, and advanced French, Italian, and Spanish courses at the University of Toronto for metaphorical content. Not even one of the textbooks examined had set aside a chapter, unit, or section dealing with metaphorical concepts as such. These did occur in dialogue samples, model sentences, and the like. But even in such form these textbooks showed a very low metaphorical density. By simply counting the total number of target language sentences used in the textbooks, tagging them as either metaphorical or literal, and computing a metaphorical density (percentage), it turned out that the average metaphorical density for the ten textbooks taken together turned out to be less than 10%. In other words, not only are students not taught anything about metaphor explicitly in textbooks, but textbook authors seem to shy away from any kind of utilization of metaphor.

Since students are also exposed to so-called 'authentic materials' (readings and realia) which are, of course, imbued with metaphorically structured discourse, it follows that students do not develop MC by osmosis. It would seem that metaphorical competence, like grammatical and communicative competence, must be extracted from the continuum of discourse and held up for students to study and practice in ways that are similar to how we teach them grammar and communication.

4 Implications. This last consideration leads me to the general implications that the notions of metaphorical competence and conceptual fluency hold for SLA research and SLT methodology in my view. First, these notions are in no way mutually exclusive of grammatical and communicative competence. It is quite likely that all three competencies constitute overlapping layers in discourse programming. We now know quite a lot about how the grammatical and communicative layers operate; the time has come to look at how and where the metaphorical layer fits in.

Second, is metaphor cognitively more salient and versatile than literal, propositional discourse? Research on so-called anomalous strings (e.g. *Colorless green ideas sleep furiously*), for instance, has shown that the metaphorizing capacity forces people to extract meaning from virtually any well-formed combination of words (e.g. Pollio and Burns 1977, Pollio and Smith 1979). If people are required to interpret such strings, then they will do so, no matter how contrived the interpretation might appear. This suggests that metaphorical thinking is a dominant and ever-present option in discourse, and that literal thinking might actually constitute a special, limited case of communicative behavior. In the absence of contextual information for an utterance such as 'The murderer is an animal,' we are immediately inclined to apply the metaphorical mode in interpretation. It is only if we are told that the so-called 'murder' was committed by a biological animal that a literal interpretation becomes possible. This is probably due to the fact that literal speech is tied to the verbalization of the finite universe of ACTUAL WORLDS, whereas metaphor extends discourse into the infinite universe of POTENTIAL WORLDS.

Third, an important question for SLA research would seem to be: to what extent do the conceptual domains of the native and target cultures overlap and contrast (Danesi and Di Pietro 1990:54–56)? The notion of conceptual fluency, therefore, provides SLA research with a convenient category for viewing certain aspects of interlanguage behavior that cannot be explained in other ways, such as, for example, the common observation that student-produced discourse texts seem to follow a native-language conceptual flow that is 'clothed,' so to speak, in target language grammar and vocabulary.

For SLT methodology, perhaps the most obvious question is the following one: Is it possible to delimit the 'conceptual world' in such a way that it can be incorporated into the modus operandi of classroom teaching? Is it possible, in other words, to develop instructional techniques and materials for imparting MC in ways that parallel how SLT has utilized theories of grammar and communication to impart linguistic and communicative competence respectively?

In a fundamental sense, this is the question that has been asked since the turn of the present century, when SLT came to be forged as a 'science'. And, indeed, SLT has responded to the challenge of translating grammatical and communicative theories into pedagogical and instructional ideas, models, and practices. So, if the research on metaphor is any indication of the significance of metaphor to discourse, then there is no reason to believe that it will constitute an impossible task to translate the findings on metaphor into pedagogically usable insights and principles.

Essentially, the study of MC and conceptual fluency implies that context is tied inextricably to verbalization: that is, contextual and situational cues undergird the form and content of discourse. In an SL classroom environment, this implies, first and foremost, that the teaching format or 'script' will have to simulate as closely as possible the culturally appropriate conditions and processes that characterize the discourse of the SL. This may mean something as self-evident as utilizing common situations and functional themes as the basis for constructing the frames in which to present oral patterns to be repeated and memorized, or something as radically new as describing the cultural models, à la Lakoff and Johnson, that underlie the discourse patterns of the SL.

5 Concluding remarks. In this paper I have attempted to argue that the study of MC should be included on the agenda of SLA research in classroom environments. If nothing else it has some intriguing possibilities for studying classroom SLA from a perspective that is radically different from traditional approaches. The pilot studies described here have suggested that the typical classroom SL learner has virtually no access to the conceptual system of the SL even after three or four years of study. If MC is an intrinsic feature of discourse, as a large amount of research in cognitive science seems to suggest, and if it is virtually nonexistent in student discourse, then the implications for SLT are rather obvious. Among other things, the materials used, the content of the curriculum, and the instructional focus will have to be reevaluated in the light of MC. Actually, the line of work known as contrastive rhetoric (e.g. Kaplan 1978, Piper 1985, Leki 1991) has for a quarter of a century attempted to put what I have called MC on the agenda of SLT. But, its approach has been limited to SL reading, not to SLT as a whole.

In previous work (Danesi 1986, 1988), I have suggested that MC is as teachable as grammatical or communicative competence. Suffice it to say here that SLT should investigate the possibility further of incorporating MC into its modus operandi. The work of Lakoff and Johnson and others has shown that there is systematicity to metaphorical concepts. The process of learning this system is, arguably, identical to the one enlisted for learning grammar and communication. To ignore metaphor is to ignore the conceptual system that underlies native-speaker discourse. The true sign of proficiency, as a matter of fact, is the ability to metaphorize in the new language.

REFERENCES

Beck, B. 1982. Root metaphor patterns. Semiotic Inquiry 2.86–97.

Black, Max. 1962. Models and metaphors. Ithaca: Cornell University Press.

Danesi, Marcel. 1986. The role of metaphor in second language pedagogy. Rassegna Italiana di Linguistica Applicata 18.1–10.

Danesi, Marcel. 1988. The development of metaphorical competence: A neglected dimension in second language pedagogy. Italiana, ed. by A. N. Mancini, P. Giordano, and P. R. Baldini, 1–10. River Forest: Rosary College.

Danesi, Marcel. 1989. The role of metaphor in cognition. Semiotica 77.521–31.

Danesi, Marcel. (in press) Metaphorical competence and classroom second language learning. Romance Languages Annual.

Danesi, Marcel, and Robert J. Di Pietro. 1990. Contrastive analysis for the contemporary second language classroom. Toronto: OISE Press.

De Cunha, Dawn. 1991. Metaphor comprehension and second language acquisition. Doctoral Dissertation, Ontario Institute for Studies in Education.

Dundes, Allan. 1972. Seeing is believing. Natural History 81.9–12.

Hoffman, Robert R. 1983. Recent research on metaphor. Semiotic Inquiry 3.35–61.

Johnson, Janet. 1989. Factors related to cross-language transfer and metaphoric interpretation in bilingual children. Applied Psycholinguistics 10.157–77.

Johnson, Janet. 1991. Constructive processes in bilingualism and their cognitive growth effects. Language Processing in Bilingual Children, ed. by E. Bialystock, 193–221. Cambridge: Cambridge University Press.

Johnson, Mark. 1987. The body in the mind: The bodily basis of meaning, imagination and reason. Chicago: University of Chicago Press.

Kaplan, Robert D. 1978. Contrastive rhetoric: Some hypotheses. ITL: Review of Applied Linguistics 39-40.61-72.

Kelly, L. G. 1969. Twenty-five centuries of language teaching. Rowley, MA: Newbury House.

Kövecses, Z. 1986. Metaphors of anger, pride, and love: A lexical approach to the structure of concepts. Amsterdam: Benjamins.

Kövecses, Z. 1988. The language of love: The semantics of passion in conversational English. London: Associated University Presses.

Kövecses, Z. 1990. Emotion concepts. New York: Springer.

Lakoff, George. 1987. Women, fire, and dangerous things: What categories reveal about the mind. Chicago: University of Chicago Press.

Lakoff, George, and Mark Johnson. 1980. Metaphors we live by. Chicago: Chicago University Press.

Leki, I. 1991. Twenty-five years of contrastive rhetoric: Text analysis and writing pedagogies. TESOL Quarterly 25.123-43.

Mininni, Giuseppe. 1986. L'uso della metafora nell'educazione linguistica. Rassegna Italiana di Linguistica Applicata 18.23-40.

Nuessel, Frank. 1991. Metaphor and cognition: A survey of recent publications. Journal of Literary Semantics 20.37-52.

Perrine, L. 1971. Four forms of metaphor. College English 33.125-38.

Piper, D. 1985. Contrastive rhetoric and reading in second language: Theoretical perspectives on classroom practice. Canadian Modern Language Review 42.34-43.

Pollio, H., and B. Burns. 1977. The anomaly of anomaly. Journal of Psycholinguistic Research 6.247-60.

Pollio, H., and M. Smith. 1979. Sense and nonsense in thinking about anomaly and metaphor. Bulletin of the Psychonomic Society 13.323-26.

Pollio, H., J. Barlow, H. Fine, and M. Pollio. 1977. The poetics of growth: Figurative language in psychology, psychotherapy, and education. Hillsdale, NJ: Lawrence Erlbaum Associates.

Richards, I. A. 1936. The philosophy of rhetoric. Oxford: Oxford University Press.

Savignon, Sandra J. 1992. Problem solving and the negotiation of meaning. Problem Solving in Second Language Teaching, ed. by C. Cicogna, M. Danesi, and A. Mollica, 11-25. Welland: Le Soleil.

Sontag, Susan. 1978. Illness as metaphor. New York: Farrar, Straus & Giroux.

Sontag, Susan. 1989. AIDS and its metaphors. New York: Farrar, Straus & Giroux.

Titone, Renzo. 1968. Teaching foreign languages: An historical sketch. Washington, DC: Georgetown University Press.

Wheelwright, P. 1954. The burning fountain: A study in the language of symbolism. Bloomington: Indiana University Press.

Winner, Ellen. 1982. Invented worlds: The psychology of the arts. Cambridge: Harvard University Press.

Perspectives on communicative language teaching: Syllabus design and methodology

H.G. Widdowson
University of London

I want to discuss pedagogy as a pragmatic activity. Let me key in my argument with a slogan: every course is a discourse. Teaching and learning a language is a joint interactive enterprise which is enacted in classroom encounters and can be discussed, therefore, with reference to factors which are involved in speech events, or communicative uses of language in general. There is, of course, a difference in that in pedagogic discourse, there is always an ulterior motive, another agenda apart from that of appearances, whether this is hidden or not, namely that whatever discourse is enacted is accountable to a didactic purpose. No matter how communicatively effective or socially meaningful the classroom discourse is, it fails unless it achieves the objective of language learning. The classroom has to provide a satisfactory context of instruction. Whether and to what extent it approximates to normal or authentic contexts of use outside the classroom is a contingent matter.

Every course is a discourse. But we need to note, then, that the discourse is of a didactic kind and has to be designed to meet a learning purpose. We need to note too that the term COURSE is ambiguous. It can mean a projected plan of work, a syllabus, a sequence of objectives, a schematic construct recorded as a text for the teacher to refer to. But it can also mean the set of activities that go on in class, the actual discourse derived from this text which is interactively enacted between the participants in the classroom encounter. The didactic directing of this activity is what I shall refer to as methodology. So the syllabus is that part of a course which serves as a schematic frame of reference, and the methodology is the procedural achievement of outcomes relevant to learning. Just as with the achievement of pragmatic meaning in other discourses, communication in the classroom is a matter of actualizing particular behaviour in reference to more general conceptual categories. The syllabus can be seen as a model of competence, and methodology as the directed realization of this competence as performance, so directed that it will be effective in the acquisition of the competence which it realizes.

Two questions arise. Firstly, on what principles should this syllabus as a model of competence be designed? How are its components to be defined? Second, how is the syllabus model to be activated as performance, as classroom discourse which will serve the necessary didactic purpose of inducing language acquisition?

SYLLABUS first. The most obvious answer to the question of what should be modelled here is the COMMUNICATIVE competence of the native speakers of the target language. Since communication in the target language is what learners are aiming for, then THAT is what needs to be specified as the objective. This seems reasonable enough. But there are problems, and developments in language pedagogy over the recent past can be seen as different attempts to resolve them.

There is, to begin with, the problem of what exactly we are talking about under the heading of COMMUNICATIVE COMPETENCE. Dell Hymes, as we all know, identified four constituent elements compounded within the term communicative: the possible, the feasible, the appropriate, the attested; and, for good measure, distinguished two elements within competence as well: knowledge AND ability. Once the original Chomskyan concept, which covered only knowledge of the possible, was thus extended, a bewildering profusion of competences was subsequently proposed. Now these models were presented in the form of constituent structure diagrams, with nodes spreading out from nodes down to an array of distinct elements each hanging on the end of a terminal branch. The difficulty about such analysis, of course, is that it fragments what is for the language user, and what has to be eventually for the language learner, a unity of interdependent parts. The question is: what are the RELATIONSHIPS between the different elements which have been analysed out in this way? How are they variously compounded or synthesised? We cannot tell from the hierarchical diagram, for no direct relationship can be shown between the elements at the end of each branch: they are only connected by analysis through the superordinate nodes.

Two kinds of problem arise from this subcategorization of competences. One has to do with its VALIDITY as a model of language use. It cannot be assumed, it seems to me, that a component of competence which is isolated and made static in this way has the same character when it is involved with other components as a moving part, so to speak, in the communicative process as a whole. By subjecting it to separate, decontextualized analysis, you formalize it beyond its normal function in relation to other components. To take one fairly obvious example. Everybody modelling communicative competence seems to accept that linguistic competence, as conceived by Chomsky, can be carried over intact as a component. But if one is talking about the ability to access knowledge of language as appropriate to different contexts of use, which Chomsky idealizes out of consideration, it is surely likely that we need a very different concept of linguistic competence, a RELATIONAL concept, one which keys in with the other components. Such a concept would, as I have argued elsewhere, give greater prominence to lexis rather than syntax and to the memorization of preformulated expressions, phrase kits ready made for speedy assembly, rather than the algorithmic analysis into rules.

The other, related, problem has to do with the UTILITY of this model of multiple competences for syllabus design. A syllabus is, as I have already indicated, a schematic construct of what is to be taught; it is, therefore, the projection of a sequence of events. But in reference to which components of communicative competence are these events to be defined? This question has to do with implicational relationships between components which, I have suggested, models of communicative competence fail to indicate.

Consider then the matter of the definition of syllabus units. The question here is: which components of knowledge and ability have to be given prominence as needing to be TAUGHT, and which can be relegated to subordinate status on the grounds that they will be LEARNED contingently by natural implicational consequence. Before the concept of communicative competence made its appearance to complicate our world, the answer seemed to be self-evident. The teachers' objective was to get students to know the rules of grammar, and they did so by exercising them in the ability to compose sentences. Once this grammatical competence was taught, it provided students with the necessary and sufficient potential, and they would learn for themselves how such potential could be realized as appropriate communicative behaviour, as and when occasions arose. It is often suggested that this structural approach, this focus on form, set out to confine learning to the formal properties of language and had no concern for communication. But that is not the case. The assumption was that students would not only learn what was taught but would go beyond the input, would learn FROM teaching, and that the analytic nature of their knowledge would guarantee maximal applicability in use.

It was the questioning of this assumption of implicational consequence that led, of course, to the notional/functional syllabus. The component that was now given prominence was the sociolinguistic, or that branch of it which was labelled illocutionary, and this focussed not on the linguistically possible but on the socially appropriate. Does then the definition of syllabus units as notions/functions provide a more effective teaching investment for learning returns? Does a knowledge of a range of speech acts and the ability to act appropriately on such knowledge necessarily implicate the acquisition of other components of communicative competence? The evidence suggests not. It appears that it does not of itself provide an adequate investment for the development of either linguistic or discourse components.

Perhaps then it is discourse competence which provides us with the basis for syllabus units: perhaps teaching THAT will lead to the comprehensive learning we are looking for. A supposition that it might has led to the proposal that such units should be defined as problem-solving tasks, which necessarily engage students in discourse enactment, in the negotiation of meaning, for their solution. These tasks may in varying degrees draw on the content and procedures of other curriculum subjects. It is this focus on syllabus design which is currently in fashion, of course, and it has the persuasive commendation of a number of people working in second language acquisition research.

There are, however, certain things about defining a syllabus in terms of tasks that need to be noted. To begin with, it appears that, as with notions and functions, tasks on their own do not provide the necessary and sufficient conditions for the acquisition of all components of communicative competence. Tasks need to be so contrived that there is some focus on form beyond the natural requirement of the task. The language needs to be noticed (Schmidt 1990), the input needs to be enhanced (Sharwood Smith 1991, White et al. 1991). This will not, of course, be news to most teachers. What they will find surprising is that anybody should ever have thought otherwise.

The second point has to do with the nature of a syllabus. If it is to be the schematic construct of what is to be taught, then the units, however defined, have to be ORDERED in some way, and that order is also implicational in character. Thus the placing of a particular unit in sequence implies that its successful teaching is dependent on preceding units and not on succeeding ones, as far as learning is concerned. Now this is a matter of judging the implicational relations in language learning, not in language use. And the two are not the same. How the components of competence interrelate in actual use, which is what I have been discussing so far, may be very different from the way they are most effectively interrelated in the process of learning. One of the claims of SLA is that the implicational order for teaching in a syllabus should be based on the natural learning order. But to the extent that this has been established, it has only been in reference to the linguistic component of competence, and mainly only the grammatical component at that. Very little has been revealed to us about the process of acquisition of other components, the lexical, the textual, the sociolinguistic, the discoursal, the strategic, and so on, all of which are implicated in the pragmatic use of language for problem-solving. The only element of communicative competence that SLA can give any guidance on (leaving aside the question of how far we should put our trust in such guidance) is in respect to the sequence of linguistic forms. But then if we have no reliable principle for ordering the tasks for teaching, how can they figure in a syllabus? The same sort of question can, of course, be posed in respect to notions and functions as well. Even if we had reason to suppose that notions/functions or tasks had implicational value for the acquisition of other elements of communicative competence and were therefore a good learning investment, we have the difficulty of knowing how they would be arranged in some order which would be effective for the process of learning itself.

And there is a further point. Tasks are intended to activate discourse on the assumption that this will implicate all other aspects of communicative competence. But the specification of tasks in a syllabus cannot alone do this. As I have indicated before, the syllabus is an inert text, a static plan. Only when the plan is put into action, only when there is a discourse realized in reference to the text can there be any language using or learning at all. And this action in our case is classroom action, the directed behaviour of students. The question arises, then, as to how these matters concerning the teaching and learning of language and communication relate to the business of methodology.

METHODOLOGY then. Methodology, as I have defined it, is the directed discourse of the classroom which realizes the text of the syllabus as actual behaviour. The discourse is directed towards a didactic purpose and succeeds in its purpose to the extent that students internalize the text of the syllabus, that is to say, acquire the components of competence, the elements of knowledge which have been specified as its units. But notice that the discourse that is enacted must not only FACILITATE the acquisition of this knowledge, but also ACTIVATE other components of competence which are not explicitly specified but assumed to be contingently learnable by implication. It is the classroom discourse which creates conditions for such contingency learning. Thus, for example, if the syllabus units are specified in terms of grammatical elements, then methodology has to contrive a discourse which will realize these in relation to other components (speech acts or tasks or whatever) so that their communicative potential is learned as well. Conversely, if the syllabus units are defined in reference to a different component of competence, then grammar will need to be given focus in the methodology. Thus syllabus and methodology are complementary, and I am not convinced that it matters, in principle, how the responsibility is distributed. The essential point is that they need to be dynamically, and dialectically, related.

What I AM convinced of is the need for contrivance and the need for the teacher to take responsibility for the direction the discourse takes. It is the teacher who steers the course. This brings us to the question of the roles that the participants take in the classroom encounter. Over recent years there has been a good deal of persuasive advocacy of natural instinctive learning and a corresponding distrust of teacher authority. The traditional roles of the classroom protagonists have been called into question.

It is, I think, helpful to consider these roles in reference to distinctions originally proposed by Goffman (1981) and elaborated on by Levinson (1988). As both point out, discourse enactment is not a simple dyadic affair. At both ends of the process there is complexity. There is, to begin with, the possibility of plurality of incumbency, particularly at the receiving end. So it is typically with classroom discourse: there is a single incumbent in the teacher role, but a plurality of incumbents in the learner role. And with the plurality, of course, comes variety, different personalities, attitudes, learning styles, and so on which the single teacher cannot possibly take separate account of. Teaching is necessarily directed at a collective incumbent. The input that it provides must in some degree be communal, no matter what allowance is made for individual intake.

But it is not only that the participant roles in discourse may have multiple incumbents. The roles themselves may be complex. At the producing end, for example, Goffman distinguishes the ANIMATOR, the person who gives actual substance to what is said (the 'sounding box' as he called it) from the AUTHOR, the person responsible for the wording of the message (in his terms 'the agent who scripts the lines'.) It is easy to see, I think, that different kinds of discourse direction can be characterized in reference to this distinction. Learners who are drilled in pattern practice, for example, are obviously acting as animators only, mouthing the script which has been dictated by textbook or teacher. The teacher herself may, indeed, be animating the textbook without taking very much authorial initiative. It is obvious that casting the learner in the role of animator is consistent with a transmission view of pedagogy, and this has now, in the minds of many at least, been discredited. It is also obvious that for many teaching situations, particularly where multiple incumbency is in evidence in large and heterogeneous classes, anything other than animation is difficult to manage. Nevertheless, current progressive thinking favours learner authorship—that is to say, it allows learners the initiative to write their own scripts, and not to be dictated to. And authorship in this sense is enhanced, it is believed, by group work, which, of course, reduces the incumbency problem by replicating the producer role and so provides the opportunity for learners to participate in discourses of their own making. But if the teacher is then no longer author, what role does she have? Does it mean that to relinquish the author role, the teacher ceases to have authority over the discourses enacted in class? I do not think so. For we have yet to consider the third participant role that Goffman mentions.

The producer of a message may be the author of its wording, the agent of the script, but may nevertheless be acting on behalf of another party, expressing their views and values and not his own: a speechwriter, for example, composing a script at the behest of another, whether that other animates it or not; a defence lawyer, putting eloquence and learning at the service of the defendant in the dock, who never animates the words of his own case. The point about the speechwriter and the lawyer is that they are both producers not of direct but DIRECTED speech. They are, as authors, mediators, not motivators. They are not, to use Goffman's term, PRINCIPALS.

What then does this have to do with the roles of teacher and learner? My argument is that the discourse of learners is also directed, and that pedagogy requires that it should be. For all the talk about the change that we have witnessed in pedagogic thinking whereby teacher authority has apparently yielded to learner autonomy, the learner role is nevertheless pedagogically ascribed. Learners may not be constrained to be only animators, they may be allowed leeway to assume more authorial responsibility, but the teacher still retains the role of principal. That is to say, learner activity is always in some degree controlled. This is what I mean by directed discourse.

Now there is, of course, directed discourse in the contexts of actual communication in social life, where the roles of participants are restricted in authorial initiative, where people are positioned to their disadvantage. Indeed, it is the purpose of critical discourse analysis to reveal such practices, seen as exploitation and the exercise of power. Surely, then, to commend such directed discourse in the classroom is to cramp the learners into submission and to repress individual initiative.

I do not think so. Teachers as principal motivators in the Goffman sense can exercise their authority benignly as guidance which allows for individual initiative: they do not have to exercise it malignantly as constraint which stifles it. In other words, the teacher role can be authoritative without being authoritarian. And in my view it needs to be. Learners of language, like learners of anything if it comes to that, need to be instructed in the limits which give their freedom meaning, in the rules and conventions which define the language they are learning. The teacher knows what these are. The learner does not. Once the limits are known, then they can of course be breached, the conventions can be exploited in all manner of ways. The point is, I believe, that learners can only assert their own authority if they first submit themselves to the authority of others. I started with one slogan and I end with another. It is a variant of the familiar injunction 'If you can't beat them, join them.' It is: 'If you want to beat them, join them first.'

REFERENCES

Goffman, Erving. 1981. Forms of talk. Oxford: Basil Blackwell.

Levinson, Stephen C. 1988. Putting linguistics on a proper footing: Explorations in Goffman's concepts of participation. Erving Goffman: Exploring the interaction order, ed. by Paul Drew and Andrew Wootton, 161-227. Cambridge: Polity Press.

Schmidt, Richard W. 1990. The role of consciousness in second language learning. Applied Linguistics 11, 2.129-58.

Sharwood Smith, Michael. 1991. Speaking to many minds: On the relevance of different types of information for the L2 learner. Second Language Research, 7, 2.118-32.

White, Lydia, Nina Spada, Patsy M. Lightbown, and Leila Ranta. 1991. Input enhancement and the L2 question formation. Applied Linguistics 12, 4.416-32.

www.ingramcontent.com/pod-product-compliance
Lightning Source LLC
LaVergne TN
LVHW090757070826
844660LV00022B/1010

* 9 7 8 0 8 7 8 4 0 1 2 7 7 *